DYSTOPIA:
A NATURAL HISTORY

MW00648584

Born in France, and educated in Canada and the UK, **Gregory Claeys** is Professor of the History of Political Thought at Royal Holloway, University of London. A historian of British radicalism and socialism from 1750 to the present, he is the author of eight books and editor of some fifty volumes, mostly of primary sources. He has written studies of Robert Owen and Owenism, Thomas Paine, and John Stuart Mill, as well as of utopianism. He has been visiting professor at the Australian National University, Keio University, Tokyo, the University of Hanoi, and Peking University.

Dystopia: A Natural History

A Study of Modern Despotism, Its Antecedents, and Its Literary Diffractions

GREGORY CLAEYS

OXFORD

UNIVERSITY PRESS

OXFORD

UNIVERSITY PRESS

Great Clarendon Street, Oxford, OX2 6DP,
United Kingdom

Oxford University Press is a department of the University of Oxford.
It furthers the University's objective of excellence in research, scholarship,
and education by publishing worldwide. Oxford is a registered trade mark of
Oxford University Press in the UK and in certain other countries

© Gregory Claeys 2017

The moral rights of the author have been asserted

First published 2017
First published in paperback 2018

All rights reserved. No part of this publication may be reproduced, stored in
a retrieval system, or transmitted, in any form or by any means, without the
prior permission in writing of Oxford University Press, or as expressly permitted
by law, by licence or under terms agreed with the appropriate reprographics
rights organization. Enquiries concerning reproduction outside the scope of the
above should be sent to the Rights Department, Oxford University Press, at the
address above

You must not circulate this work in any other form
and you must impose this same condition on any acquirer

Published in the United States of America by Oxford University Press
198 Madison Avenue, New York, NY 10016, United States of America

British Library Cataloguing in Publication Data
Data available

Library of Congress Cataloging in Publication Data
Data available

ISBN 978–0–19–878568–2 (Hbk.)
ISBN 978–0–19–882047–5 (Pbk.)

Links to third party websites are provided by Oxford in good faith and
for information only. Oxford disclaims any responsibility for the materials
contained in any third party website referenced in this work.

In Memoriam,
István Hont (1947–2013)
an abundance of warmth and light

Acknowledgements

Readers may recall Orwell's observation that 'Writing a book is a horrid, exhausting struggle, like a long bout of some painful illness' ('Why I Write', 1946). Thankfully I have had some skilled intellectual physicians to help me through the moments when I thought I might succumb to this one. In particular, a very special thanks is due to Artur Blaim, Michael Levin, Lyman Tower Sargent, and Dan Stone, who made invaluable comments on parts of the manuscript and have greatly improved the final version. I am also grateful to Antonis Balasopoulos; Mosab Bajaber; David Bradshaw; Brentford FC and its fans for helping me see how the beautiful game is like war but so much better; Justin Champion; Janice Cullen; Zsolt Czigányik; José Maria Perez Fernandez; Justyna Galant; Diletta Gari; Sam Hirst; Anna Hont; Thomas Horan; Jessie Hronesova; Mark Jendrysik; Marta Komsta; Tom Moylan; Duncan Kelly; Andrew Milner; the Museum for the Political History of Russia, St Petersburg; Patrick Parrinder; Mark Preslar; Emine Şentürk; James Somper; Sandy Stelts at Penn State University Library; Henry Tam; Fátima Vieira; Luisa Hodgkinson and the interlibrary loan team at Royal Holloway, University of London; the London Library; the British Library; and the Orwell Archive, University College London, especially Mandy Wise. In Cambodia I am particularly grateful to the staff of the Documentation Center of Cambodia (DC-Cam), including its director, Youk Chhang, and Deputy Director, Eng Kok-Thay, and Dalin Lorn; and at the Tuol Sleng Genocide Museum, Keo Lundi. Parts of the argument have been presented at conferences or seminars at Budapest, Cambridge, Durham, Granada, Grand Forks, Krakow, Lisbon, London, Montreal, Newcastle, Oxford, Pittsburgh, Prague, Sewanee, the European University, St Petersburg, São Paulo, the University of Sussex, and Timişoara. I am grateful to audiences for their feedback, and especially to members of the Utopian Studies Society (Europe) and the Society for Utopian Studies (North America). The support of the Leverhulme Trust was indispensable. I am thankful to the Salem Press for permission to reprint passages from 'Huxley and Bolshevism', in M. Keith Booker, ed., *Aldous Huxley's Brave New World: New Critical Essays* (Salem Press, 2014), pp. 91–107. At Oxford University Press I am grateful to Cathryn Steele and Hollie Thomas. Elizabeth Stone was an astute and helpful copy-editor. As always, my wife and family have been supportive and endlessly patient. Finally, thanks to Christopher Duggan, whose life was cut short tragically before the book was finished, for twenty years of friendship and encouragement.

Table of Contents

List of Illustrations

PART I

THE THEORY AND
PRE-HISTORY OF DYSTOPIA

1

Rethinking the Political Dystopia

The Group and the Crowd

We do not believe, we are afraid.
(Eskimo shaman)[1]

[F]ear, my good friends, fear is the very basis and foundation of modern life. Fear of the much touted technology which, while it raises our standard of living, increases the probability of our violently dying. Fear of the science which takes away with one hand even more than what it so profusely gives with the other. Fear of the demonstrably fatal institutions for which, in our suicidal loyalty, we are ready to kill and die. Fear of the Great Men whom we have raised, by popular acclaim, to a power which they use, inevitably, to murder and enslave us. Fear of the War we don't want and yet do everything we can to bring about.
(Aldous Huxley, *Ape and Essence*, 1949)

Hell is other people.
(Jean-Paul Sartre, *No Exit*, 1944)

INTRODUCTION: RETHINKING DYSTOPIA

The word 'dystopia' evokes disturbing images. We recall ancient myths of the Flood, that universal inundation induced by Divine wrath, and of the Apocalypse of Judgement Day. We see landscapes defined by ruin, death, destruction. We see swollen corpses, derelict buildings, submerged monuments, decaying cities, wastelands, the rubble of collapsed civilizations. We see cataclysm, war, lawlessness, disorder, pain, and suffering. Mountains of uncollected rubbish tower over abandoned cars. Flies buzz over animal carcases. Useless banknotes flutter in the wind. Our symbols of species power stand starkly useless: decay is universal.

Or: we see miles of barbed wire broken by guard towers topped with machine guns and searchlights; the deathstrips and minefields; the snarling guard dogs; the eyes of the haunted gaunt faces of the skeletal half-dead staring out of deep sockets aghast at their ill-deserved fate; corpses piled up like logs, grimacing skulls frozen in the last moment of madness.

---

[1] Quoted in Stephen Wilson, *The Magical Universe: Everyday Ritual and Magic in Pre-Modern Europe* (Hambledon, 2000), p. xvi.

Or: grim streets dominated by giant portraits of the Leader witness lengthy queues for food of weary ill-clad workers as revolutionary announcements of norms exceeded in the production plan blare out from a thousand loudspeakers.

Or: a proliferation of mushroom clouds indicates humanity's end through nuclear war.

Or: roaring planes fly overhead dropping bombs which burst among us, as men in gas masks stride over mangled corpses to stick bayonets into us or incinerate us with flamethrowers.

Or: human society resembles an ant heap in which mammoth cities are dominated by vast teeming slums and immense skyscrapers which are separated by walls from elite compounds guarded by menacing security forces.

Now the black and white newsreels give way to colour: dystopia's is blood-red. Violent explosions interspersed by screams of terror deafen us and rock the earth: this is the sound of dystopia. Burning flesh, cordite, sweat, vomit, urine, excrement, rotting garbage: this is the stench of dystopia. But what really reeks is stark naked barbarism: the perfumed scents of civility are but a distant memory. We have reverted to savagery, animality, monstrosity. And then, perhaps mercifully, the end comes.

* * * *

Visions of the apocalypse are at least as old as 1000 BC, when, in Norman Cohn's rendering, the triumph of chaos over order defined the Egyptian 'Prophecies of Neferti', which foretold of the complete breakdown of society. The 'great no longer rule the land', the 'slaves will be exalted'. Crime, robbery, and murder are rampant. The desert encroaches. The Nile turns blood-red by the corpses floating in it.[2] The Greek term, *apokalypsis*, unveiling or uncovering, indicates the revelation of mankind's destiny.[3] Many variations on it come down to us through the ages. Once they were the preserve of millennialists who heralded the final punishment of sin and the dawning of a new Divine era. Now such nightmarish scenarios occupy an increasingly prominent position in our vocabulary and our mental world, but without the hopeful outcome promised by theology.

Most of what we associate with 'dystopia' is thus a modern phenomenon, wedded to secular pessimism. The word is derived from two Greek words, *dus* and *topos*, meaning a diseased, bad, faulty, or unfavourable place. It first probably appeared in the mid-eighteenth century, but was not widely used until the twentieth. It has some awkward cousins, like Jeremy Bentham's 'cacotopia', or 'evil place'. In common parlance, the word functions as the opposite of 'utopia', the bad place versus what we imagine to be the good place, the secular version of paradise.

Yet it is readily apparent that such a stark juxtaposition leaves much to be desired. Utopia*nism*, in Lyman Tower Sargent's well-known description, has three 'faces', the

---

[2] Norman Cohn, *Cosmos, Chaos, and the World to Come: The Ancient Roots of Apocalyptic Faith* (Yale University Press, 1993), pp. 19–20; The 'Admonitions of Ipu-Wer', as described in Robert Gnuse, 'Ancient Near Eastern Millennialism', in Catherine Wessinger, ed., *The Oxford Handbook of Millennialism* (Oxford University Press, 2011), pp. 236–7.

[3] Cohn, *Cosmos, Chaos and the World to Come*, p. 163.

literary, communal, and ideological.[4] But we do not normally speak of dystopian*ism*, and we recognize no dystopian ideologies as such. The noun *dystopia* is often used synonymously with dystopian literature. However, as Ruth Levitas points out, 'Dystopias are not necessarily fictional in form; neither predictions of the nuclear winter nor fears of the consequences of the destruction of the rain forests, the holes in the ozone layer, the greenhouse effect and the potential melting of the polar ice caps are primarily the material of fiction.'[5] The adjective *dystopian* implies fearful futures where chaos and ruin prevail. So there are non-literary, empirical usages of the term.

Most commonly, from both literary and historical viewpoints, dystopia is identified with the 'failed utopia' of twentieth-century totalitarianism, treated in Part II.[6] Here it typically means a regime defined by extreme coercion, inequality, imprisonment, and slavery. Often this is described as some concept of collectivism run wild, though some include conformist tendencies in liberal societies which encourage egalitarian repression and intolerance.[7] Many authors, however, simply equate 'totalitarianism' with 'dystopia'. Thus, to Steven Rosefielde, Stalinism was simply an 'infernal dystopia', and dystopia itself, particularly 'the communist dystopia', is defined as: 'The antithesis of Utopia. A hellish state brought about by attempts to construct unrealizable ideal systems.'[8]

This indicates three main, if often interrelated, forms of the concept: the political dystopia; the environmental dystopia; and finally, the technological dystopia, where science and technology ultimately threaten to dominate or destroy humanity. Amongst these types, it is the totalitarian political dystopia which is chiefly associated with the failure of utopian aspirations, and which has received the greatest historical attention. This will accordingly be our chief concern in this book. The other two types will come into sharper focus in Part III.

We can see from the outset, however, that each of these types of dystopia might be understood as independently aligned to ideas of utopia in some way, perhaps in earlier periods, or as running parallel at a number of levels. One modern incarnation of the political dystopia, for instance, might be conceived as originating in part in the same year, 1516, that Thomas More's *Utopia* appeared, when the first 'ghetto' for Jews was created in Venice (the word being derived from an area where waste was stored). The conquest of the New World—adverted to by

---

[4] Lyman Tower Sargent, 'The Three Faces of Utopianism Revisited', *Utopian Studies*, 5 (1994), 1–37.

[5] Ruth Levitas, *The Concept of Utopia* (Syracuse University Press, 1990), p. 195.

[6] Thus Michael Geyer, for instance, writes of the 'utopian' and 'dystopian' dimensions of Nazi ideology (Geyer and Sheila Fitzpatrick, *Beyond Totalitarianism: Stalinism and Nazism Compared* (Cambridge University Press, 2009), p. 36), while Maurice Meissner writes of the 'utopian and dystopian elements' in Maoism: *Marxism, Maoism and Utopianism* (University of Wisconsin Press, 1982), pp. 184–211, and contrasts 'Mao's utopia' to 'Mao's dystopia' (p. 209). Norman M. Naimark writes of Hitler's 'racial dystopia' (*Stalin's Genocides* (Princeton University Press, 2010), p. 5).

[7] An early instance of this trend is noted in David Riesman's *The Lonely Crowd* (Yale University Press, 1950).

[8] Steven Rosefielde, *Red Holocaust* (Routledge, 2010), pp. 14, 246, 257. Here the term is specifically linked to the idea of an 'anti-utopia', and described as first being denominated a dystopia by John Stuart Mill (p. 16). Pol Pot's regime is also described as a 'dystopia' (p. 118), and his methods, indeed, as 'dystopicide', meaning 'the unpremeditated, but nonetheless culpable consequence of blindly trying to "storm heaven"' (p. 119).

More—simultaneously held out the promise of remaking one part of humanity while enslaving another. Or a utopia of opulence and consumption might be understood as generating a dystopia of scarcity and environmental degradation.

But the relation between utopia and dystopia may be more intimate still. Modern readers who peer closely into More's paradigmatic text discover much about which to be alarmed. Like the snake in the Garden of Eden, dystopian elements seem to lurk within Utopia. The country, we are informed, was founded by civilizing its barbarians and then artificially isolating a peninsula by transforming it into a fortified island.[9] Utopia remains an imperial power. When overpopulated it sends out colonies, seizing the uncultivated land of indigenous peoples, and driving out 'any who resist them'.[10] Well-paid mercenaries keep enemies at bay, the Utopians' much-vaunted contempt for gold, silver, and jewels here standing starkly in contrast with the great value their wealth has when expended on slaying their enemies. Utopia's peace and plenitude now seem to rest upon war, empire, and the ruthless suppression of others, or in other words, their dystopia.

Then there is the virtuous society of Utopia itself. Here we discover that suppressing vice requires extraordinary regulation and surveillance. In Utopia there are

> no wine bars, no pubs, no whorehouses. There are no opportunities for wickedness, no hiding places; there is no scope for conspiring in secret. They are always under the observation of their fellow citizens and have no choice but either to work as hard as the next person, or else engage in respectable pastimes.[11]

We cannot travel outside our neighbourhood without passports. We must wear the same plain clothes. We must exchange our houses every ten years. We cannot avoid labour. We all go to bed at the same time (8 p.m.), and never, under penalty of slavery, with someone else's wife or husband. We have religious freedom, but we cannot deny that the soul dies with the body, since 'but for the fear of punishment, they would have nothing but contempt for the laws and customs of society'.[12] In More's time, for much of the population, given the plenty and security on offer, such restraints would not have seemed overly unreasonable. For modern readers, however, Utopia appears to rely upon relentless transparency, the repression of variety, and the curtailment of privacy. Utopia provides security: but at what price? In both its external and internal relations, indeed, it seems perilously dystopian.

Such a conclusion might be fortified by examining selectively the tradition which follows More on these points. This often portrays societies where (in the words of the eighteenth-century French communist Étienne-Gabriel Morelly), 'it would be almost impossible for man to be depraved, or wicked'.[13] This is achieved both through institutions and mores, which underpin the common life.[14] The passions

---

[9] It is commonly described as isolated, 'a lonely island somewhere in the vast expanse of the ocean' (Gerhard Ritter, *The Corrupting Influence of Power* (Tower Bridge Publications, 1952), p. 70): the reverse is the case.

[10] Thomas More, *Utopia*, ed. David Wootton (Hackett Publishing Co., 1999), p. 103.

[11] Ibid., p. 108.   [12] Ibid., p. 147.

[13] Quoted in Frank Manuel, ed., *French Utopias* (Schocken Books, 1971), p. 100.

[14] In Morelly's case, all property aside from that required for daily needs, pleasure, and work was to be public, and all citizens were to be maintained and employed by the public, contributing according to their strength, talents, and age.

are regulated and inequalities of wealth and distinction are minimized. Needs, vanity, and emulation are restrained, often by prizing equality and holding riches in contempt. The desire for public power is curbed. Marriage and sexual intercourse are often controlled: in Tommaso Campanella's *The City of the Sun* (1623), the first great literary utopia after More's, relations are forbidden to men before the age of twenty-one and women before nineteen. Communal child-rearing is normal; for Campanella this commences at age two. Greater simplicity of life, 'living according to nature', is often a result: the desire for simplicity and purity are closely related. People become more alike in appearance, opinion, and outlook than they often have been. Unity, order, and homogeneity thus prevail at the cost of individuality and diversity. This model, as J. C. Davis demonstrates, dominated early modern utopianism.[15] And utopian homogeneity remains a familiar theme well into the twentieth century.

Given these considerations, it is not unreasonable to take as our starting point here the hypothesis that utopia and dystopia evidently share more in common than is often supposed. Indeed, they might be twins, the progeny of the same parents. Insofar as this proves to be the case, my linkage of both here will be uncomfortably close for some readers. Yet we should not mistake this argument for the assertion that *all* utopias are, or tend to produce, dystopias. Those who defend this proposition will find that their association here is not nearly close enough. For we have only to acknowledge the existence of thousands of successful intentional communities in which a cooperative ethos predominates and where harmony without coercion is the rule to set aside such an assertion. Here the individual's submersion in the group is consensual (though this concept is not unproblematic). It results not in enslavement but voluntary submission to group norms. Harmony is achieved without, in the Millian sense, harming others.[16]

Readers whose interest is chiefly literary may not in any case share these anxieties. They will rightly assume that the most common use of 'dystopia' is synonymous with the 'dystopian novel', which portrays an extremely negative or evil fictional state usually dominated by fear. Here George Orwell's great work, *Nineteen Eighty-Four*, remains paradigmatic. This is treated in Part III. But Orwell's presence can be detected throughout this book. One of his chief messages, the value of a dialogue between history and literature, is central to my effort here to synthesize the literary and historical approaches to the concept. Part I also takes up another central Orwellian theme, the threat to individuals posed by groups, in demonstrating the centrality to dystopia of approaches drawn from group psychology, sociology, and the history of religion. These are presented here with a brief overview of the prehistory of the modern dystopia.

* * * *

To place groups at the centre of our analysis as such is to recognize the proximity of some types of utopia to some types of dystopia. Both utopia and dystopia conceive

---

[15] J. C. Davis, *Utopia and the Ideal Society: A Study of English Utopian Writing 1516–1700* (Cambridge University Press, 1981).
[16] On Mill's definition of harm see my *Mill and Paternalism* (Cambridge University Press, 2013).

of ideal harmonious groups which privilege close connections between individuals and the unity and interdependence they exhibit. A key question here is how inclusive or exclusive this exchange of benefits is. Typically, the collectivist dystopia assumes two main forms: the internal, where coercion pervades the privileged main group; and the external, where coercion defines the relationship to outsiders as a means of upholding the main group, who are, however, free of most of the repression inflicted upon outsiders. Stalinism, we will see, typifies the first type, and More's Utopia the second. In both cases, however, equality and plenty are enjoyed by some groups at the expense of others.

The crucial question here is how many are involved on each side. The more universal the system of benefits, the more utopian the society. A glib observer might posit that a utopia was a society surrounded by a wall designed to keep others out, and a dystopia one intended to keep its inhabitants in. Yet it is an abuse of language to propose that societies where 51 per cent of the population live a privileged life by oppressing the other 49 per cent are 'dystopias'. Most societies, on the basis of gender alone, let alone the accumulation of property, would have to be called dystopian as a consequence. Many majorities are willing to sacrifice minorities for their own well-being. But we can certainly see the case for treating some dystopias as utopias of the equal few based upon the oppression of the many.

Another way of approaching this question is to privilege the human relationships at work. How well people get along is a key marker of their anxiety or sense of well-being. We may be at ease with one another in a markedly hierarchical society, secure in our places if prosperity and tolerance prevail. Alternatively, we may be anxious, paranoid, and fearful in an egalitarian society where nonconformity is suppressed. So we might portray the utopia/dystopia relationship in terms of a spectrum of anxiety, with relative peace, friendship, and the absence of fear at one end, matched by anxiety, paranoia, and alienation on the other.

Yet it is not impossible that these extremes still share common features. Both utopias and dystopias normally, though not universally, exhibit a collectivist ethos. People sacrifice their individual interest to the common good. Social solidarity trumps selfish individualism. In the utopian case this 'enhanced sociability', as it is termed here, is voluntary and freely engaged in.[17] It is regarded as an acceptable price to pay for avoiding unrest and extreme inequality. In dystopia, however, these bonds more often appear as what Leszek Kołakowski calls 'compulsory solidarity'. Here they are coerced, and even contingent upon the enslavement of others.[18] This coercion fundamentally erodes all that is truly valuable in solidarity. And yet, to confuse matters further, both types also intermingle in various complex ways.

At its bleakest, then, the collectivist dystopia usually exhibits an extreme ethos of sociability centring on a fervent devotion to the common good, which is, in reality, despotic rather than consensual. In striving constantly to render each sufficiently self-sacrificing, this despotism generates a fear which penetrates deep into the

---

[17] See my 'News from Somewhere: Enhanced Sociability and the Composite Definition of Utopia and Dystopia', *History*, 98 (2013), 145–73.
[18] Leszek Kołakowski. *The Death of Utopia Reconsidered* (Cambridge University Press, 1983), p. 237.

individual personality, and which dominates everyday life, sometimes for decades or longer. It is exacerbated by perceived failures to achieve the norms of self-sacrifice. These processes, in turn, are often linked with dystopia's obsession with enemies, and its determination to eliminate them, or at least neutralize their threat, while simultaneously creating them anew as a means of justifying the power of the regime. This, at least, is the hypothesis with which we can commence.

* * * *

In the twentieth century, such a condition of universalized fear was certainly intensified by the immense destructiveness of overly rapid modernization, or so several prominent examples in Part II—the USSR, China, Cambodia—suggest. But as a psychological state, dystopia may also be conceived to be humanity's starting point. We may view ourselves as a mentally fragile species today. But many of us have far less to fear than our ancestors. This book is subtitled 'a natural history' in part because it is often concerned with the emotional substrata of behaviour, and how the relationship between a few key emotions and the types of society we live in evolves. It suggests that we collectively progress from natural to socially compounded forms of fear. At first all the natural world is populated by threatening gods, monstrous beings, and malevolent spirits; hence our attention in Chapter 2 to monsters, the primordial symbols of evil both without and within. Many of these gradually disappear. Others are reinvented, or rediscovered as inner monstrosity, or replaced in later modernity by fear of the science and technology we have created, of the recreation of our selves in the image of our machines, and of their eventual domination over us. But the fear remains constant, if fluctuating, even if its objects vary.

Anthropology is thus a logical starting point here. Our 'natural', original psychic state is one of constant mental anxiety. A materially defined world is broadly predictable. A magical one is fraught with contingency. At our peril we fail to respect and propitiate the powers which lie in forests, dells, and springs, or to safeguard from evil spirits, by blessings, amulets, and sacrifices, our seed, crops, animals, and houses. In Ernest Crawley's words, 'in the thought of many peoples man's whole environment is more or less full of the agencies or influences of evil'.[19] To Lucien Lévy-Bruhl, 'primitives' attribute causation to the operation of unseen powers.[20] Plants, trees, stones, animals are all conceived as 'endued with mystic attributes' and linked by a single spiritual principle. The differentiation between humans and animals is slight, and many animals are assumed to take human form, and vice versa. Animism, the belief in spirit beings, is pervasive in the early stages of humanity. 'Primitives' have no sense of the 'miraculous' or the 'impossible'. Illnesses, death, and injuries are never 'natural', and are often blamed on witchcraft, or on the displeasure of the dead, who are usually conceived as still living in ethereal form (as they also are in More's Utopia).

---

[19] Ernest Crawley, *The Mystic Rose: A Study of Primitive Marriage and of Primitive Thought in Its Bearing on Marriage* (Watts & Co., 1932), p. 14.
[20] Those whose mental world is dominated by magical assumptions would be more suitable, for this would include Europeans and other 'civilized' peoples until quite recently.

A far wider range of behaviour, Bronisław Malinowski insists, is thus regarded as 'sacred' and 'hedged round with prohibitions and special rules of behaviour' than in later modernity. All of life's great events—birth, adolescence, marriage, death—are ritualized initiations (into and out of groups). Eating, worshipping, marriage, menstruation, sexual intercourse, pregnancy, childbirth, illness, cultivating food, dying, and being buried have usually been surrounded by restrictions and rituals of many kinds.[21] So much of daily life is ritualized that 'the social' and 'the religious' become virtually identical. Thus, the 'savage . . . perpetually lives in a world of mysticism and ritualism'.[22]

Here the power of faith, the wish to keep all this glued together, or 'clean', not tainted by evil, represents an immense emotional investment. Our life is frequently structured around and always contingent on it, for we cannot bear chaos. We are persistently challenged by threats of death, injury, illness, and affliction. Witch doctors are particular sources of terror in most early societies.[23] Anxiety about the purification required to avoid or free oneself from magic spells is ever-present.[24] Many of the Dayaks of Borneo, for instance, appear to live 'in perpetual dread of what we call fate', believing themselves to be 'constantly subjected to malevolent influences'. Most rites are an attempt to neutralize them.[25] The knowledge that one has inadvertently violated taboo has killed many—as if struck dead on the spot.[26] This is not a happy existence. Entire societies may thus serve as dystopian proto-types of paranoia and aggression. The unfortunate Dobu Island people of New Guinea described by Ruth Benedict, poor and with few natural resources, are a study in relentless, ill-tempered hostility. Singular in their obsessive paranoia, fear of witchcraft, and almost complete lack of trust for one another, they are (or were) almost uniformly 'lawless and treacherous'. Recent converts from cannibalism, their aversion to laughter is, or was, notable.[27]

Other Prototypes of Dystopia: Militarized Societies, Slavery, Despotism, Prisons, and Diseased Spaces

Besides the more malevolent types of early society, five other models pertinent to the modern collectivist political dystopia merit mention. The first are highly militarized or war-centred societies, like ancient Sparta. According to its famous

---

[21] Freud's great concern here was in the proximity of taboo prohibitions and neurosis: *Totem and Taboo: Some Points of Agreement between the Mental Lives of Savages and Neurotics* (Routledge & Kegan Paul, 1960), p. 26.

[22] Bronisław Malinowski, *Magic, Science and Religion and Other Essays* (Free Press, 1948), pp. 1, 7.

[23] Lucien Lévy-Bruhl, *How Natives Think* (George Allen & Unwin, 1926), pp. 65, 263–301; Lucien Lévy-Bruhl, *The 'Soul' of the Primitive* (George Allen & Unwin, 1928), pp. 232–60, 254.

[24] Lucien Lévy-Bruhl, *Primitives and the Supernatural* (George Allen & Unwin, 1936), pp. 5, 20–1, 227–65; Lévy-Bruhl, *The 'Soul' of the Primitive*, pp. 15–58.

[25] Lévy-Bruhl, *Primitives and the Supernatural*, p. 21.

[26] As Freud instances: *Totem and Taboo*, p. 21.

[27] Ruth Benedict, *Patterns of Culture* (1934; Routledge & Kegan Paul, 1952), pp. 94–124, here 94, 120. For a revised assessment, see Susanne Kuehling, *Dobu: Ethics of Exchange on a Massim Island, Papua New Guinea* (University of Hawaii Press, 2005).

founder, Lycurgus, Sparta's citizens were nominally equal, dining together, disdaining trade and luxury, gold and silver (like Utopia's inhabitants), and using only iron money. Their raison d'être was conquest, the earliest form of organized sadism. According to Plutarch, 'All their education was directed toward prompt obedience to authority, stout endurance of hardship, and victory or death in battle.'[28] Feeble infants were abandoned to die on the hillsides. Children were raised in common. Young males were given only one cloak a year to wear, slept on beds of rushes, and were taught to steal food. They were also subjected to annual ritual public beatings, and were forbidden to practise inferior trades, cultivation being left to their slaves, the helots. Foreigners were banned from the country. The numbers involved here were remarkably small, perhaps 9,000 citizens with an army of 6,000 in Lycurgus' time.[29] The time frame of Sparta's greatness (fifth–third century BC) was relatively brief. But Spartan equality provided a vital precedent for Plato, More, Harrington, Rousseau, Robespierre, and many other later writers.

A second prototype for the collectivist dystopia is slavery. Like war, slavery has been ubiquitous throughout history. The ancient Chinese, Indians, Babylonians, Assyrians, Persians, Egyptians, Greeks (*c.*15–40 per cent of the population), Romans (30–40 per cent in the early Christian era), and Nordic and Teutonic peoples all had large slave populations. Millions of slaves were created in the Spanish, Portuguese, Dutch, French and British conquest of the 'New World', and almost as quickly killed off. (In the Spanish Americas, for example, as many as half the slaves working the Potosí silver mines died during an average week's work.)[30] Perhaps 20 million Africans—as much as a fifth of the continent's population—were seized to cultivate the southern American Spanish and Portuguese and northern American British colonies, and then the United States prior to the Civil War (when about one-third of the South's population were slaves). East Africa was another active slaving region. In the late nineteenth century, the immense African Congo, where as many as 10 million may have died, was held as a private rubber-plantation slave fiefdom by the Belgian King, Leopold. Here, extreme brutality, beating, and severing hands as punishment were common, as was the taking of hostages to secure rubber supplies. Nazi Germany and the USSR under Stalin, as well as several other modern regimes, can be described as slave states, even as consciously reintroducing the principle.[31] 'State slavery' has thus been seen as 'one of the characteristic features of 20th-century totalitarianism'.[32]

Thirdly, political despotisms, a lamentably common form of regime, are key antecedents for totalitarian dictatorship. Their governing principle is usually described as fear or terror.[33] Aristotle first proposed the juxtaposition of regimes based

---

[28] Plutarch, *Moralia* (15 vols, William Heinemann, 1968), vol. 3, p. 237.
[29] W. G. Forrest, *A History of Sparta 950–152 BC* (Hutchinson, 1968), p. 45.
[30] Sheldon Watts, *Epidemics and History: Disease, Power and Imperialism* (Yale University Press, 1997), p. 91.
[31] Eugene Victor Walter, *Terror and Resistance: A Study of Political Violence* (Oxford University Press, 1969), p. 5.
[32] Jules Monnerot, *Sociology of Communism* (George Allen & Unwin, 1953), p. 13.
[33] See Corey Robin, *Fear: The History of a Political Idea* (Oxford University Press, 2004), pp. 27–160.

on friendship to those rooted in fear and estrangement which we will adopt here. He recognizes that 'in tyranny there is little or no friendship', and that despotism involved inverting friendship and adopting 'every means for making every subject as much a stranger as possible to every other'.[34] In the early modern period, Machiavelli advised princes that it was better to be feared than loved. Hobbes described the use of fear as an instrument of control as well as of social bonding. He also viewed the state of nature—here another dystopian model—as one of 'continual fear and danger of violent death', which vindicated the necessity of despotism to keep the peace.[35] Bodin believed the threat of violence underlay the masses' subservience to the privileged.[36] Montesquieu was the first prominent eighteenth-century theorist to define terror as the ruling principle of despotism.[37] In the later nineteenth century, Herbert Spencer would conclude that fear of the living was the root of all political control, and fear of the dead of all religious control.[38]

Classical despotism was the rule of a single tyrant. The prototype of modern despotism, we will see in Chapter 3, came when, under the 'Terror' of Robespierre and Saint-Just in 1793–4, the word 'terror' came to be understood as embodying a legitimate instrument of the defence of the general will or popular sovereignty, of the many rather than the few. The terror of 'the people' came quickly to be seen as more all-encompassing and psychologically demanding than that of the single autocrat. But it is also much more justifiable, resistance to the vast majority seeming more perverse, unreasonable, and insulting than resistance to a tyrant. Many would thus associate 'popular' terror with totalitarianism. But a soft form of an analogous pressure to conform seemed also to emerge naturally in democracies. Alexis de Tocqueville in *Democracy in America* (1836–40) thus saw the mass of individuals in a democracy as succumbing to a 'tyranny of the majority' in matters of opinion in particular.[39] John Stuart Mill agreed that, 'even in what people do for pleasure, conformity is the first thing thought of; they like in crowds'.[40] Here it was not the threat of punishment by the state but rather a constant but moderate anxiety, mostly respecting the disapproving opinions of others, which provided a social rudder. The extreme and moderate forms of fear thus oscillate across the modern period. More recently, we seem to be swinging back in the former direction; Joanna Bourke claims that fear has become 'the emotion through which public life is administered'.[41] The language of the 'War on Terror' constantly brings this message home to us.

---

[34] Aristotle, *Nicomachean Ethics*, 1161b; Robert Conquest, *Reflections on a Ravaged Century* (John Murray, 1999), p. 82.
[35] Thomas Hobbes, *Leviathan* (1651), pt 1, chs 10, 13.
[36] Arno J. Mayer, *The Furies: Violence and Terror in the French and Russian Revolutions* (Princeton University Press, 2000), p. 99.
[37] Baron de Montesquieu, *The Spirit of the Laws* (Hafner Publishing Co., 1949), p. 81.
[38] Herbert Spencer, *Principles of Sociology* (3 vols, D. Appleton & Co., 1905), vol. 1, p. 437.
[39] Alexis de Tocqueville, *Democracy in America* (2 vols, Longmans, Green & Co., 1875), vol. 1, pp. 262–5.
[40] John Stuart Mill, *On Liberty* (1859; 3rd edn, Longman, Green, Longman, Roberts & Green, 1864), p. 110.
[41] Joanna Bourke, *Fear: A Cultural History* (Virago, 2005), p. x.

Fourthly, prisons often feature in the popular association of dystopia with torture, forced labour, and the death camp. Auschwitz is its most singular embodiment. The ghetto is its antechamber. British camps in South Africa during the Boer War and German camps in South-West Africa during the Herero extermination mark the birth of these incarceration systems. But within societies, armies, military academies, and some schools and religious bodies are run along similar lines. In Erving Goffman's phrase, prisons and mental asylums, which often resemble one another, are 'total institutions' whose inmates lead a 'formally administered' life. Uniformity, depersonalization, group discipline, and the sublimation or loss of identity usually define such organizations. Their 'totalizing' character is indicated by the barriers which prevent departure and intercourse with the outside world, and the nearly complete surveillance of the population, whose lives are wholly structured by their governors.[42]

Michel Foucault suggested that the enlargement of such ideals to comprise the nation-state increasingly resembling a prison and aiming at universal behavioural reform coincides with the emergence of a 'political utopia' of supervision and punishment. His analysis focused upon Jeremy Bentham's Panopticon proposals, though Bentham's National Charity Company scheme, which would have involved draconian treatment of half a million poor, was harsher. Foucault writes of the early nineteenth-century emergence of the 'Utopia of a universally and publicly punitive society in which ceaselessly active penal mechanisms would function without delay, mediation or uncertainty; one law, doubly ideal because perfect in its calculations and engraven on the minds of each citizen would stop, at their very origin, all practices of illegality.'[43] The resemblance of such a system of control to Utopia is clearly more than merely superficial. Its success is bound up with the development of the modern state, the idea of sovereignty, the mutation of ideas of *lèse-majesté* into *lèse peuple*, and the extension and magnification of both individual and collective guilt. Yet the prison is of course not the death camp. Punishment precedes reform, and is not merely intended as the prelude to murder. Torture is incidental rather than programmatic. The prison may imply what we will here term *carcerotopia*, or the prison state. But it usually falls well short of achieving it.

Fifthly, the rigid ostracism of diseased populations from healthy offers another dystopian prototype. Lepers were amongst the first so confined. In ancient Egypt, some eighty thousand were detained in 'Avaris', the City of Mud.[44] European regulations stipulating the clothing to be worn by lepers, and removing their property and rights, date from as early as 1000. Sometimes lepers were subjected to a ceremony in which their heads were sprinkled with earth to signify that they were dead to the world. They were then either isolated or driven into the wild. From *c.*1090 to the mid-fourteenth century, such efforts focused in Europe on the

---

[42] Erving Goffman, *Asylums: Essays on the Social Situation of Mental Patients and Other Inmates* (Doubleday & Co., 1961), p. xiii.
[43] Michel Foucault, *Discipline and Punish: The Birth of the Prison* (Penguin Books, 1979), pp. 174, 273.
[44] Percy Burgess, *Born of Those Years: An Autobiography* (J. M. Dent, 1952), p. 32.

'Great Hunt' for lepers. It then shifted, as we will see in Chapter 2, to Jews, heretics, and witches.[45]

These categories of the excluded were thus interwoven and overlapping. Monks and priests condemned for sorcery were made to wear a peaked Jew's hat or a yellow Jew's badge in some locations to cement the association.[46] The excluded were also subject to a key but fluctuating sociobiological discourse on 'disease'. In 1321, for instance, lepers were rumoured to be poisoning wells in league with Jews, and aiming to kill all Christians.[47] Jews were also often associated with plague.[48] By the fifteenth century, Jews had also become widely associated with witchcraft. However, resentment of their commercial success and wealth was often a factor too.

Fear of groups we see as threatening wavers with fluctuations in majority sentiment across time. A history of collective anxiety is a subset of mankind's emotional history. If 'collective neurosis', in Michael Barkun's estimation, is too strong a term to define a constant state, 'ages of anxiety' nonetheless clearly exist when stress and paranoia come to the boil.[49] Dystopia is thus intimately interwoven with discourses about 'crisis'. In the medieval and early modern eras, worries about plague, fire, witches, war, and heresy tend to predominate. Then there are apparently two cycles of deeper fear—'apparently' because the greater documentation available skews the evidence. The first coincides with the Reformation, the erosion of feudalism, the emergence of the nation-state, prolonged warfare, and growing inequality and urbanization.[50] The breakdown of the medieval order from *c.*1400 to 1650 witnessed the decline of the Church's authority and feudal hierarchy. The drift of population from countryside to cities coincided with various epidemics and crop failures. These underpinned much of the substantial unrest of this period, including the witch-hunting mania. From the fourteenth through to the eighteenth centuries, it has been asserted, 'fear was all-pervasive and omnipresent within society', with Europeans experiencing 'unprecedented levels of anxiety and pessimism'.[51] (Much of the world was, of course, being conquered by Europeans in this period, producing a substantial export market for this anxiety.)

In the early nineteenth century, the Malthusian spectre of overpopulation then came to haunt debates about social progress. Increasingly sharp anxieties about international economic competition were shaped by the new language of political

[45] Watts, *Epidemics and History*, p. 49.

[46] Joshua Trachtenberg, *The Devil and the Jews: The Medieval Conception of the Jew and Its Relation to Modern Antisemitism* (Yale University Press, 1943), p. 67. In 1215, the Fourth Lateral Council ordered Jews and Muslims to wear distinctive clothing. Prostitutes were forced to wear a red cord, and a few years later repentant heretics were made to wear two yellow crosses. Some accused of witchcraft bore similar symbols.

[47] Robert Michael, *Holy Hatred: Christianity, Antisemitism, and the Holocaust* (Palgrave Macmillan, 2006), p. 79.

[48] Susan Sontag, *Illness as Metaphor* (Penguin Books, 1987), p. 74.

[49] Michael Barkun, *Disaster and the Millennium* (Yale University Press, 1974), p. 147.

[50] The connection between utopianism and the origins of nationalism is explored in Phillip E. Wegner, *Imaginary Communities: Utopia, the Nation, and the Spatial Histories of Modernity* (University of California Press, 2002), pp. 45–61.

[51] Penny Roberts and William G. Naphy, 'Introduction', in Naphy and Roberts, eds., *Fear in Early Modern Society* (Manchester University Press, 1997), p. 1.

economy and its productivist emphasis on utility, output, and efficiency. From the 1870s, Social Darwinism redefined this language of competition by suggesting the inevitability of the 'survival of the fittest', an ideal which would suffuse both twentieth-century fascism and communism. Nationalism and imperial rivalry helped to intensify these feelings of antagonism. The first of these, in particular, formed a new type of large-group identity to help compensate for the unsettling process of modernization and breakdown of traditional order. Allied with two newly minted concepts, race and class, these provided the potential for deep antagonism. Urbanization and rapid technical innovation also proved very unsettling. World War I then demonstrated that, just as science and technology provided humanity's greatest triumphs, its collective angst ironically also reached a crescendo.

Holy Terror: Religion and the Uses of Guilt

If the history of fear tells us something about how dystopia functions, that of guilt is equally important as a component in any natural history of the painful emotions. To Søren Kierkegaard, the prototype of Western 'dread' was the Christian doctrine of Original Sin.[52] To believers, it describes an inescapable condition which is the inherited fate of all humanity: this life is but a painful preparation for the better world to come. To non-believers and Pelagians (Christians who deny the concept) it is merely a metaphor for explaining evil.

Sexuality, of course, looms large in the story of Western guilt, and remains entangled with it, through the witch persecution craze in particular right through the totalitarian epoch. Although, in the Christian creation myth, eating the fruit of the Tree of Knowledge provided the pretext for Adam and Eve's expulsion from Paradise, it was sexual desire which came subsequently to be seen as the great obstacle to salvation. Either way, sex was linked to disobeying God and seen as detracting from our devotion to him—an association we will revisit in Stalinism. This was earliest expressed most forcefully by Augustine (354–430), who renounced his own youthful libertinism with a vengeance which still echoes down the ages. The battle for complete sexual renunciation in Christianity commenced as early as AD 40–50, and was in some instances linked to millenarian preparation.[53] The result was a cult of purity that exalted virginity, most notably in the idea of the virgin birth of Christ and the cult of the Virgin Mary. Lust came to be seen as a loathsome expression of human weakness, and the very epitome of sin. In men, the 'loss' of semen came to be seen as degenerative, even indicating the diminution of one's soul. Luther, amongst others, would vindicate marital intercourse as an essentially harmless sin. But most Christians who equated sin with lust were driven towards a contempt for the body and an abiding fear of desire as such.[54]

---

[52] S. Kierkegaard, *The Concept of Dread* (Princeton University Press, 1957), pp. 23–46.

[53] Peter Brown, *The Body and Society: Men, Women and Sexual Renunciation in Early Christianity* (Faber & Faber, 1989), pp. 33–40.

[54] Jean Delumeau, *Sin and Fear: The Emergence of a Western Guilt Culture 13th–18th Centuries* (St. Martin's Press, 1990), p. 1. Bossuet believed that Jesus never laughed (p. 296).

So desire was restrained as far as possible. The need to procreate was hemmed in by restrictions. The times and ways were highly regulated. Intercourse was prohibited entirely on Christian feast days, when it was probably most likely to occur. There were 273 of these in the seventh century, reduced to 140 in the sixteenth. (Some thirty days a year were complete holidays, besides Sundays.) The positions permitted were limited, some authors insisting that only one was sinless. The fifteenth-century writer Osimo deemed even marital intercourse sinful unless no pleasure was involved. The Church decreed that some clothing be retained for decorum's sake, and that intercourse take place only at night. Various penalties were imposed for violating these rules. Intercourse involving a forbidden position attracted ten days' penance on bread and water, with four days' penance imposed for having sex on a Sunday, with the advice to those who did so that their children would be lepers and epileptics.[55] For those who failed this test, a twelfth-century monk imagined a ladder of iron in Hell, which was 365 cubits high and had to be ascended and descended continuously.[56] Misogyny was doubtless both cause and consequence here. Men were encouraged to hate women for inflaming their own sinful desires. Women were cloaked with shame by the very definition of their gender and Eve's original act of disobedience.

From the thirteenth century to the present, then, the natural history of guilt exhibits a gradual augmentation of the fear of death and an intensification of guilt. Anxiety from without was provided by the plague, Turks, Jews, heretics, witches, and the like. But this was increasingly supplemented by self-inflicted ideological, and essentially masochistic, terror from within. Now, as Jean Delumeau puts it, in addition 'to the "fear", the "dread", the "terror" and the "fright" occasioned by external perils of all kinds (natural or human), Western civilisation was afflicted by two supplementary and equally oppressive causes of alarm: the "horror" of sin and the "obsession" of damnation'. Small wonder that scenes of torture proliferated in medieval painting throughout this period. Led by the iconography of the Crucifixion itself, they were embellished by the many varieties of painful martyrdom of the saints so graphically portrayed and described.[57]

* * * *

The discussion so far indicates that, while retaining many natural fears, we progressively adopt others which are socially formulated. This appears to be at least partially a function of the increasing predominance of groups in our lives. Like all animals, we are individually sensitive to threats in our environment. When individuals feel *en masse*, they express these fears differently, and the numbers involved usually magnify and intensify their feelings. An early observer, Charles Mackay, described this in terms of a 'moral epidemic'.[58] Today it is sometimes

---

[55] Jeffrey Richards, *Sex, Dissidence and Damnation: Minority Groups in the Middle Ages* (Routledge, 1991), pp. 29–30; Brown, *The Body and Society*, p. 439.
[56] Arturo Graf, *The Story of the Devil* (Macmillan & Co., 1931), p. 184.
[57] Delumeau, *Sin and Fear*, pp. 3, 215, 27, 242.
[58] Charles Mackay, *Memoirs of Extraordinary Popular Delusions* (3 vols, Richard Bentley, 1841), vol. 1, p. v.

referred to as mass psychogenic illness. This may reveal itself as group panic when threats become unduly severe, even to the mimicking of physical convulsions.[59] A state of mass hypnotism or suggestion is even more common. Here the concept tends usually to be applied to individuals, as psychology. As social or group psychology, concepts like 'mass psychoneurosis' (Ernest Jones) or 'sociogenic illness' might apply.[60] The thrust of the idea is that peoples can go mad, just like individuals, at least temporarily, but are even harder to diagnose and cure, and, of course, to restrain.

Some may, however, gain from such collective derangement. In every social context power relations come into play. So here the social constructions of group fears can be, in the words of David Altheide, relatively easily 'manipulated by those who seek to benefit'.[61] This is particularly the case where enemies exist or are created. Defining 'our enemy', as the Nazi jurist Carl Schmitt notably asserted, is a central part of political life. The state as such is a unit bonded by the hostility of one group to others. What is crucial, however, is not the enemy but the idea of the enemy, the concoction of what inspires hatred.[62] Political fear has been defined as 'a people's felt apprehension of some harm to their collective well-being', typically, in our times, from terrorism, crime, moral decay, nuclear war, or environmental catastrophe.[63] Its manipulation is very well established. Anatoli Rybakov puts into Stalin's mind the idea that 'Hatred of the enemy is the most powerful idea because it creates an atmosphere of general fear.'[64] It was said of Hitler (a teetotaller) that hatred was 'like wine . . . It intoxicated him.'[65] Societies at war naturally generate hate; '*If you don't hate enough, you're going to be beaten*', wrote an observer of the vicious Pacific war in 1945.[66]

Real enemies will do well enough here. Jews, Muslims, blacks, women, foreigners have all played the role. But the best enemy, we will see, is the (mostly) imaginary enemy.[67] Here, hatred, functioning to unite the group, can be more easily manipulated. Wielded properly, however, any such hatred can be therapeutic and cleansing. It can provide intense bonds of fellow feeling, as many studies of combat fraternity affirm. In dystopia, such hatred centres upon group antagonism of the type we have briefly introduced. Yet hatred of the other is interwoven with

---

[59] Hysteria is usually studied only as an individual derangement. See, e.g., Ilza Veith, *Hysteria: The History of a Disease* (University of Chicago Press, 1965). Elaine Showalter defines it as 'a mimetic disorder' which 'mimics culturally permissible expressions of distress' (*Hystories: Hysterical Epidemics and Modern Culture* (Picador, 1977), p. 15).

[60] E.g., Judith Pintar and Steven Jay Lynn, *Hypnosis: A Brief History* (Wiley-Blackwell, 2008); Ernest Jones, *On the Nightmare* (The Hogarth Press, 1931), p. 164; Showalter, *Hystories*, p. 23.

[61] Quoted in Frank Furedi, 'Towards a Sociology of Fear', in Kate Hebblethwaite and Elizabeth McCarthy, eds., *Fear: Essays on the Meaning and Experience of Fear* (Four Courts Press, 2007), p. 21.

[62] Carl Schmitt, *The Concept of the Political* (University of Chicago Press, 1996), pp. 26ff.

[63] Robin, *Fear*, p. 2.   [64] Anatoli Rybakov, *Fear* (Hutchinson, 1993), p. 512.

[65] Quoted in Robert S. Robins and Jerrold M. Post, *Political Paranoia: The Psychopolitics of Hatred* (Yale University Press, 1997), p. 281.

[66] Osmar White, *Green Armour* (George Allen & Unwin, 1945), p. 287. All italics in quotations are in the original, unless otherwise noted.

[67] Irenäus Eibl-Eibesfeldt, *Love and Hate; On the Natural History of Basic Behaviour Patterns* (Methuen & Co., 1971), pp. 101, 161.

love of the group, as we saw hatred of carnal desire was linked to the supposed need to devote oneself wholly to God. This feeling becomes most acute when wedded to paranoia. What is termed persecutory paranoia often involves 'a deep distrust of others and a strong tendency to deny their own hostility and project it onto others'. In politics it is a 'constant feature' which may be expressed in terms of grandiosity, hostility, fear of the loss of autonomy, projection, and delusional thinking.[68] It may occur when a frightened group of people exaggerates the size and strength of its enemies. They thus displace their anxieties onto another group (e.g. Jews or witches) which embodies their fears. Political paranoia has been described as characteristic of the late twentieth century. But as a response to crises it exists in many earlier forms.

GROUP PSYCHOLOGY AND DYSTOPIA

The Group Goes Wild: The Crowd

Collective fears like hatred are usually expressed, experienced, and defined by groups. These are rarely mere assemblages of individuals. They usually have a life, an identity, an organic and even a spiritual existence of their own. They also have their own psychology. Their egos often need massaging. They are by definition narcissistic, fond of self-preening, and readily prey to flattery.

Nonetheless, groups also vary greatly. People assemble for many purposes, amongst them work, play and celebration, ritual worship, and political affirmation. 'Group' is a relatively neutral term that describes such often harmless associations which satisfy our routine demands for sociability, reassurance, and sustenance. 'Mass', 'crowd', and 'mob' are more emotive terms. They imply the more invidious aspects of collective association and identity: fury, violence or lawlessness, irrationality, extreme emotionality, or uncontrolled movement, a proneness to delusion, and a pronounced susceptibility to manipulation by charismatic leaders. In these forms they play a central role in this book: the crowd is one ancestor of the collectivist political dystopia. This section will thus consider the main nineteenth- and twentieth-century theories of the crowd, focusing on Gustave Le Bon, Sigmund Freud, and Norbert Elias, as well as some sociological approaches. We will attempt to differentiate here between how groups function generally, how particularly intolerant and destructive groups arise, and how the mentality of the mass has been conceived to differ from that of individuals. We must then try to measure how close the group is to the crowd in principle, and what this implies for any definition of dystopia.

Le Bon's Crowd: The Savage Returns

We will see that the period of the 'Terror' (1793–4) during the French Revolution is usually regarded as having established one paradigm of modern despotism. The theory of the crowd as political actor, which emerged after the French Revolution,

---

[68] Robins and Post, *Political Paranoia*, pp. 5, 12, 41.

thus has a direct bearing on how we conceive of dystopia. Here, for many later commentators, the crowd often becomes the 'mob', irrational, aggressive, easily manipulated, ever larger and more threatening, and hell-bent on plunder and levelling. The antithesis of 'civilization', it carries along all before it, sweeping aside restraint. (Yevgeny Zamyatin, whose *We* is discussed in Chapter 5, described being 'submerged, awash in the crowd, drunk with it', during the 1905 Revolution: that is how it feels.)[69] It was, effectively, a monster which, once unleashed, could destroy society. Or it might alternately herald its rebirth as a new form of humanity throwing off the shackles of centuries.

The French Revolution commenced in early 1789 with an outbreak of rural panic often termed the 'Great Fear'. Fuelled by harvest failure, rising food prices, and widespread resentment of feudal dues and the privileges of chateaux dwellers, this spontaneous anarchy induced swarms of beggars to sweep through the countryside. Throughout France, Jews were attacked, and forced to cancel debts. Popular suspicion of aristocratic plotting and the arming of urban bourgeois intensified the atmosphere.[70] To hostile observers like Edmund Burke, a revival of medieval sectarian frenzy had unleashed 'cannibal appetites' which threatened civilization itself.[71] The ensuing course of the Revolution led many to associate modern revolutionism with mob fury universalized, if not the reawakening of some 'wild', monstrous, or primitive self. 'Meal-mobs' demanding bread and 'growing into mobs of a still darker quality' are at centre stage in Carlyle's great history of the Revolution.[72] For later nineteenth-century commentators, the image of the threatening, savage crowd bent on mindless (or even worse, vengeful) destruction was further exacerbated by the sanguinary collapse of the Paris Commune of 1871. This fused images of communism, the mob, and political murder. From these events, fuelled also by both Social Darwinism and the 'discovery' of the unconscious, came the first inklings of crowd psychology.

By far the most definitive account of these themes was Gustave Le Bon's *The Crowd: A Study of the Popular Mind* (1896). It produced the 'most influential school of modern crowd psychology', and would remain the starting point for most discussions of the relationship between individual, group, crowd, and mob for much of the next century, especially in relation to totalitarianism.[73] Le Bon defined the elite's fear of the masses and the privileging of rational individuals as central themes. 'The most gigantic' of experiments, the French Revolution, had inaugurated a definitively modern 'era of crowds' where opinions became 'the supreme

[69] Yevgeny Zamyatin, *A Soviet Heretic*, tr. Mirra Ginsberg (Quartet Books, 1991), p. 10.
[70] See Georges Lefebvre, *The Great Fear of 1789: Rural Panic in Revolutionary France* (NLB, 1973), and Clay Ramsay, *The Ideology of the Great Fear: The Soissonais in 1789* (Johns Hopkins University Press, 1992).
[71] Edmund Burke, *The Works of the Right Hon. Edmund Burke* (12 vols, John C. Nimmo, 1899), vol. 3, p. 420.
[72] Thomas Carlyle, *The French Revolution: A History* (2 vols, Chapman & Hall, 1898), vol. 2, p. 225.
[73] Sigmund Neumann, *Permanent Revolution: The Total State in a World at War* (Harper & Brothers, 1942), p. 113; Serge Chakotin, *The Rape of the Masses: The Psychology of Totalitarian Political Propaganda* (George Routledge & Sons, 1940), pp. 34–6.

guiding principle in politics'. Animated by furious resentment, the majority, once passive, submissive, cowering, now awakened, like some sleeping giant, to wreak revenge upon its oppressors. Le Bon assumed that a new set of psychological characteristics now emerged which had 'never been of such moment as at present'. Individuals might be rational and civilized. Crowds were atavistic and primitive. Always 'unconscious', their power was always destructive. The crowd was not merely a large number of individuals. It exemplified a 'collective mind' where the 'sentiments and ideas of all the persons in the gathering take one and the same direction, and their conscious personality vanishes'. It represented species identity in its quasi-original form, and thus humanity at its crudest. A passionate egalitarianism animated crowds possessed by 'nothing less than a determination to utterly destroy society as it now exists, with a view to making it hark back to that primitive communism which was the normal condition of all human groups before the dawn of civilisation'. Limiting hours of labour, nationalizing mines, railways, factories, and the land, 'the equal distribution of all products, the elimination of all the upper classes for the benefit of the popular classes, &c, such are these claims'.[74] The Greek myth of an original equality and pure golden age, remembered in the Roman festival of the Saturnalia, where social roles were reversed and the rich waited on the poor, recalled still again in the medieval Carnival, now became secularized and immanent, and set the agenda of modern politics.

The crowd's definitive mood was ecstasy. Le Bon strikingly delineated the psychological roots of its outlook and the dynamics underlying its momentum and trajectory. Its pulsating psyche he thought resembled a collective hallucination, fed and directed by imitation, suggestibility, or 'mental contagion'. (Think of how laughter or yawning spreads.) These processes were seemingly governed by 'the *psychological law of the mental unity of crowds*'. The 'collective mind' weakened the individual's judgement, suspending the verdicts of conscience, and encouraging a 'sentiment of invincible power which allows him to yield to instincts which, had he been alone, he would perforce have kept under restraint'. Contagion transmitted such qualities through a process akin to hypnosis or sleepwalking. By suggestibility 'an individual may be brought into such a condition that, having entirely lost his conscious personality, he obeys all the suggestions of the operator who has deprived him of it, and commits acts in utter contradiction with his character and habits'.[75]

Curiously, thus, a condition of mass disobedience and revolution both produced and required an extraordinary degree of mass submission. But mass hypnotism was also analogous to mass atavism. Individuals lost the sense of their civilized self, becoming 'a barbarian—that is, a creature acting by instinct'. The 'savage,

---

[74] Gustave Le Bon, *The Crowd: A Study of the Popular Mind* (T. Fisher Unwin, 1896), p. xvii. On Le Bon see Louis A. Nye, *The Origins of Crowd Psychology: Gustave Le Bon and the Crisis of Mass Democracy in the Third Republic* (Sage Publications, 1975); Susanna Barrows, *Distorting Mirrors: Visions of the Crowd in Late Nineteenth-Century France* (Yale University Press, 1981); and Jaap van Ginnekin, *Crowds, Psychology and Politics 1871–1899* (Cambridge University Press, 1992).

[75] To Arthur Koestler, we become 'de-personalised', more or less surrendering our independent personalities (*The Ghost in the Machine* (Hutchinson, 1967), p. 248). Some psychologists term this 'de-individuation'.

destructive instincts' emerged as 'the inheritance left dormant in all of us from the primitive ages'. Charismatic leaders also played a role here. Le Bon suggested that those chiefs or leaders who arose in this context tended to be 'morbidly nervous, excitable, half-deranged persons who are bordering on madness'. Individual men in the French Convention might have been 'enlightened citizens of peaceful habits'. United as a crowd, however, they 'did not hesitate to give their adhesion to the most savage proposals, to guillotine individuals most clearly innocent, and, contrary to their interests, to renounce their inviolability and to decimate themselves'.[76]

The main characteristics of crowds were impulsiveness, mobility, irritability, credulity, and suggestibility, a tendency to exaggeration, intolerance, servility in the face of great authority, and a compelling sense of the power of numbers. Crowds imagined in terms of, and were easily rendered subservient to, images, which were quickly transmitted, like a collective hallucination. They were readily swayed by strongly symbolic words like 'liberty'. The more often such terms were repeated, mantra-like, the more ingrained they became on the unconscious. Eventually, as fixed ideas, they no longer needed any connection to reality. The most dangerous qualities latent in mass hypnosis and reversion were thus quasi-religious, the imagination run riot. They included a proneness to intolerant fanaticism, which Le Bon called 'necessary accompaniments of the religious sentiment'.[77]

Here, then, we have the first indications of what we will examine at length in Part II as the 'secular religion' hypothesis respecting totalitarianism. 'The Jacobins of the Reign of Terror', Le Bon proposed, 'were at bottom as religious as the Catholics of the Inquisition, and their cruel ardour proceeded from the same source.' The crowd 'demands a god before everything else'. 'The Reformation, the massacre of Saint Bartholomew, the French religious wars, the Inquisition, the Reign of Terror' were thus 'phenomena of an identical kind, brought about by crowds animated by those religious sentiments which necessarily lead those imbued with them to pitilessly extirpate by fire and sword whoever is opposed to the establishment of the new faith'.[78] Le Bon also addressed the 'criminal crowd'. His focus here was upon the massacre, often with great brutality and torture, of some 1,500 imprisoned aristocrats in Paris in September 1792, and the accompanying deaths of many other 'enemies of the people', including some fifty children aged between twelve and seventeen.[79] He would later come to see socialism as one form of the new religion arising from the ashes of the old, and to warn that 'If a new belief—Socialism, for example—were to triumph to-morrow, it would be led to

---

[76] Le Bon, *The Crowd*, pp. 119, 13.   [77] Ibid., pp. 62ff.   [78] Ibid., p. 69.
[79] The Paris Commune of 1871, for Le Bon, exhibited similar behaviour. He extended this analysis in *The Psychology of Socialism* ((T. Fisher Unwin, 1899) and *The Psychology of Revolution* (T. Fisher Unwin, 1913). In 1921, he also warned of the consequences of offering 'the Hebraic myth of the promised land' to the frustrated masses (*The World in Revolt: A Psychological Study of Our Times* (T. Fisher Unwin, 1921), pp. 162–3).

employ methods of propaganda like those of the Inquisition and the Terror.'[80] Both Hitler and Mussolini were influenced by his views.[81]

Amongst Le Bon's contemporaries, those concerned with the criminal mentality, such as Enrico Ferri, author of *The Criminal Crowd*, pursued parallel themes. To the criminologist Scipio Sighele, the crowd was the basic form of social group, whose psychological principles extended from very temporary unions to the state, and included the sect, which was distinguished by its choice of members.[82] Another Italian, Pasquale Rossi, described the evolution of groups in an ascending process of progressive stability and differentiation.[83]

Another notable contribution was the French social theorist Gabriel Tarde's *L'Opinion et la Foule* (1901). This described a new science of social psychology emerging from the study of group behaviour. Here Le Bon was criticized for not separating this adequately from crowd psychology.[84] Tarde thus used 'public' more neutrally than 'crowd', defining it 'as a purely spiritual collectivity, a dispersion of individuals who are physically separated and whose cohesion is entirely mental'. This public only arose after the invention of printing, and had to be distinguished from earlier 'fairs, pilgrimages, tumultuous multitudes dominated by pious or belligerent emotions, angers or panics'. Distant from one another, individuals could nonetheless form groups by reading about the same phenomena. One specific quality here was 'the mutual contagion of sentiments among the assembled individuals'. This, for example, explained its greater patience or impatience contrasted to individuals. Tarde classified crowds into expectant, attentive, demonstrating, and active. Attentive crowds, exhibiting a kind of group narcissism, were often fascinated by their own gathering: 'the crowd itself... serves as its own spectacle. The crowd draws and admires the crowd.' Demonstrating crowds were easily animated by crude symbols and slogans endlessly repeated. Mere assemblages of people were to be distinguished from groups animated by a common goal or faith. The nascent public, moreover, was essentially still 'a church apart' united by mass reading of the Bible, until the further inventions of the railway and telegraph created a modern literary and political public.[85]

Here, clearly, there may be a relationship between the sense of 'spiritual collectivity' created by the close proximity of one type of crowd and the wider communal identity of even a nation. The former may be deliberately wedded to the latter in various ways, notably when the crowd is oriented around nationalistic ideals. Hence, Tarde writes of 'nations dominated by the spirit of crowds', which exuded intolerance in particular. Now defined largely by newspapers, 'publics' emerged

[80] Le Bon, *The Psychology of Revolution*, pp. 26, 213–15; Le Bon, *The Psychology of Socialism*, pp. ix–x.
[81] George L. Mosse, *The Nationalization of the Masses: Political Symbolism and Mass Movements in Germany from the Napoleonic Wars through the Third Reich* (Howard Fertig, 1975), p. 12.
[82] See Scipio Sighele, *La Fou Criminelle. Essai de Psychologie Collective* (Félix Alcan, 1901).
[83] See Robert E. Park, *The Crowd and the Public and Other Essays* (University of Chicago Press, 1972), pp. 13–14.
[84] Barrows, *Distorting Mirrors*, p. 183.
[85] Gabriel Tarde, *On Communication and Social Influence* (University of Chicago Press, 2010), pp. 277–9.

from groups because of 'an increasing need for sociability, which necessitates the regular communication of the associates by a continual current of common information and enthusiasm'.[86] This line of thought would later be taken up by Jürgen Habermas and others. The assumption that a 'yellow' press could level and manipulate popular consciousness, so dominant in our own time, however, was already present.

At this time, the psychology of hypnosis was also developed to explain mass group behaviour. Writing in 1898, Boris Sidis concluded of the relation of hypnotism to the unconscious, that: 'Man is a social animal, no doubt, but *he is social because he is suggestible....* Blind obedience is a social virtue. But blind obedience is the very essence of suggestibility, the constitution of the disaggregated sub-waking self.' The 'social gregarious self' was thus identical to 'the suggestible unconscious self': to be sociable was, as such, to be receptive to others. Mimeticism, the desire to be like others, is essential to social experience. Its effects were easily magnified. Mental 'epidemics' were consequently more 'normal' than pathological. Society and such epidemics were in fact 'two sides of the same coin'. (The Jekyll and Hyde of group and individual selves coexist permanently, albeit in a constant state of tension and mutual resentment.) The medieval world suddenly becomes familiar to us: it is only our own prehistory. We might easily step back into it. The Crusades, the French Revolution, demonophobia, witch-hunts, dancing manias, all become incidents of 'social suggestibility', or 'individual hypnotization written large'.[87]

The line between religion and politics now becomes blurred in an undifferentiated group mentality. Suggestion is 'intrusion into the mind of an idea; met with more or less opposition by the person; accepted uncritically at last; and realized unreflectively, almost automatically'. Suggestibility is not confined to the hypnotic or hysterical states, but is 'normal'. Its objects are most powerfully realized by repetition, and by making the last impression wherever possible (something often verified in studies of the impact of TV commercials on voting behaviour). 'Social suggestibility' explained financial panics, stampedes, and revivalist 'mental epidemics', where jumping, shrieking, rolling about, or talking in tongues occur. Demonomania, believing oneself possessed by a demon, is described as a special form of paranoia, 'the decomposition of personality ... the formation of new personalities within the depths of the subconscious'. In all these, 'the gregarious, the subpersonal, uncritical self, the mob self, and the suggestible subconscious self' were 'identical'.[88] There is little sense here of a categorical typology of different groups. Sidis distinguished between the suggestibility of the crowd and that of the mob. Yet so little distance seemingly remains between 'normal' and 'abnormal' states, the conscious or waking and the un- or subconscious or 'subwaking' self, that we rightly wonder whether a more rational concept of 'normality' still has any purchase.

---

[86] Ibid., pp. 279–92 (from *L'Opinion et La Foule*, 1901).
[87] Boris Sidis, *The Psychology of Suggestion: A Research into the Subconscious Nature of Man and Society* (D. Appleton & Co., 1924), pp. 15–16, 283, 310–11, 326–7.
[88] Ibid., pp. 297–364.

Later psychologists pushed this narrative in various directions. In the early twentieth century, Robert Park developed Le Bon's account of the crowd's emotionality, baseness, irrationality, suggestibility, and lack of critical capacity. Park saw the 'sect, religious or political' as 'a perpetuation and permanent form of the orgiastic (ecstatic) or expressive crowd'. To him, 'all great mass movements tend to display, to a greater or less extent, the characteristics that Le Bon attributes to crowds'.[89] In *Instincts of the Herd in Peace and War* (1916), Wilfred Trotter discussed a primary instinct towards 'gregariousness' which made individuals feel 'incomplete' when separated too far from the herd. It produced altruism as well as other qualities. Trotter rejected the negative connotations of 'suggestibility', though Freud took him to task for downplaying the role played by leaders.[90] Carl Jung contributed ideas of unconscious archetypes present from the primitive period which might explain various forms of aggression.[91] With a nod to Le Bon and Tarde, Graham Wallas' *Human Nature in Politics* (1908) insisted that the persistence of irrationality in public life had been insufficiently explored. Conceding that 'Political emotions are sometimes pathologically intensified when experienced simultaneously by large numbers of human beings in physical association', he went on to define the 'empirical art of politics' as consisting 'largely in the creation of opinion by the deliberate exploitation of subconscious non-rational inference'. He also forecast that 'The future of international politics largely depends on the question whether we have a specific instinct of hatred for human beings of a different racial type from ourselves.' (He thought we probably did not, but that 'general instincts modified by association' could account for the phenomenon.)[92]

Modern social psychology dates from William McDougall's *The Group Mind* (1920). Here, groups are the most elementary forms of collective association.[93] McDougall thought the greater the degree of 'mental homogeneity' or shared identity or interest the group possessed, the more likely it was that a 'group mind' would emerge. The intensification of emotions was particularly notable here, as was the concomitant pleasure of the loss of self and individuality in group identity. Leaders exercised a kind of telepathy over the group.[94] The group's apparent omnipotence empowered the individual merged within it. It also permitted blind obedience to acts which might be unthinkable individually, but which the cruder intellectual outlook of the group's mentality sanctioned. The most malevolent exhibitions of these characteristics might be avoided, however, by allowing some higher intellectual functions to be performed by certain group members.

[89] Park, *The Crowd and the Public*, p. xii.
[90] W. Trotter, *Instincts of the Herd in Peace and War* (T. Fisher Unwin, 1916), p. 33; Sigmund Freud, *Group Psychology and the Analysis of the Ego* (Bantam Books, 1960), pp. 64–5.
[91] See Robert Eisler, *Man into Wolf: An Anthropological Interpretation of Sadism, Masochism, and Lycanthropy* (Routledge and Kegan Paul, 1951).
[92] Graham Wallas, *Human Nature in Politics* (Constable & Co., 1919), pp. ix–x, 53.
[93] William McDougall, *The Group Mind: A Sketch of the Principles of Collective Psychology* (Cambridge University Press, 1920). See also F. C. Bartlett, *Psychology and Primitive Culture* (Cambridge University Press, 1923).
[94] McDougall, *The Group Mind*, pp. 28–30.

Freud and Later Group Psychology

Le Bon's 'brilliantly executed picture of the group mind' was crucial to Sigmund Freud's articulation of the parallels between individual and crowd behaviour. The familial form of love relationship which characterized the individual's attitude towards the group, and particularly its father figure, greatly interested Freud.[95] *Group Psychology and the Analysis of the Ego* (1921) often substituted 'group' for Le Bon's 'crowd', with disturbing implications. For the Freudian group is as alarming a beast as the Le Bonian crowd. Freud thought individuals acting as group members regressed to a more primitive, emotional, childlike, and suggestive state.[96] Conscience, or social anxiety, the fear of public opinion, tended to disappear, supplanted by, in Le Bon's phrase, a thirst for obedience.[97] But Freud thought Le Bon had understated the key role played by leaders. These often cast a hypnotic spell over the group, and focused individual identification, both with others and the group.

How far group thought and identity reflected the unconscious, and whether this involved a reversion to a primitive social form, or some mixture of the two, were questions left unanswered. However, the essential malevolence of group association seems undisputed. For Freud, the group permitted the individual to 'throw off the repressions of his unconscious instinctual impulses', allowing the release of 'all that is evil in the human mind'.[98] Led 'almost exclusively by the unconscious', the group was 'impulsive, changeable, and irritable', and felt omnipotent. Its extreme credulousness was exaggerated by a receptiveness to readily transmissible images and to extremism generally. Groups love obedience, which, unlike dissent, reinforces cohesion. They want to be ruled by and to fear their masters. They respect force and are contemptuous of weakness. They thus give free rein to suppressed brutality, cruelty, and destructiveness.[99] A theory of sadomasochistic behaviour emerges easily here. So does a theory of destructive groups in which a controlling masculine father figure results in a love of the leader which is not merely submissive but entices the worst characteristics out of his followers.[100]

In all these features, the group mind behaved in a manner analogous to the primitive mind, exhibiting both infantile and neurotic characteristics. The most primitive form of society, Freud thought, taking up a suggestion of Darwin's, had been composed of a 'horde ruled over despotically by a powerful male'. This was the same figure Nietzsche had anticipated as the Superman of the future. Freud wondered how 'suggestion', 'imitation', or 'contagion' functioned in groups, and regarded suggestibility as 'an irreducible, primitive phenomenon, a fundamental fact in the mental life of man'. He suggested that the libido, conceived as love, an

---

[95] Quoted in Michael Billig, *Social Psychology and Intergroup Relations* (Academic Press, 1976), p. 11.

[96] Subsequent psychology agrees in seeing the infant as lacking a sense of individuality: see W. J. H. Sprott, *Human Groups* (Penguin Books, 1963), p. 23.

[97] On this theme see Erich Fromm, *On Disobedience and Other Essays* (Routledge & Kegan Paul, 1984).

[98] Freud, *Group Psychology*, pp. 76, 9.   [99] Ibid., pp. 13–15.

[100] See, e.g., Christina Wieland, *The Fascist State of Mind and the Manufacturing of Masculinity* (Routledge, 2015), esp. pp. 109–26.

intense emotional tie, rather than any 'herd instinct', might be 'the essence of the group mind'. Two instances seemingly demonstrated this, the Church and the Army. In both, father figures united the group and focused its love, also reflecting it back to members of the group. When the group disintegrated, however, panic occurred and 'a giant and senseless fear' was 'set free'. Freud did not link this to a pathological state of paranoia or of collective neurosis. But, like Le Bon, he thought that a 'socialistic tie' which succeeded existing religions might produce 'the same intolerance as in the age of the Wars of Religion'.[101]

Freud developed these themes in several later works. In *The Future of an Illusion* (1928), the 'illusion' being religion, the crowd reveals the primitive 'memory traces of earlier generations', the instincts lurking beneath the thin veneer of everyday 'civilised' life. The group (or crowd?) was again demonized—literally, in the sense that it evoked monstrous behaviour. Individuals might be refined and cultivated. In crowds, they quickly reverted to the primitive type. This was analogous to the relationship between the restraining Superego and the wilful Id, with the Ego mediating between the two. Crowd feeling and group identity also had religious dimensions. Freud thought a secular faith might emulate the imaginary father figure in earlier religions. The rescue fantasy of a Messiah returning to restore a golden age of purity and innocence might also be replayed. Expelling religion from European thought could be accomplished only 'by means of another system of doctrines [which] would from the outset take over all the psychological character-istics of religion—the same sanctity, rigidity and intolerance, the same prohibition of thought—for its own defence'. But Freud also clearly hoped that such non-religious illusions might be corrected, as the phase of infantile obsessional neurosis was eventually superseded.[102] In *Civilization and Its Discontents* (1929), he posited that a 'primary' ego-feeling coexisted in many people with a later, more individu-ated ego, 'like a kind of counterpart to it'. The former 'much more inclusive, indeed . . . all-embracing' feeling, he thought paralleled the 'oceanic' sense of the infinite, which Romain Rolland thought the root of all religious sentiment.[103]

* * * *

This entire trend of thought demonized the crowd, rendering or recalling it as atavistic if not monstrous, and, even more threateningly, transferring some of its attributes to groups in general. It also elevated an ideal of rational individual conscience, behaviour, and restraint to a peak of moral and epistemological primacy. The crowd, especially when panicked, assumes certain qualities which are latent or repressed in individuals, such as emotional intensity, infantilism, the suspension of critical faculties, and a diminished sense of responsibility, the 'primitive', in a word. Collective action draws these out. At one level, therefore, the crowd becomes the individual's uninhibited emotional psyche writ large. I may be able to, or feel compelled to, repress my feelings and contain any anxieties. The crowd invites their

[101] Ibid., pp. 69–71, 21, 27, 31, 36, 39.
[102] Sigmund Freud, *The Future of an Illusion* (Anchor Books, 1964), pp. 49, 84, 71.
[103] Sigmund Freud, *Civilization and Its Discontents* (W. W. Norton, 1961), p. 15.

release, relieving these pressures. Alone, I am reasonable; in the crowd, I am emotional. Why should I not love the crowd, since it removes this stress of individuality? The crowd becomes our alter ego, our uninhibited self, releasing our subliminal repressed passions, including the Id's supreme fantasy of unrelenting desire and power. A veritable gift from Heaven, it may induce exuberant pleasure. But it may also work negatively. If we are alarmed and distressed, merging in a crowd which mirrors our mentality may contagiously magnify each individual's worries a thousandfold.

So crowds are not deviant as such, for they may magnify pleasure as well as alarm. For Sighele, however, criminality and delinquency were the starting point for describing the lawless crowd's behaviour. These qualities might be invariably atavistic in the sense of returning us to the instinctive and unrepressed. If they are the Id unleashed, so to speak, we see how easily we can construct affiliations between the crowd, the criminal, and the primitive. To Sighele and Tarde, the collectivity, even when acting as jury or committee, invariably produced results inferior to the individual's from a moral and intellectual standpoint. Here, the group as such was regressive, pulling all down to the lowest common denominator. To Sidis, however, this was essentially a physiological process like hypnosis. The idea that reason somehow slumbers during this process, and is suspended temporarily by the power of suggestion, indicates clear parallels between individual hypnosis and crowd behaviour.[104]

The crowd, in this account, doubtless has a specific history, which is driven by urbanization and population growth in particular, though this process needs to be clearly delineated. Where specific crowds exhibit the qualities of the general type, as in the Colosseum of ancient Rome, or large armies in earlier times, modern crowds seemingly now come to define society as such. 'Mass society' *is* modernity, a process beginning in earnest in the mid-nineteenth century and intensifying through the present. Driven by the feeling of equality, and a religiosity associated with the original myth of equality and its notional prospect of return, its mentality is highly prone to contagion and susceptibility. It is fuelled by technological developments, and especially mass communications like social media, which magnify its leading features, and, most prominently, the sense of the group's strength. The larger the crowd, the more powerful the sense of equality and, equally, of loss of self, of release of anxiety, of the abrogation of responsibility, and of the feeling of immortality in the life of the species group.

While Nietzsche and his followers foreshadowed this trend, in the twentieth century a positive antagonism to the crowd as mass group was perhaps best expressed in José Ortega y Gasset's *The Revolt of the Masses* (1930). This lamented the 'accession of the masses to complete social power' and the loss of those qualities associated with 'nobility'. Both are assumed to underpin the great crises facing modern civilization. To Gasset, this was partly a function of growing numbers: the more densely packed the mass, the more organic and species-like its behaviour.

---

[104] Sidis, *The Psychology of Suggestion*.

Allied to numbers and density was the levelling which revolutionism produced, and the inflated sense of self-worth which constant flattery of the mob induced. The masses were unthinking, unreflective, vainly prone to think themselves perfect, and apt to violence. Syndicalism, Bolshevism, and fascism were their natural expression. Force alone commands respect: this is the revenge of barbarism. War is glorified as the testing ground of virtue and manhood and (in Schmitt's phrase) 'the existential negation of the enemy'.[105] The state, the embodiment of legitimate force, here epitomizes mass aspiration and violence combined. 'All for the State; nothing outside the State; nothing against the State', was Mussolini's slogan. Here 'hyper-democracy' expresses the mass's desire to impose its aspirations and desires on all, regardless of consequence, and vengefully conscious of its mediocrity.[106]

Gasset's later works explore the profound sense of alienation intrinsic to modern identity, the 'I' juxtaposed to the 'Other'. He draws out the fear felt by the individual self lying at the heart of the idea of the 'social', and its implication that we can never subordinate all others to our will. With this comes the deduction that the 'genuine', authentic self (at any rate the safest) exists only in solitude. Here the naked ego basks narcissistically in its own perfection, unimpeded by the obstruction others represent. By contrast, the social self consists in 'mere conventionality or falsification', and social life as such degrades and endangers each individual ego.[107] We will return to this proposition shortly.

The implication of much of this line of thought was that population growth and increasing urban density encouraged the crowd to embrace entire societies. The result is the claustrophobe's nightmare realized. Such congestion breeds stupidity, violence, regression, primitivism. The emergence of the concept of 'mass society' describes this. 'The mass state is an historically unique phenomenon', Hans Speier proclaimed, as World War II commenced, introducing a now-neglected but important study by Emil Lederer. Where mere multitudes of people were psychologically heterogeneous, crowds possessed a sense of potential inward unity. This very unity intensifies their emotional anxiety and alertness. It reinforces the tendency of the individual in the crowd to 'cease thinking' and 'criticizing the emotions', and predisposes them to action when natural lethargy might prevail. A chief tendency of the crowd is to suspend credulity, increase conformity, and release inhibitions in a manner 'similar to intoxication'.[108]

Yet Freud's supposition that all masses represented a reversion to the primitive herd, as well as his theory of the libidinal linkage of masses to leaders and each other, are both challenged here. For if modern individuals are more rational, why have crowds not emulated this tendency and evolved in type? The crowd is not the 'primitive herd . . . in reality it is modern man turned emotional'. A *Bund* or communion might emerge from a crowd whose leaders aimed at a more prolonged

[105] Schmitt, *The Concept of the Political*, p. 33.
[106] José Ortega y Gasset, *The Revolt of the Masses* (George Allen & Unwin, 1972), pp. 9, 42–3, 56, 70–1, 93, 14.
[107] José Ortega y Gasset, *Man and People* (George Allen & Unwin, 1959), p. 99.
[108] Emil Lederer, *State of the Masses: The Threat of the Classless Society* (W. W. Norton, 1940), pp. 10, 14, 18–19, 33.

association and a closed membership. 'Born out of social turmoil and intellectual responsibility', modern dictatorship, 'the state of masses or crowds', resulted from the failure of particular crowds to dissolve back into groups once their initial rationale had been realized. Crowds are now substituted for society. But crowds are not identical across space and time. They possess distinctive identities. Particular crowds are animated by particular emotions shaped by time and place. Those of the 1930s in Germany derived from the war, revolution, depression, and social collapse, all of which brought unparalleled revolutions in political, social, and psychological life.[109]

Small groups cannot solve great problems: crowds muster courage, a sense of will, and self-sacrifice. These modern masses are not an undifferentiated 'herd' but possess epochally defined qualities, and are manipulated by techniques not formerly available. Now 'spontaneity and reason in society are displaced by mass-emotions and terror'. Every crowd 'feels ... totalitarian' insofar as it is 'psychologically, a whole, apart from or beyond which no other social being exists or has a right to exist'. Its unity, which 'springs from emotion, has no structure and precludes reasoning', reason being replaced by propaganda which sustains heightened emotional intensity through focus on the 'enemy'. This gives it *Zielstrebigkeit*, or a consciousness of purpose, and here a leader is crucial. Inchoate feelings, which might simply explode like a dam bursting, are now sharpened, focused, and given meaning and a much more sustained energy. Lesser loyalties fall to the wayside. The mass state—here Hitler and Stalin share much—is 'built upon the eradication of groups', and 'enslaves man by delivering him to his emotions'.[110] Here we see both the strength of totalitarian groups and the mechanism of their inner working, the surrender to the primitive.

Lederer thus portrays the emotional strength of the crowd as greatly magnified when other groups into which it might have been dissolved have been eradicated by totalitarian regimes. The power lies in numbers, and in the vaunted fictitious unity they exhibit. The crowd or mass as a dictatorship thus inevitably 'is bound to destroy society', in the sense of small, voluntarily formed groups whose differentiated and contradictory loyalties threaten society's existence. The psychology of groups mirrors that of individuals insofar as both possess emotional and irrational substrata. (There is no sense here of groups as threatening because they represent an irrationality lacking in the individual, or of some groups having proto-totalitarian tendencies.) Here, Lederer stressed, citing Le Bon, that the crowd, 'obsessed by ideas', 'feels its power because of the great numbers; the feeling of responsibility disappears; the individual, subject to contagion and exposed to suggestion, ceases to be an individual and becomes an automaton, not directed by his own will'. Yet Le Bon, crucially, thought Lederer had failed to distinguish between the process of revolution, when massacre might occur, and the violence exerted by dictatorships aiming to maintain power. So the roles of personal leadership and propaganda need to be added to the Le Bonian formula to account for Hitler's successes. No leader, no group. Yet equally, no group, no leader. Totalitarianism here is centrally derived

[109] Ibid., pp. 10, 35.   [110] Ibid., pp. 65, 30–5, 38, 45, 217.

from the psychology of mass society: 'The totalitarian state is the state of the masses; it is different from any state which is based on, and accepts the existence of, social groups.' The masses support the dictator, who usurps power less than simply embodying the crowd's will, passions, and ideas. Hence it was often said that fascism created Mussolini, rather than vice versa.[111]

Finally, two other important twentieth-century writers who analysed the destructive power of crowds also merit mention: Erich Fromm and Elias Canetti. Fromm's *Escape from Freedom* (1941) focused on the idea that totalitarian dictatorships were not simply imposed from above, but were willingly embraced from below. To Fromm, freedom was psychologically sometimes 'a burden, too heavy for mankind to bear, something he tries to escape from'. Submitting to authority relieves us of uncertainties, the pressure of making choices, and of assuming responsibility. Fromm emphasized the irrational aspects of submissiveness, but also the strength of the desire to belong in a culture increasingly prone to moral isolation. We seek group affiliation proportionately to the alienation modernity inflicts upon us. As the fluidity of individual association supplants the family, church-, and village-centred life of the earlier periods, the need for new associations becomes ever more pronounced.[112]

To Fromm, the 'paradise' of our original primary bonds cannot, however, be recaptured. But if the intensity of individuation, or the 'emergence of the individual from his original ties', was directly linked to the search for new bonds of security, these in turn weakened both freedom and the integrity of selfhood. Submission to powerful individuals in particular releases us from responsibility and anxiety about our ability to control our lives. The growth of modern individualism has, in fact, placed increasingly heavy burdens of self-responsibility upon our fragile psyches. These burdens sometimes become unsupportable. So we exchange autonomy for security. Yet this same security also induces a sadistic urge to dominate others, which is inherited from our feeling of powerlessness and loneliness. Masochism may result from the desire to lose ourselves in the group and to escape the demands of freedom. Sadism comes not from the wish to inflict pain, but to establish superiority over others. This cements our position in the group by proving our own worthiness, and also compensates neatly for our previous sense of inadequacy. Group psychology again proves to be the chief entry point for explaining the disturbed behaviour of the moderns.[113] Modernity, indeed, comes to appear increasingly marked by group pathology.

Fromm's *The Anatomy of Human Destructiveness* (1973) linked the sadistic desire to have 'absolute and unrestricted control over a living being' to the 'authoritarian character' studied by Theodor Adorno and others.[114] Fromm's description of the

---

[111] Ibid., pp. 65, 228–9. The *Bund* concept is juxtaposed to *Gemeinschaft* and *Gesellschaft* by the sociologist Herman Schmalenbach.

[112] Erich Fromm, *Escape from Freedom* (Holt, Rinehart & Winston, 1941), pp. 6, 36.

[113] Ibid., pp. 23–4, 151–2, 157.

[114] Erich Fromm, *The Anatomy of Human Destructiveness* (Fawcett Crest, 1973), pp. 318–22. See T. W. Adorno, Else Frenkel-Brunswik, Daniel Levinson, and Nevitt Sanford, *The Authoritarian Personality* (Harper, 1950).

strong emotionalism of the moment, the utter subversion of normal moral restraints, and the sense of absolute collective righteousness all echo Le Bon's account of the crowd. Yet Fromm felt that this did not explain why some reactions of this type are markedly more brutal than others. Nor did it account for routine or institutionalized cruelty, or the transformation of defensive forms of aggression into more malignant types. An instinct to swarm is not evidently an instinct to destroy. The group—even the crowd—is not in itself destructive, however atavistic it may be. 'Malignant aggression', rather, can be explained by historical patterns of (often ritualized) bloodlust, and the emergence of both spontaneous and systematic cruelty in specific circumstances. Group trauma or emotional shock releases sublimated or repressed tendencies which then erupt volcanically until the energy of the group is spent.[115]

One of the most innovative studies of the subject, Elias Canetti's *Crowds and Power* (1960), sees the crowd as an experience in which an elemental fear of touch is transcended and transmuted into an organic collective being and feeling. Close proximity melts the invisible barriers of personal space. Temporarily we are liberated from the oppressive weight of the ego-self and its moral demands. The alarm of isolation is lost as we submerge ourselves in the equality of fellow feeling. The noisy destruction of symbols of oppression may express our collective feelings of 'animal force and passion'. This is integration, by contrast to which panic reveals or provokes the disintegration of the crowd. Like the Dionysian cult, the Roman Saturnalia, and the medieval Carnival, where a remembrance of original equality is expressed, Canetti's crowd is hell-bent on abolishing difference. It is defined by four traits: the desire to grow; a persistent equality (even defining the crowd as 'a state of absolute equality' and insisting that it is 'for the sake of this equality that people become a crowd'); a love of density; and the need for a direction.[116] Canetti identifies five emotional types of crowds: the baiting crowd, a variant on the hunting pack which may engage in collective killing; the flight crowd, avoiding a threat; the prohibition crowd, which refuses to do something previously done by individuals, such as striking; the reversal crowd, seeking revenge on notional superiors, typically in a revolution; and the feast crowd, intent on consuming an abundance by equalizing indulgence and pleasure. Crowds can be deliberately formed for religious purposes (the Crusades, the festival, the pilgrimage). Crowds pitted against each other, in sport or war, are termed double crowds, and possess a different dynamic. Small groups within crowds which precipitate larger numbers are called crowd crystals. A chief historical ancestor of the crowd is the more limited 'pack', a term with sinister implications in English given its associations with hunting and war.

To Canetti, the nation may also emulate religions, particularly during war, when customs, traditions, politics, and literature 'become its faith'. Most nations regard themselves as 'chosen' by their deities to inherit the earth, and ignore the parallel

---

[115] On the linkage of trauma to dystopia see Michael S. Roth, *Memory, Trauma, and History* (Columbia University Press, 2012), pp. 87–103.
[116] Elias Canetti, *Crowds and Power* (Penguin Books, 1992), pp. 16–17, 19, 24, 32.

claims of others. They naturally 'want aggrandisement, and substantiate their claim with the fact of their increase'.[117] Other groups are therefore automatically excluded or disqualified, and become antagonists. But 'nation' is too abstract an entity for most to grasp. Individuals identify with crowds or crowd symbols rather than with 'nations'. Nonetheless, the latter share much in common with crowds. Both are like organisms: they have density, growth, openness, cohesion, rhythm, and discharge. Different nations identify with different definitive crowd symbols: the English with the sea; the Germans their army; the Swiss their mountains; the Jews their Exodus from Egypt; the Spanish the matador, the French their Revolution, with its associated symbols of the Bastille, the tricolour flag, Marianne, the shouts of 'liberté, egalité, fraternité', and so on. (How archaic some of these symbols seem today!) By identifying with flags, music (especially the anthem, patriotism's soundtrack), drums, uniforms, colours, marching in step, individuals merge in heady emotionality into a mass in which enthusiasm for the whole envelopes or transcends subjective identity. The slogans, Long live the King! (the leader, the revolution . . .), echo through every mind. The god(s), where relevant, are invoked. The name of the nation is incanted repeatedly until it becomes a hypnotic mantra, welding the individual and the collective together by repetition. God–nation–patriotism are fused. The now-organized, coherently defined crowd emboldens each individual. In the mass, each finds, and strives to achieve still more, power, as well as a liberation from the enslaved, cell-like shell of their individual weakness. Finally, we feel free—of ourselves.

* * * *

The revolutionary upheavals which agitated the modern world for two centuries after 1789 have formed the backdrop to this section. Most were revolts in the name of greater egalitarianism. Most involved substantial crowd activity, more or less spontaneously at the outset, and then orchestrated as manifestations of loyalty. Most who addressed these phenomena were hostile to them. By the mid-twentieth century, treatments of the crowd by Le Bon and many of his successors thus came under sustained criticism for their overtly anti-plebeian bias and hostility to the revolutionaries' principles and methods. Historians like George Rudé emphasized that riots were often reasonable protests by the emerging democracy of 'the people' against injustice, hunger, and want. The people usually sought to retrieve lost rights or, invoking 'moral economy' constraints, to reinstate former prices, or to prevent the confiscation of common land, wage reductions, or unfair taxes. In E. P. Thompson's well-known formulation, following Marx, these actions expressed a working class forging its collective consciousness, and thus also a 'people' becoming a 'class'.[118] Here, crowds are heroic more than anarchic, as much themselves terrorized by oppression and hunger as terrorizing in revenge. Aspiring to just and humane ideals, they are driven to desperation by extreme despair.[119] Those who stormed the Bastille

[117] Ibid., pp. 197–8.
[118] E. P. Thompson, *The Making of the English Working Class* (Victor Gollancz, 1963).
[119] See George Rudé, *The Crowd in History: A Study of Popular Disturbances in France and England 1730–1848* (John Wiley, 1964); George Rudé, *The Crowd in the French Revolution* (Oxford University Press, 1959).

were not criminals but ordinary craftsmen, shopkeepers, and journeymen, seeking not to loot but to claim representation, liberty, the rights of man. When they craved bread, as they often did—again in 1917—they increasingly sought a system which would give it to them cheaply.[120] Le Bon's postulates were thus condemned as 'overdrawn, tendentious, and misleading'.[121] Another historian, Henri Lefebvre, similarly assailed Le Bon in his account of the 'great fear' which pervaded the French countryside in the summer of 1789.[122]

Eric Hobsbawm's phrase, 'primitive rebels', captures this alternative approach to crowd psychology succinctly.[123] Such claims do not alter our description of the temporary mentality that characterizes the agitated group, or the collective outlook which may define the 'group mind'. But they greatly affect our sense of its moral object as 'some elementary form of 'natural' justice'.[124] Revolutionary activity becomes the concentrated physical as well as moral outrage at prolonged and systematic injustice. Retribution is justified by the cruelty of exploitation and oppression. The revolutionary crowd thus becomes more 'revolutionary' than 'crowd'. Much of the taint of atavism now disappears.

No (Wo)Man is an Island: The Primacy of Groupishness

The foregoing account has suggested that group psychology, focusing on the crowd, is central to defining dystopia. But not all groups are or act like crowds. In this section we need to consider more precisely how individuals relate to groups generally, in what manner groups resemble crowds, and how the privileging of the rational autonomous individual hinted at by Le Bon and others—a central issue, we will see, in dystopian literature—emerges from analyses of this relationship. This is initially and perhaps most crucially a question of identity: we mostly define who we are through the groups we belong to, and they then shape how we act. The group does not provide the same ecstatic emotional release as the crowd, and the blissful merging of 'I' into 'We'. Groups can certainly give us much by way of release from anxiety. Yet they may also take much away in exchange. Just how this all occurs needs to be clarified if we are to understand how the tension between collectivism and individualism develops in the modern period, and comes to define the dystopian.

Groups and Identity

Our lives are dominated by belonging to groups. Yet how we join and associate with them is often a surprisingly unselfconscious process. Clearly all groups offer cooperation, without which the simplest tasks would defeat us. All promote

120 Rudé, *The Crowd in the French Revolution*, pp. 180, 196.
121 Rudé, *The Crowd in History*, p. 257.
122 Henri Lefebvre, *The Great Fear of 1789: Rural Panic in Revolutionary France* (NLB, 1973).
123 Eric Hobsbawm, *Primitive Rebels: Studies in Archaic Form of Social Movement in the 19th and 20th Centuries* (Manchester University Press, 1959).
124 Rudé, *The Crowd in History*, p. 238.

sociability and provide approval, without which the self cannot function. All suggest a purpose in life—perhaps sociability itself—which individual identity may not provide. Although a formal equality of membership may mask a steep hierarchy (which most may nonetheless welcome and respect), all groups have what Fredric Jameson describes as a utopian function in providing collective solidarity.[125] This is what Aristotle meant by describing us as 'political animals'—though the polity is not the chief of groups as such. This need is also implied by the later language of the 'herd instinct' and 'group mind'. So intense is this desire that, as we will see, we can even conceive that the power of suggestion, the basis of modern mass psychology, is born from our wish to be loved by the group. 'Groupishness' is one (admittedly awkward) term which defines this need for association.[126] More precise than 'natural sociability' or 'the herd instinct', it alerts us to the peculiar dynamics of *how* we associate, not merely why.

Establishing and maintaining 'groupishness' is thus a full-time activity and a major preoccupation for most of us. The desire for 'belongingness' or 'withness', extending Erving Goffman and Abraham Maslow, is central to most assertions of identity and most rituals.[127] Our 'We' commences with similar physical characteristics, place of residence, and history. We belong with varying degrees of passion and commitment to neighbourhoods, sports clubs, towns, regions, sects, religions, nations, and so on. Our work 'team' makes claims upon our energies and loyalties. We are born into or inherit many such affiliations, or, like supporting 'our' football teams, nearly so. Who we think we are relative to others, where we belong in terms of age, sex, language, class, and so on—our 'social identity'—remains a core part of our existence.[128] In Ferdinand Tönnies' terms, every group offers us a fragment of *Gemeinschaft*, or basic unity with others. In Elias' phrase, every group provides a different 'We–I balance'.[129] All function in different ways to provide us with a socially constructed definition of the self. Like it or not, 'I' am produced by 'we'.

Groups cannot, however, be conceived of as mere aggregates of individuals. The latter, rather, are born out of the group over many centuries. Anthropologically, our 'original' identity is defined by an 'almost organic' solidarity with the group, in

[125] Sprott, *Human Groups*, p. 27; Fredric Jameson, *The Political Unconscious: Narrative as a Socially Symbolic Act* (Routledge, 1983), p. 281 (partly in reference to the ultimate ideal of a classless society). Hierarchy and equality indeed evidently balance each other in many groups.

[126] Wilfred Bion, *Experiences in Groups* (Tavistock Publications, 1961), p. 131. 'Communalism' is another possibility.

[127] See N. Kune, *The Need to Belong: Rediscovering Maslow's Hierarchy of Needs* (Paul H. Brookes Publishers, 2011), Susan T. Fiske, *Social Beings: Core Motives in Social Psychology* (John Wiley, 2010), and Harold R. Isaacs, *Idols of the Tribe: Group Identity and Political Change* (Harvard University Press, 1989). These awkward terms are sadly in need of a synonym. 'Belongingness', which is included in Maslow's famous hierarchy of needs, is often defined as referring to the feeling of being an essential or important part of a group. Being integral to the group, or needed, is closer to my meaning here, hence fellowship, intimacy, or even kinship serve as rough but still insufficient synonyms. Sociability and gregariousness also do part of the work.

[128] Erving Goffman, *Relations in Public: Microstudies of the Public Order* (Penguin Books, 1971), p. 227; Rupert Brown, *Group Processes: Dynamics within and between Groups* (Blackwell, 2000), p. 2.

[129] Norbert Elias, *The Society of Individuals* (University College Dublin Press, 2010), pp. 176–88; Ferdinand Tönnies, *Community and Civil Society*, ed. José Harris (1887; Cambridge University Press, 2001), pp. 22–62.

Lévy-Bruhl's formulation. 'The member of a primitive clan might express his identity in the formula "I am We"', argues Fromm, 'he cannot yet conceive of himself as an "individual".' This process of individuation only occurs, in Europe, when individuals cease being identified with their social role in the hierarchy.[130] Historically, 'I' am most often the family, clan, or tribe. Even in the Athenian and Roman republics, 'the fact of belonging to a clan, or a tribe or state, played an inalienable role in the human self-image'.[131] Hence, the family, village, and neighbourhood are often treated as 'primary' or 'natural' groups.[132]

Yet there is much variation here. At one extreme, certain tribes lack even the personal pronoun 'I' in their language: there is only 'we'. At the other, a highly differentiated society may permit or even encourage a sharp divergence of 'the psychological patternings of the individual people who grow up within it'.[133] But there is also a clear spectrum of orientation from an individualistic or 'I-self' or a group, family, or 'we-self', Alan Roland argues.[134] In societies dominated by the 'we-self' (to Roland, Japan and India), self-esteem depends on the honour and reputation of the groups individuals belong to, particularly the family, usually regarded as the most important bond of all.[135] 'Individuals' may also be conceived not as single persons, but as seamlessly wedded to their ancestors. They are thus several people at once. A strict hierarchy is common. To the Bantu, like Hegel's Oriental despot, only the chief is born free, while no two men are born equal, their rank being determined by the position of their family within the tribe.[136] Traditionally defined reciprocal responsibilities and obligations may nonetheless coexist alongside intense emotional intimacy and very private selves.[137] This offers a protective web which inhibits fanciful impulses towards rebellious behaviour.

The 'we-less I', as Norbert Elias terms it, is thus a psychological latecomer to the process, and perhaps only an ideal postulate, even an impostor.[138] Elias suggests, indeed, that *'Society not only produces the similar and typical, but also the individuality.'*[139] Some social stages do favour 'individualisation, the greater emphasis on the I-identity of the individual person, and the detachment of that person from the traditional groupings'.[140] Yet if the later moderns tend to conceive of 'identity' in individual terms, this detachment is much less complete than we often assume. 'I' am to a large degree still a composite personality in which inherited and adopted group identities loom large. Though the numbers are evidently increasing,[141] few of us

---

[130] Lévy-Bruhl, *Primitives and the Supernatural*, p. 209; Erich Fromm, *The Sane Society* (Routledge & Kegan Paul, 1956), p. 61.

[131] Elias, *The Society of Individuals*, p. 141.   [132] Sprott, *Human Groups*, p. 57.

[133] Ibid., p. 59.

[134] Alan Roland also describes a 'spiritual self' as a third variant, in *In Search of the Self in India and Japan* (Princeton University Press, 1988), pp. 289–311.

[135] Sprott, *Human Groups*, p. 60.

[136] Lévy-Bruhl, *The 'Soul' of the Primitive*, pp. 59–86, 123, 185, 201–2.

[137] This also helps explain why 'utopianism' is relatively less prevalent in such societies: they already possess most of its key elements, particularly a stronger group identity. It also suggests that utopianism is a response, in part, to growing European individualism.

[138] Elias, *The Society of Individuals*, pp. 178–9.   [139] Ibid., p. 58.   [140] Ibid., p. 161.

[141] Judging by the numbers of people wearing headphones and staring at their mobile phones in public, the preference for digital over human interaction, and the increased tendency to live alone. But

are defined by what we might term hyperinteriority, meaning living in one's own self-bubble, self-absorbed, myopic, solipsistic, atomized, even autistic, though we will refer to this viewpoint later on. Only rarely do we concede that 'a truly individual sense of identity', in Fromm's phrase, is superior to the 'substitutes'—if this is what they are—of nation, religion, class, and occupation.[142] Usually we belong to groups before we see ourselves as unique individuals, and remain 'individuals' most of the time as a function of being group members.[143] When 'I' attempt to escape this process, it is always at the risk of increased alienation and ostracism—for no groups tolerate rejection lightly.

Conceived historically, then, 'individualism' is a recent construct. Tocqueville reminds us that 'Our fathers did not have the word individualism, which we have forged for our own use, because in their day there was no such thing as an individual who did not belong to a group and could see himself as standing absolutely alone.'[144] Western culture, Fromm stresses, 'went in the direction of creating the basis for the full experience of individuality', though this was achievable only by a minority.[145] For most of history, therefore, the 'individual' is in some respects a mere ideal type or theoretical construct, and is more properly the 'individual member', in Pierre Turquet's telling phrase.[146]

Yet, from another angle, individualization represents, in Elias' phrase, 'a process of civilisation' where personal selves are conceived as rising above the group's more primitive instincts towards a higher morality, which prizes individuals as such rather than as group members. This notionally permits greater universality of judgement and cosmopolitanism in principle.[147] This is what John Stuart Mill, who gave the process a leading role in the advancement of civilization, called 'individuality'.[148] It is clearly a basis of that toleration upon which a pluralist society depends. For the weak 'I' must tolerate where the strong 'We' need not. (And is probably more likely to: for while the group, exulting in its strength, is contemptuous of weakness, the individual, powerless in isolation, may commiserate with it, thinking: this could be me too.)

This privileging of the rational individual, implied in nearly all crowd psychology, offers an extraordinarily serious challenge to the historical and psychological primacy of the group. Often regarded as the founding text of philosophical anarchism, William Godwin's *Enquiry Concerning Political Justice* (1793) was amongst the first works to express this. Godwin prized individuality above all else because he thought the search for 'universal benevolence' relied upon a maximal strengthening of our private judgements. All groups now appear to corrode and

---

even here there is a modified form of sociability which substitutes the distant imaginary group for real immediate people. Nonetheless, a form of technoholism is evident in the compulsive need to check one's mobile phone (350 times per day, on average).

[142] Fromm, *The Sane Society*, p. 62.

[143] See the notable scene in the Monty Python film, *The Life of Brian*, where the crowd shouts in chorus, 'we are all individuals'.

[144] Alexis de Tocqueville, *The Ancien Régime and the French Revolution* (Cambridge University Press, 2011), p. 91.

[145] Fromm, *The Sane Society*, p. 60.

[146] C. Fred Alford, *Group Psychology and Political Theory* (Yale University Press, 1994), p. 40.

[147] Elias, *The Society of Individuals*, p. 111.   [148] Mill, *On Liberty* (1859), ch. 3.

warp individual judgement, and fleeing from virtually all cooperative endeavours, including marriage and playing in orchestras, is a logical consequence. After Godwin, Max Stirner's *The Ego and Its Own* (1845)—one of the young Marx's chief targets—proclaimed the militant egoism of the intellectual.

This viewpoint is captured in Jean-Paul Sartre's famous phrase, 'hell is other people'. To extreme individualists, championing the primacy of unique autonomy, the group is the enemy. Another radical 'aristocratic' individualist, the 'free spirit' Nietzsche, is easily positioned here. As Le Bon and Freud attested, all groups are thus inherently repressive. They may raise us above our weak selves and momentarily release us emotionally by embracing us in the immensity of their power. But their main everyday function is procrustean: they cut us to size in order to suppress our deviations from the norm, and socialize us (through regressive infantilization) by way of suppressing our individuality.[149] 'Conform or else' is their message.

Here, fear *of* the group may thus profoundly affect our demeanour towards and behaviour within it. Often seething with envy, competition, even hatred within itself, the one thing the group agrees on is obedience to its norms. It is often intensely intolerant of deviance or nonconformity. The group, as such, is a bully. Bullying, be it ever so subtle, is the group's normal mode of operation. Here it mimics the crowd. Its capacity to shame and embarrass us is practically unlimited. We may term this pressure *groupism*. The tyranny of the group can be overwhelming. It appears in many guises. It is the root of our chief moral concepts. Thus, Jon Elster argues, the disapproval or contempt of others operates chiefly through shame and guilt.[150] Shame is simply the fear of the group. The sense of sin is the fear of the group. Its powers have long been recognized. 'Compared with the contempt of mankind', Adam Smith famously asserted, 'all other evils are easily supported.'[151] Mill agreed that in 'all departments of human affairs, regard for the sentiments of our fellow-creatures is in one shape or other, in nearly all characters, the pervading motive'.[152] It is this search which gives us *amour propre*, in Jean-Jacques Rousseau's formulation, or the form of self-love dependent on the opinions of others, and which makes us live inauthentically through their opinions of us.[153]

This pressure, then, is the essence of the collectivist mentality generally. It penetrates our innermost selves. Really successful groups, Arthur Koestler wrote, produce a closed

---

[149] In Elias' reckoning, the 'internal opinion of any group with a high level of cohesion has a profound influence upon its members as a regulating force of their sentiments and their conduct': Norbert Elias, *The Established and the Outsiders* (University College Dublin Press, 2008), p. 24. But he rejects the 'view, widespread today, that a sane individual may become totally independent of all his or her we-groups and, in that sense, totally autonomous' (Ibid., p. 25).

[150] Jon Elster, *Strong Feelings: Emotion, Addiction, and Human Behavior* (MIT Press, 1999), p. 87, 98–102.

[151] Adam Smith, *Theory of Moral Sentiments* (Henry G. Bohn, 1853), p. 83.

[152] John Stuart Mill, *Collected Works* (33 vols, Routledge & Kegan Paul, 1965–91), vol. 10, p. 411 ('Utility of Religion').

[153] Jean-Jacques Rousseau, *The Social Contract and Discourses* (J. M. Dent, 1973), p. 70. 'In becoming sociable and a Slave he becomes weak, fearful, servile; and his soft and effeminate way of life completes the enervation of both his strength and his courage' (*Discourse on the Origins of Inequality*, ed. Roger D. Masters and Christopher Kelly (University Press of New England, 1992), p. 24).

system in which each member 'carries a private Iron Curtain inside his skull, to protect his illusions against the intrusion of reality'.[154] At the very least, it produces what we might, in an Orwellian vein, call *groupthink*. Its demands that we be 'normal', the flip side of the desire for acceptance, can be enormous. The more anxious the group is about its cohesiveness, the more paranoid it is about its enemies, the more bullying will occur. Secure and relaxed, the group will tolerate greater deviance.

The function of the group is thus to imprison us; we possess free will only insofar as we are individuals (and suffer from its exercise in equal measure). An ideal individualist 'society', by contrast, would thus be akin to that described in Daniel Defoe's *Robinson Crusoe* (1719) (until Friday arrives), a fantasy of personal self-rule, or perhaps of domination over nature. This would extol the hyperinteriority of self-absorbed existence, not oppressed or dictated to by others, perhaps also functioning as the pure Protestant conscience. Less preposterous than it may appear, this argument will need to be addressed here in due course. We can call this fantasy of the groupless self '*my-opia*'—the pun works well. The inauthenticity of the crowd/group self/selves, and the surrender of freedom its adoption entails, as an existentialist might describe it, thus remains a haunting possibility.[155]

Without doubt, groups are aware of this threat and do their best to counter it. But we might equally plausibly contend that there is no inner 'authentic self' as such, and that what we imagine this is, is only a later contrivance bolted onto existing group selves. In most societies, at any rate, the 'I' is thus unimaginable without the 'we', or what Erving Goffman calls the 'with', the 'party of more than one whose members are perceived to be "together"'.[156]

* * * *

Groups start with a couple. Yet the couple is an odd group indeed. (Indeed, it is sometimes explicitly an anti-group, as with Orwell's Winston and Julia.) And three is not a crowd either. So to Wilfred Bion, the group proper commences minimally with three people, two alone forming a merely personal relationship. In most traditional societies, marriage means incorporating into another group. So the group prototype is the family unit, later the basis for many forms of utopian affective association. As in religion ('God the Father . . .'), in many so-called intentional communities a charismatic father figure (Robert Owen, John Humphrey Noyes) presides, or a group of elders. Thus, the language of paternalism typically suffuses the group experience. The adopted father, mother, and the brethren reflect our primal experience as children of our first 'community', seeking nurture and

---

[154] Koestler, *The Ghost in the Machine*, p. 262.

[155] '[F]rom the moment that I become pre-occupied about the effect I want to produce on the other person, my every act, word and attitude loses its authenticity': Gabriel Marcel, *Homo Viator: Introduction to a Metaphysic of Hope*, tr. Emma Crauford (Victor Gollancz, 1951), p. 17, and quoted in reference to George Orwell, in Michael Carter, *George Orwell and the Problem of Authentic Existence* (Croom Helm, 1985), p. 79. The opposite hypothesis is that 'Hell is the state of the soul powerless to come out of itself, absolute self-centredness, dark and evil isolation, i.e. final inability to love' (Nicolas Berdyaev, *The Destiny of Man* (The Centenary Press, 1939), p. 351).

[156] Goffman, *Relations in Public*, p. 41.

protection. Then, as equals, we address each other as 'brother' and 'sister', proclaiming our closeness and mutual duty.

As soon as we step outside the family's cocoon, other groups assail us from every direction. The clan identity of our ancestors is always a basic reference point. But there are times when leaving family for substitute 'fictive kin'—friends we choose—is a great improvement. Endeavouring to find our way in life, particularly in modern cities, we then encounter gangs, clubs, cliques, factions, parties, sects, movements, churches, and societies ad infinitum. Each association possesses an organic existence and a history. From village, region, or nation to humanity, multiplied by gender, age, race, religion, ethnicity, language, caste, estate, class, and other factors, a complex multidimensional spectrum of identities defines who we are or aspire to be, or are not allowed to be. How these identities interact varies enormously according to time, place, history, where we enter each, and much more.

The process by which all this occurs is a familiar one. Individuals are mostly silent on their own. Two people meet and converge in a quasi-magnetic, mesmerizing, telepathic, electrical, even quasi-sexual manner (as some variously conceive).[157] They may touch to affirm social proximity. Beginning to converse, they soon find a common emotional meeting ground where each acknowledges the other's worth.[158] A third alters this dynamic, and so on. But then, the numbers varying according to context, quality is overwhelmed by quantity. When groups reach a certain size, our ability to function as individuals is increasingly constricted. Size clearly counts: we are impressed and swayed by numbers when we assemble.[159] The larger the group the stronger we feel as members and the more likely we are to agree with it, and to sympathize less with the weak or outsiders.

Most of the time, however, our direct interactions with the group chiefly involve an assertion of belonging. This aims at inducing a profound and—literally—warm sense of emotional satisfaction in the expression of groupishness. Sameness is central here. Scanning the faces of others seeking recognition, we place a premium on similarity and familiarity. As Fred Alford puts it, originally 'the question of whom I can trust and rely upon is answered by answering the question "Who is like me?"'[160] So the badges of sameness are central to the rituals of mutual embrace. Each group structures and evokes emotions, extending its friendship, attracting our loyalty, by sympathy, positively as well as negatively, often by cliquishness, through pain of exclusion in return for demonstrations of loyalty. Each offers a system of the symbolic exchange of honours and recognition (horizontally) or a reciprocity of loyalty (vertically).[161]

---

[157] E.g., J. Lionel Tayler, *Social Life and the Crowd* (Leonard Parsons, 1923), p. 181.

[158] Some later accounts still assume the dyadic group of two to be the basic social unit: see, e.g., John W. Thibault and Harold H. Kelley, *The Social Psychology of Groups* (John Wiley & Sons, 1959), pp. 80–99.

[159] These effects interested Georg Simmel. See *The Sociology of Georg Simmel*, ed. Kurt H. Wolff (Free Press, 1950), pp. 105–80.

[160] Alford, *Group Psychology and Political Theory*, p. 43.

[161] This approach is associated with Pierre Bourdieu, e.g., *Outline of a Theory of Practice* (Cambridge University Press, 1977).

Yet the search for sameness is interwoven with a desire for differentiation which makes competitive tension ever-present. Every glance assesses superior, equal, inferior. Rivalries, often petty, sometimes bitter, even murderous, often define the dynamics of the group. The less successful, always resentful of those who surpass them, will employ gossip, bickering, backbiting, innuendo, and sabotage to try to reduce their enemies back to the average level or lower. All ask constantly: am I in or out of this group? Where am I in it? Who is up and coming and who can I choose to ignore? Why has X surpassed me in prominence? What can I do about it?

Each assertion of belonging is also thus an effort to define our niche within the group, and preferably to advance our position and prestige.[162] For all groups are about power as well as belonging. Every assertion of equality is thus simultaneously one of inequality. The bosses smirk in their superiority. The peons—perhaps pee'd on too often—retreat to the securer shadowy fringes at the edges of the group. Nonetheless, they swivel at the entry of the great and influential, who bask in their deference. While lesser luminaries sit on the sidelines, placing bets on which subgroups will ascend, which way the wind is blowing, and preparing their moves accordingly, the ambitious move to the centre, constantly jockeying for position. The real social climbers, indeed, may be seen interacting only with the group's leaders, and disdainfully ignoring the rest. They know which side of the bread the butter is on, and, better still, who churns it.

Regardless of our position within it, and the steepness of its hierarchy, the group *qua* group proclaims an equality of fraternity: that is, its magic. Slowly the group draws us into its protective cocoon, extending its acceptance, an iota or more of inclusive identity, a measure at a time. We revel in the secret handshake, the shared ceremony, the uniform, the sense of being 'in' and 'cool'. We buy the brand name, and imitate others' clothing. We talk the talk, *groupspeak*, or our own team jargon, to express belonging—'speaking Bolshevik' the communists would call this. We hammer our identities home to ourselves endlessly and obsessively, glancing in the mirror first thing in the morning and thinking 'British!' or 'Presbyterian' or 'Aryan' or 'Communist' or 'real Man' or 'True Believer' (or whatever—insert your own identity here), with a smirk of approval, then spend all day long thinking 'British' (or whatever) on every conceivable occasion, but especially those requiring reassurance or self-assertion. If we are lucky, the group responds with applause which warms our souls (but excites jealousy on the sidelines). Such acclaim strengthens our yearning to belong, to revel in the purity of the group's identity, to share in its largesse and longevity. Our craving for acceptance is almost limitless. At the most extreme we may become completely subsumed under the group—one recent terrorist suspect, stopped for an identity check, offered the Qur'an to a policeman.

What most groups offer us, then, is chiefly protection or security. All groups of any size also aim to create, shape, and sustain a common mentality or 'group mind'. To Bion, groups ideally seek to instil a sense of common purpose; to offer common

---

[162] Adler, Horney, and others have seen this as a narcissistic need; see Abram Kardiner, *The Individual and His Society: The Psychodynamics of Primitive Social Organization* (Columbia University Press, 1939), esp. pp. 13–77.

recognition to members; a sense of the boundaries of the group and its relation to other groups; to absorb new members; to permit freedom from too rigid or exclusive boundaries between internal subgroups; to value individual contributions to the group and allow for individual mobility within it; and to offer the means of coping with discontent. Bion distinguishes between three main emotional types of groups: fight–flight groups, where the group is organized to deal with an enemy; dependency groups, which rely overwhelmingly on a powerful leader; and pairing groups, who expect a messiah and millennial change. To Earl Hopper, groups aim primarily to furnish coherence, integration, and relatedness. Their greatest fear is psychological disintegration, and groups dominated by this are termed incohesion groups. And yet, paradoxically, we may gain great solace from belonging to groups dominated by paranoia. Here our problems are reduced to a few simple propositions and one powerful emotion.[163]

Every group defines itself by the excluded as well as the included. To determine who these outsiders are, groups require explicit boundaries which are commonly defined by ideas of purity and impurity. To the anthropologist Mary Douglas, ideas of the sacred, purity, defilement, pollution, fear of contagion, and desire for purification, are central to social life.[164] A hygienic world-view thus dominates some societies at some times. We fear the taint of ideas by suggestion. René Girard instances the Greek sense that the body of someone who had hung themselves was impure: self-murder might be contagious.[165] In Barrington Moore's formulation, some groups establish an ideal of moral purity and its opposite, pollution, both for self-justification and to express antagonism to enemies.[166] Just as an obsessive fear of dirt (mysophobia or germophobia) may generate (or flow from) an individual neurosis, and demand constant cleansing, its social equivalent (here termed *sociogermophobia*) invites isolation and persecution. Think of the Nazis' perceived need to pin a yellow star on Jews: what does this do psychologically for non-Jews? It focuses blame. It intensifies otherness. It awakens fears of the invisibility of alien bodies. And yet it reassures by displacing internal anxieties outwards onto others, thus alleviating our own stress.

So the purpose of belonging to many groups (not all) is to enhance the worth of some while reducing that of others.[167] This is analogous at one level to drawing a line between the sacred, within the group, and the profane, outside it, which Émile Durkheim regarded as the basis of religion.[168] The basic emotion we associate with the group is the feeling of security. This stems from a feeling of belonging, but it

[163] Bion, *Experiences in Groups*, pp. 25–6; Robins and Post, *Political Paranoia*, pp. 83–8, 94–9.
[164] Mary Douglas, *Collected Works*, vol. 2: *Purity and Danger: An Analysis of the Concepts of Pollution and Taboo* (Routledge, 2003).
[165] René Girard, *Violence and the Sacred* (Johns Hopkins University Press, 1977), p. 29.
[166] Barrington Moore, Jr, *Moral Purity and Persecution in History* (Princeton University Press, 2000).
[167] Hence, cosmopolitanism can really only be achieved through the threat of extraterrestrial invasion.
[168] Émile Durkheim, *The Elementary Forms of the Religious Life* (Allen & Unwin, 1915), pp. 36–41.

may also be security *against* outsiders. Hatred may result from threats to the bonds of love, or the group's core identity, which intensifies mere dislike or contempt.

How we define enemies and how we treat them are often contingent on our relative levels of confidence or anxiety. The more alarming external conditions are, the more hostility results, and the more rigid and all-consuming is the individual's relation to the in-group, and antagonism to the out-group. Under extreme and prolonged pressure the herd instinct may trump all desire for individuation, to the point of absolute submission to the group. Fear and hatred are particularly closely interwoven when the group's existence is imperilled by crisis. For we hate intensely only when we fear deeply. So the most destructive groups are also the most paranoid.

Yet there are many unanswered questions as to how antagonism and hostility towards 'enemies' may define groups. Surprisingly, the vocabulary of group psychology is somewhat sclerotic just where that of individual psychology is profuse. The reason for this is that it is much easier to condemn individuals for 'abnormality' than it is to accuse the group, which (at the least) after all defines the norms and is thus the highest court of appeal thereon. Yet it is anomalous that behaviour which we would regard as neurotic or even psychotic in an individual can be emulated, transferred, modified, or magnified within the group, and accepted as valid and proper, humane and civilized.

Thus we need to know how, in particular, the extraordinarily important process operates by which obsessive concern with the purity of the group (sociogermophobia) is generated and maintained, and finds parallels in individual psychology and in ritualized forms of obsessive cleanliness. Here, some groups, like the nation and some sects, are conceived as a living organism threatened by 'disease', 'parasites', or 'poison'. A struggle to 'purge' the illness results. The targets may be defined as monstrous or less than human. This language and these concepts, we will see, pervade the mass murders of the twentieth century. But they have so many antecedents that they appear to be universal responses to social threats. They may also demonstrate not only hostility to outside groups but hostility to older forms of sociability within the society itself. These define many, though not all, totalitarian societies, which are marked by individual isolation and a false sociability we have identified as compulsory solidarity. In this regard, at least, they parallel the spectrum of individual disorders often classed as autism.

In exchange for being 'one of the club', many groups may thus offer us an 'other'—the foreigner, the heretic—to be loathed and detested as 'dirty' and 'unclean', perhaps hated enough to be destroyed. Hostility to enemies, or negative groupishness, while not essential, commonly strengthens in-group identity. Such antipathy, as described by Gordon Allport, typically ranges from antilocution, or speaking ill, through avoidance, discrimination, to physical attack, and finally extermination.[169] Even if we commence on the lowest rung of the ladder, membership as such in these groups flatters us by raising us above 'them'. We feel

---

[169] Gordon Allport, *The Nature of Prejudice* (Addison-Wesley Publishing Co., 1954), pp. 39–49.

strengthened by our sameness, distinctiveness, or uniqueness, by the juxtaposition of 'us' to 'them'. We are young and they are old. We are white and they are black. We are male and they are female. We are left and they are right. All of which mostly amounts to: we are right and they are wrong.

The strength of these convictions is proportionate to the size of the group. The larger it is, and the more protection it offers, the more self-subsistent and closed to the outside world it is, and the more it offers its adherents. The larger the 'We' is, the greater is the apparent strength and virtue, the collective spirit of the group or *esprit de corps*. Here we most easily experience Le Bon's ecstasy, the compensatory emotion which counterbalances our natural anxiety and alienation. By contrast, 'I', a mere speck in the cosmos, can never hope to muster such powers (except in the fantasy of the superhero: hence its popularity). The group's personality provides us with an alter ego much braver than our private persona. How strong we feel when we roar with the crowd! ('Hurrah!' is the group's anthem.) And how much stronger when a microphone, camera, phone, or computer reaches millions. Consequently, our lives are frequently organized around maximizing these sentiments. For the honour of belonging to some groups, we will often gladly die—or kill.[170] The promise of immortality here may be literal or figurative—we go to Heaven by sacrificing ourselves, we are assured, or we live on as a 'hero' in group memory. (Think of the fervour of the Japanese Kamikaze pilots, many types of cult, or the instant paradise-seeking suicide bombers of the Taliban and ISIS.)

Our desire for large-group identity in particular may well be encouraged by modernity. Tocqueville's *Democracy in America* revealed a close relationship between individual isolation and alienation in a nation of restless aspirant immigrants, and propensities towards conformity. Such conformity then acts as a counterweight for our growing isolation. Individuation as such, in the positive sense intended by J. S. Mill, amongst others, may seem doomed to fail accordingly.[171] Similar trends a century later would negate individuality even more intensely. 'Fascism, Nazism and Stalinism have in common that they offered the atomized individual a new refuge and security', wrote Fromm. 'These systems are the culmination of alienation. The individual is made to feel powerless and insignificant, but taught to project all his human powers into the figure of the leader, the state, the "fatherland", to whom he has to submit and whom he has to worship.' This 'new herd identity' 'rests on the sense of an unquestionable belonging to the crowd'. Yet 'this uniformity and conformity are often not recognized as such, and are covered by the illusion of individuality'.[172] Here, therefore, the group virtually swallows the individual up: 'I' shrinks into 'i'. But was the loss of this alienated self really so great? What the latter receives in return may well seem worth the price.

---

[170] Orwell once commented that most men would 'die "for their country" rather more readily than they will go on strike for higher wages' (*A Patriot after All 1940–1941* (Secker & Warburg, 2000), p. 178).

[171] Under the rubric of 'individuality': Mill, *On Liberty* (1859), ch. 3.

[172] Fromm, *The Sane Society*, pp. 237, 62.

With groups, every relationship between 'I' and 'We' (which here must be upper case, even more than 'I') is thus complex. In the first instance, however, each such encounter in later modern societies, where the pressure exists to sacrifice our carefully cultivated individuation, involves what we can term *identity transferral*. Here we cede part of the individual 'I' to the group in return for being empowered by associating with the greater strength of the collective 'We'. In each case of identity transferral we submit to the group's norms in return for an enhanced identity, 'We', which is stronger than our individual ego-identity. We can term this process *horizontal vicarious enhancement*. That is to say, our sense of individual power and self-worth are increased by identifying with the strength of the mass of other equal members of the group, by living through its greater powers and generic virtues and assimilating some of them to ourselves—imbibing them, so to speak, through the ether.

Just how much individual identity we cede here depends on various factors. Groupism demands different sacrifices of our 'individual' identity to behavioural conformity. The most malignant, for our purposes, stress that while 'We' in the abstract (Christians, the People, the Proletariat, etc.) are pure, 'I' in the concrete may be sinful and polluted. So here we purify ourselves by confessing, and by associating with others who redeem us. Even small groups—particularly of young males—may challenge us to 'prove' ourselves (i.e. our masculinity) by performing extreme deeds.

The larger the groups and the more inflated their pretensions, however, the more intense their pressures are. Hence, religion and nationalism, the largest and most potent forms of 'imagined communities', in Benedict Anderson's phrase, act most strongly upon us.[173] For these groups have the power to grant us (we feel—of course, at one level this is all illusory) absolution, immortality, omniscience, and omnipotence. But to gain such qualities we must give much in return. The more we feel we will gain, indeed, the greater the sacrifice we are willing to make. We are stirred by the sight of *our* flag, the sound of *our* national anthem, the image of *our* leader. (Put the stress where you like.) We go into battle with the flag hugged against our breast like an amulet. Tears come to our eyes as these symbols evoke an all-consuming desire for patriotic self-sacrifice by the association of the symbol with the feeling of 'We' or 'us-ness'.[174] This provides a key insight into the more destructive aspects of dystopian collectivism (but also group survival generally). For to gain all we are also willing to give everything. We concede that the group's collective survival may entail our individual sacrifice. For its greater glory, and particularly the attainment of some idea of immortality or Heaven, or where a transcendental or eternal principle is introduced into the equation, anything may be permissible.

* * * *

[173] Benedict Anderson, *Imagined Communities: Reflections on the Origin and Spread of Nationalism* (Verso, 1991), p. 6.
[174] See Th. Ribot, *The Psychology of the Emotions* (Walter Scott, 1897), pp. 172–86.

We have seen so far, then, that size is everything in the functioning of group dynamics. Small groups are rarely threatening or dangerous, and may well permit a wider range of nonconformity. Normally they cannot, but even more importantly do not want to, create dystopia by the abuse of their power. (Cults or sects, which may do so, are usually a bit larger.)[175] Studies show that the larger they are, however, the less power each individual has within them, the more intimidated and inhibited most are, and the more likely it is that an ethos of subordination develops.[176] The group of the nation virtually demands that we think like it. Hence, utopias tend to be modelled on villages or small towns, and an ethos of proximate trust and acquaintance sometimes called 'neighbourliness'.

This also provides, as we saw in the case of Thomas More, the transparency which makes wrongdoing difficult. To the nineteenth-century utopian writer James Silk Buckingham, for instance,

> if a man lived in a village or in the open part of a large town, where all his movements were seen and known, he would be a much better man than in a crowded and crooked-lane neighbourhood; and if a man did wrong under such circumstances, no one would speak to him; he would find the place unsupportable, and would be compelled to go away.[177]

On an intermediary scale, in villages and neighbourhoods, mutual acquaintance renders such visibility possible, and juvenile delinquency, spousal and child abuse, and many other evils can be combated more easily.[178]

But this transparency is much more difficult to achieve on a large scale, and where privacy is highly valued. To Bertrand de Jouvenel, therefore:

> The small society, as the milieu in which man is first found, retains for him an infinite attraction; he undoubtedly goes to it to renew his strength; but ... any attempt to graft the same features on a large society is Utopian and leads to tyranny. With that admitted, it is clear that as social relations become wider and more various, the common good conceived as reciprocal trustfulness cannot be sought in methods which the model of the small, closed society inspires; such a model is, in the contrary, entirely misleading.[179]

Surveillance must assume much more ominous forms on a larger scale, then, even if its function remains the same. The counterbalancing elements of trust and familiarity are no longer present. Often fear takes their place. By contrast to the village image of utopia, thus, dystopias are often modelled on nations and nationalism. Orwell, as we will see in Chapter 7, thought the term 'nationalism' precisely captured the dystopian mentality. And, in the twenty-first century, the surveillance society based on GPS,

---

[175] Cults can be defined as small-scale totalitarian societies: David V. Barrett, *The New Believers: A Survey of Sects, Cults and Alternative Religions* (Cassell & Co., 2001), pp. 20–1.

[176] Sprott, *Human Groups*, p. 116.

[177] James Silk Buckingham, *Letters to a Clergyman* (Chapman & Hall, 1846), p. 172.

[178] Sprott, *Human Groups*, pp. 91–4.

[179] Bertrand de Jouvenel, *Sovereignty* (Cambridge University Press, 1957), p. 136.

the smartphone, and the Internet is becoming a reality, mirrored also in the dystopian literature of our own period.

* * * *

We must also briefly consider how far the success of the group in drawing us in depends upon its leaders, who play a key role both in forming group identity and in moderating interactions between members. Leaderless groups are not unknown, and indeed provide fascinating insights into alternative group dynamics.[180] But most groups have leaders. Choosing them is where politics proper commences. Negotiating the rewards of loyalty and penalties of dissent then becomes a key activity. Groups composed only of those who think themselves leaders—intellectuals are a case in point—are as anomalous as a herd of cats. (Perhaps because they are often individualists and are often alienated, intellectuals herd rather badly. And so, we will see in Chapter 6, Huxley thought a society of Alphas would quickly collapse.)

But most of the time, through boredom, laziness, or weakness, leaders focus the group's identity. Personal loyalty is easier to grasp than group loyalty. We can touch individuals more easily. The bigger gifts leaders must press upon us are also more tangible. Leaders thus provide the second form of empowerment in the group through a process we can call *vertical vicarious enhancement*.[181] Here we gain individual strength through identifying with the particularly heroic qualities of our leaders. Their valour, their passions, their strength, become ours. Their magical quality, charisma, warms and entices us. With leaders, we experience powers vicariously in the sense that we live through the experiences or qualities of one or a few rather than engaging in or having these ourselves.

The power and function of leaders is also proportionate to the group's size. As groups increase in numbers those at their centre exercise a stronger gravitational pull, defining, shaping, and solidifying the whole, and balancing the centripetal pull of cliques which emerges at the same time. Each group needs to balance hierarchy with equality. Depending on circumstances—especially the group's size and the formality of its hierarchy, the occasion of its meeting, and its emotional trajectory and tendency, the functional division of labour, how status is assigned, and other factors—the mood may be set and transferred from dominant to subordinate members, or emerge more or less spontaneously by osmosis among relative equals. The general process of emotional receptivity is similar to Le Bon's idea of contagion, or what Freud, describing the unconscious transmission of feelings between individuals, called transference.

Places, things, and persons may also combine in the process of vicarious enhancement. In religion, the pilgrimage is the ultimate devotional statement where both the effort to arrive at and basking in the sanctity of the sacred space

---

[180] See, generally, W. H. R. Rivers, *Psychology and Politics and Other Essays* (Kegan Paul, Trench, Trubner & Co., 1923), pp. 42–7.

[181] The process, but not the concept, is hinted at in Thomas Carlyle's *On Heroes, Hero-Worship and the Heroic in History* (Chapman & Hall, 1841), to which this section is indebted.

are rewarded. Even when commanded as a penance, its success may wash away many a sin. Seeing the saint's tomb or the prophet's birthplace imbues us with a sense of holiness by a process of often intense emotional transferral. The universality of cults surrounding the bones, possessions of saints, and the like—and latterly their linear descendant, the culture of celebrity, and the phenomenon of mass hysterical adoration (like Beatlemania)—evidences this principle of vicariousness abundantly. Regardless of the type we defer to, the more gullible we are the more we grovel to touch their relics or other symbols of power, of purity, sanctity and success, to rub the statue, to grasp the cloak, to kiss the hand, in the hope that some of these qualities will (literally) rub off on us. Relics, in particular, symbolize not only saintly virtue but heavenly powers ensconced in earthly matter. How many died on the Crusades to obtain a fragment of the True Cross, or other relics with miraculous healing powers? Graves are a notable site in which concentrated energy is adored and participated in. But even worshipping the ground someone walks on as 'holy', or spiritually suffused, may be a good investment of psychic energy. Evidently the immense concentration of psychic energy in prominent and recognizable persons triggers a reflex response in others which leads them to seek instinctively to derive some part of this energy by contact.

Here, in a tendency born, it is claimed, from ancestor worship, the most primitive desires show themselves.[182] Thus, objects inherit and emit emotional intensity like radiation. The desire to touch is evidently one of the most elemental of all: think of how 'faith healing' by touching works. Its inversion, in a phobia of foreign 'infection', is at the heart of dystopian collectivism. It is seemingly rooted in an almost universal assumption of a transferable 'homogeneity in essence in all beings', as Lévy-Bruhl describes it, and of the fetishism which accompanied it in early societies.[183] But this feeling may result in slavish submission to objects, individuals, and places, all because the group demands our abject subservience.

* * * *

To later modern readers this may all be somewhat disconcerting, depressing, and disappointing. What price sociability? At the very least, as Bion tells us, individual membership in groups is often difficult. The individual 'is a group animal at war, not simply with the group, but with himself for being a group animal and with those aspects of his personality that constitute his "groupishness"'.[184] It may well be, too, as Alford has stressed, that there is 'no solution to the problem of individual and group' because 'Group members never solve the problem of coming to terms with the leader while finding a place for themselves as individuals and members.'[185] And it may be that we cannot even associate amiably without both warping the moral character of individual group members and derogating outsiders. Even if Le

---

[182] Arnold Angenendt, 'Relics and their Veneration in the Middle Ages', in Anneke B. Mulder-Bakker, ed., *The Invention of Saintliness* (Routledge, 2002), p. 27.

[183] Lévy-Bruhl, *The 'Soul' of the Primitive*, pp. 15–58. This account draws on Auguste Comte.

[184] Bion, *Experiences in Groups*, p. 131. Bion rejects the idea of a 'herd instinct' (p. 168).

[185] Alford, *Group Psychology and Political Theory*, p. 72.

Bon's 'collective mind' postulate has for some time, in some quarters, been regarded as 'untenable', the taint of the 'mob' sticks to other groups.[186]

Small wonder, then, that academic psychology often steers clear of groups, preferring to concentrate on individuals and interpersonal relations. Groups, suspected as being micro- or macro-crowds in disguise, have clearly 'received rather a bad press'. At the very least they are an embarrassment, as promoting a kind of lesser, juvenile, or primitive version of the self. Some psychologists have gone further and even intimated, only partly in jest, that we would be better off without them.[187] The larger they are, the more damaging; hence Lewis Mumford pleads for 'Small groups: small classes: small communities, institutions framed to the human scale.'[188] We have spent around five hundred years discovering or giving birth to the 'I' and then celebrating and privileging it in all manner of ways until it becomes almost synonymous with 'civilization'. Why look back, after such an enormous effort, with longing nostalgia at our primitive 'we-self'? The love we gain, it might be said, is just not worth the pain we must suffer nor the hatred we must expend to sustain it. It might be better to sink into a Stoic indifference to others (which is an improvement on mutual hostility), if we could but endure the isolation which results (which—so far—we can't).

The resulting proposition, then—implied by Le Bon, Freud, Gasset, and many others—is not that dystopian groups are pathological groups. It is that groups *as such* are dystopian. (Or at least, after the discovery and elevation of the 'I-self', have become such.) All mimic the crowd. Even the smallest may be abject tyrannies: the father may be the Great Dictator personified. And so we are back to the fantasy of my-opia.

Therefore, we must return to the proposition that 'hell is other people': this is what Sartre meant.[189] In this view, every person threatens our 'authentic' autonomy through domination. Every group encounter weakens our rationality, pollutes our morality, and threatens to force us backwards regressively towards primitivism or childishness. Every group suppresses the truth about itself. Every group suggests that wanting to be alone is deviant. Every group lays us open to the influence of clever, malevolent leaders whose charisma overwhelms our own feeble public personalities and negates all our reasonable doubts. Every group invites, then bullies us, to submit, and then perhaps affects to permit us to dominate. But this is mere pretence: it is the group who is dominating. The group pretends to release our beast, and promptly reduces it to a mouse. But *en masse* even mice are dangerous.

Some readers may regard this as an extreme caricature of sociability. Perhaps we should rephrase Sartre: to the autonomous self-willing individual capable of being rationally guided by conscience, every group is dystopian which attempts to suppress these qualities. (This comes close, we will see in Chapter 7, to Orwell's formulation.) We may also observe here that having no groups at all may ultimately

---

[186] Hadley Cantril, *The Psychology of Social Movements* (John Wiley & Sons, 1941), p. 118.
[187] Brown, *Group Processes*, p. xiv.
[188] Lewis Mumford, *The Culture of Cities* (Secker & Warburg, 1938), p. 475.
[189] Or not: Sartre frequently said that this phrase had been misinterpreted; see David Detmer, *Sartre Explained* (Open Court, 2008), p. 153. But this is what he should have meant.

imply having only one. If we must have groups, then, let us have as many as possible. (Rousseau and Tocqueville were agreed here: this is the true value of 'civil society'.) This recognizes both our dependence on groups and the importance of what we most value in group association, namely non-exploitative sociability, warmth, and affection. It avoids the elevation of the hermit into a universal type, parodying the intellectual's (very understandable) fear of the masses. It queries, at the least, the elevation of an asocial idea of autonomy to the status of a first principle, without considering the other constituents of human happiness.

So, except for hyperindividualists, the group itself is not dystopian. Hell is not, as such, other people. Hell is uncooperative, aggressive, stupid people who gang up on us. It is tempting to describe the dystopian collectivist group as one in which the satisfaction of gregariousness passes into the destructive annihilation of individuality. But a quintessential desire for sameness and equality in fact pervades most groups, and there are constructive phases of this annihilation, too. The monastic loss or sublimation of the self may be one, and here asociability is consensual. Nonetheless, we are usually unhappy outside groups. The answer to the problem of dystopian groups is thus not the elimination of groups as such. However, before we pardon and excuse many types of group activity we must clarify how groups affect our moral thinking in particular. For here we may have to reverse our judgement again.

Groupism: Ethical Exchange and Higher Morality

We have seen that the group's primary function is to strengthen us through the two forms of vicarious enhancement described. Its second function, according to Freud, Bion, and others, is to distribute responsibility amongst its members, displacing it from individuals and even consciously abrogating it.[190] This is a far more dangerous process. The group pardons, exonerates, expiates, absolves. It is our invisibility cloak. What would be wrong at the individual level becomes acceptable with the group's sanction. The gang will rape more readily than the individual. So states will murder with impunity. Moral cowardice, blaming others, and evading responsibility is second nature to us. Again groups bring out the worst in us.

Particularly important here is the often ugly process known as scapegoating (the word first appears in 1530), an age-old means of displacing or transferring guilt and sin by projecting evil symbolically upon some entity.[191] It is frequently associated with purging the 'unclean' or 'impure', and is closely linked with ritual sacrifice.[192] Objects can serve the purpose: indigenous Australians put toothache into a stone. Peoples and spiritual entities serve too: Jews, heretics, infidels, witches, demons. The Athenians kept outcasts 'as public victims at the expense of the town', sacrificing two at a time when plague, drought, or famine occurred.[193] In Albania,

---

190 See Freud, *Group Psychology*, and Bion, *Experiences in Groups*.
191 In Leviticus 16:20–2, a live goat is released into the wilderness and the sins of the people of Israel are transferred symbolically to the animal.
192 Richard Kearney, *Strangers, Gods and Monsters: Interpreting Otherness* (Routledge, 2003), p. 28.
193 Grant Allen, *The Evolution of the Idea of God* (Grant Richards, 1904), pp. 349, 353.

sacred slaves were kept in the Temple of the Moon. One was ritually speared to death each year, and the people's sins transferred to his corpse. Ugly people, dwarves, criminals, and outcasts have fulfilled the same function elsewhere.[194] In early modern England, 'sin-eaters' were paid to eat and drink over a corpse to free it from its sins by taking them over.[195] The Devil who 'made me do it'—see below— has played this role for most of European history.

The most extreme instances of blood sacrifice represent first and foremost 'an act of piety . . . to save the people from calamity and the cosmos from collapse'.[196] Such a sacrifice, according to Henri Hubert and Marcel Mauss, 'through the consecration of the victim, modifies the condition of the moral person who accomplishes it'.[197] This involves transferring moral guilt above all. The shedding of blood may offer a sacred closure for a traumatic episode in group history. In Girard's account it also serves to limit violence within the community.[198] At one level this is an immensely important, all-encompassing theme, a central feature of social life. To Richard Kearney, 'the Terror after the French Revolution; the continuation of slavery and racism after the American Revolution; the mushrooming of Moscow Show Trials after the Russian Revolution; and the Holocaust and subsequent genocides' were 'all chilling instances of the seemingly ineradicable lust to purify saints by purging scapegoats'.[199] Kearney takes up Girard's suggestion that most societies are based upon scapegoating, or ritual sacrifices of maligned others.[200] Here there is an obvious, even intimate, relationship between sacrifice, sin, and bloodshed: 'Christ's blood cleanses our sins', in one rendition.

In cultures where natural disasters are understood as the gods reacting to sin or moral deficiency this is especially common. Consider the instance of a poisoning scare in Milan in 1630, which coincided with a plague outbreak and predictions that the Devil would infect the city's water supply. Many innocent people were seized, 'confessed' under torture, implicated others, and were executed for dealing with the Devil. An 'almost incredible' number of persons confessed to such collaboration, and 'day after day persons came voluntarily forward to accuse themselves'.[201] The Romans also blamed the Christians for natural misfortunes, and there were anti-Korean riots in Japan during the 1923 earthquake. Here the lunatic fringe is never far off: flooding in Britain in 2013 was blamed by one official on the recognition of the right to gay marriage, while in Indonesia naked tourists offending mountain spirits were blamed for earthquakes in 2015.

But these are extreme instances. Groups routinely perform the same functions of moral displacement. They grant us anonymity, camouflage, and escape. They

---

[194] Charlie Campbell, *Scapegoat: A History of Blaming Other People* (Duckworth Overlook, 2011), pp. 31, 39–40.
[195] Wilson, *The Magical Universe*, p. 295.
[196] Nigel Davies, *Human Sacrifice in History and Today* (Macmillan, 1981), p. 13.
[197] Henri Hubert and Marcel Mauss, *Sacrifice: Its Nature and Function* (University of Chicago Press, 1964), p. 13.
[198] Girard, *Violence and the Sacred*, p. 7.   [199] Kearney, *Strangers, Gods and Monsters*, p. 33.
[200] See René Girard, *The Scapegoat* (The Athlone Press, 1986), e.g., p. 186.
[201] Mackay, *Memoirs of Extraordinary Popular Delusions*, vol. 1, p. 180.

cushion us from direct face-to-face personal confrontation and release us from inhibitions which constrain us when we conceive ourselves to be acting as individuals.[202] When groups provide us with a mask they allow us to feign having no free will. Thus, pointing the finger elsewhere, we can escape some or even all of the consequences of our actions. So 'we do together things that would be unthinkable when we are acting as responsible individuals. We are swept away by a contagion. We even sacrifice our own interests to those of the group.'[203] It does not matter how we rationalize this process. We may submit to a God who has a 'Plan' ('Thy will be done'), a Leader, a Party, History, or some other imperative principle with exactly the same end in mind: denying our free will. Once we are 'following orders'—the chief defence of almost every incidence of mass murder examined in Part II—we feel relieved of the burden of conscience. This soothing displacement, then, is one of the chief functions of groups. The more powerless and vulnerable we feel, the more likely we will be to utilize this device. For it neatly inverts our powerlessness, making us vehicles of the greatest powers, and thus returning power to the vacuum.

We may describe this as a process of *ethical exchange*: we give up our private ethical standards and replace them with what the group commends. It is often a poor bargain. Frequently we must close our eyes and inwardly ask whether the group's morality is really superior. We blush to think it is not, but, shamefully biting our tongues in the process, comply anyway. This is what power demands. In the most exceptional cases we claim so far to transcend everyday morality in the name of collective necessity that we can perform almost any form of action, including mass murder. We will see in Chapter 3 that the Christian conception of grace and its secular equivalents, driven by quasi-millennial expectations, prove very useful here.

Religious Groups as Paradigms of Extreme Groupism

As we have constantly been reminded in recent years, extreme conformity to the group and extreme enmity towards outsiders characterize religious groups more than any other type. (Nationalism and tribalism—Tutsis vs Hutus, for instance,—offer some obvious parallels, though.) Religious groups are usually defined by their peculiar claims to certainty and their contact with eternity and destiny through communication with the Divine. Religion, from the Latin to bind or retain, provides us with one of the most primary forms of identity we have.[204] Its spiritual fusion furnishes a unique unity of will. It exhibits such a profound, intense sense of 'belongingness' that it is tempting to suggest that the former may indeed be primarily a subset of the latter. (That is to say, the community of belief is more about community than belief.) To Durkheim, therefore, 'God' and worship arise in

---

[202] Automobiles, telephones, some animals, like pets, the Internet, and other devices can fulfil an analogous function, allowing us to say or do things in a protective sphere defined by empowering machines or anthropomorphizing animals which permit us to say and do what we would could not otherwise, because of our vulnerability. Hence road rage, and murder and rape threats on the Internet, and so on.

[203] Arnold A. Hutschnecker, *Love and Hate in Human Nature* (Skeffington, 1956), p. 177.

[204] See Isaacs, *Idols of the Tribe*, pp. 144–70.

asserting group identities. Religion focuses on rituals of group belonging. 'God' here represents an idealized (just, equal) social collectivity, usually with paternal authority ordering the family's unruliness. 'God' is the mythical head of our community. (He, or whatever, 'exists', in this sense, in our minds.) Grasping this (Feuerbach, Marx), we now bypass the metaphysical and ritual formalities of religion and discern its communitarian essence.[205] Or so materialists are prone to argue.

Religion provides a primary form of identity both physically and emotionally by defining the group by the unity of transcendental experience. This appears to validate the belief system and produces intense feelings of brotherhood. Individuals bond in religious groups by sharing a psychological state of 'effervescence', elation, and enthusiasm. The feeling is 'warmth, life, enthusiasm, the exaltation of the whole mental life, the raising of the individual above himself'.[206] We are wedded by bliss. Religious groups exhibit the clearest forms of the ritualized expression of belonging through assertions of cleansing, sustenance, and the like. The muck of 'I' is cleansed by bathing in 'We'. As E. E. Evans-Pritchard acknowledged, Durkheim believed that one of the 'psychological fundamentals' of religion was 'the elimination of the self, the denial of individuality'.[207]

Purged of its quaint mysteries, religion is thus essentially a sociological phenomenon, a special form of group.[208] Often intense desires for 'salvation' or 'at-one-ment', in Ian Suttie's term, are (at least in Christianity) forms of psychotherapy which seek a 'cure' for the soul's alienation in unifying individuals in the fellowship of believers and all eventually in the higher group of 'saved' or 'elect'.[209] Yet the religious sentiment as such, as Théodule Ribot expressed it, aims 'to unite, group, *socialise*'. Unity of belief, to Ribot, thus 'creates the religious community, as community of external and internal interest creates the civil community. Both tend to expel dissidents (internal enemies), and to conquer external enemies—in this case, the heathen.'[210] The unbeliever, the *kaffir*, the heretic, come to epitomize the Other, and evil. Many religions, much of time, demand the conversion if not extermination of 'infidels' and unbelievers. They kill on principle, hesitating only for lack of power. Because of the contagion of ideas, 'heresy' is a more intensely provocative challenge to their sense of identity than being the member of concrete 'others' like race, tribe, or nation. And so they condemn and punish 'apostasy', that most reactionary and purely emotional of all concepts, for similar reasons. 'Heresy' goes beyond difference to affront. 'Faith' is an intense basis for subjective, personal identity. Pulled up, challenged, it can cause a sense of spiritual death. And so, we will soon see, can its secular equivalents.

---

[205] Ludwig Feuerbach's *The Essence of Christianity* (Leipzig, 1841) describes the projection of an idealized Christian self as the 'essence' of Christianity. This assisted Marx's starting point in the 'Paris Manuscripts' of 1844.
[206] Durkheim, *The Elementary Forms of the Religious Life*, p. 425.
[207] E. Evans-Pritchard, *Theories of Primitive Religion* (Clarendon Press, 1965), p. 64.
[208] Durkheim, *The Elementary Forms of the Religious Life*, pp. 206–14, 425.
[209] Ian D. Suttie, *The Origins of Love and Hate* (Kegan Paul, Trench, Trubner & Co., 1935), p. 146.
[210] Ribot, *The Psychology of the Emotions*, p. 323.

Religious groups, however, assume many forms. All provide unity, spiritual bonding, hierarchy, leadership, and communion and continuity between the living and the dead. Many do so by enforcing rules which are accepted by members with little or no coercion or violence. Religious sects like the Moravians, Shakers, Dunkers, Mennonites, Amish, and Hutterites (to take a few Christian examples) have provided the most long-lived of voluntary or intentional communities, and play an essential role in the utopian tradition. They display the crucial qualities of trust and mutual acquaintance, even friendship, which distinguish the *Gemeinschaft* ideal of 'community' compared to the alienation and obliviousness of the teeming *Gesellschaft*-driven metropolis. Yet such communities may also assume cult-like features, treating their members harshly and violently, and transforming bonds based on consent to those rooted in coercion. The degree to which they do so often hinges on their paranoia and anxiety and the relationship between leaders and followers.

It is when they turn to violence and the destruction of others in asserting this purity that such groups interest us here. When, in particular, does what Richard Sennett terms a 'myth of community purity' emerge, which exposes feelings of conflict and difference? Fear commonly plays a key role here: 'in the purification of a coherent community image, fear rather than love of men's "otherness" prevails'. The repression of deviants easily follows.[211] Where violence, now glorified, comes to lubricate and hasten the process of purification, ecstasy as a religious experience may both fuel and be derived from spilling blood.[212] Now ritual sacrificial killing, at the heart of many religions, can also assume a secular form, seeking scapegoats to preserve the community of believers and providing a cathartic outcome for the perpetrators.[213] So sacrifice alleviates sin or guilt felt by the group, and affirms its identity by eradicating its 'other'. Outsiders, minorities, heretics must be symbolically if not literally crushed or 'eaten' in order to strengthen ourselves or to appease the gods.[214]

Now, the solidarity and internal cohesiveness of this group are typically fuelled by paranoia. The group's 'collective psychopathology', as Norman Cohn terms it, involves extreme enmity towards its defined 'enemy', which it threatens with persecution and extermination.[215] In extreme cases, the intensified definition of the group's purity fuels its destructiveness. A language of species, class, race, and other forms of struggle becomes central to our world-view. Thus, for Steven Pinker, 'the ideology of group-against-group struggle explains the similar outcomes of Marxism and Nazism'.[216]

---

[211] Ibid., pp. 9, 30, 36, 39, 42–3, 47.

[212] Bernd Weisbrod, 'Religious Language of Violence', in Stuart Carroll, ed., *Cultures of Violence: Interpersonal Violence in Historical Perspective* (Palgrave Macmillan, 2007), pp. 74–5.

[213] Girard, *Violence and the Sacred*, p. 93. See further Robert G. Hamerton-Kelly, ed., *Violent Origins: Robert Burkert, René Girard, and Jonathan Z. Smith on Ritual Killing and Cultural Formation* (Stanford University Press, 1987) and David Pan, *Sacrifice in the Modern World: On the Particularity and Generality of Nazi Myth* (Northwestern University Press, 2012).

[214] Some suggest that sacrifice is derived from cannibalism. A Gnostic Gospel even suggested that 'God is a man-eater': Hamerton-Kelly, *Violent Origins*, p. 175.

[215] Norman Cohn, *Europe's Inner Demons: An Enquiry Inspired by the Great Witch-Hunt* (Chatto-Heinemann, 1975), p. ix.

[216] Steven Pinker, *The Blank Slate: The Modern Denial of Human Nature* (Penguin Books, 2002), p. 157.

Justification for extreme measures is also more likely to occur when the expectation of imminent salvation, or some form of millenarian transformation, is present. Millenarianism, which in Christianity involves the expectation of Christ's return, can be a religious variant on utopia, as well as on the return to a golden age of original purity. Or, alternatively, utopia becomes the 'secular equivalent of the millennium'.[217] In such instances a search for what Sennett, following Cohn, calls 'purity of identity' is common. Here defensive patterns lead people to 'desire a purification of the terms in which they see themselves in relation to others'. They may come to believe that they, or a small group, are 'chosen' for salvation, and that outsiders are not.[218]

The idea that the world should, can and/or will be made perfect, becoming a changeless realm of undisturbed peace, is as old, in Cohn's view, as Zoroastrianism (c.1500–1200 BC).[219] Our understanding of a possible final reconciliation of order and disorder dates from Judaism, and in particular the destruction of the kingdom of Judah by the Babylonians. The exiles will have their homeland restored, and milk and honey will flow again. Yahweh's promise of a new Heaven and a new earth includes the wolf lying down with the lamb, and children playing around snakes without being harmed (Isaiah 11:6–8). Martyrs and the other elect will rise from the dead and reign on earth for a thousand years. Their capital, the holy space of Jerusalem, will be a city of pure transparent gold with walls of jasper, gates of pearl, and streets of gold, guarded by angels (Revelations 21:10–21). But first, warned Augustine, the 'New World' would have to burn away 'the world's corruptible qualities'.[220]

Modern millenarianism is often associated with the twelfth-century visionary Joachim of Fiore, who divided history into three stages, those of the Father, Son, and Holy Ghost. Joachim foresaw a great messianic leader issuing in the transition from the second to the third, paradisiacal period, where there would be no work, wealth, or poverty, and no need for food, each having evolved into a spiritual being. Then a new order of 'contemplative, spiritualized monasticism' would emerge in a kind of self-endowed grace. Thus, 'the idea of a community of the spiritually perfect who can live together without institutional authority was formulated on principle'.[221] Various groups adopted this outlook. The Waldensians (twelfth–fifteenth centuries), for example, were wandering preachers calling themselves the *perfecti*. Critical of the laxity and luxury of the clergy, they followed the Lyon merchant Peter Valdès' (or Vaudès') injunction to sell their goods and possessions

---

[217] J. F. C. Harrison, 'Millennium and Utopia', in Peter Alexander and Roger Gill, eds., *Utopias* (Duckworth, 1984), p. 61.

[218] Richard Sennett, *The Uses of Disorder: Personal Identity and City Life* (Faber & Faber, 1996), p. 130.

[219] Cohn, *Cosmos, Chaos and the World to Come*, pp. 77–115; Norman Cohn, 'How Time Acquired a Consummation', in Malcolm Bull, ed., *Apocalypse Theory and the Ends of the World* (Blackwell, 1985), pp. 21–37.

[220] Cohn, *Cosmos, Chaos and the World to Come*, pp. 141–62, 173–4, 200.

[221] Eric Voegelin, *The New Science of Politics* (University of Chicago Press, 1952), pp. 113. Joachim believed that following on the ages of law and grace, the third age of love would be one of spiritual men, and was associated with the Holy Spirit.

and give the proceeds to the poor. The *perfecti* had no homes, possessions, or wives, and called each other brothers. They were single-mindedly devoted to purity of life. Deemed heretical in 1184, they were burnt when caught.[222]

The prospect of regaining an earthly or new Jerusalem or merging with the Holy Spirit suffuses many later such heresies. The antinomian idea of the 'Free Spirit' sometimes promoted a libertinism of 'perfect freedom', including sexual license and even murder. For those who had achieved perfection in this life, sin as such was abolished, on the basis of an assumed union with God or the Holy Spirit on earth.[223] In Gordon Leff's formulation, 'Man became God, and in God's name could act with the freedom and self-justification with which God acted. He could thus do anything and whatever he did was right.'[224] Here the self-proclaimed special status of the 'saved' group may induce one of the most perplexing variations on the process of ethical exchange. The saved may claim to be in an antinomian state of grace, freed from the constraints of everyday morality. Possessed by a 'higher' truth or within sight of achieving some 'final' end, they demand the right to act in any way which will hasten this end. This state of grace and absolution may prove to be the most destructive mentality of all.

In 1936, Karl Mannheim was amongst the first to identify the sixteenth-century Anabaptists with the secularization of millenarian ideas, heralding the great utopian schemes and movements of the twentieth century.[225] There is a reasonable case, therefore, for seeing what Reinhart Koselleck termed the 'temporalization of Utopia', 'the metamorphosis of utopia into the philosophy of history', where the 'imagined perfection of the formerly spatial counterworld is temporalized' in the eighteenth century, as a process of millenarian secularization.[226]

The most important intermediary stage in this development was clearly the French Revolution. This embodied, to some, a form of secular millenarianism entailing an expectation of profound change, and the passage from a corrupt to a redeemed state. It set off a 'millennial shock wave' centred on a suddenly exploding egalitarianism, a kind of *egalomania*, which reverberated through European history for the next two centuries.[227] Here transparency is wedded to self-sacrifice: in Auxerre, it was said that 'the patriot had no privacy; he relates everything to the common good: his income, his pain, he shares everything with his brothers, and herein lies the source of the publicity characteristic of fraternal, that is, republican government'.[228] Such promises include the still-proscribed idea that the revolution

---

[222] On the name see Gordon Leff, *Heresy in the Later Middle Ages* (Manchester University Press, 1967), vol. 2, p. 448. Generally see Gabriel Audisio, *The Waldensian Dissent: Persecution and Survival c.1170–c.1570* (Cambridge University Press, 1999).

[223] Robert E. Lerner, *The Heresy of the Free Spirit in the Later Middle Ages* (University of California Press, 1972), pp. 1, 82–3.

[224] Leff, *Heresy in the Later Middle Ages*, vol. 1, p. 308.

[225] Karl Mannheim, *Ideology and Utopia* (Kegan Paul, Trench, Trubner & Co., 1936), pp. 191–2.

[226] R. Koselleck, *The Practice of Conceptual History* (Stanford University Press, 2002), pp. 85, 88.

[227] Richard Landes, *Heaven on Earth: The Varieties of the Millennial Experience* (Oxford University Press, 2011), p. 288.

[228] Eli Sagan, *Citizens and Cannibals: The French Revolution, the Struggle for Modernity, and the Origins of Ideological Terror* (Rowman & Littlefield, 2001), p. 431.

could only be wholly fulfilled if it abolished private property. The leading communist in the French Revolution, Gracchus Babeuf, aimed to abolish 'all frontiers, fences, walls, locks on doors, all disputes, trials, all theft, murder, all crime, all Tribunals, prisons, gallows, torture, jealousy, insatiability, pride, deceit, duplicity, finally all vice'—a 'classic millennial vision' of boundless felicity, in Richard Landes' phrase.[229]

Soon after, more apocalyptic visions of the future began to become increasingly frequent. The theme of the 'total end of man', Saul Friedländer argues, first emerges in a secular context in the nineteenth century.[230] Apocalyptic mentalities then proliferate rather than retreat, first with capitalistic crises and tyranny, then communist revolution, and then with threats of nuclear weapons, overpopulation, resource depletion, and climate collapse. Millenarianism having failed, Apocalypse seems increasingly plausible. But the language and logic of both are often entwined.

Conclusion

This chapter has explored the background to social and political dystopias by using both psychology and sociology to suggest a group theory of dystopia. We first explored theories of the crowd, and then the bearing these have on groups more generally. Here we distinguished between *internal dystopias*, where coercion affects the privileged as well as the rest of society; and *external dystopias*, where outsiders suffer the brunt of repression. We have noted that *groupishness*, the desire to belong to larger units, is the root concept of group identity. *Enhanced sociability*, or a sense of trust, friendship, and belonging, is what most groups offer their members. *Groupism* is the pressure to conform to the group's identity and opinions. *Groupthink* is the resulting mentality and process of collective thinking of the group as such. *Groupspeak* is its verbal expression. *Carcerotopia* is the most extreme form of prison state. *My-opia* is the fantasy which releases us from all these conformist pressures.

The functioning of the group involves three processes: *identity transferral*, where we exchange aspects of our individual identity for group identity; *horizontal* and *vertical vicarious enhancement*, where our personal sense of power is increased by identifying with the group and its leaders, *horizontal* being identification with the group or crowd, and *vertical* the strengthening individual through identifying with leaders; and *ethical exchange*, the substitution of group morality for personal morality, which offers a degree of absolution for our deeds, but usually to the detriment of toleration.

Finally, three other terms help define the peculiarities of group or crowd destructiveness. *Sociogermophobia* is a sociomedical term which describes an extreme obsession with group purity that is contingent upon demonizing outsiders

---

[229] Quoted in Landes, *Heaven on Earth*, p. 290.
[230] Saul Friedländer, 'Themes of Decline and End in Nineteenth Century Western Imagination', in Saul Friedländer, Gerald Holton, Leo Marx, and Eugene Skolnikoff, eds., *Visions of Apocalypse* (Holmes and Meier, 1985), pp. 61–83.

and is usually combined with intense paranoia.[231] It is the collective equivalent of a well-known form of obsessive-compulsive disorder, a contamination anxiety resulting in obsessive cleaning. *Secular millenarianism* denotes the idea of the 'reborn' personality, linked to antinomianism and a culture of guilt. Here the Kingdom of God is redefined in terms of secular justice and equality. It is often strongly linked to a desire to change everything, and driven by a sense of overwhelming and pervasive injustice and corruption which requires complete suppression. The 'Apocalypse' symbolically denotes the critical moment of transformation in religious millennialism. Its parallel in secular millennialism is sometimes 'revolution'. Thirdly, *egalomania* is the obsessive desire for equality or sameness (sometimes involving compulsive self-renunciation), founded in mimeticism but often driven by trauma or crisis. Following Canetti, this intense desire for equality is treated as central to crowd formation and identity. It also underpins most forms of religion. (And we might go further and identify it with social modernity as such.) Clinically, this is often diagnosed in individual cases as a form of ritualistic and repetitive behaviour observed in autism spectrum disorders, especially antisocial personality disorder. It usually describes an insistence that the individual's environment remains the same in pattern and appearance. There is no equivalent term for the parallel social 'disorder', which would be akin to a concept of 'social autism'. Historically, it is identified with Christian sectarianism, and from a secular viewpoint, modern revolutionism.

The Argument of this Book

This book is divided into three parts. Part I explores the relevance of group psychology to the theme of dystopia; and explores the role of monstrosity in the prehistory of the idea of intensely evil spaces and the relation of their inhabitants to human society. Here, the Christian Devil would emerge as the most powerful monstrous figure of all times, and would serve as a trope for persecuting heretics, Jews, and witches in particular. Part II examines twentieth-century totalitarian regimes in order to explain the mechanisms of their persecution in terms of the group theory outlined so far, and in light of the account of secular millenarianism just sketched. This is done chiefly by modifying existing theories of political religion. Part III then examines the literary refractions of twentieth-century dystopianism. Here, over two hundred literary dystopias are examined in order to formulate a chronology and scheme of classification from the genre, focusing on the period 1810–2010. These take up a much wider range of themes than only the political dystopia, though the problem of collectivism remains central to many.

---

[231] Interestingly, one early meaning of the word 'obsession' is 'hostile action by the devil'.

2

Monstrosity and the Origin of Dystopian Space

INTRODUCTION: TERATOLOGY AND DYSTOPIA

We saw in Chapter 1 that an essential part of the mechanism of persecution is the isolation of 'enemy' groups and their portrayal as an 'other' essentially different from and opposed to 'us'. Although this process would only reach its destructive apex in twentieth-century totalitarianism, it has a lengthy prehistory. In Europe, which is our main focus here, fear, hatred, and persecution of Jews, heretics, and women (as 'witches') provided important antecedents for what would follow later. But this process, too, drew upon a much older fear of the monstrous 'other', which would in turn re-emerge in many other forms in modernity, as an aspect of crowd theory, in the Frankenstein trope, even finally, we will see, in imagining the robot.

Monsters inhabit the primordial *terra incognita* of the earth. By contrast to the ideal good spaces of paradise and Heaven, they define the original dystopian space in which fear predominates. As such, they mark the beginning of the natural history of dystopia. At first they often retain animal characteristics. They embody—or disembody—our fear of death most of all. As denizens of the night they prey upon our fear of darkness. They skulk outside the city wall, or beyond the last house of the village, awaiting the extinction of the last candle. The great dark forests filled with wolves, which covered Europe for many centuries before nations and ordered spaces emerged, were also their home. With Christianity they become organized, and, led by the Devil, the greatest monster of all, they came to populate an imaginary space, hell, which became the focus of our greatest fears. Then, let loose upon the world above, they terrorized us for centuries, contributing mightily to the atmosphere of persecution whose peak was reached during the Inquisition, the prototype for totalitarian coercion. So teratology, the study of monsters, reveals that the place of monstrosity in a history of dystopian spaces is a prominent one.[1]

The Origins of Mythical Beings and Spaces: Spirits, Magic, and the Dead

Throughout most of history there have been relatively few human beings in the world and comparatively many spiritual entities. In the magical world-view,

---

[1] Two good introductions to the subject are Stephen T. Asma, *On Monsters* (Oxford University Press, 2009) and Matt Kaplan, *The Science of Monsters* (Constable, 2013).

in pre-Christian Europe and elsewhere, nature was inhabited by a tremendous number of animistic spirits, both good and evil, dwelling in fields, forests, springs, and elsewhere. Many appeared in animal form.[2] The lines between matter and spirit, living and dead, animal and human, were thus relatively porous. Ghosts, talking animals, and the spirits of inanimate objects, springs, the wind, and mountains were ubiquitous. A few of these creatures were benevolent, like the unicorn or mermaid. But most were foul-tempered and malevolent: they caused eclipses, earthquakes, famines, plagues, infestations of locusts and frogs, illness, accidents, bad weather, and much else.

As we saw in Chapter 1, the life of most peoples dominated by a magical world-view appears often to have been one of constant, terrifying paranoia respecting these threats. In most early societies evil spirits are omnipresent, lurking in the corners of houses, in ruins, wells, baths, ovens, and latrines.[3] They often seem to be angry, as if not being human is alone sufficient grounds for irritability. Doing bad is thus their *métier*. They require constant appeasement. But they do not engage with us solely on a personal basis. Often their activities are assumed to be a barometer of the moral performance, the sin and guilt, of a given group. Between them and us stands the magician, sorcerer, or priest, as guardian of the boundaries between the spiritual and everyday worlds. Their arbitration, they suggest, or promise, for a fee, protects us. This magic works when we believe fervently enough in it. For magic relies upon—indeed largely *is*—the power of suggestion. The breach of taboo can kill in most societies: we die of shame, shock, and awe, sometimes almost immediately. Such threats have been subject to easy manipulation ever since the first witch doctor—the prototype, with the storyteller, of the intellectual—realized that an easy living could be made out of preying on the gullible imagination. (Later, praying became the chief form of intercession.)

Fear of death being the most elemental of all anxieties, ghosts occupy a prominent place amongst the spirits. Canetti describes the idea of the 'invisible dead' as perhaps 'humanity's oldest conception', with images of these 'invisible crowds' being perhaps the source of religion itself.[4] Our anxieties concerning every aspect of death are omnipresent and deeply ingrained. Dying, corpses, burials, graves, skeletons, tombstones, are all mournful to see or even to contemplate. Early societies commonly assume that people are composed of both body and soul, and that the spiritual component, once detached, can wander freely. Thence it may wreak havoc on the unfortunate or guilty, even expressing random irritation with the completely innocent, perhaps in sheer resentment of the living. Ancestral spirits, in particular, might watch over us if sufficiently propitiated, as they must be in most early societies. Ghosts have often been conceived as fulfilling some specific moral task, especially revenge, or the expiation of some sin.[5] Seeing them as

---

[2] Margaret Alice Murray, *The Witch-Cult in Western Europe* (Clarendon Press, 1921), p. 12.

[3] The examples of the Ginn in Egypt, given in Ernest Crawley, *The Mystic Rose: A Study of Primitive Marriage and of Primitive Thought in Its Bearing on Marriage* (Watts & Co., 1932), p. 13.

[4] Elias Canetti, *Crowds and Power* (Penguin Books, 1992), pp. 47, 51.

[5] Keith Thomas, *Religion and the Decline of Magic* (Penguin Books, 1991), p. 712.

wish- and denial-projections, at least for much of the time, is thus plausible; they reassure us that justice and moral order exist when both are so conspicuously absent from this life.

Though these magical creatures and spiritual entities have often been conceived as living amongst us, or at least as near as the last lane of the hamlet, our sense of their monstrosity often grows in proportion to their distance from us. So the further away we imagine them to be, the more bizarre they become. But this need be no great distance. In the days of King Arthur (*c.*fifth–sixth century), for instance, 'the people of South Wales regarded North Wales as pre-eminently the land of faerie' and 'the chosen abode of giants, monsters, magicians, and all the creatures of enchantment. Out of it came the fairies, on their visits to the sunny land of the south.'[6]

Elsewhere, in most countries (at least until about the nineteenth century), forests, copses, swamps, and corresponding regions outside of inhabited areas were similarly imagined to be populated by fairies, elves, goblins, trolls, and similar 'little people'. Often seen as spiteful, when not bought off by sacrificial offerings, fairies were known to steal children, or to substitute their own offspring at the moment of birth. Most supposedly possessed magical powers, including the ability to cast spells, and to disappear, reappear, and move mysteriously, all of which, with enough vision, or hallucination, can be readily imagined. Belief in all these entities thus appears to stem from a common source.[7]

The categories of the living and the dead, indeed, are often entangled. Dwarves were commonly thought to be the spirits of darkness and the underworld, and were linked to ghosts, while elves were spirits of light and goodness. (But Scottish elves were reputed to steal newborn infants and replace them with monsters, in order to pay a tithe to the Devil.)[8] In Germanic myth, so-called kobolds, or sprites, could bring good luck to houses and even assist their occupants so long as they were fed, but might turn nasty otherwise. Other trolls and fairies included fertility spirits known as the Green Men, one of whom may have been Robin Hood's prototype.[9]

Such creatures come down to us from the earliest times. From the first written document, the Epic of Gilgamesh (*c.*2500 BC) onwards many gods had animal features or qualities. In Babylonian and Sumerian myth, beasts and demons killed babies, brought sandstorms, and attacked travellers, the sleeping, and the unwary. They crept into houses through cracks, exuding a foul smell, and leaving a poisonous slug-like trail behind them. Female demons, or *succubae* (as they were later called, from the Latin, to lie under) seduced men, cut their throats, drank their blood, and ate their flesh. They could be guarded against by protective spirits, whose assistance, however, was mitigated if an individual sinned or transgressed

---

[6] Wirt Sikes, *British Goblins: Welsh Folk-lore, Fairy Mythology, Legends and Traditions* (Sampson Lowe, Marston, Searle & Rivington, 1880), p. 3.

[7] Edwin Sidney Hartland, *The Science of Fairy Tales* (Walter Scott, 1891), pp. 336–7.

[8] Eusebe Salverte, *The Occult Sciences* (2 vols, Richard Bentley, 1846), vol. 1, p. 126.

[9] Jeffrey Burton Russell, *Witchcraft in the Middle Ages* (Cornell University Press, 1972), p. 52. Thomas mentions a guardian spirit named Puck, alias Robin Goodfellow (*Religion and the Decline of Magic*, p. 724).

taboos. Egyptian demons were sent by the gods as messengers, spreading sickness and death, and had to be propitiated and warded off by amulets. Typically, they gathered around a newborn child, wielding knives, and were fought off by suitably armed benevolent little gods and spirits. At the other extreme in size, Vedic myth described a poisonous yellow, man-eating dragon named Sruvara, supposedly capable of destroying the world.[10] The fabulous Babylonian marine beast called Labhu was said to be three hundred miles long and thirty high, and threatened to overwhelm civilization itself.[11] In Egyptian myth, a giant dragon-like snake named Apophis embodied primeval chaos, and could neither see nor hear, only scream—a pretty dull life even for a monster.[12]

In Europe, the ancient Greeks were well-nigh obsessed with fabulous races elsewhere and mythical beasts nearer home. Homer's account of the island of Charybdis (*c.*ninth century BC) described a creature who spurts out vast quantities of seawater three times daily, endangering passing ships. He told, too, of an island of sirens, who lured unwary sailors to their deaths. (The legend of Lorelei on the Rhine River recounts a similar scenario.) Homer's one-eyed cannibal kings, the Cyclops, also attained great renown. Other creatures, often begot of lustful gods, were half-human, half-goat (the Satyrs), or horse (the Centaurs), or bird (the Harpies), or bull-like (the Minotaur, the beast guarding the labyrinth at Knossos, slain by Theseus), or part-serpent (the gorgon called Medusa slain by Perseus).[13] In such cases the human diluted by animality represents violence. The beast outside mirrors the animal within. 'Demons', however, were minor assistants of the gods, who were sometimes regarded as intermediaries between them and human beings, and could serve as guardian spirits. They were occasionally linked to dreaming, though not specifically to nightmares.[14]

Some of the most famous monsters of antiquity are associated with Alexander the Great, whose very might, indeed, seems to have called forth a need for suitably ferocious opponents. In conquering Egypt he was threatened by a horde of sea-creatures, who emerged nightly to disturb the construction of his city, Alexandria. So he built statues of them so realistic that the monsters fled on perceiving them. His expedition to India was a fruitful source of reports of the marvels and strange beings encountered en route. The medieval fantasy known as the 'Alexander Romance' embellished this journey with a search for the fountain of life, and encounters with giants with hands and feet like saws, or with lion heads.[15]

This also occasioned the description of perhaps the first well-defined secular dystopia, an evil space of great proportions above ground and existing in real time, a realistic large-scale Pandora's box. Here Alexander's penetration of the Caucasus, interwoven with various biblical references, culminated in his building a great gate

[10] Norman Cohn, *Cosmos, Chaos, and the World to Come: The Ancient Roots of Apocalyptic Faith* (Yale University Press, 1993), pp. 25–6, 54, 108.
[11] David D. Gilmore, *Monsters: Evil Beings, Mythical Beasts, and All Manner of Imaginary Terrors* (University of Pennsylvania Press, 2003), p. 31.
[12] Cohn, *Cosmos, Chaos, and the World to Come*, p. 21.
[13] Freud interprets this as castration anxiety.   [14] Kaplan, *The Science of Monsters*, pp. 121–2.
[15] Richard Bernheimer, *Wild Men in the Middle Ages* (Harvard University Press, 1952), p. 88.

of iron in a high mountain pass, marking the frontier with barbaric nations, particularly the Goths, but also Scythians, Turks, and Mongols.[16] (Here we see 'Tatar' associated with both 'Tartar' and Tartarus or hell, and 'Mongol' with 'Magog'.)[17] In some variations, walls were added, and the suspect population, while never entirely enclosed, was both human and monstrous. When the legend was Christianized, these enemies were replaced by the biblical peoples Gog and Magog, who also appear in Islamic accounts.[18] They were also sometimes identified with the Jews, especially the ten lost tribes of Israel, whom some thought would be released by the Antichrist in the last days to slaughter Christians.[19] This drew upon Revelations (20:7–8), where it was recounted that after Christ had returned to imprison the 'great dragon' and 'old serpent' Satan in the abyss for a thousand years, he would return 'to deceive the nations which are in the four quarters of the earth, Gog, and Magog, to gather them together to battle: the number of whom is as the sand of the sea'. Some have interpreted Gog and Magog as guarding the gates of Eden against human return.[20] This also became possibly the first earthly dystopia graphically portrayed, when a gloss on the Alexander Romance was depicted on the Hereford map of *c.*1300, showing a zone of monsters in the region of Scythia. Walled up by Alexander, it included cannibals, griffins, and a race of one-eyed men, all destined to be released by the Antichrist, the false prophet figure goaded on by the Devil or identified with him, as described in the New Testament, and supposed to be killed by Christ.[21] Here the sheer numbers involved render monstrosity dystopian.

With the growth of the legend, the site of Alexander's Gate shifted, mostly eastwards, where, following Genesis 2:8, some supposed the Garden of Eden to be. Foreshadowing Orientalist ideas of 'the East' as a kind of alternative imagined self, this region was reputed in Alexander's time to be inhabited by many monstrous races, though India was often confused with Ethiopia. (The wall motif may have been inspired by the Great Wall of China.)[22] The peoples of these regions were not usually conceived of as civilized. Images suggesting impurity and cannibalism are common in these accounts. In some variants the peoples were confined by the gates 'because of their uncleanness. For they ate things polluted and base, dogs, mice, serpents, the flesh of corpses, yea unborn embryos as well as their own dead.' Here, thus, the excluded are sometimes unhuman or semi-human, sometimes not. But they are clearly immoral, and walled off for this reason.

---

[16] Andrew Runni Anderson, *Alexander's Gate, Gog and Magog, and the Inclosed Nations* (Medieval Academy of America, 1932), p. 25.

[17] Jean Delumeau, *History of Paradise* (Continuum, 1995), p. 88.

[18] Richard Kenneth Emmerson, *Antichrist in the Middle Ages: A Study of Medieval Apocalypticism, Art, and Literature* (Manchester University Press, 1981), p. 85.

[19] Anderson, *Alexander's Gate*, p. 36; Emmerson, *Antichrist in the Middle Ages*, p. 86.

[20] Jeffrey Jerome Cohen, *Of Giants: Sex, Monsters, and the Middle Ages* (University of Minnesota Press, 1999), p. 35.

[21] Asma, *On Monsters*, p. 88. This legend was, however, much older, and possibly Hellenistic. An earlier instance in microcosm was Pandora's box, in which the world's evils were confined.

[22] Vsevolod Slessarev, *Prester John: The Letter and the Legend* (University of Minnesota Press, 1959), p. 117 n14.

Yet, curiously, these descriptions may have been in part perhaps also an inversion of the earthly paradise ideal, where miraculous, hallowed, and sacred space was mirrored by its tabooed opposite or negation. For this was also described as an immense city reached by Alexander on the banks of the Ganges. It was surrounded by a high wall which turns out to be an impenetrable spiritual barrier and a symbol of 'insatiable longing'.[23] For perhaps the first time, the prototypes of (e)utopia and dystopia appear juxtaposed as spaces epitomizing good and evil. (But we will see that, in the most common medieval image of the ideal world, the Garden of Eden, Satan the snake is usually present, the Devil incarnate, and usually interpreted as a symbol of lust.)[24] So here, perhaps, the images merge.

The Alexander legend was augmented by a variety of other Greek and Roman accounts of monstrous peoples. The chief authorities for 1,500 years,[25] Ktesias, Megasthenes, and Pliny, depict the Abarimon people of Scythia, whose feet point backwards; the Albanians, who see better by night than day and are born grey-headed; the warrior-women race of Amazons, sometimes described as unusually lustful, though often not;[26] the Androgini ('man-woman') of Africa; and the Anthropophagi ('man-eater'), who in some narratives eat their parents when old. Other races walk upside down, on all fours; consist of bearded or hairy women (the Gorillae); have only one eye (like Homer's Cyclops); or have horns and tails (the Gegetones or Gorgones, clearly hinting at our later chief villain, Satan, who gains these attributes in the sixth–eighth centuries). The first person to describe a unicorn (undoubtedly the Indian rhinoceros), Ktesias, also portrayed the Panotii as having ears which reached their feet and conveniently served as both blankets and wings; they would still appear on medieval maps as late as the thirteenth century. (The Indians themselves thought barbarians had long ears.) Megasthenes travelled in India in the early fourth century BC, and drew extensively on local epics and legends. He told of the Hyperboreans, who lived a thousand years, and a people with dogs' ears and one eye in their foreheads (again associated by the Indians with barbarians).[27] More likely to have been real was another oddity described as a 'wild man', who had his toes growing backward, and died after being captured (see Fig. 2.1).

Other historians discussed races lacking language (Pliny's *Historia Naturalis*, AD 77, describes five such). Cave dwellers (Troglodytes), pygmies, and giants were also commonly reported.[28] The Romans were particularly enchanted with the bones of

[23] See 'Alexander the Great's Journey to Paradise', in Richard Stoneman, ed., *Legends of Alexander the Great* (J. M. Dent, 1994), pp. 67–75.

[24] Psychologists often regard the snake as a primeval penis symbol (e.g. Ernest Jones, *On the Nightmare* (The Hogarth Press, 1931), pp. 94–5). In early versions of the Garden of Eden story there was no serpent or satanic figure, and Adam and Eve simply ate from the Tree of Wisdom, realized their nakedness, and were compelled to leave the Garden and relocate in less desirable environs.

[25] See J. W. McCrindle, *Ancient India as Described by Megasthenes and Arrian* (Trübner & Co., 1877), and J. W. McCrindle, *Ancient India as Described in Classical Literature* (Philo Press, 1971).

[26] John B. Friedman, *The Monstrous Races in Medieval Art and Thought* (Harvard University Press, 1981), p. 170.

[27] A good introduction here is Rudolf Wittkower, 'Marvels of the East: A Study in the History of Monsters', *Journal of the Warburg and Courtauld Institutes*, 5 (1942), 162.

[28] These examples are from Friedman, *The Monstrous Races*, pp. 10–11.

Fig. 2.1. Indian monsters *c*.1550. © Mary Evans Picture Library 10038329.

giant creatures, and the discovery of fossil remains of what we know to have been prehistoric animals.[29] Many of the near-universal ancient legends of giants probably stem from such discoveries. The Romans were also the first to project monstrosity into space, with Lucian's *The True History* (*c*.AD 125), recounting voyages involving men from the moon and sun, and a giant sea-monster. The Roman historian Plutarch described the inhabitants of the moon as demons. But some limits to credulity were being established. Pliny thought it implausible that men might turn into wolves and back again—proof at least that the speculation existed.

Human monstrosity was also often discussed in the ancient world.[30] In many societies, one twin in a birth was sacrificed owing to the fear that it was the offspring of spirits, a dilution of the partly human.[31] The Romans regarded monstrous births as deviations from nature. Cicero, for example, thought prodigies were omens marking the will of the gods. (The English word 'monster' derives from *monere*, to warn, *monstrum* implying a portent.) The Romans indeed burnt as impure or left to die of exposure some hermaphrodites, as well as many other seriously deformed children, taking them outside the city.[32] These concerns, often focused on giantism and dwarfism, would form the prehistory of later accounts of the body. The presumed linkage between monstrous births and portents of Divine punishment

[29] See Adrienne Mayor, *The First Fossil Hunters: Paleontology in Greek and Roman Times* (Princeton University Press, 2000).
[30] Pliny, *Natural History* (10 vols, William Heinemann, 1940), vol. 3, p. 61.
[31] Lucien Lévy-Bruhl, *The 'Soul' of the Primitive* (George Allen & Unwin, 1928), p. 46.
[32] René Girard suggests that sacrifice may have been involved in the Greek equivalent: *Violence and the Sacred* (Johns Hopkins University Press, 1977), pp. 163–4.

of nations would last until at least the sixteenth century. One famous later instance of this was the birth in 1512 of a child known as the 'monster of Ravenna', which supposedly had four arms and four legs, and was assumed to presage the conquest of Italy by France. Some Romans also warned that marriages between patricians and plebeians would create monsters.[33] An obsession with an ontological purity of body and race was here thus expressed in terms of class for perhaps the first time. It would not be the last.

With Christianity came the never entirely successful attempt to impose mono-theism, and the dual problems of reconciling an omnipotent god with evil gener-ally, and concentrating this evil in one opponent worthy of such a god. Augustine described monsters as derived from Adam, and as performing a specific role at the Last Judgement. In the Christian world-view, monstrosity was thus fundamentally equated with sin, and the monstrous regions with non-Christian barbarians. Their habits—cannibalism, incest, nakedness—demanded their conversion, a world-view essential to the age of conquest which began in the fifteenth century. In the tenth–eleventh century poems known as the Vienna Genesis, the deformation of Adam's children derives from disobeying Adam's command not to eat of certain plants. Consequently, some had heads like dogs, others mouths on their breasts and eyes on their shoulders, others a single foot, 'very large', enabling them to run as 'quickly as the animals in the forest'.[34]

Besides echoing the past, here we also glimpse aspects of later modern psycho-logical explanations. For Augustine, for instance, monsters were (like everything else) part of God's plan to make us aware of sin. Monstrous races existed to remind us that the monstrosities born amongst humans were still God's creation. Christian writers also had necessarily to map the emergence of such races onto a genealogy which ran from Adam to Noah to Abraham to the present. The question as to how any land creatures not taken on board Noah's ark could have survived the Flood was a puzzling one. In the Bible, two great monsters, Behemoth on land and Leviathan ('that crooked serpent . . . the sea-monster'), appear in the Book of Job as symbols of God's power.[35] (Thanks partly to Thomas Hobbes, both later became bywords for political despotism.) Amongst other fearsome beings, the Book of Revelations described Abaddon as king of some locusts who had scorpions' tails and human heads with women's hair and lions' teeth. They had the power to hurt people for the quaintly precise period of five months (9:7–10), almost as if this had been set down in some monstrous criminal code. Genesis (6:4) mentions an ancient race of giants elsewhere described as the offspring of fallen or rebellious angels who mated with human women.[36] (In some versions, a misogynist narrative was

---

[33] Carlin A. Barton, *The Sorrows of the Ancient Romans: Gladiator and Monster* (Princeton University Press, 1993), p. 151.

[34] Friedman, *The Monstrous Races*, p. 93.

[35] Jung suggests that they are linked to the 'crude instinctive side of the libido accumulated in the unconscious'. (*Psychological Types or the Psychology of Individuation* (Kegan Paul, Trench, Trubner & Co., 1923), p. 333.)

[36] A version rejected by Augustine; Asma, *On Monsters*, p. 72. In Greek myth Zeus often descended from Olympus in animal guise to pursue human women.

Fig. 2.2. *The Deluge* (1633 engraving). © INTERFOTO/Sammlung Rauch/Mary Evans 10446662.

constructed by blaming the women for leading the angels astray in the first place; evidently they dressed provocatively and were 'asking for it' or 'brought it on themselves'.)[37] The Flood was intended to punish this wickedness. But in medieval versions of the narrative, incubae (from the Latin, to lie on top), male demons specializing in furtive sexual intercourse, took over the role of the fallen angels (see Fig. 2.2). (They were commonly reported in nunneries, 'epidemics' thereof being frequent.[38] This helped to cement the association between sexuality and the Devil, but also illustrates how the line between waking and dreaming was not recognized until very late.) The Judeo-Christian account of degeneration via sin or crime from a single perfect man fitted some classical suggestions of decline from an early golden age to an inferior iron age.[39] And so monstrosity became part of the explanation for that decline too.

Of course, a place had to be found for the Jews in this theodicy as well. A link between monstrosity and anti-Semitism is already evident by the late Middle Ages. In the thirteenth-century Ebstorf *mappa mundi*, Gog and Magog were portrayed as blood-drinking cannibals with Jewish features, both derived from and fuelling

---

[37] Neil Forsyth, *The Old Enemy: Satan and the Combat Myth* (Princeton University Press, 1987), pp. 181, 212–18. Reuben's account (109–106 BC) compares this to Adam's temptation of Eve. Both are described as using seductive makeup and hairstyles: Jeffrey Burton Russell, *Lucifer: The Devil in the Middle Ages* (Cornell University Press, 1984), p. 194.

[38] Jones, *On the Nightmare*, p. 84.   [39] Friedman, *The Monstrous Races*, p. 89.

myths of Jews eating Christian children. (There are parallels here with Catholic ritual of drinking the blood and eating the body of Christ.)[40] In Church iconography, Jews were sometimes portrayed as half-goat, half-human, and painted yellow. They were also identified with pigs. Embellishing the theme later in the fourteenth century, Sir John Mandeville likened some monsters to the ten lost tribes of the Jews who would emerge to slaughter Christians. Through the early Christian period, legends of half-man, half-animal races persisted, who were associated with both Jews and Muslims, and sometimes portrayed as horned demons or monsters.[41] Indeed, anti-Semitism as such has been defined as 'the perception of the Jew as a monster'.[42] Hence monstrosity, the first expression of radical otherness, was easily transferred to 'enemy' groups.

The Christian conquest of the more legendary creatures amongst these was a lengthy and testing process. One of the Cynocephali, or dog-headed cannibal people, named Abominable, was reputedly converted to Christianity by the Apostles Andrew and Bartholomew, and renamed Christopher. Through works like the *Wonders of the East*, by the tenth century the legend of the Cynocephalus, now the dog-headed Saint Christopher, had reached Ireland. The eighth-century *Liber Monstrorum*, described by John Friedman as 'the earliest work to give us a markedly and consistently hostile treatment of the monstrous races', introduced 'the three earthly genera that strike mankind with the maximum awe and terror. That is, the monstrous progeny of men, the numerous hideous beasts and the hideous species of dragons, snakes and vipers.'[43]

Amongst these, legends of fire-breathing dragons would come to possess an enduring popularity. The Greek word *dracos*, from which the Anglo-Saxon *drakan* comes, implies that the snake was again a prototype here.[44] But dragons were also probably derived from elephants, crocodiles, and hippopotami. They were connected with extreme weather (storms and lightning) and probably, from the Greeks onwards, to discoveries of dinosaur bones. Identified with the snake in Eden, they gradually became accepted in Christianity as a universal symbol for the Devil.[45] They were also closely identified with the heathen as early as the ninth century.[46] It was a common medieval trope for saints to do battle with dragons and defeat them, good inevitably triumphing over evil, human over animal. Medieval knights encountered many such while seeking treasure or rescuing damsels in distress. (Monsters are frequently associated with the protection of virginity too.) Heroes like Siegfried and Beowulf proved their mettle in such contests. In many traditions, dragons guard the entrance to paradise. In a fourteenth-century Icelandic narrative one defends the stone bridge which must be crossed to enter the lush land beyond. And the Norse narrator walks right through him, seemingly suggesting that such

---

[40] Bettina Bildhauer, 'Blood, Jews and Monsters in Medieval Culture', in Bettina Bildhauer and Robert Mills, eds., *The Monstrous Middle Ages* (University of Wales Press, 2003), p. 80.
[41] Fernando Cervantes, *The Devil in the New World: The Influence of Diabolism in New Spain* (Yale University Press, 1994), p. 12.
[42] Asma, *On Monsters*, p. 91.   [43] Friedman, *The Monstrous Races*, p. 149.
[44] Kaplan, *The Science of Monsters*, p. 101.   [45] Salverte, *The Occult Sciences*, vol. 2, p. 285.
[46] Carl Erdman, *The Origin of the Idea of Crusade* (Princeton University Press, 1977), pp. 278–9.

Fig. 2.3. St George killing a dragon. © Mary Evans Picture Library 10067761.

obstacles are purely symbolic, imaginary, or negligible to those who have faith.[47] Dragons who guard hoards of gold are also a staple in medieval legend. In the German *Nibelungenlied*, and the Anglo-Saxon chronicle *Beowulf*, the dragon, who appears in the Book of Revelation, or the Apocalypse of John (*c*.AD 90), symbolizes Satan. But he is also an image of the Romans' persecution of Christianity, with Nero cast as the Antichrist.[48]

The story of Saint George slaying the dragon—and later Cervantes' parody in what is often regarded as the greatest European novel, *Don Quixote* (1605)— remains perhaps the best known of these accounts. This story of a Christian from Cappadocia martyred while in the Roman army probably dates from the fourth century, though its origins lie in Greek myth. The beast in question lived in a pond in Libya and held the local town to ransom, demanding increasing numbers of sacrifices. George baptizes 20,000 people and then cuts the dragon's head off just before a beautiful princess is sacrificed (see Fig. 2.3).[49]

Most of the medieval fascination with monstrosity focused on the 'East'. Pilgrims, almost by definition bent on transcendental experiences and hugely susceptible to suggestion, speculated that the earthly paradise lay somewhere awaiting rediscovery,

[47] S. Baring-Gould, *Curious Myths of the Middle Ages* (Rivington, 1868), 1st series, vol. 1, p. 262.
[48] In *Beowulf* the monster Grendel is described directly as the 'kin of Cain' (Asma, *On Monsters*, p. 95). The whole Book of Revelation can be understood as a localized response to Roman oppression. On Nero as Antichrist, see Gregory C. Jenks, *The Origins and Early Development of the Antichrist Myth* (Walter de Gruyter, 1991), pp. 252–5.
[49] Baring-Gould, *Curious Myths of the Middle Ages*, 1st series, vol. 2, p. 34.

probably in the Middle East. On medieval maps, the Garden of Eden was often placed in Ceylon (Sri Lanka), or further north on the road to Cathay. These maps depicted twenty or more monstrous races, some also in the south, or Antipodes, lying beneath us, upside down, so to speak, and others in Africa.[50] Many are portrayed as dark in pigmentation; the Ethiopians are a prototype here. The fabled kingdom of Prester John possessed lands inhabited by 'horned men who have but one eye in front and three or four in the back'. There were pigs as large as oxen and dogs like horses, horned men, bearded men, one-eyed men, and golden men without heads twelve feet tall. Here was a Cavern of Dragons, who were quaintly invited out as guests for weddings—just the thing to make the day memorable.[51] Here too was the abominable domain of Gog and Magog, cursed by God, and inhabited by cannibals who ate human flesh 'for the redemption of their sins'. We are told, too, ominously, that not only were there 'more of them than of all other peoples', but that with 'the coming of the Antichrist they will spread over the whole world, for they are his friends and allies'. But eventually they would be defeated (hopefully).[52]

The chief source of many such accounts was the most popular medieval text after the Bible, *The Book of Sir John Mandeville* (*c.*1356). This described, inter alia, islands like Chana with rats as big as dogs; Ethiopians who had one foot so large that it could shade their body against the sun; inhabitants of the Armenian desert who had one arm and one foot, and shot a bow in pairs; desert dwellers in the land of Prester John who had horns and could not speak, but grunted like pigs; and a country where all the men were born shaped like mankind, but the males 'were born like unto dogs', with men's heads but dog's faces—possibly another extension of the wolf-man concept.[53]

Interest in the monstrous expanded considerably in the mid-sixteenth century.[54] Marco Polo located most of his monstrosities in Siberia. Others described lion-headed men, men with tusks and horses' manes who breathed fire and flame, and men fifteen feet tall with black hair.[55] In Pierre d'Ailly's account, a mountain of gold on the island of Taprobane was defended by griffons and dragons. This late, too, about the time the unicorn was being identified with the rhinoceros, dog-headed people were still reputed to inhabit India.[56] A sixteenth-century Spanish account described Devil's Island in the Aegean Sea, ruled by the giant Bandaguido. When he mated with a normal woman the result was a creature covered with hair, its back coated with thick scales, and possessing long wings made of black leather and claws. It devoured humans and other large creatures.[57] The best-known contemporary account of the subject, Ambroise Paré's *On Monsters and Marvels*

---

[50] The race of Antipodes, reported by Isodore, whose feet pointed backwards, was located in Libya.
[51] Keagan Brewer, ed., *Prester John: The Legend and Its Sources* (Ashgate, 2015), pp. 10, 69, 74.
[52] Slessarev, *Prester John*, p. 69.
[53] Sir John Mandeville, *The Travels of Sir John Mandeville* (Penguin Books, 1983), pp. 127–31, 221.
[54] Jean Delumeau, *Sin and Fear: The Emergence of a Western Guilt Culture 13th–18th Centuries* (St. Martin's Press, 1990), p. 136.
[55] Friedman, *The Monstrous Races*, p. 147.   [56] Wittkower, 'Marvels of the East', 195.
[57] *Amadis de Gaula*, Zaragoza, 1508, as described in Alberto Manguel and Gianni Guadalupe, *The Dictionary of Imaginary Places* (Alfred A. Knopf, 1981), p. 94.

(1575), offered an extensive taxonomy of birth defects, but also accepted that there existed misbegotten offspring from unions between animals and 'sodomists and atheists'.[58] So, as with the Jews, monstrosity was a useful way of tainting excluded groups closer to home.

Besides their extension to heretical deviants, we also see a persistent overlap between ideas of monstrosity and conceptions of more primitive peoples. (The word 'savage' is derived from the Romans' name for the original inhabitants of the forests of Italy, the 'Silvani' or Fauni, meaning 'favouring' wood spirits.)[59] By the fifteenth century, and for explorers like Amerigo Vespucci and Columbus, these images had shifted to the so-called 'New World'—the phrase itself is, of course, quasi-utopian—where both thought the earthly paradise might be found, and El Dorado to boot. A kind of crusading pilgrim in the tradition of Mandeville rather than Livingstone, Columbus anticipated encounters with various monsters, like one-eyed men.[60] But, in a major setback for the mythical literature, he reported to Ferdinand and Isabella no monstrous creatures, only savages.[61] The French North American explorer René-Robert La Salle was told by the Indians that 'strange, cat-headed monsters would swallow canoe and men at a gulp, and demons had their homes since the world was first made'.[62] Hernán Cortés was warned that he might encounter peoples with large ears and dog-like faces: the old myths were still long in dying.

Cannibalism was a frequent theme in these narratives. Bernal Diaz has been accused of attempting the 'transformation of the natives into monsters' by categorizing all the southern American natives as outside of humanity, defining them in terms of 'a single central quality, monstrosity, by isolating and concentrating on certain features and forms of behavior "against nature"', particularly cannibalism and sodomy.[63] Maps of the period, like that in the Doge's palace in Venice (c.1340), portrayed the interior of North America as 'Terre Incognite d'Anthropofagi'. Michel de Montaigne's essay on 'The Cannibals' (1580) vividly bears out the centrality of the human fear of being eaten to exploration and the construction of the savage 'other'. In his *Cosmographia* (1544), Sebastian Muenster classified barbarians, savages, and monsters as belonging to a similar category, cannibalism being one factor linking them, and a key practice separating both from the human.[64]

[58] Ambroise Paré, *On Monsters and Marvels* (University of Chicago Press, 1982), p. 67.
[59] Robert Eisler, *Man into Wolf: An Anthropological Interpretation of Sadism, Masochism, and Lycanthropy* (Routledge & Kegan Paul, 1951), p. 29.
[60] He hoped the profits of his voyages would assist in reconquering Jerusalem: F. Thomas Noonan, *The Road to Jerusalem: Pilgrimage and Travel in the Age of Discovery* (University of Pennsylvania Press, 2007), pp. 50–3.
[61] Friedman, *The Monstrous Races*, p. 199.
[62] *Fifty Adventures into the Unknown* (Odhams, 1938), p. 524.
[63] Beatriz Pastor Bodmer, *The Armature of Conquest: Spanish Accounts of the Discovery of America, 1492–1589* (Stanford University Press, 1992), pp. 13, 16, 60, 211.
[64] Margaret T. Hodgen, *Early Anthropology in the Sixteenth and Seventeenth Centuries* (University of Pennsylvania Press, 1964), pp. 127–8.

Yet it was sometimes unclear whether these were technically 'men' eating other men. The renowned defender of the natives, Bartolomé de las Casas, was reproached by his opponent, Juan Ginés de Sepúlveda, during a debate in Valladolid in 1550–1 for treating the natives as fully human, when, Sepúlveda insisted, they were really homunculi, or smaller semi-human beings.[65] And ironically, the natives of the Americas reacted similarly at first to their conquerors. When the Spanish invaded Mexico, Montezuma's spies described them as four-legged monsters with human bodies growing from their backs, so extraordinary was the sight of an armoured horseman.

Though its roots lay much earlier, in the late sixteenth century there began to emerge perhaps the first modern myth of the man-made monster, the 'Golem' of Prague Jewish legend.[66] Like earlier images of a golem carved in wood to act as a servant (mimicking the Egyptians' *shabtis*), this golem was created from clay by Rabbi Leyb (also Leib or Loew) to fight the enemies of the Jews, and brought to life to protect them from blood libels in particular. A veritable superhero perhaps, but in some of these versions the Golem rebelled at one point, caused chaos, and had to be destroyed by the rabbi.[67]

By the seventeenth century, monsters were temporarily in retreat. Shakespeare's *The Tempest* (1623) introduced the monster Caliban (an anagram of 'cannibal'), a half-sea, half-land creature. Perhaps the most fantastic early modern utopia, Margaret Cavendish's *The Blazing World* (1666), describes a variety of Fox-, Bear-, Geese-, and Bird-Men. Foigy's voyage to Terre Australe (1676) describes hermaphrodite Australians eight feet tall; they, somewhat ironically and rather more realistically, given their later near-extermination, refer to one-sexed Europeans, whom they would readily kill, as 'sea-monsters'. The country also contains winged horses, pigs who plough the land themselves in straight furrows (a Land of Cockaygne trope), man-eating birds the size of bulls, and tribes who are half-man, half-tiger.[68]

Encounters with sea-monsters are, of course, also fairly frequent during the age of rapidly expanding nautical exploration. In the eighteenth century we still encounter the discovery of flying creatures of various types, for instance in Robert Paltock's *The Life and Adventures of Peter Wilkins* (1751), where the narrator mates with one. Yet already naturalists are categorizing and demystifying.[69] In Captain John Holmesby's *Voyages, Travels and Wonderful Discoveries* (1759), the Academy

---

[65] See Lewis Hanke, *All Mankind is One: A Study of the Disputation between Bartolomé de las Casas and Juan Ginés de Sepúlveda in 1550 on the Intellectual and Religious Capacity of the American Indians* (Northern Illinois University Press, 1974).

[66] On the prehistory of automata, see E. R. Truitt, *Medieval Robots: Mechanism, Magic, Nature, and Art* (University of Pennsylvania Press, 2015).

[67] Yudl Rosenberg, *The Golem and the Wondrous Deeds of the Maharal of Prague* (Yale University Press, 2007), pp. xvi–xvii; Joachim Neugroschel, ed., *The Golem* (W. W. Norton, 2006), here pp. 84–5.

[68] Gabriel de Foigny, *The Southern Land Known* (1676), ed. David Fausett (Syracuse University Press, 1993), pp. 29, 98, 100, 25.

[69] See Asma's account of Linnaeus' debunking of a supposed stuffed hydra (*On Monsters*, pp. 123–5).

of Kelso contains a 'Repository of Knowledge', a room containing all types of monsters, natural prodigies, and the like. We are already on scientific ground here. Monsters are to be discovered, classified, explained, and then dismissed as mere curiosities, no longer an impediment to explorers and conquerors.[70] They no longer frighten, but delight and amaze.

Some Monstrous Types: Wild Men, Vampires, Werewolves, and Fairy Tales

Wild Men and Indigenous Peoples

Wild men and women had been reported by Herodotus as inhabiting the Libyan deserts in the company of semi-human monsters with dog's heads or eyes in their chests. Alexander was said to have burned wild men because they 'lacked reason',[71] or 'because he could not capture them alive, because they have offensive and disgusting bodies'.[72] The 'wild man' would become ubiquitous in Western medieval and early modern literature, retaining a fascinating hold over the Enlightenment imagination as a test of the premises of humanity and civility.[73] The image often represents a kind of halfway between the human and the monstrous, and an attempt to conjecture about the presence of the bestial in humankind. We should not underestimate, either, the appeal of 'natural man's' primitive freedom from the constraints of civilization, dominated by rude desire and its fulfilment. Some, drawing on Freud, view the image as derived from repressed urges rising to the surface.[74] But in the age of exploration and conquest, natural (wo)man was much more frequently the victim than the hero in this narrative.[75] Later, as wildness and savagery would come to overlap with madness, this would become the untamed desire of wildness within, in a process which Hayden White describes as despatialization and psychic interiorization.[76]

Vampires

As the undead, vampires are more obviously monstrous than wild people.[77] Infinitely mutable, they are now, portrayed as zombies, the most popular monster inherited from our early history. It is easy to see why. The combination is irresistible:

---

[70] *Modern British Utopias*, ed. G. Claeys, vol. 3, p. 73.
[71] Leif Søndergaard and Rasmus Thorning Hansen, eds., *Monsters, Marvels and Miracles: Imaginary Journeys and Landscapes in the Middle Ages* (University Press of Southern Denmark, 2005), p. 57.
[72] Lisa Verner, *The Epistemology of the Monstrous in the Middle Ages* (Routledge, 2005), p. 70.
[73] See Edward Dudley and Maximilian E. Novak, eds., *The Wild Man Within: An Image in Western Thought from the Renaissance to Romanticism* (University of Pittsburgh Press, 1972), and Michael Newton, *Savage Girls and Wild Boys: A History of Feral Children* (Faber and Faber, 2002).
[74] Bernheimer, *Wild Men in the Middle Ages*, pp. 3–4.
[75] See generally Anthony Pagden, *The Fall of Natural Man: The American Indian and the Origins of Comparative Ethnology* (Cambridge University Press, 1982).
[76] Hayden White, 'The Forms of Wildness', in Dudley and Novak, eds., *The Wild Man Within*, p. 7.
[77] A recent introduction is Erik Butler, *The Rise of the Vampire* (Reaktion Books, 2013).

the fangs, the subterfuge, the sneaking up, the lunge for the sudden bite, constant sexual innuendo, Transylvanian castles, coffins, aristocrats and 'vampish' beautiful women, and, in the late twentieth century, teenage angst and gothic chic. To some psychologists, vampires are the epitome of sexual perversion, notably sadism, incest, and necrophilia, where blood stands for semen first and foremost.[78]

Cannibalism is another origin of the idea. Drinking the blood of our enemies to acquire courage commonly occurs in primitive societies. In Greek legend, Lamia, beloved of Zeus, was condemned by his jealous wife Hera to roam the world sucking the blood of children and babies. Blood-sucking ghosts like the lamia, lemures, or strygiae were portrayed with the body of a serpent and the head and breasts of a woman, or the wings of a bird, some features of which were later integrated into witchcraft. Sometimes such beings were believed to be people who had died a violent death, and in Rome they were propitiated in religious cere-monies. Others described vampires as having sexual intercourse with living persons, assuming the guise of a beautiful woman for the seduction but awakening as a corpse.[79] This too would overlap with the witch motif. In the eighth-century Anglo-Saxon saga *Beowulf*, vampires were believed to lurk amongst ancient funeral mounds. In England and elsewhere it was commonly believed that evil men were reinvigorated by the Devil after death and sent back to the world as vampires to do his will.[80] For centuries in England a stake was driven through the heart of the corpses of suicides, who were then buried at a crossroads, to prevent their ghosts wandering at night. This too would be incorporated into the vampire legend. In the Middle Ages, the Devil was, like the vampire, often warned off by the sign of the cross being presented to him. For some reason garlic did not seem to deter Satan. Nor did the threat of daylight, the vampire's enemy.

The name 'vampire' assigned to the phenomena of the 'dead' drinking blood in order to sustain life, or having sexual intercourse with the living, or eating their flesh, however, is not more than about three hundred years old. Emerging in eighteenth-century Serbia, based on rumours of the dead who arose from their graves by night to kill, the myth of *nosferatu* resurrected age-old fears of monsters, Jews, and Turks. It can be read as symbolizing cultural, ethnic, and religious uncertainty, the scapegoat or focal point for a crowd of anxieties. Thereafter, it comes to mean many things, including a variant of Orientalism, the Transylvanian vampire being a barbaric 'Eastern' threat to civilized Europe. Witches and vampires meet halfway in children's stories like Hansel and Gretel, which has many variants. (As often as not the child-eating monster is male, like the wolf in 'Little Red Riding Hood'.)[81] Vampires were, partly, merely a variation on demonic possession. In search of virgin blood, a symbol of insatiable perversion, the vampire also opens up new images of sexuality. (Le Fanu's lesbian vampire in *Carmilla*, 1872, is a case in point.)

---

[78] Jones, *On the Nightmare*, pp. 99, 119, and generally 98–130.
[79] Dudley Wright, *Vampires and Vampirism* (William Rider & Son, 1924), pp. 141–2.
[80] Montague Summers, *The Vampire in Europe* (Kegan Paul, Trench, Trubner & Co., 1929), p. 78.
[81] Max Lüthi, *Once Upon a Time: On the Nature of Fairy Tales* (Indiana University Press, 1966), p. 66.

Werewolves

The wolf-man theme also remains a popular representation of monstrosity. One of the most feared creatures in pastoral and agricultural societies, the wolf is the archetypal hunter and symbol of bloodlust. It is also the beast frequently linked in many early societies with the sorcerer's ability to assume animal form.[82] Historically, the concept can be identified centrally with cannibalism. At the most abstract level, it simply represents human aggression. *Homo homini lupus est* (man is a wolf to man), wrote Plautus (*c.*195 BC). But we also recall that the founders of Rome, Romulus and Remus, were, of course, suckled by a wolf, and went on to found the greatest empire of the ancient world. (However, in Rome, the festival of Lupercalia on 15 February was also identified with wanton sexuality.)[83] The belief that men can transform themselves into hyenas, lions, leopards, and other creatures is not uncommon in Africa and elsewhere.

'Lycanthropy' is the technical term used to describe the belief that one is a wolf. The obsession may include eating only raw bloody meat, emitting bestial howls, and engaging in unrestrained sexual attacks.[84] It is also associated with hypertrichosis, or exorbitant hairiness, a natural malady. The near-universal wolf-man or werewolf theme has been explained in terms of fear of a regression to cannibalism (like vampirism), as well as various forms of madness.[85] This link is already evident in Greek myth. In Ovid's 'Metamorphoses', the king of Arcadia, Lycaon, served the god Jupiter a dish of human flesh in order to test his omniscience, and was turned into a wolf as punishment. This is partly explained by the Arcadians, amongst whom these myths originated, being shepherds and much afraid of wolves.

In medieval Europe, werewolves appear around the fourteenth century. Ireland was known until the eighteenth century in some quarters as 'Wolf-land', and abounded in werewolf stories. Amongst these was a curse laid by a saint upon the natives of Ossory, who were forced, two at a time, to assume the shape of a wolf for seven years for their sins, returning to human form thereafter. In folk tales, the transformation of children into wolf form by a stepmother or a husband by a wife is not uncommon.[86] In the sixteenth century, some 'werewolves' were burnt as witches.[87] In several legends people are transformed into wolves but then allowed to revert to human form if they have not tasted human flesh for a period of years.[88] Hence the wolf image, like much of monstrosity, stands for a reversion to savagery, or, in 'turning into' a wolf, giving in to the monster within. In some cases it represents an incest taboo: in Portugal it was believed that the offspring of godparent and godchild became werewolves.[89]

---

[82] Lévy-Bruhl, *The 'Soul' of the Primitive*, p. 39.   [83] Jones, *On the Nightmare*, pp. 131, 136.
[84] Eisler, *Man into Wolf*, pp. 152, 34.
[85] See Leslie A. Sconduto, *The Metamorphoses of the Werewolf: A Literary Study from Antiquity through the Renaissance* (McFarland & Co., 2008).
[86] Eisler, *Man into Wolf*, pp. 137–8.
[87] Sconduto, *The Metamorphoses of the Werewolf*, p. 200.
[88] Sabine Baring-Gould, *The Book of Were-Wolves* (Smith, Elder & Co., 1865), pp. 8–12.
[89] Stephen Wilson, *The Magical Universe: Everyday Ritual and Magic in Pre-Modern Europe* (Hambledon, 2000), p. 243.

Monsters in Fairy Tales

Many eighteenth- and nineteenth-century European children first encountered monstrosity through the medium of the fairy tale, especially those of the Grimm brothers. Children have a natural and often acute dread of the unknown, which they are nonetheless delighted to confront when suitably protected. Who has not huddled deeper into the bedclothes on being introduced to the giant at the top of Jack's beanstalk, the wicked witch of 'Little Red Riding Hood', or the mischievous imp Rumpelstiltskin? Fairyland is often associated with the world of the dead, where time stands still. Most children's tales until recently had monsters good or bad. Almost all cultures have cannibalistic ogres and giants or dragons and monsters that threaten a community. Most have tales in which a protagonist must confront and conquer a ferocious savage. The quest or combat tale is undertaken in the name of civilization or humanity against the forces of voracity or uncontrolled appetite.[90]

Yet, of course, there are deeper meanings here too. What commences as a fear of real beasts becomes socially reconstructed as general metaphors of good and evil, the popular morality play reproduced for educational purposes. Children are not always as literal as we may assume them to be. Bruno Bettelheim speculated that they might readily perceive themselves as monstrous in response to nursery stories, seeing their own misbehaviour reflected in the evil epitomized in monstrosity, and ambiguously conceding the aggressive, greedy, selfish aspects of it as part of themselves. The 'monster a child knows best and is most concerned with: the monster he feels or fears himself to be, and which also sometimes persecutes him' is never far off. For it lies within. To the psychoanalyst, the giants and ogres of yore 'reside in the unconscious' as hidden anxiety, chiefly stemming from the Id's unfulfilled and frustrated yearnings. Reveal them for what they are, and they are slain.[91] And thus Freud is the real Saint George of later modernity. And yet he too went on to acknowledge a new collective monster in the crowd, which the (Quixotic?) Le Bon had failed to slay.

The Modern Reinvention of Monstrosity

When the age of enchantment gave way (as some suppose) to that of Enlightenment and the conquest and taming of most of the unknown world, the physical domain of monstrosity first appears to shrink dramatically. Now the dragon of superstition is slain by the knight of science, or 'explained' as a dinosaur. 'Monstrous' peoples turn out to be human. 'Witches' became harmless old crones. But while credulity is dented, monstrosity does not disappear. In the nineteenth century, monstrous births, dwarfism and the like, continued to titillate, if now marginalized to the 'freak show'. After Darwin, the search for a missing link between human and ape provoked renewed interest. The possibility of dystopian monstrosity was renewed.

[90] Jack Zipes, *The Irresistible Fairy Tale* (Princeton University Press, 2012), p. 8.
[91] Bruno Bettelheim, *The Uses of Enchantment: The Meaning and Importance of Fairy Tales* (Alfred A. Knopf, 1977), pp. 7, 120–1.

Three great modern prototypes of monstrosity—and dystopia—appear in this period: Mary Shelley's *Frankenstein, or, the Modern Prometheus* (1818), Robert Louis Stevenson's *Dr Jekyll and Mr Hyde* (1886), and Bram Stoker's *Dracula* (1897), which was preceded by John Polidori's 'The Vampyre' tale of 1819. Both of the latter, like so many monsters of yore, are half-human, half-animal (the bat, in Dracula's case). In addition, android themes first emerge in several continental works, including Jean-Paul's *Machine-Man* (1783) and E. T. A. Hoffmann's *The Sandman* (1817).[92]

For social theory, Mary Shelley's creature has proven the most resilient of these efforts. While not portraying a dystopia, for the monster does not affect society as a whole or even a substantial number of people, *Frankenstein* draws on images of wild men and monsters. It is often considered the founding text of modern science fiction.[93] In the early seventeenth century, Descartes had posited that animals and humans alike were nothing more than complex machines, or automatons, and that a mechanical man-machine might be activated by magnets. Others conceded the proximity of human to animal, but conceived of both as living rather than mechanical beings. In the French philosopher La Mettrie's conception of the natural history of the soul, we have the first image of animal kind as 'a graded chain of being in which man and beast are but a link apart', a theme with which Darwin would later be centrally associated. Here a 'soul' is diffused throughout the living organism, rather than being separate from matter.[94] With Shelley the image of the mad scientist, sometimes assumed to be the philosopher William Godwin (who admired La Mettrie), and behind him Rousseau, emerges. Here the hubris of man playing god was broadly conceived as the creating of new human beings in the French Revolution, and is exposed. This links Jacobin experiments, echoing the natural sciences, to create a new egalitarian man and woman, *l'homme régénéré*, to Victor Frankenstein's creature.[95]

The most famous modern monster is born when lightening is harnessed to fashion a living creature from body parts of the dead. Too late it is discovered that the doctor's creation will become a terminally unhappy outsider, out of control. The monster, sometimes called 'demon' or 'devil', is 'born' innocent, and yet corrupted by society, in an extended commentary on Rousseau's great theme. His master refuses to create him a mate, fearing their offspring would be a race of devils. Yet Victor's creation is also his alter ego, *Doppelgänger*, or psychic other, possibly a schizophrenic self, possibly an unregulated Ego, or the subliminal passions.

---

[92] On these and similar works see Christine Woesler de Panafieu, 'Automata: A Masculine Utopia', in Everett Mendelsohn and Helga Nowotny, eds., *Nineteen Eighty-Four: Science between Utopia and Dystopia* (D. Reidel, 1984), pp. 127–46, where the gender issues are drawn out.

[93] On its context see Chris Baldick, *In Frankenstein's Shadow: Myth, Monstrosity, and Nineteenth-Century Writing* (Clarendon Press, 1987) and Jon Turney, *Frankenstein's Footsteps: Science, Genetics and Popular Culture* (Yale University Press, 1998).

[94] Leonora Cohen Rosenfield, *From Beast-Machine to Man-Machine: Animal Soul in French Letters from Descartes to La Mettrie* (2nd edn, Octagon Books, 1968), pp. xxv, 143–4; John Cohen, *Human Robots in Myth and Fiction* (George Allen & Unwin, 1966), pp. 68, 70. See Julien Offray de La Mettrie, *Man a Machine* (The Open Court Publishing Co., 1927).

[95] Julia V. Douthwaite, *The Wild Girl, Natural Man and the Monster: Dangerous Experiments in the Age of Enlightenment* (University of Chicago Press, 1992), p. 10.

Many such possibilities unfold in the two following centuries, particularly as our powers of recreating and fashioning living organisms through DNA manipulation increase. Indeed, *Frankenstein* has been described as establishing the 'governing myth of modern biology', as experimental biology came gradually to epitomize the scientific promise of human perfectibility par excellence.[96] By 1874, T. H. Huxley would suggest that all animals were 'automata' or 'conscious machines', that is to say, they 'have consciousness and no souls'.[97] The reinvention of this theme in Karel Čapek's 1920 play, *R.U.R.* (discussed in Chapter 5), which imported the word 'robot' into the English language, updates the narrative powerfully. Aldous Huxley's satire on the artificial production of human beings, *Brave New World*, would then widen perception of the inherent dangers of such experimentation, though later enthusiasm for test tube babies and cloning continued unabated.[98]

Stevenson's 1886 study of the split or schizophrenic personality, where monstrosity, chiefly insanity, lies overtly underneath, the beast within ever threatening our daily self, provides another paradigm for conceiving an intimate relationship between normality and monstrosity. Here the murderous Edward Hyde is a projection of Henry Jekyll, a pre-Jungian (consciousness versus shadow) discovery of alternative self/unconscious mind (Cain/Abel; Devil/monster) of the 'primitive duality' of 'two natures', the good and evil, or light and dark, sides, within.[99] Stoker's Dracula is, of course, a corpse by day and a vampire by night: again we have darkness and shadow, reason and passion, the eternal contrast of the 'normal' to the 'monstrous', the 'semi-demon', the 'Undead'.[100]

The great scientific optimism of the Victorians was tempered by fears of species, race, and national degeneration of various types, whose literary reflections will be treated in more detail below. As the psychologist Ernest Jones indicated, vampires, werewolves, the Devil, even incubae, were, in the eyes of demystifying materialist science, transformed in the late nineteenth century from waking 'daymares' to nocturnally projected nightmares (and linked to the 'night mare', the horse/Devil in various legends who took souls to hell).[101]

Yet, in the twentieth century, events take a surprising turn for the worse. We do not have to go far here to see the immense role the monstrous continues to play in fantasy now. From Tolkien's *The Hobbit* (1937) to the monster and alien invasion movies of the 1940s and 1950s, through to the immensely popular *Star Wars*, *Star Trek*, and *Alien* series, *Avatar*, and a hundred pallid imitations, monstrosity looms large in later modernity. Godzilla, King Kong, any number of cyborgs, robots,

[96] Turney, *Frankenstein's Footsteps*, p. 3.
[97] T. H. Huxley, 'On the Hypothesis that Animals are Automata, and its History', in *Collected Essays, vol. 1* (Macmillan, 1893), pp. 199–250, here 238, 242.
[98] See generally Cohen, *Human Robots in Myth and Fiction*.
[99] Robert Louis Stevenson, *The Strange Case of Dr. Jekyll and Mr. Hyde* (Longmans, Green, & Co., 1897), p. 114. Cain gets an early mention (p. 2). The evil Hyde is described as 'deformed' (p. 12), 'pale and dwarfish . . . hardly human' (pp. 26–7), his pleasures as 'monstrous' (p. 125), and even as having 'Satan's signature' on his face (p. 27).
[100] Bram Stoker, *Dracula* (Oxford University Press, 1983), pp. 51, 201.
[101] Jones, *On the Nightmare*, pp. 82–240, 323–4.

blobs, and other evil things from outer space have continued to fascinate modern readers and viewers.

We now see the relative decline of the satanic, admittedly. But the undead (vampires, zombies) spring back to life with renewed vigour. We see a decline in the belief in witchcraft, but a recurrent fascination with wizardry (Harry Potter). Monsters are no longer a part of God's universe, subject to negotiation with theologians, but roam freely promoting their own agendas and alternative lifestyles, modern consumers with free choice if peculiar tastes. Superheroes proliferate like mushrooms, from Buck Rogers, Flash Gordon, and Superman onwards. We see science and technology coming increasingly to the fore, but yet also the recurrent suggestion that evil without mirrors evil within. Many monster films, critics have noted, portray monsters not as in themselves evil, but as the victims of some accident. Their monstrosity leads them to disrupt or challenge (in the usual Hollywood rendition) the daily routine of suburban American life, which supreme affront demands human retribution and usually the elimination of the monsters.[102]

But now it is much clearer than ever that, as Jeffrey Jerome Cohen has observed, fear of monstrosity itself exhibits desire on our part.[103] Just as we want magic to work to circumvent the all-too-unfair rules of everyday life, so we *want* monsters to exist. So we constantly invent new ones to replace those the Saint Georges have killed off. No sooner do we dispose of one than another necessarily arises to take its place. Out goes Medusa, whose stare turns men to stone. In come King Kong and Godzilla. Dragons disappear, or are transmuted into dinosaurs, and aliens take their place. Here, in proportion to their numbers and powers, they are again dystopian.

By the late twentieth century, the image of the machine running amok replaces the Frankenstein motif. For millennia we have worried about the boundaries between animal and human, and tried (mostly) to resist our animal side.[104] Now, rather than being half-human, half-animal, we encounter another great schizophrenia of identity, as new beings are created, like androids (synthetic creatures resembling people) or cyborgs (people with mechanical parts). People become more like machines and machines more like people until, in the early twenty-first century, the boundaries of 'human' identity become increasingly blurred. Some describe these phenomena as 'post-human' and presenting a 'dehumanized dystopia', which is sometimes associated with the cyberpunk genre.[105] But the threat that not only the body, but 'humanity' itself, faces obsolescence is at least present. And this time the threat is real, not mythical or imaginary.

But we have no desire to eliminate the challenge of monstrosity as such. The device is far too useful. The monster has functioned as a kind of alter ego or mirror for humanity's self-definition and affirmation of life, and a means of reflecting on

---

[102] See Vivian Sobchack, *Screening Space: The American Science Fiction Film* (Rutgers University Press, 1997).

[103] Jeffrey Jerome Cohen, ed., *Monster Theory* (University of Minnesota Press, 1996), pp. 16–20.

[104] On the animal–human juxtaposition see Joanna Bourke, *What It Means to Be Human* (Virago, 2011).

[105] Elaine L. Graham, *Representations of the Post/Human: Monsters, Aliens and Others in Popular Culture* (Manchester University Press, 2012), pp. 85, 194.

identity and difference.[106] As scapegoats, monsters are alternative and overlapping prototypes for Jews, aliens, witches, all of whom are projections of our fears, concentrated into comprehensible entities. Their construction represents a parallel and overlapping history of ideas of antagonism, exclusion, ostracism, and destruction. Like the baddies in films, we need the giant, the dragon, the shark, the monster in order to feel heroic. So: no monsters, no heroes; no Minotaur, no Theseus. Heroes need dragons to win the maiden's heart. Maidens too need dragons: no beast, no beauty. To *do* good we must slay the dragon; to *be* good we must at least cage the monster within. What a useful, versatile idea. And, we will now see: no Devil, no God, and vice versa.

THE KING OF DYSTOPIA:
SATAN'S TRIUMPHANT MARCH

And there was war in heaven: Michael and his angels fought against the dragon; and the dragon fought and his angels.

And prevailed not; neither was their place found any more in heaven.

And the great dragon was cast out, that old serpent, called the Devil, and Satan, which deceiveth the whole world: he was cast out into the earth, and his angels were cast out with him.

(Revelations 12:7–9)

The whole world is possessed by Satan.

(Martin Luther)

No Devil, No God.

(John Wesley)

Introduction: Satan's Domain

It is difficult now for many of us to conceive a world where individuals lived in the full expectation that an immensely powerful evil being might connive to ruin their lives at any hour of the day or night. In any one of a thousand guises, he might be waiting at a crossroads outside the village, or in the marketplace, or the alehouse, a favourite haunt. And yet where would we be, and where would Christianity be, without Satan? Hell, Satan's chief residence, is the key prototype for the later concept of dystopia.[107] Yet his realm above ground was no less impressive than his character warranted. He was once described as possessing 'great courage, incredible

---

[106] Erik Buller, *Metamorphoses of the Vampire in Literature and Film: Cultural Transformations in Europe 1732–1933* (Camden House, 2010), p. 8.

[107] For a comparison, see Dennis Rohatyn, 'Hell and Dystopia: A Comparison and Literary Case Study', in Michael S. Cummings and Nicholas D. Smith, eds., *Utopian Studies 2* (University Press of America, 1989), pp. 94–101, which uses Margaret Atwood's *The Handmaid's Tale* as an example of the concept of Hell surviving 'the transition from a religious to a secular age' (p. 101).

cunning, superhuman wisdom, the most acute penetration, consummate prudence, an incomparable skill in veiling the most pernicious artifices under a specious disguise, and a malicious and infinite hatred towards the human race, implacable and incurable'.[108] His ability to penetrate the innermost recesses of the mind, and to transmute himself into any form, was believed to be extraordinary. We have seen him appear already as the great dragon. Over the centuries he would be made more powerful than any preceding monster, the true founder and Monarch Perpetual of Dystopia, the ruler of the world above as well as that below. And he would be made such by none other than the Church, in order to create an opponent worthy of the Christian God.

So who is this Prince of Demons, the Tempter, Accuser, the King of this World?[109] This section considers how images of the Devil originated and developed, and then how these were related to ideas about witchcraft, particularly in the early modern period. Our aim here is to describe the more social aspects of the central role played by Satan in scapegoating a variety of groups in Christian Europe: Jews, heretics, and witches in particular. This process will then be conceptualized in terms of the characterization of dystopian group qualities outlined above. Describing evil and producing 'enemies', it will be argued, are part of the same process of defining and purifying group identity. Here the roles of panic, paranoia, and hysteria are central in making the group hyperaggressive. These qualities defined the medieval and early modern Inquisition in particular.

Satanic History

The Devil

Satan is a slippery character whose curious story is difficult to recount. The dates of so many relevant texts and identities of their authors remain controversial at best. Inventiveness dominates the entire narrative. In the Old Testament, Henry Kelly tells us, the Hebrew word 'satan' (from the Hebrew *he-satan*, the enemy or accuser) means 'adversary', which is rendered into Greek as 'diabolos', slanderer or accuser.[110] This became *diabolus* in Latin and then 'devil' in English. 'Demon' derives from the Greek *daimonion*, or evil spirit, of whom the Greeks believed there were many, some of whom were associated with nature, others with the dead.[111]

The 'unmixed spirit of malignancy, which is the central idea of Satan' arises only with Christianity.[112] Commencing as God's servant, he emerges in the Old Testament as an agent provocateur acting independently, in Neil Forsyth's description, and indeed possessing a will of his own, in a remarkable declaration of

---

[108] Johann Weyer, *De Praestigiis Daemonum*, quoted in Richard Cavendish, *The Powers of Evil in Western Religion, Magic and Folk Belief* (Routledge & Kegan Paul, 1975), p. 195.
[109] A good start here is Robert Muchembled, *A History of the Devil: From the Middle Ages to the Present* (Polity Press, 2003).
[110] Henry Ansgar Kelly, *Satan: A Biography* (Cambridge University Press, 2006), p. 2.
[111] Russell, *Lucifer*, pp. 34, 142.
[112] Frederic T. Hall, *The Pedigree of the Devil* (Trübner & Co., 1883), p. 17.

autonomy.[113] Soon he would become the rebel par excellence. The one called Lucifer (the light-bearer, an angelic representation) or Satan, the Devil, the Prince of Darkness, epitomizes evil. He is thus the general bringer of bad things.[114] He is present at the beginning, in the Christian creation myth, as the snake in the Garden of Eden. This story was itself derived from the Hebrew tradition, in which the rather capricious Yahweh placed the first humans in the Garden of Eden, then expelled them for disobedience.[115]

This early appearance was no small success. But Satan's greatest achievements lay centuries ahead, in late medieval and early modern Europe. Here he would go from triumph to triumph, conquering vast swathes of mental territory until he could claim dominion over almost the entire world, both above and below ground.

Satan came from a diverse extended family with some odd relations—more than a few skeletons in his closet—before emerging as the Christian Devil. He has been linked to the Philistine god Beelzebub. He has Babylonian ancestry too—here, as in Celtic legend, monsters guarded the entrance to the underworld, and also threatened cities and had to be defeated by heroes. In Sumerian literature (*c.*2500 BC) Gilgamesh encountered giant scorpion men on entering the realm of the dead. In Zoroastrianism, the first absolute personification of evil emerges *c.*1200 BC in the form of Angra Mainyu or Ahriman, who battles with the forces of good for a lengthy period before being finally defeated. Here, as in Christianity, the first humans, Mashye and Mashyane, are lied to by Ahriman (who could assume animal forms, including the snake) into believing that he was the creator of the world. In a prototype of the Eden myth, they offer him an ox in sacrifice, and gain knowledge and the arts of civilization in return. But disease, hatred, strife, and death then follow.[116]

The Babylonian underworld had many minor demons, including the *annunaki*, who were custodians of the dead in hell, the *etimmu*, who were the ghosts of the dead who had died unhappy, and the *utukku*, who lived in desert places or graveyards. One demon, Lilitu, the prototype of Adam's supposed first wife, Lilith (Isaiah 34), was a barren maiden, part human and part bird of prey, who roamed the night draining men of their bodily fluids—clearly a poor choice of marital partner. (In Jewish myth, Lilith, the name possibly derived from 'lascivious', became a demon, having refused to return to Eden after mating with the archangel Samael.)[117] Demons above the ground produced plagues, nightmares, headaches, and other woes.[118]

[113] Forsyth, *The Old Enemy*, p. 121.

[114] Santa, an anagram of Satan, is now the bringer of good things. But he too was once Satan's agent, in an interesting reversal of the fallen angel theme and a further hint at the parallel histories of utopia and dystopia. The affinities go further: 'Old Nick', as Satan was sometimes called, was derived from Saint Nicholas, and also identified with the north, darkness, and cold, with driving reindeer and going down chimneys disguised with soot and carrying a sack to capture sinners (Jeffrey Burton Russell, *The Prince of Darkness* (Thames and Hudson, 1989), p. 114).

[115] For a general overview of the Eden story, see Elaine Pagels, *Adam, Eve, and the Serpent* (Vintage Books, 1989).

[116] Russell, *The Prince of Darkness*, pp. 17–22.

[117] Russell, *Witchcraft in the Middle Ages*, p. 107; Russell, *The Prince of Darkness*, p. 45; Jones, *On the Nightmare*, p. 125.

[118] Russell, *Lucifer*, p. 92.

In the Hebrew tradition, Satan emerged gradually as a spirit created by God but falling into evil ways, sometimes described as *mal'ak*, the shadow of the lord, being associated with the serpent and operating as a seducer, accuser, and destroyer with a host of demonic assistants. Satan's name may have been derived from that of one of the Watcher Angels, Satanail (the term means oppose, obstruct, accuse). 'Enoch' gives us an account of the fallen Watchers which translates easily into an idea of rebellious angels expelled by God from Heaven or descending of their own volition and punished for the evil that resulted.[119] It is also possible that some devils were modelled on inspectors and informers sent by kings to ascertain compliance with the laws in Egypt, Persia, and elsewhere, who then become 'watchers' or 'satans' who would recommend punishments for transgressors.[120] (Here we have a fine pedigree for secret policemen.)

While Asmodeus was prince of the demons, no single all-powerful devil emerges yet, or for that matter in early Christianity. The Christian devil figure thus starts out in life in the plural, and evolves into a singular Satan, with the older pre-Christian gods being demoted into demons or dying out. The assembly of the various books of the Bible is so much disputed that just how this occurred is very difficult to ascertain. Amongst the many contending narratives one triumphed over the rest, presumably, like much of the rest of the text, by the votes of a committee of theologians. A plurality of angels and other spirits were associated with the weather and the elements, and 'spirits' included various leftover demons, not all of whom have been confined 'in the place of judgment', where most (nine-tenths) had been bound by Yahweh, a tenth being left 'subject to Satan upon the earth' (Jubilees 10:1–7). Even here, however, Satan, also called Mastema, is identified semantically with 'animosity', and the possibility of a psychological interpretation remains present, with the tithe of mankind being left subject to its own ill-will rather than any externalized principle of evil.[121] By now Mastema is represented as virtually independent of the Lord, a principle of evil incarnate, demanding human sacrifices and other foul deeds.[122] A single devil, who had control over death (Hebrews 2:14) then comes to be associated with the death of Jesus.[123]

This simplifies matters considerably since it gives evil a focal point: one really bad guy is always more impressive than a host of lesser miscreants. At the same time, however, it leaves unresolved the problem of local evil and temptation, which requires a multitude of assistants or incarnations. These were provided initially, in one instance, by the ghosts of the Watcher Giants, who remained even after the giants had killed each other off (1 Enoch: 6–16).[124] (But Enoch also relates that the giants introduced metallurgy and the making of swords—shades of Rousseau!—as well as makeup and personal decoration for women, with the purpose of enticing men, resulting in fornication, godlessness, and corruption, which Noah's flood was

---

[119] Some have seen the fallen angel motif as simply opposing 'the self to God' (Christopher Nugent, *Masks of Satan: The Demonic in History* (Sheed & Ward, 1983), p. 11).
[120] Kelly, *Satan*, p. 26.   [121] Ibid., pp. 37–8.
[122] Russell, *The Prince of Darkness*, p. 39; Forsyth, *The Old Enemy*, p. 182.
[123] Kelly, *Satan*, p. 30.   [124] Ibid., p. 35.

required to sweep away.)[125] Hence, from fairly early on we have both one powerful overseer of the underworld, and a variety of subordinates more or less independently mischievous. So Judaism moved towards dualism just as Christianity would do in suggesting an independently evil principle.[126]

The physical characteristics of the Devil derive from the lengthy history of monstrosity we have already partly traced. Demons almost epitomized monstrosity. To the Greeks, the Keres had fangs and blue-black faces and drank the blood of the dying, while the lamias sought the death of children. Harpies were wind demons, gorgons, like Medusa with her unruly snake-hair, were demons of the underworld or sea, while Cerberus the dog guarded Hades, where the dead reposed. The most direct antecedent of the Christian image of Satan was the Greek pipe-playing god Pan, who embodied sexual desire as well as agricultural fertility, had cloven hooves, goat's legs and horns, a goatee, a beast's ears, and a large phallus.[127] Dionysos was also worshipped in the form of a goat in night-time festivals associated with frenzy, ecstasy, excessive wine-drinking, orgies, and animal sacrifice. Primarily attended by women, though led by a male priest, these festivals clearly prefigured medieval rituals associated with witchcraft, and may have been their chief source. The Etruscan personification of death, Charun, had a hooked nose, goatee, and wings, and sometimes had serpents growing from his body, serpent cults having been common in Babylon and elsewhere. The Roman version of Dionysos worship, the Bacchanalian festival, was associated with night-time orgies of drinking and sex, and was banned by the Senate in 186 BC.[128] Ancient fertility goddesses became later 'witches',[129] though the Devil usually remained male.

The medieval Christian Devil continued many earlier associations with sexuality and fertility generally. He was by now usually coloured red or black, and was portrayed variously as a lion, crow, raven, bat, worm, donkey, dragon, and many other animals.[130] The thunder-making Scandinavian 'hammer' god Thor probably contributed a red beard and an evil (sulphurous) odour, linked to lightning strikes.[131] By the tenth century, the Devil had begun to appear as a black man, a form often assumed thereafter, and 'black' magic became juxtaposed to alchemy and other positive magic.[132] He continued to assume animal forms widely, most commonly the serpent or dragon, the goat and the dog. From the sixth to the eleventh centuries he was commonly depicted as a humanoid imp with birds' wings and clawed feet or an old man with clawed feet and a tail. Bat wings were

[125] Valery Rees, *From Gabriel to Lucifer: A Cultural History of Angels* (I.B. Taurus, 2013), p. 203; Forsyth, *The Old Enemy*, pp. 174–5. Forsyth points out that the Greek myth of Prometheus' rebellion against Zeus in giving fire to humanity and thus both evil and civilization has interesting parallels here, as well as with the Eden myth. Both hint at a perverse wish to keep humanity ignorant and primitive, in the name of innocence. Jean-Jacques Rousseau describes metallurgy as the 'fatal secret', noting that 'for the philosophers, it was iron and corn, which first civilized men, and ruined humanity' (*The Social Contract and Discourses* (J. M. Dent, 1973), pp. 92–3).

[126] Russell, *Lucifer*, p. 183.   [127] Ibid., pp. 143, 126; Russell, *The Prince of Darkness*, p. 17.
[128] Russell, *Lucifer*, p. 156, 152.
[129] The term is used here to describe those accused of the practices associated with the term.
[130] Russell, *Witchcraft in the Middle Ages*, p. 105.   [131] Jones, *On the Nightmare*, p. 161.
[132] Russell, *Witchcraft in the Middle Ages*, pp. 45–50, 71, 75–8, 87.

increasingly common from the twelfth century. Sometimes Satan was a holy man or a giant comparable to Behemoth, or a fisherman with nets and hooks, in reference to Leviathan. He was by now usually black, increasingly ugly, often imbued with mythical sexual prowess.[133] In one notable account the Devil appears as a giant black cat who descends down a rope into a 'synagogue' or conventicle of worshippers (the common term for an assemblage of witches—the link to growing anti-Semitism is clear). His body, especially its private parts, is then kissed by them.

In the Old Testament, the Devil plays a small role only. In the New he would emerge to a position of central importance. Lucifer, the 'bringer of light', is first associated with the morning star in Isaiah 14:12. In Revelations (12:7–12) he appears as a dragon or serpent, the Devil, or Satan, cast out from Heaven with all his other rebellious followers. The greatest of the Seraphim, the angels closest to God, he is the winged fallen angel, also known as the Lord of the Flies (Matthew 10:25). Guilty of wishing to supplant God himself (but does he feel guilty?), he is expelled after an abortive revolt backed by about a third of Heaven's servants, an account lovingly embellished by Milton. (So much for the idea that Heaven, beset by civil war, is any more 'perfect' than the Garden of Eden.)

In the early centuries AD, four ideas then fuse, which become much of the basis of the later idea of Satan: the sin of the Devil as pride; the ruin of the Watchers through lust; the fall of the bright morning star from Heaven; and the descent of the Watchers for the purpose of sinning. Out of this Lucifer comes to be understood as a fallen or evil angel bringing destruction on earth, and allowed to range more or less freely until the end of the world and his own demise. Now he emerges as the chief part of the Christian explanation of evil, or theodicy. In the New Testament, Satan, in Kelly's apt phrase, thus 'comes into his own'.[134] While still associated with idolatry, even the worship of the offspring of the evil giant-ghosts, and with demonic possession, Satan not only retains his previous role as the cunning tempter and tester, and punisher of sins. He effectively becomes the governor of the world, the constant overseer of human activity. His role is essential. As Neil Forsyth puts it, 'If Satan had not already existed, the church would have had to invent him.'[135] And reinvent him, imaginatively and energetically, it did.

Hell

The idea of Hell, which provides us with the first intellectual paradigm for dystopia, has a somewhat different trajectory from that of the Devil (see Fig. 2.4).[136] Throughout the world, places where people have died have been walled off and sealed by incantations to prevent evil spirits from escaping.[137] One tradition names Hell

[133] Jeffrey Burton Russell, *Satan: The Early Christian Tradition* (Cornell University Press, 1981), p. 190; Jones, *On the Nightmare*, p. 169.

[134] Russell, *Lucifer*, pp. 197, 194; Kelly, *Satan*, p. 51.   [135] Forsyth, *The Old Enemy*, p. 317.

[136] See Alan E. Bernstein, *The Formation of Hell: Death and Retribution in the Ancient and Early Christian Worlds* (UCL Press, 1993).

[137] E.g., in the Cambodian case, Chanrithy Him, *When Broken Glass Floats: Growing Up Under the Khmer Rouge* (W. W. Norton, 2000), p. 40.

Fig. 2.4. *Hell*, Hieronymus Bosch, *c*.1500. © Mary Evans/Interfoto Agentur 10226987.

as Gehanna, from Ge-hinnom, the 'valley of wailing' outside Jerusalem, where child and fire sacrifices were made to the Phoenician deity Moloch.[138] In Zoroastrianism, the resting place of the dead is located in the middle of the earth. In ancient Greece, dead souls went to the underworld ruled by and named after the god Hades. Here, originally, they only lamented, as in Norse myth, but did not suffer. But eventually Hades became 'a pit of torment for the damned', in Russell's phrase.[139] Plato also described a hell for the wicked (Phaedo 113E). The Scandinavian Hel, from which the English term Hell derives, was, like Hades, not originally a place of punishment, and was also the name of the female deity who presided over the underworld.[140] The English word is also related to an Indo-European term, **kel*, meaning cover or concealment, from which hole, helmet, hall, cave, and dwelling are derived. Darkness and blackness are in many traditions associated with evil and death, as are whiteness and light with good. By the second century BC, with the apocalyptic writers, Hell was seen as a place of punishment, in some Jewish sects only for Gentiles for eternal damnation, but for rebellious Jews only temporarily.[141]

---

[138] Rees, *From Gabriel to Lucifer*, p. 198.
[139] Cohn, *Cosmos, Chaos, and the World to Come*, p. 140; Russell, *Lucifer*, p. 143.
[140] Russell, *Witchcraft in the Middle Ages*, p. 104.   [141] Russell, *Lucifer*, pp. 62–4, 186.

The Bible portrays Hell in various ways. The Old Testament (Numbers 16:30, Job 30:23) describes a place called Sheol beneath the earth where the spirits of both good and bad went after death. Here a gloomy eternity might be mitigated by offerings of food and drink (to the priests, of course) by those still above. In Matthew 25, Christ appears to establish the domain of a Hell of 'everlasting fire', which becomes the torture ground of 'everlasting punishment'. Here many-headed 'dragons' (Leviathan) or serpents of various kinds do foul work, notably in the Book of Daniel. In Revelations 14 and 20, those who worship 'the beast and his image' end up in the 'bottomless pit' into which has been cast, for a thousand years, 'the dragon, that old serpent, which is the Devil, and Satan'. Those lacking the mark of God on their forehead are tortured by vicious locust-like beasts for five months. After his 1,000 years in the abyss the Devil is permitted to return to his old job of practising deceit, only finally to be thrown into the Lake of Fire to be tormented 'day and night through ages of ages' (Revelations 20:9–10).[142] Angels are sometimes described as bystanders to the tortures of the damned, like real spectators at a particularly gruesome execution. Throughout these narratives the association of Satan with millenarianism is thus particularly strong. Christ's prospective return clearly implies that the Devil is not immortal, or at least that his powers will be constrained eventually. However, Christ's return indicates the end of life on earth as we know it, since the world will be destroyed. It may also imply that the Devil will be especially active prior to his defeat.

By the time of Origen (c.AD 200), Satan was starting to be reinvented as the pre-Adamic fallen angel Lucifer. He was still linked to Hell or Hades. But by being made a fallen angel the inference is avoided that there could be two permanent principles of good and evil or darkness and light. The implication that there might be some Divine goodness in Satan remains, however. The early Church Fathers believed that Satan was jealous of Adam. This produced both his and Adam's fall. This account of Original Sin was, however, identified explicitly with lust by AD 70.[143] By the third century, Satan came to be seen as sinning through pride, and was increasingly construed as the enemy of God, sometimes appearing in the guise of a pagan god. In the Patristic (Church Fathers') account, Adam and Eve's sin bound them and their descendants in slavery to Satan, to be redeemed only by the death of Christ. About this time Satan also emerges as responsible for punishing the souls of the damned in Hell. By the twelfth century, in Lombard's narrative, fallen angels or demons are described as taking the souls of the wicked daily down to Hell. A century later, in Aquinas' reconstruction, the Devil remains the cause of Original Sin, and plays some role in the commissioning of new sins. Confusingly, however, God grants his approval for these, thereby colluding in the commission of evil.[144]

In the first five centuries of Christianity a number of pre-existing features were thus consolidated into the vision of the Devil which would dominate Western

[142] Kelly, *Satan*, pp. 150, 158.
[143] In the Apocalypse of Moses, written before AD 70. Russell, *Lucifer*, p. 207.
[144] Kelly, *Satan*, pp. 230–8, 248.

thought to the present day. He was now connected with Adam and Eve's sin, with the serpent in the Garden of Eden, and with the angels who fell at the time of Noah.[145] The final stages of the creation of this 'modern' Devil links Satan to Adam and to Original Sin, which occurred when the early Church Fathers began to iron out the inconsistencies in existing accounts. Satan was first held accountable for Adam and Eve's sin around AD 100, probably by Justin Martyr. He also anticipated Satan's future fall as well as that of those angels who sinned with human women before the Flood, who are also identified with pagan gods, and especially Diana.

In many of these accounts, including the Qur'an's, the Devil's final punishment is delayed until Judgement Day. Before being thrown into the hellfire, however, it was supposed that he would roam the earth tempting mankind, in the Qur'anic account accompanied by Jinns, or lesser spirits, whom some commentators supposed to be inner hidden human qualities.[146] (In some Christian accounts, 'possessing demons' exist who inhabit human hosts and cause deafness, madness, and other discomforts. They waited patiently for humans to yawn or sneeze in order to enter their bodies, which is why we still say 'bless you' when someone sneezes.)[147]

The Hell we know and love (to fear), replete with pitchfork-wielding demons, proliferated with the spread of books and literacy and of imagery, especially in churches. Graphic descriptions of Hell were widely available by the medieval period. Overkill is evident everywhere. Respecting the seven 'deadly' sins, we see that the punishment for pride is to be broken on the wheel; for envy, to be immersed in freezing water; for the gluttonous, to be fed rats, toads, and snakes; for lust, to be smothered in fire and brimstone; for anger, to be dismembered alive; for greed, to be boiled alive in oil; for sloth, to be thrown into a snake pit. In the most famous portrayal of the period, Dante's *Divine Comedy* (written between 1308 and 1321), the journey downwards through the circles of Hell in the 'Inferno' is vivid in the extreme. From the virtuous heathen we descend to the lustful, the gluttonous, the avaricious and prodigal, the wrathful, the violent, the suicides, the blasphemers, sodomites, usurers, the fraudulent, panders and seducers, eventually to the ninth circle, the treacherous. It is a crowded place, as one might expect, yet curiously no more so, evidently, than Heaven, judging by pictures of the period (e.g. Carlo Saraceni's *Paradise*, *c.*1598). (One theologian thought that Hell must contain 100,000,000,000 damned per German square mile (*c.*7777 sq.m.), though such congestion would have left little space for any of the more elaborate forms of torture.)[148] By the sixteenth century, Hieronymus Bosch and Pieter Bruegel would provide some of the best-known illustrations of the theme, often intended, as Augustine had insisted, to instruct the less literate in the perils of sin.[149]

[145] Ibid., p. 171.   [146] Rees, *From Gabriel to Lucifer*, p. 91.
[147] Kelly, *Satan*, pp. 176–85, 210.
[148] See D. P. Walker, *The Decline of Hell. Seventeenth-Century Discussions of Eternal Treatment* (Routledge and Kegan Paul, 1964), p. 39.
[149] Russell, *Lucifer*, p. 210.

Medieval Christianity also described two other places where dead souls might reside more temporarily: Limbo and Purgatory. One part of Limbo contained unbaptized infants damned because of Original Sin. In Purgatory, the sinful did penance before being accepted into Heaven. Protestantism rejected Purgatory because trafficking in Indulgences and similar practices had eroded its moral status. If you could buy your way out, it was onerous only for the poor, whom Christianity repeatedly assured would in fact be compensated in the afterlife for their disproportionate sufferings when alive. But even those who went to Hell might become Satan's accomplices rather than his victims. A third-century theologian, Origen, who was so obsessed by lust that he castrated himself, argued that while the best souls became angels, the worst became demons. Across the ages, he thought, souls could go up and down the hierarchy of rational creatures, until all, including even Lucifer, might be cleansed of sin.[150]

The prospect of Satan regaining a place in Heaven was alarming to many. But the principle of mitigating Hell pointed to the possibility of a much more widespread if not universal salvation (the Pelagian heresy), and of a more merciful rather than a more cruel God. Writing in the early thirteenth century, Gervase of Tilbury thought there were two Heavens and two Hells, the latter earthly Hell being a kind of antechamber, like Purgatory, far from the place of actual chastisement.[151] And Hell had even more enthusiastic opponents. To the medieval commentator Eriugena, for instance, it was a metaphor rather than a real place, the expression of being alienated from God through our own desires rather than united with him, its torment only the endless realization that we have made the wrong choice.[152] The sixteenth-century Anabaptists maintained that the torture of the damned and devils was not infinite. Some asserted that there was no Hell beyond the grave, and that the souls of the wicked perished with their bodies, while those of the elect slept until their resurrection.[153] The Adamites of Bohemia believed that, in Norman Cohn's words, 'heaven and hell had no existence save in the righteous and the unrighteous respectively'.[154]

The followers of Fausto Socini (1539–1604), known as Socinians, who supported both pacifism and the abolition of capital punishment, were also renowned for attempting to limit the tortures prescribed in Hell. They too presumed that the wicked simply perished at death, and only the good were resurrected, regarding this as punishment enough for evil. The seventeenth-century English Arians, led by John Locke, also often disbelieved in eternal torment. Locke maintained that sinners would be excluded from paradise and the chance of immortality. His friend William Whiston doubted that the tortures of the damned were eternal, imagining that onlooking angels might well show mercy to degenerates, in keeping with general Divine goodness. At the Last Judgement, however, the still unrepentant wicked would be sentenced to further torment, and eventually annihilated. But Hell still did service; for Shaftesbury there was 'nothing more fatal to virtue than the weak and uncertain belief of future reward and punishment'. Yet in Pierre Bayle's

---

[150] Walker, *The Decline of Hell*, pp. 60, 13.   [151] Delumeau, *History of Paradise*, p. 37.
[152] Russell, *Lucifer*, pp. 62–91, 123.   [153] Walker, *The Decline of Hell*, p. 74.
[154] Norman Cohn, *The Pursuit of the Millennium* (Secker & Warburg, 1947), p. 233.

view it appeared unreasonable that 'men would be made to suffer merely in order to make them suffer, with no intention of profiting either the sufferer or the on-lookers', an outlook we can associate with sadism and an obsessive desire to control others. Bayle worried, too, that those who were 'persuaded that by exterminating heresies he is advancing the kingdom of God, and that he will gain the highest degree of glory in paradise' would 'trample under foot all the rules of morality'.[155]

Satan's Advance

Most of these arguments fell on deaf ears, however, and were either ignored or proscribed by the Church. Far from weakening, the Devil's strength increased for some 1,500 years. Monotheism bred a monster as great as, if not indeed, in its everyday manifestations, even greater than God himself. Once this genie was let out of the bottle, putting it back was well-nigh impossible. Demonomania would eventually spread like a dark cloud across the landscape, blighting the lives of millions in a kind of spiritual holocaust. By the Middle Ages, the 'entire range of human unhappiness' was now ascribed to Satan as the author of all evil. The 'terror increased as time went on', proven in part by the great proliferation in art, decoration, tales, and sermons of ever more grotesque and monstrous evil spirits.[156]

Pleasure-seeking, much more acceptable in the classical world, became widely stigmatized in the early centuries of Christianity, as in later Puritanism. So as the Lord became increasingly repressive, much more work was available to his nemesis. Tertullian (*c.*170–220), for instance, condemned as diabolical not merely public entertainments but also baths, taverns, races, and theatres (the acting of a part representing Satan's empty lies). Even entertainment in private was idolatrous, for provoking passions hostile to reason. All luxuries and vanities were rooted in 'the veneration of the works of Satan instead of the works of the Lord'.[157] Origen (182–254) brought together the images of Satan, Lucifer, the King of Babylon, and the Dragon of Leviathan or Revelation, and portrayed Christian life as a constant unending struggle against the powers of darkness.[158]

In medieval folklore, the wily Devil becomes the constant tempter, seducing the unwary, playing cards and gambling, punishing vain women and naughty children. He entices, beguiles, allures, in a thousand ways. Adept at assuming disguises, he was particularly fond of tempting saints. Indeed, with such thespian talents the Devil truly missed his calling: he appeared as a beautiful woman to Saint Andrew, as a nun as well as a pilgrim to Saint Nicholas, as a black child to Saint Anthony, a black man to Saint John the Almoner, and an angel to Saint Juliana, and as Moses and a variety of saints. Outwitting him was no easy task. But that was the test of the saint.[159] (Or the would-be saints: Martin Luther, clearly a poor prospective

---

[155] Walker, *The Decline of Hell*, pp. 172, 78, 184.
[156] Russell, *Witchcraft in the Middle Ages*, pp. 110–12.
[157] Russell, *Satan*, pp. 143, 214, 99–101.   [158] Russell, *The Prince of Darkness*, p. 79.
[159] Voragine, *The Golden Legend of Jacobus de Voragine* ([*c.*1290]; Longmans, Green & Co., 1941), pp. 14, 19, 23, 99, 121, 166, 406.

dinner guest, turned and farted frequently at the Devil to drive him off.)[160] For
most, the message was that the mere lustful glance, the mug of ale, the casual curse,
recurrent idleness, might invite eternal damnation, the constant burning but never
consuming fires. Where pleasure was, Satan was. He was the guest of honour at
every party, and the ultimate party-pooper.

In this period, pacts or compacts with the Devil become increasingly common,
eventually being dominated by the Faust legend (a favourite of the young Hitler).
So too did the idea of diabolical possession, or the Devil taking over a person. Such
behaviour was probably the result of extreme obsession or compulsive behaviour
and/or repressed desires. Medieval people became 'obsessed by the Devil and his
demons', in Russell's account, as the counterpart of the growing role played in
both daily and spiritual life by the Virgin, the saints, Christ, and God, and then
the joining together of all other previously disparate evil principles under one
homogenous rubric. Pre-Christian religions and popular folk beliefs were slowly
amalgamated into the system as heresies. The old gods, now demobilized, were
demonized along with the spirits of pre-Christian paganism. Elves, fairies, and little
people were now enlisted in Satan's army. Minor demons like the 'little people',
leprechauns, elves, and other nature spirits, were often associated with him. Eventually demons were reshuffled and ranked into three types: the leading fallen angels
being the worst, followed by pagan gods, and finally fairies and kobolds. Some were
thought to be human souls bound to the world after death for some reason. A host
of motley and disorderly mercenaries were thus rearmed. Kitted out in one uniform
under unified command, they now posed a renewed and clearly dystopian threat.[161]

By the Middle Ages, Satan had become an immensely potent, even popular
character, the stock-in-trade villain (with demons assisting) of the *Golden
Legend*, the collection of saint's and martyrs' lives which outsold even the Bible.
By now it was commonly assumed that men and women could be possessed by
demons or Satan, resulting in illness, deformation, or madness. Racy accounts of
virtuous maidens rescued from rapine by the sign of the cross made good reading,
especially when, to pound the point home, they went on to become nuns, Beauty
defeating not only the Beast without but also that within. It was also assumed that, by
sorcery, demons could gain worldly booty and pleasure besides. At every deathbed
Satan awaited the exit of the soul, ready to pounce. Half-human, half-animal,
everyone knew what he looked like, for the iconography portraying him was
universal.

The spectre people feared usually had horns, cloven hooves, the forked tail, an
(often black) monstrous visage, a hairy, monstrous, or deformed body, the grimace
of wickedness, fire and brimstone beneath.[162] Medieval cathedrals were resplendent
with gargoyles illustrating these characteristics. Yet, coming from the other

---

[160] Carlo Ginzburg, *The Night Battles: Witchcraft and Agrarian Cults in the Sixteenth and
Seventeenth Centuries* (Routledge & Kegan Paul, 1983), pp. 135, 124; Jones, *On the Nightmare*,
p. 176. On the anal aspects of diabolism see Norman O. Brown, *Life against Death: The Psychoanalytic
Meaning of History* (Vintage Books, 1959), pp. 202–33.
[161] Russell, *Witchcraft in the Middle Ages*, pp. 57, 69, 102, 217.
[162] Kelly, *Satan*, pp. 219, 285, 295; Russell, *Witchcraft in the Middle Ages*, p. 113.

direction, the monstrous and the human also grow ever closer in this period, with the Devil himself coming increasingly to be seen in recognisably human form, and demons too. The best monsters, eventually, would be the most humanoid: bugs and lizards, even dragons, do not really cut the mustard. This humanization of the monstrous clearly paves the way for the witchcraft craze.

Satan advances from strength to strength as we move from the eleventh to the fourteenth centuries. His hand was seen in the apocalyptic effects of the Black Death (bubonic plague) between 1347 and 1349, which killed a third of Europe's population. By 1430, the population had fallen by as much as three-quarters below the level of 1290. Much of this was interpreted in terms of Divine retribution for sin. Famine, climate change, and crop failures exacerbated anxiety and a growing obsession with pain and death.[163] Few secular explanations existed for most of these events. In times of intense anxiety, the simplest explanations often come out on top. So the Devil now became accountable for every imaginable woe from plague and famine to storms, sudden death, marital discord, illness, and insanity. For most people he was much more 'real' than God or Christ, and certainly a great deal closer. His presence thus possessed, as Keith Thomas puts it, 'a reality and immediacy which could not fail to grip the strongest mind'.[164]

Heresy played a vital role in the Devil's progress. From the early medieval period onward, theologians magnified his earthly powers by making 'heretics' his allies and agents. This was worrisome given the number of schisms the Church produced and the many forms of 'paganism' it had to contest.[165] Yet, as we have seen, it exactly fitted the Church's strategy of multiplying its opponents by way of self-justification. All resistance to established Church power, every challenge to the God monopoly, thus easily became transformed into 'heresy'. This, however, often merely involved rejection of the Church's corruption, wealth, and worldliness. The celebration of poverty, the primitive teachings of Christ and his apostles, opposition to an ecclesiastical hierarchy, even communism—eventually the greatest heresy of all— thus came to form an evangelical ethos hostile to the Church. In the eleventh and twelfth centuries, this gave rise to attitudes and habits of dissent, and correspond- ingly of persecution in the name of purity and uniformity.[166] Like the emerging centralized states of the twelfth century, the Church also sought to suppress deviance within smaller communities in order to enforce its own authority.[167] The most notable heretics identified with Satan were the Bogomils and Cathars, for whom the body as such was evil and the Devil the ruler of the material world.[168]

---

[163] Jeffrey Richards, *Sex, Dissidence and Damnation: Minority Groups in the Middle Ages* (Routledge, 1991), pp. 14–15.

[164] Thomas, *Religion and the Decline of Magic*, p. 560.

[165] A key study here is Norman Cohn, *Europe's Inner Demons: An Enquiry Inspired by the Great Witch-Hunt* (Chatto-Heinemann, 1975).

[166] R. I. Moore, *The Origins of European Dissent* (University of Toronto Press, 1977), p. ix.

[167] See R. I. Moore, *The Formation of a Persecuting Society: Power and Deviance in Western Europe, 950–1250* (Blackwell, 1987).

[168] Russell, *Lucifer*, pp. 188–9. The general association lasted until the twentieth century (Norman Cohn, *Warrant for Genocide* (Eyre & Spottiswoode, 1967), pp. 42–3).

With the Manichees and Waldensians, some of whom had masses in honour of Lucifer and became known as 'Lucifer[i]ans', these now became the servants of the Devil.[169]

Magic and sorcery were now also increasingly associated with the Devil. So-called high magic was linked both to science and to the occult sciences, including alchemy, astrology, and particularly divination, or ascertaining the course of fate, through examining dreams, tea leaves, dead bodies, and many other phenomena invested with hidden meaning. Low magic included attempts to manipulate the weather, or to wound or cast spells on others. Sometimes such efforts were linked to the pre-Christian gods, to agricultural fertility cults, or to local spirits like elves, gnomes, leprechauns, and fairies. The Anglo-Saxon word *wicca* denoted one who divined or cast spells. By manipulating the powers of nature, many believed individuals could be made sick, or made to fall down or injure themselves in some other way. Christians notionally regarded all magic as evil because it relied on evil spirits and abused the powers of nature against God. Yet, of course, magic and religion were interwoven in a variety of ways. For Christianity had boldly taken over certain broad assumptions from the magical world-view. Prayers functioned as incantations. The transubstantiation of bread and wine into the body and blood of Christ involved an essentially magical act or symbolic ritual human sacrifice. Miracles and wonders reflected the ability to transform one's individual life dramatically.[170] The Church sought not to abolish but to monopolize these quasi-magical assumptions and practices.

The sense of the Devil's power and presence was evidently strengthened by the Reformation, after which the Antichrist, 'the beast', was increasingly identified by Protestants with the papacy, but also with the Anglican clergy, secular authority, and mortal sin generally.[171] The legend of the Antichrist, the incarnation of evil, a man or seven-headed dragon linked to the Devil, who would claim to be Christ but would eventually be killed by him, can be dated to at least the tenth century.[172] Stuart Clark has written that 'the Antichrist loomed as a threat and, occasionally, an obsession over the whole of the religious life and thought' of the sixteenth and seventeenth centuries.[173] By the 1560s, there were some 100,000 copies of 'devil-books' circulating in Protestant Germany. In England, over a hundred works exposed the work of the Antichrist between 1588 and 1628.[174] This controversy deepened the sense of personal sin and of the pervasiveness of evil in the world, and generally regarded revelry as a certain sign of both. Theatres, fairs and carnivals, pleasure gardens, and other assemblies deemed prurient would suffer as a result.

[169] Cohn, *Europe's Inner Demons*, p. 36; Gordon Leff, *Heresy in the Later Middle Ages* (Manchester University Press, 1967), vol. 2, p. 477.
[170] Russell, *Witchcraft in the Middle Ages*, pp. 6–11.
[171] Christopher Hill, *Antichrist in Seventeenth-Century England* (Oxford University Press, 1971).
[172] Emmerson, *Antichrist in the Middle Ages*, p. 7.
[173] Stuart Clark, *Thinking with Demons: The Idea of Witchcraft in Early Modern Europe* (Oxford University Press, 1997), p. 336.
[174] Nugent, *Masks of Satan*, p. 91.

In England, the Devil, now 'a greater reality than ever', became the 'prince and God of this world', in John Knox's words. To return to one quote with which this section began, 'No Devil, No God' (John Wesley) (or 'No Christ, no Anti-Christ, no Heaven, no Hell') we now see clearly how both Catholic and Protestant Churches became the greatest devil's advocates. The cleric Hugh Latimer assured his audiences that the Devil and a multitude of invisible evil spirits filled the air around them. The prevalence of diabolism, or devil obsession, is undisputed. So it was reported that demons 'appear to men in divers shapes, disquiet them when they are awake; trouble them in their sleeps, distort their members; take away their health; afflict them with diseases'.[175] The old fear of black magic was now being at least partly transmuted into a new fear of Satan. The sense of sin, and fear of its consequences, was now more powerful than ever. And, as far as we can tell, people were more miserable than ever as a result, and probably no more virtuous, which probably made them more miserable still. So the lives of millions were blighted pointlessly.

The logic of this conquest is now quite obvious. The Church was the Devil's best friend, for its very existence depended on his evil-doings. The further Christianity advanced and consolidated its authority, the more evil it had to create to justify its existence. Its increasing vigilance and efficiency effectively created more heretics, as pre-Christian deities (Diana and other fertility goddesses were favourites) were added to the ranks of demons, and both were increasingly linked to witches. More evil then 'existed' because the Church insisted on its reality, and because people in turn were cajoled into believing what they were told about such subjects. Hence the paradox that the Devil grew in power proportionately with that of the Church and Christianity generally.[176]

The Devil, Race, and the Jews

Portraying the Jews as Satan's agents was common in medieval Christianity. Strenuous efforts were made to cement these associations. A hooked nose was added to some medieval portrayals of Satan, and horns and a tail to those of Jews. Jew badges were added to the Devil's cloak, while Jews were depicted serving the Devil in Hell.[177] By the third century they were seen not only as opposing Christianity, but as the very inversion of Christian virtues, with both heresy and sin coming to be identified as 'Jewish'.[178] Jews epitomized the pollution taboo and obsession with cleanliness we touched on earlier: 'filthy Jew' is a common epithet used against them. Here what is described as contamination obsessive compulsive disorder (OCD) in individuals becomes sociocompulsive fear collectively. The

---

[175] Thomas, *Religion and the Decline of Magic*, pp. 561–2.

[176] For a good instance of this, see Ginzburg, *The Night Battles*, pp. 89, 153, where a 'benandante', fighting witches in order to secure a good harvest, is himself accused of witchcraft.

[177] Joshua Trachtenberg, *The Devil and the Jews: The Medieval Conception of the Jew and Its Relation to Modern Antisemitism* (Yale University Press, 1943), pp. 26, 30.

[178] Robert Michael, *Holy Hatred: Christianity, Antisemitism, and the Holocaust* (Palgrave Macmillan, 2006), pp. 25, 69.

language of disease thus emerges early on. Jews were termed 'a plague' as early as the fourth century. By the fifth century they were called devil worshippers, and it was predicted that the Antichrist would be reborn as a Jew.

Anti-Semitism, as we have seen, erupted with the First Crusade in 1096 when Jews were broadly associated with 'infidels'. Thousands would be killed by Crusaders. Facing forced conversion, many preferred suicide. The first pogroms in Russia also date from this period. By 1144, accusations of ritual murder by Jews of Christians were circulating.[179] In 1240, the king of France contended that the Jews 'polluted [France] with their filth'.[180] The fear of contamination grew so great that cities like Avignon insisted that Jews buy anything they touched. The mere mention of the plague could bring down massacres upon them.[181] When it arrived in Europe in 1348 Jews were quickly blamed for poisoning the water, and flagellants were their leading persecutors.[182] In 1349, all the Jews of Strasbourg, some two thousand people, were burnt. Tens of thousands more died within two years, 12,000 in Mainz alone.[183]

One prominent aspect of the pollution prejudice was what Miri Rubin has described as a 'host desecration narrative'. Here, commencing in the thirteenth century, Jews were commonly accused of stealing, abusing, or otherwise polluting the communion wafer representing the body of Christ.[184] They would also be linked to sorcery, well- and food-poisoning, ritual murder and drinking Christian blood, conniving with Muslim invaders, and the murder of Christ. A sense of the dangers of being unclean, the virtues of 'purity', and of the linkage of moral to physical contagion, pervaded the period, indicating the persistence in popular superstition of much older taboos.[185]

But this hostility was also free-floating. Throughout medieval Europe, Jews, lepers, sodomists, witches, and sorcerers were common and almost interchangeable targets: witches in Hungary were sentenced to wear Jews' hats in public, while prostitutes in France were confined in a leper's house in one town.[186] Lepers sometimes alleged that Jews had bribed them to spread the disease.[187] Orgies and deviant sexual activity were frequently charged against Jews, heretics, and witches alike. Sodomists were condemned as 'monsters' and heretics.[188] These fears were sometimes generalized into a fear of foreigners and anyone 'different', which some

[179] William I. Brustein, *Roots of Hate: Anti-Semitism in Europe before the Holocaust* (Cambridge University Press, 2003), p. 53.
[180] Michael, *Holy Hatred*, pp. 51, 92.
[181] Richards, *Sex, Dissidence and Damnation*, p. 103; René Girard. *The Scapegoat*, p. 3.
[182] Cohn, *The Pursuit of the Millennium*, p. 139.
[183] Richards, *Sex, Dissidence and Damnation*, p. 104.
[184] Emmerson, *Antichrist in the Middle Ages*, p. 79; Miri Rubin, *Gentile Tales: The Narrative Assault on Late Medieval Jews* (Yale University Press, 1999), pp. 1–6.
[185] See generally Mary Douglas, *Collected Works*, vol. 2: *Purity and Danger: An Analysis of the Concepts of Pollution and Taboo* (Routledge, 2003).
[186] Richards, *Sex, Dissidence and Damnation*, p. 20.
[187] Gary K. Waite, *Heresy, Magic and Witchcraft in Early Modern Europe* (Palgrave, 2003), pp. 28–9.
[188] Merry E. Wiesner-Hanks, *Christianity and Sexuality in the Early Modern World* (Routledge, 2000), p. 87.

have associated with an age-old distrust of 'abominable' groups or dissenters within any homogeneous society.[189] By the twelfth century, persecution 'became habitual' in Europe, as institutionalized violence increasingly targeted minority groups. Whether this was primarily orchestrated from above, through bureaucratic institutionalization, or erupted spontaneously from below, renewed attention to heresy certainly fostered a climate of fear. The result was what R. I. Moore aptly terms a 'persecuting society'.[190]

The Reformation did not assuage these hostilities. Calvin condemned the Jews to Hell. Luther repeated charges of ritual murder, and insisted that baptism could not alter the Jew's errant nature. But in order to explain evil, Jews remained a 'theological necessity'. Like the Devil, had they not existed they would have to have been invented.[191] They were widely expelled: from England in 1290, France in 1306, and Spain in 1492.

Gendering Dystopia: Witches and Witchcraft

Christianity enshrined misogyny as official dogma by associating women with Original Sin, thus extending the blame heaped upon Eve for Original Sin, itself linked to taboos about menstruation and pollution as well as sexuality.[192] Women came to epitomize desire as such and thus sin as such.[193] Augustine thought the pride of loving self more than God assumed its worst form in love of women. A male-dominated monopolizing Church was also deeply suspicious of competition from women's links to magic and medicine.[194] Hence Paul prohibited women from preaching. Pollution taboos, especially respecting menstruation, may also be an origin of the sense of the female as demonic, and hence of the persecution of women as witches.

Women inevitably became objects of detestation as a result. Satan thus ought rightly to have been a woman, but for the clear need to give God a worthy or socially equal opponent. (Witchcraft neatly sidestepped this problem.)[195] Gradually, Eric Maple writes, 'women were reduced in status until their lot was little better than slavery'.[196] At the same time, both men and women were rendered miserable by having their basic desires condemned in the fiercest terms. A life haunted by the fear of sin and dominated by terror defines the psychology of dystopia.

---

[189] E.g., Cohn, *Europe's Inner Demons*, p. 1.

[190] Moore, *The Formation of a Persecuting Society*, pp. 145, 5.

[191] Trachtenberg, *The Devil and the Jews*, pp. 218, 163.

[192] Richard Godbeer, *The Devil's Dominion: Magic and Religion in Early New England* (Cambridge University Press, 1992), p. 118. See Dyan Elliott, *Fallen Bodies: Pollution, Sexuality, and Demonology in the Middle Ages* (University of Pennsylvania Press, 1999).

[193] See, generally, Wiesner-Hanks, *Christianity and Sexuality in the Early Modern World*.

[194] Augustine wrote, 'How vile, how detestable, how shameful, how dreadful' was 'the embrace of a woman' (quoted in Katharine M. Rogers, *The Troublesome Helpmate: A History of Misogyny in Literature* (University of Washington Press, 1966), p. 17). See further Jack Holland, *A Brief History of Misogyny* (Constable & Robinson, 2006) and Marianne Hester, *Lewd Women and Wicked Witches: A Study of the Dynamics of Male Domination* (Routledge, 1992).

[195] But misandry, or amongst men, self-loathing, might partly account for the popularity of the male image of the Devil.

[196] Eric Maple, *The Domain of Devils* (Robert Hale, 1966), p. 37.

One pronounced consequence of this misogyny was the early modern persecution of 'witches'. Witchcraft or sorcery had been condemned, even by death, in the Old Testament, and harmful magic was punished in ancient Greece and Rome. Later witch-hunts have been traced back to second-century accusations against Christians of ritually slaughtering babies, holding orgies, and worshipping animal divinities.[197] At this time, declining belief in the ancient religions encouraged an 'extraordinary spread of belief in demons' and their powers. Witches were believed capable of calling up demons by incantation; of entering into pacts with them for various ends; and of making sacrifices to and worshipping them.[198] They could also disguise themselves as animals (including 'shapeshifting' as werewolves and vampires) or small men. Theologians debated whether they really did this or only, as Augustine thought, produced an illusion thereof, or what we today call 'magic'.

Jews were rarely accused directly of witchcraft; witches indeed inherited many of the earlier charges against them, sometimes filling a vacuum left by the Jews' annihilation or expulsion.[199] Stories of child-theft, murder, and cannibalism were thus transferred from Jews to witches.[200] In a floating process of scapegoating, much of the imagery of the witch cult was thus indebted to the ancient religions of pre-Christian Europe and to popular images of the Jews.[201] Heretics were later accused of similar practices, which then came to focus upon 'witches'. Thus, witch-hunting was less prominent in countries where the Inquisition was most active, like Spain (where no witches were executed) and Poland, and flourished where heresy was most widespread, as in Britain.[202] Yet before 1400, belief in witchcraft was often derided by the Church, and even punished as 'pure illusion', rooted especially in dreams, in a remarkable anticipation of modern psychoanalysis.[203]

This would change dramatically when persecuting heresy became the Church's great preoccupation and witchcraft and heresy came to be seen as interwoven. Now ideas that women could fly at night or transform themselves into animals were accepted by the Church (in 1450 and 1525 respectively). In 1484, a papal bull laid special stress upon fornication with the Devil. The linkage of impotence to witchcraft was then emphasized in the *Malleus Maleficarum* or *The Hammer of Witches* (1487), written by the Dominican Inquisitor Heinrich Kramer.[204] This handbook of misogyny, worthy of Augustine, branded women as essentially 'diabolic'. It established the official definition of witchcraft, linking together sorcery, pacts with the Devil, wanton female sexuality, and threats to male sexuality. Lust was again the central issue, yet so too were class and power. Misogyny was

---

[197] Cohn, *Europe's Inner Demons*, p. xi.
[198] Russell, *Witchcraft in the Middle Ages*, pp. 13–18.
[199] Michael D. Bailey, *Battling Demons: Witchcraft, Heresy and Reform in the Late Middle Ages* (Penn State University Press, 2003), p. 143.
[200] Lyndal Roper, *Witch Craze: Terror and Fantasy in Baroque Germany* (Yale University Press, 2004), p. 43.
[201] Murray's hypothesis is here supported in part by Ginzburg, *The Night Battles*, p. xiii, though here the protection of the crops against witches is the starting point (pp. 22–3).
[202] Russell, *Witchcraft in the Middle Ages*, p. 40.
[203] And accordingly welcomed as such: Jones, *On the Nightmare*, p. 216.
[204] Jones, *On the Nightmare*, pp. 218–19, 223.

Fig. 2.5. Witches kiss the Devil's ass. © Mary Evans Picture Library 10017826.

also present: monstrosity in humans, for example, the presence of a third nipple, was often held to be proof of a witch.[205] Kramer assumed that 'truly the current increase of witches essentially goes back to the sorrowful struggle between married and unmarried men and women', and that as a result of female vengeance it was 'not surprising that there are so many witches'.[206] Class struggle was thus seemingly central here. Single women were a threat to married women, to property, and to social order. Witchcraft was one symbol of resistance to patriarchal and feudal oppression. The witch, indeed, could be seen as proto-feminist.

Eventually, the idea of the witch became organized around four categories: the practice of *maleficium*, or occult harming; being bound as a servant to the Devil; flying through the air and associating with others engaged in strange acts; and meeting with others at sabbats to have intercourse with the Devil and engage in other nefarious doings.[207] Sabbat rituals can be likened to festivals like Saturnalia and Carnival (see Fig. 2.5), insofar as the 'black mass' was clearly a satirical inversion of

---

[205] Murray, *The Witch-Cult in Western Europe*, p. 94.

[206] Lène Dresen-Coenders, 'Witches as Devils' Concubines: On the Origin of Fear of Witches and Protection against Witchcraft', in Lène Dresen-Coenders et al., *Images of Women in the 15th and 16th Centuries* (The Rubicon Press, 1987), pp. 59, 61.

[207] Cohn, *Europe's Inner Demons*, p. 147.

Catholic rituals, with witches often portrayed as dancing, making the sign of the cross backwards with the left hand, and turning backwards. The overtly sexual nature of much of this ritual has often been noted. It included flying (regarded in dream analysis as an instance of excitation), transforming men into horses to ride them (or using the broomstick as a phallic symbol thereof), and titillation and fornication of various kinds.[208] Wearing masks and imitating animals occurred in both phenomena, and also hearken back to pre-Christian practices. 'Riding with', 'calling up', or invoking, adoring, paying homage to, sacrificing to, and making pacts with the Devil and harming animals were common charges in witch trials. 'Witches' were widely associated with darkness, with various animals, with aerial flight, with invisibility, with blood-sucking, with child murder and theft, with nakedness and sexuality, with orgies and Jews, with cannibalism (linked to the belief that one gained the powers of the person eaten), and with death.[209]

By the early seventeenth century, the signs of demonic possession included speaking in unknown tongues, or revealing concealed things, or manifesting unusual strength.[210] In early eighteenth-century Hungary, witches were accused of 'destroying vineyards with hailstorms' and 'selling rain to the Turks'. Older near-universal ideas of magic also associated witchcraft with impotence, premature births, infant deaths, and illnesses and disturbances of many kinds. Amongst these, impotence was probably the chief worry to men, and infant death to women.[211] Killing and eating children, was often regarded as the chief crime of witches, and perhaps symbolized infanticide, itself sometimes the result of illegitimate birth.[212] Where a population had declined these anxieties are easily explained. A linkage to illness also remains consistent with a magical world-view inherited from the earliest times. The residual strength of magical beliefs meant that a diagnosis of a malady as caused by being haunted by a fairy or evil spirit might appear side by side with that of being 'forspoken' or bewitched.[213] In some areas, witches also supposedly caused disease, illness, crop failure, and other maladies through curses and spells. Hysteria, rooted chiefly in 'sexual aetiology', has been the predominant psychological explanation for such ascriptions.[214]

Just why all this occurred has remained controversial, though most agree that 'the essential responsibility for it unquestionably rests on the Roman Catholic Church'.[215] Witchcraft in the early Middle Ages was not generally viewed as particularly threatening. In England it was regarded as a relatively minor offence, treated in the lower ecclesiastical courts. Execution for witchcraft began around 1275, in Toulouse. Execution for heresy, however, occurred as early as 1022. As heresy and

[208] Jones, *On the Nightmare*, pp. 202–13, 260.
[209] Salic law enjoined a fine of two hundred shillings to punish witches who ate persons: Russell, *Witchcraft in the Middle Ages*, p. 59.
[210] Kelly, *Satan*, p. 305.   [211] Wilson, *The Magical Universe*, pp. 61, 139–42.
[212] Russell, *Witchcraft in the Middle Ages*, pp. 167–98; Joseph Klaits, *Servants of Satan: The Age of the Witch Hunts* (Indiana University Press, 1985), p. 53; Maria Tausiet, 'Infanticide and Its Translations in Aragón', in Stuart Clark, ed., *Languages of Witchcraft: Narrative, Ideology and Meaning in Early Modern Culture* (St. Martin's Press, 2001), p. 180.
[213] Thomas, *Religion and the Decline of Magic*, p. 219.
[214] Jones, *On the Nightmare*, p. 211.   [215] Ibid., p. 214.

witchcraft came to be more closely identified over the next five centuries, campaigns against the latter became more ferocious. From a few hundred trials in the fifteenth century, many thousands occurred from the mid-sixteenth through the late seventeenth centuries.

The total number of deaths was once estimated at over 9 million. Recent historiography suggests that, across three centuries, perhaps 90,000 witch trials took place, resulting in some 45,000 executions.[216] A mere hundred died in the worst episode of witch persecution in England, between 1645 and 1647.[217] Yet in some communities in Germany in the sixteenth century, as many as 5–7.5 per cent were executed as witches in the space of only a few years.[218] And in principle it could have been a good deal worse. For a time there was a real risk, indeed, that all women could be understood as at least potentially witches.[219] The mentality which produced a potential femicide should thus be able to tell us much about later persecutions.

The growth of witch persecution was clearly linked to the spread of Catharism (twelfth to fourteenth centuries) in particular. Catharism denounced the evils of the flesh and encouraged asceticism, as well as a strong sense of dualism and of the active working of the Devil in the world. At the other end of the heretical spectrum was the thirteenth-century libertinism of the Brethren of the Free Spirit, who contended that no evil existed because all things were God, and that lust, greed, and even incest and homosexuality could be indulged with impunity.[220] The Bohemian Adamites (*c.*1300–1400) demonstrated a clear revolt against sexual repression as such.[221] The later Anabaptists also assumed greater sexual freedom to be amongst God's injunctions.[222] Some of these heretics were also thought to believe that they had achieved something like a state of Divine grace. Amongst the propositions condemned by the authorities was the assumption that 'a man in this life can attain to such perfection that he is incapable of sinning or surpassing his present degree of grace, since to do so would make him more perfect than Christ'.[223] Similarly claiming to be imbued with the Holy Spirit, the group known as the Apostolici in thirteenth-century Italy claimed they could fornicate freely as long as it was done in the name of love. Some heretics, notably the

---

[216] Older estimates were 250,000–300,000.

[217] See Malcolm Gaskell, 'Fear Made Flesh: The English Witch-Panic of 1645–7', in David Lemmings and Claire Walker, eds., *Moral Panics, the Media and the Law in Early Modern England* (Palgrave Macmillan, 2009), pp. 78–96.

[218] For instance, 150 out of 2,750 in Rottenburg: Jon Oplinger, *The Politics of Demonology: The European Witchcraze and the Mass Production of Deviance* (Associated University Presses, 1990), p. 47.

[219] Wolfgang Lederer, *The Fear of Women* (Grune & Stratton, 1968), p. 151. 'The female stereotype was in fact so strong that in some periods the words woman and witch are almost interchangeable': Christina Larner, *Witchcraft and Religion* (Basil Blackwell, 1984), p. 61.

[220] Confessions regarding such activities have, however, been discounted; see Robert E. Lerner, *The Heresy of the Free Spirit in the Later Middle Ages* (University of California Press, 1972), pp. 11–13, 21.

[221] Russell, *Witchcraft in the Middle Ages*, pp. 118–27, 140.

[222] Claus-Peter Clasen, *Anabaptism: A Social History 1525–1618* (Cornell University Press, 1972), p. 138.

[223] Abraham Friesen, *Thomas Muentzer: A Destroyer of the Godless* (University of California Press, 1990), p. 92.

Luciferans and Adamites, also adopted the view that if all things were God, so too was the Devil, who might well be worshipped on earth.[224]

The golden age of witch-hunting was from the fourteenth to the late seventeenth century. Continental witch persecution peaked between the late sixteenth and the late seventeenth centuries, with the last European victim being burnt in 1749.[225] Some celebrated trials implicated hundreds. Torture produced more accusations, though some recanted forced confessions. In fifteenth-century Arras, some maintained that as many as a third of Christians were secret witches.[226] In Britain, most witch trials took place between 1560 and 1680, when village life became much more unsettled.[227] The social pressures evident early in this period did much to stoke an atmosphere of righteous hysteria. It was no accident that the chief protector against plague, Saint Anthony, became the patron saint most directly invoked against witches. In some areas, persecution beginning in the fifteenth century also followed severe weather and crop failure, and subsequent grain crisis, which were directly linked to witchcraft. Contemporaries worried increasingly about the wickedness of humanity, and the prospects of the end of the world. War, pestilence, earthquakes, and the flourishing of witchcraft were seen as evidence of the approaching end of the world, which was forecast repeatedly in the thirteenth and fourteenth centuries and later. Some thought the Devil's powers increased as it neared.[228]

But the perceived increase in the number of witches also increased as the opportunity of profit arose through confiscating property, and by paying witch-finders' fees—in England, the famously obsessive Matthew Hopkins, who had some three hundred hanged between 1644 and 1646, was well remunerated (and lied about it). But zeal in the cause was not in short supply either. An early medieval opponent of heresy, Conrad of Marburg, insisted that he 'would gladly burn a hundred if just one of them were guilty'.[229] The Reformation did nothing to ease the situation. Luther followed Augustine in identifying Original Sin with sexual desire, and insisted he had 'no compassion' for witches and would 'burn all of them'.[230] We will encounter this deadly enthusiasm much later.

Explaining Witchcraft
The 'Reality' of Witchcraft

The Church clearly found witches a useful ally. The more there were, the more spiritual policemen were needed, and the more money could be extracted from the devout to prove their piety. So, as Russell notes, persecution of witches did not

[224] Russell, *Witchcraft in the Middle Ages*, pp. 140–1.
[225] Prosecutions in North America were reported as late as 1823.
[226] Cohn, *Europe's Inner Demons*, p. 231.
[227] Ibid., p. 160, discussing Keith Thomas and Alan Macfarlane.
[228] Clark, *Thinking with Demons*, pp. 321–2.
[229] Cited in Richards, *Sex, Dissidence and Damnation*, p. 80.
[230] Quoted in Boris Sidis, *The Psychology of Suggestion: A Research into the Subconscious Nature of Man and Society* (D. Appleton & Co., 1924), p. 334.

Engraved for Dr. HURD's Religious Rites & Ceremonies of All Nations.

Inside View of a Goal *in the* Inquisition, *shewing the several methods of* Torture *and* Cruelty, *as exercised in presence of the* Inquisitor, &c.

Fig. 2.6. Inquisition: questioning. © Mary Evans Picture Library 10037552.

diminish the supply, which in fact increased to meet the demand.[231] Once again, then, 'enemies' proved to be friends. But how many were there really? Few now believe that an even loosely *organized* body of 'witches' of the sort described by Margaret Murray, Montague Summers, and Jeffrey Russell, especially one rooted in ancient cults, ever existed.[232] Some contemporary inquisitors, like Alonso de Salazar in 1610, concluded that the supposed confessions of witches were 'nothing but a chimera' (see Fig. 2.6).[233] Given the mixture of supposition, fantasy, wishful thinking, forgery, invention, delusion, madness, and planted confessions extracted by torture, it is easy to dismiss witch-hunting as little more than a grandiose hoax.

Yet the process of inventing witches is still a phenomenon which needs explaining. Lyndal Roper argues that 'the fantasy of witch-hood is created in a project of collaboration between questioner and accused'.[234] The degree to which the Devil

[231] Russell, *Witchcraft in the Middle Ages*, pp. 288–9.
[232] Cohn, *Europe's Inner Demons*, pp. 99–125; Thomas, *Religion and the Decline of Magic*, pp. 614–15.
[233] John Cornwell, *The Dark Box: A Secret History of Confession* (Profile Books, 2014), p. 54.
[234] Lyndal Roper, *Oedipus and the Devil: Witchcraft, Sexuality, and Religion in Early Modern Europe* (Routledge, 1994), p. 227.

or the witch 'really' existed was an outcome of these negotiations. There were, doubtless, a few people who did worship the Devil, and some organized rituals were engaged in.[235] More often, women admitted fantasies in which the Devil played a prominent, usually sexual, part. Some yearned for children when none had appeared, and feared barren old women for their capacity to bring barrenness upon others.[236] Others sought occult ways of curing or harming, and sometimes for revenge or merely excitement. Some did not draw a line between conversing legitimately with angels or God, and invoking the Devil.

What is clear, at least, is that the power of suggestion was central in this process. Individually, magic 'works' like other aspects of taboo. The assertion is made that witchcraft is practised and is effective. Some wish to emulate its effects and therefore imitate practices they have heard about. Others concede their efficacy and imagine that evils which befall them are a result. Witches thus 'exist' by the power of suggestion, and are 'real' exactly in the degree to which we believe in the efficacy of their powers. They 'really exist' where the belief that they exist causes us to suffer grievously from their supposed powers.[237] (We have already seen that dying from violating taboo is by no means uncommon.) Witchcraft thus 'could only succeed where people believed that it could succeed'.[238] It has real mental bases: Freud noted that demons were often conceived as linked to those who died recently, and thought belief in their existence to be intimately interlinked to the mourning process. But they were still 'creations of the human mind: they were made by something and out of something'.[239]

And so it is at the social level. Following a 1611 trial, for example, one inquisitor noted that witchcraft had been unknown until people began talking about it.[240] In some cases, like the notorious instance of a group of nuns who were 'bewitched' in Würzburg in 1749, suggestion could extend to substantial numbers of people, who claimed they were suffocating and had frequent paroxysms as a result of sorcery.[241] It is easy to term this mass delusion, but the real effects of such beliefs are hardly delusory. Thus, the language of suggestion is more helpful. Witch-hunting was partly a form of group hysteria, instigated perhaps by a few, but gathering momentum through contagion. Instrumentally it benefited a few, but functionally it also resulted from the needs, fears, and desires of many more.

Gender and Sexual Explanations

These needs and fears clearly focus more on gender and sexuality than any other single issue. Though some 20 per cent of 'witches' were not women, a very close

[235] Russell, *Witchcraft in the Middle Ages*, p. 21.   [236] Roper, *Witch Craze*, p. 103.
[237] A Cambodian peasant said of spirits that 'They can only act if people believe in them' (Karl D. Jackson, ed., *Cambodia 1975–1978* (Princeton University Press, 1989), p. 168).
[238] Lauran Paine, *Witches in Fact and Fantasy* (Robert Hale, 1971), p. 13.
[239] Sigmund Freud, *Totem and Taboo: Some Points of Agreement between the Mental Lives of Savages and Neurotics* (Routledge & Kegan Paul, 1960), p. 24.
[240] Joseph Perez, *The Spanish Inquisition* (Profile Books, 2004), p. 139.
[241] Ilza Veith, *Hysteria: The History of a Disease* (University of Chicago Press, 1965), p. 73.

association existed between the Devil, female sexuality, and witchcraft in Europe, though more on the Continent than in Britain.[242] It is often asserted that the 'central feature' of the witch's bond with the Devil was 'the sexual relationship'.[243] As early as the tenth century, Englishwomen were warned about having sexual intercourse with the Devil. Monstrosity lurks again here: we recall here the Old Testament legends of giants born from angelic–human intercourse. The Inquisition would maintain that: 'All witchcraft comes from carnal lust, which is in women insatiable.'[244] There is both male and female anxiety potentially at work here. Witches were often portrayed as enjoying copulation with the Devil and as having the power to 'Deprive Man of his Virile Member', an obvious instance of castration anxiety also evident in the vampire image.[245] Yet we also know that many of the supposedly sexual elements in witchcraft were only introduced by the authorities during trials, not in the original complaints. Many an overheated official imagination was probably at work here.[246]

Another factor to be considered here is the growth in numbers of spinsters and widows, especially amongst the poor, which may also have made women—the chief focus of occult harm—a special target of popular anxiety.[247] The new witches were overwhelmingly single women, often older (fifty to sixty) and poor. This group had many enemies, not least simply because they were not effectively under male control. Their mere independence represented an affront to the established order. Some were healers and/or midwives, activities women had dominated before about the fourteenth century, but which the authorities were keen to regulate and monopolize thereafter. The poor were predisposed to blame witches for a range of illnesses, such as arthritis and tuberculosis, which, ironically, some might claim to be able to cure.[248] Attractive single and experienced older women were also a threat to married women, to some married men, and to other single women. (Older women suffered an additional prejudice against age, and its associations with the fear of decrepitude and death. In simple logic, old age was identified with death, and death with the Devil.)

Widows were thus in some respects the moral antithesis of celibate women. They were the greatest temptresses of the Church itself, where enforced male celibacy within clearly heightened anxiety about female sexuality outside. Only the purest woman—the least tempting and desired as well as desiring—could pose no threat to men. (The cult of the Virgin Mary, portrayed as the female antithesis to Eve, and the widespread veneration of female saints, is thus no accident. In the *Malleus*,

---

[242] For one episode here see Roper, *Witch Craze*, pp. 82–103. It has been claimed that southern American Indian witchcraft 'is simply not concerned with sex', indicating the centrality of a Christian context here. See Mary Douglas, ed., *Witchcraft Confessions and Accusations* (Tavistock Publications, 1970), p. 198.

[243] Jones, *On the Nightmare*, p. 200.

[244] Quoted in Holland, *A Brief History of Misogyny*, p. 118.

[245] Cullen Murphy, *God's Jury: The Inquisition and the Making of the Modern World* (Allen Lane, 2012), p. 135. Cavendish, *The Powers of Evil*, pp. 47–8. In some cases witches were believed able to restore a 'member' lost through a curse: Veith, *Hysteria*, p. 64.

[246] Klaits, *Servants of Satan*, p. 58.   [247] Clark, *Thinking with Demons*, p. 107.

[248] Thomas, *Religion and the Decline of Magic*, p. 639.

witches were portrayed as explicitly rejecting the veneration of Mary.) Many women who made witchcraft accusations also appear to have had difficulties with their fathers or father figures, which have been interpreted as Oedipal in Freudian terms. Others had children who had fallen ill or died prematurely. This may make many 'confessions' an early form of psychoanalytic release of the resulting tension, which helps explain motives.[249]

Seek and Ye Shall Find: The Inquisition

Organized devil- and witch-hunting is associated with one branch of the Church in particular. If the Dark Ages were dark, it was the Inquisition which snuffed the candles out and closed the curtains through most of the following millennium. Lasting from the twelfth through the eighteenth centuries, the papal and even more the Spanish 'Inquisitions' (from the Latin, to search) provide a clear paradigm for an extensive system of persecution based upon the dual obsession of faith and heresy. Its targets were Cathars, Waldensians, Manicheans, Jews, sorcerers, and the like. Not without reason, we will see, did the Bolshevik police admire its methods. Indeed, it has been plausibly suggested that modern despotism was consciously modelled on its mentality, identifying enemies by and persecuting merely for the sake of the purity of ideas, inflicting pain in proportion to its obsession with purity, loyalty, and unity, and controlling thought on principle.[250]

The Inquisition killed some 30,000 in Spain alone over a century and a half after 1478.[251] As many as 1.5 million may have been denounced, with perhaps 340,000 trials over three centuries.[252] In some places, like Toledo, as many as a third of the population were tried between 1486 and 1499 under the first Grand Inquisitor, Torquemada. A further 84,000 people were tried throughout Spain between 1540 and 1700, with perhaps 3 per cent of these being 'relaxed' permanently, in the charming contemporary euphemism (which, in the context of being released from guilt, might make sense), namely released from the protection of the Church and turned over to the secular authorities, and if necessary put to death.[253] Here there was also a duty to denounce, and failure to do so could incur savage penalties. Over such a lengthy period, we will see, these efforts pale beside twentieth-century mass murder, though in moments of peak hysteria proportionately large numbers were affected in some areas. But an important precedent was founded: the Church's purity demanded murder on a substantial scale and institutionalized terror. Extreme intolerance of deviance, and torture to determine the purity of the soul, were established and legitimized. Classifying enemies according to belief provided a bold plan for creating necessary enemies.

[249] Roper, *Oedipus and the Devil*.   [250] Murphy, *God's Jury*, p. 23.
[251] Daniel Chirot, *Modern Tyrants: The Power and Prevalence of Evil in Our Age* (Free Press, 1994), p. 17; Toby Green, *Inquisition: The Reign of Fear* (Macmillan, 2007), p. 8.
[252] Francisco Bethencourt, *The Inquisition: A Global History, 1478–1834* (Cambridge University Press, 2009), p. 444; Perez, *The Spanish Inquisition*, p. 170.
[253] Green, *Inquisition*, p. 8.

The Inquisition's obsessive rooting out of heretical belief and diabolical practice made heresy the worst of crimes. Yet it also reflected a despotism of social custom, where, as one historian has commented, 'mere eccentricity of life was reason enough for suspicion of heresy'.[254] Denying the existence of Heaven or Hell, the virginity of Mary, the validity of the sacraments, and much else could bring a death sentence. Purity of doctrine (and of blood) and unity of society produced psychological wholeness. Diversity, doubt, and disbelief engendered anxiety. Orthodoxy was strength, heresy weakness. A fanatical obsession with control and rigid exclusion dominated the inquisitors' mental world. Persecution became a routine necessity, repression an end in itself. Where categories of victims disappeared, like converted Jews in early seventeenth-century Spain, new ones had to be manufactured, like Moriscos (Muslims) and deviant Christians.[255]

The Inquisition bred heresy by drawing attention to its importance in the same manner as an increase of police apparently breeds more crime by multiplying the number of crimes reported and criminals pursued. It thus used the power of suggestion to an extraordinary degree. Torture was used to extract confessions, which often involved naming accomplices. And therefore these had to be found. Once categories of sinners were defined they were easily found. People themselves came to conform to the expected type, 'becoming' 'witches' or 'heretics' out of guilt in particular. The quest for the guilty became a self-fulfilling prophecy. To seek was to find.

Inquisitorial proceedings typically commenced by reading an 'edict of faith' to a given population, which indicated what beliefs were likely to be deemed heretical. This sowed the seeds of doubt, and commenced the process of suggestion. By the seventeenth century, crypto-Judaism loomed large in this announcement, followed by a delineation of practices associated with Islam, Lutheranism, and Illuminism. Every new campaign began with a period of grace and an invitation, planting the seed, for people to turn themselves in. So self-denunciation became a mass phenomenon in some areas.

Once suggested, the sense of guilt became contagious, and hints of doubt were easily magnified into full-blown heresy.[256] But those who so confessed could in fact avoid only the death penalty, not many other punishments, and only after a public trial, not via private confession.[257] Priests were enjoined to report any information they could glean from the confessional, and to gather heretical books. Millions of these were burnt—10,000 in a day in Rome in 1559. Offensive passages in thousands more were detected and deleted as a vast apparatus of censorship was constructed to employ Orwell's Winston Smith's ancestors.[258] Delation, or statutory assertions of guilt, became common, and as Coulton wrote, 'no man was safe from his neighbours, his servants, or even his children'.[259] The betrayal of friends in

[254] Hoffman Nickerson, *The Inquisition* (John Bale, Sons & Danielsson, 1923), p. 74.
[255] Bethencourt, *The Inquisition*, p. 350.
[256] Edward Burman, *The Inquisition* (The Aquarian Press, 1984), p. 143.
[257] Perez, *The Spanish Inquisition*, p. 136.   [258] Murphy, *God's Jury*, p. 117.
[259] G. C. Coulton, *Inquisition and Liberty* (Heinemann, 1958), p. 292.

order to prove one's own conversion was a constant theme in such interrogations, for this too was a duty. One heretic might thus produce dozens more by way of expiation. And greed, as ever, doubtless played a prominent role. (Indeed, this entire process was, at one level, yet another colossal piratical scheme for property redistribution.) *Familiares*, or lay assistants, provided much information in return for relief from taxes and other benefits. In Valencia there was one for every forty-two inhabitants.[260] Millions of people may never have encountered the Inquisition. But for millions more, particularly its targets, it was a constant threat.

The Inquisition's success occurred in part because its 'charges' and 'crimes' were exceedingly loosely defined. Introduced in the twelfth century, the allegation of 'Suspicion of Heresy' was usually divided into three grades of light, vehement, and violent. (Its application bears a striking parallel to Article 58 of the Soviet Penal Code, we will shortly see.) It was a very difficult charge to counter. Arrest signified the presumption of guilt, and no religious consolation was permitted those imprisoned. No formal charge, indeed, was demanded, mere rumour sufficing for arrest. Nor was any substantial proof required to secure conviction, only the suspicion itself attested to by two witnesses.

The basic mode of proceeding was that 'the accused was treated as one having no rights, whose guilt was assumed in advance, and from whom confession was to be extorted by guile or force'. At the trial, the burden of proof was on the accused to prove their innocence. The entire procedure was cloaked in secrecy. Sometimes the names of accusers as well as the evidence itself were kept secret, removing virtually all responsibility from both witnesses and accusers. Preliminary proceedings were held in secret and the accused might be imprisoned and tortured for years before knowing the charges against them. Many legal rules were suspended, such as allowing testimony from underage witnesses or those convicted of a wide range of crimes, including heresy itself. Existing cautions were thrown to the winds by 'the same disposition to construe everything in favour of the faith'. Wives, children, and servants were forbidden to assist the accused by their testimony, and encouraged to oppose them. Opportunities for defence were minimal, the malice of the accusers, if they could be proven to be personal enemies of the accused, often being a sole recourse. No witness could refuse to give evidence, and torture was indeed used more freely on witnesses than the accused.

Gaining friendly witnesses was well-nigh impossible in the circumstances. Lawyers employed by the defence, moreover, had the sole duty of encouraging confessions. In a wondrous logical contortion, appeals were possible only before sentence was pronounced, for verdicts were final. (Where large amounts of property were at stake, intercession was more easily arranged.) Conversion to the faith where applicable might help; a law of 1229 allowed the death sentence to be commuted to life imprisonment in such instances.[261]

---

[260] Murphy, *God's Jury*, p. 85.
[261] Henry Charles Lea, *The Inquisition of the Middle Ages* (Eyre & Spottiswoode, 1963), pp. 318, 188–91, 200, 239.

Once arrested, confession was the key goal, though it was not necessary for conviction. Torture (by water, fire, the wheel, pulleys, the rack, and other methods) was an investigative procedure introduced virtually from the outset, and over the centuries perhaps a third of prisoners encountered such persuasion. Having, in 1252, permitted their use in furthering inquisitorial investigations, Pope Alexander IV, in 1256, gave inquisitors the right to absolve each other of any blame incurred. It was forbidden for blood to be shed or disfigurement to occur during torture—a line the Soviets sometimes drew before 1937, and one we now also still recognize, and doubtless as often violate. Yet great pain in any case accompanied the common use of the pulley and water torture.[262] The distance between psychological torture, the threat of torture (the sight of its instruments, notably), and its actual use was often very small. 'Questioned' and 'tortured' were indeed often regarded as synonymous.

Once condemned, unfortunates had to endure a public *auto-da-fé* (confession of faith) proclaiming their guilt, which was sometimes attended by hundreds. Here again we see elements of scapegoating at work. Those to be 'relaxed' wore a penitential black garment called a *sanbenito*, which portrayed flames, demons, dragons, and snakes, the symbols of Hell. They were given special caps and candles for the procession.[263] Death was a logical result of accusation, since it was believed that the 'object of the Inquisition is the destruction of heresy. Heresy cannot be destroyed unless heretics are destroyed.'[264] But death was comparatively rare, and many so condemned were actually burnt only in effigy. Those unfortunates fated to die to secure the 'purification of sins' were usually garrotted before being burnt. Those who went to the stake then had the remnants of their bones broken and burnt again for good measure, the ashes often being scattered to avoid them becoming relics. Other penances included public flogging; wearing a cross or other symbol of stigma; imprisonment; confiscation of property; or destruction of houses. Forced pilgrimages and crusades involving years of exile could also be inflicted. And guilt even extended beyond the grave: the bones of those who had died and were later judged heretics might be dug up and burnt. A little pollution is a dangerous thing.

Most of these penalties could, however, be removed by an appropriate payment in what was clearly a monumental scheme of swindling, extortion, blackmail, and robbery. This leaves the lingering suspicion that much of this gigantic enterprise had as much to do with envy and plunder as faith. (We will see parallels in Nazism and Bolshevism.) The Inquisition became an immensely profitable enterprise. But the penitent found guilty could only be reprieved, never pardoned. Each 'lived for ever on the verge of ruin, never knowing when the blow might fall, and utterly powerless to avert it'. Always 'a subject to be watched by the universal police', his 'existence from that hour was one of endless, hopeless anxiety'.[265] And the stigma of heresy might easily descend to one's relatives. Thus, the climate of fear and of enforced conformity was usually attained. In 1578, it was declared that the chief

---

[262] Perez, *The Spanish Inquisition*, p. 147.   [263] Ibid., p. 162.
[264] Lea, *The Inquisition of the Middle Ages*, p. 292.   [265] Ibid., pp. 252–3.

purpose of trials and death sentences was not to save souls but to 'ensure the public good and to strike terror into the people'.[266] This, certainly, might have been the moral that the young Stalin, ensconced in the seminary, digested from the whole story.

With its extension to the 'New World' in the sixteenth century, the first truly international system of terror commenced. Conquest and conversion were like the main course and the sweet which followed. Both God and the Devil were served up to the natives, whose devil-worshipping domain of human sacrifice, cannibalism, and sodomy had first to be abolished, without getting in the way of the main business of getting gold and glory.[267] To make Christians, however, was to make 'heretics'. Every convert, indeed, was both a former and potential heretic. In areas controlled by the Conquistadores, indigenous peoples were now subject to trial for superstition, blasphemy, heresy, and other crimes. Crypto- or secret Judaism amongst those of the conquerors who had been forcibly converted themselves was also assiduously pursued. Protestantism was closely monitored. At Mexico City in 1559, for example, a crowd of some six thousand saw an Englishman condemned for Lutheranism, while another trial here in 1649 was attended by many thousands, some coming hundreds of miles. Later, readers of Voltaire and Rousseau would be pursued. Here, as in the Old World, the Inquisition did much to foster paranoia and superstition. It thus provided, in the words of Toby Green, 'the first seeds of totalitarian government'.[268] It exists to this day.

Conclusion: Monstrosities, the Devil, and the Persecution Mania

By the early eighteenth century, witchcraft was becoming increasingly associated with madness, or at least mental disturbance, and we begin to arrive at our own hesitantly quasi-secular world-view. Demonic possession, an obsession with which seems to have reached its peak in the seventeenth century, is still officially recognized by the Catholic Church today.[269] But fear of witches and the Devil is rare in most countries where most people are reasonably well educated. These monstrosities have been tamed, and are fit at best for the imaginary zoo of human psychology. Yet the monster trope itself has become stuck in our head, where it rattles around like keys in a washing machine. We cannot rid ourselves of it: we do not want to. We will later see that it undergoes many mutations through the present day.

The point of commencing a natural history of dystopia with monstrosity should now be clear. We began here with the assumption that, in the magical world-view, large segments of the world around us are populated by threatening and intermittently evil spirits. The Christian Devil inherited a much earlier set of monstrous qualities, and many lesser evils were subsumed under his personality. Slowly the monstrous legions were made subservient to Satan. Some would reappear as symbols of evil as such, and of animality lurking within in particular. Fear of

---

[266] Perez, *The Spanish Inquisition*, p. 154.   [267] Cervantes, *The Devil in the New World*, p. 9.
[268] Green, *Inquisition*, pp. 143, 4, 8.   [269] Clark, *Thinking with Demons*, p. 390.

Satan's powers came to dominate Europeans as no fear of an ethereal being had ever done before. From the fourteenth through the seventeenth centuries, the Devil became a more powerful figure in everyday life than in any preceding or subsequent period. In turn, his existence was used to justify an immensely oppressive system of persecution which threatened all dissenters from the one true faith. This system operated to reinforce the power of one dominant group for many centuries, and to exclude and suppress women, heretics, Jews, and deviants of many types. In Part II we will consider how far this mentality pervaded the totalitarian regimes of the twentieth century, and in particular how far a new essentially religious intolerance, often appearing as a form of secular millenarianism, underpinned the morality of persecution.

PART II

TOTALITARIANISM AND DYSTOPIA

3

The Caveman's Century

The Development of Totalitarianism from Jacobinism to Stalinism

See if there be any pain like unto my pain.

(Lamentations 1:12)

Behold, I make all things new.

(Revelations 21:5)

INTRODUCTION

In both history and literature, 'dystopia' has been most frequently identified with the colossal tragedies of twentieth-century despotism. In the death and prison camps of Germany and Russia in particular, millions were murdered, often with great brutality. In perhaps the finest work of modern historical narrative, Alexander Solzhenitsyn described 'terrorism' as producing 'one of the most shameful centuries in human history', 'the cave man's century'.[1] A vast and complex literature has arisen to try to explain how mankind went so far wrong, and to avoid such calamities in the future. Within it, many and heated disagreements have arisen. Whatever we make of these attempts, we clearly cannot understand dystopia (or indeed utopia) without confronting this history. Yet at times neither historical narrative nor literary expression seem to capture the depravity of these events. We might well wonder, indeed, whether any words can do so.

Yet the attempt must be made. This chapter focuses on how the regimes usually termed 'totalitarian' used fear to create and maintain their power, and how this fear became so extreme and so destructive.[2] It focuses upon a few key examples where mass destruction occurred, most notably Stalinism, the Nazi death camp at Auschwitz, and Pol Pot's rule in Cambodia between 1975 and 1979.[3] Its aim is to establish

---

[1] Alexander Solzhenitsyn, *The Gulag Archipelago 1918–1956* (3 vols, Collins & Harvill Press, 1974), vol. 3, pp. x, 36.

[2] A more general account of this type is Daniel Chirot, *Modern Tyrants: The Power and Prevalence of Evil in Our Age* (Free Press, 1994). Recent summaries of developments are Robert Gellately, *Lenin, Stalin, and Hitler: The Age of Social Catastrophe* (Jonathan Cape, 2007) and Timothy Snyder, *Bloodlands: Europe between Hitler and Stalin* (The Bodley Head, 2010).

[3] On defining genocide, see Mark Levene, *Genocide in the Age of the Nation-State*, vol. 1: *The Meaning of Genocide* (I.B. Taurus, 2005).

how the paranoid, persecutory psychology of dystopian groups outlined in the Introduction here, and, in particular, expressions of secular religiosity, provide key insights into the mentality of these regimes and movements. Then some attempt will be made to move on from and refine these explanations. Given the enormous number of books covering these areas, it has seemed preferable, where necessary, to err on the side of the subjective voice, in letting victims (where possible) speak of their experiences, at the cost of a disservice to the army of historians who have laboured to make sense of them. Blinkered, confused, witnesses nonetheless made a kind of sense of what happened to them. In recalling it, mostly in memoirs, they present us with an undisputed immediacy of feeling and perception which later layers of hindsight often obscure. These accounts do not trump more mediated evaluations, but they do tell us more directly how dystopia works, and as importantly, how it feels.

THE CONCEPT OF TOTALITARIANISM

Modern despotism is generally distinguished from its predecessors, and from authoritarianism, or the police state, by the term 'totalitarianism'.[4] Coined in 1928 to describe the Italy of Benito Mussolini (an avid reader of Le Bon), it meant that the 'Fascist conception of the state is all-embracing; outside of it no human or spiritual values can exist, much less have value. Thus understood, Fascism is totalitarian.'[5] An early account of the phenomenon, Peter Drucker's *The End of Economic Man: A Study of the New Totalitarianism* (1939), alleged that the failure of secular Marxist rationalism resulted in a 'return of the demons' of Nazism. While accompanied by spiritual crisis, a 'despair of the masses', in which 'all traditional ideas and ideologies' were regarded as bankrupt, totalitarian revolutions were defined as little more than the 'power grab' of an ascendant new class.[6] Hitler and Stalin's alliance then 'brought out the essential similarity between the German and the Russian systems', and revealed the 'misconception' that Nazism and communism were juxtaposed entities. Their shared essence was 'complete planning'.[7]

'Totalitarianism' was then widely applied in the 1940s to Nazi Germany, though its affinities with medieval Catholicism have often been noted.[8] Early studies noted

---

[4] On the wider concept see Brian Chapman, *Police State* (Pall Mall Press, 1970).The literature on totalitarianism as such is vast. A good summary is Michael Geyer and Sheila Fitzpatrick, *Beyond Totalitarianism: Stalinism and Nazism Compared* (Cambridge University Press, 2009). Other studies include: C. W. Cassinelli, *Total Revolution: A Comparative Study of Germany under Hitler, the Soviet Union under Stalin, and China under Mao* (Clio Books, 1976), Simon Tormey, *Making Sense of Tyranny: Interpretations of Totalitarianism* (Manchester University Press, 1995), and Abbott Gleason, *Totalitarianism: The Inner History of the Cold War* (Oxford University Press, 1995).

[5] Benito Mussolini, *The Doctrine of Fascism* (Vellecchi Editore, 1936), p. 13. On the left, comparisons of Nazism with Stalinism were long regarded as invidious and were semi-officially proscribed, given what was regarded as the unimpeachable moral tendency of Bolshevism by contrast to the unmitigated evil of Nazism. This trend is now in abeyance.

[6] Peter Drucker, *The End of Economic Man: A Study of the New Totalitarianism* (Harper & Row, 1969), pp. ix, xii, 11, 22, 59–84.

[7] F. Borkenau, *The Totalitarian Enemy* (Faber & Faber, 1940), pp. 7, 12–13, 197.

[8] Pope Pius XI noted in 1938 that 'if there is a totalitarian regime—in fact and by right—it is the regime of the church, because man belongs totally to the church' (quoted in *The Guardian*, 8 March 2014, 7).

five key characteristics: 'the promise of security, action instead of program, quasi-democratic foundations, war psychology, and the leadership principle'.[9] Here, if anything, it was the popular character of the modern dictatorship which was regarded as its most distinctive attribute, and as substantiating Le Bon's postulates. As the war ended, two key studies appeared which remain influential. Friedrich von Hayek's *The Road to Serfdom* (1944) warned that all forms of planning and socialism verged on 'collectivism', threatened the demise of individualism, and opened the way to totalitarianism. All attempts at complete economic control were bound to suppress differences of opinion respecting goals, and thus to suppress dissent generally in the interests of achieving unanimity. Hayek suggested that both fascism and communism were 'the outcome of the same tendencies'. He heartily endorsed those on the left, like Max Eastman, who now proclaimed Stalinism to be worse than fascism.[10] Karl Popper's *The Open Society and Its Enemies* (1945) then traced the totalitarian mentality back to Plato, and linked Hegel and Marx as enemies of liberal democracy.

During the Cold War, 'totalitarianism' came increasingly to portray qualities shared by Stalinism, then China, North Korea, and other communist states.[11] The key studies in this period were Hannah Arendt's *The Origins of Totalitarianism* (1949) and Carl J. Friedrich and Zbigniew Brzezinski's *Totalitarian Dictatorship and Autocracy* (1956). Arendt focused upon anti-Semitism, racialism, and Social Darwinism. Assuming 'total terror' to be 'the essence of totalitarianism', she linked this to the eradication of most forms of civil association and the isolation of individuals. In turn, she regarded the 'highly atomized' nature of modern society generally as providing 'the mass basis for totalitarian rule'.[12] The standard textbook for many years, Friedrich and Brzezinski's study was concerned with structure rather than origins; its refusal to even consider the Inquisition as a precedent is notable. Totalitarianism is here defined in terms of 'an ideology, a single party typically led by one man, a terroristic police, a communications monopoly, a weapons monopoly, and a centrally directed economy'. The historical uniqueness of the combination of these characteristics is stressed. So too is the characteristic 'violent passion' for 'enthusiastic unanimity'.[13]

Commencing in 1960, three major studies by Jacob Talmon saw totalitarianism originating in Rousseau's concept of the general will as an ideal of infallible popular sovereignty. Developing in mass industrial society, this produced a consensual

[9] Sigmund Neumann, *Permanent Revolution: The Total State in a World at War* (Harper & Brothers, 1942), p. 36. Another important contemporary account is Ernst Fraenkel, *The Dual State: A Contribution to the Theory of Dictatorship* (Oxford University Press, 1941).
[10] Friedrich von Hayek, *The Road to Serfdom* (University of Chicago Press, 1944), p. 27.
[11] Geyer and Fitzpatrick, *Beyond Totalitarianism*, p. 12.
[12] Hannah Arendt, *The Origins of Totalitarianism* (2nd edn, George Allen & Unwin, 1958), pp. 3–120, 178–80, 317, 407, 464, 466.
[13] Carl J. Friedrich and Zbigniew K. Brzezinski, *Totalitarian Dictatorship and Autocracy* (Harvard University Press, 1956), pp. 5, 9–10, 54 ('Far be it from us to suggest any kind of identity between the Catholic Church and totalitarian dictatorship', p. 132). A second edition (1964) gave greater stress to popular support for such regimes. On these shifts see also Carl J. Friedrich, Michael Curtis, and Benjamin R. Barber, *Totalitarianism in Perspective: Three Views* (Pall Mall Press, 1969).

majoritarian tyranny whose most notable result was the idea of the dictatorship of the proletariat. Here, militant egalitarianism combines with a hatred of wealth, privilege, ostentation, and exploitation. Talmon's account of 'political messianism' also gives stress to 'the fanatical determination of saviours-in-a-hurry, intent in fitting an imaginary new man into an artificially contrived . . . inevitably evolved ultimate social harmony'. He further sees much of the history of the past two centuries as proceeding towards a confrontation between liberal democracy and 'totalitarian messianic democracy'.[14] The latter in turn, as John Dunn has stressed, is to be measured in particular by its 'distinctive attitude towards the *scope* of politics', with private and personal life becoming politicized, in some cases to an extraordinary degree under the tyranny of a moral absolutism wedded to a 'gratuitous trust in the self-regulating capacity of the historical process'.[15]

The genesis of totalitarianism remains much debated. As we saw in Chapter 2, anti-Semitism played a major part in European conceptions of the alien, other, and enemy over many centuries. But it did not contribute to the origins of Bolshevism (where it surfaced only late and intermittently); to Mao Zedong's takeover of China; to the Khmer Rouge Revolution in Cambodia; or to the fascism of Franco or Mussolini. Some historians give greater prominence to individual dictators, notably Stalin and Hitler, by contrast to the ideas of party or class rule, and structure or function. Many early studies concentrated on Nazi Germany as the most familiar and directly threatening instance of totalitarianism, particularly after the realities of the Holocaust became known in 1945. But it is unclear that any relationship existed between the Holocaust and German economic planning. Nonetheless, most commentators agree that totalitarian states are distinguished from other despotisms by seven features: a one-party state; the use of technology to assist the regime's exercise of power; a willingness to destroy substantial numbers of domestic enemies; the use of 'total terror' to intimidate the population; a willingness to eliminate many of the barriers between the individual and the party and/or state; a 'totalist' philosophy or ideology, often devoted to an ideal of continuous revolution; and a cult of leadership.[16]

Developments after the 1960s in the study of totalitarianism revealed gaps and weaknesses in earlier accounts. The publication of many memoirs, then the work of Alexander Solzhenitsyn and other historians, and finally, in the 1990s, the opening of Soviet-era archives, revealed the scale of Stalin's murders and the penetration of fear into everyday life. From the 1990s, when details of Mao Zedong's rule began to be revealed, it became evident that the number of deaths under Marxist–Leninist

---

[14] Jacob Talmon, *The Origins of Totalitarian Democracy* (Secker & Warburg, 1960); Jacob Talmon, *Political Messianism: The Romantic Phase* (Secker & Warburg, 1960); Jacob Talmon, *The Myth of the Nation and the Vision of Revolution* (Secker & Warburg, 1981); Jacob Talmon, *The Unique and the Universal: Some Historical Reflections* (Secker & Warburg, 1965), p. 157.

[15] John Dunn, 'Totalitarian Democracy and the Legacy of Modern Revolutions: Explanation or Indictment?', in Yehoshua Arieli and Nathan Rotenstreich, eds., *Totalitarian Democracy and After* (Frank Cass, 1984), p. 38.

[16] A thirteen-point typology is offered in Michael Curtis, *Totalitarianism* (Transaction Books, 1979), pp. 7–9. Raymond Aron reduces these qualities to five, giving emphasis to the state's monopolies: *Democracy and Totalitarianism* (Weidenfeld & Nicolson, 1968), pp. 193–4.

regimes vastly exceeded those under Hitler. This had as much to do with the longevity of these regimes as intent. Both would have murdered vastly more given the chance. Hitler had only half the time Stalin did, and war interfered with—but also accelerated—half of this.

Recent studies also indicate that Stalinism penetrated much further into the private life and the inner selves of most people than Hitler's regime did or, as importantly, sought to do. Terror was not a major part of German life for the majority under the Nazis. For this book this is of considerable significance, for we want to know how widely and deeply fear was experienced, not only how many people were murdered, and how, important though this is. The opening of Eastern European archives after 1989 also reveals that the degree of surveillance was not proportionate to bloodshed. The German Democratic Republic (GDR), for instance, became one of the most intensely scrutinized regimes of all, and yet it murdered relatively few of its citizens. The other Eastern European communist states were Soviet dependencies and equally thuggish, but also were not especially bloodthirsty. All, of course, had had at least some experience of liberal democracy, where Russia had known only autocracy. The political murder rate was correspondingly lower.[17] The general trend of these studies was to make Stalinism and Nazism appear less like one another than had usually been assumed.[18]

Descriptions of the extraordinary devastating Khmer Rouge regime (1975–9), which have only gained widespread circulation in the past twenty years, finally added not only further detail but a qualitatively new dimension respecting the most terrifying example yet known of the totalitarian mentality. This alters our perception of totalitarianism, in particular by revealing that no technological underpinning was required either for total surveillance or for mass murder. Total control of the 'media' is not an issue where none exist. Neither planning nor industrialization as such explains mass murder here. Dramatically swift modernization programmes driven by modernity or machine worship do, however, in all the communist cases. So does a language of struggle wedded to class antagonisms and other 'enemy' categories. This explanation also helps to account for the massive loss of life in Maoist China and Pol Pot's Cambodia.

While all these regimes are often described as 'dystopian', few serious efforts have been made to determine just what 'utopian' aspects of their formation might have contributed to this degraded state. So that must be a key task here. So too must an assessment of totalitarianism as a 'political religion', which seems to return us to factors unifying all such forms of dictatorship. But, this approach too can be refined to focus more particularly on the causes of mass murder. Here it is not 'religion' as such but a particular combination of mental attitudes, combined as secular millenarianism, which offer more insights into this destructiveness. But this mindset, in turn, was suffused with other categories which indicated how 'friend' and 'enemy' would be defined. Here too we must bring to bear the group psychology

---

[17] See, generally, Anne Applebaum, *Iron Curtain: The Crushing of Eastern Europe* (Penguin Books, 2012).

[18] Ian Kershaw, *Hitler, the Germans, and the Final Solution* (Yale University Press, 2008), pp. 30–5.

explored in Part I, and its unfolding in medieval and early modern European forms of persecution. Here we must also introduce the language of political economy, with its focus on utility and the valuation of human beings by their labour capacity, particularly when wedded to a Social Darwinist imperative.

We begin, then, chronologically, with the event which defines most subsequent revolutionary experiences, the French Revolution. Here, as later, we must also consider the utopian elements underpinning and unleashed by the momentum of the epoch.

THE PROTOTYPE: YEAR II OF THE FRENCH REVOLUTION (SEPTEMBER 1793–JULY 1794)

The French Revolution of 1789 had many utopian qualities, not least in imposing received French over regional dialects and other languages spoken in France; in its new calendars; in reorganizing and reclassifying France's geographical boundaries; in its radical egalitarianism; and in its quest for a new 'revolutionary' type, the reborn virtuous citizen. To many, the new doctrine of the equal rights of man symbolized an almost universally explosive desire for liberty as such, in which slavery, the death penalty, feudal servitude, and other barbarities were to be swept away in favour of a new regime of freedom, justice, and equality.

Some of these sentiments were expressed in the new festivals of the revolution, which Rousseau had encouraged as promoting patriotic zeal, and which Maximilien Robespierre thought might play a vital role in forming the 'new man', especially by deliberately mixing ranks to emphasize equality.[19] In what Mona Ozouf has termed the 'homogenization of the human condition', the desire for a uniformity of cultural outlook and practice in both space and time, or a kind of higher unity trumping local particularisms, became pronounced. Revolutionary festivals became a key means of providing the new sense of social solidarity, transferring the 'sacrality' of institutions from the Old Regime to the new. If the point of festivals was to 'put everyone on the same level', indeed, the revolution could be seen as their end point and epitome. It was, effectively, itself a festival, overflowing with effusive, spontaneous, republican egalitarianism and mutual conviviality, a banquet of friendship and *fraternité*, a celebration of group self-recognition. At Troyes, for instance, municipal authorities invited the townspeople to dine in front of the city gates to recall the 'good days of our ancestors and of the golden age', and children recited the articles of the Rights of Man. But revolutionary festivals came to be fraught with ambiguity. For while they aimed at spontaneity, they were in fact not only well organized, but so orchestrated as to exclude groups like the aristocracy. They celebrated the new France and a new ideal of citizenship. But there were also darker hints at blood sacrifice; some goddesses of Reason carried the pike and even the guillotine, the modern scalpel of social surgery. (The 'national razor' was one of

---

[19] See Bronisław Baczko, *Utopian Lights: The Evolution of the Idea of Social Progress* (Paragon House, 1989), pp. 175–222.

its nicknames.) To Ozouf this revealed that 'Utopia was a less pleasant place than had been thought', and perhaps closer to Sparta than to pastoral fantasies of joy and plenty.[20]

For many, this is nonetheless the definitive moment of the founding of modernity, where greatly intensified 'promise, accomplishment, anxiety, and disaster', in Eli Sagan's phrasing, define an entirely new epoch in human affairs.[21] It was clearly a quasi-millenarian moment. Immense, liberating change is anticipated and demanded here and now. It increasingly encompasses the whole world. It embodies desires for both freedom and equality, for progress and innovation, for eradicating the old and building the new. Human behaviour, it is presumed, will alter greatly for the better. No far-off islands, no voyages to the moon, no discoveries of vestiges of primitive simplicity now suffice to appease utopian desires. The earthly Jerusalem was not to be discovered, but to be created.

On one account, at least, the modern dystopia commences at the moment when *Euchronia*, the good time, now becomes the dominant motif.[22] It also coincides with the seizure of power of a small faction within the Revolution, the Jacobins. Those who believe Jacobinism led inevitably to Bolshevism point in particular to Edmund Burke's *Reflections on the Revolution in France* (1790) as the most prescient work of the epoch. To Burke, the architects of the Revolution had extended a radical Enlightenment hostility to religion into violent intolerance. There were hints of exclusiveness, too, in the xenophobia of some of the revolutionaries. The eleven-month 'Reign of Terror' of the Jacobin dictatorship of 1793–4 has been seen as the key precedent for twentieth-century Bolshevik (not Nazi) repression. Historians like Philippe Nemo have seen the ideas dominating this period as unabashedly 'the inheritors of the millenarian and apocalyptic collectivism of Antiquity and the Middle Ages'. To Richard Landes, their millenarian quality is indicated in the clash between perfectionist ideas and the 'bitter disappointment' which accompanies their failure to be realized—and the need to find a culprit.[23] We might certainly concede that the Jacobin regime was 'without historical precedent'.[24] Jacobinism may even have provided 'in embryo' what would 'eventually become the party' in the Leninist sense. But it never achieved the discipline, hierarchy, ideological purity, and monolithic power of Bolshevism. And Jacobin and Bolshevik terror, we will see, are hardly identical.[25]

Yet there are many qualities shared by both movements. Both combined an unwavering egalitarianism with the elevation of a new group of the virtuous and privileged. The poor, the mass, the rabble were now reminded of the promise of

[20] Mona Ozouf, *Festivals and the French Revolution* (Harvard University Press, 1988), pp. 117–18, 9, 11, 98.
[21] Eli Sagan, *Citizens and Cannibals: The French Revolution, the Struggle for Modernity, and the Origins of Ideological Terror* (Rowman & Littlefield, 2001), p. 1.
[22] Frank Manuel, *Freedom from History* (New York University Press, 1971), p. 127.
[23] Richard Landes, *Heaven on Earth: The Varieties of the Millennial Experience* (Oxford University Press, 2011), pp. 282–3.
[24] Patrice Higonnet, *Goodness beyond Virtue: Jacobins during the French Revolution* (Harvard University Press, 1998), p. 69. For the argument that they were not, see pp. 325–36.
[25] Alain Besançon, *The Intellectual Origins of Leninism* (Basil Blackwell, 1981), p. 33.

1,800 years of Christianity. Original Sin was redefined as aristocratic and monarchical oppression, and later, for Marx, by capitalist exploitation and private property in principle. In 1789 and after, 'the people' were juxtaposed to the 'aristocrats' as the 'enemy'. To some, 'the people' were narrowed further to the poorest, the *sans-culottes*. After Marx, the 'working class' became the core valued social group, and the 'bourgeoisie' epitomized exploitation and oppression. Both ideals reflected Rousseau's idea of the general will, a principle of unitary sovereignty, the rule of one group based on this principle, and an absolute certainty of opinion respecting the means required to exercise it. The unitary 'people' could not be wrong; it was, wrote Robespierre in an essay dedicated to Rousseau, 'always pure in its motives, it loves only the public good, since the public good is the interest of the people'.[26]

To later commentators such as Max Stirner and Carl Schmitt, this language was essentially religious. 'The voice of the people is the voice of God', 'the will of the people is always good', 'the people are always virtuous' (Sieyès), ditto for the proletariat, ditto again for its representative and mystical embodiment, 'Society', the party: the concept is the same. Holiness, blessedness, grace, perfection, infallibility permeate these assumptions.[27] Here Rousseau's paean to equality becomes the critical standpoint vis-à-vis modernity.

How then were virtue and terror reconciled by the Jacobins? Goodness and evil, we might imagine, make a bad marriage, almost a coupling of beauty and beast. We recoil, perplexed at the suggestion that they can somehow paradoxically share common interests, or be commensurable as ends and means. But here they are closely united. 'Virtue without terror is powerless', said Robespierre. Contemporaries indeed sometimes described his rule as the 'reign of virtue and terror'.[28] The moral logic of these arguments is implied by group psychology. 'The people' were equated with virtue, innocence, ignorance, and poverty. Each of these terms implied and gave value to the others. To prove one's goodness (or that of 'the people') it was necessary to have enemies who embodied the opposite principle. Persecuting them then proved one's own virtue. The purer the people's virtue, the more dastardly by implication was the evil of their enemies, and the more deserving they were of destruction. This produces a certain inexorability: the more virtue we demand, the more violence we require. The more 'pure democracy' pushes this narrative onwards, the fewer restraints are necessary or possible.[29] This is the dialectic of virtue and terror.

Yet this self-assertion or self-recognition of the virtuous group does not alone explain the Terror. Like the Bolsheviks, the Jacobins were a small minority threatened by many enemies. 'Terror' was thus legitimized by war and 'necessity' epitomized by 'plotting'.[30] Success depended on unity, and terror aimed at the

---

[26] Quoted in Sagan, *Citizens and Cannibals*, p. 421.

[27] Carl Schmitt, *Political Theology* (MIT Press, 1985), pp. 46–8; Max Stirner, *The Ego and Its Own* (A. C. Fifield, 1913), e.g., p. 74.

[28] Raoul Hesdin, *The Journal of a Spy in Paris during the Reign of Terror* (John Murray, 1895), p. 66.

[29] François Furet, *Interpreting the French Revolution* (Cambridge University Press, 1981), pp. 68–70, 78.

[30] See the defence of this perspective in Wilfred B. Kerr, *The Reign of Terror 1793–4* (University of Toronto Press, 1927), p. 229.

'mastery of opinion' (in François Furet's apt phrase), which resulted in the stifling of all opposition, intellectual or otherwise. Ideology clearly plays a role here. To conservative critics, the 'radicalism' of the French Revolution as such dictated the endpoint of the Terror.[31] So too does the popular character of the Revolution, and its evocation of 'unfeeling and intolerant instincts'.[32]

To explain the mentality of the Terror of September 1793–July 1794 we must briefly trace its development. Extraordinary legislation to punish counter-revolutionaries was introduced as early as August 1792. That month the Jacobins also arranged that only their members could speak in the radical Parisian clubs. (In July 1793 it became an offence to obstruct their meetings.)[33] In the autumn of 1792, panic in Paris instigated by the threat of invasion and domestic uprising produced the so-called September massacres of some 1,300 prisoners. Most of these were common criminals, but a third had been charged with political offences. Those killed were usually first judged by popular tribunals following an examination of prison records.[34] These acts were, however, not widespread, were rarely uncontrolled, and usually involved well-to-do artisans and shopkeepers rather than the very poor.[35] Far from Le Bon's irrational mob going wild, as few as 150 persons committed most of the bloodshed.[36] The Jacobins' seizure of power in spring 1793 did admittedly end the liberal principles of the Revolution, and resulted in the execution of their Girondin opponents. However, it also largely curtailed popular violence, and was indeed motivated in part by an explicit desire to do so.[37] Founded in April 1793, Robespierre's Committee of Public Safety now legitimated violence defined by principle rather than necessity. Jean-Paul Marat commenced by calling for 600 'well-chosen' heads, but by early 1791 thought that if 500,000 were removed a million others would be saved.[38]

France was now effectively a one-party state, ruled through the Jacobin clubs and their leaders. In June, the moderate Girondins were outflanked by the Jacobins and expelled from the Convention. Those still under arrest were guillotined in October. Revolutionary tribunals and military commissions punished all those deemed rebels (including anyone proposing agrarian communism). The right to defence witnesses was withdrawn in June 1794. The death sentence for armed rebellion was soon augmented by extreme penalties for hoarding food. All opposition was conflated into 'enemy'. Ignorance and purity were already being associated: this equation will

---

[31] See Harvey C. Mansfield, 'The Unfinished Revolution', in Ralph C. Hancock and L. Gary Lambert, eds., *The Legacy of the French Revolution* (Rowman & Littlefield, 1996), p. 36.

[32] Higonnet, *Goodness beyond Virtue*, pp. 2, 7.   [33] Ibid., p. 44.

[34] Where some 17,000–40,000 were directly executed, among them a mere 1,158 nobles, though thousands more died of disease and neglect.

[35] See generally George Rudé, *The Crowd in the French Revolution* (Clarendon Press, 1959). A good review of these positions is given in Mona Ozouf, 'The Terror after the Terror: An Immediate History', in Keith Michael Baker, ed., *The French Revolution and the Creation of Modern Political Culture*, vol. 4: *The Terror* (Pergamon, 1994), pp. 3–18.

[36] G. Lenotre, *The September Massacres* (Hutchinson & Co., 1929), p. 15.

[37] Brian Singer, 'Violence in the French Revolution: Forms of Ingestion/Forms of Expulsion', in Ferenc Fehér, ed., *The French Revolution and the Birth of Modernity* (University of California Press, 1990), pp. 158–9.

[38] Sagan, *Citizens and Cannibals*, p. 127.

become familiar to us here. So the educated were at great risk of catching it in the neck; 'the Republic has no need of learned men', the chemist Lavoisier was told shortly before being beheaded.[39] Without a balancing mechanism, the scope for arbitrary power expanded dramatically. Paranoia escalated. One Jacobin commented that the choice now was to terrorize or be terrorized.[40] Or both: the 'Terrorists' themselves were soon 'in constant dread of assassination' through fear of revenge, and thus even less likely to relinquish terror themselves.[41] Machiavelli's adage that terror created an equality of fear, quoted by Camille Desmoulins in December 1793, seemed proven.[42] Marat's assassination by Charlotte Corday on 13 July provoked cries for revenge. On 30 August, Royer demanded that terror be made 'the order of the day'. On 4/5 September the Convention took up these very words.[43]

One consequence, announced on 17 September 1793, was the 'Law of Suspects', which seemed to reflect Robespierre's own constant paranoia about omnipresent 'plots' and 'enemies'.[44] This, in Bronisław Baczko's words, institutionalized the 'punitive attitude and apparatus from which the Terror largely drew its force'.[45] The circle of possible 'guilt' grew ever wider. Any possible 'enemy of freedom' was deemed suspicious, including entire families of the former nobility and most émigrés (perhaps 800,000 people in total). 'Suspects' included those who consorted with moderates, who had had 'certificates of patriotism' refused to them, or who, 'having done nothing against liberty, have also done nothing for it'. Committees of Surveillance were established in each commune to draw up lists of suspects. Any hint of counter-revolutionary intent sufficed for arrest. Execution might follow without trial. A culture of denunciation commenced which effectively rendered all activity public. Private behaviour became politicized as a consequence. The implication that 'loyalty' and revolutionary zeal should not only be skin deep was obvious. The whole soul, the inner self, were also required. So another of Robespierre's colleagues, Louis Antoine de Saint-Just, insisted that:

> You have to punish not only the traitors, but even those who are indifferent; you have to punish whoever is passive in the republic, and who does nothing for it. For, since the French people has manifested its will, all that is opposed to it is outside the sovereign; all that is outside the sovereign is the enemy . . . but between the people and its enemies there is no longer anything in common but the sword.[46]

The guillotines began to work overtime. In mid-1793, some eleven people per month were being executed in Paris. By mid-1794, this had risen to 800. In some

---

[39] Graham Everitt, *Guillotine the Great and Her Successors* (Ward and Downey, 1890), p. 112.
[40] Higonnet, *Goodness beyond Virtue*, p. 47.   [41] Hesdin, *The Journal of a Spy*, p. 118.
[42] Higonnet, *Goodness beyond Virtue*, p. 181.
[43] Jacques Guilhaumou, 'A Discourse of Denunciation', in Baker, ed., *The French Revolution*, vol. 4: *The Terror*, p. 147.
[44] Stanley Loomis, *Paris in the Terror* (Jonathan Cape, 1964), p. 249.
[45] Bronisław Baczko, 'The Terror before the Terror?', in Baker, ed., *The French Revolution*, vol. 4: *The Terror*, p. 26.
[46] Ibid., p. 37.

towns, 'counter-revolutionaries' (including women and children) were shot and drowned *en masse*. Freedom of speech was at an end, along with religious liberty, the victim of the dechristianization campaign. This act, in Danton's words, 'took the initiative of terror'.[47] By the law of 22 Prairial (10 June 1794), known as the 'Law of the Great Terror', proofs 'necessary to condemn the *enemies of the people*' included 'any kind of document, material, moral, verbal or written, which can naturally obtain the assent of any just and reasonable mind'. Juries were instructed to be 'guided solely by what love of country indicates to their conscience; their aim is *the triumph of the republic and the ruin of its enemies*'.[48] All citizens were empowered to denounce and seize conspirators, whose rights of defence were greatly circumscribed in what was effectively a 'legal suspension of the rule of law'.[49] Denunciation became the most overt expression of civic virtue.[50] (False accusations made in 'good faith' could be excused by a handshake.) Not to denounce also became a crime. Every man and woman now became a police agent, responsible for guarding the Revolution. The penalty for all offences brought before the Revolutionary Tribunal was deemed to be death, and the number of monthly death sentences went up fivefold over the previous winter.

Then Robespierre, condemned by the Convention on 27 July 1794, was overthrown by other Jacobins. He was executed the following day. The laws of 10 June were repealed, and on 1 August the Law of Suspects. The Thermidorian backlash against popular rule, itself fuelled by new grievances, now began. The few remaining Girondins were also admitted back into the Convention.[51] Not only was the 'Terror' short-lived. By later standards, it was not very terrifying, and, quite remarkably, involved very little torture. By the standards of Arendt, then, for whom torture is the chief 'instrument of rule' of totalitarian regimes, this is not totalitarianism, scarcely even a pale shadow thereof.[52] Historians have also noted the regard for due process and the right of defence often present in hearings, for instance in Marseilles, and the absence of 'a haste which might indicate a search for vengeance'. Verbatim minutes and lengthy interrogations were common. This was not lawless butchery.[53] But elsewhere, as in Nantes, where 'blood-drinkers' and thieves terrorized a town of 80,000, and left the river Loire red with blood for a distance of fifty miles, it was. Here:

> [T]error was the order of the day; this town was struck by the most overwhelming stupor; a person who believed himself innocent one evening could not be certain of being recognized as such the next day; it would be difficult to paint the worry, the anxiety of mothers, of wives, when they heard the rolling of vehicles, in their

[47] Ibid., p. 28.
[48] Quoted in Georges Sorel, *Reflections on Violence* (Free Press, 1950), p. 125.
[49] Higonnet, *Goodness beyond Virtue*, p. 131.
[50] See Colin Lucas, 'The Theory and Practice of Denunciation in the French Revolution', in Sheila Fitzpatrick and Robert Gellately, eds., *Accusatory Practices: Denunciation in Modern European History, 1789–1989* (University of Chicago Press, 1997), pp. 22–39.
[51] See Bronisław Baczko, *Ending the Terror: The French Revolution after Robespierre* (Cambridge University Press, 1994).
[52] Hannah Arendt, *On Violence* (Allen Lane, 1970), p. 50.
[53] William Scott, *Terror and Repression in Revolutionary Marseilles* (Macmillan, 1973), pp. 336–7.

neighbourhoods, at eight o'clock in the evening; it seemed to them that they and their husbands were going to be snatched from their homes to be plunged into the Cells. This was the fear of Nantes . . . [54]

In particularly prominent cases, such bloodshed visually defined an essential element in the revolutionary experience, the modern ritual scapegoat sacrifice, or cleansing by blood. This was the case with the spectacle of public guillotining, especially of Louis XVI and Marie Antoinette in early 1793. Atavism is also evident in the use of cannibalistic metaphors—the ultimate objectification and dehumanization of persons, as well as the ultimate symbol of revenge, and of the neutralization and absorption of the strength of one's enemy.[55] The guillotine itself was sometimes described as 'hungry'. Some nicknamed the Jacobins '*buveurs du sang*', drinkers of blood.[56] In a popular print, the executioner held up Louis' severed head, with the inscription, 'may an impure blood water our fields'.[57] The swift descent of the guillotine symbolized an essentially religious public sacrifice which was intended to provide a 'life-affirming, transcendent experience'. Regicide was a beginning, but the principle could easily be extended to large groups. Sacrificial violence could now be linked to redemption, to catharsis (a purification or cleansing), to martyrdom, and to expiation, or purifying that which has become defiled.[58] As Colin Lucas has emphasized, the very act of collective execution concentrates guilt upon the individual while absolving the collective, and promoting contagion at the same time. This sense of collective deliverance is a gasp of relief and release from anxiety as well as an expression of vengeance and retribution.[59] All these themes would re-emerge in later revolutionary movements. At their most extreme, they implied that revolutionary violence was central to moral regeneration, could hasten it, and might even be viewed as proportionate to its success.

The Terror, then, indisputably established a paradigm of repression in which hysteria induced a targeting of 'counter-revolutionary' 'enemies of the people' who were defined by suspicion alone. Theoretically, the movement in this process from identifying genuine enemies to denouncing mere suspects marked a fatal political degeneration. Indisputably, the power of the new regime rested upon its ability to create and manipulate fear, especially through threats and rumours of suspects and plots. Violence and blood were cleansing, a step towards salvation, palpable evidence of the eradication of evil.[60]

Shortly after Robespierre's fall, his close colleague Jean-Lambert Tallien distinguished between two forms of terror defining this period: one respecting actions,

---

[54] Quoted in Baczko, *Ending the Terror*, p. 153.

[55] Eli Sagan, *Cannibalism: Human Aggression and Cultural Form* (Harper Torchbooks, 1974); pp. 5, 20, and, generally, Sagan, *Citizens and Cannibals*.

[56] Landes, *Heaven on Earth*, p. 277.   [57] Sagan, *Citizens and Cannibals*, p. 347.

[58] Jesse Goldhammer, *The Headless Republic: Sacrificial Violence in Modern French Thought* (Cornell University Press, 2005), pp. 64, 15.

[59] Colin Lucas, 'Revolutionary Violence, the People and the Terror', in Baker, ed., *The French Revolution*, vol. 4: *The Terror*, pp. 59, 62.

[60] But the mere sight of the death carts commonly caused pregnant women to faint, and people began to move away from its location, and to close their shutters as the carts moved by (the mob sometimes breaking their windows in revenge): Hesdin, *The Journal of a Spy*, p. 99.

the other persons. The latter generated 'a habitual, generalized, trembling, an external trembling which affects the innermost fibers, which degrades man and reduces him to the brute'. It was 'the destruction of all physical forces, the disorientation of all the moral faculties, the disintegration of all ideas, the subversion of all the affections. It is a true disorganization of the soul . . . an extreme, total, condition.' Such terror, Tallien emphasized, 'breaks all links, destroys all the affections, defraternizes, isolates, demoralizes'. For success it needed to 'suspend a penalty over each action, a threat over each word, a suspicion over every silence; a trap must also be placed under every step, a spy in every house, a traitor in every family'. It needed thus to 'be everywhere, or it must be nowhere'.[61] France thus became divided 'into two classes: *the one that frightens and the one that is frightened,* the persecutors and the persecuted'.[62]

Such aspirations clearly exceeded the boundaries of 'legitimate' terror required simply to keep the regime in power. They passed, rather, into a condition of existential angst in which doubt, like Christian guilt, was omnipresent in principle, and required no 'real' manifestations to be validated. By a kind of circuitous logic, terror was now almost an end in itself, the 'normal' response to a 'normal' condition. And that condition was essentially defined by the ubiquity of guilt. So that curiously, while 'the people' were utterly innocent and virtuous, real people often fell well short of this ideal. Indeed, here we witness again the tyranny of the imagination: the more virtuous the abstract idealized 'people' became, the harder it was for actual human beings to live up to expectations. This was their failing, or sin, and for this they could be punished or cured without regret. In stepped the physicians of the Revolution. The people needed, Georges Couthon thought in regard to Lyon's anti-Jacobin uprising, 'strong republican medicine', 'a purge; a vomit and an enema'.[63] Sociogermophobia was clearly at work.

Despite its psychology, the Terror did not produce mass murder in 1793–4. Throughout France, about 42,000 were killed, somewhat under half being artisans or peasants (so, in a population of 28 million, about 1 in 666, or 0.00015 per cent). Perhaps 500,000 were imprisoned during 1793–4, or about 1 in 56. Another 300,000 were placed under house arrest. There were great disparities between regions. In over a third of departments fewer than ten people were guillotined.[64] (In the Civil War substantial numbers also died, some 250,000, for instance, in the Vendée alone.) These are not large figures proportionately compared to twentieth-century murder. Violence was also largely directed against resistance and not class enemies as such.[65]

[61] Quoted in Baker, *The French Revolution*, vol. 4: *The Terror*, p. xiv.
[62] Quoted in Baczko. 'The Terror before the Terror?', p. 31, and Baczko, *Ending the Terror*, pp. 49–60.
[63] Quoted in Sagan, *Citizens and Cannibals*, p. 476.
[64] Alan Forrest, 'The Local Politics of Repression', in Baker, ed., *The French Revolution*, vol. 4: *The Terror*, p. 82.
[65] Russia's population was about 150 million in 1917. Michelet estimated that, under the Inquisition, 20,000 had been killed in 16 years in one Spanish province alone (Arno J. Mayer, *The Furies: Violence and Terror in the French and Russian Revolutions* (Princeton University Press, 2000), p. 150). Rosemary O'Kane argues that both terrors produced an approximately equal proportion of victims (*The Revolutionary Reign of Terror: The Role of Violence in Political Change* (Edward Elgar, 1991), p. 94).

Yet the Terror institutionalized a virtually unprecedented form of government which, Arendt emphasizes, bore little resemblance to the control required to conquer political power.[66] Technology played no role in its success; government by fear may rest on intimidation fomented by rumour and hearsay as much as actual violence.[67] But was this process the accidental and regrettable creature of circumstances beyond anyone's control, a slippery slope down which none desired to plunge? Or was it 'an integral part of revolutionary ideology'?[68] The answer is both. The Revolution resulted from popular feelings of despair, of a lack of perceived alternatives, of residual envy of privilege, of fear bred from war, tumult, and famine. A class war was commenced which inevitably produced civil war. As Burckhardt emphasized, the temper of the times could be likened to a 'fever' in which fanaticism (disease and symptom) became the norm.[69] Barbarism surfaced easily in these circumstances. Sometimes murders were accompanied by the spectacle of beheading, the placing of heads and various organs on pikes, and their parading through the streets. These acts were, however, not unknown under the *ancien régime*, and may have helped to turn public opinion against the violence.[70] And such violence was still more instilled by hunger and focused accordingly on the price of bread.[71]

Hence, these circumstances were driven from both above and below. The identification of revolutionary virtue solely with Jacobinism played a role. Terror was also shaped by the personalities of its leaders, like Robespierre, Saint-Just, and Marat. Doubtless Jacobinism was a 'fundamentalist' and 'sectarian utopian' response to modernity more generally. The social egalitarianism underpinning Jacobinism was, in turn, partly the effect of a quasi-religious revival already underway in Britain, America, and elsewhere, and fuelled by movements against slavery and other forms of inhumanity. It was thus a revolt against privilege born of Christianity.[72] Its conception of virtue was doubtless, to a degree, also indebted to a secularized form of millenarianism. It owed something to appeals to return to the purity and goodness of the state of nature, with its original rights and uncorrupted humanity, and to the sociability of nascent society Rousseau promoted (which indeed, for Saint-Just, implied the savagery of the Franks and Teutons).[73]

* * * *

The events of the French Revolution centrally defined many nineteenth-century revolutionary movements. 'Cells' or small groups were a prototype of underground

[66] Mayer, *The Furies*, p. 112.

[67] E. K. Bramstedt, *Dictatorship and Political Police: The Technique of Control by Fear* (Kegan Paul, Trench, Trubner & Co., 1945), p. 1.

[68] Furet, *Interpreting the French Revolution*, p. 62.   [69] See Mayer, *The Furies*, p. 38.

[70] Singer, 'Violence in the French Revolution', p. 162.

[71] Ferenc Fehér, 'Introduction', in Fehér, ed., *The French Revolution*, p. 6.

[72] These are associated with 'anti-modern' and 'anti-Enlightenment' qualities by S. N. Eisenstadt, in *Fundamentalism, Sectarianism and Revolution: The Jacobin Dimension of Modernity* (Cambridge University Press, 1999), here esp. pp. 89–93. There is useful discussion of these points in John Gray, *Black Mass: Apocalyptic Religion and the Death of Utopia* (Allen Lane, 2007).

[73] Miguel Abensour, 'Saint Just and the Problem of Heroism in the French Revolution', in Fehér, ed., *The French Revolution*, p. 137. See, generally, Barrington Moore, Jr, *Moral Purity and Persecution in History* (Princeton University Press, 2000), pp. 59–104.

activity in the 1830s in groups like the Society of the Seasons, led by Auguste Blanqui.[74] In Russia, professional revolutionaries plotted to overthrow Tsarist tyranny, and drew upon ancient doctrines of the legitimacy of tyrannicide. Their fanatical dedication was epitomized in the activities of the first person to advocate conspiratorial violence as a means of arousing and educating the masses rather than of seizing power. Sometimes called the 'first Bolshevik' (a view Lenin himself shared), Pyotr Tkachev (1844–1886) followed the Jacobins and Blanquists in urging a revolutionary vanguard. He was contemptuous of the mentality of the Russian masses, of the constraints of bourgeois morality, of liberal parliamentarism, and of any post-revolutionary political opposition which might obstruct progress. The supra-moral revolutionary millenarian type was wedded to a fanatically pro-crustean egalitarianism which we have termed egalomania. Tkachev believed the Revolution would introduce a new age of perfection where 'all people were unconditionally equal, when there would no longer exist between them the slightest difference, neither intellectually, morally, nor physically'.[75] Logically, this involves reducing all to the lowest common denominator for which identicality is possible. The revolutionary's role here was central. A parallel with theomania, where all forms of lesser love are seen as detracting from God, is obvious. Tkachev insisted that 'he is no revolutionary if he pities anything in this society' and that it was 'even worse for him if he has any kindred, intimate, or amorous relationships'. Even 'the slightest competition' with revolutionary goals was impermissible.[76] By implication, here, maximum violence produces both maximum equality and maximum love of humanity. It is a fatal equation.

Widely regarded as the practical 'founder' of modern terrorism,[77] Sergey Nechayev (1848–1882) is often quoted for his assertion that 'The Revolutionary knows only one science—destruction . . . Day and night he may have only one thought, one purpose: merciless destruction'; 'For him exists only one pleasure, one consolation, one reward, one satisfaction, the reward of revolution.'[78] For Nechayev, all sentiments, including family life, love, friendship, and honour, needed to be subordinated to 'a single cold passion for the revolutionary cause'. This might require killing 'with his own hands anyone who stands in the way of achieving it'.[79]

---

[74] See, generally, James H. Billington, *Fire in the Minds of Men: Origins of the Revolutionary Faith* (Temple Smith, 1980), and Gregory Claeys and Christine Lattek, 'Radicalism, Republicanism, and Revolutionism: From the Principles of '89 to Modern Terrorism', in Gareth Stedman Jones and Gregory Claeys, eds., *The Cambridge History of Nineteenth-Century Political Thought* (Cambridge University Press, 2011), pp. 200–54.

[75] Besançon, *The Intellectual Origins of Leninism*, pp. 153, 160.

[76] Albert L. Weeks, *The First Bolshevik: A Political Biography of Peter Tkachev* (New York University Press, 1968), pp. viii–ix, 5, 87–8.

[77] E.g., David C. Rapoport and Yonah Alexander, eds., *The Morality of Terrorism: Religious and Secular Justifications* (Columbia University Press, 1989), p. 70.

[78] Quoted in Oscar Ja'szi and John D. Lewis, *Against the Tyrant: The Tradition and Theory of Tyrannicide* (Free Press, 1957), p. 136, and E. V. Zenker, *Anarchism: A Criticism and History of the Anarchist Theory* (Methuen & Co., 1898), p. 137. The character of Raskolnikov in Dostoevsky's *Crime and Punishment* is based upon Nechayev.

[79] Quoted in Vladimir Tismaneanu, *The Devil in History: Communism, Fascism, and Some Lessons of the Twentieth Century* (University of California Press, 2012), pp. 93–4.

Nechayev indicates the re-emergence of the antinomian living in a state of grace. The end to be achieved is 'final' and complete, and trumps every other consideration. Faith is essential to salvation, and justifies action which transcends 'bourgeois' morality. This type, now recast as the secular millenarian, or professional revolutionary, would become central to the self-image of Bolshevism, 'part of Communist everyday life'.[80] Here, membership in the new priesthood of the Communist Party offered absolution and salvation in an atmosphere of pitiless missionary zeal. The paradoxical idea that the 'urge of destruction is at the same time a creative urge' was thereafter developed by the leading anarchist Michael Bakunin.

Marx and Engels varied in their appraisal of such methods. In 1844, Engels thought that 'the vengeance of the people will come down with a wrath of which the rage of 1793 gives no true idea. The war of the poor against the rich will be the bloodiest ever waged.'[81] Twenty-five years later, he wrote to Marx, saying that terror consisted not in the rule of those who inspire terror, but of those who 'themselves are terror-stricken', and 'mostly of useless cruelties perpetrated by frightened people in order to reassure themselves'.[82] But their contemporary, Karl Heinzen, viewed tyrannicide as 'the chief means of historical progress', and, extending the principle, justified the murder even of thousands, at any time or place, in the higher interests of humanity.[83]

BOLSHEVIK TERROR AND THE GULAG SYSTEM

Following the Bolshevik Revolution of 1917, the USSR was ruled briefly by V. I. Lenin (1870–1924). Then followed Joseph Djugashvili, better known as Joseph Stalin (1879–1953), the 'man of steel'—whose very name is communist industrial modernity incarnate. He was rightly dubbed the 'Genghis Khan of the Russian Revolution' by fellow Bolshevik Nikolai Bukharin—a rather backhanded compliment, perhaps. For a time, the Revolution shone as a great beacon of freedom against despotism, and a logical extension of the American and French struggles for liberty. It symbolized the faith in which much of the vibrant idealism of the twentieth century was invested, and promoted the most potent secular religion of the epoch. Its promise was that of the most perfect society ever known. Lenin aimed at a utopia in which 'the *subjection* of one man to another, of one section of society to another, since people will *grow accustomed* to observing

---

[80] Igal Halfin, *Stalinist Confessions: Messianism and Terror at the Leningrad Communist University* (University of Pittsburgh Press, 2009), p. 352.

[81] *Karl Marx-Frederick Engels Collected Works* (50 vols, Lawrence & Wishart, 1975–2004), vol. 4, p. 580.

[82] Engels to Marx, 4 September 1870, in *Marx-Engels Collected Works*, vol. 44, p. 63.

[83] 'If you have to blow up half a continent and pour out a sea of blood in order to destroy the party of the barbarians, have no scruples of conscience. He is no true republican who would not gladly pay with his life for the satisfaction of exterminating a million barbarians' (Carl Wittke, *Against the Current: The Life of Karl Heinzen* (University of Chicago Press, 1945), pp. 73–5).

the elementary conditions of social existence *without force and without subjection*.[84]
To many, the Christian paradise seemed upon the horizon, and plays like
Mayakovsky's *Mystery-Bouffe* (1918) showed the regime's fall giving way to the
promised land.[85]

In practice, a repressive system of what one keen observer called 'impersonal
brutality' was the norm from the outset.[86] Morality as such was dictated by and
deduced from the proletarian class struggle, and imposed by historical necessity.
Complete lawlessness, in effect, defined the new regime. The extensive slave labour
camp system is associated chiefly with Stalin's rapid industrialization programme,
which began in 1929. But Lenin's chief lieutenant, Leon Trotsky, had already used
the term 'concentration camp' in 1918, and the first opened after the 'Decree on
Red Terror' of 5 September 1918.[87] An obsessive desire to modernize is here one
great culprit. But the one-party scheme endorsed by Marx in 1848 implied that no
legitimate opposition could exist in the new system, which ostensibly represented
the overwhelming majority, the proletariat (in fact a very small class in Russia). The
Bolsheviks were also a tiny party of perhaps 8,000 members in 1917. So the
Revolution took place neither in a highly advanced country where a high mass
standard of living was easily attainable, nor in one where the proletariat was an
overwhelming, impoverished majority awaiting the severing of its chains.

The proletariat was thus the new group-in-waiting, self-defined by its antagonism
to other classes. But it was itself too unwieldy to do the job of revolution. Lenin is
chiefly associated with the view that if the proletariat could not make this revolution,
a vanguard party might. As early as 1907, he suggested that the Bolsheviks should be
professional revolutionaries. He banned factions within the Communist Party in
1921, and soon succeeded in identifying the Party rather than the working class with
the struggle for communism. The Party now became a quasi-sacred group. In the
eyes of one sympathetic critic (who lost the faith in 1933), 'Lenin and all his followers
clung to the consecrated idea of the Party' with 'ecclesiastical wolf-pack fervor'.[88]
With the Bolsheviks' consolidation of power and the elimination of their opponents,
like the Socialist Revolutionaries, already in 1918, came the view that their policies
were infallible, and disagreement with them unthinkable. But then people had to be
made to agree. That prolonged violence and terror would be required was obvious to
many. But this was nothing new. Russia had endured a lengthy period of terror
throughout the late nineteenth century. Some 9,000 officials were killed in 1905–7
alone, and banditry, extortion, and bank robbery (one of Stalin's specialties) were
integral to the struggle. This was bound to promote a certain amount of thuggishness,

[84] V. I. Lenin, *The State and Revolution* (2nd edn, Communist Party of Great Britain, 1925),
p. 107.
[85] James von Geldern, *Bolshevik Festivals 1917–1920* (University of California Press, 1993),
pp. 66–71.
[86] Eugene Lyons, *Assignment in Utopia* (George G. Harrap & Co., 1938), p. 76.
[87] Mikhail Heller and Aleksandr Nekrich, *Utopia in Power: The History of the Soviet Union from
1917 to the Present* (Hutchinson, 1986), p. 66.
[88] Max Eastman, *Love and Revolution: My Journey through an Epoch* (Random House, 1964),
pp. 228–9.

and a weakened sense of the already fine line between crime and revolutionary morality. In Stalin's case they certainly 'left a distinctive mark on his style as a state leader'.[89] 'If you live among wolves', he would later say, 'you must behave like a wolf.'[90] He certainly lived up to the motto.

In general, this was a no-holds-barred struggle from the outset. The entire revolutionary experience from the 1870s was permeated by an ethos of extreme violence with few discernible limits. Writers like the Maximalist Ivan Pavlov proposed eliminating the entire 'unethical' 'race' of 'monsters', the government, bureaucracy, and police, including their families, by 'the best altruists', the terrorists—virtue and terror wedded again.[91] Even in the early days of 1917–18 some thought the Revolution required killing a million 'opponents'.[92] Lenin insisted that revolutionary dictatorship involved the use of 'force over and against the bourgeoisie', which was 'not bound by any laws' (see Fig. 3.1).[93] Molotov thought he was harsher than Stalin; he took a particular interest in having priests shot, evidently asking for a daily report on the numbers. In 1922, he insisted that it was necessary to 'teach these people a lesson' where the hoarding of wealth was concerned, and that the 'greater the number of representatives of reactionary clergy and reactionary bourgeoisie we succeed in executing for this reason, the better'.[94] He proposed the 'complete abolition' of the bourgeoisie (*burzhuaziya*) in *The State and Revolution* (1917).[95] But while he complained that 'when we are reproached for cruelty, we wonder how people can forget the most elementary Marxism', he also reproached a Chekist for urging executions on a class basis alone, without any proven opposition to the regime.[96]

So the bourgeoisie was to go. But did 'complete abolition' mean 'execution'? The ambiguity of this phrase would prove crucial to the future course of communist history. Hints about eliminating the bourgeoisie were already present in Marx. Did Lenin mean the bourgeoisie as a *class*, metaphorically, which implied depriving them of their property, and making honest labouring citizens of them? Or did he mean 'bourgeois' *people, physically*—their persons? Millions of lives depended on this distinction, and were wasted ignoring it. It often eluded the less educated, whom Stalinism assiduously sought to promote. But physical extermination was easily implied early on: the old order implied evil, and its taint might stick to your fingers. The spirit of the moment indicated total solutions, and no restraint: head-splitting, not hair-splitting. Lenin thought the title 'Commissariat for Social Extermination' a fitting name for a new Justice Ministry, 'exactly what it should be; but we can't say that'.[97] Trotsky saw terror as the regime's most potent weapon, and defended the necessity for 'absolute ruthlessness'.[98] In a famous exchange, he

---

[89] Anna Geifman, *Thou Shalt Kill: Revolutionary Terrorism in Russia, 1894–1917* (Princeton University Press, 1993), p. 256.
[90] Stephen Kotkin, *Stalin*, vol. 1: *Paradoxes of Power, 1878–1928* (Allen Lane, 2014), p. 155.
[91] Ibid., pp. 20–1, 82.   [92] Heller and Nekrich, *Utopia in Power*, p. 53.
[93] V. I. Lenin, *The Proletarian Revolution and Kautsky the Renegade* (Modern Books, 1929), p. 18.
[94] Richard Pipes, ed., *The Unknown Lenin* (Yale University Press, 1996), pp. 11, 154.
[95] Lenin, *The State and Revolution*, p. 46.
[96] Robert Conquest, *The Great Terror: Stalin's Purge of the Thirties* (Macmillan, 1968), p. 544.
[97] Orlando Figes, *A People's Tragedy: The Russian Revolution 1891–1924* (Pimlico, 1997), p. 536.
[98] Leon Trotsky, *My Life* (Grosset & Dunlap, 1960), p. 161.

PARLAMENTARISMENS FALD (ANTON HANSEN)

— Hvorfor maser I saadan paa — lad os dog sidde ned og tale om Tingene!

Fig. 3.1. Crowd tramples bourgeois, 1919. © Mary Evans Picture Library 10012144.

excoriated the German communist Karl Kautsky's condemnation of the Bolsheviks' adoption of 'forms of barbarity, which even the most fantastic of revolutionary romancers could scarce have expected'.[99] The 'desperation' of fomenting the first proletarian revolution had necessitated 'severe measures of State terror'.

[99] Karl Kautsky, *Terrorism and Communism* (George Allen & Unwin, 1920), p. 1.

'Repressions' remained 'a necessary means of breaking the will of the opposing side' while class society—the living hell—persisted.[100]

Lesser measures were thus hardly an option. But many factors combined to drag Soviet society downwards. Barbarism and brutality quickly emerged to dominate the Bolshevik mentality. Revolution and the Civil War (1918–21) made everyone accustomed to bloodletting, especially amongst the young, who came to know little else. Those who felt themselves weak and downtrodden were encouraged to vent their feelings of envy, and to find (in Nadezhda Mandelstam's words) in 'atrocities and crimes . . . the illusion of strength'.[101] Shooting the opposition became necessary out of expediency. The bourgeoisie, Trotsky insisted, 'cannot be terrorised by the threat of imprisonment, as it does not believe in its duration'.[102] Exile was generally not acceptable. So killing prevailed. The 'basic elements of the Stalinist regime—the one-party state, the system of terror and the cult of the personality' were thus 'all in place by 1924'.[103]

Hard People

Founded by Lenin in December 1917, the chief agency of Soviet repression was the CHEKA (Extraordinary Commission for Combating Counter-Revolution and Sabotage). Lenin insisted that 'a good Communist must be a Chekist', and urged the need to find 'truly hard people' to fulfil its mission.[104] During the 1920s, CHEKA's leader was the once-pious, sin-obsessed ex-Catholic Felix Dzerzhinsky (the character of Augustine leaps to mind). He had spent half his life in prison and called his work 'organized terror'.[105] His functionaries were hardened former Tsarist prisoners well aware of the weaknesses which had permitted their own survival.[106] Later succeeded by the State Political Directorate (GPU) (1922–3), then the Joint State Political Directorate (OGPU) (1923–34), the People's Commissariat for Internal Affairs (NKVD) (1934–46), then the Ministry for State Security (MGB) (1946–54), and finally the Committee for State Security (KGB) (1954–91), its emblem was a sword striking down a serpent—back to Saint George. Nominally it reported to the Political Bureau (Politburo) of the Central Committee of the Communist Party. But in fact, by 1930, it was wholly under the control of 'the Boss' (*Khozyain*), Stalin. A state within a state, a law unto itself (or

---

[100] Leon Trotsky, *The Defence of Terrorism* (Labour Publishing Co., 1921), pp. 54, 52.
[101] Nadezhda Mandelstam, *Hope Abandoned: A Memoir* (Collins & Harvill, 1974), p. 522. This remains perhaps the finest memoir of the Soviet period.
[102] Trotsky, *The Defence of Terrorism*, p. 55.   [103] Figes, *A People's Tragedy*, p. 807.
[104] The phrase is repeated in Victor Kravchenko, *I Chose Freedom: The Personal and Political Life of a Soviet Official* (Robert Hale, 1947), p. 289. This is one of the best contemporary accounts of the purges from the inside.
[105] Bernard Bromage, *Man of Terror: Dzherzhynski* (Peter Owen Ltd, 1956), p. 29; John K. Dziak, *Chekisty: A History of the KGB* (Lexington Books, 1988), p. 13. Recent studies include Wendy Z. Goldman, *Terror and Democracy in the Age of Stalin* (Cambridge University Press, 2007), Paul Hagenloh, *Public Order and Mass Repression in the USSR, 1926–1941* (Johns Hopkins University Press, 2009), Norman M. Naimark, *Stalin's Genocides* (Princeton University Press, 2010).
[106] Figes comments that 'One can draw a straight line from the penal rigours of the tsarist regime to the terrorism of the revolutionaries and indeed to the police state of the Bolsheviks. As Flaubert put it, "inside every revolutionary there is a policeman"': *A People's Tragedy*, p. 124.

lawlessness unto itself), the 'organs' (*Organy*), as they were colloquially called, became, in the eyes of one functionary, the 'main pillar' of the Party's 'edifice of power'. By the late 1920s they had become 'a kind of Praetorian Guard exclusively devoted to safeguarding the personal interests of Stalin and his clique'. Consequently, the entire regime rested upon fear, though its intensity fluctuated.[107] Consciously superior to mere Party members, GPU operatives 'felt themselves to be the masters of the country, and they let you know it'.[108] They were the real rulers, the group within the group (the Party) within the group (the proletariat). And as the 'saviours of the revolution' they were on a historic mission, their 'immense privileges' being thus regarded as but 'feeble rewards for their activities'.[109]

Death to the Bourgeoisie

The Soviet Constitution adopted in July 1918 distinguished between the 'toiling and exploited people' and 'parasites' and others, including former functionaries, traders, landowners, and their dependents, who were outcast and disenfranchised. The latter, and also their offspring, polluted by blood, were not only stigmatized, but denied many basic rights. A basic, binary divide between us and them, friends and enemies, the elect and the damned, immediately defined Soviet society, which invited the violent exclusion of 'class aliens'. The 1918 decree 'On Red Terror' justified disposing of 'counterrevolutionary rabble, without having to defer to anyone's authority at all'. Its targets were anarchists, non-Bolshevik socialists, the bourgeoisie, former Tsarist officials, priests, and others. Criticism of its methods was prohibited in December 1918. The CHEKA had carte blanche: the gloves were off in the class war.

As for numbers, the sky was the limit. Grigory Zinoviev (shot in 1936) thought the Party might 'get rid of' or 'annihilate' 10 million of Russia's 100 million people through 'our own socialist terror'. The language of redemptive sacrifice wedded to millenarianism is everywhere evident. 'Let blood flow like water', wrote one CHEKA newspaper, insisting that 'only through the death of the old world can we liberate ourselves forever from the return of those jackals', the bourgeoisie.[110] A decree of 13 May 1919 expropriated all bourgeois property, everything useful being seized by the Chekists for themselves. Some Chekists corralled 'bourgeois' women into brothels, used cocaine, and drank lakes of alcohol.[111]

---

[107] Georges Agabekov, *OGPU: The Russian Secret Terror* (Hyperion Press, 1975), pp. x, 249.

[108] Alex Weissberg, *Conspiracy of Silence* (Hamish Hamilton, 1952), p. 17. This is one of the better memoirs of the purges.

[109] Anton Ciliga, *The Russian Enigma* (George Routledge & Sons, 1940), p. 48.

[110] Gellately, *Lenin, Stalin, and Hitler*, p. 53; Stéphane Courtois, Nicolas Werth, Jean-Louis Panné, Andrzej Paczkowski, Karel Bartošek, and Jean-Louis Margolin, *The Black Book of Communism: Crimes, Terror, Repression* (Harvard University Press, 1999), pp. 75–6, 79, 102.

[111] Courtois et al., *The Black Book of Communism*, pp. 103–4. Yet shootings were also often witnessed by numbers of officials who evidently revelled in the prospect: so reports Agabekov, *OGPU*, p. 7, describing executions as the 'treat of treats' for some officials.

The bloodshed was staggering. Tens of thousands were executed for belonging to 'the possessing classes', including women and children seized as hostages. Some were shot in front of crowds of workers. In an article entitled 'Red Terror', the Bolshevik Karl Radek (executed in 1939) explained that this 'instilled mass intimidation more effectively than could have been accomplished even by five hundred executions carried out apart from working class participation'. Punishing individual bourgeois who had not opposed the regime was justified on the grounds that 'it may intimidate the rest'. Murder by the thousand or ten thousand, in one account 'as though we were exterminating parasites', was proposed. 'We are out to destroy the bourgeoisie as a class', proclaimed an article of November 1918, adding that whenever a bourgeois was arrested the key question was their class origin, upbringing, and education, not opposition to the government. There was thus no need to 'look for incriminating evidence showing whether he has opposed the Soviet, with arms or with words', explained an article in Kazan on 'Red Terror'.[112] 'We are not waging war on individual persons. We are exterminating the bourgeoisie as a class', reiterated a CHEKA founder, emphasizing that class origin, not guilt of anti-Soviet activity, should determine the outcome of investigations.[113] 'Death to the bourgeoisie' was on the wall of the Kiev torture chamber (see Fig. 3.2).[114]

The bourgeoisie was not, as such, a large class in early Soviet Russia, and this vengeance might have ended by some natural limitations. But 'bourgeois' was an elastic category, and rapidly became a metaphysical construct. It might mean anyone with a small amount of property, as *kulak* would shortly imply for the peasantry. The *Valuta* campaign aimed at channelling into the state's coffers—or its employees' pockets—anyone who had access to gold, jewellery, foreign currency. Having employed others or lent neighbours money, even having meat in the kitchen pot, could bring condemnation without the need for questioning. Soft hands—the mark of Satan—could sometimes justify execution.[115] So being calloused was everywhere advantageous.

The Civil War drove the violence of the revolution inexorably towards greater bloodshed. Perhaps 8–10 million perished in it, and at least 200,000 fell as victims to Red Terror.[116] By 1923, as many as 2 million executions may have occurred (compared to *c.*14,000 under the Tsars from 1866 to 1917). Much of the bloodletting was random, ill-directed, and imprecisely defined, simply the 'howling of the mob' released from the shackles of civilization.[117] Some Bolsheviks thought it did not matter. This, surely, was what the catharsis of revolutionary release from oppression was all about: the people's revenge. With inspired insight, the Commissar of Justice, Nikolai Krylenko (shot in 1938), asserted that, 'We must execute not only the guilty. Execution of the innocent will impress the masses even

---

[112] Visiliy Mitrokhin, ed., *'Chekisms': Tales of the CHEKA: A KGB Anthology* (The Yurasov Press, 2008), p. 33.
[113] Quoted in Tismaneanu, *The Devil in History*, p. 5.
[114] Sergey Petrovich Melgounov, *The Red Terror in Russia* (J. M. Dent, 1926), pp. 165, 30, 33, 37, 39–40.
[115] Ibid., pp. 137–8.   [116] Kotkin, *Stalin*, p. 405.
[117] Mandelstam, *Hope Abandoned*, p. 299.

A torture-chamber at Kiev, with " Death to the Bourgeoisie ! " scrawled across a wall.

Fig. 3.2. 'Death to the Bourgeoisie', Sergey Petrovich Melgounov, *The Red Terror in Russia* (J. M. Dent, 1926).

more.'[118] For killing the innocent is indeed perhaps the essence of this form of terror, combining both randomness and the implication that in fact no one *was* innocent anyway. Such elegant simplicity, wedded to the arrogance of certainty, prevailed throughout.

Chaos presided as a result. During the Red Terror, the CHEKA shot people whose names were not even known, and against whom no accusations had been recorded. It condemned people to death it had never even seen. It executed some convicted of drunkenness or petty theft. Cases of mistaken identity were common. At the Butyrka prison in Moscow a man was mistakenly shot when his name was mispronounced.[119] In Odessa, a 'counter-revolutionary' named Chonsir could not be found, so eleven men of the same name were arrested after perusing the telephone book. Two were finally shot after torture indicated that one was probably guilty.[120] The other must have wished he had not owned a telephone or paid his

[118] Quoted in Landes, *Heaven on Earth*, p. 335.
[119] Tatiana Tchernavin, *Escape from the Soviets* (Hamish Hamilton, 1933), p. 79.
[120] Melgounov, *The Red Terror in Russia*, pp. 145, 148, 152, 154–5.

bill on time. But, of course, that would have been defined as 'bourgeois', and thus he was guilty anyway. 'Nine grams of lead' was the only just recourse.

Repression increased massively after Stalin's rise to power at the end of the 1920s. Scrutiny now passed to beliefs and outlook, to 'bourgeois' or 'anti-Soviet' ideas or even 'feelings'. Any 'bourgeois' might be suspected of 'political unreliability and ideological deviation'.[121] The intelligentsia (engineers, doctors, students, etc.) was singled out for 'special treatment'.[122] After 1928, the Politburo was proletarianized. Hatred of the educated became fiercer. They were now proportionately possibly the most executed group—as later in China and Cambodia.[123] Metaphors of biology and disease became increasingly common in describing categories of enemy.[124] Class origins were regarded as essentially inherited, as virtually ontological, even if infection by ideology was commonly associated with condemnation on the basis of social origin.[125] Yet a new class of engineers, functionaries, and managers would arise from the ashes of the old educated class. Stalin had made them, and by and large they supported him.[126]

'Liquidating' the *Kulaks*

After 1917, some wealthy peasants were expropriated or collectivized in the name of both ideology and more efficient larger-scale production, following the United States in particular. Lenin declared in 1918 that 'the final struggle with the kulaks has now begun'. Concentration camps were set up in August that year to confine them, along with 'priests, White Guards, and other doubtful elements'.[127] But this process proceeded painfully slowly. By 1928, only 2 per cent of the peasantry had been voluntarily collectivized. The regime experimented with market forces by allowing private trade during the New Economic Policy (NEP) period (1921–8), giving many peasants the opportunities most revolutionary movements had promised them since the mid-nineteenth century. Then commenced the long-term heavy industrialization programme of the first Five-Year Plan (1929–34, in principle).[128] Stalin thought the

---

[121] Sheila Fitzpatrick, *Everyday Stalinism: Ordinary Life in Extraordinary Times. Soviet Russia in the 1930s* (Oxford University Press, 1999), p. 12.

[122] Lev Razgon, *True Stories* (Ardis, 1997), p. 217; Freda Utley, *The Dream We Lost: Soviet Russia Then and Now* (The John Day Co., 1940), p. 241. The word 'special' always had ominous overtones: 'special operation' meant shooting people; 'special corridor', solitary confinement cells; 'special tribunals' examined political cases; 'special destinations' were camps where you were told you would be killed quickly.

[123] Melgounov, *The Red Terror in Russia*, p. 140.

[124] Quoted in Tismaneanu, *The Devil in History*, p. 40, which notes that the Soviet ideologist Andrei Zhdanov wrote in 1945 that 'the "biological" approach to people is very widespread among us, when the existence of some not entirely "convenient" relatives or other, frequently long dead, is made a criterion of the political loyalty of the worker'.

[125] Fitzpatrick, *Everyday Stalinism*, p. 129.

[126] One case study which stresses this is Stephen Kotkin, *Magnetic Mountain: Stalinism as a Civilization* (University of California Press, 1995), p. 5. The 'new class' hypothesis was explored in this period by Milovan Djilas in particular: *The New Class: An Analysis of the Communist System* (Thames & Hudson, 1957).

[127] Courtois et al., *The Black Book of Communism*, pp. 72–3.

[128] It was completed in four, producing the slogan, 2 + 2 = 5.

USSR was fifty to a hundred years behind the West, and vowed to close the gap in a decade. Increased agricultural exports were crucial to importing new technologies and exceeding Western standards of living in consumer and other goods within a generation or less. Thus was the Soviet utopia to be created.

But to achieve it, Russia had to 'starve itself great'.[129] Stalin was exceedingly impatient. History had not called: it was shouting, as if time was running out. Stalin wanted to drag an essentially medieval country, where memories of serfdom (abolished only in 1861) still lingered, rapidly into the twentieth century. The peasantry— the majority of the population—seemingly obstructed this vision. 'Rich' peasants, the leading 'wreckers' of the entire communist project, were the serpents in paradise; in 1926, some 6 per cent sold perhaps two-thirds of Soviet grain.

So-called *kulaks* had perhaps two horses or cows, or employed others. In poorer villages many so classified had little more than the average farm labourer. Often ambitious, skilled, and industrious, they made up as many as a third or even, in some areas, like southern Russia, half the peasant population. But *kulak* (the word means 'fist', in the sense of grasping or greedy) was, like 'bourgeois', a relaxed category. Eventually, one observer wrote, it came to mean little 'more than victim'.[130] Large numbers had simply resisted collectivization. (When war broke out in 1941, thousands joined the 'German devils' (as they were often called) for the same reason, and were later condemned—and still are—as Nazis, when they were only anti-Stalinist.) The added category of '*subkulaks*', poorer peasants, widened the reach of the collectivizing state. Gradually they were dehumanized, described as 'cattle, swine, loathsome, repulsive', the quintessential 'enemies of the people', mere 'scum' (Stalin's view, in Khrushchev's words). Propaganda pictures depicted them as ape-like subhumans, and some threatened to 'make soap out of the kulak'. 'They are not human beings, they are kulaks', wrote one woman activist of her attitude at the time.[131] Anyone who helped them became a *podkulachnik*, a person aiding the *kulaks*. This was clearly a case of class genocide.

A new campaign against the *kulaks* commenced on Christmas Day 1929. Stigmatizing them as 'petty bourgeois', and estimating them at 5 per cent of the rural population, Stalin called for their 'liquidation' 'as a class'. This expression was less susceptible to ambiguity than 'elimination', and was interpreted literally by many thugs in the provinces.

The initial campaign lasted a mere sixty-five days. Several million were killed and perhaps 5 million deported, including children. (Elderly parents were often simply expelled from their villages.)[132] Up to 10 million were affected. As many as 15–20

[129] William Henry Chamberlin, *Russia's Iron Age* (Duckworth, 1935), p. 108.

[130] W. G. Krivitsky, *In Stalin's Secret Service* (1938; Enigma Books, 2000), p. xix.

[131] Robert Conquest, *Reflections on a Ravaged Century* (John Murray, 1999), p. 94; Lynne Viola, *The Unknown Gulag: The Lost World of Stalin's Special Settlements* (Oxford University Press, 2007), pp. 6, 35; Robert Conquest, *The Harvest of Sorrow: Soviet Collectivisation and the Terror-Famine* (Pimlico Books, 2002), pp. 20, 129.

[132] Kotkin, *Stalin*, p. 724; George Kitchin, *Prisoner of the OGPU* (Longmans, Green & Co., 1935), p. 274.

per cent of the peasants were 'liquidated' in some villages.[133] None were actually charged with anything—they were simply exiled, with one hour's notice or even less. Many killed their animals rather than be collectivized, and some their children rather than letting them starve. As famine enveloped them, they ate 'cats, dogs, field mice, birds', horse manure, and tree bark.[134] The Ukraine was surrounded by NKVD troops and no food was allowed in. Some 6 million died. (By contrast, Russia's losses in World War I were 1.5 million dead.) 'The Kingdom of Antichrist has come', one observed.[135] It was a reasonable enough description.

By the late 1930s, *kulaks* represented over half of those 'purged'.[136] Millions were transported to Siberia or Kazakhstan in unheated cattle trucks. Dumped in barren wastelands as 'special settlers', many lived in holes in the ground with branches covering them. In the depths of winter, warm clothing and shoes were removed from them.[137] Sometimes the men were taken but their families were left behind.[138] Hundreds of thousands simply vanished. In a single year, 1933, 152,000 settlers died and 246,000 fled.[139] Again, too, there was astonishing, haphazard arbitrariness. A seventy-five-year-old woman with a deaf-mute son, for instance, was deported as a 'merchant' because she lived from selling the milk of one cow. A neighbour was taken with her, mistaken for a family member, because he shared her room in their communal apartment.[140]

Amongst this mayhem there was also a fair amount of simple murder. Large numbers were simply shot. Eventually the CHEKA's trademark method of disposal would be the single seven-kopek bullet to the back of the head, usually in prison basements. It was delivered where possible by surprise. But even executions could seem merciful. Those incarcerated found CHEKA prisons much worse than their Tsarist antecedents. (And why not? The latter had held the enemies of privilege, who were morally innocent as such. The former were the enemies of the people, morally unalterably culpable. The logic was inexorable.)

* * * *

Stalin's seizure of power in the late 1920s commenced twenty-five years of fearsome dictatorship. From this time, groups targeted by the regime included the bourgeoisie; the *kulaks*; the merchant classes; priests; intellectuals, whose destruction 'as a class' was proclaimed in 1930;[141] foreigners (including 100,000 Chinese);[142] ethnic minorities (especially Jews and Poles); members of non-Bolshevik political parties, like the Mensheviks (the nearer in doctrine to the

[133] Lyons, *Assignment in Utopia*, p. 280; Viola, *The Unknown Gulag*, p. 3.
[134] Kravchenko, *I Chose Freedom*, p. 113.   [135] Viola, *The Unknown Gulag*, p. 33.
[136] Courtois et al., *The Black Book of Communism*, p. 147.
[137] Utley, *The Dream We Lost*, p. 51.   [138] Kravchenko, *I Chose Freedom*, p. 104.
[139] Lewis Siegelbaum and Andrei Sokolov, eds., *Stalinism as a Way of Life: A Narrative in Documents* (Yale University Press, 2000), p. 97.
[140] Nicolas Werth, *Cannibal Island: Death in a Siberian Gulag* (Princeton University Press, 2007), pp. 50, 97–8.
[141] Tchernavin, *Escape from the Soviets*, p. 39.
[142] Arrested as Japanese spies: F. Beck and W. Godin, *Russian Purge and the Extraction of Confession* (Hurst & Blackett, 1951), p. 110.

Bolsheviks the greater the hostility);[143] from 1935, leftist 'Trotskyists', in opposition from 1923–7 (following Stalin's sidelining of his great opponent, who was exiled in 1929); former Tsarist officials; and anyone 'oppositional' who resisted the government in any way.[144] Anyone deemed a 'class enemy element', or 'former' person of non-proletarian origin, was suspected. Some forty-eight non-Party leading engineers were shot without trial in 1930 for 'wrecking' food supplies. ('Proofs' against them were offered the following year.)[145] A hopelessly defective economic system created many failures which had to be blamed on individuals, because the system could not be wrong. 'Scapegoatism is all-pervading in Russia', noted Franz Borkenau in 1940.[146] Many were disfranchised in this period, meaning they could then only work as unskilled labourers and lost their food rations, while their children were denied schooling. Millions lost their jobs and were driven to begging and starvation. But workers were targeted too. Strikes and agitation in the factories were punished severely, with workers rejecting starvation wages sometimes being shot in large numbers. Often, class position overlapped with nationality to a considerable degree, with Ukrainian and Kazakh *kulaks* suffering particularly greatly. The suicide rate rose steeply, as people 'broke down in the general atmosphere of strain and fear'.[147]

Then came the Party purges. Signed or anonymous statements as to loyalty were solicited. Commissions of three or four loyal members examined the 'evidence', which might be a loose remark, a relative discovered to be a 'class enemy', the vaguest hint of 'deviation', or failure to toe the line at the right moment. Those called in before the Board were not told of the charges against them. They appeared, handed their Party cards to the chairman, and recited their life story, which had the 'confession of sins, near-sins and mistakes as the chief purpose'. Then they were interrogated for any inconsistency, any lack of purity of class or ideal, any wavering of enthusiasm for Comrade Stalin. This 'ordeal might last half an hour or an entire evening', and took place in front of an audience who were quick to sense weakness. By early 1934, some 200,000 Party members had been expelled. Some millions more had been severely traumatized.[148]

In the Party purges, the chief accusation was often 'Trotskyism' (see Fig. 3.3). Whereas in the 1920s a Trotskyist had meant someone who thought like Trotsky, the latter had, by the late 1930s, become virtually a devil figure, 'an iconic synonym of evil', a 'primordial enemy', lacking only horns and a tail, whose name itself became taboo. 'Trotskyism' accordingly became 'a fundamental quality of the soul', synonymous with 'heresy' under the Inquisition, a 'trope' which could be fitted to nearly any 'enemy' activity.[149] By 1937, it was simply 'a collective noun referring to

[143] Socialists and Social Democrats were derided as 'social fascists' from the late 1920s onwards.

[144] These have been estimated at about 10,000–15,000 in a party of 1 million: Alexander Barmine, *One who Survived: The Life Story of a Russian under the Soviets* (G. P. Putnam's Sons, 1945), p. 165.

[145] Vladimir V. Tchernavin, *I Speak for the Silent: Prisoners of the Soviets* (Hamish Hamilton, 1935), pp. 76–84, 175.

[146] Borkenau, *The Totalitarian Enemy*, pp. 228–9.

[147] Tchernavin, *Escape from the Soviets*, p. 51.   [148] Kravchenko, *I Chose Freedom*, p. 134.

[149] J. Arch Getty and Oleg V. Naumov, *The Road to Terror: Stalin and the Self-Destruction of the Bolsheviks, 1932–1939* (Yale University Press, 1999), p. xiii.

Fig. 3.3. Leon Trotsky as enemy, 1928. © Mary Evans Picture Library 10081705.

everything that has to be destroyed'. So, logically, 'every citizen who does not love his motherland is a Trotskyist'. Victims of the purges were by now being denounced as what Igal Halfin terms 'a set of vaguely defined evil creatures, obsessed with the desire to reverse History', and reviled as 'monsters' and 'evilmongers'. By 1937, 'the Stalinist utopia structured itself around an incessant struggle against vaguely specified deadly foes'. Now, within 'NKVD discourse, it made no sense to distinguish between truth and fiction'. What mattered was only identifying the ever-mutating 'source of pollution'.[150]

This onslaught began by using the murder of the Leningrad Party Chief Sergei Kirov in December 1934 as a pretext. While never proven, this was probably on Stalin's order: Kirov was popular with the opposition and a growing rival. It may also have been in imitation of Hitler's successful Blood Purge in June. A spiral of destruction of unparalleled ferocity and 'implacable war against all those who had ever disagreed with Stalin' had begun.[151] The desire for intensified loyalty and for rooting out deviation reached new heights of frenzy.

This peaked with the 'Great Terror' or *Yezhovshchina* (after the new NKVD boss, Yezhov, a drunkard who, Stalin himself later claimed, often signed off

---

[150] Halfin, *Stalinist Confessions*, pp. 126, 203, 432, 203–4, 193, 249, 255, 8.
[151] Barmine, *One who Survived*, p. 249.

execution lists of innocent people).[152] This began in early 1936 and ended in early 1939. Its apex came in August 1937. Stalin, evidently anticipating a fifth column threat in a coming war, but also consolidating his dictatorship, called for 'mass operations of repression of *kulaks*, criminals, and other anti-Soviet elements'. About 1.8 million Party members were expelled, 'and in most cases expulsion meant concentration camp or worse'. Millions who escaped the purges 'were maimed in their minds and wounded in their spirits by the fears and the brutalities amidst which they lived'.[153] The 'whole country was numbed by fear—it affected everybody without exception', recalled Nadezhda Mandelstam.[154] As many as 8 million were arrested over a two-and-a-half-year period.[155] Anyone who, even in 'his thoughts . . . threatens the unity of the socialist state' was a target.[156] The term 'enemies of the people' now entered everyday discourse. Cells 'were crowded to bursting'. The courts sat twenty-four hours a day. Cases might take seven minutes: the judges too had a production quota to meet.[157] Ten-year sentences were routine until 1 October 1937, when twenty-five-year terms were introduced.

Stalin's 'Great Purge' supposedly exposed a vast conspiracy enveloping every area of Soviet life. In reality, it consisted of a 'vast cycle of frame-ups by Stalin and his entourage'.[158] Targets now included both 'rightists' and leftist 'Trotskyites', and even 'one-eighth Trotskyites', echoing blood language.[159] 'Suspect' national minorities were 'a key group singled out now'. (During the war newly occupied territories like the Baltic States and eastern Poland were particularly badly hit.)[160] Intellectuals everywhere were sitting ducks. The Party and army were particularly hard hit in 1937.[161] About a third of the Party's membership, around a million people, were arrested between 1936 and 1939, most being executed.[162] Initially a quota was established to shoot 76,000. This was later quintupled.[163] Much of the diplomatic corps was recalled and shot without trial.[164] The military lost about 40,000 officers, or half its senior commanders, evidently because Stalin feared

---

[152] Halfin, *Stalinist Confessions*, p. 352. This incisive account is the best recent analysis of the broader subject. Stalin himself signed nearly four hundred such lists in 1937–8, containing thousands of names (Conquest, *The Great Terror*, pp. 259–60).

[153] Kravchenko, *I Chose Freedom*, p. 303.   [154] Mandelstam, *Hope Abandoned*, p. 576.

[155] This figure is from Weissberg, *Conspiracy of Silence*, p. 1.

[156] Quoted in Tismaneanu, *The Devil in History*, p. 8. Another Chekist wrote that 'we are trying to exterminate the bourgeoisie and the kulaks as a class' (Courtois et al., *The Black Book of Communism*, p. 103).

[157] Evgenia Semyonova Ginzburg, *Into the Whirlwind* (Collins/Harvill, 1967), pp. 109, 130.

[158] Conquest, *The Great Terror*, p. xii.

[159] Courtois et al., *The Black Book of Communism*, p. xviii.

[160] At least a million Poles were taken to the USSR, including virtually everyone with a university education. In Lithuania, the NKVD lists of those to be deported comprised 700,000 out of a population of 3 million: [Zoë Zajdlerowa], *The Dark Side of the Moon* (Faber & Faber, 1946), pp. 50–1.

[161] Hagenloh, *Public Order*, p. 1. See further Vadim Z. Rogovin, *1937: Stalin's Year of Terror* (Mehring Books, 1998).

[162] Anna Larina, *This I Cannot Forget: The Memoirs of Nicolai Bukharin's Widow* (W. W. Norton, 1993), p. 17.

[163] Adam Hochschild, *The Unquiet Ghost: Russians Remember Stalin* (Viking Penguin, 1994), p. 192; Werth, *Cannibal Island*, pp. 189–90.

[164] Barmine, *One who Survived*, pp. 19–20.

a coup. (But no conspiracy existed.)[165] This proved a near fatal move when Germany invaded in 1941, though anyone who warned of the prospect was, of course, arrested.[166] (Astonishingly, more officers were executed or died in the camps than would be killed in the war itself: Stalin shot 1,000 generals, while 600 were killed in action.) At the moment of their arrest, officers had their medals removed from their uniforms and their epaulets cut away: guilty until proven innocent.[167] Accounts of the trials were broadcast over loudspeakers in the streets, constantly denouncing the 'traitors', 'spies', and saboteurs. This raised the public's sense of anger and paranoia, and made crowds edgy, nervous, and panicky.[168] Even in private no one 'dared discuss what was happening... Any mention of the purge was imprudent; it might lead to some avowal of emotion or opinion.'[169] In this atmosphere, political offences were regarded 'as a contagious disease' which anyone might catch.[170]

The most intense public moment of this epoch was the 'show trials' of 1936–8, the subject of Arthur Koestler's famous *Darkness at Noon* (1940),[171] discussed in Chapter 5. Here the targets were Stalin's main rivals. These trials have been described as analogous to classic ritual sacrifices, the few being chosen to die for the good of the many.[172] The accused were charged with an absurd range of crimes, including spying for various countries (Trotsky had been linked to the Gestapo in 1936 as well as British Intelligence); conniving at assassinating Lenin in 1918; inserting glass into butter; spoiling eggs; breeding anaemic horses; and spreading plague amongst pigs. Their ultimate aim was supposedly 'restoring capitalism' and 'the power of the bourgeoisie'.[173] The old Bolsheviks Kamenev, Bukharin (who in 1936 had said the NKVD ruled the country rather than the Party), and Zinoviev, were all tortured before their trial. They and fifteen others were condemned to be shot, many of their relatives soon following. Thereafter, those condemned had necessarily to be erased from the files and deleted from the encyclopaedias, becoming 'unpersons', to preserve unsullied the myth of purity and virtue.

From the late 1930s onwards the Party also commenced rewriting the history of everything since the revolution. Now it 'deliberately stood history on its head, expunging events and inventing facts... to conform with the version of affairs presented by the blood-purge trials and the accompanying propaganda'. Books, articles, and museum artefacts which contradicted the new truths 'disappeared throughout the country', along with living witnesses. So 'falsification without measure or limit', in Victor Kravchenko's words, became the aim.[174]

---

[165] Conquest, *The Great Terror*, p. 207.   [166] Ibid., p. 229.
[167] A. V. Gorabatov, *Years Off My Life: The Memoirs of General of the Soviet Army* (Constable, 1964), p. 109.
[168] Anatoli Rybakov, *Fear* (Hutchinson, 1993), p. 367.
[169] Barmine, *One who Survived*, p. 250.
[170] Gustav Herling, *A World Apart* (William Heinemann, 1951), p. 87.
[171] Arthur Koestler, *Darkness at Noon* (Jonathan Cape, 1940).
[172] Nigel Davies, *Human Sacrifice in History and Today* (Macmillan, 1981), p. 16.
[173] *Report of the Court Proceedings in the Case of the Anti-Soviet 'Bloc of Rights and Trotskyites'* (People's Commissariat of Justice of the USSR, 1938), pp. 5, 33, 206–7, 330, 332.
[174] Kravchenko, *I Chose Freedom*, pp. 304–5. See George Orwell, *Our Job is to Make Life Worth Living, 1949–50* (Secker & Warburg, 2002), pp. 68–9.

At the height of the purges, some 680,000–800,000 executions occurred, around 1,000–1,500 a day. Relatives were usually told that the victims had received ten years' imprisonment without right of correspondence. Some waited decades for their return. Another 300,000–400,000 were forced into exile.[175] But the net was cast ever more widely. Eventually, about half the urban population was on NKVD suspect lists.[176] Most of the rest would logically have found their way there too in due course. It made sense: having more names made it easier to fill quotas. Thus millions of 'eggs' were broken with nary an omelette in sight.[177] But even the NKVD itself was not spared; between 1936 and 1938 some 20,000 of its members were shot or imprisoned, including some 7,000 investigators.[178] They knew too much; they were dangerous. They might prove infectious. And yet eyewitnesses reported that many such faced their fate 'with relative calm', feeling that their deaths contributed to saving the regime as a whole—'an astonishing manifestation of Caste-feeling', in Anton Ciliga's words—a triumph of groupishness, we might say.[179]

Arrest

The mental world of the 1930s is difficult for us to comprehend. The unguarded word, the misplaced glance, the overhasty smile, the hint of political disagreement, insufficient zeal, an innocent meeting with a friend under suspicion, the failure to applaud loudly or long enough, now implied grave consequences. By the late 1920s, suspicion pervaded every corner of Soviet life. Every economic failure engendered a new search for 'wreckers', spies, nationalists, 'cosmopolites' (e.g. Jews), Trotskyites, Whites, and untold further 'anti-Soviet' and 'counter-revolutionary' bodies. Enemies proliferated like flies. Every 'successful' uncovering of 'spies' by one Chekist unit encouraged others to go further in order not to fall behind or appear unenthusiastic. So 'plots' begat more 'plots', and more 'laws' begat more 'criminals'. Entirely new areas of social life were now criminalized. The death penalty was extended to those who merely belonged to organizations deemed hostile.[180]

It is a challenge to recapture just how paralysing this system was. To be taciturn in public meetings was risky. Solzhenitsyn recounts how, during the 1937 purges, a group applauding a Party leader's speech feared the first to stop clapping would be arrested for disloyalty. They clapped and clapped for ten minutes, until their hands were raw. The first to stop was indeed arrested, and was told by his interrogator that the moral of the story was never to be the first to stop clapping.[181] But over-zealousness in the wrong cause could be equally dangerous. Anxiety intensified as

---

[175] Oleg V. Khlevniuk, *The History of the Gulag* (Yale University Press, 2004), p. 165, gives the figure of 681,692. The population at this point was about 169 million, giving an execution rate of about one in twenty-four.

[176] In Poland, by 1954, a third of all adults were on suspect lists: Applebaum, *Iron Curtain*, p. 294.

[177] 'Where is the omelette?', Orwell once said, in reference to the 'standard formula' of Stalinist apology (*I Belong to the Left 1945* (Secker & Warburg, 2001), p. 342).

[178] Halfin, *Stalinist Confessions*, p. 228.   [179] Ciliga, *The Russian Enigma*, p. 96.

[180] Gellately, *Lenin, Stalin, and Hitler*, p. 55.

[181] Solzhenitsyn, *The Gulag Archipelago*, vol. 1, p. 70.

millions weighed every public moment as a judgement on their inner selves, and
that at a time when the Party line, the determinant of one's outlook on nearly every
subject, wavered daily on numerous issues. One's choice of words could matter a
great deal; 'uses irony' was recorded by a GPU agent of a deported intellectual in
1922.[182] By 1937, 'physiognomism', as Halfin terms it, or reading faces, gestures,
even skin textures, became an exact science. One writer claimed he could recognize
a Trotskyist 'by the alien glitter in his eyes'.[183]

So it was vital for the inner and outer selves, the 'innermost essence' and the
'Party face', to be fused. Complete transparency needed to exist, and interiority to
be banished, replaced, by 1937, by the 'New Man', utterly focused not just on the
Party, but its blameless leader.[184] Perfection incarnate, the latter should be referred
to not as 'Comrade Stalin', but only as 'Comrade Stalin, the beloved leader of the
Soviet proletariat', or some similar title. Universal surveillance, observing and being
observed, now became necessary. 'Every toiler in our country must become a
security agent', claimed a Soviet leader in 1937.[185] As interrogations aimed to
uncover 'conspiracies', anyone who knew a suspect became a suspect. Even reading
about 'counter-revolutionary organisations' in the paper got one unfortunate fifteen
years, for this counted as 'knowledge'.[186] So in principle only hermits were above
suspicion. But hermits, of course, were anti-social/Soviet elements by definition,
and Robinson Crusoe's ruminations would certainly have counted as bourgeois
propaganda.

Alice in Wonderland seems reason incarnate compared to this topsy-turvy world.
Who was arrested and why became increasingly random as a result of both accident
and design. Absurdities abounded. Enemies had to be found. It mattered little
where. A popular joke in the 1920s and 1930s recounted how a group of rabbits
applied to enter Poland at the frontier, after the GPU had ordered the arrest of all
camels. 'But you are not camels!' came the response, which met with, 'Try telling
that to the GPU.'[187] Another joke ran: the guard asks a prisoner what his sentence
is. The answer: twenty-five years. The guard asks, 'what did you do?' The prisoner
says, 'nothing'. The guard's answer: 'You are lying, prisoner; the sentence for
nothing at all is ten years.'[188] (Such jokes normally attracted a three- to ten-year
sentence. The joke within the joke was that bad jokes got the lesser and good ones
the greater penalty.) So to try to make 'sense' of this system is the wrong approach:
its very strength lay in being random, unpredictable, and nonsensical. Intensified
absurdity was the essence of true terror.

But many were arrested through bad luck rather than bad humour. Mere
proximity could invite arrest. By 'such innocent means as a handshake, a breath,
handing someone anything, [or] a chance meeting on the street', others were

[182] Kotkin, *Stalin*, p. 440.   [183] Halfin, *Stalinist Confessions*, p. 210.
[184] On this theme see Raymond A. Bauer, *The New Man in Soviet Psychology* (Harvard University Press, 1952).
[185] Halfin, *Stalinist Confessions*, pp. 250, 210–11.
[186] Razgon, *True Stories*, p. 172.   [187] Fitzpatrick, *Everyday Stalinism*, p. 218.
[188] Alexander Dolgun, *Alexander Dolgun's Story: An American in the Gulag* (Alfred A. Knopf, 1975), p. 211.

implicated.[189] Numbers of people who simply happened to be at markets or railway stations were caught up in the net. In the early 1930s, arrests of 'socially harmful elements' in Moscow, Leningrad, and other large cities, usually anyone not tied to a fixed job, led to the rounding-up of the elderly, blind, invalid, retarded, thousands of Gypsies, and many whose papers were quite in order. Thousands were resettled in the barren eastern wastelands with virtually no food or tools, hundreds of miles from the railway. Hundreds of thousands simply vanished into the taiga, marshes, and desert, sometimes eating each other in desperation. Arrest also led to relatives and friends, even friends of friends, being arrested. Consequently, it did not pay to have friends. (Though real friends would stand the test of terror, and in this sense friendship 'became an ultimate value, produced in resistance struggles in the Soviet Union'.)[190]

It thus paid to cross the corridor or street to avoid suspects. But it was unwise to move about too often. People went out to shop, and then vanished, 'vaccinated' or 'immunized', in NKVD disease-speak.[191] People avoided speaking of those arrested, and, in offices—shades of taboo—avoided looking at their empty desks, as if a glance might prove infectious.[192] Having books by 'enemies of the people' was grounds for arrest, so people took to cutting out chapters and sections written by those taken away, while the state engaged in the same activity on a much larger scale, purging the libraries from 1930 onwards—even the works of Marx and Engels.[193] For years no schoolbooks were available because every new edition had to be pulped when 'enemies' were discovered. Even banknotes had to be withdrawn when their signatories were arrested (to solve this awkwardness new rouble notes in 1938 had no signature at all.)[194] Having photographs of 'enemies', even one's own family members, was dangerous.[195] People were often confused as to why they were arrested; a sixty-five-year-old woman sentenced to ten years as a 'traktist' (Trotskyite terrorist) wondered in camp why old women were accused of abusing tractors.[196]

Most incomprehensibly frightening of all, perhaps, were the arrests and executions resulting from quotas. This, more than anything else perhaps, made the entire 'machine of destruction' seem an 'autonomous mechanism into which a monstrous program had been fed . . . outside the power of man to control it'.[197] (Who but the Man of Steel could make such a machine?) All Soviet industry was governed by quotas defined by the Plan. So the State Planning Commission, assigning the

[189] Solzhenitsyn, *The Gulag Archipelago*, vol. 1, p. 75.
[190] Oleg Kharkhordin, *The Collective and the Individual in Russia: A Study of Practices* (University of California Press, 1999), p. 319.
[191] Joseph Berger, *Shipwreck of a Generation: The Memoirs of Joseph Berger* (Harvill Press, 1971), p. 45; Halfin, *Stalinist Confessions*, p. 203.
[192] Tchernavin, *I Speak for the Silent*, p. 73; Halfin, *Stalinist Confessions*, p. 251.
[193] Siegelbaum and Sokolov, eds., *Stalinism as a Way of Life*, pp. 82–4.
[194] Beck and Godin, *Russian Purge*, p. 32.
[195] 'Counter-revolutionary publications' had been banned since 1923, but the full-scale destruction of 'unhealthy literature', which involved burning mountains of books—24 million volumes in a single year—began in the late 1930s. Lists of banned literature were themselves pulped, and librarians were sometimes forbidden to consult them: Halfin, *Stalinist Confessions*, pp. 204–8.
[196] Ginzburg, *Into the Whirlwind*, p. 138.   [197] Mandelstam, *Hope Abandoned*, pp. 568, 614.

numbers required to fulfil the Plan, and always so insanely rushed that it wasted millions of rubles, helped set the numbers to be arrested. It produced enemies like any other commodity, inefficiently. Percentages of estimated numbers of spies, wreckers, and *kulaks* were laid down from the late 1920s for each Soviet district.[198] Even writers were affected. Some desperately orthodox ones found themselves particularly unfairly arrested when the quotas were issued only by numbers and not names.[199] Not fulfilling any norm risked arrest and, at least, unemployment.[200] A specific number from each category had to be arrested. This was where the pressure really mounted on the police. Merely enquiring about someone arrested, or being a neighbour accidentally present, could entail arrest if the quota had not been filled. Yet an ideal of mechanical efficiency dominated here too. When the quota was reached, often arrests and shootings stopped, no matter how many were left, and whether they were 'guilty' of anything or not.

But sadly there was no safety here either. Names were 'kept in reserve against a shortage', like corn in a granary.[201] If the quota was filled in one category, say 'Trotskyists', prosecutors could transfer your charge to another, perhaps 'bourgeois nationalist', where a shortage existed, to meet demand there.[202] Or if the 'politicals' quota was not met, those arrested on ordinary criminal charges might be reclassified. At the height of the purges all these tendencies increased. After the Kulak Operation of August 1937 began, in Smolensk, 7,000 were ordered arrested and 1,000 were executed, irrespective of 'guilt'.[203] Animated by the Stakhanovite spirit of overfulfilling any plan, zealous units in some regions demanded an increase in execution quotas. The Politburo in October 1937 demanded 63,000 more executions. Local NKVD branches, often acting on hearsay, were free to 'raise or lower the numbers' as they pleased. In Moscow, a quota of 200 per day was introduced on 29 January 1938.[204] It was always safer to be overzealous. So the Ossetia Chekist Zabolovsky, granted a quota of 500 to be shot, asked for it to be increased to 750. It was.[205]

A host of regulations poured forth to assist the need for arrests. Wearing dirty clothes in the street became illegal in Stalingrad in 1938, as did storing food between the inner and outer windows of apartments.[206] Sharing ideas with those convicted meant 'sharing moral and criminal responsibility' for their acts.[207] Knowing foreigners—many specialists were working in the USSR at this time— or refusing to return from trips abroad for any reason were almost certain tickets to the camps. Writing letters to friends abroad was sufficient to be arrested. Many in

---

[198] An example is given in Getty and Naumov, *The Road to Terror*, pp. 475–6.
[199] Berger, *Shipwreck of a Generation*, p. 43.
[200] 'The more they arrested, the better they lived': Hochschild, *The Unquiet Ghost*, p. 78.
[201] Mandelstam, *Hope Abandoned*, p. 574.
[202] In the case of the Tartar biologist Julia Karepova: Ginzburg, *Into the Whirlwind*, p. 105.
[203] J. Arch Getty and Roberta T. Manning, eds., *Stalinist Terror: New Perspectives* (Cambridge University Press, 1993), p. 192. See generally Paul R. Gregory, *Terror by Quota: State Security from Lenin to Stalin* (Yale University Press, 2009).
[204] Mayer, *The Furies*, p. 658; Robert Conquest, *Inside Stalin's Secret Police: NKVD Politics, 1936–9* (Macmillan, 1985), p. 57.
[205] Solzhenitsyn, *The Gulag Archipelago*, vol. 1, p. 71.
[206] Fitzpatrick, *Everyday Stalinism*, p. 34.   [207] Ginzburg, *Into the Whirlwind*, p. 131.

the Foreign Ministry, whose job it was to cultivate such contacts, died because of them. Ideologically false science was also dangerous, and true science was commonly fatal. Thirty-five agronomists were shot in 1933 for causing weeds to grow. Members of the Meteorological Corps were arrested for predicting weather harmful to crops. Twenty-seven astronomers were killed after their sunspot research was deemed unMarxist. The 1939 census takers were shot for showing a decline in population after the purges. (Their replacements 'correctly' estimated a higher false number.) Filing an accurate productivity report, if it was below the norm set, could merit arrest. Even referring to the catastrophic famine of 1932–3, in which more than 6 million died, could get one five years in the camps. (Blaming the authorities for it incurred a death sentence.)[208] 'Espionage' after 1941 could include being a prisoner of war (POW) in another country, or knowing someone who knew someone employed by a foreign power. A peasant who stopped to gawk at a seaplane in Leningrad, never having seen one before, was swept up: spy![209]

The list goes on. Possession of Western newspapers: ten years. Listening to foreign broadcasts: twenty-five years. Undermining 'sacred hatred' of the enemy in war: twenty-five years.[210] One of Kamenev's few surviving relatives was convicted for having an 'aesthetic approach to literature': ten years (but he also called Stalin a dictator).[211] A 110-year-old woman got ten years for claiming that she had read bad things about Lenin in the Gospels.[212] A Pole named Gerling was convicted in part because he was assumed to be a relative of one Goehring.[213] One man, reporting having seen an American film starring Robert Taylor, was convicted with associating with a known US agent, one R. Taylor. Another, who adored Stalin, got twenty-five years for dreaming the leader had died, then telling his wife how upset it had made him. She got ten for 'failure to denounce' him. In one case a girl reported a young man for anti-Soviet views. He got twenty-five, plus five years' exile and five years' deprivation of political rights. Then she got the same—for 'associating with known subversives'. Some prisoners thought this very funny: some justice existed after all.[214]

'Sabotage' and 'wrecking' were the most common charges covering a million mishaps in a system industrializing and collectivizing at breakneck speed. That wondrous tool, capable of convicting anything, Article 58 of the Criminal Code of 1927, covered these. Its idea of 'counter-revolutionary', it has been said, covered every 'conceivable form of human behaviour'.[215] 'Sabotage', whose definition was extended in 1936, could include any mistake at work, in an industrial system where even fatal accidents were common. 'Revealing State Secrets' included mentioning the name of a civil airport or of any Gulag prisoner. A professor faced espionage charges for noting the depth of the river Dnieper in a textbook. The range of topics

[208] Chamberlin, *Russia's Iron Age*, p. 154; Conquest, *Reflections on a Ravaged Century*, p. 96.
[209] Anne Applebaum, ed., *Gulag Voices: An Anthology* (Yale University Press, 2011), p. 7.
[210] Lev Kopelev, *No Jail for Thought* (Secker & Warburg, 1977), p. 10.
[211] Hochschild, *The Unquiet Ghost*, p. 88.
[212] Larina, *This I Cannot Forget*, p. 53.   [213] Herling, *A World Apart*, p. 3.
[214] Dolgun, *Alexander Dolgun's Story*, pp. 208, 32, 169.
[215] [Zajdlerowa], *The Dark Side of the Moon*, p. 24.

regarded as secret included details of transportation, contagious diseases, factory output, and the quality of production. A 'spy' could be anyone photographed near a foreigner, or who lingered too long near a factory. 'Acts' of treason were not necessary for conviction, either. 'Intents' or even 'contacts leading to the suspicion of espionage' sufficed.[216]

Errors at work were particularly liable to prosecution, and workplace denunciations of private misbehaviour, inadequate enthusiasm, or the wrong class outlook were encouraged.[217] Any sentiment deemed likely to 'weaken Soviet power', even in private conversation, courted incarceration. The more preposterous the allegation, the more likely it was to stick. Stealing two spools of thread ('state property'): seven years.[218] A mentally ill deaf-mute who could not even sign: ten years for counter-revolutionary propaganda.[219] A tailor who stuck a newspaper with a pin to the wall through a picture of Kaganovich: ten years; a saleswoman noting bars of soap on the only piece of paper available, which had Stalin's portrait on it (shops rarely had paper bags): 58:8; terrorism, ten years; a peasant who threw an axe at a rival at a drunken party and missed, but hit a portrait of Stalin: eight years; a shepherd who swore at a cow, 'You collective-farm whore': fifty-eight!, and so on.[220] 'Failure to denounce' was 58:12. 'Sabotage' for shoeblacks included cleaning shoes with bad polish to encourage complaints about the leather.[221]

Every taint of foreign association was dangerous. Philatelists, numismatists— 'ists' in general perhaps—were suspect. Esperanto speakers were at risk. Someone who praised the variety of fruit in Greece compared to the USSR was arrested.[222] A photographer was executed for claiming that pre-revolutionary developing paper had been better. Praising the superiority of any foreign product, indeed, was grounds for a 58:10 charge: one man got ten years for saying Soviet cars were inferior to American at a time when the higher Soviet bureaucracy favoured the latter.[223] Attempting to flee the USSR attracted a penalty of five to ten years, the reasoning being that foreigners would learn about Soviet life, which constituted espionage. (But wanting to leave the USSR also implied betrayal of its ideals.)[224] Idealistic young foreign communists, however, got three, five, or eight years for trying to get *into* Russia.[225] From 1934, twelve-year-olds were held responsible for not reporting their parents' treason. From 1935, children were treated as adults

---

[216] Solzhenitsyn, *The Gulag Archipelago*, vol. 1, p. 64.
[217] Cynthia Hooper, 'Terror of Intimacy: Family Politics in the 1930s Soviet Union', in Christina Kaier and Eric Naiman, eds., *Everyday Life in Early Soviet Russia* (Indiana University Press, 2006), pp. 61–92.
[218] Kopelev, *No Jail for Thought*, p. 242.
[219] Unto Parvilahti, *Beria's Gardens: Ten Years' Captivity in Russia and Siberia* (Hutchinson, 1959), p. 114.
[220] Solzhenitsyn, *The Gulag Archipelago*, vol. 2, p. 293; Beck and Godin, *Russian Purge*, p. 44.
[221] Beck and Godin, *Russian Purge*, p. 111.
[222] Sarah Davies, *Popular Opinion in Stalin's Russia: Terror, Propaganda and Dissent, 1934–1941* (Cambridge University Press, 1997), p. 5; Fitzpatrick, *Everyday Stalinism*, p. 208.
[223] Dolgun, *Alexander Dolgun's Story*, p. 329.
[224] Tchernavin, *I Speak for the Silent*, pp. 138–9; Kazimierz Zarod, *Inside Stalin's Gulag: A True Story of Survival* (The Book Guild, 1990), p. 47.
[225] [Zajdlerowa], *The Dark Side of the Moon*, p. 131.

where such crimes were concerned, and twelve-year-olds earned the death sentence. Hundreds of thousands had roamed the streets as vagrants after 1917 and they became the core of the criminal class in the camps, the wildest of the wild. One arrest begat another with the regularity of an infection. And so millions disappeared, half of them '58's'. Perhaps 10 per cent of the population were guilty only of belonging to the wrong class, or being related to someone who had been arrested (which usually got you five to eight years).[226]

From Arrest to Prison

The path from suspicion to arrest often proceeded via denunciation. 'A single anonymous denunciation and your fate is sealed!'[227] 'Proofs' were not obligatory; 'Where class instinct speaks, proof is unnecessary', said a Kiev scientist (who was later arrested).[228] In the early days, trials in 'People's Courts' aimed at 'revolutionary justice', and hearsay by debtors, lunatics, aggrieved neighbours, or former servants, and, commonly, anyone themselves suspected of anything, might secure conviction.[229] Nadezhda Mandelstam recalled that before '1937 there had to be some element of truth'. Thereafter, almost any fantasy sufficed.[230] The course of events, the shortages, the overcrowding, the suspicions, made many more enemies than life might normally occasion. Invariably the process worked like a kind of pyramid scheme. Each person arrested, hoping to save themselves, implicated many more. One person could easily incriminate hundreds. In principle, indeed quite logically, everyone was suspect. Every human being was an enemy in a revolution made only for angels. Not just the bourgeoisie, but every worker, fell short of perfection. (The only reason, indeed, that everyone was not arrested, which was perfectly defensible in principle, was that it was impracticable. So the policy was 'to pick up those who came to hand, as a lesson to the rest'.)[231] Every fifth person working in offices was reckoned to be an NKVD informer, and perhaps 5 per cent of the nation as a whole.[232] Once locked into the system they too could not escape without the threat of the camps, and many were driven to early graves 'by insomnia, self-disgust, and horror'.[233] So they watched, listened, denounced.

The knock on the door could come any time. Several generations learned to wince at the sound of a doorbell, or of car tyres on the street outside, or of the heavy clomp of late night footsteps on the stairs. By the late 1920s, many families kept a suitcase of warm clothing in readiness.[234] In the late 1930s, many could scarcely

---

[226] Conquest, *The Harvest of Sorrow*, pp. 315, 306, 300.

[227] Ivan Solonevich, *Escape from Russian Chains* (Williams and Norgate, 1938), p. 185.

[228] Beck and Godin. *Russian Purge*, p. 29.   [229] Figes, *A People's Tragedy*, p. 534.

[230] Nadezhda Mandelstam, *Hope against Hope: A Memoir* (Collins & Harvill, 1971), p. 131.

[231] 'The whole point of terror is that people are arrested at random in order to instil fear into everybody else': Mandelstam, *Hope Abandoned*, p. 571.

[232] Conquest, *The Great Terror*, p. 281; Stephen F. Cohen, *The Victims Return: Survivors of the Gulag after Stalin* (I.B. Taurus, 2011), p. 101.

[233] Mandelstam, *Hope Abandoned*, pp. 567–8.

[234] The Soviet comic Vladimir Khenkin even joked: 'I heard a vigorous knock at my door. *So I took my little suitcase and went to open the door.*' (Lyons, *Assignment in Utopia*, p. 346). He lived until 1953.

sleep amidst such fears. Still, arrest might come like a 'bolt of lightning which has scored a direct hit on you . . . an unassimilable spiritual earthquake'. The shock drove many insane.[235] Insolent jackbooted security men entered, with cowed civilian witnesses (required by law) hovering in the background. Night-time was favoured as disguising the volume of arrests and catching victims in a state of slumber and confusion.[236] The moment of arrest was one of guilt, doubt, bewilderment, uncertainty, overpowering emotion. This was, many suspected, the anteroom between life and death. Yet sometimes, in an overheated atmosphere of constant threat and recrimination, arrest brought relief and even happiness.[237] Apartments were often searched for hours on end. Much was destroyed or trampled on. Looting—'expropriation of excesses'—was common, even kitchen utensils and clothes being confiscated.[238] Deprived of their belt to prevent them from hanging themselves, the dazed victims might gather a few possessions together, which were later nearly always stolen. Indeed, this was a police prerogative: apartments themselves, where desirable, were not uncommonly taken over by interrogators. Whole blocks sometimes changed hands several times in the 1930s. This was a fine incentive: even Chief Prosecutor Vyshinsky took over the prime *dacha* of a suspect shortly after arresting him.[239]

Those arrested were usually transported to jail in large furniture-moving-style vans labelled 'bread' or 'meat' or 'Drink Soviet Champagne' (the irony of promoting commodity sales in the capitalist manner while transporting class enemies is exquisite; what genius thought this up? A NEP man?) Their new home was the last many ever saw. For many, its anteroom was a single box-like cell occupied prior to the first body search. Moscow's infamous Lubyanka prison, with its appropriate rooftop statue of the Parcae, or Greek Fates, who cut the threads of mortal life, had, ironically, housed an insurance company, which also subsisted on calculating the value of lives. Now it was nicknamed the 'Government Terror' (*Gos Uzhas*). This Leviathan swallowed thousands.[240]

In the supercharged moment of personality transformation, arrest brought an almost immediate transition from Soviet citizen to 'enemy of the people' (*vragi naroda*). The higher the prisoner's former rank in society, the more startling was the mutation from everything to nothing. Those who *knew* themselves to be 'class enemies'—priests and the like—were probably more resigned to their fate, especially if they were guilty of 'concealment of social origin', such as denying possessing a university degree. Tens of thousands taken as 'hostages' from 1918 onwards likely did not see themselves as such. Nor were the immense numbers who merely knew someone who knew someone who had been on a list, or who had been

[235] Solzhenitsyn, *The Gulag Archipelago*, vol. 1, p. 3.

[236] But arrests on the street, at the railway station, in shops, or while at work, even on the operating table, were common enough. And in 1945–6 whole trainloads returning from Europe were arrested *en masse* without any pretence of ritual.

[237] Solzhenitsyn, *The Gulag Archipelago*, vol. 1, p. 14.

[238] Lev Kopelev, *The Education of a True Believer* (Wildwood House, 1981), p. 10.

[239] Rybakov, *Fear*, p. 338. He died peacefully in 1954.

[240] Chamberlin, *Russia's Iron Age*, p. 158; Dolgun, *Alexander Dolgun's Story*, p. 10.

raked in on some quota sweep. Or the generals and administrators and factory managers whose individual failings were perhaps negligible at best. But accidentally accusing innocents was never a serious concern. Lenin had no qualms about suggesting that 'one out of every ten idlers' might 'be shot on the spot'.[241] His principle that arresting a hundred innocents was better than letting one guilty person escape was heeded widely; Stalin, more modestly, thought it right to 'report people if you are right only 5 percent of the time'.[242]

The general principle seems to have been, as often as not, guilty until (an unlikely event) proven innocent. For like the Party whose infallibility it embodied, 'the NKVD did not make mistakes'.[243] So 'to be accused was to be condemned'. One member of the Academy of Sciences arrested in 1937 was told that the fact that 'you may be innocent does not play a role. If you are arrested we will find you guilty of something—we cannot undermine the authority of the NKVD.'[244] But in any case, while common criminals might be saved and rehabilitated, members of any kind of real or suspected opposition could not. Like the sinners punished by the Puritans, for whom dominion was founded on grace, they 'being unsaved ... had lost the common rights of humanity'.[245] The stigma of class origin, inherited by children, was also as ineradicable as Original Sin. This resulted in disfranchisement, lack of educational opportunities, jobs, medical care, and most vital services. Thus, ironically, as Sheila Fitzpatrick writes, people 'tainted by social origin or political history were, in practice, almost invariably disqualified as objects of reclamation. To be eligible for reforging, you had to have committed real crimes.' Those whose only crime was being born were lost from the outset.[246]

* * * *

After arrest came interrogation. The experience of the first interrogation cell, Solzhenitsyn recalled, was like 'nothing in your entire *previous* life or your whole *subsequent* life'.[247] They could be crowded or empty, hot or cold; there were many variations. Sometimes inmates were jammed so closely together that they could scarcely move hands or legs. In the Lubyanka, sixty men were packed into 'the kennel', a space fifteen by fifteen feet, for a week or more.[248] (Try to imagine this: 225 feet...) This was not uncommon elsewhere either.[249] Some prisoners were held in chains, some in cells six inches deep with water. With overcrowding every movement, every use of the toilet, getting up, washing, and so on, had to be strictly regulated by the inmates themselves. In some cells several hundred prisoners covered with lice were forced to stand all day.[250] Some prisoners, like the American

[241] Gellately, *Lenin, Stalin, and Hitler*, p. 61.   [242] Gregory, *Terror by Quota*, p. 268.
[243] Elinor Lipper, *Eleven Years in Soviet Prison Camps* (Hollis & Carter, 1951), p. 51.
[244] Halfin, *Stalinist Confessions*, p. 464.
[245] R. A. Knox, *Enthusiasm: A Chapter in the History of Religion* (Clarendon Press, 1950), p. 133.
[246] Fitzpatrick, *Everyday Stalinism*, p. 79.
[247] Solzhenitsyn, *The Gulag Archipelago*, vol. 1, p. 180.
[248] Conquest, *The Great Terror*, p. 278.
[249] E.g. thirty-five packed into a space of two by three metres in Lvov: Edward Buca, *Vorkuta* (Constable, 1976), p. 14.
[250] Tchernavin, *I Speak for the Silent*, pp. 122, 200–1.

Alexander Dolgun, were alone, and were prevented from sleeping or lying down during the day. 'The prison smell' was everywhere: one of 'ammonia, damp, urine, dirty bodies, a touch of the smell of death'.[251] Where other prisoners were present, one was always a stool pigeon. The interrogator's first task was 'to convince their prisoner that he was no longer a human being and anything could and would be done to him'.[252] His object vis-à-vis the prisoner was 'the complete disintegration of his individual personality', a process which ends, after all the torment, with the person 'reborn' with a 'newly-assembled personality'.[253]

Endless questioning, night after night, sometimes eighteen hours on end, six days a week, often without food, the interrogators changing shifts like a 'conveyor belt', or 'production line' (*konveer*) were common. (How appropriate to 'scientific socialism'—a mechanized confession process.) After two weeks 'you hardly know your own name'.[254] After sixty-one days (another American, here in Budapest), sometimes sixty-five hours continuously, you are 'reduced to such a state of despondency' that you confess to anything.[255] You make up any story, no matter how preposterous, to gain a few hours' rest. But then your story has become truth, and you have incriminated yourself. This might go on for four to five months or more. So some astonishing stories were dreamt up on the spot, like creating artificial volcanoes to blow up the USSR.[256]

Then there were constant confrontations with friends and acquaintances or fellow workers brought in as witnesses, themselves swearing to anything to save themselves and their children, to the point where no friendship seemed to have any value except those made in prison itself. But dystopian sociability too was often defined by betrayal.[257] In the cells people would converse, and then the next day be confronted by any indiscretion. A 'kind of group psychosis' resulted, where people who, a moment earlier, had been on good terms with neighbours, 'suddenly saw them as potential stool-pigeons and provocateurs'.[258] Importuning the GPU about conditions was fruitless; one complainant was told that 'There are no human beings here . . . only humble guardians of the revolution. There's no room for sentiment here. Our tools against enemies of the State are pain and death. The sooner you realize it the better.'[259]

Those arrested, sometimes the cream of Soviet society, were surprised to be told that 'enemies are not people', and that they would be treated like scum.[260] And they were. The 'dross of humanity is an impediment to its progress. So we must eliminate it ruthlessly', they were informed.[261] There was some restraint in Soviet

[251] Dolgun, *Alexander Dolgun's Story*, pp. 28–9, 25.   [252] Razgon, *True Stories*, p. 284.
[253] In Herling's brilliant account (*A World Apart*, pp. 65–7).
[254] Joseph Scholmer, *Vorkuta* (Weidenfeld & Nicolson, 1954), p. 9; Halfin, *Stalinist Confessions*, p. 121.
[255] Robert A. Vogeler, *I Was Stalin's Prisoner* (W. H. Allen, 1952), p. 141.
[256] Beck and Godin, *Russian Purge*, p. 46.
[257] Ginzburg, *Into the Whirlwind*, p. 80: 'There are no more fervent friendships than those made in prison.'
[258] Ibid., p. 126.   [259] Kravchenko, *I Chose Freedom*, p. 157.
[260] Ginzburg, *Into the Whirlwind*, p. 54.
[261] Iulia de Beausobre, *The Woman Who Could Not Die* (Victor Gollancz, 1948), p. 55.

torture before the early 1930s.[262] In June or July 1937, 'special methods'—beatings and very painful torture—became routine for many from the outset.[263] Perhaps nine-tenths were then tortured through the 1940s.[264] Those who 'actually had something to confess usually had an easier time'.[265] An abundance of cruel tortures were meted out (by women too) to extort confessions.

Each local CHEKA seemingly had its own chosen speciality. Over fifty types have been catalogued, including constant beatings, sometimes for days on end; pulling out fingernails; using acid; insects, especially legions of bedbugs; blinding with light; the 'white cell', where everything was painted bright white; near-drowning in cesspools; hanging in excruciating positions; confinement for hours on end in 'standing cells'; kneeling for up to forty-eight hours; great heat which made blood ooze through the pores of the skin; intense cold; crushing the genitals with a boot; burning with cigarettes; confinement in cramped spaces or punishment cells, sometimes damp or awash in water, sometimes overheated, sometimes freezing; weeks of sleep deprivation; endless thirst and hunger; extreme humiliation; crushing prisoners together in confined spaces, sometimes three per square metre, for weeks on end; a barrage of lies and threats; and much more. In Kiev they fixed a tube to the victim and heated it, allowing maddened rats to eat their way through. (Did Orwell know this?) Gold teeth were usually extracted from the dead (or living), to enrich executioners paid by piece rate. Frequently drunk or drugged, a fair number of executioners, to their credit as human beings, subsequently went mad.[266] The worst methods were freely practised in 1937–8, the less extreme throughout the Soviet period. It is difficult enough to write of them, much less to imagine them. One who experienced them reflected: 'Think of the worst agony you can imagine, multiply it by a million times, and you may approach what I went through.'[267]

* * * *

Following interrogation came the inevitable confession. Extracting these, particularly in 1937, proved surprisingly easy. Prisoners, seized by 'psychological madness', enveloped by an inward-looking persecution mania, often embellished absurd accusations with 'fantastic details'. Prosecutors knew most if not all of this was 'a grotesque invention'. But an *Alice in Wonderland* atmosphere pervaded the entire proceedings.[268] Confessions had to occur. They were the raison d'être of the entire process, the proof of its rectitude. Those who did not confess faced the greatest

---

[262] Halfin states that it was not 'widely used in 1936' (*Stalinist Confessions*, p. 141).

[263] Ginzburg, *Into the Whirlwind*, p. 62.   [264] Berger, *Shipwreck of a Generation*, p. 159.

[265] Leona Toker, *Return from the Archipelago: Narratives of Gulag Survivors* (Indiana University Press, 2000), p. 66.

[266] Melgounov, *The Red Terror in Russia*, pp. 177–8, 198, 201–3. Kravchenko mentions rats in prisons, but not their use in torture (*I Chose Freedom*, p. 447).

[267] Kravchenko, *I Chose Freedom*, p. 447.

[268] Weissberg, *Conspiracy of Silence*, pp. 305, 310. A good account of this process is Igor Halfin, 'Stalinist Confessions in an Age of Terror: Messianic Times at the Leningrad Communist Universities', in Michael D. Gordin, Helen Tilley, and Gyan Prakash, eds., *Utopia/Dystopia* (Princeton University Press, 2010), pp. 231–49.

chance of being shot; indeed, they were often given the choice between the two.[269] Interrogators who failed to elicit confessions were in no small danger of becoming victims themselves. The act of confession, even only to an interrogator, satisfied the public demands of the concept of the hypertransparent society. Many who believed themselves innocent fell prey to their own suspicions when confronted with knowing someone else who had been arrested and who had 'confessed'.[270] Once people did confess, they were in the hands of the regime, which could now use them as it pleased. This solved the 'most incomprehensible of Soviet enigmas', the demand for confessions to 'crimes' which not only had not been, but sometimes even theoretically could not have been, committed.[271] From 1937, when torture became the norm in interrogations, confessions from one or other motives came more speedily. In other sectors of Soviet production, shoddiness might get you shot for underperformance. Here, shoddy confessions were positively encouraged. No absurdity was too unreasonable to submit: mass delusion and fantasy reigned with the enthusiasm of Alice's Queen of Hearts.

Some of this was possible because, by the late 1920s, the USSR had become an almost completely closed society where there was no way of knowing what was real or practised elsewhere or how others viewed the Soviet system. Commonly, prisoners were not told why they had been arrested, to encourage them to admit to any 'crime' they might have committed. First they were asked why they thought they had been arrested, a technique supposedly based on studying Inquisition manuals.[272] From the outset, 'guilt' was chiefly a function of class origin, education, and upbringing, 'the questions which must determine the fate of the accused', according to one Chekist. The entire process was embodied in the will of the Party. 'If it is necessary to shoot you', one investigator insisted, 'then you will be shot even if you are altogether innocent. If it is necessary to acquit you, then no matter how guilty you are you will be cleared and acquitted.' For, in reality, *the heart of the matter is not personal guilt, but social danger*.[273] Like the Revolution itself, therefore, the end was everything, the means unimportant. One investigator informed his victim in 1938: 'I know that everything in the written protocol is a pure fable. Still, you must accept the charges. The international situation demands that.' 'If you love the Party', another was told, 'you must sign the investigation protocol.' Other investigators said that making false confessions would help convict real criminals. So Party members readily signed ridiculous confessions if it was 'really needed in the interests of the Party and the Revolution'.[274]

Yet here, ironically, once you were arrested, even when utterly innocent, you ceased to be harmless. You knew 'how rotten the system was' and had to be kept

[269] Tchernavin, *Escape from the Soviets*, p. 107.
[270] 'The mere awareness of this deprived him of the will to defend himself and resist': Mandelstam, *Hope Abandoned*, p. 575.
[271] Ciliga, *The Russian Enigma*, p. 154.
[272] Conquest, *The Great Terror*, p. 306; Roy Medvedev, *Let History Judge: The Origins and Consequences of Stalinism* (Vintage Books, 1973), p. 264.
[273] Solzhenitsyn, *The Gulag Archipelago*, vol. 1, pp. 96, 146, 282.
[274] Halfin, *Stalinist Confessions*, p. 151–3.

inside.[275] Examining magistrates were well aware that few, if any, they were condemning were in fact guilty of any offence. But the system's failures could only be blamed upon enemies. Therefore enemies had to be found. The best confessions named dozens if not hundreds, who often went to their deaths on the basis of a single accusation. Confessions were commonly made up, sometimes without prisoners ever seeing them or even talking with prosecutors. Material was added to those which had been signed. Some accused signed blank pages which were later filled in by their interrogators. Several prisoners genuinely felt a sense of guilt and gladly confessed in the hope of forgiveness. Others thought themselves innocent, but everyone else guilty: for how could so many mistakes be made? Some thought 'innocence' was genuinely in the eyes of the Party, which, lacking any other moral compass or reference point, defined guilt.[276] In a culture so obsessed with labour, to find anyone innocent clearly implied so much wasted resource. In a culture so steeped in guilt, repentance and atonement were, in any case, a relief, and echoed centuries of Christian practice.

Psychologically, the purpose of this process was to ensure that 'the dialectic of inner and outer selves was resolved' so that 'the new, self-transparent individual' was ready to be judged. Here a confession could appear as an 'awakening, a conversion, the adoption of the proper, dialectical view of oneself', a reconciliation of personal and historical narratives. So the most fulfilling denunciation was self-denunciation, the best confession heartfelt confession, a complete surrender begging the Party's forgiveness, knowing it to be all-wise, all-seeing, omnipotent, and immortal. With luck, this might bring psychological release from the unbearable weight of guilt, or the confidence of martyring oneself in the cause or of joining the 'community of the saved' who had 'seen the light', in the Stalinist rewriting of Gnostic theories of transforming people into spiritual beings. This ethereal implication was useful, for the ideal Soviet personality was to be as transparent as the society was intended to be, each aspect mirroring the other, with no space for an inner enemy to hide.

The process Halfin describes as a 'conversion' occurred when interrogator and accused fused in a unified world-view. Here the accused conceded the necessity for their metaphysical 'guilt' because the Revolution demanded it, and then joyfully accepted the higher sacrifice and exoneration this represented, which united them with the conquerors of evil.[277] Thus confession could come as an overwhelming relief in which 'you cleanse your soul of some sort of trash' by speaking 'sincerely and truthfully'.[278] So the 'end' of totalitarianism was fulfilled in two senses, with utterly voluntary compliance even to the death sentence. No more coercion was required, no more 'totalitarianism', no discipline enforced from without, only inner dedication. To *want* to confess, to open oneself to cleansing and healing, was where the Party and

[275] Berger, *Shipwreck of a Generation*, p. 253.
[276] J. A. C. Brown, *Techniques of Persuasion: From Propaganda to Brainwashing* (Penguin Books, 1963), pp. 209–10.
[277] Halfin, *Stalinist Confessions*, pp. 105, 417, 154, 194–5.
[278] Jochen Hellbeck, *Revolution on My Mind: Writing a Diary under Stalin* (Harvard University Press, 2006), p. 110.

the individual could see eye to eye. Winston Smith, we will see in Chapter 7, would gratefully reach this moment. A true confession appeased both sides simultaneously. It dissolved the schizophrenia of the private and public selves. 'When I committed counterrevolutionary deeds', the USSR's most able commander, Marshal Tukhachevskii, confessed, 'I was pitting myself against myself.'[279] The one true self who emerged here was shot shortly after midnight, on 12 June 1937.

This process was a peculiar one for Party loyalists in particular. Millions swallowed up in the maw of this behemoth felt compelled to keep faith in the cause. While betraying them, they apologized to their friends with the excuse that Party discipline needed to be retained.[280] Communism represented a higher moral standard for humanity, and ironically this implied a higher cost could be exacted for failing to meet it. (Here again we see how virtue and terror interact.) Party members were accordingly expected to exercise great self-control and selfless dedication to the cause of proletarian class struggle. By 1929, after the liberalism of the NEP period, even the use of tobacco and alcohol was discouraged. Female comrades were looked down upon if they wore lipstick or affected bourgeois hairstyles (this changed temporarily during a liberal phase in 1934).[281] Party members lived transparently, under constant scrutiny.[282] Any shortcomings required a constant recourse to confession and repentance. Efforts to create a 'totally new type of human being', as Lenin's wife Nadezhda Krupskaia put it, were bound to create great tension in individual identity.[283]

So good communists were encouraged to attest to their crimes if they had faith in the Party.[284] A surprising number (perhaps) shouted 'long live Comrade Stalin' just before being shot, until this was (in some places) prohibited.[285] (What was the penalty for disobedience?) Even after the purges had taken thousands, imprisoned Party members assured themselves that it was all for the good of the cause. And how many in the camps would cry when they heard of Stalin's death?[286] Or, like Marshal Rokossovsky, who had eight teeth knocked out by the NKVD in 1937, would refuse to turn against Stalin after 1956, claiming 'for me, Comrade Stalin is sacred'.[287] For those to whom, like the Leningrad history professor Grigorii Zaidel, 'life outside the Party would be nightmarish torture'—the demotion from comrade to citizen being unbearable—accusations of oppositionism in 1934 called into question an entire being and way of life.[288] People of a 'Party-komsomol [Communist Youth] character' saw such expulsions as 'something between death

---

[279] Halfin, *Stalinist Confessions*, pp. 33, 111, 214.   [280] Conquest, *The Great Terror*, p. 158.
[281] Ibid., p. 449; Beck and Godin, *Russian Purge*, p. 24.
[282] A term derived from the French Revolution (Fitzpatrick and Gellately, *Accusatory Practices*, p. 10).
[283] Quoted in Igal Halfin, *Terror in My Soul: Communist Autobiographies on Trial* (Harvard University Press, 2003), p. 8.
[284] Conquest, *The Great Terror*, pp. 128–33; Nanci Adler, *Keeping Faith with the Party: Communist Believers Return from the Gulag* (Indiana University Press, 2012), pp. 49–50.
[285] Halfin, *Stalinist Confessions*, p. 247.
[286] 'Whoever has doubts about the Party is no longer a communist' was a common belief: Artur London, *The Confession* (William Morrow & Company, 1970), p. 17.
[287] Cohen, *The Victims Return*, p. 67.   [288] Halfin, *Stalinist Confessions*, p. 82.

and civic extinction'.[289] To be ostracized by arrest and expulsion was, in Bukharin's words, to be 'isolated from everybody, an enemy of the people, in an inhuman position, completely isolated from everything that constitutes the essence of life'.[290]

Many thus confessed out of a sense of duty. Some thought they were serving the cause of 'proletarian humanism' and 'communist morality'. Some felt guilty because of their anxiety about being thought guilty. The true Bolshevik was 'ready to believe that black was white, and white was black' if need be, 'if the Party required it', as one put it. So if an omniscient and infallible Party said they were guilty they *were* guilty. Some even complained of being treated too lightly for having, for instance, 'objectively' been 'Trotskyists'.[291] 'Objectively', of course, the Party was always right, the line was always right, because it represented history's march forward towards justice and goodness. For if this power had a metaphysical purpose, it was to embody such goodness.

Much of this seemed plausible to Party members because the Party was such a peculiar organization. It needs thus to be understood as a group as such. Like a secret society or priesthood, it had its own rituals and language, full of elusive allusions which had to be read carefully to determine the current 'line'. The Webbs noted the 'mass conversion to the creed of Lenin' and described it as a 'new religion' like Comtean Positivism.[292] It possessed a history, a metaphysics, a martyrology, a set of sacred texts, and a strong sense of common endeavour. It was a complete, hermetically sealed, self-sufficing, and all-explaining world-view, less a religion, perhaps, than the first meta-religion, for it also purported to unmask religion as a sham and to replace it by real, immanent history. It was consciously constructed as an ideal group with the capacity to grant a wholly meaningful life. It was thus difficult not to slip into what was termed the 'communist conceit' of being the 'chosen people'.[293] *Partiinost*, the 'sense of party', or partyness, was better than family, above blood, nobler, more exalted, more all-encompassing, akin to 'human-ness'.

In order to grasp this we must imagine for a moment that loyalty to nation, class, religion, ethnicity, locality, one's football team, and so on are all rolled into one— think of the intensity! Membership was often conceived of as 'birth' or 'rebirth', and its loss as akin to 'social death', worse for some even than death itself. Most members underwent something like a spiritual conversion in becoming communists. This was indeed, as Jochen Hellbeck has written, 'the founding experience for a Communist', whose life was accordingly categorized into 'an early phase marked by backwardness, passivity and lack of consciousness and a mature, active, and conscious phase induced by exposure to the teachings of the Communist Party'.[294] Wherever possible, 'spiritual breaks' from the past were encouraged, especially from unacceptable class

[289] Solonevich, *Escape from Russian Chains*, p. 269.

[290] Quoted in Fitzpatrick, *Everyday Stalinism*, p. 19.

[291] London, *The Confession*, pp. 316, 313, 110 (quoting Kierkegaard), 144, 393.

[292] Sidney and Beatrice Webb, *Soviet Communism: A New Civilisation* (2 vols, Longmans, Green & Co., 1941), vol. 2, pp. 699, 896; vol. 1, p. 392.

[293] William G. Rosenberg, ed., *Bolshevik Visions: First Phase of the Cultural Revolution in Russia* (University of Michigan Press, 1990), pp. 39–40, 94; Adler, *Keeping Faith with the Party*, pp. 33, 36.

[294] Hellbeck, *Revolution on My Mind*, p. 319.

viewpoints. Children were to be taught 'to nurture an absolutely instinctive reaction of passionate hatred toward our class opponents'.[295] Achieving a true Bolshevik outlook could require an arduous spiritual odyssey if the distance implied by class origin or past associations was considerable. In a regime where all other organizations were insignificant, and every privilege which made life pleasant resulted from Party membership, the sense of self-worth associated with belonging to it was thus extraordinarily powerful, beyond even normal religious affiliation. This was, indeed, one of the most extraordinary groups ever deliberately created. It epitomized group-ishness. If the Bolsheviks aimed 'to collectivise the self', this was the result.[296]

* * * *

After confession came what passed for a trial. Sentences ('administrative penalties') were often determined by directives (that of 1937: ten years, twenty years, execution by shooting; that of 1943: twenty years, death by hanging; that of 1949: twenty-five years for everyone). They were delivered as an assembly line of shoddy judgements. The 'trial', at least in the late 1930s, when hundreds of thousands were being processed daily, might last two minutes, and 'everyone understood it was a farce'.[297] Sometimes there was no trial at all, only 'extra-judicial procedures'. Abolished in 1917, the death penalty was reintroduced in 1918, increasingly used after 1930, and extended to twelve-year-olds in 1935. It was applied in perhaps 10 per cent of cases. Normally the worst sentence was twenty-five years. But some special categories of prisoners were not tried but given unlimited sentences by three-person committees. People could also be exiled without any criminal charge whatsoever. Curiously, there were no professional executioners, and sometimes prosecutors were even drafted in to do the job.[298]

Following the verdict, which besides incarceration often included confiscation of all property and deprivation of rank or title, the sentence commenced. Thousands condemned to the 'supreme measure', 'the highest decree', 'to be sent to the moon', 'to the left', 'to be written off the books', 'to spend seven kopeks', waited lengthy periods for these metaphors to materialize.[299] Consumed by fear, some 'turned gray in three or four days before their cellmates' eyes'.[300] For the rest, a lengthy journey commenced. The living and the dying were crammed together for weeks in rail carriages, some labelled 'special equipment'. Some spent long weeks in holding camps, where nationalities often banded together. Thieves helped each other, politicals helped each other, priests helped each other.[301] Group identity was vital to survival. Tens of thousands never reached their destination. One overburdened ship bound for the frozen north got caught in the ice floes. The following spring its 12,000 inmates were all dead.[302]

* * * *

[295] Rosenberg, *Bolshevik Visions*, p. 45.   [296] Halfin, *Stalinist Confessions*, p. 430.
[297] Solzhenitsyn, *The Gulag Archipelago*, vol. 1, pp. 291, 293.
[298] Krivitsky, *In Stalin's Secret Service*, p. 126.   [299] Tchernavin, *I Speak for the Silent*, p. 159.
[300] Solzhenitsyn, *The Gulag Archipelago*, vol. 1, p. 453.
[301] Walter J. Ciszek, *With God in Russia* (Peter Davies, 1965), pp. 112, 123, 167.
[302] Robert Conquest, *Kolyma* (Macmillan, 1978), p. 26.

'An Empire based on slave labour':[303] The Gulag
'Whoever is not in prison—will be there; whoever was in prison—will return
there'

(Soviet saying, 1929).[304]

*'[T]he GPU in the USSR is not simply a state institution, it is actually a state
within a state.* The GPU has its own troops, its own navy, millions of its own
subjects (the prisoners in camps), its own territory where Soviet authority and
laws do not function. The GPU issues its own currency, forbids its subjects to
use Soviet currency and does not accept it in its stores. The GPU proclaims its
own laws for its subjects, has its own jurisdiction and prisons. It . . . maintains
its own industry, parallel to Soviet industry.'[305]

Then came the camp.[306] This was not for punishment, for the term was removed
from the Soviet vocabulary and replaced by 'measures of social defense'.[307] Compared to the prisons where all were held prior to sentencing, here there was 'military
discipline and martial law'.—'For refusal to work, the dungeon, and for a second
offense—shooting.' Here the life of a horse was worth that of ten men—and why
not? Horses never became Trotskyites.[308]

The acronym 'Gulag' stands for chief administration of corrective labour
camps. As the extract above indicates, the camps were a world apart from Soviet
reality. In the state inside the state prison, *carcerotopia* (or OGPUtopia) perhaps
a third of the working class were slaves in all but name. Entire industries,
including forestry and gold and uranium mining, were run by convicts. Some
14 million were at work in 1938.[309] Not all prisoners were remote; some were
in the centre of Moscow, building flats. There were many types of camp, from
extreme punishment and hard labour (*katorga*) camps, where inmates wore
chains and had no mattresses at night, to relatively mild ones. All had punishment blocks or 'Stalin villas' attached to them which were 'virtually death
camps'.[310] Some camps, like Tayshet, held as many as 100,000 inmates in the
1940s. At the Vorkuta mine camp complex above the Arctic Circle, a million
were still labouring when 'the wisest of the wise, the greatest of all geniuses, the
most brilliant of all commanders' died in 1953.[311] Tsar Nicholas I had deemed
it unsuitable for exiles. But even Vorkuta had its own special hell, the isolation
camps on the island of Novaya Zemlya, 150 miles further north, from which no
one returned.

Aside from the condemned classes already mentioned (chiefly the bourgeoisie
and *kulaks*), the Gulag system did not aim at outright murder. There were output
norms to consider, despite the never-ending supply of labour. The administrators

---

[303] Buca, *Vorkuta*, p. 39.   [304] Tchernavin, *I Speak for the Silent*, p. 37.
[305] Ibid., p. 281.
[306] A good survey of Gulag memoirs is Toker's *Return from the Archipelago*.
[307] Heller and Nekrich, *Utopia in Power*, p. 219.
[308] Kitchin, *Prisoner of the OGPU*, pp. 46, 115.
[309] Ciliga, *The Russian Enigma*, p. 250; Beck and Godin, *Russian Purge*, p. 74.
[310] Lipper, *Eleven Years in Soviet Prison Camps*, p. 166.
[311] Kopelev, *No Jail for Thought*, p. 33.

were also greedy and loved power.[312] Common criminals (*urka*) mostly ran the huts. They had no sympathy for 'politicals', though they usually refused to collaborate with the administration. Those who collaborated, the *suki*, were in constant tension with those who refused, the *blatnoy*. As with rival nationalities, Balts, Germans, Jews, Poles, Ukrainians, and the rest, divide and conquer was the basic method of rule. (Anti-Semitism was common enough, but aside from the real Nazis, Germans prisoners were often friendly with the Jews.)[313] Teaching prisoners not to 'defend or support each other' was 'precisely the goal of the authorities'.[314] Within these groups there was some solidarity. Outside there was little. Sadism was hardly unknown, but did not occur on a murderous scale. At Vorkuta, for instance, beating was rare, and guards and prisoners often reached an accommodation.[315] Yet abuse of prisoners was common. They were exposed for hours or days to swarms of mosquitoes or gnats which could actually darken the skies, or were beaten, or crippled by frostbite. You might end up in a punishment cell lying down, scarcely able to move, *for six months*.[316] Or not even be able to lie down, but to be bent, hunched forwards, for days, until you were crippled. Or be shot for any reason, or none at all. (Dum-dum bullets were used for maximum damage.) In some random cases hundreds were killed. Sometimes the executioners shared the same fate in the next purge.[317] Self-inflicted wounds were also not uncommon: you lasted longer in the hospital.

For millions, the camps became a death sentence inflicted by poor diet and hygiene, oppressive labour, appalling living conditions, and the fierce climate. Isolation was common—the many lumber camps were often hundreds of miles from anything but trees. 'Starvation was routine': the size of the food ration—a few hundred grams of so-called 'bread' and a watery substance, 'tea'—was the measure of life and death, though this diet, of course, assured death anyway.[318] Many camps made that described in Solzhenitsyn's classic *A Day in the Life of Ivan Denisovich* (1962), which has been called 'surely the most important book published in the Soviet Union in modern times',[319] appear like 'one in which you could happily have spent a lifetime'.[320] A few months in, many turned inmates into *dochodiagi*, walking corpses weighing as little as thirty-five kilos who begged or licked spilt food from the floor.[321]

---

[312] Solzhenitsyn, *The Gulag Archipelago*, vol. 3, p. 221; vol. 1, p. 152: 'The passion for gain was their universal passion.'

[313] Scholmer, *Vorkuta*, p. 91. A number of former Gestapo and SD (Sicherheitsdienst) employees reached high positions in Vorkuta, including some convicted of killing Jews under the German occupation (p. 96).

[314] Varlam Shalamov, *Kolyma Tales* (W. W. Norton & Co., 1980), p. 90.

[315] Buca, *Vorkuta*, p. 81; Scholmer, *Vorkuta*, p. 151; during the famous strike here in 1953 many soldiers took the side of the strikers (p. 223).

[316] Solzhenitsyn, *The Gulag Archipelago*, vol. 2, p. 418.

[317] See Janusz Bardach, *Man is Wolf to Man: Surviving the Gulag* (Scribner, 2003), p. 201, for a case at Magadan.

[318] Ibid., pp. 133, 234. Others point out that the care of the ill was much better in the Gulag: Berger, *Shipwreck of a Generation*, p. 198.

[319] Kopelev, *No Jail for Thought*, p. 267.   [320] Mandelstam, *Hope Abandoned*, p. 612.

[321] 'If you have never experienced real hunger it is impossible to say how you would behave', remarked Buca (*Vorkuta*, p. 130). This was his own weight (p. 152).

Poor nutrition and hygiene produced skin diseases, scurvy, dysentery, and eventually death. Vermin, stench, and overcrowding were normal.

The mortality rates thus defy belief. Vast ill-conceived and hastily pursued projects swallowed millions. The death rate in the worst camps was *c*.30 per cent per annum, with an average of *c*.18 per cent.[322] The White Sea–Baltic Canal, on which 500,000 laboured and which proved both unnecessary and inadequate, alone claimed 250,000 lives. In one camp of 600, only a solitary prisoner remained after six years. Entire campfuls of new arrivals died within weeks. In Narym, in 1930–1, 8–12 per cent of the children died *per month*. Twenty-eight thousand—*every single one*—expired at the infamous coal mines of Vorkuta within a year. Here mass deaths were the norm from 1942–7 in particular. In the quarries of Spassk in 1948, *zeki* (ordinary convicts) worked at 35°C below zero in summer clothing. Few lasted longer than two months. A hundred a day died during winter.[323] The intellectuals and upper classes, the least fit, died first. It did not matter: queues of new inmates were usually forming behind them. Soviet modernity was constructed from their bones. There was little pretence of re-education here: work was the thing. (A Gulag slogan was the biblical 'He who does not work shall not eat.')[324]

Most camps employed prisoners in mining, canal digging, road and railway building, and tree felling, in appalling conditions. Again the quota, production norms, the idea of production itself, of humanity defined by productivity, directed everything. No fulfilment, no humanity. This was Social Darwinian 'fitness' personified. Within each type of camp, treatment also varied according to the offence, with common criminals enjoying many privileges, and counter-revolutionaries, especially 'Trotskyists', suffering the harshest conditions. *Katorga* convicts sentenced to the severest forms of labour, often in the mines, were transported in chains. Known solely by their numbers, they were permitted a blanket only after three years of good conduct.[325] Even by Gulag standards the mortality rate in such conditions was extraordinary. At Stalin's insistence 'the "coddling" of prisoners was stopped in the labour camps in 1937, and the death rate soared'.[326] During the war, when camp conditions deteriorated markedly, some *zeks* were able to volunteer for the front in the hope of eventual freedom. They then found that their sentences were increased at the war's end.

In this terrifying narrative, the vast gold-mining region of Kolyma in the Arctic Circle, one of the most isolated regions on earth, occupies a special place. Here, where the temperature once reached -97.8°C, 'the central aim was to kill off the prisoners'. For fulfilling impossible work norms, rations were not adequate even when full (800 grams of not always edible bread daily). When prisoners faltered, rations were reduced to 500 and then 300 grams, which meant a speedy death. (At Auschwitz, we will see in Chapter 4, it was 350 grams per day, but soup

[322] Courtois et al., *The Black Book of Communism*, pp. 226–7.
[323] Solzhenitsyn, *The Gulag Archipelago*, vol. 3, pp. 10, 63.
[324] Lipper, *Eleven Years in Soviet Prison Camps*, p. 255. See 2 Thessalonians 3:10: 'this we commanded you, that if any would not work, neither should he eat'.
[325] Lipper, *Eleven Years in Soviet Prison Camps*, p. 169.
[326] Conquest, *Inside Stalin's Secret Police*, pp. 49–50.

sometimes appeared at lunch.) In a month, the healthiest were reduced to wrecks. During the short summer, prisoners were tormented by mosquitoes the size of wasps and the camps were like 'Auschwitz without ovens'. In face of this almost everything else seemed soft. Here, where there were many intellectuals and scientists, administrators and Party officials, the entire area was controlled directly by the NKVD. The death rate early on (1932–3) reached 98 per cent in some areas. Often it averaged 20 per cent per annum. Shootings occurred at Kolyma for many reasons or none; there were c.26,000 in 1938.[327]

In the camps, amnesia was the recommended therapy for the new self shorn of most of its humanity. Wherever you were, numbers replaced names, as many as three per person, several inches tall, prominently sewn onto caps, trouser legs, and backs. They were, one recalled, 'the prime symbol of our slavery, of our demotion from human being to object'.[328] Remembering one's previous life only invited despondency. Only a rigorous 'discipline of oblivion', which also eliminated hope for the future, made everyday life tolerable.[329] Yet the hint was offered, in the oft-repeated slogan, that 'Through hard labour you become free.' This *might* mean that you *might* live if you got the full rations which fulfilling your daily labour might norm gain you.[330] (It might also mean that hard work would kill you, thus freeing you from life's responsibilities.) Little by little people were 'ground down by inhuman forms of life' until, for many, 'normal notions of good and evil, of what is permissible and what is not' disappeared. People would kill for a piece of bread, and did. If they had twenty-five-year sentences, they might only get a few months more, having already reached the maximum. It made murder seem reasonable, and forgettable, in the circumstances. Anyway, there was constant fear of 'new blows', transfers to worse camps, more severe punishments, more calloused guards. There was indeed 'plenty to be afraid of'.[331] But sometimes mutual aid did occur; camp 'friendships were about one thing: trust'.[332] So, paradoxically, we see that they do tell us something about utopia.

From early on, the main rationale for the camps was economic. In a grim parody of the capitalism it aimed to supersede in the name of humanity, millions endured vastly worse conditions here than under capitalism in order to attain the paradise of modernity at breakneck speed. Communism had to prove itself the superior economic system. Like the Americans whose technology they so admired, the Bolsheviks were also obsessed with work as redemption and salvation. The USSR was, to a substantial degree, a slave state, *carcerotopia*, or in Eugene Lyons' words, a 'dungeon'.[333] The largest proportion of those arrested provided slave labour.[334]

[327] Conquest, *Kolyma*, p. 58.
[328] Hochschild, *The Unquiet Ghost*, pp. 237, 262, 281; Adler, *Keeping Faith with the Party*, p. 132; Dolgun, *Alexander Dolgun's Story*, p. 275.
[329] Terence Des Pres, *The Survivor: An Anatomy of Life in the Death Camps* (Oxford University Press, 1976), pp. 185–7.
[330] Dolgun, *Alexander Dolgun's Story*, p. 130.
[331] Evgenia Semyonova Ginzburg, *Within the Whirlwind*, (Collins/Harvill, 1967), pp. 13, 69–70.
[332] Bardach, *Man is Wolf to Man*, p. 208.   [333] Lyons, *Assignment in Utopia*, p. 524.
[334] Lipper, *Eleven Years in Soviet Prison Camps*, p. vii; Courtois et al., *The Black Book of Communism*, p. 417.

The 'leading idea of the Archipelago—*forced labor*' was suggested by Lenin by December 1917. The combination of revenge, paranoia, and an all-consuming need for slave labour, especially to develop the north and Siberia, guaranteed the system's expansion until Stalin's death. And even fifteen years later, some claimed that, for political prisoners, things were 'just as horrific as in Stalin's time'.[335]

There is little agreement, however, on the total numbers involved, for no one knows. In 1916, under the Tsar, there were about 142,399 prisoners.[336] By 1930, there were some 660,000. Then expansion came: to as many as 5 million in 1932, perhaps 7 million in 1939, with 15 million incarcerated between 1930 and 1937, most of whom died in camps.[337] By 1939, perhaps 8 million, 9 per cent of the adult population, were in the camps. By now the NKVD had swallowed some 18 per cent of the national budget, and provided about 20 per cent of all labour.[338] Others estimate that the largest prison camp system ever known comprised over 2 million in 1941 (1 per cent of a population of 196 million), and over 5 million in 1945 (2 per cent of 170 million), falling to 2.4 million in 1953, with 2–3 million prisoners dying over some twenty years.[339] Some 20 million or one-eighth of the population may have been arrested during the 1930s, and 4–7 million shot or died while imprisoned between 1935 and 1941.[340] Others estimate a minimum of 5 per cent and maximum of 10 per cent of the population were incarcerated.[341] At the upper end are estimates of 50 million deaths (compared to 20 million killed in World War II).[342] A further 1.5 million returning Soviet POWs and soldiers who had experienced life outside the USSR were sent directly to the camps from 1944 onwards (those who were not shot straightaway).

These figures have tended to decline somewhat in recent decades. Solzhenitsyn estimated about 50 million prisoners. Others propose 20–25 million, or up to 15 per cent of the population, with 14–18 million imprisoned between 1929 and 1953; another 6–7 million being deported; and 1.75–3 million dying between 1930 and 1953, or around 1 per cent of the population. Some 4–5 million children probably passed through the camps.[343] Some eyewitnesses thought as many as 80 per cent of prisoners died there.[344] A recent study gives about 3.4 million deaths in total by shooting, in camps or on the way to them.[345] Other recent estimates give an average of 1.3 to 2.4 million in the camps per annum from 1936 to 1953,

335 Anatoly Marchenko, *My Testimony* (Pall Mall Press, 1969), p. 3.
336 Heller and Nekrich, *Utopia in Power*, p. 219.
337 Utley, *The Dream We Lost*, pp. 241, 253–4; Ivan Solonevich, *Russia in Chains* (Williams & Norgate, 1938), p. 21.
338 Heller and Nekrich, *Utopia in Power*, p. 316.   339 Conquest, *Kolyma*, pp. 16–17, 227.
340 Arthur Koestler estimated some 20 million out of a population of 170 million: *The Yogi and the Commissar* (Jonathan Cape, 1945), p. 186.
341 Edwin Bacon, *The Gulag at War: Stalin's Forced Labour System in the Light of the Archives* (Macmillan, 1994), pp. 36–7.
342 Berger, *Shipwreck of a Generation*, p. 248.
343 Applebaum, *Gulag Voices*, p. ix; Cohen, *The Victims Return*, p. 29.
344 Buca, *Vorkuta*, p. 285.
345 Steven A. Barnes, *Death and Redemption: The Gulag and the Shaping of Soviet Society* (Princeton University Press, 2011), pp. 1–2; Adler, *Keeping Faith with the Party*, p. 4.

indicating that one adult in six spent time in a camp.[346] This suggests that one member of every family was jailed—and far more amongst the educated classes. Others suggest 8–15 million prisoners in the immediate post-war period.[347] As many as 9 million Ukrainians died from 1917 to 1953, in camps or otherwise—small wonder that so many hated Stalin enough to support the German invasion in 1941.[348] Perhaps 12–30 million were consumed in total outside the wars. Twenty million killed in the camps and purges is a compromise figure often given.[349]

* * * *

If by chance you survived all this and served out your time, you were hardly 'free'. Not infrequently prisoners were not released on time, but years later. Like Kafka's K., you were only 'provisionally free', and liable to rearrest at any magistrate's whim.[350] So too 'liberty' often meant 'deprived of exile', forbidden to return home, without the right to live in any of the 135 largest cities in the country or have any kind of decent job.[351] Nearly all, leaving the camp gates, stopped a few paces later to wait for the guards to catch up with them, by force of habit.[352] Once they proceeded, the shock of 'freedom' killed not a few. Others were run over by buses or died in drunken accidents. The nightmares and paranoia would continue for years.[353] Isolated, shunned, both feared and afraid, confused, ex-prisoners were often exiled in remote areas, often still at hard labour under NKVD surveillance. Once 'we had been declared enemies', it was evident, 'the state would ever assert the right of the stronger and trample us, crush us, squash us, until the day we died'. Many doubtless felt that they were 'no longer a human being' after 'every imaginable human feeling' had been purged from them.[354]

The camp system was not abolished until 1960, and its extent not revealed even to the Party until Khrushchev's famous 'secret' speech at the 1956 Party Congress. Despite all the bitterness, some former prisoners remained devoted to the Soviet system, unable and/or unwilling to abandon their basic lifelong beliefs, some proud

[346] Bacon, *The Gulag at War*, p. 24; Nicolas Werth, 'The Crimes of the Stalin Regime', in Dan Stone, ed., *The Historiography of Genocide* (Palgrave Macmillan, 2010), pp. 403–4 (who gives 20 million as the total number of prisoners, and 1.8 million deaths in the camps). But other estimates put the number much higher, with a grand total of probably 20–30 million. Steven Rosefielde gives 13–20 million prisoners for 1929–53, but the total dying in the Gulag at only *c.*1.6 million (*Red Holocaust* (Routledge, 2010), p. 20). Rudy Rummel (*Lethal Politics: Soviet Genocide and Mass Murder since 1917* (Transaction Publishers, 1990)) estimates 62 million deaths between 1917 and 1987, of which 55 million were Soviet citizens. Getty and Naumov, *The Road to Terror*, pp. 587–94, suggest *c.*3.5 million deaths through execution or 'custodial mortality'. Martin Malia accepts 20 million deaths (*The Soviet Tragedy: A History of Socialism in Russia, 1917–1991* (Free Press, 1994), p. 263). By contrast, about 20 million died in total in World War I, and 26.5 million Soviets in World War II.
[347] Conquest, *The Great Terror*, p. 317; Heller and Nekrich, *Utopia in Power*, p. 493.
[348] Scholmer, *Vorkuta*, pp. 114–15.
[349] Solzhenitsyn, *The Gulag Archipelago*, vol. 2, p. 10. Solzhenitsyn here posits 66 million as a possible figure.
[350] Franz Kafka, *The Trial* (Everyman's Library, 1992), p. 173.
[351] Solzhenitsyn, *The Gulag Archipelago*, vol. 3, pp. 407, 446.
[352] Ciszek, *With God in Russia*, p. 217.   [353] Cohen, *The Victims Return*, p. 74.
[354] [Zajdlerowa], *The Dark Side of the Moon*, p. 106.

of remaining 'Leninists' in defiance of Stalin.[355] Others lived in constant fear the rest of their lives, even long after release. For the authorities knew well that anyone who had been arrested had a grudge against the system and was thus a potential enemy of the people. Their arrest itself had made them such.[356]

Terror and Everyday Life

The piercing searchlight of suspicion pointed by the CHEKA and its successors reached so far into Soviet society that few corners were left unilluminated. In twenty-four years of terror, 'every family, in both the countryside and the cities' was affected.[357] Daily life for anyone under suspicion was like living 'under floodlights in glass houses equipped with loud speakers'.[358] In the late 1930s, in particular, the entire population seemed divided into the 'absolutely loyal' and the 'counter-revolutionary', and most people felt themselves to be under observation.[359] The threat of imminent or inevitable arrest hung over most of Soviet life like the blackest imaginable cloud, creating a climate of 'perpetual fear' and achieving the 'complete intimidation of the people'. Thousands lived, the eyewitness Eugene Lyons recorded,

> in a state of chronic terror, their little suitcases always packed, though they worked diligently and avoided even facial expressions which might cast doubt on their loyalty. To awaken in their own beds in the morning was a daily miracle for such people. The sound of a doorbell at an unusual hour left them limp and trembling.[360]

Trust—the chief factor in a calm and satisfying life, the definitive quality of utopia— was almost entirely eradicated. 'The loss of mutual trust is the first sign of the atomization of society in dictatorships of our type, and that is just what our leaders wanted', wrote Nadezhda Mandelstam.[361] 'Fear sat deep within us', remembered Lev Razgon. 'No personal qualities could provide the necessary immunity to that constant anxiety.'[362] Fear indeed has been described as 'the foremost factor of life in the Soviet Union': this one frozen emotion epitomized dystopia.[363] Enveloped in cocoons of self-protection, individuals often abandoned all types of mutual assistance. 'Fear had devoured kindness, compassion, conscience, everything in people', wrote Anatoli Rybakov.[364] Nerves had already started to unravel in the 1920s. Then came the hastening retreat into interiority, peeling away layer after layer of sociability until—the desired effect—one was socially naked, stripped bare. Plucked: all the easier to devour. And the Man of Steel was insatiably hungry.

By 1938, half the urban population were on NKVD suspect lists.[365] The USSR was now a Chekist state: theoretically the Party ruled, but in 'practice we were helpless pawns in a game played by a police regime according to rules of its own

---

355 For some examples, see Adler, *Keeping Faith with the Party*.   356 Rybakov, *Fear*, p. 418.
357 Cohen, *The Victims Return*, p. 33.
358 Lyons, *Assignment in Utopia*, p. 602.   359 Rybakov, *Fear*, p. 113.
360 Lyons, *Assignment in Utopia*, p. 347.   361 Mandelstam, *Hope against Hope*, p. 95.
362 Razgon, *True Stories*, p. 256.   363 Lipper, *Eleven Years in Soviet Prison Camps*, pp. vi–vii.
364 Rybakov, *Fear*, p. 371.   365 Beck and Godin, *Russian Purge*, p. 202.

making'.[366] In that year, Anastas Mikoyan (known as 'the survivor'—he died in 1978) reiterated the need for every Soviet citizen to become an NKVD operative.[367] And indeed mutual surveillance became 'the reliable bedrock of Soviet power'.[368] Five per cent of the population (but a far larger percentage of educated people) had been arrested by the time the NKVD Chief Yezhov was overthrown and executed in 1940, with perhaps 3 million killed during 1937–40.[369] Such astonishingly large numbers were taken in some places—a *quarter* of Leningrad's population during the mass arrests—that virtually everyone must have been perpetually afraid.[370]

Terror and purge generated a new language which eventually pervaded Soviet life. Terms like 'unmasking enemies', 'suppressing criticism from below', 'wreckers', 'Trotskyist centre', 'family circles', 'lickspittles', 'diversionists', and 'toadies' provided a new sense of alienation and antagonism.[371] Enemies were 'neutralized' or 'liquidated', in newspeak jargon. 'Innocence' became an empty category where all were suspect. (Even babies with the wrong class pedigree were, after all, 'guilty'.) Indeed, the logic of the system made it difficult to conceive that it was possible to be innocent even in principle. Solzhenitsyn wrote that 'the very concept of guilt' had been 'repealed by the proletarian revolution'.[372] But equally it was also replaced by universal guilt. Any hesitation in zeal, a moment of slacking, a tired mistake, being late to work, was evidence of inadequacy. Who was *not* guilty of not performing at 100 per cent efficiency and not fulfilling unattainable work norms? Unyielding loyalty to the Party line was of little avail if that line changed suddenly and without warning, making one a counter-revolutionary 'anti-Party' element. 'Anti-Soviet' sentiments might lurk below the mask of consciousness, eating the body away like a disease. And so, if like the academic Trofimov, it was found that 'he always had Trotskyism buried in him', like some secret virus, it had to be rooted out and purged.[373]

Failure to consult the Party line on any public issue was thus dangerous—a teacher was chastised for not condemning the 'Trotskyist platform' in dealing with the issue as to whether pupils should bring their lunch to school. Similar perils resulted when the Party line on lipstick, jewellery, makeup, and Christmas trees changed in 1936.[374] Souls could be disloyal, feelings anti-revolutionary, dreams most treacherous of all. Stalin vowed in 1937 that 'anyone who by his actions or thoughts—yes, even thoughts! encroaches on the unity of the Soviet state' should be destroyed.[375] So 'thoughtcrime', in Orwell's later term, indeed existed. The daily toll taken in alcohol, drugs, bad temper, general anxiety, and ill-feeling was enormous. Plagued by his own demons, Stalin has himself been portrayed as a victim of events, reacting to circumstances rather than orchestrating mass murder.

---

[366] Kravchenko, *I Chose Freedom*, p. 172.
[367] Simon Sebag Montefiore, *Stalin: The Court of the Red Czar* (Phoenix, 2007), p. 263.
[368] Kharkhordin, *The Collective and the Individual in Russia*, p. 110.
[369] Conquest, *The Great Terror*, p. 317. Yezhov wrote: 'Tell Stalin that I shall die with his name on my lips': Getty and Naumov, *The Road to Terror*, p. 553.
[370] Solzhenitsyn, *The Gulag Archipelago*, vol. 1, p. 13.
[371] See Goldman, *Terror and Democracy in the Age of Stalin*, p. 8.
[372] Solzhenitsyn, *The Gulag Archipelago*, vol. 1, p. 76.
[373] Halfin, *Stalinist Confessions*, p. 203.   [374] Beck and Godin, *Russian Purge*, pp. 19, 24.
[375] Quoted in Halfin, *Terror in My Soul*, p. 11.

Particularly after his wife's suicide, he too suffered psychologically from the system, though this did not stem the flood of death warrants.[376] It is difficult to shed a tear for those who carried them out. Nonetheless, we may recall, in assessing the fear it produced, the brutalizing effects upon them as well. Had Soviet psychiatry not itself been part of the system, its expansion would have outstripped any plan set.

Stalinism thus penetrated deeply into 'ordinary life':[377] 'Fear by night, and a feverish effort by day to pretend enthusiasm for a system of lies, was the permanent condition of the Soviet citizen.'[378] This was quite intentional. As early as 1924, Lenin's wife, Nadezhda Krupskaia, warned that 'We must strive to bind our private life to the struggle for and the construction of communism.' 'Everyday life is not a private affair', exhorted *Pravda* in 1938, 'it is the most crucial zone of the class struggle.'[379] The casualties of this struggle included much of what makes life worth living. Humour had already 'disappeared altogether' by the 1920s—the Dobu would have felt quite at home. By the late 1920s people began to shy away from all political conversations, then from associating with anyone who had been arrested or was suspected, then from intellectuals. To glance at someone in the street who was under suspicion—an unperson—was to court suspicion. So people looked away. By the late 1930s Moscow's citizens were 'walking the streets like automatons, their already dead eyes glazed by the worst terror in the country'. Some came to 'fear strangers like the plague'.[380] To an impressive degree, evidently, people simply stopped talking entirely.[381] Many doubtless regretted that, perhaps voluble in vodka, they could not. 'Chatterers' who told anti-Soviet jokes or gossip (58:10, usually five to ten years) filled the cells in 1937. Privacy, Halfin writes, was regarded as a 'bourgeois fetish', and good Bolsheviks were proud to proclaim, 'I never seclude myself in the shell of personal life.' Less good Bolsheviks, however, like the genuine Trotskyist Victor Serge, complained that, 'We lived in a house of glass, our least gestures and remarks spied upon.'[382] Zamyatin, we will see, would have smiled in bitter irony.

Though, Nadezhda Mandelstam recalled, working-class homes seemingly enjoyed greater freedom of speech, people soon learned to hold their tongues (see Fig. 3.4).[383] The Soviet Union became a nation of 'whisperers', in Orlando Figes' apt phrase.[384] Even in Moscow's prisons it was forbidden 'to speak above a whisper'.[385] Joseph Berger thought, 'While Stalin was alive there had been a complete paralysis of public opinion. No two people could speak freely to each other; few indeed had courage enough to face even their own opinions.'[386] 'We live in a country where everyone around us wears a mask. Trust no one, no one, with your thoughts', one

---

[376] Robert Thurston, *Life and Terror in Stalin's Russia, 1934–1941* (Yale University Press, 1996), pp. 227–8.
[377] See generally Fitzpatrick, *Everyday Stalinism.*   [378] Conquest, *The Great Terror*, p. 278.
[379] Hellbeck, *Revolution on My Mind*, p. 87.
[380] Mandelstam, *Hope Abandoned*, pp. 123, 98, 50.   [381] Rybakov, *Fear*, p. 303.
[382] Halfin, *Stalinist Confessions*, p. 429.   [383] Mandelstam, *Hope against Hope*, p. 336.
[384] Orlando Figes, *The Whisperers: Private Life in Stalin's Russia* (Allen Lane, 2007).
[385] Margarete Buber, *Under Two Dictators* (Victor Gollancz, 1949), pp. 31–2.
[386] Berger, *Shipwreck of a Generation*, p. 238.

Fig. 3.4. Keep Your Tongue Behind the Teeth! (1941 Soviet poster).

victim of the purges recalled. 'Everlasting distrust' and 'everlasting Soviet suspicion' characterized all relationships:[387] 'Everybody was afraid of everybody else: not even the "safest" person was immune.'[388] Seeing 'a potential informer in every neighbour and every colleague', the sense of a private sphere or self shrivelled perceptibly.[389] Even deep and genuine friendships ended when people realized that they might have to report on each other. Isaak Babel wrote that a man only talked 'freely to his wife—at night, with the blankets pulled over his head'.[390] People who had telephones put pillows on them in case there were microphones. At night they sat in the dark—whole towns—rather than draw attention to themselves. In public they could be seen trembling. It was a condition sometimes 'bordering on dementia', Nadezhda Mandelstam recalled: 'We all became slightly unbalanced mentally—not exactly ill, but not normal either: suspicious, mendacious, confused and inhibited in our speech, at the same time putting on a show of adolescent optimism.'[391]

[387] Kravchenko, *I Chose Freedom*, pp. 165, 450; Tchernavin, *I Speak for the Silent*, p. 7.
[388] Mandelstam, *Hope against Hope*, pp. 300–1.   [389] Mandelstam, *Hope Abandoned*, p. 570.
[390] Conquest, *Reflections on a Ravaged Century*, p. 111.
[391] Mandelstam, *Hope against Hope*, pp. 33, 320, 360, 88.

'Wearing the mask', even the 'thick mask', thus became an institutionalized part of Stalinist life for anyone with a past to conceal, and many others too.[392] Forged documents attesting to 'good' class origins were common. Male Party members were enjoined not to take wives from an 'alien class', as if blue blood might dilute red.[393] (The ontology of class parallels that of race elsewhere.) Privacy was also reduced by building new housing blocks in which family units shared a communal kitchen, or by other contrived communal arrangements. (The less fortunate, particularly in the new industrial towns, lived in barracks.) Many disliked forced sharing, as well as, particularly for women, who were cooking for others, caring for their children, cleaning their mess.[394] But less privacy meant less heresy. Even dreams were not safe: the optimal success of the regime came when people dreamt recurrently that their best friends were tearing them apart.[395] After 1937, people stopped meeting almost entirely, and the regime's goal of isolating people from one another was virtually met.[396] The only place left 'where people can express their feelings sincerely and openly', wrote one observer, was in prison—and then only in select groups.[397] So to gain an iota of liberty one had to lose everything else.

'Resignation, silence, and decay' became the demeanour of *Homo Sovieticus*, the New Man. Here, truly, was Frankenstein's creature, dying, like Mary Shelley's, of lack of sociability. A profound schizophrenia between public and private personas developed. Betrayal, corruption, dishonesty, and universal suspicion were pervasive. 'Nobody in Soviet society was inherently trustworthy', writes Steven Barnes.[398] Not only were there informers everywhere. A culture of blame also pervaded the entire society, the result of politicizing all social institutions, and of assuming the infallibility of the Party. Every mistake was regarded as intentional sabotage. 'Accidents' did not happen. (Ironically, thus, the Soviet system relied at its core on a conception of free will rather than behavioural determinism.) The lie became 'a form of existence', a 'continuing basis of life'.[399]

Soviet life was typified by an 'atmosphere of suspicion, insincerity, secrecy, and cliquishness'.[400] The constant need to praise the regime created what Jon Elster has called a 'culture of hypocrisy', where everyone is aware that no one is sincere in their praise of the regime but no one can halt the process.[401] 'Falsehood had become the morality of the society', wrote Anatoli Rybakov. 'People lied at every turn. And no one objected. They were all tricked and deceived. Fear had been beaten into them

---

[392] Alex Inkeles and Raymond A. Bauer, *The Soviet Citizen: Daily Life in a Totalitarian Society* (Harvard University Press, 1959), p. 289.
[393] Rosenberg, *Bolshevik Visions*, p. 38.
[394] Robert G. Wesson, *Soviet Communes* (Rutgers University Press, 1963), p. 216.
[395] Berger, *Shipwreck of a Generation*, p. 77. Reinhart Koselleck comments on the penetration of Nazi terror into the dreamworld in *Futures Past: On the Semantics of Historical Time* (Columbia University Press, 2004), pp. 209–16.
[396] Mandelstam, *Hope against Hope*, p 34.   [397] Ciliga, *The Russian Enigma*, pp. 137, 184.
[398] Barnes, *Death and Redemption*, p. 54.
[399] Solzhenitsyn, *The Gulag Archipelago*, vol. 2, p. 646.
[400] Lipper, *Eleven Years in Soviet Prison Camps*, p. 46.
[401] Jon Elster, *Strong Feelings: Emotion, Addiction, and Human Behavior* (MIT Press, 1999), p. 96.

all.'[402] Intellectuals parodied the plan meant for them as implying five conditions: 'Don't think. If you must think, don't talk to yourself. If you must talk to others, don't write. If you must write, don't print. If you must print, deny it the next day.'[403] Brave were the few, in such circumstances, who kept diaries as a means of nurturing the garden of the inner self. In the late 1930s, thousands, it was said, were consigned to the flames.[404] The atmosphere of suspicion created lasts to this day, when a wariness of strangers and openness of disposition is still common in Russia, which (visitors are informed) derives from this period.

The most personal and intimate relationships were, of course, also a casualty of this process. Family loyalties in particular broke down because of the principle of familial responsibility. Introduced in 1918, it meant that entire families might be arrested as hostages or accomplices. Being related to a 'traitor' became a criminal offence. But this meshed well with other Soviet aims. A conscious aim of destroying the family as the 'basic cell' of capitalist society was evident in 1930, though by 1936 there was a retreat from this policy.[405] Even so, the Bolsheviks, already anticipating the eventual disappearance of the 'bourgeois' family, aimed to reform marital relations more radically than did the Nazis.[406] Getting more women into the workforce and saving by communal cooking and childcare were key motivations. But as the Commissar for Education, A. V. Lunacharski, stressed in the 1930s, it was also necessary to replace ideas of 'my children' and 'our parents' with less possessive descriptions born out of communal care.[407] Putting the Party first, of course, also invited the risk of being denounced by one's children: Pavlik Morozov became a model citizen, with parks named after him, for denouncing his *kulak* father for 'sabotage', namely selling false documents to exiled *kulaks*. (He was martyred when his grandfather and uncle shot him in revenge.)[408]

Love could not long subsist in such a climate. Early flirtations with sexual liberation were short-lived. The 'free love' ethos associated with Alexandra Kollontai's wish to wed 'eros to . . . comradely solidarity' (still emphasizing both the necessary centrality of love to sex and the need to avoid separating the 'loving pair from the collective') was soon supplanted by a more puritanical approach to sexuality. By the mid-1920s, promiscuity, in the spirit of August Bebel's famous pronouncement of sex being akin to drinking a glass of water, was becoming pronounced. Soon reaction set in to what was evidently a great thirst. A professor, Aaron B. Zalkind, formed a theory of revolutionary sublimation which stressed the need for 'class energy' to focus on constructive activity rather than 'the dope of sex'. Indeed, Zalkind alleged that 'every joy must have a productive purpose', taking the productivist discourse to yet another extreme. Evidently no Lothario, Bukharin warned that 'great variety in this

[402] Rybakov, *Fear*, p. 669.   [403] Chamberlin, *Russia's Iron Age*, p. 330.
[404] Hellbeck, *Revolution on My Mind*, p. 4.
[405] Kotkin, *Magnetic Mountain*, pp. 158, 179.
[406] See Claudia Koonz, *Mothers in the Fatherland: Women, the Family and Nazi Politics* (Jonathan Cape, 1987).
[407] H. Kent Geiger, *The Family in Soviet Russia* (Harvard University Press, 1968), p. 48.
[408] Michael Burleigh, *Sacred Causes: Religion and Politics from the European Dictators to Al Qaeda* (HarperPress, 2006), p. 92.

area will take too much energy, feeling and intellect from a person', and hinted that 'purely physiological grounds' were the best basis for sexual intercourse. Sexual activity which failed to promote 'the growth of collectivist feeling' now became suspect.[409] (Short of orgies, what could?) This aim clearly disturbed some intimate moments. 'It is so difficult to think about . . . proletarian needs during sexual intercourse', one student wrote in 1927, echoing the new puritan line that 'the perfect New Man was sexless'. By the mid-1930s, the idea of 'love for love's sake' had become 'treasonable', since it detracted from 'the sole purpose of human existence: service to the state'. By 1937, Party agencies actually proposed banning sexual intercourse and replacing it with artificial insemination.[410] Yet in other areas the Bolsheviks' feminist credentials were impeccable. They aimed to destroy the bourgeois, patriarchal family model based on property holding and to supplant it with equality between husband and wife, and (unlike the Nazis) the full integration of women into production. Here they anticipated many developments elsewhere regarded as progressive.[411]

These intrusions into private life represent a massive campaign to eradicate feelings which might be devoted to the Party and its goals. We should be wary, however, of seeing totalitarian aims as inevitably successful. Studies of popular opinion at the height of Stalin's Terror indicate that, while a discourse of fear and violence emanated from official sources, the population took some of this in its stride, and sometimes mocked and parodied the regime. The unaffected were indifferent or, particularly when much-resented and highly privileged Party and police officials were themselves being purged, supportive. Historians have recently stressed that terror from below emanated from the 'social revolution' of 1917, and 'was an integral element of the social revolution from the start'. Plebeian hatred of privilege, Figes emphasizes, was used by the Bolsheviks to fuel the revolution. Popular slogans like 'loot the looters' produced widespread plunder of the property of the Church and the wealthy.[412] Some, untouched by accusation or arrest, would remain diehard supporters of Stalin for decades, as attested by the widespread genuine mourning at his death in 1953.[413] Others retreated into 'cowardice, the paralysis of initiative, the irresponsibility of local leaders'.[414]

Surveillance also needs to be separated from terror. As Fitzpatrick points out, the GDR was the most watched-over state in the Soviet bloc, but was relatively free of terror from the 1970s onwards.[415] In the USSR, after the Red Terror, the 1930s

[409] Ibid., pp. 63–7, 84–8; Halfin, *Terror in My Soul*, p. 129. The cue here may have been taken from Lenin, who, conversing with Clara Zetkin, rejected the 'glass of water theory' as 'completely unmarxist' and urged 'self-control, self-discipline'. Warning of 'orgiastic conditions' and intoxication through 'sexual exaggeration', he emphasized 'no weakening, no waste, no destruction of forces' (Webb and Webb, *Soviet Communism*, vol. 2, p. 1056).
[410] John Rodden, *The Politics of Literary Reputation: The Making and Claiming of 'St George' Orwell* (Oxford University Press, 1989), p. 205; Halfin, *Stalinist Confessions*, p. 223, which is contrasted with the very real and extensive debauchery of many of Stalin's inner circle, especially his secret police chiefs.
[411] On this process see Rosenberg, *Bolshevik Visions*, pp. 61–125.
[412] Figes, *A People's Tragedy*, pp. 812, 525.
[413] For this view see Thurston, *Life and Terror in Stalin's Russia*, esp. pp. 137–63.
[414] Davies, *Popular Opinion in Stalin's Russia*, pp. 7–8, 108, 123.
[415] It has been estimated that the Czech communist regime murdered no more than two hundred persons. By contrast, about 30,000 probably died in Bulgaria from 1944 to 1989; and between

and 1940s were extremely difficult periods. Indisputably, suspicion pervaded everyday life. A shortage of housing meant cramped conditions, constant surveillance by neighbours and informers, insults, arguments, and persecution of all sorts. Feuds lasting decades occurred. Nervousness and mental illness could not but increase under such circumstances. 'Hooliganism' erupted onto the streets outside, where petty crime was common.[416] Poverty, scarcity, corruption, speculation, black marketeering, and rationing added to the regime's woes. By the 1930s, the 'system' was based on complex exchanges for everything from food and shoes to medical care and holidays. '*Blat*' (pull) or 'connections' became the only way to acquire anything useful. Everyday life was extremely insecure for most.

Yet family life proved remarkably resilient under this assault.[417] Far from declining, the sense of family solidarity, if anything, strengthened during the Soviet period. For millions, Stalin lived on 'inside us' for decades after his death. With the recent rehabilitation of Stalin as millions of Russians sank into poverty, this was, for some, no bad thing.[418] Yet 'totalitarianism' failed where personal loyalty proved resilient.[419] Total state control was never achieved. 'Individualism'—if this is the correct term—was preserved in various forms, perhaps even in the act of confession. A specifically Soviet individualism was also consciously created by the regime and by people themselves.[420] Nonetheless, forty years after Stalin's death, millions 'back from *there*', the name still unpronounceable, still looked over their shoulders every day. The 'Great Silence' about all this, in Adam Hochschild's phrase, persisted down to the 1980s. Today the movement called Memorial tries to keep their memories alive, or let them out in order finally to bury them. In Kolyma, the land of mass graves, children gather blueberries growing in skulls.[421]

Explaining Stalinism

Just why the Bolshevik Revolution degenerated so far has been much debated. Scarcely ever has a nation inflicted so much horror upon itself for so long. Many circumstances explain this debacle. Amongst these, ten merit prominence.

The first was the circumstance of the revolution itself. Seldom have events conspired to thwart such a rebellion against tyranny. World War I, and before it the Russo-Japanese War of 1905, were disastrous for Russia. The international army united to defeat Bolshevism included British, French, Czech, Japanese, Italian, American, Romanian, Greek, Polish, and Chinese troops. White (anti-Bolshevik)

60–300,000 in Romania (Benjamin Valentino, *Final Solutions: Mass Killing and Genocide in the Twentieth Century* (Cornell University Press, 2004), p. 75).

[416] Fitzpatrick, *Everyday Stalinism*, pp. 190, 48.

[417] See generally Paul Ginsborg, *Family Politics: Domestic Life, Devastation and Survival 1900–1950* (Yale University Press, 2014), pp. 397–434.

[418] Cohen, *The Victims Return*, p. 80.

[419] Sheila Fitzpatrick, 'Everyday Stalinism: Ordinary Life in Extraordinary Times', in David L. Hoffmann, ed., *Stalinism* (Blackwell, 2003), p. 161–78, and Fitzpatrick, *Everyday Stalinism*, p. 140; Inkeles and Bauer, *The Soviet Citizen*, p. 211.

[420] Kharkhordin, *The Collective and the Individual in Russia*, pp. 2–8, 251–3.

[421] Hochschild, *The Unquiet Ghost*, pp. xxii, xxiv, 43.

successes during the Civil War were bloody and substantial. Unlike the Nazis, the Bolsheviks were a very small minority and were initially widely unpopular. Their paranoia and constant sense of panic was therefore deep-seated and ingrained into the mentality of the Party, which feared conspiracies constantly from the start. The Bolsheviks' minority mentality and popular hatred of privilege and oppression fused in promoting violence.[422] Terror is a logical strategy where one does not have the upper hand and has to cow one's enemies. It results from weakness; that was the Bolshevik catastrophe in one reflection. Real, complete power does not require violence of this type. The ever-wider expansion of police activities effectively enveloped the entire society, and universal suspicion prevailed. The language of war pervaded Soviet life for most of its history: everything was a 'struggle', including that on the 'ideological front'. This contest was no holds barred. The restraints of civility were soon lost.

Secondly, the mentality of the professional revolutionary was violent and unforgiving. Many Bolsheviks had endured forty years of underground work and imprisonment. A military and criminal ethos dominated their outlook. To the many ordinary criminals in their ranks, 'crime' merely meant repaying the exploiting classes. No line between revolutionary activity and 'crime' thus existed. This was perhaps the most important turning of all on the revolutionary road. Expropriating the expropriators was not theft and not morally wrong. Paranoid and consummately dedicated to their cause, the Bolsheviks were habitually secretive and conspiratorial. Many thuggish habits associated with this mentality proved impossible to relinquish. The 'cult of violence' became 'central to the Bolshevik self-image, an end in itself rather than the means'.[423] As with the Nazis, pity came to be seen only as weakness, the prime Social Darwinist sin. 'Bourgeois humanism' was a vice. 'With the rest of my generation I firmly believed that the ends justified the means', wrote the ardent communist Lev Kopelev (born 1912), who participated in the anti-*kulak* campaigns on the 'grain front'. He continued:

> our great goal was the universal triumph of Communism, and for the sake of that goal everything was permissible—to lie, to steal, to destroy hundreds of thousands and even millions of people, all those who were hindering our work or who could hinder it, everyone who stood in the way'. 'Relativist morality'—'whatever helps us is good, whatever helps the enemy is bad'—raised a species of immoral craftsmen of death.[424]

Thirdly, this (a)morality was underscored by the very nature of the Communist Party. The Bolshevik Party as a sacrosanct group bestowed the hallowed privilege of Party membership, symbolized by the sacred card, every communist's most prized possession, a primary symbol of power which conferred a sense of invincibility and immortality on its holder.[425] It exemplified exactly what we have previously termed 'groupishness', and what Orwell, we will see in Chapter 7, would call 'nationalism'.

---

[422] Dziak, *Chekisty*, p. 21.   [423] Figes, *A People's Tragedy*, p. 505.
[424] Kopelev, *No Jail for Thought*, pp. 11, 13; Kopelev, *The Education of a True Believer*, p. 226.
[425] Kopelev, *No Jail for Thought*, p. 19; Lev Kopelev, *To Be Preserved Forever* (J. B. Lippincott, 1977), p. 19.

Partiinost, 'partyness', the morality of the group, defined the best and worst of Bolshevism, the highest idealism and the most cynical realism, intermixed in bewildering ways in every member. 'Bolshevik partyness', 'an almost mystical concept', required the ability to do 'precisely as required by the Party at any given moment', and 'to think and act only in the interests of the Party under any and all circumstances'. If 'the party demands it', insisted Iurii Piatakov in 1928, 'I will see black where I thought I saw white . . . because for me there is no life outside the Party or apart from agreement with it.'[426] 'A true Bolshevik', he added, 'has submerged his personality in the collectivity, "the Party", to such an extent that he can make the necessary effort to break away from his own opinions and convictions, and can honestly agree with the Party—that is the test of a true Bolshevik.' (He was shot in the 1937, despite probably having passed the test.)[427] The revolutionary type was defined by purity, frugality, and utter dedication to the cause. Once in, there was no return: 'one could not simply "leave" the Party'. The only way out was expulsion, purge, the life of a 'political leper', 'distrusted, barred from promotion, rounded up as a potential "enemy of the people" in time of crisis', with the 'concentration camp or worse as the inevitable end'. Suicide often seemed the sounder course.[428]

Fourthly, a sense of absolute rectitude and 'entire self-righteousness' pervaded Bolshevism. An extraordinarily powerful form of idealism, the secular equivalent of a crusade of the poor, it embodied an extremely intolerant sectarian movement.[429] Party members routinely reported having not had 'the slightest doubt that the party line was right'.[430] Its end was regarded as so utterly important—the earthly paradise, the culmination of all human history—that any means were 'necessary' to achieve it. 'Revolutionary expediency' produced a 'sin against humanism' by justifying anything.[431] Capitalism epitomized the evils of war and exploitation, and even more, every wrong turn in human history since the creation. The most important of these, Rousseau had indicated, was private property in land, and for Marx, in the means of production generally. Every effort was justified to eradicate it. The most 'total' element in the totalitarian formula was this simple moral postulate: there was one cause of human misery and one solution. Private property and exploitation caused war and poverty, the most fundamental human problems. Any obstacles to such an obviously immensely beneficial movement—little short of the salvation of humanity—were thus intolerable. So 'revolutionary legality was higher than moral legality'.[432] The similarity between medieval ideas of heresy and inquisitional persecution and the official Soviet mentality is obvious. Bolshevik 'purging' of 'Trotskyists' was exactly analogous to Christian persecution of heretics.

Fifthly, even if the 'dictatorship of the proletariat' had never been clearly explained by Marx, the new regime was, in principle, a 'dictatorship', and hardly temporary at that. It would last until the final stage of communism had been

---

[426] Quoted in Malia, *The Soviet Tragedy*, p. 227.
[427] Quoted in Landes, *Heaven on Earth*, pp. 335–6.
[428] Kravchenko, *I Chose Freedom*, pp. 132–4.
[429] The phrase is Chamberlin's: *Russia's Iron Age*, p. 18.
[430] Ginzburg, *Into the Whirlwind*, p. 11.   [431] Berger, *Shipwreck of a Generation*, p. 272.
[432] Adler, *Keeping Faith with the Party*, p. 33.

reached. This mirage appeared ever elusively over the horizon, only to retreat on inspection, but remained the supreme justification for everything that happened after 1917. After competing political parties were abolished in 1921–2, a one-party state thereafter existed, in which opposition was impermissible, even in principle. For to revelation there can be no opposition.

Sixthly, the CHEKA was never seriously restrained. Lev Razgon wrote that 'for the Cheka men there was no God and therefore all was permitted'.[433] Organizational imperialism here also helps to explain the growing power of the secret police.

Seventhly, the CHEKA assumed early on, as one henchman boasted, that 'exterminating the bourgeoisie as a class' was a key task.[434] Murdering people who had been successful over many centuries was thus justified. This, with the 'liquidation of the kulaks' and campaigns aiming at the 'total extermination of the educated class in Russia', represented a massive onslaught against the propertied, skilled, and educated.[435] It virtually guaranteed the survival of the 'least fit', the least educated, and most docile and opportunistic. Most party functionaries were not well educated or terribly bright. That was why they were successful: these were suspect qualities. But this did little to help the system succeed.[436]

Eighthly, undoubtedly a very low ethical starting point was inherited from the Tsarist regime, though it had never been even remotely as murderous as the new would become, killing only a few thousand for political offences before 1917.[437]

Ninthly, Stalin's rapid modernization programme after 1928 was underpinned by a paranoia about Russia's backwardness. This justified any measure by simple technological jealousy, or modernization anxiety, a kind of collective penis envy (my rocket is bigger than your rocket . . .) In 1931, Stalin detailed Russia's many defeats by the Mongols, the Turks, the Swedes, the Poles, the Japanese, explaining that 'all beat her for her backwardness . . . That is why we must no longer be backward.' The glittering appeal of technological modernity, and the cherished dream of 'overtaking and outstripping America', were essential to Bolshevism's self-image. This sense of Russian weakness underpinned Stalin's nationalism.[438]

Tenthly, Soviet propaganda aimed at fulfilling only the Party's will, not telling the truth about anything. This made dissimulation and hypocrisy nearly universal. The lack of any sense of objective truth was fatal on many levels. For Orwell, we will see in Chapter 7, this was perhaps the deepest flaw in the entire system.

* * * *

These factors, while they help to explain early Soviet policy, do not justify the terror of 1934–9. This did not result from revolution, war, economic imperative, or political crisis. It certainly reflected the will of one man, however. So finally, of course, there is Stalin's personality to consider: 'even by satanic, let alone human,

---

[433] Razgon, *True Stories*, p. 285.   [434] Courtois et al., *The Black Book of Communism*, p. 8.

[435] Tchernavin, *Escape from the Soviets*, p. 88.   [436] Berger, *Shipwreck of a Generation*, p. 265.

[437] Five Decembrists were killed in 1825, and five executed when Lenin's brother attempted to assassinate the Tsar. The entire Tsarist prison system held about 200,000 convicts—about as many as died in the White Sea–Baltic Canal project of 1931–3.

[438] Chamberlin, *Russia's Iron Age*, pp. 40, 64.

standards', remembered Evgenia Ginzburg, 'it was impossible to be more cruel'.[439] In a personal dictatorship, the blame for these catastrophes finally rests with Stalin. The Man of Steel had an astonishing memory for detail, but was nonetheless a mediocre if monstrously egotistical petty criminal with no sense of restraint or humanity. In all things Stalin's desire for power dictated his course of action. He early learned how far ruthlessness contributed to self-advancement and how much absolute and self-abasing loyalty could be demanded from his followers.

Stalin's and his lieutenants' chief aim was to institutionalize terror to rule more thoroughly than any preceding regime. Stalin supposedly preferred Party members to be loyal because of fear, not conviction, 'because convictions can change; fear remains'.[440] If, as Koestler expressed it, Soviet life began as 'a world of diffuse insecurity, of floating apprehension', it worsened dramatically.[441] Nations can back away from temporary dictatorships, even despotism. Under Stalin this could never occur. If the 1937 purges had continued they might have engulfed most of the population. But this was not necessary. The purges successfully cowed the populace into abject submission to Stalin's despotism.[442]

Nonetheless, the degeneration of communism in the USSR was not entirely Stalin's doing. Lenin 'set the intolerant tone of the new regime and relentlessly pursued a widening circle of enemies'. He 'pressed for terror as much as, and probably more than, anyone'.[443] Counterfactual history may be in vogue, and possibly Trotsky or Bukharin might have altered the course of history, certainly by slowing the pace of industrialization. Nonetheless, the Bolsheviks suspended the basic freedoms of speech, political organization, assembly, and demonstration. A revolution based on minority rule and an unquenchable desire for unanimity could only ultimately be held by force. 'Rights' was a bourgeois concept to which no Bolshevik subscribed on principle.

Perhaps the most outstanding feature of Soviet terror was its attempt to become all-encompassing. The Catholic Inquisition provided a model worth emulating. But its unwillingness or inability to torture and murder on a vastly grander scale prevented the search for total control from becoming total violence. In the USSR, the lack of any conception of necessary limits is remarkable, as is the persistent obsession with and ruthless pursuit of 'enemies'. Paranoia was a psychological motif of Stalinism. So was bloodthirstiness. So was the random, erratic, and wholly arbitrary process of arrest, interrogation, confession, and conviction. Anyone could be arrested at any time for anything or nothing. The most frightening thing, perhaps, was that the system finally failed to function in any rational manner. It fell victim to its own logic: in order to succeed, an entire population might perish. Where has any idea exercised greater tyranny? And so an immensely noble experiment degenerated into one of the most ignominious regimes humanity has ever constructed. Imposed on the areas of Eastern Europe occupied by the USSR at the end of World War II, it finally collapsed in 1989–91.

---

[439] Ginzburg, *Within the Whirlwind*, p. 361.   [440] Weissberg, *Conspiracy of Silence*, p. 501.
[441] Arthur Koestler, *The Invisible Writing* (Collins, 1954), p. 57.
[442] Conquest, *The Great Terror*, p. 467.   [443] Gellately, *Lenin, Stalin, and Hitler*, pp. 7, 10.

4

Totalitarianism from Hitler to Pol Pot

NAZI GERMANY AND THE 'FINAL SOLUTION'

Despite the similarities implied by the term 'totalitarianism', Nazism differed from Stalinism in many ways.[1] After its defeat in 1918, Germany endured famine, chaos, revolutionary upheaval, then an economic depression which saw its banks fail in 1931 and its middle classes wiped out amidst the chronic political instability of the Weimar Republic. When Adolf Hitler's National Socialist Party came to power in 1933 his military wing, the Sturmabteilung (SA), and then his secret police force, the Gestapo, began to intimidate and imprison Social Democrats, communists, trade unionists, homosexuals, Gypsies, some clergy, 'anti-socials', and other dissidents. Germany's self-proclaimed saviour promised to lead his nation out of chaos by overturning the humiliation of 1918. Revanchism was the spirit of the times. Hitler, the ne'er-do-well failed artist, the histrionic Wagnerian, a man jam-packed with resentment, and consumed by persecution mania, was its incarnation. He was a master at conjuring hatred out of fear. He knew well how far flattery could assuage the bruised national ego. Amidst apocalypse he promised salvation—but only if Germany's enemies were eliminated. Fed the carrot of racial supremacy, beaten by the stick of threatened annihilation, Germans responded warmly to his flattering invitation to rise above mere nationhood and become the master race.

This mood, of course, had many antecedents. The phrase, the 'Third Reich', had millenarian overtones.[2] It hinted at the immortality which group membership promised, as Hitler wrote of 'the nothingness and insignificance of the individual human being and of his continued existence in the visible immortality of the nation'.[3] Affinities with earlier episodes of mass hysteria are also evident. The former Nazi Hermann Rauschning, wrote in 1940 that 'National Socialism is the Saint Vitus' dance of the twentieth century.'[4] ('Vitality' was, of course, an oft-noted and seductive Nazi quality.) Nazism also has monstrous qualities linked to Le Bon's mob: Neumann likened it to the biblical Behemoth, epitomizing 'a non-state, a

---

[1] For a general overview of approaches to the regime see Ian Kershaw, *The Nazi Dictatorship: Problems of Perspective and Interpretation* (Arnold, 2000).

[2] An early instance is F. A. Voigt, *Unto Caesar* (Constable & Co., 1938), pp. 51–75.

[3] Quoted in Tzvetan Todorov, *Facing the Extreme: Moral Life in the Concentration Camps* (Henry Holt & Co., 1996), p. 158.

[4] Hermann Rauschning, *Hitler Speaks: A Series of Political Conversations with Adolf Hitler on His Real Aims* (Thornton Butterworth, 1940), p. 249.

chaos, a rule of lawlessness and anarchy'.[5] A long legacy of anti-Semitism and a more recent, vicious form of Social Darwinism were also brought into play. Hitler the Redeemer-Messiah portrayed a world dominated by the stark choice between racial apocalypse—the destruction of the superior Aryan type—and racial salvation—the supremacy of the German *Volk* over all others. Building, as we have seen in Chapter 2, upon a long history of anti-Semitism, as well as the colonial extermination of the Herero peoples in the German colony of South-West Africa between 1904 and 1909, the Nazis began to persecute Jews systematically.[6] Eventually they would kill almost 6 million.[7]

Just why and how this occurred has been the subject of more controversy than any other event in history, and rightly so. Our concerns here are limited to outlining how the peculiar group mentality of the Nazis contributed to their murderousness. We must then briefly trace the forms their persecution took, focusing on the Holocaust, and especially the death camp at Auschwitz. We can then examine how Stalinism paralleled and departed from Nazi genocide, before later considering how explanations for both, and especially the theory of political religion, help us to comprehend their violence.

* * * *

The key to Hitler's success lay in his ability to portray Germany as a people, nation, and race in crisis, to express its fantasies and anxieties as a kind of combined spirit medium, father confessor, and psychoanalyst, and then to reconstruct its collective personality in an image of 'superior' unity and harmony, which was, nonetheless, based upon the conquest, enslavement, and extermination of 'inferiors' outside the group. Utopia for Germany was to be dystopia for everyone else. More than anything else, thus, Nazism from the outset embodied a new ideal group, 'a community of living beings who are physically and mentally alike' (in Hitler's words). The idea of *Volksgemeinschaft*, the community of the whole people, was the core of Hitler's 'utopian vision'.[8] This entity was to be 'judged solely by the degree of the goodness of its own institutions for its own people'. To Hitler, it required an 'infallible herd-instinct which comes from unity of blood'.[9]

This 'Aryan' instinct involved the insistence that (as the 'Nazified don' Werner Sombart put it): 'There is a super-individual Something to which man is to sacrifice himself . . . the concrete idea that appears in the group *(Verband)*.' Here, 'community

[5] Franz Neumann, *Behemoth: The Structure and Practice of National Socialism* (Victor Gollancz, 1942), p. 5.
[6] See David Olusoga and Casper W. Erichsen, *The Kaiser's Holocaust: Germany's Forgotten Genocide* (Faber & Faber, 2010). Here there were concentration camps, extermination by labour, the prohibition of mixed race marriages, and even medical experiments on prisoners.
[7] The literature here is enormous. A good overview is Ian Kershaw, *Hitler, the Germans, and the Final Solution* (Yale University Press, 2008). On the historiography, see Dan Stone, *Constructing the Holocaust: A Study in Historiography* (Vallentine-Mitchell, 2003), Dan Stone, *Histories of the Holocaust* (Oxford University Press, 2010), and Dan Stone, ed., *The Holocaust and Historical Methodology* (Berghahn, 2012).
[8] In Kershaw's phrase: *Hitler and the Final Solution*, p. 55.
[9] Quoted in Wickham Steed, *The Meaning of Hitlerism* (Nisbet & Co., 1934), pp. 40, 42.

is not *an* assembly of individuals but a primary "Whole" of which individuals are merely members or partial emanations'. The 'thing of root importance, the vital point of the Nazi attitude', an acute contemporary observer, Aurel Kolnai, emphasized, was that 'blood' here meant 'not so much Race in the purely biological sense, as the subjectivist conception of a *peculiar breed of men*, claiming, by virtue of its very peculiarity, to be a law unto itself, and ultimately to the whole world'. It was a group par excellence, the 'absolute standard of its own conduct . . . the absolute subjectivity and sovereignty of a closed social group—is indeed the moral charter of the new Germany': 'Humanity as the supreme standard of human conduct is eliminated.' Deduced from the assumption that man was 'a beast of prey', its ethics could be expressed in a single, simple, ingenious aphorism: morality is what strengthens the group. Internally the nation was composed of 'moral kinsmen' (the phrase of the Nazi Wilhelm Stapel). With one 'morality for outward and one for interior use', 'what is valid for one people will be altered when applied to the "stranger"'. War would embody the exemplary external ethics of this new group. Destruction of enemies and slavery of the rest of the lower peoples were necessary consequences.[10] Cleansing the society of alien influences—Jewish, 'negro', and Bolshevik—also followed.[11]

The harbinger of the 'New Age' was to be the Nazi Party, 'the hierarchical Order of a secular priesthood', in Hitler's phrase.[12] Even more than the Bolsheviks, this group needs to be understood as defined by and bonded closely with its enemies. 'The greatness of every powerful organization which embodies a creative idea lies in the spirit of religious devotion and intolerance with which it stands out against all others, because it has an ardent faith in its own right', reasoned Hitler. In this cause, the feeling of hatred, 'more lasting than mere aversion', was crucial in attracting the masses.[13] National Socialism also portrayed itself as a utopia of state–nation–race–community. Its unifying concept was a *völkisch* ideology of group identity which drew upon Teutonic and Nordic peasant mythologies, and a confused melange of romantic images of heroic knights, the Holy Grail, a cult of sport and health, and a pure and virtuous Germanic race. Bolted on was some socialist ideology: Hitler's 'German Ideal State' included demolishing the slums and building adequate housing for the workers.[14] This anti-capitalist component was, however, specifically fused into anti-Semitism. To this was added, as the Party's name suggested, an intense nationalism and anti-Bolshevism. These provided the '"we" experience', as Kolnai termed it.[15]

[10] Aurel Kolnai, *The War against the West* (Victor Gollanz, 1938), pp. 30, 36, 53, 66, 70, 89, 196, 293–4. Kolnai terms this a return to the 'tribal mind' (p. 31), citing Lévy-Bruhl on the individual here living only through the community, never 'apart from it', a reversion he thought 'far more horrible than original barbarism', and which derived 'directly from the inner tensions, hardships and failures encountered by that civilization in the arduous course of its development' (p. 32).

[11] Jost Hermand, *Old Dreams of a New Reich: Volkish Utopias and National Socialism* (Indiana University Press, 1992), pp. 102–7, 171–263.

[12] Ibid., pp. 200, 237. See David Redles, 'National Socialist Millennialism', in Catherine Wessinger, ed., *The Oxford Handbook of Millennialism* (Oxford University Press, 2011), pp. 529–48.

[13] Adolf Hitler, *Mein Kampf* (Hurst & Blackett, 1939), pp. 294, 283.

[14] August Kubizek, *Young Hitler: The Story of Our Friendship* (Mann, 1973), p. 126.

[15] Kolnai, *The War against the West*, p. 440.

The Nazi dream was, nonetheless, more indebted to Hitler's personality than its Stalinist counterpart, and less focused on the Party as such. Hitler's delusions of grandeur rested on hyperbole, primitivism, irrationality, boorish self-promotion, egotism, fear of infection, sexual deviance, a childish fixation on blood, and plain simple-mindedness. He has been described as having 'disliked any physical contact with people', and projecting this antisocial personality disorder onto the German people. An isolated youth and lonely man, an architect and *artiste manqué* who hated his father, was obsessed with his mother, was probably masochistic and possessed a profound urge to dominate, he is a psychoanalyst's dream if everyone else's nightmare.[16] As a persecuted Austrian, seeking the larger group, he knew what it was to crave the embracing, protective folds of the *Volksgemeinschaft*. Possibly doubtful about his own racial purity, he imagined the purity of the Aryan type as an antidote. Obsessed with cleanliness, he projected his self-loathing and anxiety upon the Jews. Unable, it seems, to have normal sexual relations, he insisted he could only 'marry' Germany—the ultimate group identity possible. His Jekyll, announced by 'convulsions of weeping in all emotional crises', was matched by a Hyde of unwavering ferocity and mercilessness.[17] To him, 'barbarian' was 'an honourable title', and there was 'no such thing as truth, either in the moral or the scientific sense', only the sovereignty of the will, as Nietzsche (whose works he presented to Mussolini) had taught, and especially of the 'will to power' of the *Volk*.[18]

Nietzsche's *Übermensch* idea thus represented another affectation of living in a state of grace 'beyond good and evil', where a 'transvaluation of all values' enabled 'free spirits' to define as 'good' only 'all that enhances the feeling of power'.[19] To Hitler, Spartan 'racial laws' had served 'the natural process of selection'.[20] The message of the trenches was 'that life is a cruel struggle, and has no other object but the preservation of the species'.[21] The 'Nordic-Aryan' was true, pure, noble, strong, honourable, worthy: a conquering military elite. Hitler hoped 'to see once more in the eyes of pitiless youth the gleam of pride and independence of the beast of prey'.[22] His Social Darwinism, wedded to the racialism of Gobineau and Houston Stewart Chamberlain, equated strength with nobility. It also glorified violence and war as creative forces underpinning social and racial renewal.[23]

---

[16] Kubizek, *Young Hitler*, p. 117. Jonathan Glover, *Alien Landscapes? Interpreting Disordered Minds* (Harvard University Press, 2014), pp. 297–9. See further Daniel Pick, *The Pursuit of the Nazi Mind: Hitler, Hess and the Analysts* (Oxford University Press, 2012), pp. 128–52.

[17] Hitler had many compulsive-neurotic symptoms and was obsessed with cleanliness, dirt, and pollution. This has been linked to his fixation on blood (Elie A. Cohen, *Human Behaviour in the Concentration Camp* (Jonathan Cape, 1954), pp. 222–3).

[18] Rauschning, *Hitler Speaks*, pp. 27, 87, 220, 267; *Hitler's Table Talk 1941–1944*, ed. Hugh Trevor-Roper (Weidenfeld & Nicolson, 1953), pp. xxi, 720.

[19] Friedrich Nietzsche, *The Twilight of the Idols . . . The Antichrist* (T. N. Fouis, 1911), pp. 128, 139.

[20] Michael Burleigh, *The Third Reich: A New History* (Pan Books, 2000), p. 382.

[21] *Hitler's Table Talk 1941–1944*, p. 44.

[22] Robert Eisler, *Man into Wolf: An Anthropological Interpretation of Sadism, Masochism, and Lycanthropy* (Routledge & Kegan Paul, 1951), p. 35. Eisler thought that the 'very title "Führer" denotes the leader of the hunting lupine pack of his followers' (p. 169).

[23] Hermann Rauschning, *Germany's Revolution of Destruction* (William Heinemann, 1939), p. 29; Kolnai, *The War against the West*, p. 178.

Hitler was thus typecast to lead the Le Bonian crowd. 'Mass suggestion and persecution mania', the journalist Wickham Steed reported in 1934, were combined in him to an astonishing degree.[24] The most powerful orator of his age, a man of great charisma capable of holding audiences in a trance for hours, he achieved 'complete rapture and ecstasy', a friend reported, when publicly describing his prophetic mission to lead Germany from servitude to freedom.[25] Hitler knew well how to make 'mass suggestion' so potent that 'thought is eliminated'. The 'bigger the crowd, the more easily it is swayed'. The crowd wanted 'the strong man', not a 'grant of liberal freedom; they often feel at a loss what to do with it and even easily feel themselves deserted'. 'Mass demonstrations on the grand scale not only reinforce the will of the individual but they draw him still closer to the movement and help to create an *esprit de corps*', Hitler recognized. For while in his workplace he might feel 'very small indeed', when

> he should enter a vast assembly for the first time and see around him thousands and thousands of men who hold the same opinions . . . he is gripped by the force of mass-suggestion which comes from the excitement and enthusiasm of three or four thousand other men in whose midst he finds himself.

Thence,

> if the manifest success and the consensus of thousands confirm the truth and justice of the new teaching and for the first time raise doubt in his mind as to the truth of the opinions held by himself up to now—then he submits himself to the fascination of what we call mass-suggestion.[26]

And so the Nazi cult made Hitler Germany's strongman. He was 'deliberately and unceasingly held up to the masses as a deity' and 'treated functionally and pragmatically as God. People pray to him; people greet in his name as they did in the name of God.'[27] His birthday and the heroic incidents of his life (like the Munich *Putsch*) were fêted annually on a vast scale.

The Nazi movement, particularly the Hitler Youth, emulated the Führer's ideal of bullying brutality, fitness, and mindless obedience. The Party also provided all the paraphernalia of religion in unifying symbols like the swastika, armbands, portraits, flags, banners, uniforms, and heroic songs. To emphasize inclusivity amongst members, a rigid hierarchy was balanced by an ethos of egalitarianism

---

[24] Steed, *The Meaning of Hitlerism*, p. xvi.
[25] Quoted in Richard Landes, *Heaven on Earth: The Varieties of the Millennial Experience* (Oxford University Press, 2011), pp. 357–8.
[26] Rauschning, *Hitler Speaks*, pp. 209–10; Sigmund Neumann, *Permanent Revolution: The Total State in a World at War* (Harper & Brothers, 1942), p. 117; Hitler, *Mein Kampf*, pp. 397–8. Christina Wieland comments on this passage that 'this exhilaration and joy is only possible because the murderousness of the group is directed outside the group' (Christina Wieland, *The Fascist State of Mind and the Manufacturing of Masculinity* (Routledge, 2015), p. 143). Hitler added: 'A man who enters such a meeting in doubt and hesitation leaves it inwardly fortified; he has become a member of a community.' 'Magic' here can also be taken much more literally: see Dan Stone, 'Nazism as Modern Magic: Bronislaw Malinowski's Political Anthropology', *History and Anthropology*, 14 (2003), 203–18.
[27] Rauschning, *Germany's Revolution of Destruction*, p. 37; Bronisław Malinowski, *Freedom and Civilization* (George Allen & Unwin, 1947), p. 312.

and common sacrifice. Nazis boasted that 'genuflections' and class arrogance 'had been completely eliminated among us in the Party'.[28] A sense of equality—the 'socialist' element in the Nazi ideal—was also shared by many carried along in the current of everyday life. People did not have to join the Party or use the *Hitlergruss* (Heil Hitler!—a hundred times a day or more) or express other symbols of belonging to benefit psychologically from the new sense of national health and prosperity which was soon evident after 1933.

The ethos of public service associated with Party work was thus widely welcomed. Many Germans were oriented towards local work and organizations rather than towards Hitler himself. Donations to the Winter Relief Fund (1933–45), for example, though sometimes resented as a 'voluntary' tax, made everyone who wore its coveted badge feel a part of the national renewal. Propaganda, and in particular the powerful unifying medium of the radio, helped to forge popular unity. The proliferation of uniforms underscored the sense of common endeavour and homogeneity of experience. The Nazis loved marching in step for hours on end, observed Hermann Rauschning, because it killed thought and made 'an end of individuality' by accustoming people to 'a mechanical, quasi-ritualistic activity until it becomes second nature'. The great rallies thus had the effect of creating a 'sense of primitive community through functional integration'.[29] By torchlight, the sight of thousands of massed uniformed men, captured so vividly in Leni Riefenstahl's film of the Nazis' 1934 Nuremberg Rally, was awe-inspiring.

Nazi Germany and 'Totalitarianism'

Unlike Stalin, Hitler needed no dictatorship to retain power. With 37 per cent of the vote, the Nazis were the largest party in 1932. (Over 40 per cent of its supporters were aged eighteen to thirty.) In March 1933, after the Communist Party had been suppressed, the Nazis achieved 43.9 per cent—well over what brings most democratic governments to power. By the late 1930s, Nazi achievements in foreign policy and in bringing about full employment, prosperity, improved wages, subsidized holidays, and social security were enthusiastically endorsed by most Germans. A palpable sense of relief, regeneration, and renewed national unity defined German public and private life during the mid- and later 1930s as the shame of humiliating defeat was washed away.[30] After the onset of an initially unpopular war in 1939, the victories were swift and stunning. The Nazis would thus probably have won any election from the mid-1930s right up to 1945.

Reconciling this popularity with the prevalent image of Hitler's Germany as a 'totalitarian' dictatorship is difficult. The language is present: Hitler regarded terror as the 'most effective political instrument', stressing that the 'important thing is the

---

[28] Theodore Abel, *Why Hitler Came to Power* (Harvard University Press, 1986), pp. 242, 244.
[29] Rauschning, *Germany's Revolution of Destruction*, p. 51.
[30] Peter Fritzsche, *Life and Death in the Third Reich* (Harvard University Press, 2008), pp. 11, 17, 38, 63.

sudden shock of an overwhelming fear of death'.[31] Nonetheless, recent scholarship calls 'into question the long-held notion that terror was ubiquitous in Nazi Germany'.[32] Wartime Allied propaganda, and post-war German unwillingness to confront the degree of popular consent to Nazism, assisted the view that the Gestapo had ruthlessly terrorized Germany under Hitler. But this is scapegoating again. In fact, while obviously a dictatorship and intensely hostile to its antagonists, Nazi Germany was internally a much less totalitarian state than Stalin's USSR. Far from being a strictly regimented society where the population cowed under systematic terror, few were affected by extreme measures until the very end of the war. Even then, the regime was not an 'all-out police state'.[33] '[M]ost Germans did not live in fear', and terror as a means of controlling Germans played only a minor role in the regime.[34]

There were many reasons for this. Hitler's Germany was not paranoid generally, and did not endure a civil war like that fought by the Bolsheviks. Unlike fears based upon class categorization under Stalinism, which affected many Soviets, those based on race were negligible to most Germans. Once fixed, racial differentiation was much more manageable than that based on class. For most were usually permanently in or out on racial grounds, whereas class proved much more flexible. A highly industrialized state like Germany did not need to sacrifice millions of its own citizens in breakneck modernization schemes. (During the war it sacrificed millions of other people in its industries.) Germany's successes up to 1943 also meant that there was far less pressure to root out 'wreckers', spies, and the like, as well as to create the hyperzealous ideal type sought in the image of 'Soviet' man and woman. The general level of paranoia was thus much lower than in the USSR. 'Crimes' like listening to foreign radio broadcasts were thus punished much less severely than under Stalin. The vast majority of Germans also remained unaffected by either the Gestapo or the Holocaust. Hitler ruled largely by consent rather than coercion. Fear was not necessary to feed anti-Semitism, though it remains controversial as to how many knew about the mass murders perpetrated by the regime (some of which were so unbelievable that reports were simply disregarded). The accusation of collective collusion in and guilt for his policies hence persists.[35]

The once-prevalent assumption that Nazi Germany was a 'gigantic torture chamber', then, no longer prevails.[36] Compared to the People's Commissariat for

[31] Adolf Hitler, *The Speeches of Adolf Hitler 1922–39* (2 vols, Oxford University Press, 1942), vol. 1, p. 196; Rauschning, *Hitler Speaks*, p. 90. The only thing, Hitler said, 'more important than terrorism is the systematic modification of the ideas and feelings of the masses' (p. 275).
[32] Eric A. Johnson and Karl-Heinz Reuband, *What We Knew: Terror, Mass Murder, and Everyday Life in Nazi Germany: An Oral History* (John Murray, 2005), p. 349.
[33] Nikolaus Wachsmann, *Hitler's Prisons: Legal Terror in Nazi Germany* (Yale University Press 2004), pp. 3, 372–3.
[34] Johnson and Reuband, *What We Knew*, pp. 329, 341–4, 354, 360.
[35] A starting point here is Eric Voegelin, *Hitler and the Germans* (University of Missouri Press, 1999).
[36] Jacques Delarue, *The History of the Gestapo* (Macdonald, 1964), p. 91, quoting Robert Jackson, a Nuremberg Trial prosecutor.

Internal Affairs (NKVD), the Gestapo was a small organization, with about 1 officer for 10–15,000 inhabitants. During the war it actually shrank. Many cities had fewer than fifty Gestapo officials. Essen had 43 to cover 650,000 people, while northern Bavaria in 1943–5 had only 80–100 informers. In the entire country, only 32,000 employees in late 1944 were responsible for a population of some 70 million. With a rate of probably one paid informer to every official this was a very small percentage (1 in 200 or 0.5 per cent) of what the German Democratic Republic (GDR) would achieve (some 2.5 per cent of the population were informers).[37] Gestapo functionaries were often normal policemen, if reliable Nazis. Some were pathological persecutors of the regime's enemies. But they were not omnipresent, and the power of the state over the individual was far from total. Fewer than 2 per cent of the population probably ever had dealings with them, or were accused of any crime—far less than the proportion of Soviet citizens affected by Stalin. Only 17 per cent feared a 'run-in' of some kind.[38]

Perhaps 16,500 non-Jewish Germans were executed under Hitler from 1933 to 1944, including those from annexed territories, with some 11,000 of these during wartime (compared to 680,000–800,000 under Stalin in 1937–8 alone).[39] Another 77,000 were murdered for resistance activities. About 3.5 million were imprisoned in camps (thus one in twenty). Conditions generally were better than in the USSR, and inmates (at least early on) were often released fairly quickly. The number of denunciations was also relatively much fewer. Germans did not perceive the secret police as 'all-powerful or even as terribly threatening to them personally'.[40] A third of denunciations, indeed, involved personal conflicts. Well aware of this, the Gestapo pried only reluctantly into private lives.[41] Nor did it usually pursue family liability—for instance for military desertion—unless clear opposition to the regime was indicated.[42] Hitler's outlook may have been marked by a 'fanaticism and even intolerance with which its exclusive rightness is professed by its adherents'. His followers may have claimed that: 'There are no longer any private people. All and every are Adolf Hitler's soldiers, and a soldier is never a private person.'[43] But such rhetoric fell far short of practice. In fact, the 'totalitarian' paradigm does not fit here very well.

For most people, 'normal' life thus prevailed up to the middle years of the war. In many niches 'neither the propaganda nor the terror were totally effective'.[44] Young

---

[37] Robert Gellately, *The Gestapo and German Society* (Clarendon Press, 1990), pp. 44, 62.

[38] Eric A. Johnson, *Nazi Terror: The Gestapo, Jews, and Ordinary Germans* (John Murray, 1999), p. 174.

[39] The statistics are Richard Evans', as cited in Johnson, *Nazi Terror*, p. 315. These include some annexed territories including Poland: the majority of executed were non-Germans. This gives a rough average of 1 execution under the Nazis for every 4,848 people, and under Stalin, for 1937–8 alone, 1 in 24, or 200 times as many. A comparison of total executions under Stalin for the same period would bring a much higher ratio, while factoring in the Holocaust would reduce the ratio to *c.*1:3. Other accounts give *c.*12,000 as the number of German citizens executed.

[40] Johnson and Reuband, *What We Knew*, p. 348; Johnson, *Nazi Terror*, p. 262.

[41] Johnson and Reuband, *What We Knew*, p. 350.

[42] Nicholas Stargardt, *The German War: A Nation under Arms* (The Bodley Head, 2015), p. 455.

[43] Kolnai, *The War against the West*, pp. 164, 169.   [44] Johnson, *Nazi Terror*, p. 15.

people were integrated into the Nazi world-view through the Hitler Youth and BDM (League of German Girls). Family life was largely unchanged, indeed, if anything, was more avowedly traditionalist after the libertine atmosphere of Weimar. Women's entry to university was restricted. It was proposed that smoking be restricted to males, and makeup was condemned as decadent—but this was, Sigmund Neumann noted, 'the first battle National Socialism lost'.[45] (Some noted a 'thinly veiled contempt for the female' in Nazi ideology.)[46] Population growth and racial purity were obviously encouraged. Despite fierce persecution of some groups, religious worship was not proscribed either. Terror was thus very selective, and relative freedom—for a police state—the norm for the majority.

Yet many minorities had cause for fear. Diaries from the period note the founding of concentration camps, arrests, and violence.[47] Social Democrats, communists, homosexuals, and many clerics and sectarian Christians, such as the Jehovah's Witnesses, were punished not as racially 'unworthy', but as 'asocial' or 'parasitic'. Later, eugenics profiling targeted certain types of criminals, prostitutes, alcoholics, and drug users, and some victims of diseases, like TB. The mentally ill and handicapped (even war veterans) were regarded as an economic burden. Some 400,000 were sterilized as mentally or physically feeble (but many countries did this). The first German euthanasia programme (so-called 'T4') for eliminating 'mental defectives' branded them 'beings' or 'creatures' instead of people.[48] In one rehearsal for the death camps, about 270,000 were murdered.[49] Franz Stangl, heavily involved in this programme from 1940 to 1942, went on to become Commandant of Sobibór and then Treblinka.[50]

Nonetheless, there is another sense in which Nazi Germany did achieve a measure of totalitarianism. Its attack upon individualism in the name of a higher communal group without doubt degraded intellectual and moral life in the insistence that the personality was nothing and the *Volk* all. To Kolnai:

> [F]ascist philosophy, by overshooting the mark, destroys the idea of Community. Men form no community, for they do not commune; they are supposed to be, and are treated as, cells of a definite social Body sovereign in its aims, with a hierarchy of equally definite sub-sections of relative 'wholeness' to which, like soldiers to their superiors, they are committed both in their individual and in their collective existence.

---

[45] Neumann, *Permanent Revolution*, pp. 191–2.

[46] Kolnai, *The War against the West*, p. 224.

[47] Fritzsche, *Life and Death in the Third Reich*, p. 37.

[48] Michael Burleigh, *Ethics and Extermination: Reflections on Nazi Genocide* (Cambridge University Press, 1997), p. 119.

[49] Fritzsche, *Life and Death in the Third Reich*, p. 114. For a summary of this programme see Burleigh, *Ethics and Extermination*, pp. 113–41, and Michael Burleigh, *Death and Deliverance: 'Euthanasia' in Nazi Germany* (Cambridge University Press, 1994), for a more extended account. This programme was ended when Hitler, jeered by a crowd when his train was held up by mental patients being taken away, ordered it closed: Gitta Sereny, *Into that Darkness: From Mercy Killing to Mass Murder* (Andre Deutsch, 1974), p. 59.

[50] Sereny, *Into that Darkness*, p. 59.

True community, in this view, requires the expression of *Gesellschaft*, where multiple associations emanating from private life reflect multiple personalities. The subordination of the self to a higher sovereign entity is not 'community', but akin to Kołakowski's 'compulsory solidarity'. The Nazis believed, Kolnai insisted, 'not in a congregation of Egos, but rather in a primary *We*, full of reality and positively identified as a unique body with its particular "selfhood". This is what the term "We experience" denotes.' But this experience 'only marks the state of mind which corresponds logically to tribal self-assertion. It emphasizes the effacement of personality and the supreme subjectivity of the closed group.' This 'We' 'is an enlarged Ego engulfing personality and defying the world, strictly limited in its closed and "shaped" historical identity and uniqueness, and yet virtually unlimited as regards the extent of its claims to unfolding and conquest'. It was epitomized in the idea of a *'Bund'* as 'a closed and dominating body'. This is exactly what we defined in the Introduction as the dystopian group.[51]

Anti-Semitism

We have seen in earlier chapters that the Jews had long been identified with the Devil, plague, and other misfortunes. Fear of Jews, as opposed to dislike, was both greater and more common than is often acknowledged; the historian Jules Michelet wrote in 1846 of 'a race of men . . . reared . . . in terror of the Jews' because of their role as moneylenders.[52] After a brief period of enlightened toleration, anti-Semitism became pronounced in Germany in the late nineteenth and early twentieth century. At least nineteen proposals for the physical extermination of the Jews were made between 1861 and 1895, though by marginal rather than mainstream groups.[53] Anxiety about biological swamping of 'fit' races and individuals by the burgeoning 'unfit' led Nazi ideology to take up, with a vengeance, a number of 'negative' eugenics strands from late nineteenth-century thought. These were wedded to a half-baked Nietzschean evolutionary doctrine respecting the need for a purified master race ready for world conquest.

Anti-Semitism became one defining attitude of the genuine Nazi, the 'secret sign and binding mystery' which separated careerists and hangers-on from true believers. The Nazis were less a political party than a character type: *'To be a Nazi means to be a definite type of human being.'* Lack of scruple here marked the type.[54] Anti-Semitism was a crucial component in the *Volksgemeinschaft* ideal: the Other or outer which defined the pure and inner, the alien or wall defining the group's boundaries. Generalized hatred, of course, had its uses. To Franz Borkenau, in 1940, Nazism was 'simple concentrated hate . . . The Nazis hate everybody and everything.'[55] This could be applied to any group; as the Nazi Gerhard Günther

---

[51] Kolnai, *The War against the West*, pp. 72–3, 75, 91.

[52] Jules Michelet, *The People* (Whittaker & Co., 1846), p. 11.

[53] Daniel Jonah Goldhagen, *Hitler's Willing Executioners: Ordinary Germans and the Holocaust* (Little, Brown & Co., 1996), pp. 71–7.

[54] Sebastian Haffner, *Germany: Jekyll and Hyde* (Secker & Warburg, 1940), pp. 77–80.

[55] F. Borkenau, *The Totalitarian Enemy* (Faber & Faber, 1940), p. 137.

put it, 'The foreigner—the stranger—is not a fellow-man for the Horde, the Tribe, he is a cause for superstitious shudder and abhorrence.'[56] Hitler too would write of his generic 'hatred for the promiscuous swarm of foreign peoples', 'incest incarnate', in the Vienna of his youth.[57] But the specific focus of antagonism was the Jews. The 'World Jewish Conspiracy' became Hitler's chief 'other' or antithesis. The group in negation, an object at once of fear and hatred, 'our misfortune', in the frequently quoted nineteenth-century slogan (*'Die Juden sind unser Unglück'*), was an obstacle which had to be eliminated.

Though less than 1 per cent of the population in 1933, the 520,000 German Jews thus became the focus of all the resentment and guilt stemming from World War I, the Versailles Treaty, and the economic depression. Old and new languages of exclusion now merged. 'Redemption' from this 'evil' power, the 'Jewish world enemy' bent on destroying Germany, referred both to a 'Jewish capitalist' and 'Jewish Bolshevik' enemy, and 'the aspiration of the Jewish people to become the despots of the world'.[58] Hitler described the Jew as 'a parasite, a sponger who, like a pernicious bacillus, spreads over wider and wider areas according as some favourable area attracts him'. The Jew was a 'vampire' or 'anti-man', lower even than the beast, 'a creature outside nature and alien to nature'. These 'men of Satan' were the ideal anti-group, combining as they did the monstrous and satanic, economic resentment, and long-standing historical and racial enmity.[59] This, Dan Stone stresses, resulted in a prejudice which was as much 'mystical antisemitism' as the 'applied biology' of 'scientific' or eugenicist racism. The Jews were a kind of 'counter-race', a symbolic inversion of Germanness, rather than a free-standing entity in a racial hierarchy.[60] They were, in fact, the monstrous other.

The depth and intensity of feeling against the Jews thus had 'a decidedly metaphysical and religious character' in its opposition to 'the cruelty of the anti-Christ . . . worshippers of all that in the Christian tradition is called Satanic'.[61] Propaganda made them a wholly alien 'other', symbolized by the yellow star, in one of the purest examples known to us of what in the Introduction we termed sociogermophobia. After 1933, every major element in European hysteria over the past thousand years was piled on randomly for effect. The Christian and monstrous components overlapped here. In the political religion of Nazism, the Jews again played the age-old role of the Devil as embodying evil, with the Nazis pitted against them as mankind's redeemers.[62] A children's book of 1936—the appropriate intellectual level for their ideology—literally termed Jews the offspring

[56] Kolnai, *The War against the West*, p. 148.
[57] Hitler, *Mein Kampf*, p. 115; Kubizek, *Young Hitler*, p. 185.
[58] Hitler, *Mein Kampf*, p. 538; David Pan, *Sacrifice in the Modern World: On the Particularity and Generality of Nazi Myth* (Northwestern University Press, 2012), p. 8. It has been estimated that some 50 per cent of the membership of revolutionary parties in Russia in 1903 was Jewish: Anna Geifman, *Thou Shalt Kill: Revolutionary Terrorism in Russia, 1894–1917* (Princeton University Press, 1993), p. 32.
[59] Hitler, *Mein Kampf*, pp. 254, 274, 538; Rauschning, *Hitler Speaks*, p. 238.
[60] Stone, *Histories of the Holocaust*, p. 2.
[61] Borkenau, *The Totalitarian Enemy*, pp. 138, 140.
[62] Norman Cohn, *Warrant for Genocide* (Eyre & Spottiswoode, 1967), p. 180.

of the Devil.[63] Hitler described them as descended from 'veritable devils', and Goebbels as 'incarnate devils'.[64] The outer monster was hinted at: 'The category of human being was no longer applicable' to Jews, one murderer later wrote: they had become monsters.[65] The propagandist Julius Streicher even asserted that an Aryan woman who had married a Jew bore him an ape.[66] And the Hyde-like inner monster was present too: some took the Jews psychologically to represent 'a distortion, a shadow, the dark side of human nature', not only different from but opposite to the German. Reduced to this infantile level, the logic of elimination was simple. Hitler explained in 1943,

> if the Jews did not work, they were shot. If they could not work, they had to succumb. They had to be treated like a tuberculosis bacillus, with which a healthy body may become infected. This was not cruel, if one remembers that even innocent creatures of nature, such as hares and deer, have to be killed, so that no harm is caused by them.[67]

It is customary to see the Holocaust as the inevitable outcome of these ideas, but there were many intermediary stages. After 1933, Jews were rapidly excluded from most professions and often plundered of their property, which they were forced to sell quickly for a pittance. The 'Law for the Protection of German Blood and Honour' of 1935 prohibited interracial marriages. The mere presence of Jews was seen as 'sufficient to contaminate public baths and even park benches'.[68] So, from 1935–6, Jews were prohibited from frequenting swimming pools and bathhouses. (A Nazi paper rejoiced after Jews were banned from a seaside resort that 'it's just us now', *unter uns* being the closed circle of insiders.)[69] The public pogrom of Reichskristallnacht (9 November 1938) unleashed a wave of violence against Jews. Their passports were stamped with a 'J', and all men had the middle name of 'Isaac', and all women 'Sarah', assigned to them, thus homogenizing the identity of the negative group. Non-Jews could lose their jobs for meeting or talking with Jews. The fortunate few were forced into exile. Many more were jailed and finally murdered. From 1942, even their pets were killed: 'Jewishness' had seemingly been transferred to them by proximity, pollution, or taboo (or negative vicarious enhancement). Proposals were made to sterilize by X-rays 2–3 million Jews who might be retained for labour. This sums up quite adequately the prevailing mentality, which Michael Burleigh describes as a 'conflation of Jews, criminality, Bolshevism and subhumanity'.[70]

These measures were consensual, to a degree later conveniently forgotten, when scapegoating Hitler and the Party became the norm. 'The Nazi regime is undoubtedly a tyrannical autocracy', observed Borkenau. 'But at the same time it is

[63] Goldhagen, *Hitler's Willing Executioners*, p. 411.
[64] James M. Rhodes, *The Hitler Movement: A Modern Millenarian Revolution* (Hoover Institution Press, 1980), p. 45.
[65] Goldhagen, *Hitler's Willing Executioners*, p. 280.
[66] Burleigh, *The Third Reich*, p. 291. Elsewhere he portrayed Jews as 'poisoned mushrooms' in a book of that title (*Der Giftpilz*, 1938).
[67] Burleigh, *The Third Reich*, pp. 770–1.
[68] Primo Levi, *The Drowned and the Saved* (Abacus Books, 1988), p. 103.
[69] Fritzsche, *Life and Death in the Third Reich*, pp. 68–9.
[70] Burleigh, *The Third Reich*, p. 338.

Fig. 4.1. 'Jews Not Wanted'. © Everett Collection/Mary Evans 11000408.

undoubtedly mob rule.'[71] In the mid-1930s, hundreds of anti-Semitic meetings took place. Thousands of Jews were beaten and humiliated. Signs were widely posted, even outside large cities, saying 'Jews are not welcome here' (see Fig. 4.1). Even Protestant Church leaders asserted that Jews were the 'born enemies of the world and of Germany' and urged that the 'severest measures against the Jews be adopted and that they be banished from German lands'.[72] Many Germans voluntarily engaged in both random and organized violence against Jews in the early years of the regime, egged on by a 'narcissistic ethno-sentimentality' (in Burleigh's phrase) and the constant flattery of being praised as the master race.[73] But popular participation in oppressing these *Volksfeinde* was not always universal. (In conquered areas after 1941 popular anti-Semitism was very common.) There was sometimes considerable embarrassment and shame about local pogroms, complaints by non-Jews about the wearing of the yellow star, and even protests at some deportations of Jews.[74]

Hitler had long proclaimed his intention of making Germany *judenrein*, or free of Jews. His dislike and fear of the eastern Jews, whom conquest soon rendered his property, was particularly pronounced. In a Reichstag speech of 30 January 1939,

---

[71] Borkenau, *The Totalitarian Enemy*, p. 151.
[72] Goldhagen, *Hitler's Willing Executioners*, p. 112.
[73] Burleigh, *The Third Reich*, p. 812.
[74] Fritzsche, *Life and Death in the Third Reich*, pp. 137, 255–6; Stargardt, *The German War*, p. 242.

he threatened them with 'annihilation' if another world war occurred.[75] He often referred back to this 'prophecy', which in retrospect, of course, seems a clear enough signal of intention.[76] The onset of war in 1939 accelerated the general atmosphere of brutality. Hitler ordered the elimination of Poland's intelligentsia, arguing that Poland could not have two ruling classes (Stalin would shortly do the same for his area of control). Plans were detailed for turning the entire conquered east into one mass slave labour camp governed by resettled ethnic Germans.[77] A system of forced labour was also imposed on the other conquered peoples of Europe.

The occupation of Poland then represented what Peter Longerich calls the 'decisive step towards a racially motivated policy of annihilation'.[78] Now system, structure, and function pushed the logic of extermination even where no direct orders were evident. Expulsion, relocation to Madagascar or 'Lublinland' or further east, forced emigration, ghetto imprisonment, now all gave way to killing and a plan of grand territorial cleansing (30 million in some estimates) in preparation for German settlement. First Jewish men were shot, as potentially hostile to the occupation. By mid-1942, women and children were routinely included. Even in late 1941, the 'biological extermination of the whole of Jewry in Europe' was being explained by Alfred Rosenberg as the new policy. The overcrowding of ghettos and the difficulties encountered in mass shootings militated towards a more efficient 'final solution', which was in place by mid-1942.[79] In February 1942, Robert Ley, the Labour Front leader, proclaimed in a speech in the Berlin Sportpalast (capacity 14,000), the largest public arena in the capital, that 'Jewry will and must be exterminated. That is our holy mission. That is what this war is about.'[80] Only the deaf could claim not to have received such a clear message.

Once the invasion of the USSR began in 1941, mass murder began in earnest. The ferocity with which 'ordinary' German special units or Einsatzgruppen conducted an unprecedented campaign of killing with gruesome cruelty (plundering all the way) has been well documented.[81] Here, 'mercy' meant shooting Jews straight away. But, shot in pits by drunken soldiers and policemen, many were still alive as the next corpse fell on top of them. Furthermore, 'Jewish' and 'Bolshevik' were often regarded as synonymous—and not only by the German invaders. An explosion of local resentments, ethnic, political, religious, historical, hastened the descent into barbarism. The oldest prejudices would resurface; the Romanian leader Antonescu would proclaim 'Satan is the Jew.'[82] A general writ enjoining the destruction of the Jews and thus ridding Germany, as the Commandant of

[75] Jeffrey Herf, *The Jewish Enemy: Nazi Propaganda during World War II and the Holocaust* (Harvard University Press, 2006), p. 3.
[76] Kershaw, *Hitler and the Final Solution*, p. 111.   [77] Burleigh, *The Third Reich*, p. 442.
[78] Peter Longerich, *Holocaust: The Nazi Persecution and Murder of the Jews* (Oxford University Press, 2010), p. 143.
[79] Ibid., pp. 181, 220, 226, 302–3, 314.
[80] Richard Evans, *The Third Reich at War* (Penguin Books, 2008), pp. 256, 269.
[81] Goldhagen, *Hitler's Willing Executioners*, pp. 203–82.
[82] Evans, *The Third Reich at War*, pp. 220, 231. The Romanians killed as many as 380,000 Jews, more than any other country except Germany (p. 233).

Auschwitz, Rudolf Hoess, explained it, of its 'relentless adversaries',[83] was probably given orally by Hitler to Himmler, perhaps during summer 1941, but more likely in December.[84] Hitler also intended to enslave the Central Asian 'hordes', with the educated and ideologues being murdered as a matter of principle.[85]

With Jews, the logic now became simpler: the more who were killed, the more who had to be killed. The larger the number of Jews in the territories of the advancing German armies, the greater the pressure to kill them. The more who were murdered, the more revenge was feared by the Germans. They were thus driven to kill still more, and to see all Jews as a threat, until total extermination seemed the only feasible solution. Resettling them, perhaps a real option until 1941, now seemed increasingly pointless. Forced into ghettoes, Jews began dying of hunger, overwork, and disease.

But the systematic process of murder, mainly by shooting, was erratic, makeshift, and time-consuming. The shooters were often 'besmirched with blood, brains, and bone splinters'. Executing women and children one at a time was also demoralizing. Some actually relished the work. But many broke down under the shame and horror of the task. A large number began drinking to excess every day. In one group, about a dozen out of 500, told of the task before them, were allowed to 'step out' and avoid the killing. A former cigarette sales representative shot only one old woman and gave up, his nerves 'totally finished from this one shooting'. But those who did so faced the wrathful disgust of their colleagues. Few could bear to 'lose face' this way: 'no one wants to be thought a coward'. They also risked 'isolation, rejection, and ostracism—a very uncomfortable prospect within the framework of a tightly knit unit stationed abroad amongst a hostile population'. Some commanders were too distressed to bear the sight, and sent their men off without accompanying them. Shooting infants and small children was particularly difficult for most, especially those with children of their own.

Once the brutalizing process began, all this became easier.[86] Nonetheless, the executioners sought a less traumatic, more sanitized, and less personal form of

---

[83] Rudolf Hoess, *Commandant of Auschwitz: The Autobiography of Rudolf Hoess* (Phoenix Press, 2000), p. 153. But this account is, of course, suspect for any number of reasons. Hoess himself estimated the number murdered at 2.5 million (p. 193). Others go as high as 3 million. Eichmann put total Jewish deaths at 6 million. Other estimates go as high as 7.5–9.5 million (Cohen, *Human Behaviour in the Concentration Camp*, pp. 10, 28).

[84] Hoess, *Commandant of Auschwitz*, pp. 132, 161, 183; Burleigh, *The Third Reich*, p. 648; Hannah Arendt, *Eichmann in Jerusalem: A Report on the Banality of Evil* (Faber & Faber, 1963), pp. 72, 78–9, 94–5.

[85] Some 5 million Soviet prisoners of war (POWs) died in German captivity. About 12 million civilians perished during the invasion (7 million of them Ukrainians), out of about 24–29 million Soviet citizens killed.

[86] Christopher R. Browning, *Ordinary Men: Reserve Police Battalion 101 and the Final Solution in Poland* (HarperCollins, 1992), pp. 14, 62, 65–6, 71–2, 82, 112, 140–1, 162, 185. Special instructions had been given for the 'spiritual care' of those involved in these shootings, whereby 'the impressions of the day are to be blotted out through the holding of social events in the evenings'. As early as November 1941, one entire Schutzstaffel (SS) hospital was devoted to treating men who had broken down from executing women and children (Burleigh, *The Third Reich*, p. 604).

murder. For this, a mechanism was already in place: the concentration camp. But it too needed to be refined and perfected.

The Concentration Camps

Concentration camps 'represent the extreme of the totalitarian regime: they are its quintessence, its most intense and concentrated manifestation'.[87] The first such camp in Germany, founded at Dachau in 1933, was for punishment, not extermination. Eventually, there were some 1,000 large and perhaps 15,000 smaller camps, through which some 10 million would pass, with perhaps 2–3 million surviving.[88] First extensively and systematically described in Eugen Kogon's well-named *The Theory and Practice of Hell* (1950), they held an average of about a million persons during the war.[89] Many were unlike traditional prisons in several respects. The most infamous at the war's end, Bergen-Belsen, was largely a holding camp, where disease rather than gas was the chief cause of death. In the five extermination camps, however (Chełmno, Bełżec, Sobibór, Treblinka, and Auschwitz-Birkenau), no one was meant to be healed, trained, or reformed, made whole, or reintegrated into society, or even just confined. This is not, as is commonly assumed, a prison model writ large. For Wolfgang Sofsky, 'the institution of the concentration camp resembles a social leprosarium, exaggerated to a murderous level, where all who had been excluded from the *Volksgemeinschaft* were isolated and then murdered'.[90] It thus represents the extension of an obsession with group purity and the threats of mental illness and racial and personal impurity. Sociogermophobia was the Nazi psychosis.

A Place beyond Hell: Auschwitz

Amidst the infinite horrors of the camps, one place outweighs all the rest in significance. This is the one true Hell that has ever been created on earth (indeed something rather worse), the 'island of death', the Auschwitz-Birkenau camp in annexed Poland, where over a million were murdered. The chief accounts of Auschwitz stress that much of what occurred there is virtually beyond comprehension to those who did not experience it, and practically impossible to convey in words. Survivors asked, 'What term does justice to physical, psychological, and moral annihilation, experienced in wretched shame?'[91] We can, then, speak here of the language of Hell, but still we fall well short in our description. That of dystopia, too, fails us here. Auschwitz tells us as much about humanity as it does about

---

[87] Todorov, *Facing the Extreme*, p. 28.
[88] Eugen Kogon, *The Theory and Practice of Hell: The German Concentration Camps and the System behind Them* (Octagon Books, 1973), p. 227.
[89] Johnson and Reuband, *What We Knew*, p. 353.
[90] Wolfgang Sofsky, *The Order of Terror: The Concentration Camp* (Princeton University Press, 1997), pp. 277, 209–10.
[91] Paul Steinberg, *Speak You Also: A Survivor's Reckoning* (Penguin Books, 2000), p. 19.

National Socialism. It proved, and still proves, our capacity to sink to hitherto unplumbed depths. And yet we must make an effort to understand it.

* * * *

The camp system at Auschwitz had three interwoven purposes: to provide short-term labour; to break down personality and dehumanize the inmates; and to kill them *en masse* in the gas chambers. Labour here was mostly a pretext, for death was nearly guaranteed. The destruction of the prisoners' humanity was a clear object. But this was mostly a sadistic exercise: their murder was the real point.

Killing the Body: Death by Work

The Auschwitz entrance gate, graced with the bitterly ironic slogan 'ARBEIT MACHT FREI', symbolized the grim reality of the actual truth: work might buy you a little time, but it would kill you, and thus 'free' you, in the second, ironic, and much more meaningful implication of the phrase, only of your earthly burdens.[92] You remained a slave no matter how much you worked. The average life expectancy was 2–3 months, exactly the time the Germans had estimated prisoners would last on rations of *c*.1,600 calories a day.[93] Work was only a pretext, or a delaying mechanism, because the murder rate was not rapid enough. In some camps, repetitive tasks like digging ditches and then filling them in again were imposed just to clarify the point.

Besides immediate extermination, death by starvation was thus the lot of most inmates. Half-dead, mere emaciated skeletons barely alive, souls almost without bodies, some weighing a mere twenty-eight kilos, the so-called *Muselmänner* had the effect of showing how close human beings could become to being both dead and merely animals without being either. They provided a constant reference point between life and death for the living. Such torture required no violence as such, but was essentially suggestive. 'This is you in a week or a month', these visions of decrepitude proposed: 'your fate too is inescapable'. Often diseased, the *Muselmänner* suggested contagion and weakness. In an ideology which used images of health and racial purity, such contamination justified extermination.[94] The living dead thus proved that their own fate was deserved.

'Here There is No Why': The Destruction of the Soul

In Wolfgang Sofsky's words, Auschwitz was a novel experiment to reduce 'social life, the foundation of any human selfhood, below the animal minimum. It does not suffice with obedience and subjugation, but strikes people in their entirety,

---

[92] The slogan originated with the I. G. Farben chemical firm, which had a large factory at Auschwitz.

[93] Rations in the Lodz ghetto at this point were *c*.800 calories per day (Primo Levi, *Moments of Reprieve* (Abacus Books, 1987), p. 166).

[94] 'We have exterminated a bacterium because we do not want in the end to be infected by the bacterium and die of it', said Himmler: Rhodes, *The Hitler Movement*, p. 50.

their social, mental, and physical existences.'[95] The process of disintegration was akin to plunging ever deeper in medieval images of the circles of Hell. By methodical, planned, deliberate measures, people descended by steps through trauma, suffering, violence, and indignity to land in that monstrous half-human, half-animal state which weds the worst of both beings. Many prisoners were subjected to such abuse and horror that they would reflect that 'there are infinitely worse things than death' (here a woman forced to sit upon a refuse heap, covered with worms and loathsome insects, which she had hated since birth). 'No stretch of the imagination, no power of the written word' can convey the plight of frozen naked women, 'living corpses', covered with lice and forced to lie in their urine and excreta for two months. Those on the freezing death marches in the final weeks of the war became 'really no longer human beings in the accepted sense. Not even animals, but putrefying corpses moving on two legs.'[96] Survivors describe 'the death of feeling, the death of thought, then the death of the man'. 'Our flesh and bones melt away, our teeth loosen, our guts liquefy, our wounds fester, and we die, we die, we die', one recalled. Others observed the 'transformation into a different variety of human being, no longer *Homo sapiens* but "extermination-camp man"'.[97] Reducing human beings to 'the bottom', to the lowest condition it was possible for a person to sink, or below what most could even conceive to sink, was so effective as to exceed the bounds of an older language, and perhaps to demand a new one.[98]

In such circumstances, the loss of one's 'real' or old personality occurs quickly. Disorientation is extreme. Adaptation to a new 'camp personality' takes place. But even here an 'acute depersonalization' or displacement occurred in which people felt that their own life and events around them were happening to others rather than themselves.[99] This defence mechanism then gave way as weakness produced depression and resignation. The feeling of powerlessness and alienation was overwhelming for most. The sense of a downward spiral and increasingly desperate struggle for survival trumped even fear. One of the best-known Auschwitz survivors, Primo Levi, would later reflect that there was no time for fear in everyday camp life. The quest for survival predominated over everything else.[100] Life was a four-letter word: food. The merest whiff or sight of it produced a 'ruthless and unscrupulous' animal-like sensation.[101]

Dehumanization occurred from many causes. Group nakedness enforced the absence of psychological protection. In their huts, inmates, both dead and alive, were jammed densely together in stench and filth. Here, with 'the compression of

---

[95] Sofsky, *The Order of Terror*, p. 281.

[96] Reska Weiss, *Journey through Hell: A Woman's Account of Her Experiences at the Hands of the Nazis* (Vallentine-Mitchell, 1961), pp. 103, 188–9, 211.

[97] Steinberg, *Speak You Also*, pp. 62–3, 73.

[98] See Primo Levi, *If This is a Man* and *The Truce* (Penguin Books, 1979), pp. 32–3: 'our language lacks words to express this offence, the demolition of a man . . . no human condition is more miserable than this, nor could it be conceivably so'.

[99] Cohen, *Human Behaviour in the Concentration Camp*, p. 116; Bruno Bettelheim, *The Informed Heart: The Human Condition in Modern Mass Society* (Thames & Hudson, 1960), pp. 115–19.

[100] Myriam Anissimov, *Primo Levi: The Tragedy of an Optimist* (Aurum Press, 1998), p. 131.

[101] Cohen, *Human Behaviour in the Concentration Camp*, pp. 132, 139.

human masses into the narrowest spaces', where they 'constantly saw, smelled, and touched one another, they were deindividualized and turned into an opaque mass of flesh'.[102] They were constantly preyed upon by vermin which infested beds and clothes. Large numbers succumbed to diseases like typhus and typhoid. Forced crowding with unrelated persons increased the sense of weakness, of contagion from immediate contact, of violence, of the need to establish some zone of safety around oneself. With virtually no space between individuals, and all privacy eradicated, in the lowest form of sub-social association, any sense of an intimate lone self was quickly lost. Instead, an intense mutual hatred and 'brutal indifference' prevailed.[103] Soon the personality was utterly broken down and an essentially 'subhuman' entity created. Fear, humiliation, torment, torture were here not aimed at regulating behaviour but at destroying the personality by eradicating every aspect of civility (especially cleanliness) which distinguishes a humane existence. And 'in this soul-destroying process animal instincts gained the upper hand'.[104] Eventually, Levi comments, comes the 'death of the soul', when a person breaks under pressure.[105] What remains is then only a shell, the phantasm or illusion of humanity, not an automaton, not an animal, but the shadow of a human being, a kind of monster created in reverse by disassembly.

As we saw in the case of the Stalinist purges, absurdity was one means used to achieve dehumanization. One could die quite arbitrarily at nearly any time of day or night for the slightest infraction of the rules, or for none at all, or for 'infractions' of 'rules' which did not exist. So Levi found when he was refused permission to eat a piece of frozen ice; he enquired why he should not and was told, '*Hier ist kein Warum*' (there is no why here).[106] This is a post- or pre-rational world. Reason suited human beings, not you: this was the clear message. As if the utter arbitrariness of punishment were not sufficient, an atmosphere of insane cynicism had to be added, almost as a parody on terror itself. The point was pointlessness.

The demented gallows humour of some aspects of camp life is well exemplified by the slogans gracing public spaces. One sign Himmler ordered hung at Buchenwald read: 'There is one path to freedom. Its milestones are called obedience, industry, honesty, order, discipline, cleanliness, sobriety, the willingness to sacrifice, and love of the fatherland.'[107] Here, too, 'My Country—Right or Wrong'. And on one steel gate (which could also be seen from the inside), painted bright red, 'To Each His Own' (*Jedem das Seine*), a motto embodying justice drawn from Roman law—extremely paradoxical, obviously ironical, perhaps intentionally absurd, a regular logical labyrinth. At Treblinka, where some eight hundred thousand were murdered by engine exhaust fumes from a captured Soviet tank, many died within twenty minutes of arriving, and entire trainloads within two hours. Here too the Nazis could not resist mocking their victims, even in death: a Hebrew

---

[102] Hermann Langbein, *People in Auschwitz* (University of North Carolina Press, 2004), p. 68.
[103] Sofsky, *The Order of Terror*, p. 320. [104] Weiss, *Journey through Hell*, p. 121.
[105] Levi, *The Drowned and the Saved*, p. 42.
[106] Levi, *If This is a Man* and *The Truce*, p. 35: Anissimov, *Primo Levi*, p. 115.
[107] David A. Hackett, ed., *The Buchenwald Report* (Westview Press, 1995), p. 57.

inscription hung over one gas chamber entrance reading, 'This is the gate through which the righteous enter.' (The 'road to Heaven' on the way 'up the chimney' or 'going to Saint Peter' were common expressions for the path to the gas chambers.)

Everywhere, thus, there was a deliberately instilled feeling of senselessness. Jews who were constantly reminded that labour alone brought redemption clung to the hope that their labour power would not be squandered, discovering too late that their destruction trumped any value they had to the war effort. Prisoners who were nursed back to health in the primitive hospital were sometimes gassed directly after recovery. (Others, even with only minor illnesses, were killed by injection almost immediately.)[108] Those 'selected' and condemned to be gassed sometimes received double rations the night beforehand. The provision of bands playing marching music for work parties, the theme tunes of death, lent a sense of the bizarre and macabre to the proceedings; 'infernal', Levi calls it.[109] Those on the spot, even afterwards, sometimes found the facts unbelievable, and denied their possibility, assuming such allegations to be 'just propaganda'.[110] (Ironically, just speculating on the existence of the gas chambers out loud risked an immediate death sentence.)

The Beginning: Enumerization

Destruction at Auschwitz commenced with transportation in deportation trains from every corner of Europe. Often this involved lengthy journeys without food or water. For 1,600 from Corfu it was 20 days, standing until enough died (5–10 per cent). On arrival, the cattle wagons thus disgorged an already decrepit cargo.[111] As they emerged, prisoners were overwhelmed by feelings of powerlessness, shame, guilt, and terror. From July 1942, 'selection' at the larger Birkenau camp took place straightaway, next to the tracks which brought carriages in. SS doctors chose about 20 per cent as suitable for labour. The rest were gassed more or less immediately. Nearly all the rest, even the few babies who had survived so far, were then tattooed.[112] This process made them feel 'as if we were transformed into stone' and looked like 'dangerous-looking, insane criminals'.[113] The tattoo was like branding animals, or making people objects, like factory equipment. The tattoo number was their new identity.[114] Its significance was obvious. One inmate recalled: 'From that moment on, I ceased to be a human being. I stopped feeling,

---

[108] Perhaps 30,000 by late 1943. See Langbein, *People in Auschwitz*, p. 34.

[109] Levi, *If This is a Man* and *The Truce*, pp. 56–7; 'the expression of . . . the resolution of others to annihilate us first as men in order to kill us more slowly afterwards'.

[110] Donald L. Niewyk, ed., *Fresh Wounds: Early Narratives of Holocaust Survival* (University of North Carolina Press, 1998), p. 375.

[111] By contrast, some wealthy Jews reached Treblinka in normal railway carriages with full service.

[112] The SS were also tattooed, though only with their blood type.

[113] Niewyk, *Fresh Wounds*, p. 358; Ber Mark, *The Scrolls of Auschwitz* (Am Oved Publishers, 1985), p. 197.

[114] Shlomo Venezia, *Inside the Gas Chambers: Eight Months in the Sonderkommando of Auschwitz* (Polity Press, 2009), p. 41.

thinking. I no longer had a name, an address. I was prisoner no. 55 908.'[115] This number had to be used in every encounter with authority. As Bettelheim recounted, 'for a Jewish prisoner it would go: "Jewish prisoner number 34567 most obediently prays to be permitted to (whatever the request was)."'[116] Losing one's name, Sofsky notes, is 'among the most far-reaching and profound mutilations of the self'.[117] Self-respect relies on a sense of an individual self existing to respect. No one respects a number, unless, amongst prisoners, it was low and denoted survival.

Disrobed in public, their clothing confiscated, possessions stolen, and heads shaven, new inmates were quickly 'almost dehumanised with terror'. Their first glimpse of other prisoners made them think these were 'surely all lunatics', for so they appeared.[118] Some, like Elie Wiesel, were told directly by the SS that the choice was either 'work or the crematory'.[119] Others selected for work were informed by other prisoners that their relatives had been killed immediately. Some were not fed or given water for days after arriving.[120] The wretched diet soon ravaged their bodies, and cannibalism would eventually occur. Food distribution, on which life depended, was itself a specialized form of torture. Starvation rations were commonly and instantaneously denied for many infractions. Dysentery was rife. The few toilets were rarely accessible. Most of Auschwitz-Birkenau stank of urine and excrement. Prisoners frequently walked in and even slept in both. Sometimes prisoners were forced to lie in their excrement, or had their heads pushed into toilet bowls, provoking mental breakdown. In the huts, excrement was often mixed with pus, vomit, and blood. On various death marches it was forbidden to go to the toilet at all, so prisoners were covered with urine and excreta. This 'excremental assault' aimed at producing a sense of defilement. It succeeded.[121]

Uni(de)formity and Group Identity

Prisoners were 'clothed' in torn, ill-fitting, filthy striped uniforms thrown at them, often insufficient even to cover their bodies. Upon these their number was sewn. The chief variations were the symbols worn on uniforms denoting categories, which might include national origins ('F' for French, for example). At Auschwitz this was most typically two yellow triangles (or yellow with another colour, usually red) for the chief *Rassenfeind*, the Jews. Red triangles denoted political prisoners, pink for homosexuals, purple for Jehovah's Witnesses, black for 'asocials' and prostitutes, green for criminals, and so on. The reds and the greens had positions of power here, and even predominated in particular sub-camps. Rivalry between 'politicals' and criminals was common. Sometimes, where nationalities could band together (like

---

[115] Sofsky, *The Order of Terror*, p. 82. This was the number of Krystyna Żywulska, a Polish political prisoner.
[116] Bettelheim, *The Informed Heart*, p. 132.   [117] Sofsky, *The Order of Terror*, p. 84.
[118] Weiss, *Journey through Hell*, pp. 36–8.
[119] Elie Wiesel, *Night* (Penguin Books, 1981), p. 50.
[120] Weiss, *Journey through Hell*, pp. 44, 47.
[121] Terence Des Pres, *The Survivor: An Anatomy of Life in the Death Camps* (Oxford University Press, 1976), p. 57.

the Czechs or Salonika Greeks), these symbols provided an important bond and means of survival. This was true of POWs (Russians, Yugoslavs) too, as well as communists and co-religionists. (It was also a source of division exploited by the SS, and even Jews came to see one another as opposed nationalities rather than co-religionists, the modern group trumping the ancient.)[122] The little camaraderie existing in Auschwitz, Primo Levi notes, was 'confined to compatriots, and toward them it was weakened by minimal life conditions'.[123] All others were 'foreigners' and 'enemies'.[124] Others have noted that limited solidarity emerged only where there was enough to eat, as in the *Sonderkommandos*.[125]

Thus, despite this intense competition, the camps were not miniature versions of 'mass society', for they harboured too many inequalities.[126] Nazi pseudo-scientific race theory provided a hierarchy. A small aristocracy of mostly Aryan prisoner officials, the *Prominente*, enjoyed privileges, authority, even the power to kill. As representatives of the *Herrenvolk* German prisoners ranked high here, with criminals and political prisoners leading them. Jews and Slavs were at the bottom. But here too distinctions existed. Having a low camp registration number proved knowledge of the secrets of longevity, which might rub off on others. Newcomers with laughably high numbers were treated with disdain and contempt as wholly ignorant of how to survive. Whole cohorts of national intakes were instantly recognizable by their number ranges. At a glance, a 200,000, otherwise a tangled mass of bones and decrepit flesh, is a Frenchman from the Vosges.[127] So a primitive solidarity might emerge.

Any possibility of mutual assistance was limited, however, by the harsh conditions which prevailed. But complete atomization was avoided through group identities which might mitigate the initial shock and trauma of camp existence and provide a shred of hope for survival. Even resistance was possible through strong religious or ideological beliefs, a counter-identity powerful enough not to be destroyed here. Jehovah's Witnesses and other groups attained a degree of psychological stamina few could match and many envied. Yet other zealots probably undermined those around them. A rabbinical judge present at one crematorium perversely insisted, invoking the ultimate metaphysical scapegoat, that 'We are here to do God's mission. God wants it this way', insisting that even the little children killed were guilty of sin and 'tainted from their mothers' milk'.[128] (Primo Levi's reply: 'If there is an Auschwitz, then there cannot be a God.') Yet it was impossible to survive without collaboration and moral compromise. And Levi noted that the 'harsher the oppression, the more widespread among the oppressed is the willingness to collaborate with the power'.[129]

---

[122] Langbein, *People in Auschwitz*, p.13.   [123] Levi, *Moments of Reprieve*, p. 67.
[124] Primo Levi, *The Reawakening* (Little, Brown & Company, 1965), p. 14.
[125] Venezia, *Inside the Gas Chambers*, pp. 100–1.   [126] Sofsky, *The Order of Terror*, p. 153–5.
[127] Levi, *The Reawakening*, p. 20.
[128] Gideon Greif, *We Wept without Tears: Testimonies of the Jewish Sonderkommando from Auschwitz* (Yale University Press, 2005), p. 318.
[129] Anissimov, *Primo Levi*, pp. 181, 144.

Daily Life

'Hell' is the nearest fictional analogy or imaginary construct we have to Auschwitz. Most accounts of Auschwitz call it a 'hell on earth'.[130] In Chełmno, where the first experiments with gas began in December 1941, and 400,000 Jews died, the lorries in which prisoners were 'processed'—gassed with carbon monoxide—were called 'hell-vans'. A *Sonderkommando* diary retrieved from Auschwitz after the war described the Germans as a nation of 'Satan's servants'.[131] George Steiner calls it 'hell made immanent'. Others term it 'a strange planet', 'the next world', 'the hinterland of death', 'time overstepping its boundaries' (all by Yehiel Dinur, an inmate). One account saw the Nazis' efforts as 'Satan's work of elimination'.[132]

Yet this language is strangely inadequate to the task. Reality trumps the imagination. Bosch's and Dante's 'Hell', and every other, pale beside these tortures, more numerous and varied than anything idle monks and imaginative inquisitors could conceive.[133] Here human ingenuity indeed surpassed even the powers of imagination. Of Primo Levi's first day in Auschwitz, his first hours in a barracks, after a four-day journey without water, he later wrote:

> This is hell. Today, in our times, hell must be like this. A huge empty room: we are tired, standing on our feet, with a tap which drips while we cannot drink the water, and we wait for something which will certainly be terrible, and nothing happens, and nothing continues to happen.

Yet Hell, we might respond, at least had a purpose, was a rational construct, occupied a fitting place in a theory of cosmic justice, served as a mechanism to uphold everyday morals. By contrast, Auschwitz was defiantly senseless, obstinately meaningless. The camp was (Levi again) 'not a punishment', only 'a manner of living assigned to us, without limits of time, in the bosom of the Germanic social organism'.[134] A Nazi doctor who witnessed the gassing wrote in his diary that 'Compared to this the Inferno by Dante seems to be as a comedy.'[135] Another eyewitness agreed that 'such unspeakable vileness... made Dante's *Inferno* appear like a pleasure garden'.[136] And another (Franz Stangl): 'Dante come to life.'[137] The moderns of course aim to excel. What earlier theologians, monks, poets, and painters could not even imagine, the Nazis actually created. So we need a new concept here: Hell will not suffice.

Daily life was a chronic, unrelenting struggle. Time was managed as cruelly as space. A frenzied rising at 4:00 or 4:30 (an hour later in winter) commenced a routine of cleaning, dressing, eating, roll-call, assembly, work, all interspersed with panic and violence. Morning and evening roll-calls were a form of torture on their own. Standing for hours on end frequently killed the weakest. Even the dead

---

[130] Mark, *The Scrolls of Auschwitz*, p. 15.
[131] Yisrael Gutman and Michael Berenbaum, eds., *Anatomy of the Auschwitz Deathcamp* (Indiana University Press, 1994), p. 524.
[132] Mark, *The Scrolls of Auschwitz*, pp. 16, 178.   [133] Ibid., p. 198.
[134] Levi, *If This is a Man* and *The Truce*, pp. 28, 89.
[135] Cohen, *Human Behaviour in the Concentration Camp*, p. 238.
[136] Filip Müller, *Eyewitness Auschwitz: Three Years in the Gas Chambers* (Ivan R. Dee, 1979), p. 133.
[137] Sereny, *Into that Darkness*, p. 157.

needed to be present to make up accurate numbers, however. So, still compelled to obedience, they too were laid out on the ground to submit in supine silence to the power of their murderers. Corpses hanging from the gallows in the *Appelplatz* hinted at the close proximity of death. The constant fear of 'selection' of those deemed unfit to work haunted prisoners.[138] Standing at attention, marching in an orderly fashion, saluting in the regulation manner, responding verbally to orders, were all strictly regimented. Marching to work could be rendered more macabre by enforced singing, or more difficult by being ordered at double-time. Work itself, frequently accompanied by violence, 'was always terror time', in Sofsky's phrase.[139]

And always one had to be vigilant. Everything precious, which was everything—clothes, food, shoes—could be stolen in an instant. No angels, one's fellow inmates: 'All are enemies or rivals.' Even sleep was a torment, the constant daytime dream of food driven by ever-present hunger and thirst transmuted into a collective nightmare of food not quite possessed, water vanishing before one's eyes, vainly provoking mass salivation.[140] But *could* there be 'nightmares' in Auschwitz? *Could* any mere *dream* be worse than this reality? One survivor wrote that in camp he did not awaken fellow prisoners having nightmares, knowing that 'no matter how bad the dream may be, reality was worse'.[141]

In winter, a desperate biting cold killed thousands. Random savage beatings and a hundred forms of ritual humiliation were routine.[142] Those who did not understand German, or at least the crude camp variant like that used with children and animals, died soonest. Everyone who did not move at double-time for every task risked a beating. ('Faster, faster' was a word which echoed for decades after in prisoners' memories.)[143] The constant babel of mostly incomprehensible languages was infinitely confusing but also hinted at life and death. Merely sealing space off as such, of course enabled surveillance and control. Rigorously organizing time within this space minimized individual flexibility, mobility, or freedom. Symbols of violence were everywhere: barbed wire, guard towers, electrified fences, gallows, armed guards, the death strip with warning signs ('Danger of Death!'—more irony in a death camp), minefields, loudspeakers and searchlights, aggressive dogs.[144] (Below being subhuman was sub-animal: so in the camps police dogs were fed much better and treated much better.)[145] Crematoria, too, were often seen and always smelled, the sickly-sweet odour of flesh hanging around the camp for miles around.

---

[138] 'Selection', 'transfer', 'special' all being synonyms for murder.
[139] Sofsky, *The Order of Terror*, p. 77.   [140] Levi, *If This is a Man* and *The Truce*, pp. 48, 67.
[141] Des Pres, *The Survivor*, p. 75.
[142] This regime was much worse under Rudolf Hoess than his successor, Lt-Col. Liebehenschel. The latter was reportedly appalled by conditions at the camp and ordered an immediate cessation of capital punishment. But he stayed only six months and when Hoess returned so did his regime. See Langbein, *People in Auschwitz*, p. 45.
[143] Langbein, *People in Auschwitz*, p. 67.
[144] Wiesel noted: 'Danger of Death. Mockery: was there a single place here where you were not in danger of death?' (*Night*, p. 51).
[145] One SS man shot his dog for nestling in a prisoner's lap: an extreme form of 'defilement' indeed (Burleigh, *The Third Reich*, p. 204). Elinor Lipper records the case of a Gulag prisoner who petitioned to be granted the status of a horse so that he could have more food and time off work (*Eleven Years in Soviet Prison Camps* (Hollis & Carter, 1951), p. 226).

Everyday Violence

Violence permeated life in Auschwitz. Universal terror and fear reigned, categorized (according to one inmate) by segregation, debasement, humiliation, and extermination.[146] Death might be drawn out. But it could also come quickly, by beating, shooting, drowning, being buried alive, or other forms of murder. New prisoners were commonly beaten on arrival, to teach them the principles of the place. Intellectuals, especially those wearing glasses, were a favoured target, the symbol of educated privilege denoting the distance—the greater, the more rewarding— which violence could force an individual to fall.[147] The slightest deviation from clothing regulations, sleeping rules (only a thin shirt was permitted), bed-making, or the placement of personal possessions was punished by block administrators, themselves usually prisoners. Public floggings, enforced standing for hours, assignment to deadly work in mines or quarries, punishment details of various types, random beatings, and murder were all routinely inflicted. Dachau contained 'dog cells' where prisoners could only lie down and were made to bark for their food.[148] Auschwitz too contained one-metre-square 'bunker' punishment cells where as many as four prisoners might be crammed. The penalty for many infractions, including lying down on the ground, was often death. Guards were actually encouraged to shoot prisoners 'attempting to escape', earning rewards thereby.[149]

Prolonging violence by using alternating methods of torture, and allowing for brief periods of recovery, maximized pain. Exacting pain and ingeniousness in brutality were also a source of both competition and amusement amongst the guards. (Laughter, indeed, accompanied many of the more perverse tortures, particularly those involving humiliation.) A sense of individual responsibility for such acts was avoided by the feeling of group and organizational responsibility. Violence, in turn, demonstrated a proof of belonging, and extreme violence, of outstanding dedication. Abstaining from cruelty in such circumstances was considered abnormal, and guards were punished for exhibiting any kind of pity.[150]

Some of this had a rational point, if the concept applies here. Many punishments were designed to encourage work or prevent escape. Random violence also superseded the need for permanent surveillance, which was impossible.[151] And yet because extermination was already a very labour-intensive process, violence which might have occurred did not. Much subterfuge was used to lure victims to the gas chambers and to avoid panic and time-wasting. The progression of prisoners to a supposed delousing shower was the main such ruse. Speeches were sometimes made

---

[146] Kogon, *The Theory and Practice of Hell*, p. 30.

[147] Also in Dachau: Bruno Bettelheim, *Surviving and Other Essays* (Thames & Hudson, 1979), p. 12. Bettelheim noted that the SA and SS 'hated most those prisoners who came from the professional or otherwise well-educated middle classes', indicating the intensity of class resentment: *The Informed Heart*, p. 206.

[148] Kogon, *The Theory and Practice of Hell*, p. 207.

[149] Sofsky, *The Order of Terror*, p. 57.

[150] One had a sign on his desk reading 'Compassion is weakness': Langbein, *People in Auschwitz*, p. 282.

[151] Sofsky, *The Order of Terror*, pp. 260, 192.

about the future Jewish state. Inmates were assured that those who worked would save their lives. Prisoners were told that they would be reunited with their possessions.[152] The need to murder thus curiously limited the need for violence.

In an essay, 'Useless Violence', Primo Levi suggests that the Nazi camps utilized 'widespread useless violence, as an end in itself, with the sole purpose of creating pain'. No justification for this derives from any Superman or master-race ideal. This cruelty was systematic, and the accompanying humiliation was as complete and ritualized as could be devised. Levi points to public nakedness, the lack of eating utensils, lengthy roll-calls, enforced bed-making, the tattooing of prisoners' numbers on their arms, and similar activities as all essentially pointless, and designed merely to torment. Levi doubted that many of the guards were psychopaths or sadists: they had simply been educated to accept the normality of violence. Their brutality in turn made their work as executioners easier.[153] Often the most violent were *Kapos*, who headed labour details, or *Blockälteste*, hut leaders, themselves prisoners defending their privileges with violence.

The cruelty which dominated everyday life in Auschwitz was astonishing. Everyday beatings were understood, Levi relates, 'as an incitement to work, a warning or punishment'. Some guards, however, used pain 'to produce suffering and humiliation'.[154] Many rules, like the nearly impossible tasks of ensuring smooth beds or clean shoes, were pointless, and designed only to harass the prisoners and to prove the power relationship among the SS, prisoner warders, and the prisoners. Death on the gallows was often by strangulation, to prolong the agony.

To Sofsky, the routine torment of camp life, however, was not the result of a specially sadistic group of SS guards being in charge. Uncontrolled violence driven by pleasure in tormenting others was rare. Camp violence was routine, almost bureaucratized, a part of the job description. Excessive violence simply for its own sake, 'terror per se', only to prove one's power, did, of course, occur.[155] Trials and memoirs reveal many cases of extreme sadism, for instance of children being smashed against walls.[156] Some remember all the SS guards as sadists, and later recalled them as being 'excited' by killing.[157] Indisputably, many if not most were gratified in some manner through their brutality.[158] For Arendt, this sadism,

---

[152] The Potemkin-village-style railway station at Treblinka, with its flower boxes, station clock painted to read 3:00, and other gaily painted artifices, is perhaps the most striking illustration of these ruses. See Jean-François Steiner, *Treblinka* (Weidenfeld & Nicolson, 1967), p. 162.

[153] Levi, *The Drowned and the Saved*, pp. 83, 101.   [154] Ibid., p. 55.

[155] Sofsky, *The Order of Terror*, pp. 223–4.

[156] Bernd Nauman, *Auschwitz: A Report on the Proceedings against Robert Karl Ludwig Mulka and Others before the Court at Frankfurt* (Pall Mall Press, 1966), p. 123. Wilhelm Boger was the murderer here.

[157] Greif, *We Wept without Tears*, p. 278; Nauman, *Auschwitz*, p. 130. See the summary of SS character in Gutman and Berenbaum, *Anatomy of the Auschwitz Deathcamp*, pp. 267–362.

[158] Hoess, *Commandant of Auschwitz*, p. 117, even admits this, while, of course, denying that his own behaviour was anything other than utterly professional, and insisting that he 'had a heart' and 'was not evil' (p. 181). Some, apparently ironically, but in fact quite consistently, were completely repulsed by being touched with the blood of victims they shot, and would even kill nearby inmates if they had been (Venezia, *Inside the Gas Chambers*, p. 78).

'basically sexual', was a dominant 'human factor' at Auschwitz.[159] Some non-German and some Jewish *Kapos* were also notoriously cruel, and indeed were often chosen for this quality. Doubtless, many were, like their SS masters, little men who were 'nobody and suddenly had power' and a life of relative luxury.[160] Some few, usually politicals, stand out for their relative humanity. But for many their survival depended upon appearing to be zealous, so their beatings were much worse when the SS were near.[161]

Below this level of Hell was another deeper layer. The infamous medical experiments engaged in by 'the most hated man in the world', as he became, Josef Mengele, are so gruesome as to defy understanding. Here, the wanton torture of children, especially twins, in the name of 'racial science', included unnecessary surgery, amputations, injections with diseases, and attempts to change eye colour. To dystopia, Mengele has bequeathed one formidable image: in his office was a wall of eyes, 'pinned up like butterflies'. 'I thought I was dead and already living in hell', a witness later recalled.[162]

The SS Guards

The concentration camps were administered by an elite military force, the SS, or Schutzstaffel (protection squadron), who were supposed to possess greater personal dedication to Hitler than ordinary Wehrmacht units. The SS saw itself as a small elite governing a much large class of slaves who could only 'work and obey'.[163] The organization, with its imitation runic symbol of the lightning strike (⚡⚡), was conceived in another woeful instance of misbegotten romanticism as a sacred order or voluntary nobility akin to the Teutonic knights. Its obsessive fixation upon death and destruction, and its symbol, the naked skull or death's head, with

[159] Hannah Arendt, in Nauman, *Auschwitz*, pp. xxvii–iii. For evidence of this, respecting Hoess, see *Commandant at Auschwitz*, pp. 92–7, and, respecting ritual flogging in particular, Klaus Theweleit, *Male Fantasies* (Polity Press, 1989), vol. 2, pp. 301–9. Torture by hitting the genitals was particularly associated with sadism (Nauman, *Auschwitz*, p. 259). This explanation is, however, somewhat circuitous, de Sade being chiefly associated with the idea of sexual pleasure being gained from the pain of others. To assert with Freud that sadism is rooted in *eros* is thus, to some degree, only to say that sadism is what de Sade practised, and to leave open the possibility of other forms of sadism. The desecration of female corpses at Auschwitz, particularly the cutting off of breasts, suggests that misogyny is a related motive here (Nauman, *Auschwitz*, p. 271). Aspects of SS medical experimentation also had sexual overtones (Cohen, *Human Behaviour in the Concentration Camp*, p. 87). Some prisoners also reported that guards had told them they beat women savagely because the sight of them aroused erotic feelings which went unfulfilled (Weiss, *Journey through Hell*, p. 168). Incidents of rape were extremely common during the killing campaigns on the Eastern Front, while the pornographic quality of some Nazi propaganda, especially Streicher's *Der Stürmer*, has often been commented on. On the background to the theme, see Edward Glover, *War, Sadism and Pacifism: Further Essays on Group Psychology and War* (George Allen & Unwin, 1946). This is, however, chiefly concerned with the death instinct in relation to war.

[160] Langbein, *People in Auschwitz*, p. 151.

[161] Gutman and Berenbaum, *Anatomy of the Auschwitz Deathcamp*, p. 56. See the portrait of Mietek in Müller, *Eyewitness Auschwitz*, pp. 40–1.

[162] Gerald L. Posner and John Ware, *Mengele: The Complete Story* (Queen Anne Press, 1986), pp. 34, 277. Mengele killed some prisoners specifically because of their eye colour.

[163] Kogon, *The Theory and Practice of Hell*, p. 15.

crossbones, became perhaps the most enduring of all Nazi emblems. The SS shared all of the characteristics of the classic dystopian group, building its own identity upon hatred and the merciless oppression of others, and measuring its own worth by their degradation.

While the banality of their everyday routine of extermination is often stressed, SS camp guards were also notoriously brutal. For a new race of supermen, however, they were curiously inferior. Often maladjusted, frustrated, unsuccessful, and lonely, possessed of a deep sense of personal inferiority requiring constant compensation, their educational attainments were 'far below average' (only a fifth to secondary school level).[164] It is easy to see how the smart uniform and arrogant cruelty appealed to these misfits. Many saw camp service as a way of avoiding front-line duty. Corruption (embezzlement, shakedowns, theft, etc.), despite stringent penalties, was also rife up to the highest ranks—indeed, encouraged by Hitler.[165] Often guards collaborated with the 'green' criminal prisoners, who, in so many respects, they resembled.[166] Inside the camp, most services could be bought at a price.

Below the Lowest Circle of Hell

Descending within Auschwitz, one still worse, unimaginable, 'much more tragic, much more horrible' level remains to be plumbed.[167] This was the experience of the seven hundred to a thousand *Sonderkommando* prisoners, who oversaw the gassing of prisoners, the removal of their corpses from the gas chambers, and their final disposal.

First they stood mutely by or assisted as prisoners were told they needed disinfecting before beginning work. They had to beat those who were reluctant to enter the 'showers' and had to be forced down the concrete steps underground, to stand in rows of three to five. Inside they supervised prisoners, now often weeping copiously, as they entered the changing room, where they were told to remember the hook number where their clothes were placed. They then herded them onwards, as if on a conveyor belt headed for the ovens. Women went first, then men, to the 'Disinfection Room', the name itself a precise description of their sociomedical relation to the German Reich, the room—but it is the humour which is sick—was adorned with slogans like 'cleanliness brings freedom'.[168] If the *Sonderkommando* was not active enough here, they risked being shoved in themselves by the SS.[169] Meanwhile, a vehicle marked with a Red Cross symbol—still more grim humour—conveyed the Zyklon B gas canisters to the building (see Figs. 4.2 and 4.3). An SS

[164] Ibid., pp. 258, 266.

[165] Weiss, *Journey through Hell*, p. 34; Rauschning, *Hitler Speaks*, pp. 90–1. A few were arrested by the Gestapo for this offence.

[166] They were described at Buchenwald as corrupt 'through and through' (Hackett, *The Buchenwald Report*, p. 122).

[167] Langbein, *People in Auschwitz*, p. 202.

[168] The SS men trained to use the gas were called 'disinfectors': Langbein, *People in Auschwitz*, p. 285.

[169] But see the disavowal of this claim: Greif, *We Wept without Tears*, p. 56.

Fig. 4.2. Gas chamber, Majdanek concentration camp. © Gregory Claeys.

Fig. 4.3. Gas chamber complex (destroyed) Auschwitz-Birkenau concentration camp. © Gregory Claeys.

man emptied the pellets down small chutes. Within fifteen minutes all inside were dead. A German doctor announced 'the business is done'. As many as 3,000 were killed at a time in one room, up to 24,000 a day in peak periods, often within a few hours of arrival.[170]

A sight surpassing 'the worse nightmare' now confronted the *Sonderkommando*.[171] As the gas rose, the strongest, in their last moments of life, clawed their way to the top, trampling upon and crushing the bodies of the weak, and of women and children. What the *Sonderkommando* saw when the doors were opened can scarcely be described. Wading through the last crystals of Zyklon B, they had to wrench apart the entangled naked corpses, fused together by the effects of the gas, covered with blood, urine, and excrement, their vessels having burst through internal haemorrhaging. Their faces were contorted with agony, the flesh torn and mangled from the final struggle to ascend the heap of bodies in search of air.

Hauling the corpses out, the *Sonderkommando* now extracted gold teeth, broke off fingers to detach rings, and searched orifices for hidden valuables.[172] Women's hair was sheared; at least six goods-wagons' worth, some sixty tons in total, was sent away for use as felt socks and stockings. (Seven tons, now almost all grey, remained when liberation came.)[173] Then came the laborious pitchforking of corpses into the crematoria, when the bodies sometimes 'sprang to life' from the heat. Small wonder that some later thought that 'the dead were perhaps luckier than the living; they were no longer forced to endure this Hell on earth, to see the cruelty of men'.[174]

Almost every remaining trace of existence disappeared in twenty minutes, at the rate of a thousand an hour or more, sometimes twenty thousand a day. In outside pits, the 'worst of all' of even these jobs was that of the ash team, who had to climb into the pits and shovel the still-hot ashes, amongst which were many half-burnt body parts, into heaps.[175] Streams of liquid human fat surrounded them. Sometimes civilian technicians, more engineers of death, looked on, taking detailed notes to see how less coke might be used to burn bodies, and what combination of corpses, young and old, skeletal and less so, burnt most rapidly, to the greater triumph of science and efficiency in this factory of death.

---

[170] Hoess, *Commandant of Auschwitz*, p. 192, estimates 9,000. The initial use of Zyklon B had been for disinfection.

[171] Of the sight when the gas chambers were opened, one *Sonderkommando* member later wrote that 'Nobody can even imagine what it was like' (Venezia, *Inside the Gas Chambers*, p. 65). At Treblinka, we are told, 'Under the effect of the heat the belly of a pregnant woman burst like an over-ripe fruit, expelling the foetus, which went up in flames' (Steiner, *Treblinka*, p. 278). At Treblinka, 700,000 bodies had to be exhumed from mass graves and burnt.

[172] Five to ten kilos-worth a day; Greif, *We Wept without Tears*, pp. 195, 223; Müller, *Eyewitness Auschwitz*, p. 68. The removal of teeth was delegated to one person alone, at least one was a genuine Czech dentist, others were Greeks: a hell within a hell within a hell (Greif, *We Wept without Tears*, pp. 112, 197). The gold was often stolen by SS officers.

[173] Gutman and Berenbaum, *Anatomy of the Auschwitz Deathcamp*, pp. 260–2.

[174] Venezia, *Inside the Gas Chambers*, p. 62. With the cruellest of ironies, Rudolf Hoess described the 'callous' and 'dumb indifference' with which these tasks were carried out (*Commandant of Auschwitz*, pp. 152, 199).

[175] Müller, *Eyewitness Auschwitz*, pp. 138–9.

At the very end, too little gas was used, and many were thrown into the crematoria still alive.[176] The ashes were often used for agricultural fertilizer (even the dead could be made to work), or scattered in the Vistula as 'fish food'. Inconceivably, for the mentality again defies belief, fat was manufactured into soap, stamped 'RJF'—*Reines Juden Fett* (pure Jewish lard), the most perfectly brutal symbol of the 'cleaning' the Nazis intended. Bars were actually handed out to some prisoners (Hungarian Jews, who constituted almost a third of Auschwitz's victims—437,402 people). Some were also kept as souvenirs by guards.[177] Each body thus became simply a unit or resource from which value could be extracted: 'not only human labor but the total person became [a] commodity'.[178] The total net profit for the Reich per inmate, counting nine months' labour each, clothing, dental gold, and personal possessions, was estimated by the SS themselves (who subtracted the cost of cremation) at about £500.[179]

Some, amazingly, survived these most gruesome of tasks not only physically but psychologically. How they did so, like so much of the process itself, almost defies comprehension. Work like this, one recalled, compressed a lifetime's suffering into a day.[180] Some *Sonderkommando* members begged to be killed on the spot rather than do the work.[181] At least one (Rudolf Vrba) tried to enter the gas chambers to die along with others. Some prayed as they went about their work, perhaps for forgiveness, perhaps for mercy, perhaps to save a small piece of their own conscience, as likely for a quick end to their own lives. These Jews could warn no one of their impending fate, not even, in one case, their own mother.[182] Yet unendurably intense emotions of despair and anguish were soon suppressed. For survival was otherwise impossible. Unhappiness is a luxury of the free.[183] And, decently housed, some in dormitories above the crematoria, they ate and drank to their heart's content.[184] And soon the work came to seem 'absolutely normal, as if life were like that'.[185] Some would even sit on corpses during a brief meal break. Humanity's capacity for cruelty seems matched only by its ability to adjust.

Explaining Auschwitz

The Germans, indeed, were often called monsters, even, as individuals, 'a monster conscious of his monstrosity'.[186] Yet to speak of the monstrosity of the Holocaust is, as we have seen, perhaps a misnomer, an insult to monsters, a displacement or denial, yet another scapegoat. If the Holocaust is, in Zygmunt Bauman's phrase, a 'test of modernity' which proves that 'we do not yet have as yet enough civilization',

---

[176] Niewyk, *Fresh Wounds*, pp. 315–16.

[177] Weiss, *Journey through Hell*, p. 154; Posner and Ware, *Mengele*, p. 161.

[178] Bettelheim, *The Informed Heart*, p. 243.

[179] That is, 1,630 marks, or $745 in 1994 (Gutman and Berenbaum, *Anatomy of the Auschwitz Deathcamp*, p. 262); Kogon, *The Theory and Practice of Hell*, p. 269.

[180] Greif, *We Wept without Tears*, p. 121.   [181] Müller, *Eyewitness Auschwitz*, p. 17.

[182] Greif, *We Wept without Tears*, pp. 35, 60–1.   [183] Anissimov, *Primo Levi*, p. 154.

[184] In Crematoria I [II] and II [III]. Elsewhere inmates lived on the ground floor.

[185] Greif, *We Wept without Tears*, p. 231.   [186] Cited in Todorov, *Facing the Extreme*, p. 136.

it also tests humanity generally.[187] Monsters devour us, but not on an industrial scale, and rarely by category. They loll about too much to be methodical. They also lack that wanton cruelty and perverse intelligence required to actually mock their victims while killing them: only humans can do this. We should speak rather, then, if the words permit, of the humanity of the Holocaust, for such cruelty is unparalleled amongst monsters. And to speak of the human, in modernity, is to speak of the machine, and of humans made machine-like.

A deficiency of humanity thus seems inadequate to explaining everyday violence at Auschwitz. What is both most frightening and most puzzling about this scenario is its normality, rather than its extreme cruelty as such. For the Reserve Police Battalion 101, heavily involved in the Polish killings in 1942–3, 'mass murder and routine had become one', as otherwise 'ordinary men', in Christopher Browning's phrase, became converted into mass killers.[188]

The SS, however, were trained to be violent, and expressed their identity through violence: a sociological explanation here trumps a psychological one. These torturers, who hid so successfully after the war behind the veneer of duty, like Mengele, proclaiming themselves mere functionaries following orders, included many foul individuals. But, on the whole, the guard cohort should probably be characterized primarily in terms of the 'fearsome, word-and-thought defying *banality of evil*' (an interpretation often associated with Hannah Arendt).[189] Their work often involved 'administrative massacres' organized by 'desk murderers',[190] where violence and murder became so unexceptional as to scarcely need mentioning.

Here, the quintessential villain is the 'drab functionary' (in Levi's description of Rudolf Hoess), driven to mass murder by circumstances. Here we encounter lonely, disturbed, marginal, and alienated people, but not those who, as such, enjoy murder or inflicting pain.[191] Most such men and women were not sadistic killers, and probably would not have been had it not been for the war.[192] They were not devils. They differed, indeed, so little from most of the rest of us that, as the publishers of Eugen Kogon's classic study of the camps commented, we see no monsters in its mirror, only a more familiar carnivalesque image of our own distorted selves.[193] Some, like Hoess, were automatons who worshipped hierarchy, order, and the *Führerprinzip*, and who saw no objection to killing the Reich's

---

[187] Zygmunt Bauman, *Modernity and the Holocaust* (Polity Press, 1989), pp. 6, 13.

[188] Browning, *Ordinary Men*, pp. xix, 57–9, 62. These middle-aged inhabitants of Hamburg were raw recruits. Their non-commissioned officers (NCOs) were often party men (p. 47). This is a classic small-unit study of the mentality of the exterminators.

[189] Arendt, *Eichmann in Jerusalem*, p. 231. The theme is explored in Olaf Jensen and Claus-Christian W. Szejnmann, eds., *Ordinary People as Mass Murderers: Perpetrators in Comparative Perspective* (Palgrave Macmillan, 2008).

[190] Hannah Arendt, in Nauman, *Auschwitz*, pp. xxvi, xx.

[191] Hoess, *Commandant of Auschwitz*, p. 19.

[192] Hackett, *The Buchenwald Report*, p. 23; testimony of an Auschwitz doctor-prisoner: 'There were few sadists. Not more than 5 or 10% were pathological criminals in the clinical sense. The others were perfectly normal men who knew the difference between right and wrong. They all knew what was going on' (Nauman, *Auschwitz*, p. 91).

[193] Kogon, *The Theory and Practice of Hell*, p. 11.

'relentless adversaries', the Jews.[194] They regarded commands from above as akin to Divine mandates to perform one's duty conscientiously, unquestioningly, without moral qualm, with 'perpetual self-mastery and unbending severity'. Signs of weakness and sentimentality were treated as vestiges of an outdated 'bourgeois' world-view which Hitler sought to supersede.[195] Doubtless, had the SS not been so keen to kill them off, they would have seen some kinship here with their NKVD counterparts. Each could admire the demonic, nay, the human, professionalism of the other, and revel in their mutual contempt for ordinary decency.

Arendt described Adolf Eichmann's 'banality' in order to assert that he was not some kind of 'monster' but an undistinguished and poorly educated man whose talents in ordinary life would not have taken him far.[196] A thuggish dictatorship, however, offered unlimited opportunities for those driven by grudges, resentments, frustrations, disappointments, and compound feelings of inadequacy as well as ruthless ambition and, above all, a love of power. (But this hardly describes Hitler, who united exceptional talents with enormous psychological problems.) Admittedly, leadership was an important component in the Nazi catastrophe generally. Yet there are no leaders if there are no followers, amongst whom could be numbered a fair proportion of 80 million Germans, themselves beset by a sense of national anxiety and the feeling that they must 'annihilate their enemies or be annihilated'.[197]

For Auschwitz and the rest of the murderous process to happen, many passions had to collide and coincide. A 'metaphysics of punishment', as David Rousset called it, existed, which viewed all of the Reich's enemies as abstractly 'evil' and their extermination as a process of expiation which aimed at the 'total disintegration of the individual'. So the 'purpose' of punishment was never reform, but only punishment as such. Many hatreds and resentments were entangled in these acts, including anti-Semitism (Ukrainian guards were often noted for this); xenophobia, anti-intellectualism and class resentment; the sense of superiority of the master race over mere animals, or even 'dirt' or 'vermin';[198] as well as misogyny and probably other deeply rooted phobias, like fear of infection. Sixty to seventy per cent of the guards were ethnic Germans from Eastern Europe (*Volksdeutsche*), many with a first language other than German, and doubtless feeling an acute need to prove their group loyalty—to out-German the Germans. The flip side of sadism in many cases, psychologists have supposed, was a masochistic desire of submission to the Führer, with all this entailed.[199] Mass murder, of course, required copious infusions of alcohol to disguise the sense of shame, revulsion, and disgust naturally felt. Yet even the subsequent desire to 'humanize' mass murder (for the perpetrators) by making it more anonymous in the gas chamber was still not perfect. Thus, it was reported of those who executed Russian POWs at Buchenwald, that 'these brutish

---

[194] Evans, *The Third Reich at War*, p. 305.
[195] Hoess, *Commandant of Auschwitz*, pp. 86–7. When he first witnessed corporal punishment at Dachau, Hoess later claimed later he found the experience extremely unpleasant (p. 66).
[196] Arendt, *Eichmann in Jerusalem*, p. 49.　　[197] Ibid., p. 47.
[198] David Rousset, *A World Apart* (Secker & Warburg, 1951), pp. 63–4, 87, 91.
[199] Langbein, *People in Auschwitz*, pp. 280, 273.

SS murderers were always drunk throughout the drama'.[200] (Some SS actually committed suicide after engaging in mass murder, and others went mad.)[201] Many SS doctors officiating at the selections at the Auschwitz ramp were also upset by the process.[202] Thus these were not 'monsters' either, for monsters feel no guilt.

So even the SS, it seemed, could not fashion the perfectly disciplined, emotionless mass murderer, possessing an ethos of absolute obedience. For absolutely remorseless mass killing only a machine will do. The imposition of constant terror upon others, for anyone not themselves pathologically sadistic, is too destructive for the average psyche. This barbarism has been explained as less a function of individual cruelty or ideological determination than the complete absence of moral norms governing one's actions.[203] The delegation of cruelty to prisoner warders added a masterly touch to the situation. This spared the SS some potential unpleasantness, while breaching the dividing line between Nazis and inmates, permitting yet another sense of anxiety to foster.

Conclusion: National Socialism as External Dystopia

How much more ingeniously cruel, then, was the concentration camp system than the images of Hell and the Devil we examined in Chapter 2! Satan was a papier-mâché, almost comic opera character by comparison with a Himmler, an Eichmann, a Heydrich, or a Hoess. No mere Devil could have heaped vile sadism upon sadism in the way human beings did. To Christians, envisioning Hell had a purpose: controlling and reforming behaviour. Auschwitz aimed only to impress a sense of overwhelming power as sadistically as possible, and then to murder. Herein lay no chance of salvation, of redemption, of reward for good behaviour. Hopelessness was the order of the day. Humanity was never able to imagine anything so evil as this, before it happened. And now these images are, or must be, forever burned into our consciousness. Those who somehow imagine that these events never happened, or are a function of 'symbols' and 'interpretation', or of accident, or of 'system' and 'orders', rather than just being murder—more scapegoats, should simply put themselves for a moment in the place of the victims. Most of these hair-splitters, too, as we have seen, might well have suffered the same fate.

Why all this occurred has troubled every thinking person since 1945. Just how much was planned, and when, and why what happened when, are immensely important questions. It is not an exaggeration to state that the meaning of 'humanity' depends on how they are answered. Hatred of the Jews mainly motivated the Holocaust.[204] But the word 'hatred', conveying passionate intensity, seems insufficient to explain both the magnitude and manner of the killing in a notionally civilized society. The basic plan was indisputably Hitler's. It could not have been

---

[200] Hackett, *The Buchenwald Report*, p. 239.   [201] Hoess, *Commandant of Auschwitz*, p. 148.
[202] Gutman and Berenbaum, *Anatomy of the Auschwitz Deathcamp*, p. 327. Joseph Mengele was one of the few exceptions.
[203] Sofsky, *The Order of Terror*, p. 115.   [204] Ibid., p. viii.

conceived or carried out without him. His servants, especially the SS, bear responsibility for the manner of its implementation. Whether or not most Germans actually hated the Jews or others who were exterminated or not, they nonetheless turned a blind eye to the potentially murderous solution hinted at from *Mein Kampf* onwards. The fact of dictatorship does not explain this. Nor does Hitler's derangement. Nor does the progress of the war, which hastened the mass murder of the Jews. Nor does mere greed and resentment. (The 'moral monster', as Gitta Sereny calls him, Franz Stangl, who presided at Treblinka, later said of the Jews, his 'cargo', that the Nazis 'wanted their money'.)[205]

Other factors thus play a role here, including paranoia, the mentality of a slave state, and a collective 'authoritarian personality', which fed the aggression and destructiveness of the regime.[206] But the central issue, anti-Semitism, resulted from a crisis of national identity, and the simplistic, childish desire to blame others for our misfortunes, to kill the scapegoat. Insufficiently self-confident to be self-sufficient, the Nazi idea of group identity required a devil figure as its antithesis. The Jews provided the best historical example to hand. Hitler himself was the paradigmatically alienated individual in search of a higher unity to which to attach himself. He acknowledged wishing to give his followers 'the feeling of absolute domination over a living being'.[207] The sense of group identity he instilled combined feelings of superiority and a lust for power with a craving for submission. But this did not result in the totalitarian treatment of most Germans. The enemy here was chiefly external. Killing Jews came to be seen as an expression of the life force of their killers. To kill was to affirm the right, the virtue, the purity of the group. Here is where destruction and creation, virtue and terror, meet face to face, and the paradoxes of apparent contradiction dissolve.

These were the ingredients of Freud's theory of group behaviour and of Fromm's theory of sadism. Fromm describes the psychology of Nazism in terms of an authoritarian predisposition which was fuelled by economic and political factors. 'It seems that nothing is more difficult for the average man to bear than the feeling of not being identified with a larger group', Fromm observed, noting that one of Hitler's successes was the identification of Nazism with Germany.[208] The crude flattery of the people as such, their linkage with a 'master race' and exalted destiny, wedded the spirit of blind obedience to the leader to a contempt for lesser races and minorities. The advantages of a national over a class ideology are obvious here. National Socialism doubtless made a majority feel good and proud rather than anxious and alarmed. Class was not divisive where labour and capital were supposedly in alliance and businessmen were described as natural rulers.[209] The social utopia defined by being a member of the 'master race' was effortlessly empowering,

[205] Sereny, *Into that Darkness*, pp. 201, 101, 367.
[206] Cohen, *Human Behaviour in the Concentration Camp*, pp. 241–6.
[207] Quoted in Erich Fromm, *Escape from Freedom* (Holt, Rinehart & Winston, 1941), pp. 222–3.
[208] Ibid., p. 210.
[209] Robert A. Brady, *The Spirit and Structure of German Fascism* (Victor Gollancz, 1937), pp. 265–94.

if you were born to it.[210] Had nation and race not overlapped here so substantially a very different outcome might have occurred.

CHINA

The Chinese Revolution of 1949 led by Mao Zedong followed a century of humiliation at the hands of Western imperialists, a prolonged civil war, and nearly fifteen years of brutal Japanese invasion. The revolution brought peace, but at great cost. No Chinese Solzhenitsyn has yet stepped forward to chronicle in voluminous detail the violence which resulted or the labour and punishment camp system (*laogai*) which was created.[211] About a thousand large camps, containing some 13 per cent of detainees, were established, and many smaller ones. Their population of *c.*2 million during the 1950s suffered terrible conditions, with mortality rates reaching 10 per cent per month.[212] There were perhaps 8–9 million prisoners in 1960; still a low incarceration rate compared to the USSR.[213] In 1992, the estimated total prisoner population was some 3–4 million, with the number of political prisoners unknown. Labour for profit rather than reform became the norm from the late 1970s onwards, especially after Deng Xiaoping assumed power in 1978 and dramatically altered China's path of development. About 50,000 prisoners were reported as being held in labour camps in early 2013.

Overall death rates are less clear for the *laogai* than the Gulag. The lowest estimate gives approximately 30–50 million politically motivated arrests, chiefly for 'counter-revolutionary activity', with 10–15 million executions. The highest gives some 30–50 million deaths.[214] Between these are estimates of 20 million deaths, with *c.*50 million imprisoned up to the mid-1980s.[215] Perhaps 1–2 million executions occurred between 1949 and 1951 out of a population of 550 million, which is proportionately similar to killings under the Jacobins and Bolsheviks.[216]

---

[210] On the utopian aspects of National Socialism see Hermand, *Old Dreams of a New Reich*.

[211] One personal account is Harry Wu and Carolyn Wakeman, *Bitter Winds: A Memoir of My Life in China's Gulags* (John Wiley & Sons, 1994).

[212] R. J. Rummel nonetheless compares this favourably with the Gulag system, with an estimated death rate of *c.*20% per year from the 1930s through the 1950s (*China's Bloody Century: Genocide and Mass Murder since 1900* (Transaction Books, 1991), p. 231).

[213] Frank Dikötter, *Mao's Great Famine: The History of China's Most Devastating Catastrophe, 1958–62* (Bloomsbury, 2010), p. 291.

[214] Hongda Harry Wu, *Laogai: The Chinese Gulag* (Westview Press, 1992), pp. 21, 70; Kate Saunders, *Eighteen Layers of Hell: Stories from the Chinese Gulag* (Cassell, 1996), p. 1.

[215] Stéphane Courtois, Nicolas Werth, Jean-Louis Panné, Andrzej Paczkowski, Karel Bartošek, and Jean-Louis Margolin, *The Black Book of Communism: Crimes, Terror, Repression* (Harvard University Press, 1999), pp. xviii, 498–9.

[216] Figures as low as 710,000 have been cited. Frank Dikötter suggests that about two million people were killed by 1951 (*The Tragedy of Liberation: A History of the Chinese Revolution, 1945–57* (Bloomsbury, 2013), p. 100). Rummel, *China's Bloody Century*, pp. 219–46, gives about 15 million from 1949 to 1959, with a further 10.7 million from 1959 to 1966, and 7.7 million during the Cultural Revolution, or a total of 33.4 million. Rummel also gives a figure of 61.9 million killed in the USSR (p. ix). Benjamin Valentino suggests 10–46 million deaths from 1949 to 1972 (*Final Solutions: Mass Killing and Genocide in the Twentieth Century* (Cornell University Press, 2004), p. 75).

Mao himself asserted in 1948 that a tenth of the peasants (about 50 million people) 'would have to be destroyed'. (In 1957, he said that the sacrifice of 300 million or even a billion people was justified so long as socialism was achieved.) Others spoke of 30 million 'necessary' executions.[217] This mentality was clearly inherited in part from Bolshevism: imperfect citizens get in the way of the perfect state when the latter becomes the true end of the revolutionary process. The paradox that murder on this scale may not be classified as 'genocide' may leave some readers bewildered.[218]

From the outset, 'class enemies' were key targets. No criminal code existed until 1980, nor any limit on the party's dictatorship. Arrest usually implied guilt. Once accused, 'enemies of the people' were shunned even if they were not arrested. There were no rights of appeal.[219] The entire population was classified into good, middle, and bad classes, soon to be reduced to the inherited status of good (red) or bad (black, the traditional colour of monsters). Marriages between individuals of different classes were proscribed. In the countryside, violence targeted landlords, some 10 per cent of the population. About 15 per cent of these were executed, 25 per cent sent to camps, and the other 60 per cent put to forced labour. The Korean War exacerbated suspicion of strangers and foreigners (most of whom, barring the Russians, were expelled in 1951). Hostility to the educated classes was common. Mao boasted in 1957 that he had already killed 400,000 'intellectuals'.[220]

Arrests without trials and imprisonment without specified sentences were common. Sometimes years were spent in solitary confinement. Often prisoners were not freed after completing their sentences. Emulating Stalin, arrest quotas were imposed. Mao initially dictated a quota of one per thousand for imprisonment, though this was often exceeded.[221] Quotas for the arrests of 'rightists' and 'counter-revolutionaries' during the Anti-Rightist Campaign, when half a million intellectuals were arrested, were, for example, for one university department, about 10 per cent, and in other work units, 5 per cent. Amongst intellectuals it was reported that 'everybody was denouncing others and was denounced by others. Everybody was living in fear.' Thousands of books were burned, and the number of titles deemed 'progressive' declined. In custody, torture and near-starvation were routine until the 1980s, with real famine in the years when the outside society suffered it too.[222]

Like the Bolsheviks, the Chinese communists aimed to produce a 'new people'. Maoism has been described as 'millennial' insofar as it assumed that, through

[217] Rummel, *China's Bloody Century*, p. 223.

[218] See Jean-Louis Margolin, 'Mao's China: The Worst Non-Genocidal Regime?', in Dan Stone, ed., *The Historiography of Genocide* (Palgrave Macmillan, 2010), pp. 438–67. Hence 'mass killing' may be a less troublesome concept: see Valentino, *Final Solutions*, pp. 9–29.

[219] Rosemary H. T. O'Kane, *The Revolutionary Reign of Terror: The Role of Violence in Political Change* (Edward Elgar, 1991), pp. 198–200.

[220] Daniel Chirot, *Modern Tyrants: The Power and Prevalence of Evil in Our Age* (Free Press, 1994), p. 200.

[221] Thus, 4,500 were executed in 1959 and 4,000 in 1960, by quota, out of 213,000 arrested and 677,000 publicly humiliated in 1959 (Dikötter, *Mao's Great Famine*, p. 291).

[222] Wu and Wakeman, *Bitter Winds*, p. 31; Zhisui Li, *The Private Life of Chairman Mao* (Chatto & Windus, 1994), p. 216.

massive human effort, a near-perfect social stage was attainable.[223] A nationwide scrutiny of beliefs began, which continued for decades. One likened this to a 'carefully cultivated Auschwitz of the mind'. To a greater degree than under Stalin, China's prisoners were encouraged to reform through 'struggle' sessions and by accepting 'correct ideas'. Meditation, confession, and repentance were constantly encouraged. The basic aim, one foreign prisoner wrote, was to convince individuals their ordinary lives were 'rotten and sinful and worthy of punishment' compared to 'the police's conception of how life should be led'.[224] More than in the USSR, thought was believed to be the determinant of action, and efforts to reshape ideas thus came to the forefront of party activity.[225] The goal of imprisonment was thus 'thought reform' in accordance with Mao Zedong's ideas. This involved acknowledging one's 'crime' by confessing. So posters read: 'Have you confessed today?' Thought reform was intended to instil a sense of guilt. What Robert Jay Lifton called 'revolutionary immortality' involved 'an effort to create so pure and intense a national environment as to render immortal the revolution itself and the individual's participation in it'.[226] 'New socialist' personalities would be forged through labour. 'Re-ed' (re-education) inmates were sometimes even instructed to greet each other with the words, 'have a good reform'.[227] These methods are widely regarded as having been very effective.

Violence in China was driven in part by Soviet-style modernization. It peaked first after 1949, during the Land Reform Movement, when 95 per cent of the peasant population was reorganized into communes, abandoning houses, workplaces, even spouses. As many as 70 million, more than 10 per cent of the population, may have died in this period. Then came the purge of the Party in 1950–1 and the Anti-Rightist Campaign of 1957. By 1956, most of the countryside had been collectivized, with dire results.[228] By 1958, some 26,000 military-style 'people's communes' existed, of up to 20,000 families each. The communes aimed to provide free food, medical care, and shelter, with communal dining replacing private kitchens in 1958. Daily meetings and constant haranguing through loudspeakers were the norm.

Then, from 1958 to 1962, came the greatest catastrophe of modern Chinese history, the 'Great Leap Forward', with its vast irrigation projects and disastrously obsessive local steel production campaigns. (Steel being, of course, the great symbol of modernity here.) Like the Ukraine in the 1930s, forced collectivization and grain requisition had devastating consequences. As much as 40 per cent of all housing was destroyed. Violence 'became a routine tool of control' in the countryside,

---

[223] Scott Lowe, 'Chinese Millennial Movements', in Wessinger, ed., *The Oxford Handbook of Millennialism*, pp. 318–19.

[224] Courtois et al., *The Black Book of Communism*, pp. 501, 510.

[225] Frederick T. C. Yu, *Mass Persuasion in Communist China* (Pall Mall Press, 1964), p. 4.

[226] Abbott Gleason, *Totalitarianism: The Inner History of the Cold War* (Oxford University Press, 1995), p. 98; Robert Jay Lifton, *Thought Reform and the Psychology of Totalism: A Study of 'Brainwashing' in China* (Penguin Books, 1967), p. 7.

[227] Saunders, *Eighteen Layers of Hell*, p. 84. For a fictional portrayal of the atmosphere, see Yan Lianke, *The Four Books* (Chatto & Windus, 2015).

[228] Dikötter, *The Tragedy of Liberation*, pp. x–xii, 47, 49, 97, 100, 183, 192, 238, 245.

accounting for up to 10 per cent of all deaths, or as many as 2.5 million people. Half of cadres are estimated to have beaten regularly, often to please their bosses. Torture, mutilation, and burying alive were common. Many executions took place—and still do—in public. After mass rallies and ritualized humiliation, several hundred were often shot at once, in stadiums filled with tens of thousands. Crowds were urged to curse and malign the victims, and praise the party. The *laogai* system also grew in this period, with about 8–9 million being incarcerated by 1960 (still a lower rate than the USSR). But worst of all was the resulting famine, 'one of the most deadly mass killings in human history', when perhaps 45–55 million died (in a population of 682 million, about one in fourteen people).[229]

The Cultural Revolution

The most protracted phase of mass violence in China took place in the early stages of the decade-long Cultural Revolution (1966–76). The Party later admitted some 100 million people, an eighth of the population, suffered persecution in this period. The later leader Deng Xiaoping, a prominent victim himself, said at least a million had been killed by mobs.[230] The campaign was conceived by Mao partly to extend egalitarian ideals widely perceived as hampered by bureaucracy, partly to ensure that proletarian 'red' trumped bourgeois 'expert' in every area of life, but mainly to reinforce Mao's authority over the Party. It was marked by an egalitarian and puritanical revolt against luxury and ostentation as well as a youth rebellion against traditional forms of authority—China's version of Europe's 1968: one of its slogans was the wondrously perplexing 'Overthrow everything'.[231]

As an exercise in mass agitation, the Cultural Revolution was unparalleled in Soviet experience, except perhaps early in the October Revolution. 'Big-character' wall-poster campaigns in every workplace exhorted people to expose 'demons', 'ghosts and monsters', bourgeois 'rightists', 'capitalist roaders', and 'counter-revolutionary revisionists'.[232] Rumours of conspiracies soon abounded. Local government and other organizations found their leaders, aims, and methods called into question. Much of this challenge came from young Maoists known as Red Guards. Violence against both people and things was restrained at first, and central authorities indeed regularly warned against 'indiscriminate beatings and kill-ings'.[233] But as the revolution gathered momentum, peaking between 1968 and 1971, the police were generally told to ignore 'excesses'. Intellectuals were again a

---

[229] Dikötter, *Mao's Great Famine*, pp. 292–2, 298, 300, xi. Earlier estimates go as low as 10 million (Rummel, *China's Bloody Century*, p. 247). See also the authoritative account offered in Yang Jisheng, *Tombstone: The Untold Story of Mao's Great Famine* (Allen Lane, 2012), which gives a range of 36–45 million dead (p. x).

[230] Anne F. Thurston, *Enemies of the People* (Alfred Knopf, 1987), p. xvi; Rummel, *China's Bloody Century*, p. 262.

[231] Li, *The Private Life of Chairman Mao*, p. 482.

[232] Jack Chen, *Inside the Cultural Revolution* (Sheldon Press, 1976), p. 222.

[233] Yang Su, 'Mass Killings in the Cultural Revolution: A Study of Three Provinces', in Joseph W. Esherick, Paul G. Pickowicz, and Andrew G. Walder, eds., *The Chinese Cultural Revolution as History* (Stanford University Press, 2006), p. 118.

special target: 'bourgeois scholar tyrants' were the butt of many accusations.[234] Many lost all their possessions and were imprisoned. Universities closed for nearly ten years. About 10,000 intellectuals were killed in Shanghai alone, and some 10 per cent of teachers nationally were persecuted. Local bureaucrats seem to have been responsible for many murders, though others were spontaneous.

The Cultural Revolution also represented a ferociously destructive onslaught on one of the world's most distinguished civilizations. Indeed, it assailed the very idea of respect for history, which seemingly epitomized China's past humiliation and painful lack of progress. 'Old' and 'bad' became virtually synonymous. Following Lin Biao's invocation to 'strike down all ghosts and monsters' and 'eradicate all old ideas, old culture, old customs and old habits of the exploiting classes', the destruction began.[235] The smashing of the 'Four Olds' began in Beijing on 19 August 1966. Within days, the city was placarded with posters, slogans, and proposals invoking the new spirit. 'Old' personalities (bourgeois, counter-revolutionary, rightist, etc.) were one target. Old *things* were destroyed by the millions. The physical records of three thousand years of culture, tombstones, monuments, and the like, were smashed into dust.[236] Within a month, some two-thirds of Beijing's historic sites had been razed, including temples, frescoes, archways, and statues. The Imperial Palace was protected only by Zhou Enlai's direct intervention. A frenzy of renaming buildings, streets, restaurant dishes, and even personal names took place. Portraits of Mao were put up in place of religious icons. Similar destruction occurred throughout China. Wutai Mountain, a sacred Buddhist complex, was derided as 'the home of demons and spirits', and its sixty temples were pillaged.[237] The old dystopian space was symbolically reconquered. So, appropriately, a culture which reverenced the old excessively inverted this with equal enthusiasm.

But if the old was bad, this did not make the new good. For this often symbolized decadence and weakness. Capitalist novelties were thus similarly attacked. Symbols of other adolescent rebels, 'Hong Kong-style haircuts', cosmetics, jeans, and T-shirts, indeed anything perceived as foreign, were targets.[238] Families could be arrested for having 'bourgeois' possessions or anything 'Western'. Keeping cats or birds and cultivating flowers were spurned as destructive of 'revolutionary energy'.[239] Those who spoke foreign languages faced arrest as spies. A new style of 'forced modernity' dominated by military themes and the war against Japan was created in art and theatre.[240] Xenophobia, revolutionary purity, and a militarized society fused.

[234] Barbara Barnouin and Yu Changgen, *Ten Years of Turbulence: The Chinese Cultural Revolution* (Kegan Paul International, 1993), p. 71.
[235] Ibid., p. 97.
[236] In Beijing, 4,922 out of 6,843 designated historical sites were damaged or destroyed: Barnouin and Changgen, *Ten Years of Turbulence*, p. 98.
[237] Yan Jiaqi and Gao Gao, *Turbulent Decade: A History of the Cultural Revolution* (University of Hawaii Press, 1996), p. 73.
[238] Ibid., p. 65; Chen, *Inside the Cultural Revolution*, pp. 226–7.
[239] Courtois et al., *The Black Book of Communism*, p. 523.
[240] The idea is that of Paul Clark, *The Chinese Cultural Revolution: A History* (Cambridge University Press, 2008), pp. 249–62.

Much of the Red Guard assault on its enemies was much more public than its Stalinist counterparts. A simple scheme of colour coding was followed. Everyone was classified into the 'Red Five category', including workers, poor and lower middle peasants, soldiers, revolutionary cadres, and 'revolutionary martyrs' (meaning their dependents), and the 'Black Five category' of landlords, rich peasants, counter-revolutionaries, bad elements, and rightists.[241] Ostracism of 'blacks' was common; their marriage with 'reds' became nearly impossible. To be identified as 'black' invited murder or confiscation of property. (One-third of Beijing's residences were affected.)[242] Suspected 'counter-revolutionaries' could be beaten, even to death. Charges by Red Guards often occurred at public meetings where large crowds taunted their victims as 'ox ghosts and snake spirits' or 'freaks and monsters'.[243] Then they hit them. The accused were paraded through the streets wearing dunce caps, with placards around their necks, and were repeatedly spat upon. Then they were taken to 'struggle sessions' where they might be tortured or even killed. One could be denounced as a counter-revolutionary for not appearing sufficiently zealous. This was particularly important for those moving upwards in the social hierarchy, and so, thought some, 'it was a combination of ambition and fear that made people so cruel'. 'Re-education through labour' meant sending millions of people into the countryside to experience peasant life. The sense of collective guilt increased. The intriguing story is told of a man wrongly arrested who had the same name as the person sought. After some months he confessed to the charges made against him. But when released, after the mistake was discovered, he found it difficult to leave the camp because of his feeling of guilt.[244]

This episode gives us a good insight into the extraordinary psychology of this period, which often parallels, in secular form, the millenarian mentality. China experienced an emotional explosion of volcanic proportions in this period. Its intensity is unparalleled in history, not only because of the numbers involved, but equally the degree to which these compounded and drove the sense of collective identity and endeavour. Here, apparently, the shock and trauma of the humiliations of Western imperialism and Japanese conquest, pent up for generations, were released with torrential force. There is here, as elsewhere, a powerful sense that, after deep and extensive trials and suffering, a much better world should result as spring must follow winter. With this, too, came an intensified anger and irritation at all who stood in its way.

The colour coding of this experience is extraordinary. Novelty and change were epitomized by 'redness'. 'Red' stood for an intensely enhanced sociability where idea, emotion, and colour were powerfully fused. Participants in the enormous rallies seemed 'transported far beyond the conditions of normal life', and momentarily 'felt themselves beyond ordinary morality. They belonged to a glorious

---

[241] Jiang Jiehong, *Red: China's Cultural Revolution* (Jonathan Cape, 2010), p. 99.
[242] Jiaqi and Gao, *Turbulent Decade*, p. 77.
[243] Thurston, *Enemies of the People*, p. 90. The 'ox-ghost' was a mythical monster with fangs who ate people.
[244] Saunders, *Eighteen Layers of Hell*, pp. 79, 37, 80.

collective and were elevated to an entirely different world defined by the colour red.'[245] So profound was the obsession with 'redness' that, for a time, until many accidents forced a reversal, red became the colour for 'go' on traffic lights. Beijing was renamed 'The City of the East is Red'. Houses and shops by the thousands were repainted red. Walls were covered with red slogans. Badges, armbands, clothes, and books followed. Rituals of dress, language, posture, and other collective behaviour thus demarcated new (and young) from old, revolutionary from reactionary, red from black.

The Mao Cult

Mao's extraordinary personality cult played a key role in focusing the group identity and ethos of loyalty of the Red Guards. But the phrase 'personality cult' does scant justice to the personal and group experience of leader worship. Devotion to the living is different from revering the dead (later the embalmed corpse in its reliquary would have to do). The sense of vicarious empowerment is much more direct. Mao's portrait was utterly inescapable. Nowhere in history has one image dominated so many minds at once. The Great Red Father, 'Emperor' Mao, the Communist Superego, was everywhere. Observers noted 'Mao's unavoidable scrutiny from his portraits on the walls of classrooms, assembly halls, and elsewhere. The great gaze was examining every single thought or action, at any time, anywhere.'[246] Mao statues sat on household altars in rural areas. Every newspaper and journal bore a likeness. (But accidentally sitting on these reproductions invited a death sentence.) Carrying a large framed portrait of Mao hung around the neck became popular—the bigger the better: suffering proved loyalty.[247] Pledges of devotion before the portrait in the workplace every morning became *de rigueur*, and often confession before it in the evening too. Badges were ubiquitous, and grew in size in proportion to one's loyalty. Wearing one was mandatory. Some 2.8 billion Mao badges were forged, of at least 50,000 varieties. In many, the golden rays of a holy, enlightened halo, the 'red sun', emanate from the Chairman's head. By osmosis, objects too were Maoified: the Chairman's doctor related that when Mao gave a gift of mangoes to a factory, workers filed by the fruit, placed on an altar, in veneration. When it rotted the flesh was boiled and everyone drank a small spoonful of the water. Finally a wax replica was made and that too was venerated. Mao 'seemed delighted by the story'.[248]

No less ubiquitous were the Chairman's works, 40 billion copies of which were distributed—fifteen for every citizen. Everyone carried the 'Little Red Book', the Bible of Mao's sayings. Excerpts were often read for as long as an hour in groups every morning, even while working in the fields or on a moving bus. No occasion existed for which a suitable Mao homily could not be mustered. Quotations appeared on 'towels, pillows, wooden furniture, wine bottles, medicine wrappings,

---

[245] Jiehong, *Red*, p. 116.   [246] Ibid., p. 14.
[247] Chen, *Inside the Cultural Revolution*, p. 219.
[248] Li, *The Private Life of Chairman Mao*, p. 503.

wallets, toys, and candypaper'. A discourse of loyalty focused on flattery of Mao and comparing each individual's behaviour with the Chairman's. Campaigns like the 'Three Loyalties' (loyalty to Mao, to Mao Zedong Thought, and to Mao's proletarian revolutionary line), and the 'Four Boundlesses' (boundless worship, boundless hot love, boundless belief, and boundless loyalty) carried the message to a billion people. Assertions of loyalty even accompanied such mundane acts as selling goods or answering the phone ('Wish Chairman Mao eternal life!' or 'Serve the people!' were suitable greetings, which might be answered by 'comprehensively' or 'thoroughly'.)[249]

During the thirty years of Maoism, the system of official propaganda penetrated deeply into everyone's life. Insecurity was heightened by the constant shifting of expectations, sudden reversals in party line, and the rebranding of groups as 'oppressive' or 'useful'. The peasantry, small bourgeoisie, and even intellectuals were reclassified at various times. Much of the violence resulted from economic failures as well as the frequent renewals of class struggle against landlords, 'rightists', and others. The sharp movement away from these aims in the 1980s brought a surprisingly swift reversal of many of their assumptions, though China remains divided as to how to weigh these legacies.

'ABOLISH EVERYTHING OLD':
CAMBODIA UNDER POL POT

April is the hottest, cruellest month in Cambodia. But in April 1975 the temperature and degree of cruelty came to exceed those of Hell itself. Imagine an entire nation in which every family has had someone murdered—perhaps seven or eight relatives or more. That was the catastrophe of the Pol Pot regime in Cambodia, the world's first 'auto-genocide' (in Jean Lacouture's term).[250]

No revolution was ever born in more calamitous circumstances. Decades of conflict and a brutal five-year civil war with many atrocities on both sides preceded this debacle. Then, from 1975–9, between a fifth and a third of Cambodia's population, some 1.7–2 million people, or nearly 1,500 a day, died of famine, neglect, overwork, or murder by the Khmer Rouge.[251] The rule of 'Angkar', as it was soon universally called, epitomized a nearly undiluted collectivist mentality, trumping even Stalinism and Maoism in its ruthless suppression of every quality deemed hostile to the pure peasant ideal of labour and virtuous innocence which it sought to universalize.

The chief architect of this disaster was *bong thom*, 'Brother Number One' or 'Big Brother', the French-educated Saloth Sar (1925–1998), best known by his *nom de*

---

[249] See Daniel Leese, *Mao Cult: Rhetoric and Revolution in China's Cultural Revolution* (Cambridge University Press, 2011), esp. pp. 149–252, here 191, 211–13.

[250] Discussed in David Chandler, *Voices from S-21: Terror and History in Pol Pot's Secret Prison* (Silkworm Books, 2000), p. v.

[251] The regime was overthrown by Vietnamese invasion in 1979, after which some pro-Vietnamese Khmer Rouge remained in government. The party itself was outlawed in 1994.

guerre, Pol Pot. He was a talented and charismatic teacher whose highest degree was a certificate in carpentry. From a fairly well-to-do background, Pol Pot was converted to communism while studying in France in the 1950s. There is little evidence of intense or profound study of the sacred texts when it came to applying them to Cambodia, though he remained close to Mao on many issues.[252] Once in power he became imbued with wild schemes to restore Cambodia to the greatness of the Angkor Wat period (twelfth–sixteenth centuries).

Pol Pot was obsessed with the purity and superiority of the Khmer race. He particularly admired the Jarai and Bunong minorities of the far north-east, who had no money and shared their food.[253] Yet he also said that 'we wish to do away with all vestiges of the past': this was the principle of rebirth.[254] Initially, Pol Pot concealed his identity as leader. Few knew his name before 1978. But by then busts of him were displayed in the four or five main ministries in Phnom Penh. A plan was then hatched to erect a giant statue of him in Phnom Penh on the site of the ancient temple mound of Wat Phnom. Grandiosity exploded just as Pol Pot's power evaporated. In the wider nation, quite possibly beyond his own knowledge and gratification, he now became the supreme embodiment of Angkar. As proud of his achievements as he was paranoid of their opponents, he was later quoted as saying that the revolution was the 'work of God, for it is too imposing for mere humans . . . of great and purest character, unprecedented in the millenary history of our country'.[255] And mere humans indeed proved woefully inadequate to the task.

From the day Cambodia's capital, Phnom Penh, fell, 17 April 1975, panic, paranoia, haste, and hatred suffused almost everything the Khmer Rouge attempted. They began introducing their communist utopia with unparalleled rapidity, consciously attempting to surpass their chief supporter, Mao's, efforts. Most of the scowling soldiers who entered the city early that morning were very young, uneducated peasants from the far reaches of the countryside where 90 per cent of the population lived. They had endured great hardship throughout their struggle. To them, Phnom Penh, swollen by refugees to 2 million inhabitants or more, some four times its pre-war population, symbolized the old regime's corruption, burdensome taxation, and decadent enthrallment to the tawdry charms of the colonizers and imperialists. They resented, disliked, or feared nearly everything about it. Hence, virtually all its inhabitants were seen as 'enemies'. (Curiously, the soldiers were ordered as they entered the city not to touch anyone, or only with a rifle barrel.)[256] Under the pretext that the Americans were about to bomb it, and promising its inhabitants that they could return in three days, the city was swiftly evacuated. In fact, the Khmer Rouge aimed, at least initially, to eradicate the influence of urban modernity as such in Cambodia by, as some put it, 'cleansing'

---

[252] David P. Chandler, *Brother Number One: A Political Biography of Pol Pot* (Silkworm Books, 1999), p. 32. Cadres were often lectured on 'Max-Lenin' [sic].

[253] Rithy Panh, *The Elimination* (The Clerkenwell Press, 2013), p. 183.

[254] Ibid., pp. 144–5.

[255] Elizabeth Becker, *When the War Was Over: The Voices of Cambodia's Revolution and Its People* (Simon & Schuster, 1986), p. 168.

[256] Panh, *The Elimination*, p. 29.

or 'cleaning out' the cities as well as purging the physically and morally unfit, including the handicapped.[257] At most, the capital held 40,000 people during the next four years. Grass grew in the streets, and many public buildings were destroyed.[258]

Within hours on 17 April, factories, schools, and monasteries were closed. About 20,000 hospital patients, some wheeled along by their relatives, were turned into the streets by soldiers.[259] (Most doctors—502 out of 550—as well as nurses, would later be killed.) The Khmer Rouge gave the impression that 'they loathe everything modern'.[260] There were bonfires of furniture, one onlooker being told by a cadre that 'furniture represents class and therefore it must disappear'.[261] Televisions and refrigerators were smashed, not because they were machines, but because they symbolized foreign dependence. Thus they were 'contaminated' by having 'allowed foreign countries to invade Cambodia, not just physically but also culturally'.[262] Columns of people streamed into the countryside, those with cars driving until they ran out of petrol or had their vehicles seized by soldiers. The streets out of the capital were lined with abandoned cars, uniforms, helmets, TV sets, and other personal possessions. (Three vivid dystopian symbols: Pin Yathay describes a Mercedes being demolished, the metal cut into strips for making knives, the rubber tires cut up for shoes: modernity deconstructed, literally. Then: the National Bank is blown up, and useless banknotes floated through the streets for days. Some used them for toilet paper. Finally: the National Library, emptied of books, becomes a pigsty, the pigs replacing the books.)[263]

Within three days, the heat and a shortage of water began to take effect on the vast processions out of Phnom Penh. The ill and weak, the young and the old, succumbed most quickly by the roadside. Some 20,000 died. People, sometimes entire families, were seen hanging themselves from trees by the wayside or drowning themselves in rivers. At checkpoints, all books were confiscated as containing 'imperialist thoughts', and destroyed. Driving licences and dictionaries were burnt as 'relics of feudal culture'.[264] Literacy as such seemed to symbolize exploitation and oppression. But looting was also common. Watches were usually the first item plundered—'*Angkar* suggests that you happily offer him your watch', soldiers would say—curiously in a land where time was moving so swiftly backwards.[265] Some took several, as if this might advance their mastery of the process. It was a mild if grim foretaste of what was to come. And every other town, village, and

---

[257] John Barron and Anthony Paul, *Murder of a Gentle Land: The Untold Story of Communist Genocide in Cambodia* (Reader's Digest Press, 1977), pp. 37, 76.

[258] François Ponchaud, *Cambodia Year Zero* (Holt, Rinehart & Winston, 1978), p. 21.

[259] In Kampong Chhnang hospital, patients were taken by truck eighteen miles into the forest and dumped: Jon Swain, *River of Time* (Heinemann, 1995), p. 167.

[260] Chanrithy Him, *When Broken Glass Floats: Growing Up under the Khmer Rouge* (W. W. Norton, 2000), p. 182; Swain, *River of Time*, p. 147.

[261] Ponchaud, *Cambodia Year Zero*, p. 45.

[262] Loung Ung, *First They Killed My Father* (Harper Perennial, 2006), p. 58.

[263] Pin Yathay, *Stay Alive, My Son* (Silkworm Books, 2000), p. 74; Panh, *The Elimination*, p. 61.

[264] Pin Yathay, *Stay Alive, My Son*, pp. 74, 50.

[265] Moeung Sonn with Henri Locard, *Prisoner of the Khmer Rouge* (Editions Funan, 2007), p. 60.

hamlet captured in the previously unoccupied zones now suffered the same fate of forced evacuation, perhaps 4 million in all.[266]

'Year Zero' commenced. A new world was to be created virtually without precedent in the old, as epitomized in the slogan, 'Abolish everything old, replace it with everything new.'[267] Within days there were 'no prisons, no courts, no universities, no money, no jobs, no books, no sports, no pastimes'. Private property was abolished. The love of money being the greatest sin of all, money immediately became useless.[268] An atmosphere of extreme paranoia and mistrust descended. Here, truly, ignorance was regarded as strength. Hatred of education was perhaps unparalleled in history. (To enforce the point, again with grim revolutionary humour, being sent for 're-education' became a common synonym for murder— that was how the chief torturer, Kang Kek lew, or Duch (pronounced 'doyk'), used the term: nothing like death to wipe the slate clean.)[269] 'We were destroying the old world in order to build a new one', Duch insisted.[270]

But, of course, everyone and everything was tainted with the old, and liable to destruction. Schooling and books were regarded as corrupting. The National Library and those of the universities were almost completely destroyed, along with hospital medical libraries. Thousands of books were thrown into the Mekong or burnt. Diplomas, 'the invisible signal', were deemed useless. Only manual labour, 'the visible signal', was honourable. ('The spade is your pen, the rice field your paper', ran one slogan.)[271] But a large proportion of the educated had only emerged from illiteracy in the last fifteen years. Often born of the peasantry themselves, they were the first generation of Cambodia's intelligentsia.

Besides the privileged Khmer Rouge elite, the new society was divided into three categories. Poor peasants and a handful of urban workers from areas previously occupied for some years by the Khmer Rouge were deemed 'Old' or 'base' people (*mulethan*). These possessed full 'rights', which were chiefly meaningful in terms of food rations, and soon, the right to eat privately. (Some later reported that they included the right to kill 'New People'.) Next came a less privileged group called 'candidates'. The wealthy and the urban refugees were usually known as 'New People', 'depositees', 'April 17 people', or 'people of 1975'.

Some assurances were offered that New People could 'build ourselves up and graduate into a higher group'.[272] But soon the Khmer Rouge came to regard virtually all, but especially non-peasants, as the irredeemably corrupt 'infected' 'enemy'.[273] Told to 'purify themselves', they had no political rights, poorer rations,

[266] Barron and Paul, *Murder of a Gentle Land*, p. 127.

[267] Henri Locard, *Pol Pot's Little Red Book: The Sayings of Angkar* (Silkworm Books, 2004), p. 272.

[268] Most, thereafter, were permitted to own what could be held in a single bundle of clothes, a plate, spoon, and drinking cup. Paper money was later printed but never circulated.

[269] Swain, *River of Time*, p. 258.

[270] Panh, *The Elimination*, p. 259. This invaluable book by the maker of the film, *S-21*, recounts a series of interviews with Duch.

[271] Barron and Paul, *Murder of a Gentle Land*, pp. 20–1; Locard, *Pol Pot's Little Red Book*, p. 96.

[272] Chum Mey, *Survivor: The Triumph of an Ordinary Man in the Khmer Rouge Genocide* (DC-Cam, 2012), pp. 29, 32.

[273] François Bizot, *The Gate* (The Harvill Press, 2003), p. 109.

suffered under far more strenuous labour conditions, and were frequently relocated. Pol Pot lamented in a speech to selected cadres in 1976 that 'some of the comrades behave as if all the new people were enemies'.[274] But he did little to dispel the sentiment. Indeed, it is possible that their extinction as a group was planned in principle from the outset. New People were essentially 'war slaves', and were sometimes referred to as such.[275] New and Old People were forbidden to inter-marry.[276] The New could never advance in principle, though the carrot of moral re-education was dangled constantly before them. There were also subgroups here, with former professionals being regarded as particularly corrupt.

'Old people', by contrast, embodied the pure type of the propertyless peasant dignified by manual labour. They alone possessed an uncorrupted self. The less educated the better: this was a clearly a variation on the Noble Savage ideal which Pol Pot may have misappropriated from Rousseau. A Party document actually stated that 'people who pilot our helicopters can't read a great deal. Formerly to be a pilot required a high school education—twelve to fourteen years. Nowadays, it's clear that political consciousness is the decisive factor. It shows us our line is correct.'[277] Youth was also crucial. Many cadres were twelve years old or even younger. 'Clay is molded while it is soft' was an Angkar slogan. Many were 'spoon-fed on hate', in Jon Swain's phrase.[278] Knowing nothing but discipline and orders, these youths killed the more readily, without hesitation or remorse, or restraint of sentiment.

Expelled to the countryside, sometimes into remote jungle areas without shelter, the entire urban population was turned forcibly to agriculture, and especially rice production. (Later, when small factories were opened by the Khmer Rouge in Phnom Penh, Angkar preferred to import peasants for the work, keeping former factory workers on the land.)[279] Soon they were organized into cooperatives of 700–1,000 families supervised by Old People and guarded by soldiers. Huge irrigation schemes were begun, designed to restore the grandeur of the medieval Khmer kingdom. Official barter was restricted to ten-family production units. Labour teams were subdivided by age, marital status, and gender. Some were broken down into individual tasks in order to 'atomize' workers.[280] Now 'numbers were more important than anything': water, rice, fertilizer, 'everything was gauged . . . Everything began with the numbers and nothing had any value except in numbers.'[281] Written permission was required to leave any area, and travel was sometimes restricted to groups of three. An astonishingly punitive work regime was

---

[274] *Pol Pot Plans the Future: Confidential Leadership Documents from Democratic Kampuchea, 1976–77*, tr. David P. Chandler, Ben Kiernan, and Chanthou Boua (Yale University Southeast Asia Studies, 1988), p. 206.

[275] Haing S. Ngor, *Surviving the Killing Fields: The Cambodian Odyssey of Haing S. Ngor* (Pan Books, 1989), p. 202.

[276] Chirot, *Modern Tyrants*, pp. 223–4.   [277] *Pol Pot Plans the Future*, p. 160.

[278] Locard, *Pol Pot's Little Red Book*, p. 17; Swain, *River of Time*, p. 44.

[279] A plan to develop heavy industry already existed in 1976: *Pol Pot Plans the Future*, pp. 98–100.

[280] Ben Kiernan, *The Pol Pot Regime: Race, Power and Genocide in Cambodia under the Khmer Rouge, 1975–79* (2nd edn, Yale University Press, 2004), p. 167.

[281] Panh, *The Elimination*, p. 142.

begun, with laziness regarded as 'the worst crime by the Angkar'.[282] 'It is the wish of the Party that socialism be built quickly', Pol Pot contended, adding that, 'If we are not strong and do not leap forward quickly, outside enemies are just waiting to crush us.'[283]

Daily life became an unrelenting regimen of work and more work, with the aim of producing a 'Super Great Leap Forward'. Sports, laughing, and singing were usually prohibited. Traditional festivals were replaced by revolutionary celebrations. Women's attractiveness was deliberately concealed, since, an Angkar slogan explained, 'Physical beauty hinders the will to struggle.'[284] Jewellery was regarded as 'a capitalist item which poisons society completely'.[285] Even haircuts were rendered identical to purge 'the corrupt Western concept of vanity'. Few pastimes were permitted in the little 'free' time available. But time taken from Angkar could never be 'free', but was for lesser duties. A uniform attire was imposed of black clothes, a red *krâma* scarf, and rubber sandals. Town dwellers, told that 'bright colours only corrupt your mind', burnt their colourful clothes or dyed them black.[286] So this became, literally, the blackest of all dystopias.

Without provisions, tools, skills, or seed, hundreds of thousands of ill-prepared city dwellers died of famine, disease, and the climate in the first year. Only 'full rights' people had adequate rations and could grow their own food. New People often starved. But all were valued only in proportion to their labour, and the ill and disabled were often killed. Rice was hoarded and exported to China to pay for weapons even as the basic ration was sharply reduced. As famine advanced, people were reduced to eating insects, lizards, snakes, tree roots, and leaves. Since the Party assumed the country only needed 1–2 million people to achieve self-sufficiency there was little sympathy for their plight. Thus, Pin Yathay was told at a political meeting that only a million people were needed 'to continue the revolution. We don't need the rest. We prefer to kill our friends than keep the enemy alive.'[287] Entire villages starved and were abandoned. Some who resorted to cannibalism were condemned as 'ogres', the flesh-eating demons of Khmer mythology.[288] 'Purification by the survival of the fittest' became the rule of the day.[289] By late 1976, it was becoming increasingly clear that mass starvation was a deliberate policy.

The regime was basically divided into two factions in this period. In the eastern provinces, where the Khmer Rouge wore khaki uniforms and leant towards the exiled monarch Prince Sihanouk, the regimen was more benign. In areas west of the Mekong, the harsher, more Maoist Pol Pot faction wore black. With a long history of slavery, Cambodia became the first modern state to enslave virtually its entire population. Surrounded by minefields to prevent escape, it was the purest dystopia

---

[282] Ung, *First They Killed My Father*, p. 135.   [283] *Pol Pot Plans the Future*, pp. 21, 24.
[284] Ung, *First They Killed My Father*, p. 158; Sonn with Locard, *Prisoner of the Khmer Rouge*, p. 149.
[285] Sathavy Kim, *A Shattered Youth: Surviving the Khmer Rouge* (Maverick House, 2010), p. 81.
[286] Ung, *First They Killed My Father*, p. 59.   [287] Yathay, *Stay Alive, My Son*, p. 167.
[288] Ibid., p. 150.
[289] Paul Hollander, ed., *From the Gulag to the Killing Fields: Personal Accounts of Political Violence and Repression in Communist States* (ISI Books, 2006), p. 471.

of all, 'an open air prison', carcerotopia. Within this were secret prisons: the knowledge of their very existence could be cause for execution.[290]

Angkar

The chief aims of the Party organization were to eradicate all opposition to Pol Pot and the inner party of perhaps a dozen people, and to instil undivided loyalty to Angkar. Known colloquially as *Anka Loeu*, or Angkar, the 'higher organization' or 'the law', it was associated with the Buddhist *Dhamma*, epitomizing wisdom and far-sightedness. Buddhist antagonism to material possessions and family ties, submission to a higher discipline, and the confessing of faults were also drawn upon. While it represented all the cadres and authority in general, it was often conceived and described in quasi-mystical terms, as, for instance, having 'no smell, no weight, no colour'. This mysteriousness was driven by obsessive secrecy, 'Secrecy is the key to victory' being a common slogan.[291] In propaganda sessions it was said that 'Angkar is all-powerful', and was 'the savior and liberator of the Khmer people'.[292] 'Master of the waters, master of the earth', possessed, in a popular saying, of 'as many eyes as a pineapple', it saw and knew everything. It was never wrong, and dictated the people's destiny. But it might alter at any time, and was 'not to be predicted'.[293] Those who disobeyed were told that a Juggernaut-like 'wheel of history' would crush them: this god image was not evidently a wheel to be grasped with human hands.[294] To allow flexibility and maintain secrecy, and because so many cadres were illiterate, commands were almost always given verbally. Locally, power was usually given to the least educated as being the 'purest'. The young soldiers thrived on their power of life and death.

Within Angkar, however, whatever the effects of decades in the jungle, revolutionary equality dissipated rapidly. Within days, perhaps hours, of 17 April 1975, but probably well beforehand, some were more equal than others. (Bizarrely, 'Equal Comrade' indeed became a title of high respect.)[295] Small but psychologically significant badges of rank began to sprout. Corruption also set in almost immediately. In Phnom Penh, a few higher cadres moved into French villas along the Mekong river and had access to imported foreign luxuries, chauffeur-driven cars, life-saving Western medicines, and the like. In some areas, bribery was relatively negligible until 1978 or so, when the regime began to disintegrate. In others, lower cadres benefited from outset from the constant confiscation of everything valuable from 'Old people', and from black market exchanges, especially in rice. Their rank was often marked by one or more pens, even four. (The warden of the infamous

---

[290] Kim, *A Shattered Youth*, p. 184.
[291] Locard, *Pol Pot's Little Red Book*, p. 128. This was emblazoned above the gate of Tuol Sleng prison. Duch explained that 'There are four secrets: I don't know, I didn't hear, I didn't see, I'm not talking' (Panh, *The Elimination*, p. 237).
[292] Ung, *First They Killed My Father*, p. 125.
[293] Hollander, *From the Gulag to the Killing Fields*, p. 468.
[294] Him, *When Broken Glass Floats*, pp. 14–15.
[295] Ngor, *Surviving the Killing Fields*, p. 275.

Tuol Sleng or S-21 prison in Phnom Penh had two.) These were prominently displayed on the outside of the breast pocket, like medals, 'to show off their status and intelligence'.[296] Silk *krâma* scarves were also worn by higher cadres. Some wore more fashionable coloured clothing under their black uniforms, but usually only at night, discretely revealing a collar to flaunt their vanity.[297]

For the masses, 'Angkar' stood for a more extreme attack on privacy and individualism than anything ever attempted anywhere on this scale. This was compulsory solidarity indeed. An 'absolutely clear collectivism', the Party stated, implied the eradication of 'capitalist vestiges', including 'privateness' as such. If the collectivist path were followed, cadres were told, 'imperialism can't enter our country. If we are individualists, imperialism could enter easily.'[298] A 'high spirit of collectivity' was thus required. New People were told to have 'no sense of individuality at all'.[299] They were taught to renounce all possessions, to have only one 'container', their stomach, and to aim to be like a grain of rice in a large pot, utterly identical, an image whose irony, in the midst of starvation, must have seemed especially bitter.

The collective was exalted proportionately. An unmitigated love of Angkar was encouraged, with no displacements through love of self, family, sexual attraction, or attachment to objects or property. Angkar warned, 'Do not harbor private thoughts!'[300] Angkar reminded people constantly to forget everything about life before 17 April 1975. Indeed, nostalgia itself was criminalized as 'memory sickness', and people were punished for recalling the past.[301] Displays of affection were banned, along with 'arguments, insults, complaints and tears'. 'Feelings' were generally associated with 'individualism' and condemned. The word 'freedom' was equated with selfishness, individualism, and 'the absence of morality', or used in the sense of a garden being free from weeds.[302] Or, as an Angkar saying, 'Comrade, you are very free!', went, it could mean that accusation was imminent, 'free' here meaning thinking independently of Angkar. ('If you want liberty, why not die at birth?', one slogan ran.)[303] Thus, an informer reported that in areas under Khmer Rouge control, 'All which is not revolutionary or which is harmful to the revolution is condemnable, forbidden', with the aim of '"taming" a man to become a "machine" (*un robot, un automate*)'. Under the 1976 Constitution—the sole legal act of the regime's four-year rule—religious belief was permitted. But 'reactionary' religions were banned, and all religions were regarded as reactionary.[304] 'Instruction sessions' involving self-criticism or 'self-reproach' and mutual criticism, after the

---

[296] Yathay, *Stay Alive, My Son*, p. 179.   [297] Kim, *A Shattered Youth*, p. 121.

[298] *Pol Pot Plans the Future*, pp. 108, 156.

[299] Timothy Michael Carney, ed., *Communist Party Power in Kampuchea (Cambodia): Documents and Discussion* (Department of Asian Studies, Cornell University, 1977), p. 29; Kim, *A Shattered Youth*, p. 19.

[300] Bizot, *The Gate*, p. 294.

[301] Kim, *A Shattered Youth*, pp. 75, 88; Sonn with Locard, *Prisoner of the Khmer Rouge*, p. 149; Barron and Paul, *Murder of a Gentle Land*, p. 199.

[302] Bizot, *The Gate*, p. 296.

[303] Locard, *Pol Pot's Little Red Book*, p. 296; Panh, *The Elimination*, p. 120.

[304] Carney, *Communist Party Power in Kampuchea*, pp. 40, 47; Yathay, *Stay Alive, My Son*, p. 192.

Buddhist term *rien sot*, meaning 'religious education', were held several times weekly or even nightly.[305] They often ended with the ritual formula, 'I humble myself so that Angkar can purify me, criticize me, and educate me to be even more submissive.'[306] To acknowledge any flaws publicly was dangerous, but so too was silence. So, as one S-21 interrogator confessed, 'You never know if you are "correct".'[307]

In 'history's fiercest ever attack on family life', and in a culture where kinship is extremely important, most families were broken up.[308] This 'negation of intimacy' has been described as aiming to establish 'feelings of distance between people' in order to 'build up an initial basis of hate'.[309] Angkar itself replaced the family, and it became permissible to speak not of 'my wife' but only of 'our family'. The very word 'family' was redefined to mean only 'spouse', excluding children, who now belonged to Angkar.[310] The word marriage was eliminated, and replaced by 'arranging a family', the purpose of which was to produce 'pure' children. A 1978 radio broadcast, 'Who are "We"?' clearly delineated all those characteristics which made up 'us' and 'the enemy'.[311] Here we see the dystopian group par excellence, in virtually its purest form.

For all New People, from early 1976, a new phase of 'socialist revolution' commenced. Communal eating was enforced and private cooking prohibited. Unrelated men and women were made to stand at least three metres apart during conversations, and were not allowed to travel together.[312] Forms of address were altered to abolish hierarchy and emphasize equality. Angkar often chose spouses, usurping the traditional role of parents. In group marriages of up to 600, the vows taken included achieving rice production norms and loyalty to Angkar. The evening of these weddings, guards were placed outside couples' rooms to ensure the marriage was consummated. (Yet, curiously, in an isolated instance of humanity, husbands were also forbidden to beat their wives or scold their children. And even more ironically, some were told not to quarrel.)[313]

Children were often sent to distant workplaces or barracks, and raised in common as the sons and daughters of Angkar, the 'dad–mom' of the people.[314] In principle, they were supposed to be educated from ages five to nine, but this often meant only a few hours a day learning revolutionary songs. They were punished for showing affection to their parents, and taught not to love them, but

---

[305] See Bizot, *The Gate*, pp. 53, 63, 110, for a list of parallels.

[306] Yathay, *Stay Alive, My Son*, p. 131.   [307] Chandler, *Voices from S-21*, p. 27.

[308] Ben Kiernan, in Kim Depaul, ed., *Children of Cambodia's Killing Fields* (Yale University Press, 1997), p. xi.

[309] Robert J. Sternberg and Karin Sternberg, *The Nature of Hate* (Cambridge University Press, 2008), p. 187.

[310] Kiernan, in Depaul, *Children of Cambodia's Killing Fields*, p. xi.

[311] Alexander Laban Hinton, *Why Did They Kill? Cambodia in the Age of Genocide* (University of California Press, 2005), pp. 213–14.

[312] Courtois et al., *The Black Book of Communism*, pp. 597–8, 605, 609.

[313] Yathay, *Stay Alive, My Son*, p. 120; 'Angka doesn't allow people fighting each other' (Ngor, *Surviving the Killing Fields*, p. 127).

[314] Karl D. Jackson, ed., *Cambodia 1975–1978* (Princeton University Press, 1989), p. 164.

only Angkar. 'Familyism', or missing one's family, became a crime punishable by death. Slogans insisted that 'Your love for Angkar must be boundless.'[315] Children were trained to spy on adults, and all were urged to 'secretly observe the slightest deeds and gestures of everyone around you'.[316] Sometimes young soldiers were even encouraged to kill their parents. In the countryside, informants crawled under the bamboo stilts of houses 'lurking like a demon' to listen carefully to night-time conversations.[317] Even the slightest wrong word could 'get one sent to Angkar' or to 'carry the bed of Angkar', meaning executed. So husbands and wives stopped speaking, even in bed. 'Only the deaf and mute will survive', warned a nineteenth-century Cambodian apocalyptic prophecy. And so it was: this form of enforced sociability, like Stalin's, ended by destroying virtually all sociability whatsoever.

The Killing Fields

Death hovered everywhere in these years. 'Keeping you is no gain, destroying you is no loss', New People were constantly told. 'A person suffering from the sickness of the old society must be cured with Lenin's medicine!' ran one slogan.[318] So anyone regarded as irredeemably corrupted by the old regime or by 'imperialism' was likely to be killed. The only foreigner captured by the Khmer Rouge to survive, François Bizot, thought that the regime had decided to release no prisoners by 1971.[319] Frequent denunciations and the search for 'bad backgrounds' quickly produced a sense of 'massive despair and hopelessness'.[320] As in China, autobiographies were demanded from the entire population to ascertain class origins, and were often used to compile 'enemies' lists.[321] Within a short time, 'Fear dominated life, and immediate death was constantly at hand.'[322] The aim of the revolution was described in terms of 'seething with anger against one class, about striking and destroying that class'. But this group was astonishingly large, and indeed came close to describing all urban dwellers at the time of the revolution, New People being derided as 'parasites' for whom 'no development is possible'. 'You can build Socialism only if you have Socialist people' was a widespread assumption.[323] But few such angelic personages appeared.

Instead there were enemies everywhere. The worst purges began in 1977. The antagonist, at once, of both the two great superpowers of the epoch, Democratic Kampuchea, as it was known, felt hemmed in on every side and penetrated by traitors and spies in every crevice. Xenophobia and class hatred became so intense and guilt so universal as to extend even to seeing the 'enemy' as, in principle, within each person, a truly diabolical conception. This enemy, 'the imperialistic habits of our hearts', was invisible. Eventually, 'all the people were enemies of and obstacles

---

[315] Bizot, *The Gate*, p. 106.   [316] Locard, *Pol Pot's Little Red Book*, p. 114.
[317] Him, *When Broken Glass Floats*, p. 81.   [318] Panh, *The Elimination*, p. 121.
[319] Bizot, *The Gate*, p. 274.   [320] Chirot, *Modern Tyrants*, p. 224.
[321] Craig Etcheson, *After the Killing Fields: Lessons from the Cambodian Genocide* (Praeger, 2015), p. 111.
[322] Henry Kamm, *Cambodia: Report from a Stricken Land* (Arcade Publishing, 1998), p. 126.
[323] Bizot, *The Gate*, pp. 156, 184–5, 292.

to the Khmer Rouge government'.[324] A genocidal logic thus existed from the outset, which insisted that 'All we need to build our country is a million good revolutionaries', the rest, by implication, being largely superfluous. Some even said that since the revolution only needed 'pure' people, if only two Cambodians were left 'uncontaminated' and all the 'diseased' were destroyed, a new nation could still be built.[325] (But bad luck if one of these turned out to be an 'enemy'.) A regime 'obsessed with the notion of purity' of race, nation, and class thus combined to produce an intense cultivation of Khmer identity paralleled by an equally intense vilification of her supposed enemies.[326]

Few groups of this size can ever have been defined by such hatred of their opponents. Even the Khmer national anthem spoke of the blood of 'unrelenting hatred' covering the towns and plains of Kampuchea. (The tune is not catchy either.) Non-Khmer ethnic groups were 'seen as an obstacle to a utopian agrarian society'. All languages other than Khmer were declared illegal.[327] The regime targeted Cambodia's Cham (Muslim) inhabitants fairly systematically after 1978, killing as many as half for refusing to eat pork and then for rebelling when this was forced on them.[328] Then came the Vietnamese minority, or those with 'Khmer bodies and Vietnamese minds', and to a lesser degree Thai and Chinese.[329] But almost everyone became a suspect. Traitors (*Kmaing*), Angkar said frequently, were everywhere, and since anyone who displeased Angkar was an enemy this was indeed the case. The word was itself sometimes used simply as a synonym for New People.[330]

The murders began with officers of the former regime, in some accounts anyone above the rank of corporal. In Phnom Penh they were executed almost immediately on 17 April 1975. Their severed heads littered the streets.[331] Civilian officials were also sought out. These totalled perhaps 250,000 people. Then followed their relatives. Then a prime target was 'intellectuals', who were regarded as irredeemably corrupted by alien, colonial, Western influences. Wearing glasses was regarded as 'a sign of intelligence' by soldiers, and invited execution from the first days of the regime. (Others thought wearing glasses was condemned because this was 'vain', for style alone.)[332] Admitting to having tasted chocolate could also risk arrest. Smooth hands, small feet, and light skin were dangerous (the peasantry were darker and the pre-war prejudice against darker skin was now reversed). Most who spoke a foreign language or who had any education after the age of twelve were arrested. Town dwellers who had 'known modern life' risked arrest.[333] Many in disguise were lured out with the promise of employment in the cities and then killed.

[324] Panh, *The Elimination*, p. 194; Kim DePaul, ed. *Children of Cambodia's Killing Fields*, p. 118.
[325] Hollander, *From the Gulag to the Killing Fields*, p. 463.
[326] Nic Dunlop, *The Lost Executioner: A Story of the Khmer Rouge* (Bloomsbury, 2005), p. 136.
[327] Farina So, *The Hijab of Cambodia: Memories of Cham Muslim Women after the Khmer Rouge* (DC-Cam, 2011), pp. 54–6.
[328] Ysa Osman, *The Cham Rebellion: Survivors' Stories from the Villages* (DC-Cam, 2006), p. 132.
[329] A hundred thousand were killed in one border area in six days (Dunlop, *The Lost Executioner*, p. 175).
[330] Kim, *A Shattered Youth*, p. 245.   [331] Jackson, *Cambodia 1975–1978*, p. 86.
[332] Ngor, *Surviving the Killing Fields*, p. 139.
[333] Peter Maguire, *Facing Death in Cambodia* (Columbia University Press, 2005), pp. 26–7.

Fig. 4.4. Tuol Sleng prisoners. © Tuol Sleng Genocide Museum.

Other targets included young men with long hair, diplomats, landlords, and monks. Idealists lured back or returning from abroad to assist the revolution were usually taken directly to Tuol Sleng as 'outsiders' and executed (see Fig. 4.4). Anything deemed 'foreign' was outlawed. 'Ancients' who were friendly with 'New' People courted punishment. New People could not laugh without risk. (The Dobu would have approved.) Any complaint against Angkar could result in being led into the forest for execution. Families of suspects were often arrested on the collective responsibility principle and that of blood guilt by education or association. An underlying culture of blood revenge or *kum* led, however, to fear of retribution from the children of victims, and a heightened sense of revenge, thus perpetuating the killing. 'The blood debt must be repaid by blood' was another Angkar slogan.[334] Every arrest produced 'strings' of associated guilty parties, for this was the point of arrest. By the end, one interrogator, himself forced to confess, asked whether if Angkar 'arrests everybody, who will be left to make a revolution?'[335] In and outside S-21 women were sometimes raped, one Khmer Rouge injunction being 'rape women deemed enemies of Angkar'.[336]

Despite elaborate confessions being demanded, the reform of prisoners was usually deemed impossible. 'Comrades under arrest were enemies, not men', said Duch, who was 'obsessed with purity'.[337] The fact of arrest was a presumption of guilt. Indeed, the Angkar concept presumed universal guilt, under the assumption

---

[334] Hinton, *Why Did They Kill?*, pp. 45–95; Panh, *The Elimination*, p. 55.
[335] Dunlop, *The Lost Executioner*, p. 175.   [336] So, *The Hijab of Cambodia*, p. 88.
[337] Panh, *The Elimination*, pp. 67, 181, 251.

that 'Only a newborn is free from stain.' (Prisoners were sometimes referred to as 'damned souls'.)[338] Those arrested were 'enemies, not people', in the words of Duch. One leader, Ieng Sary, confessed that 'we all had an enemy within ourselves'. To some, this was the stain of 'bourgeois' or 'Vietnamese' tendencies.[339] In the new cooperatives Angkar estimated that at least half the population were 'enemies'.[340] So the pattern of arrest–accusation–execution was common. (Typical slogans here: 'You can arrest someone by mistake; never release him by mistake', and 'Better to arrest ten innocent people by mistake than free a single guilty party!')[341] Often there were no trials, only confessions following barbaric torture, which had been routinely practised in Cambodia for many generations. Three denunciations as a 'CIA agent' or (as the USSR was Vietnam's main supporter) a 'KGB agent' (or, not uncommonly, both) were sufficient to justify arrest. In some districts, quota systems existed where percentages of enemies had to be arrested and destroyed.[342]

But to save the burden of courts and police, executions often occurred without charges ever being made. 'Angkar kills but never explains' became one of the sayings of the epoch.[343] Humane treatment was seen as 'weakness'. Finally, in 1978–9, a spy mania then led the party to begin to destroy large numbers of its own members. Pictures of such 'victims', ironically, are mostly what modern visitors to Tuol Sleng see exhibited on the walls, and whom they commiserate with. But these are themselves often the killers.

Prisons and isolated as well as mass graves soon spread throughout the country. Some said every field had a skeleton or more. Eventually, some 117 prisons were constructed, and around 343 mass killing sites established. 'Everyone was cowed' by the constant fear of execution.[344] Stealing food—in the midst of famine—most commonly occasioned the death penalty. There was also, by 1977, real resistance to the regime, and many escape attempts. But death could be imposed for sexual 'misconduct' (even with one's own spouse or by male soldiers having relations with New women); for refusing to marry a soldier; for drinking alcohol; or for criticizing shortcomings in government or arguing with the authorities. Any fault at work, any grumbling, shirking, sickness, scavenging for food (even insects and plant roots) could invite death. Sometimes preceded by paper summons, villagers were ordered to report to Angkar. Then, usually at night, in the wild, outside villages, they were murdered. In less than four years as many as 25 per cent of the population died, with New People making up about 40 per cent of the total.

Amongst the dead, some 200,000 to 1 million were executed. Here the mundane use of exceptional brutality is chilling. Babies were frequently killed by being swung against trees. Some soldiers even claimed that 'It is very easy to kill children;

---

[338] Chandler, *Voices from S-21*, p. 118.
[339] Bizot, *The Gate*, pp. 143, 201; Chandler, *Voices from S-21*, p. 102.
[340] Meng-Try Ea, *The Chain of Terror: The Khmer Rouge Southwest Zone Security System* (DC-Cam, 2005), p. ix.
[341] Bizot, *The Gate*, p. 209.   [342] Jackson, *Cambodia*, p. 201.
[343] Courtois et al., *The Black Book of Communism*, p. 608.
[344] Michael Vickery, *Cambodia 1975–1982* (George Allen & Unwin, 1982), p. 58.

we only have to tear them apart.'[345] Few prisoners were shot: only advanced nations could afford the luxury of the seven-kopek solution. So most executions were carried out with iron bars or bamboo clubs or throat-cutting to save bullets.[346] Public executions in front of children sometimes happened. Many witnesses reported the mutilation of the sexual organs of female corpses, and the removal of foetuses from murdered pregnant women.[347] Sometimes victims were simply tied to trees and left to die. Organs of the dead, especially the liver, pancreas, and gall bladder, were sometimes cooked and eaten, to gain courage and inspire fear in others, or to use in traditional medicine.[348]

Extreme and devious torture was common in Tuol Sleng. This was the only area in the capital with full-time electric power, a beacon, so to speak, of illuminated darkness of the blackest hue. Its interrogators and torturers regarded their work as crucial to the entire course of the revolution (and indeed their destruction in many ways was). Here, four-fifths of the 14–20,000 murdered (less than a dozen survived) were Khmer Rouge themselves, many eastern zone, supposed pro-Vietnamese cadres. The executioner-in-chief was the irritable Maoist former schoolteacher Kang Gouek/Kek Eav, aka D(e)uch, who was finally sentenced to life imprisonment in 2010 in the first Cambodian genocide trial. Interrogators here worked in 'political', 'hot', and 'chewing' units ('like a dog chews on a bone'), depending on the degree of torture required. Guards were expected to be paragons of virtue 'like monks in the pagoda'. All spied on each other, and many were themselves killed, sometimes for the slightest error, or for failing to extract confessions. In one team only one of twelve survived.[349] Even Duch himself was described as 'ruled by fear'.[350]

Once admitted, inmates were always termed 'guilty'. They were often referred to in extremely derogatory terms, women prisoners being called 'female animals' while Vietnamese were denoted 'black dragons who spit poison'. Nearly all confessed to absurd accusations after sufficient torture and being kept lying in rows thirty to a room with virtually no food, often for several months. Then they were 'smashed to bits' and, initially, buried nearby. Later, as numbers increased, they were taken by truck to Choeung Ek outside Phnom Penh. Here, to the deafening sounds of a generator and loudspeakers playing revolutionary music, they were murdered with cart-axles, axes, clubs, hoes, or bayonets, and their throats then cut with sharp palm fronds. Killers were reported as happily going about their tasks, having been told they were facing the regime's enemies. They gladly fulfilled their sense of duty, and the need to prove their loyalty, to gain honour, and avoid losing face, to cement

---

[345] Hinton, *Why Did They Kill?*, pp. 265–71; Kamm, *Cambodia*, p. 128.

[346] But if we think clubbing to death merely the result of primitivism, the same thing happened in Bulgaria in the 1950s: Courtois et al., *The Black Book of Communism*, p. 421.

[347] Locard, *Pol Pot's Little Red Book*, p. 258.

[348] Sonn with Locard, *Prisoner of the Khmer Rouge*, p. 204.

[349] Dunlop, *The Lost Executioner*, pp. 130, 155, 173; Jackson, *Cambodia*, p. 198; Maguire, *Facing Death in Cambodia*, pp. 58–60, comments that the 'climate of fear, paranoia, and distrust at S-21 had few equals during the twentieth century'. But as many as 60,000 were killed at centres like Wat Kokoh.

[350] Bizot, *The Gate*, p. 115.

their own identity, and, of course, to avoid being executed themselves. In the countryside they often worked only for fifteen days or so in any one area. When they left, ghosts and evil spirits were often reported as appearing. Many who survived suffer recurring nightmares, paranoia, estrangement, hypervigilance, and other symptoms to this day.[351]

Explaining Angkar

The Pol Pot genocide is difficult to comprehend. Cambodia was transformed into a mass graveyard where even today the summer rains bring bones to the surface everywhere. 'In the scope of repression', it has been written, 'Cambodian Communism surpasses and differs radically from all other forms of Communism.'[352] This 'murderous utopia' (in Pin Yathay's description) was the first society to engage in collective suicide or auto-genocide, where the largest proportion of the members of a society met death at the hands of its regime. Yet some reject this label, insisting that the crimes of the Khmer Rouge were 'incontrovertibly human', even that 'the twentieth century reached its fulfilment in that place; the crimes of Cambodia can even be taken to represent the whole twentieth century'.[353]

Collective psychosis seems a mild if appropriate term to describe the mental world of the Khmer Rouge. This is much more sinister than what Freud, in *Civilization and Its Discontents*, termed 'communal neurosis'.[354] It is madness, but it is also the madness of reason, the tyranny of an idea, the pure and ferociously equal 'We'. The regime was dominated by 'continual fear'.[355] No despotism, perhaps, has ever aspired to such a completely pure collective mentality, or failed its people so dismally. In this case, the experience was exacerbated by a malevolent interpretation of the doctrine of karma, which led many to fatalistically assign blame for their present fate to conduct in their past lives.

In the Cambodian case, a schizophrenic division of the mind into the pure idea and the impure real personality rendered the idea the supreme tyrant. This idea was religious and utopian. It was excessively obsessed with purity of class, race, and blood, and with promoting a pure peasant type of idealized virtue and innocence. It drew upon Buddhist ideals of self-renunciation, celibacy, and poverty in aspiring to create a new priesthood aiming at greater virtue than any beforehand (for the old monks had been mere 'parasites'). So, in a constant ritual of purification it demonized towns, education, and everything foreign to an unparalleled degree. A perfectionist ideology driven by a hatred of the modern, the Western, and the privileged here combined with murderous results. The murderers themselves fell victim to this process much more frequently than in any other case examined in this

---

[351] Beth van Schaack, Daryn Reicherter, and Youk Chhang, eds., *Cambodia's Hidden Scars: Trauma Psychology in the Wake of the Khmer Rouge* (DC-Cam, 2011), p. 94.
[352] Courtois et al., *The Black Book of Communism*, p. 579.
[353] Panh, *The Elimination*, pp. 110–11.
[354] Sigmund Freud, *Civilization and Its Discontents* (W. W. Norton, 1961), p. 110.
[355] Ponchaud, *Cambodia Year Zero*, p. 183.

book. Constant fear of being punished or killed for insufficient zeal haunted guards and supervisors, driving them to greater violence.

The bloodthirstiness of the regime was also a self-sustaining process which grew seamlessly out of the Civil War, as well as a legacy of repressed violence 'in the blood' and instilled in part by being 'rigidly concerned with keeping face'.[356] Much of the time there was virtually no moral, customary, or legal restraint on violence and murder. But there was also a deliberate policy of murder from as early as 1971, at least in Tuol Sleng: 'Whoever was arrested must die', Duch recalled the day in 1999 he was finally identified by Nic Dunlop.[357]

But the entire system was self-propelling. The more people the regime arrested, the more mostly imaginary 'enemies' it identified for subsequent arrest. The more people it killed, the more enemies it made (their relatives especially, in a country dominated by *kum*, or retributive vengeance). So the more people it killed, the more it had to kill. Once confined in secret prisons, prisoners had to be killed to avoid telling of what they had seen. This logic was relentless and inexorable: violence bred counter-violence in an incessant cycle which was not ended by but actually fuelled by death, creating a 'vengeful, bloodthirsty people'.[358] And so on in retribution. 'I want to eat them up', was how the intensity of animosity was expressed by one against the Khmer Rouge.[359] 'We are going to be eaten', said one victim shortly before nearly being executed.[360] And here we see why 'eating' as an expression of total destruction was projected onto the Jews for so many centuries. Cannibalism is one of dystopia's most prominent symbols.

The Pol Pot genocide thus stands as a unique instance of human barbarity which was clearly coupled to an equally uniquely intense collectivist mentality. The suggestion that Khmer rule, particularly in its antagonism to individuality, was analogous to Nazi Germany or Stalin's Russia, is highly misleading.[361] The entire nation became a death camp to a much greater degree and far more rapidly than had ever occurred elsewhere. Almost everything conspired against a successful outcome of the revolution. Instead, Cambodia became carcerotopia incarnate.

Five key features thus stand out here as primary causes: the youth of the Khmer Rouge killers, who had never been socialized to anything other than 'absolute hate' for 'enemies';[362] the almost complete lack of education of many; the disastrous circumstances in which the communist takeover occurred; the continuing paranoia in the next few years; and the extreme egalitarian ideology of Angkar. To these should be added an obsession with work to the detriment of all other activities; antagonism to the family as well as individual identity; a strong and pervasive sense of guilt at failing to reach the level of perfection demanded by the system, justifying

---

[356] Swain, *River of Time*, p. 5; Ngor, *Surviving the Killing Fields*, p. 449.
[357] Dunlop, *The Lost Executioner*, p. 274.
[358] Kim, *A Shattered Youth*, p. 100; Ung, *First They Killed My Father*, p. 205.
[359] Dunlop, *The Lost Executioner*, p. 289.
[360] Barron and Paul, *Murder of a Gentle Land*, p. 67.
[361] O'Kane, *The Revolutionary Reign of Terror*, p. 30.
[362] Sonn with Locard, *Prisoner of the Khmer Rouge*, p. 94.

near-universal punishment and even the desire for it; and a pre-existing cultural history of vengeful violence.

Just how much of this catastrophe was planned and how much emerged from the constant disasters of Khmer Rouge policy is a moot point. The Khmer Rouge never escaped the mentality of warfare, which is all most had ever known. 'Everything was seen in terms of a constant struggle', Nic Dunlop has written, where the only distinction was between the 'front-line battlefield' and the 'rear battlefield'.[363] This was the model of the militarized society par excellence, without any transition to civilian rule, brutal war being simply followed by equally brutal military administration. Soldiers kill first and foremost, and this remained the basis of the Khmer Rouge mindset. 'Peace' was simply war by another name.

Nonetheless, what remains perhaps most disturbing about the Cambodian catastrophe is the ease with which a society was almost completely destroyed in a remarkably short time, and the intensity of prejudice against education, learning, and modernity as representing 'class'. This most tragic of societies relapsed into something worse than barbarism and more like collective insanity, and saw the most ruthless repression of every pleasant feeling in a few weeks. In its bloodlust and hatred it remains the most dystopian of all modern regimes. Here was an entire nation resembling Auschwitz in almost everything but the poison gas used for mass murder.

Addendum: North Korea

Less is known about the North Korean communist system than any other dictatorship we have examined in this book.[364] Headed by the 'Great Leader' Kim Il-Sung (1912–1994) from 1948 (named 'Eternal President' after his death), then by Kim Jong-Il ('Dear Leader'), and now (2011–), Kim Jong-un, the nation is now the most isolated and repressive regime in the world. Some 2.1 million people (*c*.12 per cent of its 1977 population) have been killed or died in prison there. At least another 2 million died of famine in the 1990s. Here too we see the same Stalinist cycle of arrest, the confiscation of possessions by the secret police, long periods of incarceration in extraordinarily severe conditions, disease, public executions, mass death by starvation.[365] Perhaps 1 per cent of the population were political prisoners in 2013. The death penalty has been imposed for listening to South Korean radio, amongst other activities. A cult of personality has been created which would have embarrassed Stalin, with rumours circulated that the first Kim created the world, while the second could control the weather. (But, as we have seen, to say something ridiculous once may appear laughable. Repeat it a thousand times and it begins to appear like gospel truth.) The state is the most militarized nation in the world, with 9.5 million under arms, or one soldier for every twenty-five citizens. Here too

[363] Dunlop, *The Lost Executioner*, p. 147.
[364] A recent study is Bruce Cumings, *North Korea: Another Country* (The New Press, 2004).
[365] See Kang Chol-hwan and Pierre Rigoulot, *The Aquariums of Pyongyang: Ten Years in the North Korean Gulag* (Atlantic Books, 2006).

distinctions between a core class, a wavering class, and a hostile class, those of 'tainted blood' who stand no chance of social advancement, have become central to the state's treatment of its citizens.[366]

ERADICATING THE 'OTHER': EXPLAINING TOTALITARIAN GENOCIDE

The genocides of race and class described in this section stemmed from several sources.[367] For communist regimes, the most obvious factor was the obsessively rapid pace of industrialization under Stalin and Mao in particular. This resulted in absurdly unrealistic demands for productive increases and a hypercompetitive atmosphere in the race to surpass capitalism. This in turn guaranteed failure and produced accusations of deliberate 'wrecking'. Hence, too, the most advanced industrialized socialist countries, notionally totalitarian, were much less violent. (So Marx was right about the need for revolution to occur here first.) The Nazis, Stalinists, and Pol Pot also shared an extreme cult of work and antagonism towards 'parasitism'. All employed slave labour on an immense scale. The largest single number of deaths, the famines resulting from enforced Soviet collectivization, especially in the Ukraine, and in China's 'Great Leap Forward', derived from failed economic policies. Here, 'letting die' overlaps with principled murder. Here the number of deaths was proportionate to the degree to which the old society was to be altered (namely, almost completely).[368]

In the communist dictatorships in particular, class hatred compounded by paranoia also underpinned persecution. Antagonism towards the educated characterized most Marxist regimes, and especially the Khmer Rouge. Extreme nationalism implied the suppression if not extinction of racial or ethnic minorities. Scapegoating of the Jews in particular underlay Hitler's greatest crime. But the pattern of anti-Semitism had been shared with misogyny and hostility to other minority groups for many centuries. Stalin, by contrast, killed many more of those who were notionally supporters of his system. René Girard's hypothesis that ritualized sacrificial violence also functions to limit violence within the community thus seems to help explain Nazism, but is less illuminating vis-à-vis Stalinism's more unlimited appetite for bloodshed. Stalinism thus represents the type of an internal dystopia far more than Nazi Germany, whose external dystopia was largely imposed by the ruling group on outsiders. Here, 'totalitarianism' obscures funda-mental divergences of outlook, policy, and effect.

While Nazi–communist comparisons may seem invidious, murder by class category, if more destructive, was no 'better' or 'worse' than that by race. Hatred of class, race, and religion manifests itself in very similar ways: how we describe a powerful enemy makes little difference. The loss of every single human life in any of

[366] Barbara Demick, *Nothing to Envy: Real Lives in North Korea* (Granta, 2010), pp. 27–8.
[367] For an overview of approaches to the subject, see Stone, *The Historiography of Genocide*.
[368] This is the general conclusion of Valentino, *Final Solutions*, pp. 73–5.

these circumstances is a tragedy. Blaming and then punishing large groups for the existence of exploitation and the loss of wars did not improve any of the societies we have studied here. The killing and letting die of so many (100–150 million or more) over a few short decades (1930–80), indeed, simply greatly undermines our sense both of progress as a civilization and as human beings. The Holocaust was a uniquely awful event in its combination of torture and intent of extermination. It was, perhaps, unique also in the sense of Germany's higher development and notionally higher ethical starting point compared to less complex societies, implying that 'civilization' deepens our general moral responsibilities. This might place a greater moral burden on Hitler's Germany than, say, Pol Pot's associates.

But every other genocide is also unique after its own fashion. We cannot call Stalin's starvation and murder by overwork by the millions less cruel than the gas chambers: how many, like Varlam Shalamov, who served seventeen years for a deviation in literary criticism (praising an émigré writer), would envy those who had simply been executed?[369] Yet we have seen in this chapter that an intention to exterminate was present on both sides, where entire, sometimes floating categories (bourgeoisie, *kulaks*, Trotskyites) were doomed to disappear. Under Stalin, however, the total numbers were far higher, and many more were tortured. So genocide is genocide, whether Jews or *kulaks* are the victims: class is as important a group as ethnicity, race, or religion, though it is often underplayed in definitions of mass murder. But a murder is a murder whether 'progress' is served or not. And when the state kills, a murder is nonetheless a murder.

All the movements we have considered here, whether focused on race, gender, or class, relied on scapegoating an 'other' like monsters, witches, women, and the Devil, which, by dehumanizing people, came simplistically to epitomize evil.[370] Sometimes, as with Jews, the bourgeoisie, and *kulaks*, the 'other' epitomized greed, privilege, and inequality. Sometimes, as in the case of witches, lust was the key sin. There are clear antecedents in medieval and early modern Europe for the horrors of the twentieth century. The history of scapegoating was continued here through large-scale sacrifices of the unworthy in the name of the future ideal state. Impure groups had to be sacrificed both to atone for past sins (especially greed) and to avoid future ones. Paranoia drove the perception of these groups as enemies, but the intellectual rationale for their sacrifice lay elsewhere, in the idea of the purity of the group and its renewal or 'cleansing', a quasi-religion of the purified organism which owed much to Social Darwinism. Wedded to this outlook, too, was a language indebted to classical political economy, which demonized the idle or 'unproductive' as lacking the right of subsistence from a common stock, an outlook restated most dramatically in T. R. Malthus' *An Essay on the Principle of Population* (1798). This productivist discourse, valuing people only by their labour, fetishizing 'output' by measuring the worth of societies only by steel, concrete, machinery, and capital

---

[369] Varlam Shalamov, *Kolyma Tales* (W. W. Norton & Co., 1980), p. 73.

[370] On the debate over what 'humanity' became in the Holocaust context see Dan Stone, 'The Holocaust and "The Human"', in Dan Stone, *The Holocaust, Fascism and Memory* (Palgrave Macmillan, 2013), pp. 49–63.

accumulation, could easily be linked to discourses on the 'asocial', 'parasitic', and 'unfit', and applied to criminals, 'deviants', 'degenerates', the poor, and many other categories.[371]

The common features of the Stalinist and Nazi dictatorships led them to be called 'totalitarian'. Both systems were contemptuous of law, which both regarded as (in Burleigh's words) an 'obstruction on the road to utopia'. Both deliberately confused objective guilt with subjective intent, exaggerated the dangers posed to the *Volk*, nation, or party by opponents, criminalized race (Germany), and class (the USSR, China, Cambodia), and 'erased distinctions between ordinary and political crime, while criminalising harmless utterances'. Both used networks of informants to report dissent and instil paranoia, and relied on denunciations from ordinary citizens. In both systems, outcomes were often predetermined after accusations were made, and individual rights were virtually non-existent.[372] Anything was permitted which justified creating the ideal community, the mythical *Volk*, or the march of history towards the classless communist society, the new golden age. The leader as executive fusing with the judiciary easily imposed these ideals by will (the *Führerprinzip*, the Superman as messiah, in Germany; Lenin, Stalin, and Mao in the USSR and China).[373] But pressure from below was also vital. Compared with earlier dictatorships, one contemporary wrote, what distinguished fascism and communism was 'the conscious support of large disciplined masses of followers, whom they are constantly strengthening in the faith by injecting new doses of propaganda'.[374] Both Nazism and Stalinism were consensual dictatorships to an impressive degree, both because many gained by their existence, and because the alternatives often looked even worse.

Red Terror versus Brown Terror

Besides the universalistic utopian appeal of the Soviet experiment as opposed to the nationalism of the Nazis, other major variations nonetheless existed between Nazi and communist dictatorships. Perceptions of these have themselves undergone alteration. In the 1930s and 1940s, the totalitarian paradigm, to most observers, was Nazi Germany. It was relatively rare to assert, as Franz Borkenau did in 1940, that 'Russia is infinitely more totalitarian than Nazi Germany', referring both to the purges and the disasters of the Five-Year Plans.[375] Until the late twentieth century, much more was known of Hitler's crimes than of Stalin's. As the main enemy in World War II, Hitler was much more feared and, especially in popular culture, demonized. The discovery of the Holocaust alerted the world to the most terrifying mass murders ever to take place. Asked to compare this with Stalin's crimes, many

[371] On the latter category see Elof Axel Carlson, *The Unfit: The History of a Bad Idea* (Cold Spring Harbor Laboratory Press, 2001).
[372] Burleigh, *The Third Reich*, pp. 162–6.
[373] 'The Messiah of humanity is Lenin' was a typical believer's formulation, here in 1929, reported by Arthur Koestler: *Arrow in the Blue: An Autobiography* (Collins, 1952), p. 185.
[374] William Henry Chamberlin, *Russia's Iron Age* (Duckworth, 1935), p. 130.
[375] Borkenau, *The Totalitarian Enemy*, pp. 227–8.

observers find the former '*much* worse', albeit without being able to say exactly why, or resting judgement solely upon 'feelings'.[376] In part this is because images of Bergen-Belsen, Auschwitz, and Buchenwald dominated the ending of World War II, and became central to our consciousness of it and to its justification. Until the mid-1960s, we knew much more about the Holocaust than communist genocide. During the war, 'Uncle Joe' was so far sanitized as to achieve a benign portrayal in the Western press. The notionally more 'civilized' Nazis, too, methodically slaughtered millions who posed no threat to their existence, while the USSR, while prone to hysterical paranoia, actually had many and powerful enemies from 1917 onwards, and could legitimately play David to capitalism's Goliath.

As details of Stalin's slaughter began emerging in the 1960s, however, a shift occurred in which theorists of totalitarianism came increasingly to condemn Brown and Red Terror as equally despicable. Soon numerical calculations tipped the balance even further against Stalin. In terms of the total numbers murdered, leaving wartime military casualties aside (which is also problematic), Stalin killed and let die (in famines) at least 15 million people and possibly twice as many. Hitler killed 6 million Jews and at least 5 million other civilians, mostly Slavs and mostly during the war. But there were many more communist regimes, and they lasted much longer than Hitler's twelve-year rule. If we combine the various communist regimes, especially Mao's, we get figures of about 100 million or so killed under communism, and at most 25 million under Hitler, outside of war. Add wartime casualties (another 70–80 million), factoring in famine and other related events, and we have a death toll approaching 200 million. (The world's population was 2.3 billion in 1940: so these twentieth-century movements cost in total perhaps 8.5 per cent of all human lives in this period.) Such bloodshed was not utterly without parallel—there are always Genghis Khan's tens of millions of victims to contend with. But seven hundred years later one might have expected more from humanity.

Had the Nazi regime lasted longer, its death toll would doubtless have been vastly larger, for its plans for eastward expansion projected ethnic cleansing by murder much further. In terms of the treatment of domestic populations, Stalinism was doubtless a more destructive form of rule *internally*, and more obviously an internal dystopia, by comparison with Hitler's chiefly external dystopia. The Gestapo 'were still bound, if ever so loosely, to the judicial traditions of a civilized country', and did release accused persons.[377] Even those supreme unfortunates tortured by both the Gestapo and the NKVD, like many of the German communists Stalin obligingly handed over during the Molotov–Ribbentrop Non-Aggression Pact (1939–41), generally thought the Soviets the greater evil, though not necessarily by much.[378] (During the 1939–41 period the NKVD even assisted the Gestapo with training and targeting selected Jews and foreign communists for Gestapo arrest, later excused by a 'Jewish fascist' argument.) Some thought the

[376] Robert Conquest, *Reflections on a Ravaged Century* (John Murray, 1999), p. xii.
[377] Margarete Buber, *Under Two Dictators* (Victor Gollancz, 1949), p. 184.
[378] Alexander Solzhenitsyn, *The Gulag Archipelago* (3 vols, Collins & Harvill Press, 1974), vol. 1, p. 145. For one such account, see Buber, *Under Two Dictators*. Many died at Auschwitz.

Soviet camps worse because of the long slow lingering death they usually implied.[379] But, of course, they had no gas chambers.

A much larger percentage of the Soviet population was affected by Stalinism than Germans were by the Gestapo or their concentration camps. This was equally the case in Maoism and under the Khmer Rouge, where a reductionist and essentialist ideal of moral purity based on class prevailed, itself a variation on the contrast of virtue to corruption already central to the French Revolution. In everyday life, the difference was even greater. Far more people were naturally on the 'inside' in fascism, where class struggle was proclaimed to be extinct.[380] One might suppose that this would have mitigated aggression against those on the 'outside', but it did not. Contempt for Jews and Poles alike by educated members of Germany's eastern administration, for instance, was extreme, and ideas of exterminating both peoples entirely were commonly floated.[381]

The judgement of the greater domestic severity of Stalinism has to be weighed against the uniqueness of both the intentions and implementation of the Holocaust.[382] The mentality which calculated human life in terms of Reichsmarks and pfennigs, and which turned body fat into lard and skin into lampshades, is unparalleled in a civilized country. (It has parallels, albeit very limited, only amongst Pol Pot's cannibals.) The Soviet Gulag system differed from Auschwitz in several ways. As with Hitler, thousands died on transports even before reaching any camp, and hundreds of thousands died in conditions of extreme hardship and overwhelmingly severe labour. As with Hitler, criminal gangs dominated the Gulag camp administration. Stalin ruthlessly eliminated some national minorities. The tortures inflicted in Auschwitz had no parallel within the Gulag system, despite widespread Soviet pre-trial use of torture to extract confessions from arrested persons.

There is something fiendish in Nazi brutality, however, which is lacking in its NKVD counterpart. Torture in the Lubyanka aimed at eliciting a confession. Torture in Auschwitz was simply meant to degrade. While millions died in the Gulag, the Soviet Union never constructed extermination camps as such, or aimed at what Primo Levi calls the 'finality' of 'erasing entire peoples and cultures from the earth'.[383] (Although, to the bourgeois or *kulak*, and the Kolyma miner, this may seem like hair-splitting.) The psychological aims of the Gulag were much less ambitious. In many areas of the north and Siberia far fewer internal controls were necessary, for the environment virtually guaranteed that prisoners would not stray far from their camps. The Gulag was an inefficient slave state, the Nazi camps an efficient scheme of mass murder. 'Exterminating by labour', regarded by Goebbels as the best means of dealing with concentration camp prisoners, was a specific Nazi

---

[379] Edward Buca, *Vorkuta* (Constable, 1976), p. 222.
[380] Michael T. Florinsky, *Fascism and National Socialism* (Macmillan, 1936), pp. 118–54.
[381] Götz Aly and Susanne Heim, *Architects of Annihilation: Auschwitz and the Logic of Destruction* (Weidenfeld & Nicolson, 2002), pp. 127–9.
[382] See generally Alan S. Rosenbaum, ed., *Is the Holocaust Unique? Perspectives on Comparative Genocide* (2nd edn, Westview Press, 2001).
[383] Levi, *If This is a Man* and *The Truce*, p. 391.

concept.[384] Nazi prisoners tended to be the victims of racial prejudice first and foremost, Soviet prisoners of class prejudice, and then simply of paranoia. In both systems, slave labour played a major role. But it was more central to the Gulag, which was effectively a slave appendage to a slave state, and where most who perished died of overwork, not of murder.[385] (But again, to the dead, what is the difference?) The Gulag's guards were also much less sadistic than Hitler's SS. For Levi, Nazism represented 'a general atmosphere of uncontrolled madness ... unique in history'.[386] 'Collective madness' was a less predominant part of the Soviet landscape.

And yet, the physical extinction of the well-to-do bourgeoisie and peasantry and educated classes obsessed every communist regime studied in this chapter, from Lenin onwards, and notably also in China and Cambodia. These classes were persecuted as much as the Jews, and they died in large numbers. This murder, on this scale, has rightly been termed 'class genocide'. It is certainly analogous to what Hitler attempted against the Jews.[387] The fact that these victims were not gassed *en masse* does not mitigate the determination to kill most, if not all, of them. Millions who suffered the death sentence by overwork in the Gulag would have seen little difference in Hitler's and Stalin's ways of killing, or in the general aim of exterminating one's opponents.

* * * *

One of the main concerns of this section has been to explore how terror functioned on an everyday basis in these regimes, and how, as Sofsky puts it respecting the Nazi camps, 'a social form of power crystallized that was essentially different from the familiar types of power and domination'.[388] Here, modernity brought its own special perverse logic and cruelty. Here, terror was organized in a manner previously unknown, not only in scale, but in routinization and standardization. Insofar, at least, as the Nazi camps aimed at extermination, they departed from traditional forms of despotism and the exercise of absolute power. Their aims were not repression and obedience. Their cruelty and sadism were essentially pointless and arbitrary, proof merely of absolute power over others. If it had a 'point', this was only that it was the obverse side of that masochistic tendency to absolute subordination to authority which so singularly marked the Nazi mentality. Work was rarely, as it was in the Gulag, a means to an end of construction or production. In Auschwitz, it was an accessory means of extermination, 'not so much a question of work output as one of senseless torment'.[389] The intense struggle of prisoners against each other to secure the means of survival also compounded the terror exerted from the institution itself. From the de-individualization of the person,

---

[384] Gutman and Berenbaum, *Anatomy of the Auschwitz Deathcamp*, p. 51.

[385] This was rarely the case in Tsarist prisons, even in Siberia, where conditions were much more benign and the workload was onerous rather than murderous (Fyodor Dostoevsky, *The House of the Dead* (William Heinemann, 1915), p. 19).

[386] Levi, *If This is a Man* and *The Truce*, p. 395.

[387] Vladimir Tismaneanu, *The Devil in History: Communism, Fascism, and Some Lessons of the Twentieth Century* (University of California Press, 2012), pp. 37–9, and, generally, Courtois et al., *The Black Book of Communism*.

[388] Sofsky, *The Order of Terror*, p. 13.   [389] Hackett, *The Buchenwald Report*, p. 50.

through the creation of walking skeletons, barely alive, to the moment of death, the Nazi camp system contrived to create an unparalleled system of terror not only on a scale but of a qualitatively different kind from any known beforehand.

Within Nazi Germany, then, race proved to be a more all-encompassing and lenient form of national categorization than the more elastic idea of class in Stalinism. Stalinism was more destructive because it lasted longer; because it emerged from circumstances of civil war, foreign invasion, and extreme paranoia; and because hatred of the bourgeoisie and the *kulaks* and then even of suspect Party members too imperilled a great proportion of the domestic population. By contrast, in Nazi ideology, the *Volk* constituted a large, relatively constant and naturally loyal 'insider' group. The 'Other' conceived of as within is here more threatening than the 'other' outside. When the Other looks like us and is close to us, too, it appears more ubiquitous, more threatening, more likely to pollute and infect us. When ideas make one heretical, too, the risk of universal suspicion becomes greater. The nearer the ideal approaches to perfection, too, the more will fall short of it, until all appear deficient. Class became so fluid a category that 'liquidation' seemed its logical dissolving category; what mattered more than 'objective' categories was what people thought.[390] But 'bourgeois' and 'Trotskyite' also simply came to mean 'other' or 'enemy', a term of abuse, and, more than 'Jew', came to be seen as a transferable attribute simply connoting 'evil'. Stalinism also set itself against the institution of the family, and the militant anti-individualism of several forms of communism made nearly everyone 'enemies'. Here, extreme collectivism resulted from paranoia in particular. In principle, then, Stalinism and its imitators had more 'enemies' than Nazism did. But real resistance to Soviet rule in a restive empire populated by many minorities was also much more substantial than internal opposition to Hitler. The random nature with which paranoia dictated arrests here combined with a principled opposition to 'enemy' groups. Hence, more needed to be murdered, or at least neutralized.

Secular Salvation: The Political Religion Hypothesis

It is often contended that the contingent aspects of both the Nazi and Soviet revolutions cannot themselves explain their genocidal actions. Such hatreds, such bloodlust, surely spring from deeper sources. Metaphysics, theology, and psychology are sometimes called in at this point. Underlying factors have been sought in the frailties of human nature, the fractiousness of modernization, and elsewhere.[391] In one of the most extreme explanations, Leszek Kołakowski has even suggested that Nazism and Bolshevism are evidence of the 'Devil in history' or that 'the Devil incarnated himself in History'. This is not very helpful. But if the resulting 'radical evil' is meant metaphorically rather than literally, taking the 'Devil', for example, to

---

[390] Sheila Fitzpatrick, *Everyday Stalinism: Ordinary Life in Extraordinary Times: Soviet Russia in the 1930s* (Oxford University Press, 1999), p. 122.
[391] See my 'When Does Utopianism Produce Dystopia?', in Zsolt Czigányik, ed., *Utopian Horizons: Utopia and Ideology: The Interaction of Political and Utopian Thought* (CEU Press, 2016).

be merely an incarnation of Le Bon's crowd, or thinking in terms of monstrosity within, it is less implausible.[392]

A more rationalist approach to both dictatorships portrays them as embodying secular or political religions. Such a description, however, might be negative, neutral, or positive in implication. As Jameson argues, it is not the case that this is necessarily to the discredit of either religion or Marxism (in the Stalinist case), where an empirical description of phenomena and psychic states is concerned.[393] More important is the implication that a quasi-religious fanaticism, and thus a deeper and more virulent form of hatred, wedded to secular ends, results from secular religious premises.

This section will explore this hypothesis with a view to linking it to the discussion of dystopian groups in Part I. To do so, however, requires a more precise delineation of those features of these phenomena which have been most conducive to mass murder. Not all religions are genocidal, and there is no reason to presume that all secular religions are either. (Mass consumerism—shopping, also a religion of sorts—might, after all, be considered here.) Marxism often, as Koestler suggests, presents a 'closed system' like Catholicism or Freudianism. As a 'grandiose enterprise in wishful thinking', its 'religious mystique' may have been primarily responsible for its intolerance. But intolerance does not spell the extermination of millions.[394] 'Religion' may not be the central issue here, either, so much as something beneath it, of which it is the expression. So we must go beyond merely acknowledging the parallels between 'religion' and totalitarian mass movements. We need to know what psychological principles unite them: this may provide a meta-theoretical account of 'millenarianism', which unites its 'religious' meanings with their secular equivalents by exploring the psychological origins of both.

* * * *

Political religion has been defined by Emilio Gentile as 'the sacralization of a political system founded on an unchallengeable monopoly of power, ideological monism, and the obligatory and unconditional subordination of the individual and the collectivity to its code of commandments'.[395] Secular religions were first described as fundamental to democracy by Rousseau, and in some instances are regarded as a normal component of it.[396] Their rise has often been associated, in Talmon's words, with the 'decline of the religious sanction', particularly the belief in Original Sin.[397] In this view, Enlightenment anti-clericalism fuelled scepticism.

---

[392] Quoted in Tismaneanu, *The Devil in History*, pp. 18–19, 47.

[393] Fredric Jameson, *The Political Unconscious: Narrative as a Socially Symbolic Act* (Routledge, 1983), p. 275.

[394] Koestler, *Arrow in the Blue*, pp. 230–1; Max Eastman, *Love and Revolution: My Journey through an Epoch* (Random House, 1964), pp. 644–5.

[395] Emilio Gentile, *Politics as Religion* (Princeton University Press, 2006), p. xv. A good discussion of some problems associated with the concept is Dan Stone's 'The Uses and Abuses of "Secular Religion": Jules Monnerot's Path from Communism to Fascism', *History of European Ideas*, 37 (2011), 466–74.

[396] A good review of the hypothesis is Emilio Gentile, 'The Sacralisation of Politics: Definitions, Interpretations and Reflections on the Question of Secular Religion and Totalitarianism', *Totalitarian Movements and Political Religions*, 1 (2000), 18–55.

[397] Jacob Talmon, 'Utopianism and Politics', in George Kateb, ed., *Utopia* (Atherton, 1971), p. 93.

But it did not eradicate underlying needs for 'religion' or spiritual fulfilment, and only redirected them. Both the American and French Revolutions had powerful religious components, and can be seen as reviving Christian themes of equality, now often conceived in terms of rights, sometimes with explicitly utopian implications. This implies a wider form of egalitarianism which underpins both capitalist and communist movements, and whose strength is renewed, ironically, just as faith in the original state of human equality finally seemed to be disappearing.[398] Many later revolutions, too, have often been described as having a central religious component,[399] or as relying upon a political myth such as the fulfilment of historical inevitability.[400]

Socialism in particular had already often been portrayed in religious terms in the early nineteenth century, by Saint-Simon, Owen, and others.[401] In the 1820s, the Saint-Simonians saw the golden age as lying in the future, not the past, and constructed an elaborate new religion to accompany its introduction. Owen proclaimed a 'New Religion' of charity to suit the coming state. By 1901, Vilfredo Pareto described socialism as 'the great religion of modern times'.[402] National Socialism and Marxism, as we have seen, both echoed millenarian themes. Soviet Party discipline, with its emphasis upon self-criticism and self-perfection, was often later described as 'a form of religion'.[403] Raymond Aron termed Bolshevism 'a Christian heresy' and insisted that, 'as a modern form of millenarianism, it places the kingdom of God on earth following the apocalyptic revolution in which the Old World will be swallowed up'.[404]

The popular appeal of both Nazism and Bolshevism clearly had many parallels with religious observance.[405] Each party possessed catechisms, saint-heroes, relics, heretics, and all the other paraphernalia of religion. The vast processions, the mass quasi-worship of portraits, flags, and symbols, the touching of the Leader's clothing, possessing the soil on which He had trodden,[406] the pilgrimage to Lenin's

---

[398] For this argument see my 'Socialism and the Language of Rights', in Miia Halme-Tuomisaari and Pamela Slotte, eds., *Revisiting the Origins of Human Rights: Genealogy of a European Idea* (Cambridge University Press, 2015), pp. 206–36, and 'Paine and the Religiosity of Rights', in Rachel Hammersley, ed., *Revolutionary Moments* (Bloomsbury, 2015), pp. 85–92.

[399] E.g., Lyford P. Edwards, *The Natural History of Revolution* (University of Chicago Press, 1970), pp. 90–1.

[400] This is the line of argument, for instance, in François Furet's *The Passing of an Illusion: The Idea of Communism in the Twentieth Century* (University of Chicago Press, 1999).

[401] See Gareth Stedman Jones, 'Religion and the Origin of Socialism', in Ira Katznelson and Stedman Jones, eds., *Religion and the Political Imagination* (Cambridge University Press, 2010), pp. 171–89.

[402] In *Les systemes socialistes* (1901), quoted in Alberto Toscano, *Fanaticism: On the Uses of an Idea* (Verso, 2010), p. 204. A good introduction to the topic is Joseph Dietzgen, 'The Religion of Social-Democracy', in Joseph Dietzgen, *Some of the Philosophical Essays* (Charles H. Kerr, 1906), pp. 90–154.

[403] Artur London, *The Confession* (William Morrow & Company, 1970), p. 111. This Czech account nonetheless provides great insight into Soviet methods.

[404] Quoted in Tismaneanu, *The Devil in History*, p. 90.

[405] The Nazi case is re-examined by Neil Gregor in 'Nazism: A Political Religion? Rethinking the Voluntarist Turn', in Neil Gregor, ed., *Nazism, War and Genocide* (University of Exeter Press, 2005), pp. 1–22.

[406] Burleigh, *The Third Reich*, p. 239, in Hitler's case.

embalmed body in Red Square, all indicate a process of transferral (of holiness, strength, immortality) through vicarious horizontal and vertical enhancement. Party members recalled themselves as feeling 'chosen by History to lead my country and the whole world out of darkness into the socialist light ... we were the acolytes of a sort of materialist religion'.[407] Stalin was easily likened to a god. People who met him assumed 'an expression of religious fervour'; one woman in 1937 commented, 'I have seen Stalin. Now I can die.'[408] Pictures of leading Bolsheviks were sometimes hung in the very icon holders formerly occupied by Christian saints (or under them).[409] The constant chanting repetition of phrases, the songs and music, also indicate methods drawn from religious assemblies, though often used for secular purposes. They have been described as inducing 'a spiritual state ... that borders on bodily rapture'.[410] So we are on familiar ground here: these are religious groups.

Soviet Marxism thus became a secularized eschatology, moving forward towards humanity's collective salvation, its redemption from oppression, and the emergence of 'New' men and women. Here, 'consciousness' was substituted for 'soul', 'comrades' for 'faithful', and 'classless society' for 'paradise'. To socialists like Julius Braunthal, the movement meant 'the firm resolve to bring about nothing less than the New Jerusalem on earth in my own lifetime'.[411] That sacrifice and suffering were inherent in the process of redemption is also clear.[412] 'We were raised', Lev Kopelev recalled,

> as the fanatical adepts of a new creed, the only true *religion* of scientific socialism. The party became our church militant, bequeathing to all mankind eternal salvation, eternal peace and the bliss of an earthly paradise ... The works of Marx, Engels and Lenin were accepted as holy writ, and Stalin was the infallible high priest.[413]

Some observers have also detected more than a hint of technology worship in this cult. Eugene Lyons thought Stalinism's 'insensitive gods of statistical efficiency' which 'spawned mechanistic religions in which people are mere cogs and digits' might well be the 'revenge of the machine age'.[414] Aldous Huxley, George Orwell, and other dystopian authors, we will see later in this book, took a similar view. And few thought Nazism much different.

Yet broad comparisons of 'religion' to 'secular religion', while suggestive, do not take us very far. We need to assess this theory in greater detail if it is to be of service here. We will briefly consider the views of Karl Mannheim, Eric Voegelin, Norman

---

[407] Victor Kravchenko, *I Chose Freedom: The Personal and Political Life of a Soviet Official* (Robert Hale, 1947), p. 38.
[408] Evgenia Semyonova Ginzburg, *Into the Whirlwind* (Collins/Harvill, 1967), p. 27.
[409] George Kitchin, *Prisoner of the OGPU* (Longmans, Green & Co., 1935), p. 123.
[410] Igal Halfin, *Stalinist Confessions: Messianism and Terror at the Leningrad Communist University* (University of Pittsburgh Press, 2009), p. 5.
[411] Julius Braunthal, *In Search of the Millennium* (Victor Gollancz, 1945), p. 39.
[412] Igal Halfin, *From Darkness to Light: Class, Consciousness and Salvation in Revolutionary Russia* (University of Pittsburgh Press, 2000), pp. 5, 39.
[413] Lev Kopelev, *The Education of a True Believer* (Wildwood House, 1981), p. 249.
[414] Eugene Lyons, *Assignment in Utopia* (George G. Harrap & Co., 1938), p. 646.

Cohn, Jacob Talmon, and Michael Burleigh, before focusing upon three features of the theory which appear most germane to examining the relationship between totalitarianism and violence.[415]

Karl Mannheim's 1929 study, *Ideology and Utopia*, was amongst the first works to offer the suggestion that 'the decisive turning-point in modern history was . . . the moment in which "Chiliasm" joined forces with the active demands of the oppressed strata of society'. This moment was linked by Mannheim to Joachim of Fiore, but even more to Thomas Müntzer and the 'orgiastic chiliasm of the Anabaptists' of the early sixteenth century. Here a powerful emotional sense of 'absolute presentness' or inner psychic/emotional experience is projected outwards onto the external world, rather than Heaven. This results in an outburst of 'ecstatic-orgiastic energies' where the inner world 'takes hold of the outer world and transforms it'.[416] Regardless of the content of these goals (e.g. equality or mass slavery), the experience of projection itself retains something of the ecstasy of the initial impulse. Centrally, it is now revolutionary: this is what links it to Jacobinism and to Marx. Here, 'revolution' chiefly describes an emotional state, not a social and political event. We feel ourselves possessed by a higher entity, now History rather than God, which directs and suffuses us, and dictates the course of our domination of the outer world.

The first major account of this topic, Eric Voegelin's *The Political Religions* (1938), contended that secularization had paved the way for Nazism, too, by imbuing the *Volk* or state with absolute power, with faith therein supplanting religious belief.[417] The *Volk* thus became a higher form of mystical community or congregation. Its ersatz God, the leader or holder of sacred office, defines its 'like-mindedness', or community of equals. The Christian apocalyptic tradition proposed the possibility of spiritual renewal and the creation of a spiritual community, represented by Joachim of Fiore. It anticipated 'the perfection of the Christian ideal of existence as a this-worldly one', particularly in ideas of individual perfectibility, of unlimited progress, and of realizing some type of Enlightenment. The thousand-year Reich becomes the kingdom of Christ on earth. To Voegelin, Marxism, Nazism, and Italian fascism were all embodiments of 'immanentism'. The 'mandate of God' was now the 'mandate of history' or of 'progress' or of 'blood' or the leader. 'Science', 'scientific socialism', and 'scientific racial theory' produced the same moral mandates and metaphysical postulates as 'God' had done previously.[418]

---

[415] Burleigh, *The Third Reich*, pp. 1–23, 691–2. See also Simon Critchley, *The Faith of the Faithless: Experiments in Political Theology* (Verso, 2012); Hans Maier and Michael Schäfer, eds., *Totalitarianism and Political Religion* (3 vols, Routledge, 2007); Toscano, *Fanaticism*.

[416] Karl Mannheim, *Ideology and Utopia* (Kegan Paul, Trench, Trubner & Co., 1936), pp. 190–6.

[417] On Nazism and political religion generally see generally Roger Griffin, ed., *Fascism, Totalitarianism and Political Religion* (Routledge, 2005). Voegelin was himself described as supporting 'National Fascism' in the sense of a racial idea of community which offered a new justification for inequality (Kolnai, *The War against the West*, pp. 315–16, 472).

[418] Eric Voegelin, *Political Religions* (Edwin Mellen Press, 1986), pp. 45, 72–3. Voegelin preferred to characterize Nazism as a 'gnostic' revolution, referring to an ancient doctrine which described the world as an alien place into which mankind had strayed, and from which they had to return, and the claim of certain knowledge as to the correct path to achieve salvation. Against Voegelin, his teacher

The most influential contribution to this literature has been Norman Cohn's pioneering study, *The Pursuit of the Millennium: Revolutionary Messianism in the Middle Ages and Its Bearing on Modern Totalitarian Movements* (1947). Here Cohn vividly describes the trajectory of apocalyptic and millenarian prophecy from the eleventh through the sixteenth centuries, through medieval heretical sectarianism and egalitarian visions of the millennium modelled on Stoic ideas of the state of nature and Roman myths of the golden age. These ideas were trumpeted by an 'elite of amoral supermen' like Thomas Müntzer and John of Leyden. The 'old religious idiom' was 'replaced by a secular one' and underpinned both the idea of the 'Third Reich' and the stage of final communist society.[419] The vision of the Antichrist, the great struggle, the last days, the apocalyptic judgement, and the eventual triumph of good and the reign of Christ, appear as a colossal metaphors striding across the ages, reappearing in various guises and permutations, but clearly ingrained in the human psyche. Evil brings suffering, but eventually the worthy achieve redemption and salvation. Heretics are swept away, and the pure community remains.

We may call this grand scheme 'religion', but it is essentially a set of categories for organizing time, assuring us that justice exists, and promising the purification of society. (It also sounds perilously like the simple-minded plot of a black-and-white Hollywood 'B' movie.) And in it are shared what Fred Polak termed 'certainty-seeking attitudes towards the future', which act 'as a cause of the coercive thought models of human bondage'.[420] This implies that the sense of certainty is a key cause of coercion. If we really are absolutely right and others absolutely wrong it is pointless reasoning with them. And, given their pig-headedness, they do not even deserve the effort.

The vision of mass redemption described by Cohn appealed especially to the poor majority, whom it flattered, and whose anxiety, hopes for justice, and prejudices against outsiders were all fed by its promises. It induced and promoted their self-exaltation from the Crusades onwards, and imbued them with a sense of collective salvation. It demonized their perceived enemies, like the Jews, and, by helping to turn them against the papacy, fuelled the greatest egalitarian moment of the early modern period, the Reformation. Its communist component weds the radical Anabaptists at Münster to Marxism–Leninism. Its persecution mania links

Hans Kelsen contended, vis-à-vis Marx, that the ideal of the overcoming of alienation in communist society was not theological, but was instead grounded in the transformation of labour relations in modern industrial production: Hans Kelsen, *Secular Religion: A Polemic Against the Misinterpretation of Modern Social Philosophy, Science and Politics as 'New Religions'* (Springer, 2012), p. 187.

[419] Norman Cohn, *The Pursuit of the Millennium: Revolutionary Millenarians and Mystical Anarchists of the Middle Ages* (Paladin Books, 1970), pp. 286, 108–10. The phrase 'Third Reich' came from Moeller Van Der Bruck, *Germany's Third Empire (Das Dritte Reich)*, published in 1923. The presumption that it would 'end all strife' in particular echoes traditional ideas of Heaven (George Allen & Unwin, 1934, p. 15). The leader of the Nazi Labour Front, Dr Ley, asserted that 'the German people can become eternal only through National Socialism', and thus could not have their loyalties shared with religion (quoted in Ihor Kamenetsky, 'Totalitarianism and Utopia', *Chicago Review*, 4, 1964, 122).

[420] Fred L. Polak, *Prognostics: A Science in the Making Surveys and Creates the Future* (Elsevier Publishing Co., 1971), pp. 45–7.

them to Hitler.[421] At the same time, it generated an ideal of revolutionary leadership in the form of the heresy of the Free Spirit. This rigidly divided humanity into two groups, the saved and the unregenerate. Here the suspension of all ordinary moral norms was justified by an act of 'total emancipation' from luxury and wealth and a voluntary embrace of poverty.[422] Freedom from sin, in a state of natural liberty and innocence like that before the Fall, permitted anything one desired, including theft, free love, and, for some, bloodshed. Here we see the fun side of being saved. During the fifteenth-century Taborite or Hussite millenarian insurrection in Bohemia, which aspired to recreate a communist golden age of plenty, preachers (many were ex-priests) enjoined that no pity should be shown to sinners. All, they reasoned, were the enemies of Christ, and could be legally killed. The most extreme contended, indeed, that those who did not destroy sinners were themselves only fit for annihilation. The Anabaptists also aimed to live in a state without sin, bound by love alone. They were similarly violent, and linked destruction to self-affirmation and regeneration.[423] These, then, were 'the precursors of Bakunin and Nietzsche' and of Stalin and Hitler, for whom history offered similar absolution from guilt.[424]

Less historical and more psychological was the account offered by Jules Monnerot in 1949, which termed Marxism a 'secular religion', indeed 'the twentieth-century "Islam"', in the sense in which 'the political and the sacred are indissolubly merged'. Monnerot captured the sense in which communism was not simply conceived of as 'the highest truth' very well. Believers saw themselves as '*possessed* by something' they believed to be 'the truth', and then carried along by such a tsunami-like torrent that any sense of individual will was helpless. So, all responsibility was removed from individuals. Rational assent to 'truth' was now less important than submitting to a higher power, which fulfilled deep emotional needs. To Monnerot, Marxism's search for 'totality', and answers to all questions, marked a move in this direction. Hegel had already conceived of the highest form of knowledge as individual reunification with God. Insofar as Marx's theory of alienation encouraged a sense of each being reunified in the new society, reincarnated in a fully social, truly human, communal self akin to a state of original purity, a similar trend is evident. This desire for 'totality' and 'unity' exemplifies an essentially religious quest for salvation or redemption from sin. Monnerot provides a sophisticated account of the psychology of secular religion, which in his view essentially focuses on delusion. Possessed by *une idée fixe*, believers simply rationalize away any counter-evidence. Logic has no truck with faith, which is underpinned by a powerful and highly addictive collective passion. Rituals, processions, and litanies fuel a mutual contagion akin to 'collective intoxication' and

[421] Steed, *The Meaning of Hitlerism*, p. xviii.
[422] Cohn, *The Pursuit of the Millennium*, p. 151. See also Robert E. Lerner, *The Heresy of the Free Spirit in the Later Middle Ages* (University of California Press, 1972), and Raoul Vaneigem, *The Movement of the Free Spirit* (Zone Books, 1994), pp. 95–232.
[423] Jean Delumeau, *Sin and Fear: The Emergence of a Western Guilt Culture 13th–18th Centuries* (St. Martin's Press, 1990), p. 32; Cohn, *The Pursuit of the Millennium*, pp. 209–23.
[424] Ibid., pp. 65, 148.

hysteria. This eventually becomes an 'endemic neurosis'. (A key source here is Freud, whom we recall relied upon Le Bon in his theory of group psychology.) In the 'crowd psychological situation' the 'barriers which the personality's organisation opposes to suggestion and affective invasion are lowered, and this makes such crowd situations ideal conductors of myths'. So this is fundamentally a mass delusion. The fact that 'science' is enlisted in support of the world-view allays any doubts about logic's failure in this case.[425]

In a series of studies commencing with *The Origins of Totalitarian Democracy* (1952), Jacob Talmon identified political religion with utopianism in particular. He insisted that 'totalitarian coercion' was inevitable because the complete agreement utopianism presumes was only possible through dictatorship. Utopianism meant

> that one assumes as possible (or even expects as inevitable) an ultimate condition of absolute harmony in which individual self-expression and social cohesion, though seemingly incompatible, will be combined . . . This combination is possible only if all individuals agree. All individuals, however, do not agree. Therefore, if you expect unanimity, there is ultimately no escape from dictatorship.

'Socialist messianism' was the particular form such beliefs assumed in some quarters, but a general 'expectation of universal regeneration' was in fact a dominant feature in nineteenth-century thought as a whole.[426]

Respecting Nazism, Michael Burleigh has described Hitler as a twentieth-century incarnation of sixteenth-century Anabaptist intolerance. He terms the Nazi racial ideology, with its idealized Teuton-Germanic-Aryan type wedded to both anti-Semitism and a particularly nefarious, eugenics-driven form of Social Darwinism, a 'barbarous utopia'.[427] Burleigh emphasizes the extent to which Nazism was a 'politics of faith, purveyed by a mock-messiah', 'with its own intolerant dogma, preachers, sacred rites and lofty idioms that offered total explanations of the past, present and future, while demanding constant affirmation and enthusiasm from their own populations'. Germans 'voluntarily surrendered to group or herd emotions, some of a notoriously nasty kind'. The 'fantasy world of the nursery', with its mythical heroes, demons, and promised eternal spring, 'the dark irrationalist world of Teutonic myth, where heroic doom was regarded positively, and where the stakes were all or nothing', overcame any rational accounting of German history. To Burleigh, it was 'precisely this combination of moralising about trivia, absolute self-righteousness, and the utopian doctrine of the perfectibility of mankind through a radical "quick fix", which made the twin

[425] Jules Monnerot, *Sociology of Communism* (George Allen & Unwin, 1953), pp. 9–122; here pp. 219, 20, 125–62, and esp. 134–47.

[426] Talmon, 'Utopianism and Politics', pp. 92, 95; Jacob Talmon, *The Origins of Totalitarian Democracy* (Secker & Warburg, 1960), pp. 21–4; Jacob Talmon, *Political Messianism: The Romantic Phase* (Secker & Warburg, 1960), pp. 15, 35–124.

[427] Michael Burleigh, *The Racial State: Germany 1933–1945* (Cambridge University Press, 1991), pp. 23–43.

totalitarianisms of this century and the moralising zealots who sought to realise them so lethal'.[428]

Other authors have offered variations on this account. Following Cohn and Voegelin, James Rhodes describes National Socialism as a 'modern millenarian revolution'.[429] Hitler's thousand-year 'Third Reich' drew on an apocalyptic strain in Western thought which invested a body of saints with the mission of exterminating a principle of extreme evil, resulting in the kingdom of the Saints, the New Jerusalem. Hitler's doom-mongering rhetoric constantly warned of Germany's approaching annihilation and racial enslavement. Its 'revolution' paralleled the effects associated with baptism, conversion, and spiritual renewal in Christianity. It induced a sense of complete 'inner renewal', the elimination of vice, a passionate devotion to nationality, an intense sense of self-sacrifice to the community, and 'a boundless, all-encompassing love for the *Volk*' (in Hitler's words).[430] To Hitler, the Aryan elect, the only creative race, were to be remade as perfect. But sinners, innately destructive, like the Jews, were incapable of anything but 'the naked egoism of the individual' (Hitler again), and would suffer their just fate. The disasters of 1918–33 accounted for the growth of popular millenarian sentiment in Germany. Hitler's revelation cut through the profound disorientation of the post-war period, and showed how a new and far superior world could be created. He exploited an 'ontological' hysteria based upon 'unbearable tension' (Hitler's phrase), acute anxiety or paranoia, and the dread of annihilation or perpetual enslavement to either Jewish communism or Jewish finance capital.[431] This apocalyptic mindset, and Hitler's semi-messianic and prophetic role, with an imperialist fantasy of the advantages to be gained by enslaving millions of other people, explain the fanaticism of Nazi violence and racism. Both the Nazis and the Soviets thus inherited a millenarian mentality which made each, in their own eyes, the 'chosen' people designed to inherit the earth.

Amongst other authors addressing this theme, Emilio Gentile underscores the identification of crowd manipulation with the deployment of religious symbols in Gaetano Mosca's *The Ruling Class* (1895), as well as Le Bon's emphasis on the instinctive need for faith in some all-powerful force and the consequent willingness to offer unconditional submission to it. Gentile also supports Aron's subsequent development of these themes into an account which makes religion, or an analogous set of practices, the essence of totalitarianism. In Waldemar Gurian's view, a focus on crowd manipulation is now simply abandoned in favour of an account of the fusion of religion and politics.[432] Vladimir Tismaneanu describes Marxism as 'a

---

[428] Burleigh, *The Third Reich*, p. 812, 5, 8, 12, 197. See also Michael Burleigh, *Sacred Causes: Religion and Politics from the European Dictators to Al Qaeda* (HarperPress, 2006), pp. 38–122, and generally for the wider theme.

[429] Rhodes, *The Hitler Movement*, pp. 29–84.

[430] 'In giving one's own life for the existence of the community lies the crown of all sense of sacrifice', wrote Hitler. Goebbels insisted that: 'To be a socialist: that means to subordinate the I to the Thou, to sacrifice the personality to the whole. In the deepest sense socialism is service': Rhodes, *The Hitler Movement*, pp. 79, 109, 114.

[431] Rhodes, *The Hitler Movement*, pp. 109, 70.   [432] Gentile, *Politics as Religion*, pp. 57–67.

rationalized theodicy' where 'history replaced God, the proletariat was the universal redeemer, and the revolution meant ultimate salvation, the end of human suffering'.[433] Linked to this is an ideology, the 'New Faith', by which 'good and evil are definable solely in terms of service or harm to the interests of the Revolution'.[434] Marxist 'science' is here reduced to something like biblical prophecy. Most recently, John Gray has reiterated and expanded on many of these points.[435]

These are the general themes associated with the 'political religion' hypothesis. Superficially there is no difficulty enrolling Stalinism and Nazism under this category. However, let us examine three aspects of the theory more analytically to see whether the specific issue of violence is illuminated by them. Religiosity may produce a radical dualism which divides the world into believers and heretics, even demonizing the latter. But this does not, as such, explain the 'Holy Terror' of Nazism and Stalinism. Demonizing heretics and killing them are not the same thing. When, then, does hatred become violent? Three particular attributes of this mentality may go further in this direction: the millenarian feeling of time, the idea of antinomian agency, and the legitimation of violence as a source of redemption. We can then consider how far 'utopia' enters into this issue.

Millennium, Apocalypse, and Sacred History: The Revolution as Pretext

We have seen that the millenarian elements in both Nazism and Bolshevism are striking. The distance between the corrupt and pure needs to be underscored here. Early socialists—at least the more religiously minded amongst them—often spoke of the passage from the 'old immoral world' to the 'new moral world' (as Owenites did).[436] The world to come resembled the ancients' golden age or the Christian paradise. To writers like Arthur Koestler, a state of 'primitive communist society' was the basic reference point for modern communists.[437] In Bolshevism (as for Rousseau and Engels), private property was akin to Original Sin. Revolution might be plausibly conceived as returning to mankind's original condition of primitive equality, virtue, and justice. Hitler's thousand-year Reich was little different. Millenarian thinking and, even more, feeling, indisputably lends a sense of finality to everyday events which was shared by many professional revolutionaries and was epitomized in the concept of revolution itself. 'When the revolution comes, everything will be different' is a common sentiment derived from this mentality. Marginal change is dull and unambitious. A clean sweep is more rewarding spiritually. Why have a small piece of the pie when you can have the pie and the sky together?

---

433 Tismaneanu, *The Devil in History*, p. 227.
434 In the words of Czesław Miłosz, quoted in Tismaneanu, *The Devil in History*, pp. 127–8.
435 John Gray, *Black Mass: Apocalyptic Religion and the Death of Utopia* (Allen Lane, 2007).
436 See my *Citizens and Saints: Politics and Anti-Politics in Early British Socialism* (Cambridge University Press, 1989), which explores the tensions between theological and political models in Owenism.
437 Arthur Koestler, *The God that Failed* (Hamish Hamilton, 1950), p. 25.

Yet we can have neither, we soon discover, without first thoroughly sweeping all the rooms of our projected heavenly mansion. A radical binary world-view, much older than, but reinforced by, Christianity, is evident in these assumptions. A powerful medical-organic metaphor predominates in which the despised are described as diseased, parasites, viruses, germs, and so on, which required 'cleansing' and 'purging'. Decades spent conspiring in secret societies, constantly pursued by police agents, concentrated the revolutionary's sense of the end sought. Paranoia reinforced the certainty of its overwhelming truthfulness and importance. (And what *could* be more important than ending so much human suffering?) The 'comforts of certainty', as Furet calls them, dispel nagging anxieties.[438] Doubts are swept aside as dissenters and the faint-hearted are eliminated. (No doubters, no doubts.) Decades of pent-up anger and anxiety are focused onto a few objects of hatred. Time becomes compressed, heavily weighted down with moral significance, laden with the implications of a now-secularized sacred history and eternity. The senses of the lost golden age and the new egalitarian epoch are elided and squashed together. Any who oppose their (re-)creation are seen as simply irrational, or as merely rationally class-interested. Under Stalin, 'the enemies of the Party had to be exterminated for the good of the community', Igal Halfin writes: 'both the purges and the resistance to them ... may show in what way the messianic mentality justified, and sometimes even mandated, wide-scale extirpation of the oppositionist, the wrecker, and the spy'. This 'justified the cleansing operations as an apocalyptic event preceding the triumph of universal peace'.[439] But it is soon evident that hardly anyone is fit to inhabit the new mansion: it is too good for us.

'Revolution'—a scant two letters from 'Revelation'—thus became a heavily fetishized category. Viewed psychologically, an analogy with revivalist movements, and the experience of ecstasy as a 'peak' or 'core religious experience' (in Maslow's terms), is an exact one.[440] The emotionally addicting release of nervous energy is an ecstatic, essentially religious, experience. If religion functions partly to provide or organize transcendent experiences, to deliver us from the anxieties of an over-wrought self-identity, and 'to shake the individual in his deepest insides', all are here fulfilled in secular fashion. Now, however, the experience of the universe as 'an integrated and unified whole' is conceived in secular terms, the 'oneness' being humanity rather than an integration with nature or spiritual or transcendental entities. The mere size of the group clearly permits an extraordinary range of moral assumptions: it is humanity we are saving. No higher group exists to challenge our assumptions or offer moral arbitration. Other qualities in this experience, such as ego-transcendence, self-validation, a sense of worth and meaningfulness, and of the world as beautiful, good, and desirable, of reverence and awe, of personal honesty,

---

[438] Furet, *The Passing of an Illusion*, p. ix.   [439] Halfin, *Stalinist Confessions*, pp. 352–3.

[440] Abraham H. Maslow terms it a 'peak experience', or 'secularized religious or mystical or transcendent experiences' (*Religions, Values, and Peak-Experiences* (Ohio State University Press, 1964), p. xii). He adds that it implies that 'the sacred and profane, the religious and secular, are not separated from each other' (p. 33).

innocence, and unselfishness, and also of having free will, all make the transition from religion to politics effortlessly.[441]

The sense of having something as fundamental as universal human justice virtually at our fingertips, tantalizingly close, and requiring only a final great surge of effort to achieve, then, is a powerful motive here. We may regard the lust for power as a transcendent motive nonetheless. But we should not neglect the idealism of millions. To 'liberate the world from social injustice' was the motive of one young communist.[442] Nadezhda Mandelstam describes the 'craving for an all-embracing idea which would explain everything in the world and bring about universal harmony in one go' as the reason 'why so many people willingly closed their eyes and followed their leader'.[443] To Bolsheviks, the word 'revolution' came virtually to invoke a 'second coming', a quasi-sacred and semi-mystical transform-ation of both society and individual, the wiping of the slate and the commencement of a new beginning. To the Nazis, too, it was both an end in itself and a perpetual process of becoming, and represented a transvaluation of values. All preceding bankrupt values and institutions were now replaced by 'devotion to the revolution-ary movement for its own sake'.[444] Edward Shils paraphrases Georges Sorel in describing this as an 'ethic of crisis', which is 'resolved only by an apocalyptic transformation in which *everything* is *totally* changed'.[445] (We recall the Maoist injunction, 'overthrow everything'.) To Maslow, this corresponds to the sense of completion, ending, finality, justice, totality, total gratification, climax, or fulfil-ment.[446] It explains the perverse fascination with the Apocalypse and total destruc-tion by the promise of total renewal, and the paradox which Lifton so acutely describes as 'the orgiastic excitement of . . . destroying everything in order to feel alive'.[447] Here we see again how violence and creativity, virtue and terror, may in fact be very closely wedded indeed. To destroy the enemy is to affirm ourselves. To destroy an evil enemy is to affirm our own virtue. Blood cleanses.

The mental atmosphere of the millenarian-revolutionary moment is one of concentrated frenzy and haste which parallels the anxiety felt during catastrophes. Time is now intensified. Rather than meandering aimlessly through life we now have an acute sense of direction. The minor distractions and petty irritants of everyday existence—who would not like to dispense with these?—are rendered meaningless, and fall by the wayside. Reality may come to seem like a dream sequence, or like drowning.[448] One or more moments of acute awareness, when the

[441] Maslow, *Religions, Values, and Peak-Experiences*, pp. 34, 59, 61–8. But Maslow does not describe moral anomie as amongst these qualities.
[442] Joseph Scholmer, *Vorkuta* (Weidenfeld & Nicolson, 1954), p. 3.
[443] Quoted in Adam Hochschild, *The Unquiet Ghost: Russians Remember Stalin* (Viking Penguin, 1994), p. 71.
[444] Rauschning, *Germany's Revolution of Destruction*, p. 61.
[445] George Sorel, *Reflections on Violence* (Collier Books, 1950), p. 15.
[446] Maslow, *Religions, Values, and Peak-Experiences*, p. 93.
[447] Saul Friedländer, Gerald Holton, Leo Marx, and Eugene Skolnikoff, eds., *Visions of Apocalypse: End or Rebirth?* (Holmes & Meier, 1985), p. 15.
[448] Mary Sturt, *The Psychology of Time* (Kegan Paul, Trench, Trubner & Co., 1925), pp. 117–18, on the experience of duration.

scales fall from our eyes, and we 'truly see' for the first time, vividly mark the cathartic stages of the process of purification, like saints' tombs on the route of a holy procession. Our new visions seem much more secure, confident, vivid, and 'real' than our old world-view. 'Before' and 'after' mark the great event, the psychological rupture and transformation from corruption to virtue. This is, in Karl Mannheim's fine formulation, 'the moment of time invaded by eternity', an 'absolute presentness' in which secular history is dissolved.[449] The spirit of the moment sweeps us along. Invested with a sense of mission and all-powerful rectitude, we feel the burden of history pressing heavily upon us. We must act quickly and resolutely. We must make decisions we would normally avoid. We must subordinate the niceties of morality to pressing necessities. This is a transcendent mentality: we are absolved in and by it.

Where these experiences are wedded to fierce hatreds and our oppressors and enemies have been clearly identified, this mentality easily becomes furious with the unpurified who obstruct it. Patience, tolerance, and compromise get short shrift. Such obstructions are not minor irritants: they block our collective salvation. Disagreements with the party line are treated like religious heresy or blasphemy. Ideological challenges become psychological threats. Parallels between the Church's approach to witchcraft and the Bolsheviks' treatment of their 'Trotskyist' demonized enemies, as we have seen, are plentiful. So we have an intimate dialectic between a fervent longing for the tranquillity of the ideal community and an increasing zeal to destroy everything that impedes its attainment. To the saints, mercy only impedes the progress of the holy. It is counterproductive. So for an entire generation, as Lev Kopelev wrote:

> [T]he ends justified the means. Our great goal was the universal triumph of Communism, and for the sake of the goal everything was permissible—to lie, to steal, to destroy hundreds of thousands, and even millions of people, all those who were hindering our work or could hinder it, everyone who stood in the way. And to hesitate or doubt about all this was to give in to 'intellectual squeamishness' and 'stupid liberalism', the attributes of people who 'could not see the forest for the trees'.[450]

Redemption, Rebirth, and Grace: The Agents

Millenarian thinking requires, accompanies, and nurtures a millenarian psychological type. Jean Baechler suggests that, historically, the messiah echoes 'the shaman, the magician, the sorcerer'. Some are common brigands, recasting themselves as Robin Hoods. Others are marginalized intellectuals, or failed priests. Many come from the bottom of society—think of Stalinism after 1930—and bear great grudges against the privileged and educated, whom they slaughter mercilessly. Most have been mocked, belittled, humiliated, and have long memories where vengeance is concerned. They compensate for their inferiority complexes by being

---

[449] Mannheim, *Ideology and Utopia*, p. 193; see Toscano, *Fanaticism*, p. 93.
[450] Lev Kopelev, *To Be Preserved Forever* (J. B. Lippincott, 1977), p. 13

distinguished by their fanaticism. They are rarely half-hearted or agitated by mental reservation. Compromise is alien to their nature. They seek total change because, for them, everything in the old society is rotten. All change means improvement, the more the better. But what may be much more frightening is the ordinariness of those who implement the system they construct, who are not psychotic, but look like us, act like us, are . . .

To the millenarian, as we have seen, such change also involves a qualitative improvement in humanity's character. As early as the 1870s, Marx's critics, like Mazzini, accused the International of promoting an 'impossible utopia' in 'the notion that it is the business of revolution, not to carry on the progress of humanity, but to create humanity anew'.[451] This moment combines the experiences described in religion in terms of revelation, baptism, and conversion. In the language of religion, we are reborn. 'Our goal is the total recasting of man', wrote Trotsky, who insisted that 'The average human being will rise to the heights of an Aristotle, a Goethe, or a Marx.'[452] (Casting is usually done in a furnace, of course.) The Bolshevik Revolution aimed to build 'new men' and 'new women', a new species indeed, *Homo Sovieticus*. Hitler's master race was defined in ethnobiological terms. For both, children, now flattered for their potential, and their virtue by comparison to their parents' corruption, were to be the chief buildingblocks. (Here we see how integral youth rebellion as such is to modernity, and how far age comes to epitomize corruption rather than wisdom.) In Bolshevism, the idea of moral regeneration was rooted in an assumption that private property caused all crime. Utopia would have no criminals because it had no private property. Under Hitler, the presumption was that the newly invigorated and racially purified nation would express more powerful communal values. Here, Trotsky's image of genius does not express the new type: we are more sociable, and more orderly, a better group.

For the people to cross this threshold, however, leadership was crucial, both of the more charismatic or messianic figure, and by an elite of 'chosen' 'Saints' or inner circle of the faithful, for whom, at least at the outset, revolution is a 'vocation', in Niemeyer's term.[453] The new group acquires the attributes of the 'perfect', deriving these (by horizontal vicarious enhancement) from the virtues attributed to the 'people', the 'proletariat', the German *Volk*, and so on, and then monopolizing these qualities when these groups fail to achieve the ideal qualities attributed to them. The Comintern was described by Franz Borkenau as 'a select community, a sort of religious order of professional revolutionaries, crusaders of a materialistic faith, a selection of the most self-sacrificing, the most decided and active amongst the revolutionary intelligentsia'.[454] The revolutionary priesthood of the Nazi and Bolshevik Parties became invested with the same attributes of the supra-moral ideal

[451] *Contemporary Review*, 20 (1872), 578.
[452] Leon Trotsky, *Literature and Revolution* (University of Michigan Press, 1975), p. 256.
[453] Gerhart Niemeyer, *Between Nothingness and Paradise* (Louisiana State University Press, 1971), p. 3.
[454] F. Borkenau, *The Communist International* (Faber & Faber Ltd, 1938), p. 419.

of grace or blessedness, of purity and holiness, or being immediately favoured by God and directly under Divine guidance, as their Christian predecessors.

This feeling of being in a state of grace, clearly present in some variants on both Nazi and Marxist revolutionary practice, directly encouraged the suspension of 'ordinary' moral norms.[455] Recast as historical necessity and biological destiny, Providence could absolve and justify the use of any means to achieve this end. In one of the most chilling instances of the Bolshevik mentality in this regard, an Extraordinary Commission for Combating Counter-Revolution and Sabotage (CHEKA) functionary proclaimed the need to reject

> the old systems of morality and "humanity" invented by the bourgeoisie to oppress and exploit the "lower classes". Our morality has no precedent, and our humanity is absolute because it rests on a new ideal . . . To us, everything is permitted, for we are the first to raise the sword not to oppress races and reduce them to slavery, but to liberate humanity from its shackles . . . let our flag be blood-red forever.[456]

Antinomianism, the heresy of the Free Spirit, superseding the moral norms of the existing society, thus here follows logically from the boldly Manichean portrayal of the bankruptcy and corruption of the old society and its morals. All is thoroughly rotten. All must be swept away. 'Bourgeois' morality is part of 'bourgeois' society, which will be destroyed. 'Humanitarian' considerations are swept away with it: kindness, mercy, and forgiveness are 'bourgeois'.

An absolution from moral doubt is now central to this group's identity. The stronger this identity becomes, the less place there is for individual responsibility. The 'Party' thinks abstractly and acts concretely for each person. Following Koestler, Tismaneanu describes the 'oceanic feeling' (we recall the phrase from Freud's description of religion), 'the ecstasy of solidarity, the desire to dissolve one's autonomy into the mystical supra-individual entity of the party' as 'the emotional ground for a chiliastic type of revolutionary commitment'.[457] The intense sense of elitism which bonds the saints is fetishized into a 'fraternal comradeship of the righteous'.[458] Both the Nazi and Bolshevik Parties became a holy order, all-consuming in their demand for loyalty, all-powerful in their claims to primacy in each member's identity. 'My honour is loyalty' was the SS motto. Absolute loyalty is owed only to God in Christianity: now the Party assumes this role.

Belonging to these privileged and sacrosanct groups clearly had exhilarating, intoxicating, addictive, and magnetic qualities.[459] The release from the overwhelming weight of the past, of sin, of the humdrum world of normality, and the adrenaline-borne surge of energy it brings, is almost invariably accompanied by a

---

[455] Drawing on Paul Tillich, Ruth Levitas contends that utopia ought to be understood as a secular form of grace in the sense of a state of freedom from (original) sin: *Utopia as Method* (Palgrave Macmillan, 2013), p. 13.

[456] Courtois et al., *The Black Book of Communism*, p. 102.

[457] Tismaneanu, *The Devil in History*, p. 61.

[458] The phrase is Andrzek Walicki's: *Marxism and the Leap to the Kingdom of Freedom* (Stanford University Press, 1995), p. 473.

[459] Conquest uses 'addiction' to describe adherence to Marxism: *Reflections on a Ravaged Century*, p. 127.

sense of omnipotence. Whatever we do seems right, and, for Marxists, 'dialectics' serves as the alchemical formula of the revolution, turning dross into gold. In Georg Lukács' telling phrase, 'The conviction of the true Communist is that evil transforms itself into bliss through the dialectics of historical evolution.'[460] The emotional state of the true believer is not complicated. Despite its philosophical garb and empirical veneer, Marxism is a profoundly emotional faith, a kind of primitive Methodism for intellectuals, a form of what even Eric Hobsbawm, an insider, describes as 'mass ecstasy'.[461] Nazism was little different in this respect. No sacrifice is too great to defend such a feeling.[462]

The Morality of Finality: The Consecration of Violence as the Agency of Rebirth

These two factors, the sense of millenarian expectation and the associated idea of grace which accompanied it, underpinned the mentality which permitted the Holocaust and the Stalin's Terror to develop. Both helped to release those pent-up 'reservoirs of bloody destructiveness' which some psychologists assume lie just beneath the surface of everyday human behaviour.[463] Both were driven by the mesmerizing power of belief, the possession of the self by the Idea. Self-sacrifice inevitably follows from this mentality. To sacrifice others, one further element was also necessary, however: the consecration of violence.

In both Nazism and Stalinism, violence acquired traits associated with nobility, with the romance of the knight upon the battlefield, the slaying of the dragon (the Devil or Jew) and rescue of the virginal maiden. In Stalinism, violence embodied heroism and the heroic proletariat's struggle in an all-conquering symbol of goodness, the universal assertion of virtue against a monstrous oppressor, the bourgeoisie. In both cases, blood sacrifice epitomizes the embrace of virtue, and at some level we recognize the inexorable logic: the more blood the more virtue, or minimally, the more blood the less vice. Some assume these rituals to be an integral part of political religions as such, or at least assert, following Le Bon in spirit if not in name, that the '*sanctification of violence* as a sacred instrument of regeneration' developed logically after 1789.[464] Clearly, the fanaticism, intolerance, supposed infallibility, unscrupulousness, and proneness to persecution of their opponents of both the Nazis and the Stalinists promoted violence. Yet they do not wholly account for it, or tell us why it assumed the particular forms it did. Nor does the

---

[460] Melvin Lasky, *Utopia and Revolution* (University of Chicago Press, 1976), p. 53.

[461] Eric Hobsbawm, *Interesting Times: A Twentieth Century Life* (Abacus Books, 2002), p. 74.

[462] Sorel noted that: 'During the Terror, the men who spilt most blood were precisely those who had the greatest desire to let their equals enjoy the golden age they had dreamt of, and who had the most sympathy with human wretchedness: optimists, idealists, and sensitive men, the greater desire they had for universal happiness the more inexorable they showed themselves': *Reflections on Violence*, p. 38. See further Jack J. Roth, *The Cult of Violence: Sorel and the Sorelians* (University of California Press, 1980).

[463] Hans Toch, *Violent Men: An Inquiry into the Psychology of Violence* (Aldine Publishing Co., 1969), p. 4.

[464] Gentile, 'The Sacralisation of Politics', pp. 25, 36.

concept of totalitarianism, when applied (as Niemeyer does) to the idea that revolution aims at 'total destruction', adequately describe regimes like the Nazis, who aimed to preserve an idealized order as much as to create a new one.[465]

The most important explanation of these themes has been Georges Sorel's *Reflections on Violence* (1906), a work much influenced by Le Bon.[466] Like many Marxists and fascists—Mussolini acknowledged a key debt to him—Sorel assumed that historical necessity justified the higher moral activity of a heroic sect, opposed to any compromise with the existing exploitative order and bound together by its own solidarity. The force required to achieve this end Sorel rather paradoxically regarded as an expression of the revolt of the essential goodness of man against the radical evil of bourgeois society. Here we see, once again, why the marriage of violence to virtue is, in fact, not so paradoxical. The Marxian theory of catastrophic revolution was, like the narratives of both primitive Christianity and the Reformation, a 'myth' in which a struggle against 'Satan' was predominant. Adopting Bergson's idea of an *élan vital*, or creative life force, Sorel saw the creative moment of the revolution occurring when it broke from the bonds of habit and asserted a new self. This was a moment dominated by 'overwhelming emotion'.[467]

Here, action as such—any action—is viewed as superior to mere criticism. Activity stands juxtaposed to thought, acting to being, freedom to passivity. In a leap of faith, 'actions', when directed against some great injustice, transform themselves into 'violence'. In this assertive self-definition, violence is construed as a higher form of action and thus an embodiment of self-assertion, willpower, and moral rebirth. It becomes expressive of the noble and heroic type. (Nietzsche is another source here.) The individual is reborn while expunging evil and decadence, the more unclean, impure, and sullied, the merrier. This is the moment when revolutionary catharsis becomes individual catharsis. This rebirth, like its Christian prototypes, releases us from sin and guilt. Like a balloon untethered, we spring upwards when freed from the weight of these burdens. Killing other people actually frees us from our own burdens. It cleanses our sins by destroying the embodiment of even greater sins. We can thus do it gratefully.

Then the spilling of blood becomes ritualized as well as transformative. Sorel (quite wrongly) felt that there was 'no danger of civilisation succumbing under the consequences of a development of brutality'. Socialist violence, he thought, possessed its own internal restraining ethical standard based upon the idea of 'free producers' and the 'enlightening' qualities associated with the general strike.[468] These themes were later famously developed by Jean-Paul Sartre into a theory of violence as a creative force, writing in a preface to Frantz Fanon's *The Wretched of the Earth*, of the 'mad fury' that enabled the dispossessed to 'become men'.[469] But the violence may also imply seeking what Voegelin described as a 'pseudo-identity

---

[465] Niemeyer, *Between Nothingness and Paradise*, p. 3.

[466] Sorel termed Le Bon 'one of the most original physicists of our time' (*Reflections on Violence*, p. 152).

[467] Sorel, *Reflections on Violence*, pp. 42, 48.   [468] Ibid., pp. 186, 249.

[469] Franz Fanon, *The Wretched of the Earth* (Grove Press, 1968), p. 17. To Fanon, a similar hypothesis applied to the need to form an undamaged racial identity and overthrow an ingrained sense

through asserting one's power, optimally by killing somebody—a pseudo-identity that serves as a substitute for the human self that has been lost'.[470]

The key question here, then, is not whether modern revolutionism embodied millenarian elements, nor whether these inspired a degree of fanaticism as intense as that provoked by most religions, nor whether Marxism in particular adopted, when in power, many of the traditional forms of religion. All this is easily conceded. The bloodletting which surrounded these processes was doubtless also linked to their quasi-religiosity. But whether this is coincidence or evidence of causal linkage is another matter. The potential for modern revolutionism to become immensely murderous can be associated with Karl Heinzen in the 1850s. The deep hatred of bourgeois society which it represented remained undiminished for over a century, at least through to the movements associated with 1968.[471] When it became most murderous—against Jews, bourgeois, *kulaks*, New People—was when the logic of extermination trumped that of neutralization. The more internal the enemies were, the less they could be exiled to distant lands. The closer they were, the more dangerous they were. And the threat of impurity was most acutely felt by those most keen to be virtuous.

* * * *

The Secular Millenarianism Hypothesis Revisited

The concept of secular millenarianism discussed here suggests a model with ten components: (1) a quasi-millennial goal of harmony, peace, goodness, and plenty is proclaimed as an ideal future (communist society, the abolition of the state, the thousand-year Reich) which is akin to religious salvation and for which present sacrifices are constantly justified; (2) the proclamation of these goals is presented as a complete, final, total, and irrefutable understanding of both history and the progress of the present into the future which is defined in terms of deterministic 'laws' (of race, the economy, for example); (3) a sense of conversion to this vision is akin to the medieval idea of union with God leading to antinomianism,[472] which verges on a mystical, cathartic, or ecstatic experience for individuals; (4) an idea of 'revolution' as apocalyptic transformation from the bad old 'polluted' world to the good new pure one is promoted by an act of 'cleansing' which is intensely emotional; (5) a claim that the new world-view promotes a profound moral transformation of the individual or human nature, a moral rebirth akin to religious redemption or rebaptism, which involves expunging most vice and either returning to a condition of original virtue (e.g. the peasant of 'natural society') or creating a higher type of 'new' personality; (6) a claim that the morality required to attain the new society justifies superseding traditional morality, akin to an idea of secular

---

of racial inferiority during the struggle against colonialism. Hannah Arendt sees this as alien to Marx: *On Violence* (Penguin Books, 1970), p. 13.

[470] Quoted in Burleigh, *Sacred Causes*, p. 119.   [471] Arendt, *On Violence*, p. 65.

[472] This is identified with the concept of progress in particular in Ernest Lee Tuveson, *Millennium and Utopia: A Study in the Background of the Idea of Progress* (Harper Torchbook, 1964).

grace, and will be exercised by a vanguard or elite of secular 'saints' and/or a prophetic or messianic figure, 'whose word is Revelation' (in Koestler's phrase), and whose Apostles keep the sacred flame burning;[473] (7) the assertion is made that the new morality ('*fraternité*', solidarity, enhanced sociability) will pervade and define the new society; (8) 'enemies' become primary obstacles to achieving the quasi-millennial goal and must be eliminated as a consequence (Jews, bourgeois, *kulaks*); (9) the perfectionist assumptions of the revolutionary process promote an increasing punitive attitude towards all participants who display any signs of inadequacy; (10) the assumption is common (though not universal) that the new society, while usually more equal, would be defined by the norms of modernization established elsewhere, especially in the United States, centred on giving a priority to heavy industry and the collectivization of agriculture. (Germany, of course, had already reached this level.)

These attributes do not fit all the regimes studied here, and are indicative rather than rigid. Some suggest new problems. A major difficulty with this approach is the term 'secular millenarianism' itself. Are these phenomena 'millenarian' when they are substantially modified by the term 'secular'? God and/or Christ play no role here. This 'millennium' is always inaugurated by human beings, even if the leader sometimes appears as a *deus ex machina* (or both a history- and machine-made god). Is a return to that primitive virtue associated with the natural state, golden age, or origins of humanity, a condition assumed to have really existed rather than being merely mythical or illusory, 'millennial' or a condition of 'secular salvation'? Is the communist ideal of the abolition of property—the defining quality of Marxism—'essentially' a 'millennial' concept as such, especially when linked to ideas of virtue? (And thus, is 'communist society' a 'secular' concept?) And then what does 'secular' itself mean? Is the idea of moral rebirth as such 'religious', or a psychological assumption of another type? Should we consider a form of 'modernity psychosis', as Eli Sagan terms it, in which powerful paranoid fantasies of destruction come to be shared by large numbers, to be central to this explanation?[474]

These assumptions, and especially that of the rebirth of virtue through a kind of revolutionary baptism, do clearly mimic religion at a variety of levels. Without doubt, the metaphor and historical precedent for this sense of and longing for the immensely improved future is based in religion. The intense desire for extreme moral improvement, both individual and social, is a reaction to crisis. It may be conceived religiously, in terms of Divine or saintly virtues, and a condition akin to secular grace. To Richard Landes, for example, these are sufficient conditions to employ the concept of 'secular millennialism', describing the search for a perfect society on this earth, an idea of collective salvation, and a dynamic of apocalyptic time which follows a trajectory of enthusiasm, disappointment, and re-entry into 'normal time'.

---

[473] Koestler, *Arrow in the Blue*, p. 232.
[474] Eli Sagan, *Citizens and Cannibals: The French Revolution, the Struggle for Modernity, and the Origins of Ideological Terror* (Rowman & Littlefield, 2001), p. 331.

But this process may, nonetheless, simply be a defence reaction against social breakdown. It may be akin to the 'spiritualization of politics' which Mannheim described. The idea of 'sacred politics' or the 'sacralization of politics' places the shoe on the other foot, so to speak. This is no longer 'millenarianism', but its distinctively religious affinities are nonetheless underscored. Talmon's phrase, 'political messianism', achieves the same mixture. Another approach, usually associated with Carl Schmitt, implies that 'political theology' is an operative category here, insofar as all the concepts which make up the modern idea of the state are 'secularized theological concepts'.[475] At the very least, then, we can agree with Landes that 'the emotional drives that underlie perfectionist social thinking, whether secular or religious... share important dynamics'.[476] But these conclusions imply that we need to go beyond the language of religion to explain these aims, and to turn instead to the language of the group and its aspiration to purity.

These concepts need, moreover, to take into account the rapid forced modernization in twentieth-century Stalinist regimes and the immense dislocation this occasioned.[477] Here, a concept of 'millennial modernization' would be useful. That is to say, we invest in the concept of progress, and particularly its technological expressions, a sense of overwhelming confidence that our greatest problems will be 'solved', and that we will achieve something like the secular paradise of the utopians through science and technology. The predominance of mechano-intoxication is here everywhere obvious. Marxism became only a variant of the liberal ideal of industrial progress, albeit one even more obsessed with efficiency and productivity. Some of the catastrophes which followed doubtless resulted from a paranoid wish to avoid conquest by enemies. But many resulted from the mentality associated with an intoxication with the liberating effects of technology. As the nineteenth century ended, it was clear that the age-old dream of 'a perfect, ideal society which would really ensure universal well-being and happiness' might for the first time be realized through the Industrial Revolution.[478] Science and technology coalesced with religion in the assumption that only one solution could logically prevail to any problem. And so the machine produced machine worship. The fact that the violence associated with this process appears to be in direct proportion to the society's distance from industrialism is notable.

The strengths of the political religion analysis, then, are that it explains a good part of the collective hysteria associated with both Bolshevism and Nazism, and the linkage between a Manichaean world-view and certain forms of millenarian Christianity in the modern period. It portrays the Nazi and Bolshevik Parties as reborn sectarian emanations of an extreme Christian ideal of self-sacrifice to the common good, and as aiming to abolish egoism in the subsuming of the individual in the social. It draws out analogies between the 'totalizing' qualities of religion and those of these ideologies. It builds upon contemporary allegations that moral nihilism and

[475] Carl Schmitt, *Political Theology* (MIT Press, 1985), p. 36.
[476] Landes, *Heaven on Earth*, pp. 339–41, xvii.
[477] This, to Valentino, is also a central cause of communist mass deaths (*Final Solutions*, p. 93).
[478] Nadezhda Mandelstam, *Hope against Hope: A Memoir* (Collins & Harvill, 1971), p. 254.

hostility to Christianity played a key role in Nazi aspiration, though they were more obvious in Stalinism.[479] Its weaknesses are that it does not penetrate far enough into the psychology of religion itself, but chiefly delineates those qualities shared by religion and its secular successors.

Both religion and totalitarianism share a moral dualism which is not, as such, either 'religious' or 'political'. By positing a binary system of good and evil, inclusive and exclusive, us and other, and describing the need for the former to triumph over the latter, and then coding one's earthly enemies as evil, a recipe for inevitable bloodletting on a grand scale is virtually guaranteed. Religion can simply be seen as 'sacralized politics'. That is to say, power is distributed in such a way as to create privileged elites and masses of labourers, but a supernatural sanction is added to the obligations created by social membership. When this is driven by a compelling sense of inevitable struggle, the Social Darwinist element shared by the Nazis and Stalinists, it also receives a powerful pseudo-biological justification.

Group psychology, as we have seen throughout this chapter, assists the explanation of these processes through the history of religion. Millenarianism produces a final struggle against the forces of evil which threaten the group's identity and purity. The militarized group is best equipped to 'struggle', so all groups are militarized, and war and violence become constant and all-consuming. But the obsessive quest for purity, especially when wedded to a desire to purge impurity, is rooted in psychological phenomena in which religion is a result rather than a cause. It epitomizes one aspect of the psychopathology of society which remains too little understood.[480]

A second weakness in many, though not all, versions of the political religion hypothesis lies in presuming that the only grounds for opposing totalitarianism are religious. In Voegelin's words, 'Satanic substance can only be opposed by an equally strong religiously good force of resistance.' Here the 'secularisation of life' is the dreaded malaise which opens the door to barbarism.[481] 'Dedivinization' is equated with and held to account for 'dehumanisation'.[482] By implication, only respect for the 'godly' component in people can induce respect for them as human beings. Theologians often stress that political religion is only an *ersatz* religion, distinctly inferior to the real thing.[483] So we are told to contemplate the 'presence of God' and another world.[484] Politics in this vision must remain religious, and 'a political community cannot be defined as a profane sphere, in which we only have to deal with questions of organizations, of law, and of power'.[485]

---

[479] Rauschning, *Germany's Revolution of Destruction*, pp. 96–7.
[480] This is the conclusion of Sagan, *Citizens and Cannibals*, p. 476.
[481] Voegelin, *Political Religions*, p. 2.
[482] 'The denial of the nonexistent reality of transcending toward divine being destroys the *imago Dei*. Man becomes dehumanized. The suffering from the meaninglessness of a Godforsaken existence leads to outbreaks of concupiscent fantasy, to the grotesque creation of a "new man"—of Marx's and Nietzsche's supermen': Voegelin, *Hitler and the Germans*, p. 263.
[483] E.g., Mathias Behrens, ' "Political Religion"—a Religion? Some Remarks on the Concept of Religion', in Maier and Schäfer, eds., *Totalitarianism and Political Religion*, vol. 2, pp. 225–45.
[484] Voegelin, *Hitler and the Germans*, pp. 159, 171.
[485] Voegelin, *Political Religions*, p. 77.

But this is unhelpful both as an explanation and a cure or antidote. It ignores thousands of years of religious conflict based upon theological distinctions. It ignores that fact that many revitalized religions are extremely intolerant (Christian fundamentalism) while others are astonishingly brutal (ISIS). Undeniably, totalitarianism represented a profound crisis of values, often conceived as 'spiritual'.[486] But why should a revival of the old divisive religions, each themselves proclaiming their absolute truth and compelling total obedience from their adherents, represent a step forward rather than a regression? Seen from the perspective of group psychology, 'religion' may simply be another variation on 'politics'. Both are group self-definitions. Thus, modern (Western) politics is less the search for salvation than a restatement of the search for equality at the heart of Christianity, commencing with a redefinition of the group(s) tasked with the effort.

Religion, Utopia, and Dystopia

What can a discussion of utopia and dystopia add to this debate? Few writers distinguish between 'utopianism' and 'political religion' as aspects of totalitarianism. Both seemingly represent the search for perfectibility, which its critics regard as doomed to fail outside theology. We do not have to search far, consequently, to find the allegation that 'utopianism' underpins totalitarianism. For Friedrich Hayek, communism and fascism were only the outcome of the same statism, 'the great Utopia', which produced socialism and social democracy. Democratic utopia, 'the great Utopia of the last few generations', was 'unachievable' in principle.[487] One of the main themes of Karl Popper's *The Open Society and Its Enemies* was the contrast of 'piecemeal social engineering' to 'Utopian social engineering'. Originating with Plato, the 'utopian approach' in politics is described as aiming for an 'ideal state' and plotting a rational course for achieving it. Popper thought any differences amongst utopian engineers invariably led 'to the use of power instead of reason, i.e. to violence'.[488] Jean-Luc Domenach has written that 'the intrusion of Utopia into politics coincided very closely with that of police terror in society'.[489] Jacob Talmon insisted that 'totalitarian coercion' paradoxically resulted from utopianism, the complete agreement utopianism presumes being possible only through dictatorship.[490] To a leading historian of Bolshevism, Robert Conquest, Popper's 'culture of sanity' contrasts societies underpinned by irrational taboos which oppose all change to those which promote critical public debate and scientific reasoning. By contrast, Conquest, who comes close to describing many on the political left as simply insane, describes 'despotic-utopian' regimes as rooted in

---

[486] See, e.g., Karl Mannheim, *Diagnosis of Our Time* (Kegan Paul, Trench, Trubner & Co., 1943), pp. 12–30.

[487] Friedrich Hayek, *The Road to Serfdom* (University of Chicago Press, 1944), p. 31.

[488] Karl Popper, *The Open Society and Its Enemies* (2 vols, Princeton University Press, 1966), vol. 1, pp. 1, 157–8, 161. This definition Popper thought corresponded 'largely, I believe, to what Hayek would call "centralized" or "collectivist" planning' (p. 285).

[489] Quoted in Courtois et al., *The Black Book of Communism*, p. 492.

[490] Talmon, 'Utopianism and Politics', p. 95.

the 'archaic idea that utopia can be constructed on earth; the offer of a millenarian solution to human problems'. Here, 'utopianism' coincides with a dogmatic and essentially religious mentality, though we note the assumption of its implied overlap with millenarianism.[491]

Continuing this line of thought, Kołakowski takes utopia to imply a world-view in which 'evil is entirely done away with' and 'all human values and desires reconciled', a project bound to end in 'disastrous failure'.[492] Adam Hochschild addresses the 'more hazardous side of Utopianism', 'the faith that if only we make certain sweeping changes, then all problems will be solved', and describes how 'the promised Utopia' of the USSR 'rapidly became quite the opposite'.[493] Specific aspects of Stalinism were also described as 'the bloody implementation of a utopia', namely 'a vast enterprise of social engineering, of bureaucratic and police planning, that sought to "cleanse" and "purify" certain Soviet spaces—notably cities—by deporting them to Siberia's "garbage-can" areas'.[494] Tismaneanu describes the 'acme of radical utopianism' as an 'all-pervading technology of socially oriented murder' (referring to Stalin).[495] In Leonard Schapiro's assessment, Marx's aim, the end of the state, becomes 'the most dangerous utopia of all times', the end of legal order and triumph of naked power.[496] François Bizot, Pol Pot's captive, wrote that 'I detest the notion of a new dawn in which Homo Sapiens would live in harmony. The hope this Utopia engenders has justified the bloodiest exterminations in history.'[497] Steven Rosefielde writes that: 'The Red Holocaust is best interpreted in this light as the bitter fruit of an Utopian gambit that was socially misengineered into a dystopic nightmare by despots in humanitarian disguise.'[498] Critics of many of the phenomena we have explored in this section are thus quick to condemn 'illusory visions of utopia based on false notions of scientific certainty'.[499] But to consider 'the revolutions of 1989 the end-point of the historical era ruled by utopia' does not take us any closer to understanding the catastrophes of this epoch.[500] Nor does the view (here expressed by Martin Malia) that 'any realistic account of communist crimes would effectively shut the door on Utopia'.[501] It is easy enough to describe communist regimes as 'failed utopias'.[502] But if these are merely variations on the political religion hypothesis this tells us nothing new.

There are three related problems, then, with bracketing utopia with religion in this approach.

[491] Conquest, *Reflections on a Ravaged Century*, pp. 20, 14, xiv, 92–3, 112–13.

[492] Leszek Kołakowski, 'Need of Utopia, Fear of Utopia', in Dick Howard et al., *Radicalism in the Contemporary Age*, vol. 2: *Radical Visions of the Future* (Westview Press, 1977), p. 4.

[493] Hochschild, *The Unquiet Ghost*, p. xix.

[494] Nicolas Werth. *Cannibal Island*, p. 171.   [495] Tismaneanu, *The Devil in History*, p. 68.

[496] Leonard Schapiro, quoted in Conquest, *Reflections on a Ravaged Century*, p. 35.

[497] Bizot, *The Gate*, p. 7.

[498] Steven Rosefielde, *Red Holocaust* (Routledge, 2010), p. 240.

[499] Chirot, *Modern Tyrants*, p. 341.   [500] Tismaneanu, *The Devil in History*, p. 45.

[501] Ibid., p. 49.

[502] Arch Puddington, *Failed Utopias: Methods of Coercion in Communist Regimes* (ICS Press, 1988).

The first is that utopia is not synonymous with perfectionism.[503] It generally represents—despite overlapping with theology at various points—a guided improvement of human behaviour towards a substantially better condition, usually where society is considerably more equal and people are much better behaved. The demand to create a new human nature, baptized in the crucible of revolution, inevitably failed, as did the more extreme forms of egalitarianism. Expecting a moderate improvement in behaviour in superior circumstances may well be realistic (and has occurred). Expecting perfection invites destruction. This failure thus took place in part precisely because the assumption of change, the metaphor of rebirth, was essentially religious.

So, secondly, utopia is not synonymous with millenarianism. Nostalgia for the golden age predates Christianity, and many forms of utopianism do not require millenarian premises to be realized—More did not hint at them—and, in addition, avoid revolutionary means. Stalinism, in particular, represents a radical form of millenarianism *as well as* utopianism. But its demand for angelic rather than improved people mimics religion rather than utopia.

Thirdly, identifying utopia with communism and then with dystopia is also a misconception. Communal property holding, usually in the village and/or clan, has been the norm throughout much of human history. When voluntary, it generates successful, long-lived communities, like the Shakers or various monastic orders. Many forms of utopia, moreover, are not communistical but involve various types of cooperation or profit-sharing.

Secular perfectionism and millenarianism may lead towards dystopia, then. Utopia, as such, does not. It is quite right to describe both Nazism and Stalinism as forms of utopianism. But they are not its only forms, and they do not invalidate utopian thinking and action as such any more than the failures of the Bolshevik Revolution invalidate revolution as such. Utopianism has frequently eschewed violence, and opted instead for non-coercive free association on cooperative principles. It is by no means inevitably linked to class hatred and the extermination of the wealthy, or the insistence on remaking whole societies according to romanticized and overly perfectionist images of the working classes.

The Group Identity Hypothesis Revisited: The Redemptive Group and the Idea of Heresy

We need now to revisit the account of group identity introduced in Part I. Amongst religious organizations, we noted in the Introduction, millenarian groups have provided both the most intense and the most exclusive forms of group definition. Their senses of finality, of urgency, and of moral transcendence have been wedded to violence on various occasions. Their willingness to sacrifice this world in the name of the ideal future obliterates any considerations of everyday moral restraint.

[503] See my 'The Five Languages of Utopia: Their Respective Advantages and Deficiencies; With a Plea for Prioritising Social Realism', in Artur Blaim and Ludmila Gruszewska-Blaim, eds., *Spectres of Utopia* (Peter Lang, 2012), pp. 26–31.

The goal is final; so are the means. The future trumps the present. Such futur-ointoxication, as we might call it, guarantees intense bonds between those sharing this ecstasy. This group now defines all the rules. Its survival, that is, expansion, is now the all-consuming ideal.

The affinities between such groups and totalitarian political parties are obvious. It is easy to see why these groups might seem to be central to any definition of dystopia. Both project a form of idealized community in which powerful emotional bonds of belonging are directly proportionate to a passionate antipathy towards outsiders, non-believers, heretics, and enemies. The triggers for the intensification of these bonds—the moment when violence is legitimated—lie both in paranoia, and a redemptive sense of particular moments and of the group as such. In the cases of both Nazism and Bolshevism, paranoia was also driven by genuine threats of invasion and/or the loss of wars. This was particularly the case for Russia, having been invaded in the seventeenth century (by Poland), the eighteenth (by the Swedes), the nineteenth (by Napoleon), and twice in the twentieth century. In China, memories of Japan's invasion (1931–45) and humiliation by Western imperialism were raw and fresh to Mao's generation. Cambodia, having achieved freedom from French rule only in 1953, suffered from constant fear of foreign incursion in the 1960s and 1970s. None of these countries had liberal or demo-cratic traditions which might have offset the tendency towards despotism that such paranoia supported. In most of them—even Cambodia—extensive modernization seemed the only course to prevent new conquest. This was not, thus, an irrational response to circumstances.

We tend to associate both the successes and excesses of the Nazis and the communists in terms of their group self-definition. An astute survivor of Pol Pot wrote: 'The invention of a group within a larger group, of a group of human beings considered different, dangerous, toxic, suitable for destruction—is that not the very definition of genocide?'[504] The Nazis and SS and the Communist Party and CHEKA excelled as groups par excellence. Their combination of religious and military characteristics permitted intense emotions and the supposed exertion of supreme virtues. They offered alienated ambitious individuals an outlet for their resentments and isolation while at the same time identifying their goals with social salvation. They abolished intermediary groups precisely in order to keep their crowd mentality intact, and to prevent the retreat of its emotional force and basis back into lesser forms of association. Many happily traded personalities racked with inferiority for a share in the new collective super-entity, the 'counter-community of the estranged', in Lenin's apt term.[505] Whether the threat is the Devil, witches, Jews, the bourgeoisie, or *kulaks* matters little to the projected antagonism. All these groups defined enemies, which they then chose to destroy in order to preserve and reinforce their own identity. Killing meant saving. Eradicating vice meant reinfor-cing virtue. The group's identity and its enemies were thus mutually bound up and intertwined. When survival was deemed to depend on the destruction of these

---

[504] Panh, *The Elimination*, p. 182.   [505] Quoted in Burleigh, *Sacred Causes*, p. 76.

enemies, the process was unstoppable. Violence now became both redemptive and creative, strengthening the group by destroying its enemies.

The Pursuit of Finality: Dystopia and Totalitarianism

Finally, in what sense does 'dystopia' differ from 'totalitarianism'? We have seen that there is no one theory of totalitarianism, and many regimes fit the bill. It is challenging to assimilate the shared characteristics of Nazism, Stalinism, Maoism, and Pol Pot's Cambodia. The differences between them, indeed, particularly vis-à-vis race and class, are as striking as their similarities. We have defined the despotic political dystopia here in terms of a peculiar form of group identity in which an obsession with purity of identity becomes contingent upon an obsessive pursuit of 'enemies'. This is usually underpinned by a secular millenarian identity. These qualities may lie dormant, even harmless, the stuff of beer hall bombast, until they are triggered by external crises, and gather the force of numbers and momentum. Then, newly confident, anointed by history, they tip over into violent paranoia of the sort which characterized many of the movements examined in this chapter, and which is often held to be the key source of modern ideological terrorism.[506]

To conclude, then. The quasi-religious nature of these processes has been noted in much of the most recent literature on totalitarianism. What we have added here, firstly, is a theory drawn from group psychology which explains how dystopian groups work *as groups*, how they construct images of the 'enemy', and what historical precedents we need to address in order to see how this works. We have seen that dystopian groups thrive on suspicion, the opposite of trust. Their definition of 'enemies' is linked to ideas of group purity, as well as an interiorized conception of the guilty 'self' or some component therein. Also dominant here was a medical-organic metaphor of the group, in which 'purging' and 'cleansing' become appropriate languages expressing social paranoia. This helps to explain the 'totalizing' aspects of totalitarianism in a manner which builds on existing accounts.

Secondly, we have attempted to isolate those elements of the secular religion hypothesis which were seemingly most conducive to mass cruelty, torture, and murder in these regimes. These are described as part of a secular millennial outlook whose psychology we have briefly explored here.

Thirdly, while the concept of totalitarianism often distinguishes these regimes from earlier forms of despotism by describing their efforts to penetrate the inner psyche, our exposition of the dystopian group explains both why this is necessary and how it occurs. The modern self is often an interiorized, spiritual self with a strong sense of individual identity. The totalitarian collectivist self is simply its counterpart. As individualism intensifies, and threatens to hasten the disintegration of society, so collectivism is reinforced, and becomes more extreme, rising to the challenge of emboldened individualism, like the Devil to the deity.

---

[506] Sagan, *Citizens and Cannibals*, pp. 327–31.

Fourthly, we have provided a much more long-term historical explanation for the phenomena here described as the modernization of guilt. Secular guilt, operating successfully outside a Christian context, is central to dystopian identity. The culture of confession functions nearly universally. It was modernized when a class definition of guilt was substituted for ideas of Original Sin in a revolutionary context. Class identity was then coded as powerfully as race or ethnicity had ever been. It became, consequently, in secular form, even more powerful than Original Sin had been, and could only be expunged through ideological purity and extensive good works. Wedded to an unforgiving work ethic, and a rigid, often puritanical, priest-like idea of duty, it produced regimes to which the vast majority were simply slaves. This we have characterized as the internal dystopia, or carcerotopia. In the external dystopia these conditions were imposed on those outside the definitive group.

Undoubtedly, understanding these extraordinarily complex phenomena cannot safely be entrusted to the historian or sociologist alone. Dystopian literature has emerged as amongst the most powerful intellectual currents of our time. How its insights vary from, supplement, or fall short of the story we have examined so far must now be considered.

PART III

THE LITERARY REVOLT AGAINST COLLECTIVISM

INTRODUCTION TO PART III

This section will examine literature's contribution to our understanding of dystopia through a concentration on themes and ideas rather than literary form. We can commence with the assumption that, while much literature may aim chiefly to entertain us, dystopian fiction often has a higher purpose. But what does imaginative literature, which projects horrifying or disastrous conditions, *do* that political tracts or historical narratives cannot? Thomas More offered a neat turn of phrase to explain fiction's utility: 'the truth might slip into people's minds a little more agreeably, as if smeared with honey'.[1] Literature often does this by bringing home at the individual, emotional level experiences which, writ large, are meaningless when lost in the anonymity of historical narrative. As the saying (commonly attributed to Stalin) goes: one death is a tragedy, a million is a statistic. The novel, thus, as Margaret Atwood stresses, is 'always about an individual, or several individuals; never the story of a generalized mass'.[2] So dystopian literature is often about rational autonomous individuals lost in the Le Bonian crowd. Unlike history, fiction also allows us to move back and forth in time almost seamlessly, to break the rules of linear narrative and the disciplined recording of memory, and to flit and dip here and there as we please. This quality gives a vividness, immediacy, and intensity to literature which history usually lacks.

Dystopian novels are imaginary futures where much has gone wrong, though sometimes ways out are indicated. Rebellions by individuals and (sometimes) groups, often against collectivism, do occur, as do escapes from perilous predicaments like nuclear wars or environmental collapse. The revolts usually epitomize values with which the author wishes the reader to sympathize. Often these values are broadly 'liberal' or 'humanist'. They express profound apprehension respecting two developments in particular. Firstly, revolutionary movements in Europe and elsewhere seemingly heralded a new despotism more frightening than those they promised to overthrow. Secondly, the very sources of much mid-nineteenth-century optimism,

---

[1] Thomas More, *Utopia*, ed. David Wootton (Hackett Publishing Co., 1999), p. 167.
[2] Margaret Atwood, *Curious Pursuits: Occasional Writing 1970–2005* (Virago, 2005), p. 93.

science and technology, now appeared Janus-faced, threatening destruction and a new barbarism or the ruthless elimination of the 'unfit', while simultaneously promising improvement and happiness. Civilization was now seen as capable of degeneration as well as progression. World War I would adequately demonstrate the correctness of the first of these fears, as World War II did the second. Both technological modernity and its enemies seemingly conspired against humanity. Capitalist machines brought factories, collectivism, and a new slavery. But so did socialist machines. The unfolding task of dystopian literature was to envision these dire futures, and to suggest alternatives.

* * * *

While acknowledging the contributions of a few better-known authors, this chapter introduces about 150 texts, many not discussed elsewhere, to indicate the main trends in dystopian literature up to the mid-twentieth century. The first dystopias proper are dated from the French revolutionary period. The genre proper then commences in the 1870s and enjoys great successes through the early 1930s. We then take up, in Chapters 6 and 7, Aldous Huxley and George Orwell, the two authors who centrally define the genre in the mid-twentieth century. In the final chapter, developments from the 1950s to the present are traced through some fifty works.

The focus here will be largely upon British and American dystopian narratives. (Some reference is made to other traditions, particularly after 1917, but an exhaustive comparative study of the subject is not yet possible.) Discussing so many texts in these two traditions alone is still problematic, however. Plot summaries must be offered in the many cases of unfamiliar and often inaccessible works. A sufficient number of these are required to ground wider generalizations. Genre definitions and boundaries constantly pose problems of categorization. Various competing subgenres which broach the future from slightly different entry points emerged in the later nineteenth century: the future war novel; projected imperial collisions; and, most importantly, science fiction, which eventually engulfed the other genres. Monstrosity was reborn with both natural beings being created by scientific experiment (*Frankenstein*) and then as mechanical or organic mass-produced creatures. These would often revolt against their creators, while sometimes serving metaphorically for a working class enslaved to machines.

We need here too to separate literatures of natural disaster, Apocalypse, and cataclysm, many of which are variants on Christian millenarianism, from those of dystopia proper. Dystopian scenarios may occur before or after an Apocalypse. But, like utopia, a key aspect of dystopia's specificity is its portrayal of social and political relations. Many, though not all, dystopias imagine regimes characterized by extreme suffering, fear, and oppression. Our concern throughout this section is chiefly with these more 'realist' horrors, and with the cruelties imposed by people upon other people. We need thus to separate dystopia from the much larger genre of science fiction, in order to refine our sense of the distinctiveness of the dystopian novel. We will also need to consider dystopias which function as 'anti-utopias', some of which, however, then propose counter-utopias.

* * * *

We commence with the nineteenth-century literary dystopia. This was dominated by four themes: the progress of revolutionism and the terror it implied; the potential unleashing of scientific and technological inventions which would prove more destructive than not; the prospect of a eugenic control over parenthood and the family; and the more generalized threat of mechanization as intrinsically dehumanizing. These themes would eventually intermingle in various ways. The political dystopia commences with the French Revolution. It gathers momentum in the 1880s, and emerges with full force after 1917. From the 1870s, science and technology play an increasing role in dystopias, as we might now understand them, many texts being originally conceived as utopian.[3] In the twentieth century, dystopia then becomes dominated by two themes: the despotic collectivism associated with fascism and communism, and the domination of science and technology over humanity both here and in modernity generally. Here, three works define the genre: Zamyatin's *We* (1924), Huxley's *Brave New World* (1932), and, most importantly, Orwell's *Nineteen Eighty-Four* (1949). After the 1960s, we will see in Chapter 8, anxiety about totalitarianism gradually drops away as the confrontation of humanity with technology becomes increasingly central, with growing threats of the loss of humanity, of identity, and of free will, and then the possibility of our real extinction.

We will see throughout this section that dystopian literature was not as such reactionary, in the sense of politically conservative (but this too covers many possible positions). Its greatest example was produced by a socialist, George Orwell. But the politics of dystopia often represent a rejection of the intense collectivism which seemingly permeated not only modern revolutionism but, equally, machine civilization. Modernity seemingly came to embody many of the qualities of mechanism itself. Nationalism and socialism could easily be accommodated to, even driven by, the machine. All the great symbols of progress, the steam engine, the steamship, the railway, the tractor, automatic weapons, the telegraph, the internal combustion engine, the airplane, electricity, radiation, refrigeration, the radio, the telephone, and numerous domestic appliances, and—that perfect symbol of modernity, the equalizing machine, the handgun—were produced by science and technology. All implied complexity, control, organization, integration, discipline, subordination—in a word, efficiency. All implied an obsession with increasing productivity, and with human beings conceived primarily as agents of production. But where were individuality, freedom, the dignity of man, the great watchwords of nineteenth-century thought, to be found in the onward march of production, consumption, and power over nature? They seemed increasingly lost in the vast anonymous jungle of steel, concrete, and engines which defines modern life. Or worse still, they might be exchanged voluntarily for economic stability and the consumerist paradise. And yet if all these products, and the substitution of machine labour for human labour, were capable of alleviating humanity's burdens, surely such a price was acceptable? These questions would haunt dystopian writers, regardless of their political outlook.

---

[3] See Patrick Parrinder, *Utopian Literature and Science: From the Scientific Revolution to* Brave New World *and Beyond* (Palgrave Macmillan, 2015), and, further, Nell Eurich, *Science in Utopia: A Mighty Design* (Harvard University Press, 1967).

5

Mechanism, Collectivism, and Humanity

The Origins of Dystopian Literature, 1810–1945

We is from God, while I is from the Devil.

(Zamyatin, *We*)[1]

THE LITERARY DYSTOPIA:
PROBLEMS OF DEFINITION

We must commence by reviewing approaches to the dystopian literary genre. The term 'dystopia' was evidently coined in 1747, spelt as 'dustopia'.[2] In 1748, 'dystopia' was defined as 'an unhappy country'.[3] The next important use came in an 1868 speech by John Stuart Mill in Parliament. This termed British policy in Ireland 'too bad to be practicable', and its proponents as 'cacotopians' (after the Greek, bad place), or dys-topians.[4] The former term never really caught on. 'Dystopia' came into meaningful common usage in the late twentieth century, and then mainly in secondary literature concentrating on contemporary texts. Critics focusing on the last thirty to forty years, when science fiction swamps dystopia, not uncommonly take the latter to be a subgenre of the former. This proposal is considered below.

Determining what is distinctive about the literary genre of dystopia has proven very problematic. Immense variation exists within the genre. Some dystopias are only minimally literary, and are primarily tracts in social and political thought where conversation and monologue only frame the argument. Others offer complex plots and well-drawn characters, and display considerable emotional power, prioritizing the elaboration of subjective experience over the methodical presentation of ideas. Dystopias are not reducible to the history of ideas, then. But their

---

[1] Yevgeny Zamyatin, *We*, tr. Bernard Guilbert Guerney (Jonathan Cape, 1970), p. 165.

[2] In Henry Lewis Younge's *Utopia: or, Apollo's Golden Days*: Lyman Tower Sargent, *Utopianism* (Oxford University Press, 2010), p. 4.

[3] V. M. Budakov, 'Dystopia: An Earlier Eighteenth Century Use', *Notes and Queries*, 57 (2010), 86–8.

[4] John Stuart Mill, *Collected Works of John Stuart Mill* (33 vols, Routledge & Kegan Paul, 1965–91), vol. 28, p. 248. 'Cacotopia' did not generally stick thereafter, though it is used by Anthony Burgess (*1985* (Arrow Books, 1980), pp. 52–60) and Matthew Beaumont (*Utopia Ltd.: Ideologies of Social Dreaming in England 1870–1900* (E. J. Brill, 2005), pp. 129–68). Lewis Mumford uses 'kakotopia': *The Myth of the Machine*, vol. 2: *The Pentagon of Power* (Secker & Warburg, 1964), pp. 220–4.

contribution to it, rather than an analysis of their literary forms, is our central, though not sole, focus here.[5]

We have already seen that the concept of dystopia (here referring to literature alone) can, in several respects, be identified with the utopian tradition as such. Utopia comes into its own as a popular literary genre in the late nineteenth century. Dystopia emerges from the same set of problems: how to control industrialization, widespread poverty, the concentration of wealth, and an increasing tendency towards collectivist solutions to these issues. But in an age also characterized by growing individualism, some saw the more repressive and puritanical attributes of the older utopian tradition as part of the problem rather than of the solution. Homogeneity, uniformity, transparency and mutual supervision, abstinence from luxury, the suppression of dissent and privacy, and the intolerance of heresy figure in many early modern utopias from More onwards. Often these were conceived as the price to be paid for universal opulence and relative social equality: for the poor, the bargain may seem reasonable enough. So, collectivism, and a trend towards what Francis Russell, in a much-underrated study, termed a 'persistent policy of benevolent autocracy', thus defined many utopias from the outset. The trend continued until at least the late nineteenth century and even the twentieth.[6] But a democratic age clearly demands democratic utopias.

This uncomfortably close proximity of utopian and dystopian traits has encouraged disagreement about key definitions. Most early scholarly studies of utopia do not mention 'dystopia'.[7] The first, apparently, to do so, Glenn Negley and J. Max Patrick's *The Quest for Utopia* (1952), describing Joseph Hall's *A New World* (*c.*1605), commented that 'dystopia, if it is permissible to coin a word', might be conceived as 'the opposite of *eutopia*, the ideal society'. Here it is assumed that the concept entails both satire and an implied ideal society portrayed by negation.[8] So the anti-utopia seemingly dismisses one (degraded) form of utopia, often by parody, while implying that another (attainable or superior) variant is possible.[9] (But not all anti-utopias, of course, offer us this alternative.) From the outset, then, 'dystopia' often implies a negative condition caused by an excess of (one or other kinds of) utopian zeal. We will need to challenge and modify this assumption, however. Some dystopias are not anti-utopian, but grow out of existing trends towards dictatorship, economic monopoly, the degradation of the poor, or environmental collapse. Some seemingly reject all forms of utopianism, others only one

---

[5] For a discussion of some of these problems see Gary Morson, *The Boundaries of Genre: Dostoevsky's Diary of a Writer and the Traditions of Literary Utopia* (Northwestern University Press, 1981), pp. 69–186.

[6] Francis Russell, *Touring Utopia: The Realm of Constructive Criticism* (The Dial Press, 1932), p. 64.

[7] This includes: Lewis Mumford, *The Story of Utopia* (1922; The Viking Press, 1962); Joyce Hertzler, *The History of Utopian Thought* (George Allen & Unwin, 1923); Karl Mannheim, *Ideology and Utopia* (Routledge & Kegan Paul, 1936); Martin Buber, *Paths in Utopia* (Beacon Press, 1949); Harry Ross, *Utopias Old and New* (Nicholson & Watson, 1938).

[8] Glenn Negley and J. Max Patrick, eds., *The Quest for Utopia* (Henry Schuman, 1952), p. 298.

[9] See Morson, *The Boundaries of Genre*, pp. 115–42. But, to Morson, the parody must be of the genre as a whole and not 'a single work in the target genre'. So the anti-Bellamy parodies which present 'rival utopias' are not 'anti-utopias' as such because they do not take 'exception to utopianism *per se*'.

or other varieties.[10] We will review the most important of these approaches to the genre chronologically.

The 1950s

Writing in 1956, the anarchist (and friend of Orwell's) George Woodcock described 'Utopias in Negative' as resulting from a shift from four centuries of utopian focus on 'the hopes of men with uneasy social consciences' to a genre which 'gives shape to their fears'. Planned societies, Woodcock lamented, had 'brought little marked increase in human happiness'. This failing seemed 'to lie in the Utopian outlook itself', and particularly in the dependency of a 'free and full life' on 'social fluidity'. 'Negative quasi-utopias' are treated in terms of two categories: 'the romances in which an imaginary country is used to satirise existing society', and 'those in which conservative thinkers attack Utopian radicalism'. Before 1914, the target was often 'the collectivist idea', thereafter more its 'concrete manifestations'. But 1914 represented a watershed for both the utopians and their enemies, for now technological promise and threat seemed equally balanced. Zamyatin, Huxley, and Orwell are then seen as cut from the same cloth, projecting a possible, even probable, future emerging from the present. They differed only, Woodcock thought, in Orwell's greater pessimism, where 'even the promise of happiness is withdrawn'. Thus, the latter satirizes not only totalitarianism, but the 'Utopian form of society' as such.[11]

The 1960s

The 1960s produced the first extensive literature on dystopia. In 1961, Arthur O. Lewis delineated a range of forms of anti-utopian fiction, including reverse utopias, negative utopias, inverted utopias, regressive utopias, cacotopias, dystopias, non-utopias, satiric utopias, and nasty utopias. These are classified into three main groups: the anti-totalitarian, the anti-technological, and the satiric, or combinations of all three. Lewis defined the anti-utopian novel as a work 'depicting a society which is officially "perfect" but which is demonstrated to have flaws making it unacceptable to the author's—and presumably the reader's—point of view'.[12] In 1961, Fred Polak's fine study, *The Image of the Future*, provided numerous categories for comprehending negative utopias. These included dis-utopia, pseudo-utopia, semi-utopia, and negative utopia.[13]

The first major study of the field, Chad Walsh's *From Utopia to Nightmare* (1962), sees the genre as progressing from being a minor 'satiric fringe of the

---

[10] 'Distopia' also occasionally appears in this period, e.g. in M. Kessler, 'Power and the Perfect State: A Study of Disillusionment as Reflected in Orwell's *Nineteen Eighty-Four* and Huxley's *Brave New World*', *Political Science Quarterly*, 72 (1957), 568.

[11] George Woodcock, 'Utopias in Negative', *Sewanee Review*, 64 (1956), 81–97.

[12] Arthur O. Lewis, Jr, 'The Anti-Utopian Novel: Preliminary Notes and Checklist', *Extrapolation*, 2 (1961), 27–32.

[13] Fred L. Polak, *The Image of the Future* (2 vols, Oceana Publications, 1961), vol. 2, pp. 21–9.

Utopian output in the 19th century' to promising 'to become the dominant type today'. Walsh proposes juxtaposing utopia to dystopia or the 'inverted utopia' or 'anti-utopia' (the terms are used interchangeably) to characterize the competing genres. He insists that in defining texts as dystopias, 'a writer's intention is what counts' (but inside or outside the text?). His definition of dystopia is 'an imaginary society presented as inferior to any civilised society that actually exists'. (Today both 'inferior' and 'civilized' are regarded as fairly problematic categories, and this would also presumably render all primitive societies 'dystopian'.) Walsh adds that: 'An inverted Utopia, in its turn, is often a deliberate attack on the idea and possibility of Utopia. But it does not have to be. It may equally well be an attack on certain tendencies in existing societies.' He excludes most forms of science fiction as 'too alien to our condition'. The dystopian (chiefly conservative) 'counter-attack' is dated to the reaction to Edward Bellamy's *Looking Backward 2000–1887* (1888), and the many refutations it spawned.[14] Walsh's conclusion, following Huxley, is that one of dystopia's chief moral lessons is that: 'You can have a society aquiver with creativity—arts, sciences, technological breakthroughs, everything—or you can have a safe and stable society. You can't choose both.'[15]

The motto of Irving Howe's 1963 study, 'The Fiction of Antiutopia', might have been, 'be careful what you wish for'. Anti-utopia is described here not as a conservative outlook as such, but as emanating primarily from 'a systematic release of trauma, a painful turning upon their own presuppositions of "men of the left" like Zamiatin, Huxley and Orwell'. Having expected history to deliver utopia, what 'they fear is that the long-awaited birth will prove to be a monster', not 'progress denied but progress realized'. What resulted was a disenchantment with history in the realization that a 'transparent universe' emerges which aims to fix all categories, and eliminate surprise, novelty, and adventure. Technique and functional rationality come to trump humane values. Freedom becomes a burden, though anti-utopian plots require a few characters who express 'a spontaneous appetite for individuality'. But the idea of the personal self becomes a mere cultural artefact, the product of a liberal era, and 'susceptible to historical destruction'. Ultimately, these works express the great choice exposed by Dostoyevsky, 'the misery of the human being who must bear his burden of independence against the contentment of the human creature at rest in his obedience'. To Howe, the peculiarities of the genre lie in five qualities: positing a flaw in the perfect regime; demonstrating the predominance of 'an idea that has become a commanding passion'; being clever in the use of detail; keeping to a fine line between the probable and plausible; and 'in presenting the nightmare of history undone', permitting a sense of historical recollection, especially of 'the power that the idea of utopia has had in Western society', a kind of remembrance of the golden age now posited in negation.[16]

[14] See Jean Pfaelzer, *The Utopian Novel in America 1886–1896* (University of Pittsburgh Press, 1984). Pfaelzer claims the first dystopian text of this type appeared in the USA in 1884, with the movement peaking between 1887 and 1894 (p. 78).
[15] Chad Walsh, *From Utopia to Nightmare* (Geoffrey Bles, 1962), pp. 12, 25–8, 74–5, 148.
[16] Irving Howe, *Decline of the New* (Victor Gollancz, 1971), pp. 66–74.

Writing in 1963 in one of the most penetrating post-war accounts of the problem, George Kateb considered several 'anti-utopian' arguments. Taking utopia to be a 'dream-world . . . in which the welfare of all its inhabitants is the central concern', he identifies 'the essence of modern antiutopianism' in Berdyayev and Huxley's assumption that a revolt of 'freedom' against 'perfection' is necessary (but unlike Negley and Patrick he does not consider how and why this may be utopian as well—witness the case of Huxley). Though he does not use the concept of dystopia, Kateb describes anti-utopias as relying on three chief assumptions: the inevitability of violence in attaining utopian ends; the maintenance of such ends through oppressive regimes; and the destruction of many worthy values in the pursuit of others deemed more valuable. The anti-utopian insists that wisdom may be gained by suffering, that happiness alone is not sufficient to define the good life, that pleasure, indeed, 'needs difficulty, austerity, contrariety, comparison' to validate its very nature. Kateb challenges the idea of conditioned virtue satirized by Huxley and promoted by B. F. Skinner in *Walden Two*. Following Berdyayev, the search for perfection is a particular target. Kateb insists that: 'The way of sin, the way of experience, the way of loss of innocence, must be the way by which the generally virtuous character is formed. This is the way of the world; this is the way that Utopia eschews; but this is the better way.'[17] Where utopia strives for perfection, then, it invites dystopia. We must return to this motif later, for Orwell reached a similar conclusion respecting Wells.

Mark Hillegas' *The Future as Nightmare: H.G. Wells and the Anti-Utopians* (1967) describes the 'anti-utopia' as 'a sad, last farewell to man's age-old dream of a planned, ideal, and perfected society'. As established by Wells, this genre is 'a phenomenon of our contemporary world, no older perhaps than the governments of Hitler, Stalin, or Roosevelt'. 'Anti-utopia' is thus a subset of 'superior science fiction'. Wells' *The Time Machine* (1895) was 'the first well-executed, imaginatively coherent picture of a future worse than the present, a picture at the same time generally anti-utopian in its tendencies'. *The Island of Doctor Moreau* is Wells at his most pessimistic. Hillegas illustrates Wells' great influence on subsequent writers like Huxley and Forster. He notes that 'the anti-utopian tradition after Wells pivots on *We*', where 'social-scientific fantasy' targets communism. Thereafter, Huxley and Rand dominate the field. But even works like *Facial Justice* and *Player Piano* are described in terms of a Wellsian inheritance, as is the post-catastrophic novel in the nuclear age.[18] Several minor studies in this decade will appeal to specialist readers.[19]

[17] George Kateb, *Utopia and Its Enemies* (Schocken Books, 1972), pp. 6, 18, 129, 133, 186–7.

[18] Mark Hillegas, *The Future as Nightmare: H.G. Wells and the Anti-Utopians* (Southern Illinois University Press, 1967), pp. 3–4, 34, 36, 99, 163, 167.

[19] In 1965, Northrop Frye distinguished between the 'straight utopia, which visualizes a world-state assumed to be ideal', and 'the utopian satire or parody, which presents the same kind of social goal as terms of slavery, tyranny, or anarchy', including the works of Zamyatin, Huxley, and Orwell. These, in turn, are described as the 'product of modern technological society, its growing sense that the whole world is destined to the same social fate with no place to hide, and its increasing realization that technology moves towards the control not merely of nature but of the operations of the mind' ('Varieties of Literary Utopia', in Frank E. Manuel, ed., *Utopias and Utopian Thought* (Beacon Press, 1967), pp. 25–49). Constantinos Doxiadis' *Between Dystopia and Utopia* (Faber & Faber, 1966)

The 1970s

Dominating this period is Alexandra Aldridge's perceptive study, *The Scientific World-View in Dystopia* (1978).[20] Commenting that 'little criticism exists on the dystopian phenomenon', and nothing until after 1945, Aldridge terms dystopia 'not merely "utopia in reverse"', but 'a singular generic category issuing out of a twentieth-century shift of attitudes toward utopia'. She argues that 'the literary and philosophical tradition which in various ways generated the pure dystopias was the Utopian tradition'. Dystopia was the 'form specifically concentrating on the alienating effects of science and technology'. It aimed 'to critique the scientific world view which stimulated its Utopian predecessors and upon which Utopia, "the dream of reason", was built'. Wells, Zamyatin, and Huxley are addressed here. In all,

> dystopia always aims to critique and ridicule that world view for its adherence to
> instrumental values, its elevation of functional and collective ends over the humanistic
> and individual . . . They have criticized the replacement of a humanistic ethos with a
> scientific/technological one; their fiction assails the scientizing of society.[21]

contrasts negative spaces created in the real world (conceived particularly in terms of the city) and their fictional representations. Doxiadis observes that classifying the fictional genre 'depends on many subjective criteria—what is good and what is bad—and many objective but changing ones, on what is possible and what is impossible", and may result in describing texts in terms of the percentage of utopian or dystopian elements in them (p. 25).

[20] The terms 'anti-utopia' and 'dystopia' were still being used more or less interchangeably in the 1970s. In 1970, Robert C. Elliot described *Ape and Essence* (1948) as 'Huxley's dystopia', and termed Orwell's *Nineteen Eighty-Four* 'a true anti-utopia and dystopia' (*The Shape of Utopia: Studies in a Literary Genre* (University of Chicago Press, 1970), pp. 147, 97). Gordon Browning contended, in defining the anti-utopian form, that 'anti-utopian' writers normally did not offer 'a prophecy of doom or a warning that we must brace ourselves for a certain disaster', but rather held out the 'faith or at least hope that the situation will be improved if man will only accomplish a certain series of necessary reforms' ('Towards a Set of Standards for Everlasting Anti-Utopian Fiction', *Cithara*, 10 (1970), 18). The collection of essays edited by Peyton Richter entitled *Utopia/Dystopia?* (Schenkman Publishing Co., 1975) manages to skirt around the subject without defining it, though Walter L. Fogg suggests that 'dystopian writers project a hellish life in a hellish society' (p. 71.) E. J. Brown's *Brave New World, 1984, and We: An Essay on Anti-Utopia* (Ardis, 1976), uses 'anti-utopia' but not 'dystopia' (pp. 41, 47). Warren Wagar's *Terminal Visions: The Literature of Last Things* (Indiana University Press, 1982) juxtaposes utopia to dystopia, and dates the latter from the later nineteenth century, and especially the years from 1890 to 1914, when a shifting mental climate revealed great anxieties about the coming future. But it does not use 'anti-utopia' as a category and is not concerned with the relationship between utopia and dystopia as such, particularly in ideological terms (pp. 7, 19–20). Writing in 1977, Gorman Beauchamp noted that the dystopian novel commonly represented a protest against civilization in favour of a more 'natural' life. Here, 'utopia' is defined as 'a systematic intensification of all the repressive restraints of actual civilisation', in the flat recognition that 'happiness can be guaranteed man only at the sacrifice of his freedom'. In the twentieth century, this becomes a problem with regard to the predominance of machinery and 'a caste of technocratic Salomonians'. This underpins modern totalitarianism, which, in Beauchamp's words, 'would be impossible without a highly complex technological apparatus' (news of Pol Pot's regime had not yet filtered out of Cambodia) ('Cultural Primitivism as Norm in the Dystopian Novel', *Extrapolation*, 19 (1977), 88–96.) Taking utopia to mean 'the production of social dreams', Bronisław Baczko, writing in 1978, did not use 'dystopia', but employed 'anti-utopia' to define texts in which 'it is the very practice of social dreams that is refused' (*Utopian Lights: The Evolution of the Idea of Social Progress*, pp. 29, 144, 154–5).
[21] Alexandra Aldridge, *The Scientific World-View in Dystopia* (UMI Research Press, 1978), pp. 1, 79.

Aldridge identifies Bulwer-Lytton's *The Coming Race* as an early instance of an 'anti-utopia'. She notes the 'vagueness and contradiction in the critical literature that is reminiscent, or more accurately a continuation, of the genre problems associated with Utopia'. She echoes George Woodcock and Eugen Weber's support for Berdiaeff's view that both the genre and the mood underlying it emerged 'for the first time in the civilizational malaise generated by World War I'. She accepts Woodcock's distinction between 'contemporary anti-Utopian novels' or dystopias and the 'various negative quasi-Utopias which appeared before 1924', as well as his further contrast of the anti-Bellamy texts, 'which attack the collectivist idea rather than its concrete manifestations' and later dystopias. She criticizes Walsh, and to a lesser degree Hillegas, for not theorizing their central concepts adequately.[22] But her own definition is clearly overly centred on science and technology.

The 1980s

Krishan Kumar's *Utopia and Anti-Utopia in Modern Times* (1987) is the chief study of this period.[23] Discussing Huxley and Orwell, Kumar uses 'anti-utopia' as a 'generic term' which includes 'what is sometimes called the "dystopia"'. He observes that 'Utopias commonly contain dystopian features, unseen and unintended by their authors', and asks 'Might this not also be true of dystopias, that they contain, in however distorted and diminished a form, a Utopian impulse?'[24] Similar distinctions are employed in Kumar's *Utopianism* (1991), which describes 'the satirical strand in utopia' as eventually leading 'to the splitting off of a separate

---

[22] Ibid., pp. 10–12. The reference is to Woodcock, 'Utopias in Negative'.

[23] Three lesser studies appear early in the decade. One account, which poses the paradox of the coexistence of utopia and dystopia within a single text, is Warren W. Wooden's 'Utopia and Dystopia: The Paradigm of Thomas More's *Utopia*', *Southern Humanities Review*, 14 (1980), 91–100. More's book had already been seen, by the later sixteenth century, as 'some kind of fanciful detention camp or isolation ward for chronic malcontents and social misfits'. But the variant eutopian reading had also been established. These are described as a 'fusion of opposites' within the text (pp. 99, 108). Eric S. Rabkin, Martin H. Greenberg, and Joseph D. Olander's useful edition of essays, *No Place Else: Explorations in Utopian and Dystopian Fiction* (Southern Illinois University Press, 1983) is chiefly an introduction to the major texts, does not distinguish between dystopia and anti-utopia, and usually simply describes major works like *Brave New World* as 'dystopias' or 'bad places' (p. 1). The collection of essays edited by Everett Mendelsohn and Helga Nowotny, *Nineteen Eighty-Four: Science between Utopia and Dystopia* (D. Reidel, 1984), juxtaposes 'utopian dreams' to 'dystopian nightmares'. Nowotny also terms dystopia 'the dysfunctional version of a science and technology having fallen victim to the surplus of order and control that we have seen inherent in utopian thought'. Ingo Grabner and Wolfgang Reiter point to a contrast between the 'technologically optimist component of utopian thought' and 'the politically pessimist, "dystopian", one', while James Fleck hints at a '"dialectic" between the concepts' (pp. viii, 15, 247, 193–4.) Many studies in this period do not define their key concepts. The closest any essay in Dominic Baker-Smith and C. C. Barfoot, eds., *Between Dream and Nature: Essays on Utopia and Dystopia* (Rodopi, 1987) comes, is the suggestion that 'The ultimate refutation of Utopia is dystopia, the demonstration that Utopian visions are not just impractical, but potentially sinister' (Keith Thomas, 'The Utopian Impulse in Seventeenth-Century England', p. 43).

[24] Krishan Kumar, *Utopia and Anti-Utopia in Modern Times* (Basil Blackwell, 1987), pp. 224, 286, 447.

sub-genre, the dystopia or anti-utopia', which aimed 'to show a society marked by the extremes of folly and unreason'.[25]

Lyman Tower Sargent entered this debate with 'The Three Faces of Utopianism' (1967). Here dystopia is associated with Samuel Butler's *Erewhon*.[26] In 1975, Sargent defined dystopia as synonymous with 'anti-utopia' or 'negative utopia', which describe 'bad places'.[27] In Sargent's 'The Three Faces of Utopianism Revisited' (1994), 'dystopia' is a 'bad place' which is usually 'an extrapolation from the present that involved a warning', but excluding works published in the last thirty years. 'Dystopia' or 'negative utopia' is 'a non-existent society described in considerable detail and normally located in time and space that the author intended a contemporaneous reader to view as considerably worse than the society in which that reader lived'. 'Anti-utopia' is 'a criticism of utopianism or of some particular eutopia'. Sargent acknowledges that works intended as eutopias may appear to be dystopias. In 1994, he also suggested the possibility of using 'critical dystopia' to describe various recent (chiefly science fiction) texts possessing a socially critical content.[28] Recently, he has defined utopia, broadly conceived, as 'social dreaming' which imagines a 'good or significantly better society that provides a generally satisfactory and fulfilling life for most of its inhabitants'.[29] Dystopia might then logically involve some inversion of these qualities, a 'social nightmare' for a large number of people, or a text which readers regard with alarm rather than hope.[30]

* * * *

These definitions clarify various problems while revealing others. Nearly all dystopias criticize utopia (Orwell, Huxley), but so do many utopias (e.g. William Morris' *News from Nowhere*, which targets Bellamy's *Looking Backward*). So books opposing one type of utopia are not necessarily 'anti-utopias' or 'dystopias', or against all utopias as such. A substantial space exists between 'bad' and 'considerably worse' places—and worse than what? If authorial intention is central here, we cannot classify More's *Utopia*, where this is notoriously unclear, in these terms. But many modern (affluent, middle-class, less self-sacrificing) readers might describe More's text as a dystopia when imagining their own position there as 'worse' than their lives today. Poorer readers might not: a slum dweller will view a fantasy about living in suburbia as utopian. So categorizing readers' perspectives is awkward. They inhabit so many different societies and groups that it is unclear when and

[25] Krishan Kumar, *Utopianism* (Open University Press, 1991), pp. 26–7.

[26] Lyman Tower Sargent, 'The Three Faces of Utopianism', *Minnesota Review*, 7 (1967) 222–30, here 227.

[27] Lyman Tower Sargent, 'Utopia: The Problem of Definition', *Extrapolation*, 16 (1975), 138.

[28] Lyman Tower Sargent, 'The Three Faces of Utopianism Revisited', *Utopian Studies*, 5 (1994), 1–37; here 5–6, 8–9, 12.

[29] Lyman Tower Sargent, 'The Problem of the "Flawed Utopia": A Note on the Costs of Eutopia', in Raffaella Baccolini and Tom Moylan, eds., *Dark Horizons: Science Fiction and the Dystopian Imagination* (Routledge, 2003), p. 226. An undated version of this argument is offered in 'Theorizing Utopia/Utopianism in the Twenty-First Century', in Artur Blaim and Ludmila Gruszewska-Blaim, eds., *Spectres of Utopia* (Peter Lang, 2012), pp. 13–26.

[30] Sargent, *Utopianism*, p. 8.

where 'bad' and 'worse' apply. Further problems emerge with locating authors who move about: what is their chief reference point? The presumption is apparently that readers share the same class and/or values as authors, which is questionable. If 'better' and 'worse' here implies 'for the majority' (which Kateb asserts is a crucial point), this needs to be specified.

To J. C. Davis, thus, 'the concept of "better" is too imprecise, vague and subjective. The emphasis on "dream" carries with it difficulties of its own. For it can ambivalently mean fictional, unreal or impractical.'[31] 'Better' does not differentiate the 'ideal' from modest ameliorations, or to what class or group such improvements are directed. Hence, we must consider more precisely just *what* is 'better' here, and *for whom*. In the case of *Nineteen Eighty-Four*, for example, what if the reader was living in the USSR in 1949, where (it is argued here in Chapter 7) conditions for many were actually worse than or certainly as bad as those described as suffered by the majority in Orwell's novel? Then the latter would not be a 'dystopia'. But members of the Inner Party in the novel enjoy a standard of living well above that of the poorest, indeed the average, Briton in 1949. So their position is utopian. Such definitions are thus relative to time, place, and social position as well as to expectations about values like liberty, equality, and order, more than to authorial intention. There are also problems with texts which mix utopian and dystopian themes, or where utopias apparently exist within dystopias and vice versa, or where one succeeds the other sequentially, sometimes several times—scenarios common in the genre, as we will see.

The notable contribution of Tom Moylan to this field, indeed, consists, firstly, in alerting readers to the close proximity of utopian and dystopian scenarios within particular texts; and, secondly, in contending for substantial transformations in literary utopian/dystopian writing in the post-World War II epoch. Moylan's *Demand the Impossible: Science Fiction and the Utopian Imagination* (1986) contends that the mid-twentieth-century 'bleak dystopia' was supplanted by the 'critical utopia' from the 1970s onwards.[32] This new subgenre 'negated the negation of utopia' (i.e. the anti-Stalinist dystopia) by demonstrating an 'awareness of the limitations of the utopian tradition' and 'rejecting utopia as a blueprint while preserving it as a dream'.[33] Thus, the 'critical dystopia' describes works which authors 'intended a contemporaneous reader to view as worse than contemporary society' but which usually include 'at

---

[31] J. C. Davis, *Utopia and the Ideal Society: A Study of English Utopian Writing 1516–1700* (Cambridge University Press, 1981), p. 13.

[32] See Tom Moylan, 'Beyond Negation: The Critical Utopias of Ursula K. Le Guin and Samuel R. Delany', *Extrapolation: A Journal of Science Fiction and Fantasy*, 21 (1980), 236–53. 'Critical utopia' is noted as a category in Kenneth Roemer, ed., *America as Utopia* (Burt Franklin & Co., 1981), p. 236. 'Utopian writing in the 1970s was saved by its own destruction and transformation into the "critical Utopia"' (Tom Moylan, *Demand the Impossible: Science Fiction and the Utopian Imagination* (Methuen, 1986), p. 10). Baccolini and Moylan, *Dark Horizons* (p. 2) also describes 'the critical utopia of the 1970s'.

[33] Moylan, *Demand the Impossible*, pp. 8–11. Why a 'dream' is superior to proposals, plans or programmes, or 'blueprints' is, however, unclear. These texts in turn are defined as sharing 'a rejection of hierarchy and domination and the celebration of emancipatory ways of being as well as the very possibility of Utopian longing itself' (p. 12).

least one eutopian enclave or holds out hope that the dystopia can be overcome and replaced with a eutopia'.[34]

This again begs the question as to whether *privileged* groups in dystopias do not themselves occupy a utopian position (Orwell's Inner Party, Huxley's Alphas), where a 'majority' definition (Kateb) is not specified. (So they cannot be 'utopias' at all unless the majority live comfortably.) Just what 'contemporary society' means here is also unclear: is it the class and nation the author inhabits when the work appears? This description, moreover, might suit *Nineteen Eighty-Four* as well as *Brave New World*, since spaces and/or hope of this type are present in both works. Many, indeed possibly most, such texts, if we generalize about the genre from *c.*1870–1970, imply something similar, as we will see in this chapter. And the problem of texts which propose the status quo ante as alternative to the 'dystopia', rather than a 'eutopia', remains puzzling. The definition of dystopia as 'the narrative that images a society worse than the existing one' also exhibits the same problems with 'worse' and 'existing' as formerly, with the loss of 'substantially' further weakening the argument. A privileging of 'authentic Utopian expression', and the intimation that we should condemn any dystopia not exhibiting 'hope' is intended to underpin the argument that the 'ambiguous, open endings' of some novels 'maintain the utopian impulse within the work' by allowing 'both readers and protagonists to hope by resisting closure'.[35] A case study applying these themes is given in *Scraps of the Untainted Sky: Science Fiction, Utopia, Dystopia* (2000). Here, Moylan views *Nineteen Eighty-Four* as a 'classic' dystopia which asserts a 'militant pessimism' because there is 'no meaningful possibility of movement or resistance, much less radical change, embedded in any of the iconic elements of the text'.[36] This reading, treated in detail here in Chapter 7, dismisses the author's intentions outside the text, in this case the fact that Orwell remained a socialist while writing *Nineteen Eighty-Four*.[37]

In a 1997 study, David W. Sisk describes dystopian fiction as turning 'human perfectibility on its head by pessimistically extrapolating contemporary social trends

[34] Sargent's 'considerably' is dropped here. This is elsewhere expressed as a contrast of dystopia as representing 'militant pessimism' and 'pseudo-dystopia' as representing 'resigned pessimism', the latter exhibiting a failure 'to challenge the ideological and epistemological limits of the actually existing society' (Tom Moylan, '"Look into the Dark": On Dystopia and the Novum', in Patrick Parrinder, ed., *Learning from Other Worlds: Estrangement, Cognition, and the Politics of Science Fiction and Utopia* (Duke University Press, 2001), p. 65).

[35] Baccolini and Moylan, *Dark Horizons*, p. 7. Fredric Jameson indeed suggests that the term 'dystopia' should be reserved for 'critical dystopias' which retain a 'politically enabling stance' derived from 'Utopian ideals' (*Archaeologies of the Future: The Desire for Utopia and Other Science Fictions* (Verso, 2005), p. 198). This again privileges a Marxist outcome, and implies that the perceived intent of the concept is to browbeat Orwell in particular.

[36] Tom Moylan, *Scraps of the Untainted Sky: Science Fiction, Utopia, Dystopia* (Westview Press, 2000), p. 162.

[37] On this approach see, e.g., Sargent, 'The Three Faces of Utopianism Revisited', 8; Andrew Milner, *Locating Science Fiction* (Liverpool University Press, 2012), pp. 118–20. These categories appear to apply chiefly to science fiction texts published after 1970, and others have interpreted them accordingly, e.g., Alexander Charles Oliver Hall, 'A *Nineteen Eighty-Four* for the Twenty-First Century: John Twelve Hawks's Four Realm Trilogy as Critical Dystopia', in M. Keith Booker, ed., *Critical Insights: Dystopia* (Salem Press, 2013), p. 211.

into oppressive and terrifying societies' (implying it does not realistically reflect such societies). Here, the suppression of individual freedom is a central theme, with the control of language a primary weapon in this struggle. By the early twentieth century, 'anti-utopia' had emerged to connote 'all fictions that turn utopian dreams into nightmares'. Sisk contends that 'dystopia' is preferable to 'anti-utopia' since it actually portrays the 'bad place' rather than merely satirizing the failed pursuit of the good one. Thus, 'all dystopias are anti-utopias, but not all anti-utopias are dystopias'. (But, we will see, this is a misconception insofar as some dystopias extrapolate from the present rather than from aspirations to utopia, though it is correct if it implies that this present results from utopian ideals.) All dystopias, moreover, aim at avoiding the horrors imminent in this present: 'the mission is to motivate the reader, not merely to horrify'. This avoids the problem of classifying works according to their hope quotient. The emergence of dystopia is linked to the shift towards viewing technology as producing 'impersonalized mechanization and exploitation', and, following Aldridge, depicting this in terms of 'the advancement of the collective over the individual'.[38]

The late Erika Gottlieb's pioneering study of both East European and other forms of dystopia, *Dystopian Fiction East and West* (2001), terms the literary dystopia a 'post-Christian genre' which describes 'damnation, by an unjust society, a degraded mob ruled by a power-crazed elite', a 'dictatorship of a hell on earth', the 'worst of all possible worlds'. The focus here is less on science fiction than on real dictatorships. More than most modern studies, an effort is made to tease out the relationships between history and fiction, and to engage with the secondary literature on totalitarianism.[39]

[38] David W. Sisk, *Transformations of Language in Modern Dystopias* (Greenwood Press, 1997), pp. 2, 6–7, 11.

[39] Erika Gottlieb, *Dystopian Fiction East and West* (McGill-Queen's University Press, 2001), p. 3. Among the most recent studies, Michael Gordin and his co-editors of *Utopia/Dystopia* argue that 'dystopia is not simply the opposite of utopia. A true opposite of utopia would be a society that is either completely unplanned or is planned to be deliberately terrifying and awful. Dystopia, typically invoked, is neither of these things; rather, it is a utopia that has gone wrong, or a utopia that functions only for a particular segment of society' (*Utopia/Dystopia: Conditions of Historical Possibility* (Princeton University Press, 2010), p. 1). Introducing a volume edited in 2012, Barnita Bagchi contends that 'every successful conceptualization of utopia' has 'as its Janus face a dystopia: one (wo)man's utopia is often another's dystopia, and vice versa'. Her emphasis is on the fluid relationship between utopian and dystopian ideas whether expressed in fictional form or not. Bagchi also recognizes the existence of the 'real-life dystopia', such as Nazi Germany, even arguing that: 'The real-life context is extremely important, indeed, for utopian and dystopian thought, writing, and practice.' She thus concedes, with Kumar, that, particularly 'in twentieth-century writing, utopia and anti-utopia/dystopia are mutually dependent, complementary forms' (*The Politics of the (Im)possible: Utopia and Dystopia Reconsidered* (Sage, 2012), pp. 2–3, 6). Two publications by M. Keith Booker also merit mention. *Dystopian Literature: A Theory and Research Guide* (1994) defines 'dystopian literature' as 'in direct opposition to Utopian thought' (p. 3). In *Critical Insights: Dystopia* (pp. 1, 5, 7), Booker terms dystopian fiction 'the subgenre of science fiction that uses its negative portrayal of an alternative society to stimulate new critical insights into real-world societies'. This is contrasted to post-apocalyptic disaster narratives with little detail about the projected societies. Dystopias are also distinguished from anti-utopias, which assess the negative consequences of utopianism. 'Classic' dystopias criticize social and political practices, while 'critical dystopias' retain 'a strong utopian dimension' by offering alternatives to the conditions portrayed. (Note here the inflation of the utopian component in Moylan's description.)

Finally, Artur Blaim has recently summarized much of this definitional controversy, and emphasized the importance of differentiating between satires upon particular utopias as opposed to those targeting utopianism in general. This restores the possibility that an apparently 'anti-utopian' work can still be 'utopian' on a number of levels, while rejecting the idea that such works constitute an independent literary genre.[40]

* * * *

The foregoing discussion reveals considerable disagreement over the key terms: dystopia and anti-utopia. Considering the bewildering variety of texts being analysed by intellectual historians, sociologists, political and literary theorists, and by Marxists, liberals, and enthusiasts as well as critics of (aspects of) utopia, this is hardly surprising. We might easily sympathize with those who proclaim, out of sheer exasperation, that all 'we may safely say . . . is that dystopia is not utopia or is a flawed utopia, and that each author defines it in his or her own way', such that the 'difference between utopia and dystopia finally comes down to a matter of point of view'.[41]

But this is unsatisfactory. It is clear that not all dystopias are anti-utopian as such: many anti-capitalist and ecological novels project existing trends rather than failed efforts to create utopia. (But this may imply that the present represents a failed utopia, notably in the case of liberal capitalism.) Most importantly, perhaps, many texts criticize some utopian ideas but not others. Terming them 'anti-utopian' or fetishizing their 'utopian' or 'anti-utopian' or hopeful or pessimistic qualities tells us nothing useful about what they approve or disapprove of. Many literary discussions, moreover, contain little assessment of ideological trends or real despotisms. Few meet the arguments mounted by conservative critics of utopianism, or attempt to disentangle the various strands of utopianism present in many texts. A swamp-like jargon, aiming to exclude outsiders, sometimes impedes clarification, too. We have seen so far, however, that the concept of dystopia has generally been approached through three levels of interpretation: authorial intention; reader perception or context by juxtaposition to the author; and various types of content or historical narrative. All need to enter into any nuanced treatment of the tradition.

Science Fiction and Dystopia

Further problems arise from describing dystopian literature as a branch of science fiction. Though lunaria, or imaginary voyages to the moon, were already common in the seventeenth century, the utopian genre precedes that of science fiction by some four centuries.[42] The term 'science fiction' was not evidently used before

---

[40] Artur Blaim, 'Hell upon a Hill: Reflections on Anti-Utopia and Dystopia', in Fátima Vieira, ed., *Dystopia Matters* (Cambridge Scholars Publishing, 2013), pp. 80–91. This volume contains a number of other short essays on the subject.

[41] Derek Thiess, 'Critical Reception', in Booker, ed., *Critical Insights: Dystopia*, p. 19; Robert Philmus, 'The Language of Utopia', *Studies in the Literary Imagination*, 6 (1973), 63.

[42] The origins of science fiction are usually dated to Hugo Gernsback, who founded a magazine in 1926 and thought the correct recipe for the genre was '75 percent literature interwoven with 25 percent science'. He first used the term itself in 1929.

1851.[43] Often dated from Mary Shelley's *Frankenstein* (1818), the genre prolifer-
ates only in the late nineteenth century, and remains intermixed with other forms
of narrative.[44] By the late twentieth century, however, science fiction became so
popular as to swallow up nearby genres, including, by 1950 or so, both utopia and
dystopia combined; hence the tendency to back-date this process.[45]

Yet some authors have concluded that, leaving Wells aside, 'there has been very
little overlap between science fiction and utopia', but considerably more between
science fiction and anti-utopia (instancing Huxley, Orwell, Vonnegut, and Pohl
and Kornbluth).[46] W. Warren Wagar notes that much science fiction has 'only a
peripheral interest' in those questions of social and political organization which are
often central to utopia and dystopia.[47] Most science fiction is not collectivist in
orientation, in Patrick Parrinder's view, Wells here being the exception rather than
the rule.[48] Many studies of science fiction also explicitly ignore texts we would
regard as dystopian, though H. Bruce Franklin, for instance, defines *The Iron Heel*
as science fiction and *Looking Backward* as a novel about time travel. From a
utopian viewpoint, this seems odd; why not call More's *Utopia* a travel book? (It
was once read this way, in the Mandeville tradition.) Bellamy's book is about
projected alternative societies where 'time travel' is a literary device which enables
the projection. It has no scientific import as such. Any similar device which
performs the same function of distancing or estrangement, providing a critical
distance from the present—a key aim of these genres—would have sufficed.[49]

Many commentators thus separate utopia, dystopia, and science fiction on
broadly realist grounds. Kingsley Amis describes science fiction as 'that class of
prose narrative treating of a situation that could not arise in the world we know, but
which is hypothesised on the basis of some innovation in science or technology, or
pseudo-science or pseudo-technology, whether human or extra-terrestrial in origin'.[50] This indicates a 'realist' criterion of genre separation, if relative to time and
place. (Near-future texts are invariably more realistic.) And it remains, as Parrinder
reminds us, also relative to real science itself, which, it is sometimes claimed, is
rarely portrayed in the genre with any degree of accuracy.[51] In both cases, the
advancement of science moves themes from the domain of science fiction to that of
utopia/dystopia as their possibility becomes realizable. What is crucial is that
science is central to the narrative, as Darko Suvin indicates: '*An S-F narration is a*

---

[43] H. Bruce Franklin, *Future Perfect: American Science Fiction of the Nineteenth Century* (Oxford
University Press, 1978), p. xi.
[44] David Seed, *Science Fiction* (Oxford University Press, 2011), p. 3.
[45] Sargent noted in 1975 that utopian writing had, since the 1940s, existed 'almost solely as a sub-
type of science fiction' ('Utopia: The Problem of Definition', 142).
[46] Thomas M. Disch, 'Buck Rogers in the New Jerusalem', in Roemer, ed., *America as Utopia*,
p. 52.
[47] Wagar, *Terminal Visions*, p. 9.
[48] Patrick Parrinder, 'Science Fiction and the Scientific World-View', in Patrick Parrinder, ed.,
Science Fiction: A Critical Guide (Longman, 1979), p. 75.
[49] Franklin, *Future Perfect*, pp. 229, 269.
[50] Kingsley Amis, *New Maps of Hell: A Survey of Science Fiction* (Victor Gollancz, 1963), p. 18.
[51] Parrinder, 'Science Fiction and the Scientific World-View', pp. 67–88.

fiction in which the S-F element or aspect is hegemonic—that is, so central and significant that it determines the whole narrative logic, or at least the over-riding narrative logic, regardless of any impurities that might be present.'[52]

Thus there are major differences between, say, sixteenth-century imagined voyages to the moon, which are purely fantastic, and their nineteenth-century equivalents, where the scientific prospects had improved dramatically. Science fiction is usually described as portraying a world radically different from the present. But there are great variations in the degree to which what it projects is clearly impossible in the present, or merely varies in quality or quantity compared to the present state of scientific discovery and technological invention. To confuse matters, some parameters are in constant flux. To us, aliens and zombies remain a major dividing line, because they are imaginary. But robots, cyborgs, and androids, once fictional, now actually exist. 'Prophetic science', as Hugo Gernsback termed it, might well include both science fiction and dystopia.[53] In utopias, we might want to ask how far human nature and social organization have been stretched beyond credibility, where a future society is markedly superior *because* of its scientific and technical innovations. (To Lewis Mumford, for instance, this hardly ever occurs.) For dystopia, the question is not what the science produces, but its negative impact on humanity. So the issue is not whether we imagine ray guns, infinite power sources, or space travel. It is whether we use them as instruments of oppression and destruction.

Where science fiction becomes *political*, then, it may overlap substantially with utopia and dystopia. Here our chief concern in science fiction, Kenneth Roemer has argued, is with 'what could be', and in dystopia with 'what ought not to be'.[54] Most utopias and dystopias before 1900 do not rely on scientific and technological tropes to support their visions of future or alternate worlds. (And many often use these realistically, e.g., in relation to nuclear wars.) Thus, to Mark Hillegas, More's *Utopia* is simply 'not science fiction'.[55] Both genres share some formal themes, such as appearing to extrapolate from the author's present into the future. There is a further overlap here with both futurological speculation or projection and what are sometimes called histories of the future.[56] But merely setting a fictional work in the future does not make it 'science fiction' either. (Two early instances are Samuel Madden's *Memoirs of the Twentieth Century* (1733) and Mercier's *Memoirs of the Year 2500* (1770)). And neither does the centrality of science and technology, *where these are portrayed realistically*—as we will see. Narratives set on other planets

---

[52] Darko Suvin, *Victorian Science Fiction in the U.K.: Discourses of Knowledge and of Power* (G. K. Hall, 1983), p. 89. But Suvin appears to include texts in which 'utopian-dystopian' elements may be central as 's.f.' works (p. 95), while being completely uninterested in what these might entail.

[53] Quoted in Paul A. Carter, *The Creation of Tomorrow: Fifty Years of Science Fiction* (Columbia University Press, 1977), p. 5.

[54] Roemer, *America as Utopia*, pp. 6–7.

[55] Mark Hillegas, 'The Literary Background to Science Fiction', in Parrinder, ed., *Science Fiction: A Critical Guide*, p. 3.

[56] See, e.g., Alan Sandison and Robert Dingley, eds., *Histories of the Future: Studies in Fact, Fantasy and Science Fiction* (Palgrave, 2000).

but which are otherwise realistic hold a halfway position here: the trope does not necessarily make the critique unrealistic.

As a subgenre, then, dystopian science fiction is a shared set of the two concepts, and does not imply making either derive from the other. It includes texts with a preponderantly scientific and/or technological emphasis; that is, which are *science-centred* or *science-dependent*, but where these would generally be regarded as unrealistic or not extrapolations on current knowledge and practice. (Invariably, there will be haggling on this point. And what are we to make of texts concerned with human obsession with scientific or mechanical thinking?) This definition suits Bacon's *New Atlantis*, but not More nor Orwell's works. If 'science fiction' implies the *extremely* imaginative use of science, Orwell would certainly be excluded. 'Realism' is again central. Hence Margaret Atwood's insistence, reinforced here as the 'Atwood principle', that science fiction is 'fiction in which things happen that are not possible today', including the portrayal of 'technologies we have not yet developed'. This implies that we need to further distinguish between realistic, science-based and science fiction dystopias. It also implies a considerable distance between 'speculative fiction' and 'science fiction'.[57]

In 'Utopia and Science Fiction', Raymond Williams suggests that what is crucial is the degree to which '"science", in its variable definitions, can be an element' in utopias or dystopias. Here, dystopia might consist of a 'hell', 'a more wretched kind of life . . . existing somewhere', a 'less happy' 'willed transformation' which instigates social degeneration, 'harmful kinds of social order', or the 'unforeseen yet disastrous consequences of an effort at social improvement'; or technological transformations where 'the conditions of life have been worsened by technical development'. Science may predominate more or less in each type, in terms of how the destination is reached, described, and maintained. Strictly speaking, the 'willed transformation' is 'the characteristic utopian or dystopian mode'. This leaves open the question as to whether science-gone-wrong is intentionally or accidentally the key cause of the negative transformation. (Are bad human beings abusing science or normal human beings falling victim to it?) To Williams, most dystopias have been extrapolations from existing trends rather than fantastic projections.[58] This implies a scale or spectrum of possibilities, where the interrelationship between 'willed transformation' and science and technology constitutes one frontier between utopia/dystopia and science fiction. Andrew Milner has argued that many leading science fiction critics, however, are actually 'either hostile or indifferent' to dystopia.[59] Suvin in particular contends for a distancing between science fiction and 'the fashionable static dystopia of the Huxley-Orwell model'.[60] Some of this hostility, we will see in the case of Orwell, is simply political, and aims at rebutting a perceived antagonism towards Marxism in dystopian fiction.

[57] Margaret Atwood, *Curious Pursuits: Occasional Writing 1970–2005* (Virago, 2005), p. 85.
[58] Raymond Williams, 'Utopia and Science Fiction', in Parrinder, ed., *Science Fiction: A Critical Guide*, pp. 52–66.
[59] Milner, *Locating Science Fiction*, pp. 115–35, here 115.
[60] Darko Suvin, *Metamorphoses of Science Fiction* (Macmillan, 1988), p. 83.

Nonetheless, the collapsed genre definition, subsuming utopia/dystopia under science fiction, has many adherents. In an oft-quoted formulation, Suvin describes utopia as 'the *socio-political subgenre*' of science fiction.[61] Utopia is a 'quasi-human community where the sociopolitical institutions, norms, and individual relations are organized on a more perfect principle than in the author's community'. Dystopia portrays 'a radically less perfect state'.[62] To Suvin, 'the historically very intimate connection of utopian fiction with other forms of SF (extraordinary voyage, technological anticipation, anti-utopia and dystopia, etc.)' results from 'the cultural interpenetration of the validating intertextual category of utopian fiction (socio-politics) with the validating categories of the mentioned cognate forms (foreign otherness, technocracy or wrong politics)'.[63] This position has been accepted by Fredric Jameson, and also loosely by Moylan and Baccolini. David Ketterer sees Bellamy, Huxley, and Orwell as belonging here.[64] But Aldridge argues that 'it is a mistake to submerge the major dystopian novels of the twentieth century in the science fiction category largely because their primary emphasis is *always* on power relationships in clear sociopolitical terms'. Unlike much science fiction, dystopian literature is also *always* 'committed to a formal hierarchical system'. Moreover, 'the literary and philosophical tradition which in various ways generated the major dystopias was the Utopian tradition (including especially Utopian satire) and only to a much lesser extent the traditions of horror story, voyage literature, fantasy adventure and those other modes which (along with utopia/dystopia) converged into science fiction'.[65] The *reductio ad absurdum* of the collapsed definition is reached in the proposition that Marx, 'if implicitly and unconsciously', must be conceived as 'one of the major theorists of science fiction'.[66] (All religion is presumably 'science fiction' on the same principle.) All of these imaginative forms are, at this level, simply lesser or greater forms of the displacement of everyday life, and are always, fundamentally, concerned with humans in this world. Hence, the degree of otherness or estrangement is no longer crucial: nothing unhuman is alien to us, paraphrasing Terence's *humani nihil a me alienum puto* (nothing human is alien to me).

There are other variations on these themes. Lewis Mumford identifies science fiction with 'kakotopia', where 'the true criterion of science fiction is that the perfection it seeks rests exclusively within the realm of conceivable scientific

---

[61] Ibid., p. 38. On Suvin's categories see, generally, Parrinder, *Learning from Other Worlds*.

[62] Suvin, *Metamorphoses of Science Fiction*, pp. 35–6.

[63] Darko Suvin, *Position and Presuppositions in Science Fiction* (Macmillan, 1988), p. 84. Suvin continues: 'If in the dystopian works the closure can only be understood as a non-openness, in the utopian works the revolutionary openness can only by understood as a permanent struggle against entropic closure—whether the cosmic voyage of discovery (as in Le Guin) or left to stand on its own as the vehicle of the parable (as in Yefremov).' Cf. p. 104: 'SF will be the more significant the more clearly it emancipates itself from both classical utopia and classical dystopia as static and closed paradigms.'

[64] David Ketterer, *New Worlds for Old: The Apocalyptic Imagination, Science Fiction, and American Literature* (Anchor Press, 1974), pp. 102–18, 125–6.

[65] Aldridge, *The Scientific World-View in Dystopia*, pp. 15–17.

[66] Carl Freedman, 'Science Fiction and Utopia: A Historico-Philosophical Overview', in Parrinder, ed., *Learning from Other Worlds*, p. 96.

knowledge and technical invention; and that there is no attempt by most writers to show that this has any viable connection whatever with human welfare or further human development'.[67] Both, in other words, exemplify extreme technophilia, and especially the assumption that human social problems are susceptible to techno-logical solutions as such. Keith Booker says 'dystopian fiction can be defined as the subgenre of science fiction that uses its negative portrayal of an alternative society to stimulate new critical insights into real-world societies'.[68] To Robert Philmus, who ignores the term dystopia, 'the distinguishing feature of science fantasy involves the rhetorical strategy of employing a more or less scientific rationale to get the reader to suspend disbelief in a fantastic state of affairs'.[69] Frederick Pohl terms 'political science fiction' science fiction works which engage substantially with political issues, while acknowledging that most works in the genre do so to some degree.[70] David Ketterer distinguishes between 'fictional utopias' and 'science fictional utopias', contending that 'utopian fiction, certainly in its original form, is not generically related to science fiction'. He insists that 'the genealogy of science fiction and utopian fiction has been erroneously con-flated', even that 'utopian science fiction is a semantic impossibility' though 'science-fictional dystopias abound'.[71] Northrop Frye similarly contrasts utopias with a legal or institutional underpinning to those focusing on 'technological power', the former being 'closer to actual social and political theory', while 'the latter overlaps with what is now called science fiction'.[72] Andrew Milner stresses the temporal coincidence of the emergence of dystopia and science fiction, as well as the antipathy of many historians and theorists of science to other modes of dystopian writing.[73]

The key question here, then, may be primarily one of degree. Dystopia is distinguished by the density of its socio-political narrative and its plausible relation to the period in which it appears. Highly speculative texts, particularly respecting science and technology, push dystopia towards science fiction. Neither of the two foundational works treated in the next two chapters goes this far. In both *Brave New World* and *Nineteen Eighty-Four*, the science is not so wildly improbable as not to be an extrapolation of existing trends. This implies that while dystopia becomes progressively more identified with science fiction in the twentieth century, the two genres are not identical. In this respect, some parts of science fiction become the

---

[67] Mumford, *The Myth of the Machine*, vol. 2, p. 220.

[68] Booker, *Critical Insights: Dystopia*, p. 5.

[69] Robert Philmus, *Into the Unknown: The Evolution of Science Fiction from Francis Godwin to H.G. Wells* (University of California Press, 1970), p. vii.

[70] Frederick Pohl, 'The Politics of Prophecy', in Donald M. Hassler and Clyde Wilcox, eds., *Political Science Fiction* (University of South Carolina Press, 1997), p. 7.

[71] David Ketterer, 'Utopian Fantasy as Millennial Motive and Science-Fictional Motif', *Studies in the Literary Imagination*, 6 (1973), 81–3, 95, 99, and generally 79–101; here utopia is a 'place where everybody lives happily ever after'. Ketterer aligns writers like Bellamy with millenarianism.

[72] Frye, 'Varieties of Literary Utopia', pp. 27–8.

[73] See the discussion of these issues in Andrew Milner, 'Need It all End in Tears? The Problem of Ending in Four Classic Dystopias', in Booker, ed., *Critical Insights: Dystopia*, pp. 109–24.

telos of the utopian genre from More onwards, the science-based ideal society, which only 'comes into its own' in this incarnation.[74] Yet simply counting numbers of texts, much utopian and dystopian writing after *c.*1875 is not *centrally* about science, and, particularly, unrealistic science, or contingent on it, even if the general drift of both society and literature are towards technological predominance by the twentieth century. Science and technology may merely decorate the narrative rather than provide its foundation. If this changes after *c.*1970, or in the wake of the V2, Hiroshima, or Sputnik, we need other lines of demarcation to establish it.

* * * *

The Literary Dystopia Defined

The three main approaches to literary dystopias are through authorial intention, presumed reader context/response, and content, all of which are also interwoven with the interpreter's perspectives on the text. Critics have often been concerned with whether the societies described are 'worse' than the author's real-life society, and whether 'hope' is offered the reader to alleviate possible negative outcomes. A content-oriented definition also suggests that we need to analyse social relations portrayed fictionally, and particularly, since the central theme of the modern dystopia is despotism, the degree of oppressiveness of the regime described. Here the estrangement and isolation of individuals, and their fear of each other, are central, as well as the ways this is engineered by external, usually collectivist, authorities. Sometimes these are projections of existing political trends, or satires upon them. In the more science-oriented dystopias, technology often plays a central role in dehumanizing individuals and degrading their sociability. In science fiction dystopias, by contrast, projected scenarios go well beyond present-day science and technology, and often into much more distant futures and beyond the frontiers of plausibility.

   In what follows, then, literary dystopias are understood as primarily concerned to portray societies where a substantial majority suffer slavery and/or oppression *as a result of human action.* Privileged groups may benefit from this. Others may escape it, either to a condition of previous (preferable) normality or to something better. Some 'critical dystopias' (post-*c.*1970) also suggest that such systems might be overthrown internally. But this does not imply a 'utopian' counter-proposal, only an alternative to dystopia, which may also be the status quo ante. Following Sargent (1975), then, we can agree that 'anti-utopias' should be separated from dystopias insofar as the former reject utopianism as such, whereas the latter do not, or do so more obliquely. This definition does not privilege texts which retail 'hope', or those which propose utopian as opposed to non-utopian alternatives. But the principal deficiency in most of the secondary literature here is simply that it generalizes from too narrow a textual basis. This is the chief issue we must remedy here.

---

[74] Freedman, 'Science Fiction and Utopia', p. 93.

FROM SATIRE TO ANTI-JACOBIN
DYSTOPIA IN BRITAIN

The satirical prehistory of dystopia began as early as Aristophanes' 'Parliament of Women' and its discussion of Plato's 'Republic'. The work usually described as the first anti-utopia proper is Joseph Hall's *Mundus Alter et Idem* (1605), which is really a satire of contemporary manners cast in the form of a sea journey, in the good ship *Fantasia*, to the lands of Crapulia (gluttons), Viraginia (fault-finders), Moronia (fools), and Lavernia (thieves). This is generally accounted a source, in turn, for the most important early satire of utopianism, Jonathan Swift's *Gulliver's Travels* (1726). Its four voyages include both a biting critique of science and an anti-utopia in the depiction of Houyhnhnms, a horse species who live by the light of pure reason.

The eighteenth century saw a proliferation of satires on both utopian aspirations (such as Edmund Burke's *A Vindication of Natural Society* (1756)) as well as upon evidently degenerate trends in the present which are projected into the future. *Private Letters from an American in England to His Friends in America* (1769) and John Elliott's *The Travels of Hildebrand Bowman* (1778), for instance, call attention to the corruption of manners, the dissolution of morals, an obsession with money-getting, and the consequent confusion of social ranks.[75] Luxury is the chief enemy here: most eighteenth-century utopias, accordingly, even in the revolutionary period, are moderately primitivist and autarkic, and typically regulate consumption through sumptuary laws.[76] They correspond to republican warnings about the dangers of commercial society and a narrowing division of labour, and the debilitating effects of luxury upon the military capacity in particular. But, in their alarm not at luxury as such, but, even more, its dissemination to the lower orders, they also hint at the growing drive towards equality which would soon become central to dystopia.[77]

Only with the political controversy accompanying the French Revolution, however, do we encounter fictional anti-utopian responses to revolutionary principles which establish the pattern for later nineteenth- and twentieth-century developments. Now dystopian collapse is induced by the search for imaginary perfection, rather than the logical projection of the development of commercial society.

Several examples can be introduced here. The first is a brief (two-page) satire on Thomas Paine's *Rights of Man, A Trip to the Island of Equality* (1792). Perhaps the first English-language literary dystopia of the modern type, it is a parody of collapse growing out of revolution.[78] It portrays the island of Ulaga (Gaul, or France) in the

---

[75] See my edition, *Modern British Utopias* (8 vols, Pickering & Chatto, 1997), vol. 1, pp. xiii–xxxix, where these tests are reprinted.

[76] A good example is James Burgh's *An Account of... the Cessares* (1764), reprinted in my edition, *Utopias of the British Enlightenment* (Cambridge University Press, 1994), pp. 71–136.

[77] See my *The French Revolution Debate in Britain* (Palgrave Macmillan, 2007).

[78] It is reprinted in my edition, *Political Writings of the 1790s* (8 vols, Pickering & Chatto, 1995), vol. 7, pp. 279–81.

Behring Straits, where Paineite egalitarianism reigns. Its melancholic inhabitants wear fox-skins and live in caves. Annually they assemble to pile their pitiful possessions into a heap, whereupon a scramble to seize the best results in many being killed.

So-called anti-Jacobin novels also provided a strand of emerging satires which verge on later dystopias. Many were directed at the 'new philosophy' associated with William Godwin's *Enquiry Concerning Political Justice* (1793), at the avant-garde feminism of Godwin's wife, the author Mary Wollstonecraft, and at the alleged sexual profligacy of their unorthodox relationship. A similar motif pervades these works: revolutionary and/or 'enlightened' principles are pursued, often loose-ly described as 'perfectibility', with disastrous results. Most of the perhaps twenty such novels published on these themes parodied shifts in manners towards radical and utopian ends rather than literary dystopias as such. One of the many widely distributed Cheap Repository Tracts, Hannah More's *The History of Mr Fantom, The New Fashioned Philosopher and His Man William* (1797) was probably the most successful of these satires. Amongst the longer novels, George Walker's *The Vagabond* (1799) also merits mention. 'Dystopianism', in the sense of a 'popular discourse about fear', is sometimes used to describe 'anti-Jacobin' (radical) literary efforts of this type.[79]

In non-fiction prose, the most savage anti-utopian attack on Godwinism was T. R. Malthus' *An Essay on the Principle of Population* (1798), which assailed Condorcet, too, and indeed all aspirations to human perfectibility. In proposing the gradual abolition of poor relief (or welfare) and an implied support only for those willing to labour, Malthus, a clergyman, also proved that it was not necessary to kill God to value human beings only by their labour power: a perspective wedded to political economy was sufficient. Malthus too, however, was satirized in fiction occasionally. In Thomas Love Peacock's *Melincourt, or Sir Oran Hautton* (1818), in chapter 5, 'The Principle of Population', for instance, 'Mr Fax' asserts that: 'The cause of all the evils of human society is single, obvious, reducible to the most exact mathematical calculation; and of course susceptible not only of remedy but even of utter annihilation. The cause is the tendency of population to increase beyond the means of subsistence.'[80]

A second literary dystopia from this period—but the first full-length narrative with elaborated characters—was written by the leading anti-Jacobin John Reeves.[81] Published as *Publicola. A Sketch of the Times and Prevailing Opinions, from the Revolution in 1800 to the Present Year 1810* (1810), long believed lost, it has never been analysed previously. Reeves lambasted the obsessive 'political enthusiasm' which suggested schemes 'to form a more perfect system'. The history of British radicalism in the mid-1790s is presented, thinly disguised. Then fantasy

---

[79] Notably in Wil Verhoeven, *Americomania and the French Revolution Debate in Britain, 1789–1802* (Cambridge University Press, 2013), pp. 307–40.

[80] Quoted in Geoffrey Gilbert, ed., *Malthus: Critical Responses* (4 vols, Routledge, 1998), vol. 1, p. 169.

[81] On Reeves see Philip Schofield, 'Reeves, John (1752–1829)', *Oxford Dictionary of National Biography* (online edition, 2008).

commences. Following unrest in 1799, a commonwealth is established led by seven guardians. Chief amongst these is Publicola, clearly Thomas Paine, who is recalled from exile in France to become Chief Guardian. He urges 'equalization' of landed property, moves into the spacious premises of Somerset House in London, seizes ecclesiastical property, and disbands learned bodies. Spies and informers harass the people and the army becomes corrupted. Polygamy becomes 'if not decreed by law . . . sanctioned by the highest example'. Publicola sends his critics to Bedlam, weakens the navy, and eventually, adopting 'all the insignia of royalty', gains 'the power of an absolute monarch', including a veto over all laws. Commerce and cultivation fall steeply into decline. At the end the narrator awakens: it was all a nightmare.[82]

As Anne Mellor has argued, the period after Napoleon's defeat was often prone to a mood of despair, since further revolutions seemed in the offing despite the manifest failures of that of 1789.[83] We begin in this period, thus, to see secular versions of the Apocalypse being presented. One of these was J.-B. Cousin de Grainville's *The Last Man* (1806), subtitled in English 'A Romance in Futurity', which hints at the earth's collapse through overpopulation, though a volcanic eruption on the moon finally destroys humanity.[84] Another was Mary Shelley's *The Last Man* (1826), which has been described as a 'more or less pure example of secular eschatology'.[85] This is set in the future, with the last human dying in 2100, a global plague having struck about halfway through the book. But the idea that this is punishment for human sin is rejected, as is any promise of a perfect future for an elect virtuous few. This is thus apocalyptic fiction rather than dystopia or anti-utopia insofar as human endeavours have not caused the disaster. There is also no attempt to dwell upon the socio-political results of catastrophe. Yet it is also, like *Frankenstein*, partly a satire on the utopianism of the French revolutionary period, and on Mary Shelley's father, Godwin's, idea of the perfectibility of mankind. One character in the book thus insists that the 'earth will become a Paradise' where servitude, poverty, and disease have been conquered.[86] The very image of the plague here, indeed, suggests the limits of human endeavour: here nature resists hubris.[87]

The revival of the popular democratic movement in the 1830s, now under the name of Chartism, combined with the origins of Owenite socialism to produce a

---

[82] *Publicola. A Sketch of the Times and Prevailing Opinions, from the Revolution in 1800 to the Present Year 1810* (1810), pp. 10, 94, 103, 118, 130, 140, 144–7, 116. Publius Valerius Publicola (d. 503 BC) was a Roman aristocrat who helped overthrow the monarchy. Curiously, however, Reeves' fantasy also portrays Paine as to some degree a moderate, who is challenged by a 'staunch Republican' for wanting to keep some old laws. A later variant on the theme is Anatole France's *The Gods are Athirst* (The Bodley Head, 1913), set in the year 1794, where the painter Évariste Gamelin endures the Terror. Sympathetic to the French Revolution, *citoyen* Gamelin serves a Tribunal faithfully, sending many to their deaths after trials of three or four minutes. When the Terror passes, however, he finds himself on the other side of the Tribunal, and is denounced as a 'drinker of blood', a cannibal, a vampire, and so the guillotine claims him too (p. 274).

[83] Anne Mellor, 'Introduction', in Mary Shelley, *The Last Man* (University of Nebraska Press, 1993), p. xix.

[84] First published as *Le Dernier Homme* (Paris, 1805).

[85] Wagar, *Terminal Visions*, p. 16.   [86] Shelley, *The Last Man*, p. 159.

[87] A later instance of the genre is M. P. Shiel's *The Purple Cloud* (Chatto & Windus, 1901).

substantial amount of utopian thought, notably in communitarian schemes to repopulate the land with the unemployed urban poor. Few literary utopias or dystopias emerged out of this movement. However, one satire on the Chartist uprising at Monmouth in 1839–40 appeared as *The Island of Liberty and Equality* (1848). Here a group of colonists, led by an idealistic nobleman, divide property equally upon settling an island. Predictably, some are more diligent than others, and soon quarrelling, theft, and bloodshed put an end to ideas of 'Arcadia and the golden age', and prove that equality cannot exist 'where some are industrious and others idle'. It takes a bishop and a regiment of British soldiers to put matters to rights again.[88] An American satire on Owenism in this period portrays the pursuit of harmony in community as entailing reducing all to a common level (thus cutting all women's noses off to make them equally ugly). It assails the 'total absence of the passions' in community as resulting from treating people like machines, and governing them so thoroughly that they 'had nothing to do but to move ourselves about with all the regularity of a spinning-jenny'.[89]

In France, this period also saw the publication of Émile Souvestre's *The World as It Shall Be* (1846), which I. F. Clarke has described as 'the first major dystopia in the history of future fiction'. Although a world state exists called the Republic of United Interests, the novel is chiefly a satire on liberal political economy. Virtually all nations specialize in only one trade or occupation, with one state, for instance, making only pins (Adam Smith's famous example of the benefits of specialization). No one talks of anything but their own task. Mechanical servants have replaced human ones. The education system aims only to produce 'citizens with skills to enrich themselves', so students learn how to haggle, lie, and make risky transactions.[90] *Plus que ça change . . .*

GREAT BRITAIN: SOCIAL DARWINISM, EUGENICS, REVOLUTION, AND MECHANICAL CIVILIZATION, 1870–1914

Prior to the present day, the most important wave of English-language utopian/dystopian writing occurred between 1875 and 1914, when at least a hundred works appeared in Britain, and as many in the United States. There is some convergence in Anglo-American developments in this period. Morris' *News from Nowhere* (1890), for instance, responds to Bellamy's *Looking Backward*. Yet there were important differences in theme and emphasis on both sides of the Atlantic. Consequently, it is useful to treat each tradition separately, and then to assess their convergence.

[88] It is reprinted in my *Modern British Utopias*, vol. 8, pp. 121–258 (here pp. 160, 181).
[89] [J. R.] Paulding, *The Merry Tales of the Three Wise Men of Gotham* (Harper & Brothers, 1839), pp. 17–102.
[90] Émile Souvestre, *The World As It Shall Be*, ed. I. F. Clarke (Wesleyan University Press, 2004), pp. xi, 18, 38.

In Britain, three trends mark a distinctive dystopian turn in this period: the debate over Social Darwinism, or the application of Darwin's theory of natural selection to society, which resulted in widespread discussion of eugenic schemes to improve the genetic 'stock' of the human species; the looming threat of revolution from the burgeoning socialist movement; and the growing challenge to humanity of mechanization. By the end of this period, a movement towards science fiction proper which exhibits all these trends is discernible.[91]

Darwin to the Rescue: Evolution and Dystopia

Charles Darwin's theory of natural selection had an immense impact on utopian and dystopian writing alike. For a genre long fixated on ideas of both the distant past and remote future, an elongated species history provided by natural science was a godsend (it also sent the gods packing). A human history formerly supposed to be a few thousand years in extent could now be reimagined in terms of millions of years. The prospect that science might aid the progressive development of the human species echoed traditional concerns for perfectibility evident since Plato, and even more, Bacon.[92] One result was utopia's leap towards science fiction.[93] Another, however, was the threat that a different descent of man, not upwards from the apes, but backwards towards animality or degeneration, was also insinuated by Darwinian principles.[94] This would be woven into the idea of a primitive group self like that described in Le Bon's conception of the crowd, and linked to various types of monstrosity too.

An early instance of Darwin's influence on utopian writing came with a story of the discovery of an underground humanoid species saved from the original Flood. Edward Bulwer-Lytton's *The Coming Race* (1872) contains elements of science fiction, in the mastery of immense natural power, the Vril, and the fact that the species has grown wings. But a key theme is social: this race, more highly evolved, has outgrown the need for Darwinian competition. Cooperation is stressed, all see each other as brothers, and population is restrained. Marriages are limited to three years in the first instance. 'Automaton figures' are also widely used in work.[95]

Amongst these themes, conscious evolution through population control most evidently bridged the utopia/dystopia divide. Darwin stressed the role of sexual selection in evolution in either enhancing or retarding a given population. This underscored concerns about the poor's overbreeding, which Malthus had made central to debates about poor relief half a century earlier. But the issue now was less the degradation of the poor as such than the possibility that they would dilute the

---

[91] A recent account of British utopian literature in this period is Beaumont, *Utopia Ltd*. See also Beaumont's *The Spectre of Utopia: Utopian and Science Fictions at the Fin-de-Siècle* (Peter Lang, 2012).

[92] On some German parallels, see Peter Weingart, 'Eugenic Utopias: Blueprints for Rationalization of Human Evolution', in Mendelsohn and Nowotny, eds., *Nineteen Eighty-Four*, pp. 175–87.

[93] For this period see Suvin, *Victorian Science Fiction*.

[94] See Patrick Parrinder, *Utopian Literature and Science: From the Scientific Revolution to* Brave New World *and Beyond* (Palgrave Macmillan, 2015), pp. 97–128.

[95] Lord Lytton, *The Coming Race* (George Routledge & Sons, 1872), p. 145.

nation's pool of inherited characteristics. One obvious deduction was the need to regulate marriage and childbirth. In the mid-Victorian period, John Stuart Mill, most prominently, had mooted proposals for restraining population, including restrictions on marriage, hoping to raise working-class standards of living, and without regarding such restrictions as interfering unduly with individual liberty. The Malthusian League took up such proposals in Mill's name energetically after his death.[96]

Others inspired by Darwin were animated primarily by evolutionary rather than economic considerations. Crucial here were fears of the relative decline in the educated classes given their shrinking family sizes, which thus threatened culture and intelligence generally. These concerns were boosted immensely by the schemes proposed by Darwin's cousin, Francis Galton, under the rubric of 'eugenics'. 'Positive' eugenics schemes sought to promote the 'hereditary genius' of the few, while 'negative' variations sought to inhibit the overbreeding of the less educated.[97] (Both, however, today tend to be associated with dystopia.) Rather than leaving such matters to chance, most utopian writers agreed, they should be subject to science. Thus, Robert Ellis Dudgeon's *Colymbia* (1873) explains such policies as merely carrying out 'in a scientific and merciful manner, the process performed in a clumsy and cruel manner by nature . . . "the survival of the fittest"'.[98] Whether such proposals were in fact utopian or dystopian depends on one's perspective. Auschwitz was not the only or inevitable destination of this debate—modern genetic modification aiming at more robust health and longer life also starts here.

By the 1880s, proposals for regulating the marriages and progeny of the poor, as well as their notional betters, often under more centralized and collectivist regimes, became a favoured utopian topic and equally the butt of satire. Some works, following Mill's lead, punish the indolent who bear children, but not the unmarried poor.[99] Most recommend regulating marriage itself, usually on medical grounds, often with a view to maximizing the poor's efficiency. Thus government regulation of marriage is proposed in G. Read Murphy's *Beyond the Ice* (1894), and those with cancer or consumption cannot wed.[100] In Alex Newton's *Posterity, Its Verdicts and Its Methods: or, of Democracy A.D. 2100* (1897) a marriage certificate requires proficiency from men in their work, and cooking in women, with both undergoing physical examinations. The 'morally unsound and the mentally diseased' are prevented 'from leaving progeny'.[101] Infanticide of the deformed is often justified by excluding 'every form of life but that which is natural, healthy, and likely to grow

[96] See my *Mill and Paternalism* (Cambridge University Press, 2013, pp. 173–210).
[97] See the introduction to my *Late Victorian Utopias* (6 vols, Pickering & Chatto, 2008), vol. 1, pp. ix–xxxii.
[98] [Robert Ellis Dudgeon], *Colymbia* (Trübner & Co., 1873), p. 175.
[99] Christopher Yelverton, *Oneiros, or Some Questions of the Day* (Kegan Paul & Co., 1889), p. 30.
[100] G. Read Murphy, *Beyond the Ice: Being a Story of the Newly Discovered Region Round the North Pole* (Sampson Low & Co., 1894), pp. 120–2.
[101] [Alex Newton], *Posterity; Its Verdicts and Its Methods of Democracy A.D. 2100* (Williams & Norgate, 1897), pp. 14, 71.

up capable of taking its place in our community on an equal footing with its brethren'.[102]

Female writers held similar views. Thus in Mrs George Corbet's feminist *New Amazonia: A Foretaste of the Future* (1889), no men may hold the highest offices, and 'no crippled or malformed infants were permitted to live'. A 'medical certificate of soundness had to be procured before anyone was allowed to marry', too, 'as, above all, the State was determined to secure none but healthy subjects'.[103] In some cases, even those with defective eyesight or teeth were forbidden to marry.[104] Yet the aged often fare no better than the deformed young. In Anthony Trollope's satire on the productivist mentality, *The Fixed Period* (1882), set in the British colony of Britannula in 1980, life terminates at sixty-five so resources can be used by the most productive, and infants' birthdates are tattooed on their backs. (But the system is overthrown.)[105] In Andrew Acworth's *A New Eden* (1896) families are limited to two children and the state grants a 'discharge' at age sixty.[106] Voluntary euthanasia is available in Percy Greg's *Across the Zodiac: The Story of a Wrecked Record* (1880). Some satirical works took such themes to great extremes. In Michael Rustoff's *What Will Mrs Grundy Say? Or, A Calamity on Two Legs (A Book for Men)* (1891), for instance, euthanasia takes place for women at forty and men at fifty-five. A Matrimonial Department regulates all marriages, and no one is

> allowed to marry without a license, not merely specifying whom it is he wishes to marry, but how many children he is entitled to have. The number of licences is strictly regulated by the national requirements; no one can marry until he proves his ability to make provision for his wife and children.[107]

Besides reducing the fecundity of the lower orders, positive efforts to improve the upper classes along Galtonian lines are evident in many texts. In Kenneth Follingsby's *Meda* (1892), the world in 5575 limits family size to four children and marriages depend partly on 'educational equality'. 'By strictly adhering to this law of selection', we learn, 'the offspring of intellectual people are more susceptible to develop an improved intellectual power.'[108] In Walter Besant's *The Inner House* (1888), natural decay, crime, pain, and anxiety have all been arrested by science. But it is debated as to whether such advantages should be reserved for 'the flower of mankind, for the men strong in intellect and endowed above the common herd'. Here, too, progress is conceived as a steadily diminishing sociability, a 'tendency to solitary habits' being 'a most healthy indication of the

[102] [E. J. Davis], *Pyrna: A Commune; or, Under the Ice* (Bickers & Son, 1875), p. 106.
[103] Mrs George Corbet, *New Amazonia: A Foretaste of the Future* (Power Publishing Co., 1889), pp. 45–6.
[104] E.g., W. J. Saunders, *Kalomera: The Story of a Remarkable Community* (Elliot Stock, 1911).
[105] Anthony Trollope, *The Fixed Period* (2 vols, Bernhard Tauchnitz, 1882), vol. 1, pp. 20, 35.
[106] Andrew Acworth, *A New Eden* (Ward & Lock, 1896), pp. 48, 64.
[107] Michael Rustoff, *What Will Mrs Grundy Say? Or, A Calamity on Two Legs (A Book for Men)* (Simpkin & Marshall, 1891), p. 49.
[108] Kenneth Follingsby, *Meda: A Tale of the Future* (Printed for Private Circulation, 1891), pp. 121, 141–3.

advance of humanity'. Society is so transparent that 'We all live together: we know what each one says and thinks and does: nay, most of us have left off thinking and talking altogether.'[109]

These discussions indicate that artificially cultivating character traits was inter-meshed with a discourse about labour, productivity, and idleness, or at any rate the supposed idleness of the poor. (When socialism mirrored this discourse, it started from the idleness of the rich to contend for universal mandatory labour.)[110] To the poor, the consequences were usually dystopian. For the Victorian work ethic and its attendant profit-and-loss mentality was notoriously unforgiving. An obsession with efficiency and productivity—an anxiety to be constantly making more things and consuming them—indeed dominates many such works, if only satirically. In Henry Wright's *Mental Travel in Imagined Lands* (1878), science helps promote qualities like generosity and nobility of character. But we are also informed that 'we have not that pseudo-tenderness for human life which preserves it, however useless to itself and society. Citizenship is dependent on productiveness, and cannot be held through mere right of birth alone.'[111]

Proposals for an overtly coercive treatment of the poor thus often occur. *In the Future* (1875), for instance, envisions the poor living in 'new Laboratories, each a combination of asylum and manufactory', where they are numbered and subjected to 'never-ceasing supervision'.[112] In *Quintura: Its Singular People and Remarkable Customs* (1886), the poor are supervised by doctor-policemen, and all children are cared for by the state.[113] In *Etymonia* (1875), 'Allowance is made for everything, except mere idleness, and for this the remedy is stern', namely being 'confined to a strong room' and 'supplied with work'.[114] The 'state industrialism' system de-scribed in Frederick W. Hayes' *The Great Revolution of 1905* (1893) punishes those lacking the means of subsistence. Refusal to work in jail leads to flogging and a reduced diet, which eliminates loafers and the 'dangerous classes'.[115] In Percy Clarke's *The Valley Council* (1891), those over thirty who are not gainfully employed are simply killed.[116] Employing the poor was also often linked to concerns over immigration. In Henry Lazarus' *The English Revolution of the Twentieth Century* (1894), pauper immigration is ended, and 'The would-not-work

---

[109] Walter Besant, *The Inner House* (Bernhard Tauchnitz, 1888), pp. 22–4, 28, 31, 78, 122.

[110] On this theme see my *Machinery, Money and the Millennium: From Moral Economy to Socialism, 1815–1860* (Princeton University Press, 1987).

[111] Henry Wright, *Mental Travel in Imagined Lands* (Trübner & Co., 1878), pp. 181, 34, 41. Wright's later *Depopulation: A Romance of the Unlikely* (George Allen, 1899) dwells on the problem of the decline in numbers of the most cultured.

[112] *In the Future: A Sketch in Ten Chapters* (Hampstead, 1875), p. 7. Here one great king rules over ten European nations and aims to obliterate all distinctions of race, custom, and language.

[113] Joseph Carne-Ross, *Quintura: Its Singular People and Remarkable Customs* (J. & R. Maxwell, 1886), pp. 11, 58, 88.

[114] *Etymonia* (Samuel Tinsley, 1875), pp. 37.

[115] Frederick W. Hayes, *The Great Revolution of 1905; or, the Story of the Phalanx* (R. Forder, 1893), pp. 158–65, 291.

[116] Percy Clarke, *The Valley Council; or, Leaves from the Journal of Thomas Bateman of Canbelego Station, N.S.W.* (Sampson Low & Co., 1891).

and the criminal classes were definitely dealt with by the Penal Colonies.'[117] William Herbert's *The World Grown Young* (1892) similarly excludes foreign paupers from Britain, and prevents professional criminals from marrying.[118]

Satirists sometimes implied that the harsh implications of such measures derived from Darwinian materialism. In H. C. R. Watson's *Erchomenon; or, The Republic of Materialism* (1879), set 600 years in the future, the Americans have taken over, though Africa is covered with British colonies. At the 'Baby Farm', where all are raised in common, injured children are put to death. The dominant theme here is the callousness implied by Darwinism. While once 'Christianity, reverence for human life' seemed 'to demand the care of the sick and maimed', now 'Human nature lost some of its sweetest attributes when it ceased to care for the weak, the sick, the wounded, and was on the way to extinction.' Darwin's own descendants, indeed, are involved in scientific mating, with their offspring becoming more and more like monkeys.[119]

A later, equally biting satire of this type is Victor Emanuel's *The Messiah of the Cylinder* (1917). Here, a century on, the new republic is based on reason, mostly taken to be Wells' principles, which are linked to Darwin, Marx, and Nietzsche. Marriage is regulated with a view to maximizing productivity. A quarter of the population are not allowed to mate at all, and the rest are supervised carefully to eliminate 'defectives'. Anyone who cannot produce a standard unit of output is eliminated; when they cease to be socially profitable the old enter the 'Comfortable Bedroom'—the age of euphemisms has already begun. The 'word "productivity" was the new fetish', we are told, so 'defectives' are imprisoned in workshops for life rather than killed. Yet the system of mating under state supervision fails, and 'the galling inquisition and atrocious tyranny of Science run mad' is overthrown by the Russians, who restore Christianity. 'Eugenics', we are told, 'was the natural product of a time which, steeped in materialism, laughed at the belief in a human soul.'[120] A lighter touch is evident in Rose Macaulay's satire, *What Not: A Prophetic Comedy* (1919), where a post-war Mental Progress Act sets up a Ministry of Brains which institutes fines for those who marry unsuitably, World War I having been deemed the result of insufferable stupidity. (But the Ministry is finally torched by the crowd.)[121]

Satire ended where the real prospect of tinkering with evolution was entertained. Here the Frankenstein motif was never far distant. H. G. Wells treated this theme in various works. The purest type of eugenic dystopia was represented in *The Island of Dr Moreau* (1896), where a vivisectionist creates people out of animals, resulting in apelike 'beast-men' and many other mixtures. The implication is clearly that we

---

[117] Henry Lazarus, *The English Revolution of the Twentieth Century: A Prospective History* (T. F. Unwin, 1894), pp. 241–3.

[118] William Herbert, *The World Grown Young* (W. H. Allen & Co., 1892), pp. 43, 59.

[119] H. C. R. Watson, *Erchomenon; or, The Republic of Materialism* (S. Low, 1879), pp. 65, 87, 92, 151. In one blunt anti-Darwinian satire, monkeys take over Britain (Arthur Brookfield, *Simiocracy: A Fragment from Future History* (Blackwood & Sons, 1884)).

[120] Victor Rousseau [Victor Emanuel], *The Messiah of the Cylinder* (Curtis Brown, 1917), pp. 91, 126–7, 177, 316.

[121] Rose Macaulay, *What Not: A Prophetic Comedy* (Constable & Co., 1919), pp. 11–13, 224.

may as easily fall back into as rise above our animal nature.[122] This theme is also explored in *The Time Machine* (1895), perhaps Wells' most pessimistic work. Here the world of AD 802701 is divided into two great groups. The master race, the Eloi, are 'a real aristocracy, armed with a perfected science and working to a logical conclusion the industrial system of to-day'. An underground slave race, the Morlocks, a parody of the existing working classes, have degenerated into a near-subhuman condition. The satire here is upon communism, industrialization, the existing class system, and schemes of selective breeding. In the novella, 'A Story of the Days to Come' (1897), Wells commences with a typical modernist projection of enormous cities, flying and working machines, and artificial food. Yet beneath the superficial inventions we see that progress has also brought a palpable sense of loss. The countryside is almost abandoned, except for the giant Food Company farms. People are unaccustomed to walking, so their muscles atrophy. There is the lament that 'we have almost abolished wonder, we lead lives so trim and orderly that courage, endurance, faith, all the noble virtues seem fading from mankind'. Nor has the class system improved. In 2100 the poor live on the ground floors and in the basements of huge buildings.[123]

These themes recur in Wells' later works. The idea of species degeneration is again taken up in *The War of the Worlds* (1897), where the Martians, with their quivering lips, tentacles, and monstrous eyes, at least partially embody eugenic preoccupations with a possible evolutionary degradation into monstrosity. In *When the Sleeper Awakes* (1899), Wells leapt 200 years forward to a slave regime, 'no Utopia, no Socialistic state'. Progress has abolished disease, but the people, swayed by propaganda, are 'helpless in the hands of the demagogue and organiser, individually cowardly, individually swayed by appetite, collectively incalculable'. (He had read his Le Bon.) Science and urbanization thus assist the concentration of wealth.[124] In *Anticipations of the Reaction of Mechanical and Scientific Progress upon Human Life* (1901), Wells warned that 'the new needs of efficiency' dictated that those who did not 'develop sane, vigorous and distinctive personalities for the great world of the future' would 'die out and disappear'.[125]

Yet while his chief work of this period, *A Modern Utopia* (1905), trumpeted the need for a new leadership, the Samurai, Wells also retreated from eugenics solutions to these issues. Here there was no 'attempt to develop any class by special breeding, simply because the intricate interplay of heredity is untraceable and

---

[122] The first man is made from a gorilla and produces a 'negroid type', but there are many other mixtures of animals and humans: H. G. Wells, *The Island of Doctor Moreau* (William Heinemann, 1896), pp. 82, 117–18. Wells thought this was entirely 'within the possibilities of vivisection' (p. 218). Some of these themes are explored in John Rieder, *Colonialism and the Emergence of Science Fiction* (Wesleyan University Press, 2008), esp. pp. 97–122, and in Patricia Kerslake, *Science Fiction and Empire* (Liverpool University Press, 2007).

[123] H. G. Wells, *Tales of Space and Time* (Macmillan, 1906), pp. 167–324.

[124] H. G. Wells, *When the Sleeper Awakes* (Harper & Bros., 1899), pp. 69, 169, 236. For Wells on Le Bon, see, e.g., *First and Last Things* (Archibald Constable & Co., 1908), p. 192, *The Correspondence of H.G. Wells* (4 vols, Pickering & Chatto, 1998), vol. 4, p. 333.

[125] H. G. Wells, *Anticipations* (Chapman & Hall, 1902), p. 317.

incalculable'.[126] Later, Wells still experimented with dystopia. *The Dream* (1924), for instance, projects us 2,000 years forward in order to describe the present as a 'planless, over-populated world', 'pitiless and confused...dirty and diseased', where 'there were no such things as security or social justice as we should understand these words nowadays'.[127] *The Autocracy of Mr. Parnham* (1930) portrays a fascist-style dictator emerging in Britain just as another rises in Germany and plots an invasion of Russia. In the event, it is British meddling in Central Asia which provokes the Second World War, as Wells terms it. But Britain interferes with American shipping in China and the subsequent conflict with the United States ruins the navies of both. Europe collapses into conflict as the United States withdraws into itself. In Britain, a resistance movement arises. The regime collapses, but with the promise that the 'age of war and conquest is over', to be supplanted by a new age of equality, morality, and scientific guidance. This all turns out to have been a dream.[128]

The Darwinian revolution also brought into focus concerns about race relations in the British Empire, and doubtless fuelled racial aggression. Victorian writers generally assumed that the 'white' races were superior and were intended by God to rule the rest. Usually, as in Mill's case, some justification for conquest was provided in the excuse of raising the 'lower' races to higher civility. Such arguments were repeated in Winwood Reade's best-selling *The Martyrdom of Man* (1872), which proposed that security of property and individual rights would eventually tame the barbarians, but only 'by means of European conquest'.[129] Some texts simply posit an unspecified 'inferior race', as in *Pyrna* (1875), where an otherwise egalitarian society controls 'a subjugated, or rather a tributary, race' outside its boundaries.[130] Imperial racial utopias/dystopias—depending on which side of the conquest you were on—were often fairly pitiless. In Robert William Cole's *The Struggle for Empire: A Story of the Year 2236* (1900), the 'Anglo-Saxon race' had 'long ago absorbed the whole globe'.[131] Sometimes non-white peoples were whisked away entirely, as they had been, indeed, in Tasmania. In one such extreme fantasy, William Hay's *Three Hundred Years Hence* (1881), a billion blacks and Chinese are killed off and their lands taken over by whites.[132]

'Yellow peril' novels usually specified conflicts with the Chinese.[133] In Standish O'Grady's *The Queen of the World; or, Under the Tyranny* (1900), they slug it out with the English in the twenty-first century. Matthew Shiel published a series of

[126] H. G. Wells, *A Modern Utopia* (Collins, n.d.), p. 184.

[127] H. G. Wells, *The Dream* (Jonathan Cape, 1924), pp. 66, 152.

[128] H. G. Wells, *The Autocracy of Mr. Parnham: His Remarkable Adventures in this Changing World* (William Heinemann, 1930), p. 353.

[129] Winwood Reade, *The Martyrdom of Man* (15th edn, Kegan Paul, Trench, Trübner & Co., 1896), p. 504.

[130] [Ellis James Davis], *Pyrna: A Commune; or, Under the Ice* (Bickers & Son, 1875), p. 65, repr. in Claeys, *Late Victorian Utopias*, vol. 1, pp. 32–3.

[131] Robert William Cole, *The Struggle for Empire: A Story of the Year 2236* (Elliot Stock, 1900), p. 4.

[132] William Hay, *Three Hundred Years Hence* (Newman & Co., 1881), pp. 216–57, 335.

[133] E.g., [Standish James O'Grady], *The Queen of the World; or, Under the Tyranny* (Lawrence & Bullen, 1900).

'yellow' novels, which included *The Yellow Danger* (1898) (revised in 1929 as *The Yellow Peril*) and *The Yellow Wave* (1905). Occasionally other races win, often the Japanese or Chinese, sometimes after miscegenation or cultural degeneration leads 'whites' to become a minority. The latter are thus sometimes described as weakened by 'want of staying power, love of unwholesome food, excitement, fantastic pleasures, fondness of rapid motion, and the adoption of what was known as the strenuous life, which compelled the continual overtaxing of mind and body in a struggle to acquire wealth or political advantage'.[134] In any of these works, a victory of 'our' race suggested a utopia, and its loss, a dystopia. In other instances, however, the races are harmoniously integrated, and national prejudices have likewise been eliminated.[135] Wells would also hint at such a solution to this issue in *Anticipations* (1901).

Revolution and Dystopia

Most works hostile to the French Revolution also hinted that democratic reform masked a potentially bloodthirsty intolerance. Many early forms of socialism were not revolutionary, and aimed to reorganize society in small-scale communities. They did not inspire a widespread critical literary reaction, though they were easy satirical targets. By the 1880s, however, socialism was increasingly both revolutionary and collectivist, and anticipated new state-wide systems of organization. Combined with Social Darwinism, a peculiar melange of themes resulted in collectivist politics spilling over into collectivist eugenics. Political themes were naturally central to the anti-socialist dystopias. With the Paris Commune in mind, and, before it, Jacobin dictatorship and the Blanquist insurrectionist tradition, the scenario that revolution would induce dictatorship and social decline became the most common dystopian projection.

A socialist reign of terror is thus frequently envisioned in these near-future tales.[136] Lower wages and the ruthless destruction of individualism result in Charles Fairfield's *The Socialist Revolution of 1888* (1884). *A Radical Nightmare: Or, England Forty Years Hence* (1885) foresees Britain breaking up after a revolution. Poverty deepens, free speech disappears, and a secret police monitors behaviour.[137] In *The Island of Anarchy* (1887), anarchists and socialists are banished to an island called Meliora, where they are joined by Russian, German, Irish, and Belgian sympathizers. Here, however, their efforts collapse into violence, which ends only with the imposition of a new social contract.[138] In *'England's Downfall;' or, The Last Great Revolution*, published in 1893, the year the Independent Labour Party, aiming at communal ownership, was founded, an exodus of managerial talent results in national decline. In other works a failed socialist revolution induces a

[134] [Ernest George Henham], *John Trevena: The Reign of the Saints* (Alson Rivers, 1911), p. 13.
[135] Robert Desborough, *State Contentment: An Allegory* (Newsagents' & Publishing Co., 1870).
[136] E.g, [Alfred Morris], *Looking Ahead: A Tale of Adventure* (Henry & Co., 1892), p. 205.
[137] An Ex-M.P., *A Radical Nightmare: Or, England Forty Years Hence* (Field & Tuer, 1885).
[138] E[lizabeth] W[aterhouse], *The Island of Anarchy* (Lovejoy's Library, 1887).

return to feudalism.[139] Sometimes progressive social reform weakens the nation and invites annexation by powers like Germany.[140] Simple economic collapse is a common scenario.[141] But what if the revolution succeeded? Many dystopias described subsequent coercion, especially mandatory communal labour.[142] And if it failed? In some texts collectivism is eventually defeated, but some form of halfway house between it and the status quo ante is conceded. In *James Ingleton: The History of a Social State. A.D. 2000* (1893), the 'individualists' are first suppressed, but re-establish a constitutional monarchy where the state cares for the young and provides an old age pension.[143]

A spate of such novels appeared in the years just after the failed Russian Revolution of 1905. Horace W. C. Newte's *The Master Beast: Being a True Account of the Ruthless Tyranny Inflicted on the British People by Socialism, A.D. 1888–2020* (1907) envisions a socialist majority elected in 1906. This weakens the nation so far as to permit a German invasion. By 2020, the state assigns all work, and labour gangs feed only those who perform their assigned tasks. The family has been abolished because it nourished selfish instincts in parents. Children are educated in common, and the 'humanizing influence' of domestic life has been lost. Cockney-speaking officials wear red rosettes in their buttonholes, form a permanent voting majority, and rule as 'an all-powerful bureaucracy' 'completely indifferent to those who toiled with the sweat of their brow'. Women, who have won the vote, then had it taken away from them again, 'lack restraint' in sexual intercourse, and dress like prostitutes. Since 'freedom does not exist . . . the vast majority of men have neither hope nor interest in life', and act like 'soulless automatons, who have occasional outbursts of animalism'. In Saturnalia-like debaucheries of frenzied tumult, warehouses are plundered for food and drink and 'every kind of indulgence' results. The novel ends with an invasion by the darker races. The narrator, who writes a manifesto of rebellion against the system, flees to France. The title and crowd focus alike indicate an invocation of Le Bon's categories.[144]

Such themes clearly echoed the temper of the times. In John D. Mayne's *The Triumph of Socialism, and How It Succeeded* (1908), an elected socialist majority establishes a republic. Substantial nationalization engenders much resistance, however, and a weakened Britain is nearly invaded by Germany. Indeed, a European war results in 1912 in which France, Britain, and Russia ally against Germany.[145]

---

[139] E.g., [Morris], *Looking Ahead.*

[140] As in [John Parnell], *Cromwell the Third: or the Jubilee of Liberty* (John Parnell, 1886).

[141] E.g., An Ex-Revolutionist, *'England's Downfall;' or, The Last Great Revolution* (Digby & Long, 1893).

[142] E.g., W. A. Watlock, *The Next 'Ninety-Three, or Crown, Commune and Colony* (Field & Tuer, 1893), p. 6.

[143] 'Mr. Dick', *James Ingleton: The History of a Social State. A.D. 2000* (James Blackwood & Co., 1893), pp. 74, 160, 436.

[144] Horace W. C. Newte, *The Master Beast: Being a True Account of the Ruthless Tyranny Inflicted on the British People by Socialism, A.D. 1888–2020* (Rebman, 1907), pp. 27, 79, 81–2, 91–2, 101–2, 180–94, 222, 236, 249.

[145] John D. Mayne, *The Triumph of Socialism, and How It Succeeded* (Swan Sonnenschein & Co., 1908), pp. 8–10, 133.

In Ernest Bramah's *The Secret of the League* (1909), a Socialist Party electoral victory leads to abolishing the House of Lords, confiscating ecclesiastical property, and dismembering the empire. But discontent results in a Unity League winning a new election, bringing to power men who 'were not of the class who oppress. The strife of the past was being forgotten; its lessons were remembered. What was good and practical of Socialistic legislation was retained. So it came about that the vanquished gained more by defeat than they would have done by victory.'[146] We will encounter this *juste milieu*, neither the status quo ante nor utopia, but effectively a compromise, again.

In France, Jules Verne at this time produced his sole dystopian satire on collectivism, *The Survivors of the 'Jonathan'* (1909). Here a group of shipwrecked reformers turn out to be 'impotent on the constructive side', the majority being '[d]ocile slaves, ready to do what they were told' and easily misled by the ambitious few. They easily succumb to 'that madness so powerful, wherever crowds assemble, that, when they have once tasted violence, they never pause until drunk with destruction and bloodshed'. 'Ere long, chaos reigns.[147]

The idea that revolution might actually bring some progress thus does appear in the dystopias of this period. William Le Queux's *The Unknown Tomorrow* (1910) recounts how a socialist revolution in 1935 follows a lengthy period of economic decline. In the subsequent Red Terror, 'Death to the Rich' is a prevailing slogan. The land, hotels, and coal and food supply are nationalized, the national debt repudiated, and working hours are reduced to seven per day. Hosts of 'unnecessary inspectors' plague industry. Marriage is abolished and children become wards of the state. The result is that 'Socialism had abolished all sentiment, and nowadays in England all love, paternal affection, sympathy, and softness of heart seemed dead—killed by law.' The system is overthrown, but in 1937 the government plans reforms to improve the lives of the majority. So again (failed) utopia has pushed the social agenda leftwards.[148]

But often, more disaster results. *Wake Up, England! Being the Amazing Story of John Bull, Socialist* (1910) depicts an exodus of wealth and talent, the loss of the colonies, and the formation of 'a kind of aristocracy' in the 'despotism of a cunning officialdom'. The state becomes a 'prison-house' where 'compulsory interdependence' results in putting 'each man in fear of his comrade, and imposes a condition of things which makes for continual antagonism'. Children are reared in common and the tenderness of family life gives way to a 'completely brutalized' mentality.[149] The more satirical dystopias tend to give greater emphasis to

---

[146] Ernest Bramah, *The Secret of the League: The Story of a Social War* (Thomas Nelson & Sons, 1909), pp. 29–33, 55, 285–6. This appeared first in 1907 under the title, *What Might Have Been: The Story of a Social War*.

[147] Jules Verne, *The Masterless Man: Part One of The Survivors of the 'Jonathan'* (Arco Publications, 1962), p. 28, 103, 142–3, 191; and Jules Verne, *The Unwilling Dictator: Part Two of The Survivors of the 'Jonathan'* (Arco Publications, 1962), pp. 10, 15–17, 33, 37, 108, 132, 155, 192.

[148] William Le Queux, *The Unknown Tomorrow: How the Rich Fared at the Hands of the Poor, Together with a Full Account of the Social Revolution in England* (F. V. White, 1910), pp. 3, 64, 225, 230, 293.

[149] Edward Prince, *Wake Up, England! Being the Amazing Story of John Bull, Socialist* (St. Stephen's Press, 1910), pp. 45, 50–1, 55, 59, 119, 128.

incompetence than violence, and typically portray a socialist experiment on an island colony which eventually collapses. So in Capt. Will. J. Ward's *Shanghaied Socialists: A Romance* (1911), a vision of 'Happy Valley, in which every individual will be a man and a brother, to every other individual' goes disastrously wrong.[150] In one of the few political dystopias of this period not to take socialism as a target, the Inquisition is re-established after Home Rule in Ireland produces 'Rome Rule' in England, and 50,000 are executed for heresy.[151]

A combination of eugenics- and revolutionary-driven collectivism also emerges in British works of this period. In *Red England: A Tale of the Socialist Terror* (1909), three doctors must approve all marriages, and month-old children are taken from their parents to be raised by the state. In Horace Bleackley's *Anymoon* (1919), the British Commonwealth raises 'drone' babies in incubators, giving them different food even from workers' babies, since they are designed to have no intellects. This, however, is overthrown by a Soviet-style system in which 'none but the manual workers were of any account. Everyone else was a pariah, who might be robbed and maltreated at their pleasure.' By the end, a yearning for the old political and economic system is evident.[152]

After 1917, these themes naturally focused on Bolshevism. In John Cournos' *London under the Bolsheviks* (1919), a provisional government led by Ramsay Macdonald is overthrown by MacLenin and Trotsman. H. G. Wells is jailed as a counter-revolutionary when the task of exterminating the 'boorjooys' commences.[153] In Emerson C. Hambrook's *The Red To-Morrow* (1920), a Marxist revolution in 1948 establishes a British Socialist Republic following another war with Germany. This leads to the flight of capital, falling output, and general economic decline. The Red Army, led chiefly by Germans and Jews, pillages and shoots bourgeois prisoners. The narrators flee to Ireland to await better times.[154]

J. D. Beresford's *Revolution* (1921) recounts how the late war has left veterans feeling that 'it was all going to be different, sort of Utopia, short hours, and good pay, and everyone pals with everybody else'. But profiteering and price rises make things worse than ever. The novel follows the fortunes of a war veteran caught up in a general strike which seeks to end inheritance, nationalize the land and industry, and guarantee the right to work. There is no parliamentary majority for these measures, and the Labour Party splits on the issue. A trend towards a long-term 'equalisation of mankind' is evident. But is 'Bolshevism' the solution, especially when pushed on by 'dangerous looking' mobs instigated by the 'hero-worship' of 'an inspired demagogue'? The answer, of course, is no: the more ignorant and cruel tend to boil to the top of the pot, and the poor assume that communism means the

---

[150] Capt. Will. J. Ward, *Shanghaied Socialists: A Romance* (The Maritime Review, 1911), p. 19.

[151] [Allen Upward], *Romance of Politics: The Fourth Conquest of England: A Sequel to 'Treason'* (The Tyndale Press, 1904), pp. 13, 59.

[152] Horace Bleackley, *Anymoon* (The Bodley Head, 1919), pp. 253–62, 279, 325.

[153] John Cournos, *London under the Bolsheviks: A Londoner's Dream on Returning from Petrograd* (Russian Liberation Committee, 1919), pp. 3–6, 10.

[154] Emerson C. Hambrook, *The Red To-Morrow* (The Proletarian Press, 1920), pp. 217, 281, 307, 323.

plunder of the rich. Only the 'stubborn inertia' of habit, routine, and sloth prevents further degeneration. It becomes clear that the 'ideal of Liberty, Equality, and Fraternity, could never be reached by a change of Government' alone. As economic collapse looms, counter-revolution prevails. Yet civilization now 'seemed to be waning', and it is implied that factory labourers would no longer wish to engage in arduous work, but would prefer to return to shorter hours and a quiet life on the land, with a great decline in manufactures and international trade resulting. This seems the face of Britain's future. But is it a worse lot for the majority? On balance, perhaps not.[155] 'Barbarism' has its appeal.

A similar ambiguity defines Edward Shanks' *The People of the Ruins: A Story of the English Revolution and After* (1920). Set in 1924, this describes a series of strikes and growing antagonism towards the 'dirty bourgeois'. After a house collapses on him, a young physicist awakens in a long-overgrown ruined London in the year 2074. Some trains still operate, but otherwise technology has declined greatly after many wars, the closure of schools and universities for twenty years, and a great famine. There are no telephones and little electricity. The population of Britain has declined from 50 million to about 10 or 12 million, and the rest of the world in similar proportions (the USA has dissolved, but Canada has emerged stronger). The 'Reds' have been suppressed and something like the old class system exists. There are still wars on the Continent, but Britain has been at peace for a century, despite religious divisions, the southerners being mostly Catholic, the Welsh Methodists, and the northerners Spiritualists. Britons are much poorer. But their air is clean, and they have more space and time in which to develop. The narrator finds them 'happier than we were'. Though the streets are unsafe at night, violence is rare. Then a new civil war begins to brew between the northern and southern English, which is portrayed as a contest between barbarism and civilization. The southerners commence manufacturing artillery again, enrolling the narrator as their instructor. The northerners are defeated, but the narrator is forced to flee and commits suicide at the end.[156]

By the mid-1920s, it was becoming evident that the conflict of the epoch was shaping up to be communism versus fascism. This was played out in various literary scenarios. In Hugh Addison's *The Battle of London* (1924), it is noted that 'the Fascists saved Italy' from Bolshevism, and when in Britain the communists demand 'instant Soviet rule over the vital industries' they are met by a Liberty League of ex-officers and soldiers determined to defend the status quo. Armed insurrection occurs, but finally the Reds are defeated.[157] In I. F. Grant's *A Candle in the Hills* (1926), a pan-Gaelic movement called the Friends of Liberty overthrows the Soviet govern-ment of Great Britain, and aims at home rule for Scotland.[158] Various novels envision an eventual White victory and the overthrow of the Soviet regime.[159] In

---

[155] J. D. Beresford, *Revolution: A Novel* (W. Collins Sons & Co., 1921), pp. 26, 28, 39, 43, 46, 77, 83, 141, 198–200, 212, 239–40.

[156] Edward Shanks, *The People of the Ruins: A Story of the English Revolution and After* (W. Collins & Sons, 1920), pp. 18, 41, 70–1, 107, 110, 113, 126, 134, 163, 187, 290.

[157] Hugh Addison, *The Battle of London* (Herbert Jenkins Ltd, 1924), pp. 6, 20.

[158] I. F. Grant, *A Candle in the Hills* (Hodder & Stoughton, 1926), pp. 115, 318–19.

[159] E.g., Morris Sutherland, *Second Storm* (Thornton Butterworth, 1930).

others, a heroic narrator visits a loosely disguised Soviet Union and helps bring the system down.[160] In *The Blue Shirts* (1926), similarly, the Socialist Republic of Great Britain, founded in part by the Red Army and the Irish Republican Army (IRA), is countered by the Freeman's Union heavies of the title, possibly funded by Mussolini, who suppress the Reds and drastically reduce alien immigration.[161] Kenneth Allott and Stephen Tait's *The Rhubarb Tree* (1937) offers the prospect of a British Nazi victory within months, and the observation that 'Fascism lifts the intolerable weight of private judgment off the back of the man in the street. Hence its success. Marxism, party communism, will never defeat it. Primitive Christianity might.'[162]

By the late 1920s it was also possible to imagine that the Soviet Union would collapse following economic bankruptcy. But some authors saw it adopting American-style private enterprise in the New Economic Policy (NEP) experiment, with prosperity returning as a result. In one account, socialism along Fabian lines is tried in Britain at the same time, and then rejected after a plebiscite.[163] In another, the Proletarian State of Britain is founded, resulting in an atmosphere in which 'No man dare trust his neighbour; no man, even between the four walls of his own house, and in the circle of his own family, dare say his thoughts. Each man walked alone, greedy, suspicious, pitiless . . .' But a royalist insurrection overthrows the Proletarian State.[164] Dennis Wheatley's *Black August* (1934) projects a see-sawing back and forth in Britain between communists and fascists, following Germany's conquest of Poland and Russia's 'sinking back into a state of barbarism' after its intelligentsia is slaughtered. Here, though the victorious communists in Britain retain the monarchy and seek to distribute the unemployed throughout the empire, they are ousted. In the aftermath, industrialists promise to work for the common good (and the beer tax is abolished), thus indicating some progress.[165] But Richard Heron Ward's *The Sun Shall Rise* (1935) ends with the narrator arrested by fascists, amidst laments that communism gives too much emphasis to 'destroy-the-bourgeoisie without any thought of what is to happen when the bourgeoisie is destroyed'. Hope is expressed that a Christian form of communism might prove more successful.[166]

Even gloomier is Shamus Frazer's *A Shroud as Well as a Shirt* (1935), where the triumph of fascism brings about concentration camps, book burning and attacks on Jews, and an Anglo-German alliance against the USSR. It ends with most of London destroyed by bombing.[167] In many texts, the satires upon existing dictatorships portray some space where the regime's principles have not penetrated, which serves as a counterweight. In Rex Warner's *The Wild Goose Chase* (1937), which is broadly a satire on Soviet development (their deity is the Wild Goose) and

---

[160] E.g., Daniel O'Den, *Crimson Courage* (Frederick Muller Ltd, 1940).
[161] J. J. J., *The Blue Shirts* (Simpkin, Marshall, Hamilton, Kent & Co., 1926), pp. 161–4, 272, 278.
[162] Kenneth Allott and Stephen Tait, *The Rhubarb Tree* (The Cresset Press, 1937), pp. 9, 43.
[163] Felix J. Blakemore, *The Coming Hour* (?) (Sands & Co., 1927), pp. 165–6.
[164] Laurence Meynell, *Storm against the Wall* (Hutchinson & Co., 1931), pp. 14, 285.
[165] Dennis Wheatley, *Black August: A Novel* (Hutchinson & Co., 1934), pp. 11, 323, 332, 341.
[166] Richard Heron Ward, *The Sun Shall Rise* (Ivor Nicholson & Watson, 1935), pp. 95, 363.
[167] Shamus Frazer, *A Shroud as Well as a Shirt* (Chapman & Hall, 1935), pp. 273, 335.

the oppression of the peasantry, for instance, the 'Free State of Lagonda' exists as a kind of pastoral or Arcadian retreat where liberty prevails, and in the end the regime is overthrown.[168]

The eugenics trends of the late nineteenth century were never far away in the post-war period. Sometimes simple birth control amongst the labouring classes was projected as ensuring that 'very slowly competition for work has died out and wages risen', despite some resistance to mandatory restraints on birth.[169] Eugenics was central to Milo M. Hastings' *The City of Endless Night* (1920). In the underground city of Berlin in 2041, 300 million people live in isolation from the outside 'World State' in an 'unholy imprisonment of a race' described as 'but the logical culmination of mechanical and material civilization'. Under an Imperial Socialist regime headed by the House of Hohenzollern, all classes are bred scientifically, and 'romantic love' and family life are forbidden. Everywhere there is 'the ceaseless throbbing of the machine'. The science of applied eugenics commences during World War II with the aim of breeding superior men in the official and intellectual classes. Workers are bred separately, however, and by a combination of heredity and training most males now don't desire women and can thus work more. Again, thus, productivism is triumphant. No resistance is possible, since the 'powers of mental reaction no longer exist in German minds. We have bred and trained it out of them.' Hope lies only in the World State overthrowing 'this folly of scientific meddling with the blood and brains of men'. Eventually it does.[170]

Similar themes are explored in John Bernard's *The New Race of Devils* (1921), where German scientists aim to eliminate 'the best that is inherent in humanity' and to intensify 'latent cruelty, violence and selfishness' through artificial breeding. The prototype calls himself a 'Thing without a soul', who nonetheless acquits himself to some degree by joining a revolution, only to die in a plane crash.[171] In Francis D. Grierson's *Heart of the Moon* (1928), darker skinned peoples are kept in almost 'complete subjection' and the Wise Ones choose women for mating. The author warns that this was not civilization but 'automatization', aiming 'at the reduction of every human law to an exact formula'. Hence, 'if the Wise Ones have their way we shall cease to be men and become machines'. Control over marriage is at the centre of the scheme. The unfit are sterilized, and no one who cannot support their offspring is permitted to marry. Population levels are not allowed to exceed the provision of work and food.[172]

Extreme projections of eugenic schemes thus remain common as we enter the 1930s. In Aelfrida Tillyard's *Concrete: A Story of Two Hundred Years Hence* (1930), a lengthy period of proletarian revolution, war, and epidemics has reduced the world's population by three-quarters. Following the Great Death, 'ten years of

---

[168] Rex Warner, *The Wild Goose Chase* (Boriswood, 1937), pp. 115, 237, 438.

[169] Diane Boswell, *Posterity: A Novel* (Jonathan Cape, 1926), pp. 9. 13, 38.

[170] Milo M. Hastings, *The City of Endless Night* (1920; Hesperus Books, 2014), pp. 25, 30, 40, 47, 83, 89, 134–7, 253–5.

[171] John Bernard, *The New Race of Devils* (Anglo-Eastern Publishing Co., 1921), pp. ii, 8–9, 176, 188.

[172] Francis D. Grierson, *Heart of the Moon* (Alston Rivers Ltd, 1928), pp. 39, 67, 104–6.

madness' occur, with millions dancing to the point of exhaustion. The Age of Unreason ended when Eugenist Party revolutionaries sought to eliminate criminals, imbeciles, priests, effete aristocrats, and other defectives. After 200 years, poverty and war are finally abolished. Unhealthy children are subjected to euthanasia, and the society is divided into five classes. Yet while the society is devoted to minimizing pain, many possess 'an immense lassitude' and see no point in life. A million men a year in the United States alone ask for euthanasia, and a popular cult originating in Russia seeks race suicide. The masses have

> opportunities for a full and rich life, and they are too inert to avail themselves of them . . . The cinemas are free, but who troubles to go and look at them? Most of the houses have the teleflick, but the owners are too bored to turn it on. Who reads the books in the free libraries? Why is there always such difficulty in getting an audience at a lecture?

No one wants to work the light requisite hours, either: 'The vital energy is lacking. Nobody cares. We are becoming a race incapable of effort . . . Why should it invent?—it has invented enough. Why should it build?—there are more huge edifices than a dwindling population needs. Why should it create?—it has no vitality which clamours for expression. Why should it make more laws?—the docile rabble are over-governed already.' Here, two years before *Brave New World*, we have a clear satire on the utopia of eugenicist hedonism. Whilst the black races are described as still vigorous, the older 'European races' are 'over-refined, and, now that they felt they had pushed progress almost to its furthest limits, their will-to-live was dying down'. The answer, it is suggested, is religious revival. So our heroes retreat to an island where refugees have fled 200 years ago and Christian ritual still persists.[173] The restoration of Christianity as an alternative to Bolshevism, indeed, is a not uncommon theme in this period, through at least to the end of World War II.[174]

One of the most innovative of the eugenics-based literary projections of this period was John Palmer's *The Hesperides* (1936). Palmer thought his narrative, completed in 1932, had been confirmed in theory by Huxley and in practice by the USSR's renunciation of sexual libertinism in favour of a more traditional approach to the family. Hesperus is an earth-like planet where those who live on the outer rim and control the water supply are absolute masters of the natives in the interior. The former exhibit 'an astonishing conformity of bearing and feature' and 'live quite literally in glass houses'. While they regard eating and drinking as 'deplorable or even offensive', 'All works of benefit to the community, in other words all acts which were regarded as directly or indirectly productive, were performed in the general eye.' Their obsession with productivity extends to wishing to eradicate sleep

---

[173] Aelfrida Tillyard, *Concrete: A Story of Two Hundred Years Hence* (Hutchinson & Co., 1930), pp. 34, 40, 42–5, 110, 163, 177–85, 198, 226. Tillyard mentions *Erewhon* in her sequel, *The Approaching Storm* (Hutchinson & Co., 1932), p. 10.

[174] A late instance is Erik and Christiane von Kuehnelt-Leddihn, *Moscow 1979* (Sheed & Ward, 1946), pp. 312–14. The authors were Austrian monarchist exiles who had lived in Britain and at this time lived in the USA. He also published (under the name of Francis S. Campbell) *The Menace of the Herd* (The Bruce Publishing Co., 1943), which emphasized the similarities of Nazism and communism.

insofar as it might 'deprive the community for an appreciable portion of every day of services potentially valuable'. This system was established 2,000 years ago, when, facing species extinction, one Euthan laid down a code which 'made it a crime to think. It was get together or perish. So they got together.' Procreation became an act of public service, family life was abolished, and eugenics engineered a standard race. This, however, resulted in too many average people being produced.[175] So the educated classes in a seven-class society modified the scheme to permit personal mating, family life, and some connection with children, while still enforcing Euthan's regime upon the two lowest classes, who are bred closest to the communal system, 'unthinking devotion to routine, a complete absence of initiative, a kind of ecstatic servility which found its reward in the unwavering repetition of a necessary function'. We are told that 'the classes to which these liberties were accorded were more prolific, virile and intelligent than those to whom they were denied'. The natives of the interior, however, do not 'in their hearts accept the communal system', and still practice pre-Euthan religious rituals, thus threatening the system. The author's warnings are made most evident in two passages. The first declares that

> men do not naturally desire liberty or responsibility. No sooner do they come together than they invent prohibitions and servilities. They love discipline. They always seek to walk together. They accept and consecrate their bonds. This is always more to be feared than liberty. Man is in constant peril of losing himself merely in order to survive as a group or species. He is only served in the last resort by those who, from time to time, feeling responsibility to God alone, defy the common mind.

The second warns of the increasing

> tyranny of herds, governments, nations, sects and parties, in the standardising of our emotions and minds, in the synchronising of our pleasures. The people of earth are being driven to the doctrines of Euthan—organisation, censorship, assembly. Man stands in peril of the mass. He is exposed each minute of the day to the relentless order; Conform or Perish.[176]

Two other variations on dystopia in this period merit mention. The first is the ever-popular future war scenario. Chris Morgan's little-known *The Shape of Futures Past* irreverently surveys many such works, which become increasingly common after 1870.[177] Amongst the first is Sir George Chesney's *The Battle of Dorking* (1871), written during the Franco-Prussian War, where poorly trained English volunteers are swiftly routed by a technologically superior force. In *Cromwell the Third: Or, the Jubilee of Liberty* (1886), Britain is annexed by Germany. William Le Queux's *The Great War in England in 1897* (1894) offers the usual diatribe on Britain's lack of preparedness for conflict, and warns of the 'Great War' to come. Here, France and Russia combine against Britain after unrest in Bosnia. As Russian troops land, anarchist mobs loot the

---

[175] John Palmer, *The Hesperides: A Looking-Glass Fugue* (Martin Secker & Warburg, 1936), pp. 24, 27, 44–6, 60–3.

[176] Ibid., p. 71, 75–6, 215, 319.

[177] For this period, see esp. Chris Morgan, *The Shape of Futures Past: The Story of Prediction* (Webb & Bower, 1980), pp. 17–73.

banks and slash and burn portraits in the National Gallery in London. Eventually Britain's enemies are beaten back. But Germany gains by France's losses.[178]

This outcome, however, led nicely into a sequel, Le Queux's *The Invasion of 1910* (1906), which was translated into seven languages. Here, a German surprise attack conquers an ill-prepared Britain. Martial law is imposed, and savage reprisals are meted on resisters. The population is forced to supply the invaders, who, after a month, are expelled. The key message is that the socialists 'who had declaimed against armaments', were 'faithless friends' whose 'dream of a golden age proved utterly delusive'.[179] Germany again prevails, largely through air superiority, in H. H. Munro's *When William Came: The Story of London under the Hohenzollerns* (1913). Previously, however, foreigners and Jews have weakened Britain's sense of national identity. This narrative commences after the fact, with none of Le Queux's laborious military detail. The occupation permits middle-class life to continue, and many are portrayed as surprisingly unconcerned at the turn of events. The lower classes are heavily taxed to pay for the occupying garrison. But, we are told, to balance the 'hopelessly subservient', 'in thousands of English homes throughout the land there were young hearts that had not forgotten, had not compounded, would not yield'. They wait.[180] Late in this period, J. Bernard Walker's *America Fallen! The Sequel to the European War* (1915) depicts Germany occupying the United States in 1916 despite the defeat of German land forces in Europe and the imposition of a punitive peace treaty.[181] In the 1920s, variations on the genre included the Yellow Peril wedded to Bolshevism in a future invasion (in Reginald Glossop's *The Orphan of Space: A Tale of Downfall* (1926)).

A second new subgenre now emerging was the ecocatastrophe. An early instance is William Delisle Hay's *The Doom of the Great City* (1880), where London is engulfed by extreme weather conditions. In 'Edwarda Gibbon''s *History of the Decline and Fall of the British Empire* (1884) imperial disintegration is hastened by a shift in the Gulf Stream which makes Britain progressively colder. Eventually, polar bears roam the forests and in 2488 the king flees to New Zealand.[182]

Relapse into barbarism is also the central theme in Richard Jefferies' *After London; or, Wild England* (1885) (see Fig. 5.1). This dystopia, based on cataclysm rather than collectivist revolution, follows various wars and disasters, though the wealthy have been largely spared, having sailed away to parts unknown. The towns have been evacuated, and regular land cultivation abandoned. Wild animals inhabit

[178] William Lé Queux, *The Great War in England in 1897* (Tower Publishing Co., 1894), pp. 6, 46, 52, 327.
[179] William Le Queux, *The Invasion of 1910* (Eveleigh Nash, 1906), pp. x, 549.
[180] H. H. Munro, *When William Came: The Story of London under the Hohenzollerns* (John Lane, 1913), pp. 45, 54–6, 182, 188, 322.
[181] J. Bernard Walker, *America Fallen! The Sequel to the European War* (G. P. Putnam's Sons, 1915). Other nations projected similar trends. A German work, August Niemann's *The Coming Conquest of England* (1904), expresses resentment over Britain's territorial acquisitions, now resisted by Germany, France, and Russia. India is lost first, and finally Britain itself is conquered, and her empire is divided. But the work is an adventure story rather than a future projection.
[182] Edwarda Gibbon, *History of the Decline and Fall of the British Empire* (Field & Tuer, 1884), pp. 23, 27, 30.

Fig. 5.1. *Ruins of London*, Gustav Doré, 1870. © Mary Evans Picture Library 10022798.

much of the countryside. Some people live in small enclosures of a few hundred, in camps ruled by the eldest, and coexisting with a multitude of Romany tribes, or roam the woods. Others inhabit kingdoms, provinces, or republics, all of which are, however, corrupt and insecure, and rely on mercenaries. Slavery and servitude are common. Much of London has relapsed into swampland where the air is noxious and occasionally even bursts into flame. The plot within the story is essentially a kind of medieval romance. Little effort is made to explain how these catastrophes occurred. Even the love story barely rescues the tale, except to suggest that some measure of civility survives barbarism. So the satire on contemporary life is well disguised. There is a sense that the existing class system is 'held together by brute force, intrigue, cord and axe, and woman's flattery'.[183] A similar relapse into 'helpless and hopeless savagery' 200 years in the future is described in P. Anderson Graham's *The Collapse of Homo Sapiens* (1923), resulting from a series of wars, the use of poison gas, and flood and famine, with hopes held out for the revival of Christianity.[184]

Yet we should not assume that the yearning for primitivism, the simpler life, was a uniformly dystopian theme, either. Morris famously confessed to feeling consoled at the prospect 'of barbarism once more flooding the world, and real feelings and passions, however rudimentary, taking the place of our wretched hypocrisies'.[185] Barbarism is indicated as a favourable alternative to modernity generally in various texts of this epoch, including two works by J. Leslie Mitchell, *Three Go Back* (1932), in which a lost world/Atlantis narrative contains the accusation that 'the vicious combativeness of civilized man is no survival from an earlier epoch; it is a thing resultant on the torturing threads of civilisation itself'; and *Gay Hunter* (1934).[186]

The Threat of the Machine

Having invented the steam-engine and pioneered in many other fields, Britain was the first machine-based society. Its experience served as a prototype of what everyone else would undergo in the next century or so. Those who owned and invented the new machines, of course, were rarely those who suffered from their adverse effects. They profited from the economies in labour, time, effort, and expense: they did not find their own labour intensified, subjected to extreme discipline, and made more dangerous. Working-class Britons drawn from the countryside into the new industrial towns were often equivocal about the new inventions. The Luddites destroyed the new looms, which they feared would supersede their labour, and gave the language the term 'Luddism' to describe those who thought technological restraint the better part of wisdom. In the 1760s, the Scot Adam Ferguson had warned that the new manufacturing work-shops seemed to prosper most where 'the mind is least consulted, and where the workshop may, without any great effort of imagination, be considered as an engine, the parts of which are men'.[187] By the mid-1820s, Thomas Carlyle associated such an outcome with an 'Age of Machinery', which attempted to shape humans to the repetition, regularity, and discipline demanded by technology. Carlyle also

---

[183] Richard Jefferies, *After London* (Cassell & Co., 1885), p. 312. On Jefferies see W. J. Keith, *Richard Jefferies: A Critical Study* (University of Toronto Press, 1965).
[184] P. Anderson Graham, *The Collapse of Homo Sapiens* (G. P. Putnam's Sons, 1923), pp. 14, 28–30, 33, 92.
[185] Quoted in J. W. Mackail, *The Life of William Morris* (2 vols, Longmans, Green & Co., 1899), vol. 2, p. 144.
[186] J. Leslie Mitchell, *Three Go Back* (Jarrolds, 1932), p. 161.
[187] Adam Ferguson, *An Essay on the History of Civil Society* (1767; Edinburgh University Press, 1966), p. 183.

conceived of this as a fatalistic abrogation of moral responsibility: the machine might conquer the human will. Now, he thought, men had 'lost faith in individual endeavour, and in natural force, of any kind', and instead reposed their confidence and aspirations in institutions and collectivities. He was also insistent that a basic trend in modern society was the destruction of friendship, competition bred by commerce inducing, at best, 'armed neutrality'.[188] Some of the landed aristocracy thought the railways were ravenously devouring the landscape. Others conceded with plebeian and some Tory radicals that the new factory prisons might simply represent a more advanced form of slavery.

None of this slowed the progress of machinery. Possessing the technological edge was essential to building the world's largest empire. But always there was ambiguity. One great symbol of the day, the Maxim, or automatic machine gun, was a source of boastfulness so long as it was deployed in imperial slaughter. After 1914, used against Britons, it stood for the mindless waste of trench warfare. World War I tipped the technological balance for many observers. Now the risks of scientific and technical advancement seemingly outweighed their benefits. The nineteenth-century image of progress, and Wells' great future vision, now seemed suspect. Doubt, suspicion, scepticism, anomie, and anxiety stepped into the place of the vacuous optimism of the technophiles. Orwell would later write that World War I 'succeeded in debunking both Science, Progress and civilised man. Progress had finally ended in the biggest massacre in history, Science was something that created bombing planes and poison gas, civilised man, as it turned out, was ready to behave worse than any savage when the pinch came.'[189] It was an immense, depressing let-down for millions.

These anxieties were already notable by the 1870s. One of the earliest works to view machinery as distinctly and even inevitably threatening, Samuel Butler's *Erewhon* (1872), has been described as the 'most complete and adequate example of the inverted utopia'.[190] Butler complained that reviewers dismissed the argument in his chapter entitled 'The Book of the Machines' 'as an attempt to reduce Mr. Darwin's theory to an absurdity'.[191] To us it seems quite plausible. Butler hinted that machines might acquire consciousness, or what we today call artificial intelligence, on the analogy that 'the race of man has descended from things which had no consciousness at all'. People were, moreover, akin to machines already in many respects, responding to stimulus as if pulled by levers. 'Man's very soul', Butler ventured, was indeed 'due to the machines; it is a machine-made thing: he thinks as

---

[188] Thomas Carlyle, 'The Signs of the Times', in *Works* (30 vols, Chapman & Hall, 1899), vol. 27, p. 63; Thomas Carlyle, *Sartor Resartus* (Chapman & Hall, 1885), p. 199. His views were also influential in America: Leo Marx, *The Machine in the Garden: Technology and the Pastoral Ideal in America* (Oxford University Press, 2000), pp. 170–90.

[189] George Orwell, *All Propaganda is Lies 1941–1942* (Secker & Warburg, 2002), p. 214.

[190] Russell, *Touring Utopia*, p. 183. Lewis Mumford describes it as the first work to understand 'the full implications of automation': *The Myth of the Machine*, vol. 2, p. 193. For background see Parrinder, *Utopian Literature and Science*, pp. 82–96.

[191] Samuel Butler, *Erewhon and Erewhon Revisited* (The Modern Library, 1927), pp. viii, and generally, 223–61. The chapter first appeared under the title, 'Darwin among the Machines', and then 'The Mechanical Creation'. For an assessment of its main themes, see Herbert S. Sussman, *Victorians and the Machine: The Literary Response to Technology* (Harvard University Press, 1968), pp. 135–61.

he thinks, and feels as he feels, through the work that machines have wrought upon him, and their existence is quite as much a sine quâ non for his, as for theirs.' This, Butler thought, 'precludes us from proposing the complete annihilation of machinery, but surely it indicates that we should destroy as many of them as we can possibly dispense with, lest they should tyrannize over us even more completely'. Indeed, the servitude seemed already well underway. 'How many men at this hour are living in a state of bondage to the machines? How many spend their whole lives, from the cradle to the grave, in tending them by night and day?' Butler asked. 'Do not machines eat as it were by mannery? Are we not ourselves creating our successors in the supremacy of the earth?' If humans had evolved from lower animals, higher machines could logically succeed them. It might all be a spoof on Darwin, of course. But Butler hinted at a still darker future where machines made machines. The suggestion that 'the difference between the life of a man and that of a machine is one rather of degree than of kind' introduced a perplexing proposition into debates over progress.[192] In this vein, Morris would condemn Bellamy's view of the future as a 'machine-life'.[193]

But these themes only came fully to fruition in the early twentieth century.[194] In the fullest versions of scientific materialism, as John Gray indicates, people deny that they have any free will, and see themselves as genetically determined machines. At the most extreme projection of mechano-humanism, J. D. Bernal, in 1929, envisioned post-human cyborgs with machine bodies, with human distinctiveness virtually eliminated.[195] Lewis Mumford's *Technics and Civilization* (1934) hoped that the 'decay of the mechanical faith' might be spurred on by 'symptoms of social danger and decay'.[196] But the threat of an ever more obsessive cult of efficiency loomed ever larger. Jacques Ellul's *The Technological Society* (1954), where the replacement of politicians by technicians is a central theme, was recommended by Aldous Huxley as a key study of the problem. Here the now-familiar themes of the mechanization of the worker, the triumph of the unconscious, the emergence of mass society, and the creation of a 'universal concentration camp' are wedded.[197] Scarcely a generation later, the idea of cybernetics emerged in the writings of Norbert Wiener to describe the process by which, through advancing human–machine communication, machines might evolve beyond their human designers.[198]

---

[192] Butler, *Erewhon and Erewhon Revisited*, pp. 227, 234–5, 251.

[193] William Morris, *Political Writings* (Thoemmes Press, 1994), p. 423.

[194] A survey of key authors who treat the theme is Thomas P. Dunn and Richard D. Erlich, eds., *The Mechanical God: Machines in Science Fiction* (Greenwood Press, 1982) and Thomas P. Dunn and Richard D. Erlich, eds., *Clockwork Worlds: Mechanized Environments in SF* (Greenwood Press, 1983). Brian Aldiss' introduction to the latter, 'Robots: Low-Voltage Ontological Currents' (pp. 3–12) is especially noteworthy.

[195] J. D. Bernal, *The World, the Flesh and the Devil* (Jonathan Cape, 1970), pp. 32–46; John Gray, *The Soul of the Marionette: A Short Inquiry into Human Freedom* (Allen Lane, 2015), pp. 10, 14.

[196] Lewis Mumford, *Technics and Civilization* (George Routledge & Sons, 1947), pp. 366–7.

[197] Jacques Ellul, *The Technological Society* (Vintage Books, 1964), esp. pp. 387–412, here 397; Julian Huxley, ed., *Aldous Huxley* (Chatto & Windus, 1965), p. 98.

[198] Norbert Wiener, *Cybernetics: Or Control and Communication in the Animal and the Machine* (John Wiley & Sons, 1957). An excellent overview of the field is Patricia S. Warrick's *The Cybernetic Imagination in Science Fiction* (MIT Press, 1980). See also Langdon Winner, *Autonomous Technology: Technics-Out-of-Control as a Theme in Political Thought* (MIT Press, 1977).

By now, in most quarters, satire and hope had given way to deep alarm, with science fiction now also shifting from optimism to pessimism in the mid-twentieth century.[199]

THE USA, 1880–1914: BELLAMY AND HIS CRITICS

The United States industrialized and urbanized some decades after Britain. Its great extent, constant immigration, and expansion westwards hindered inequality and urban poverty for a time. Nonetheless, the agrarian, egalitarian, and individualist components of the American dream associated with Jefferson and Jackson were already seriously threatened by the late 1870s. The Civil War of 1861–5 had forced rapid industrialization upon the north. The immense idealism unleashed by the 1776 Revolution, combined with a powerful underlying ethos of equality, often fed by religion, invariably produced profound disappointment when the society developed in other directions. Inequality was the main problem: in 1896, seven-eighths of the nation's wealth was owned by one-eighth of the population, and, of these, 1 per cent perhaps owned more than the other 99 per cent.[200] The rich monopolized many resources, including the railways and many natural assets. They also speculated wildly in the new stock exchanges. Six financial crises from the early 1870s to the century's end, and a depression from 1893 to 1898 caused substantial problems. These included growing conflict between capital and labour, and hatred of the new financial oligarchy, but also, on the other side, diatribes against the 'foreign agitators' who criticized them. Other issues in the epoch included mass immigration (from Europe) and its prospect (from Asia); urbanization and industrialization; the United States' increasing imperialism; and the growing influence of Social Darwinism, which fuelled racism.

The utopian tradition was hardly foreign to the United States, and in the early nineteenth century both Owenism and Fourierism were satirized even as they attracted hundreds of converts to communitarianism. The first substantial nineteenth-century literary utopia published in the United States, John Lithgow's *Equality: A History of Lithconia* (1802), proposes a system of communism, mandatory universal labour (travel not being permitted without its performance), uniform housing, and an annual distribution of clothes, which later readers might identify as dystopian.[201] Joel Nydahl writes of 'a strong authoritarian bias in many early American utopian novels'.[202] A number of works also assailed

[199] Harold L. Berger, *Science Fiction and the New Dark Age* (Bowling Green University Popular Press, 1976), p. 4. This is an undervalued survey of science fiction dystopias to this point, though it takes 'dystopia' to be synonymous with 'anti-utopia' (p. xi).

[200] Kenneth Roemer, *The Obsolete Necessity. America in Utopian Writings, 1888-1900* (Kent State University Press, 1976), p. 3. This is, curiously, almost exactly the same proportion of global wealth, in 2016.

[201] Formerly attributed to James Reynolds, it is reprinted in Arthur O. Lewis, ed., *American Utopias: Selected Short Fiction* (Arno Press, 1971).

[202] Joel Nydahl, 'Introduction', in Timothy Savage, *The Amazonian Republic* (1842; Scholars' Facsimiles & Reprints, 1976), p. ix.

utopian themes before 1880. These include James Kirke Paulding's 'The Man Machine' (1826), an anti-Owenite satire which mocks Owen's environmental determinism as mechanistic; Ezekiel Sanford's *The Humours of Eutopia* (1828), which lambasts both egalitarianism and democracy; Nathaniel Beverley Tucker's *The Partisan Leader* (1836), an anti-Jacksonian tract which projects a failed federal US despotism, advocates the southern case for states' rights and anticipates the Civil War;[203] Timothy Savage's *The Amazonian Republic* (1842), a tract on the American 'sordid love of wealth', the effects of 'corporations or associations of combined capital' in undermining press freedom, and the disadvantages of a universal suffrage which brings about the rule of 'vagabonds and ruffians';[204] and James Fenimore Cooper's *The Crater* (1847), where a South Sea paradise succumbs to an excess of democracy.[205] Amongst the catastrophe novels to appear, J. A. Mitchell's *The Last American* (1889) rediscovers a ruined America in the year 2951, and dwells upon climate change in particular, though it also satirizes the progress of wealth and luxury and describes a bloody rebellion by the poor.[206]

Only in the 1880s did there occur what many American authors perceived to be an 'Armageddon of the late nineteenth century'.[207] Now some warned that the economic system faced collapse. Set in the ninety-sixth century, John Macnie's *The Diothas or A Far Look Ahead* (1883) portrays a society which has 'relapsed to a form of barbarism more frightful than even that of primitive ages'. A despotism in the United States, however, is eventually overthrown and replaced by a more egalitarian republican system which limits property.[208] Both utopian and anti-utopian writers, Frederic Jaher writes, shared in this period 'an apocalyptic version of the end of corrupt society', and differed 'more in emphasis than ideology'.[209] America had become corrupt, individualistic, materialistic, and aggressively exploitative. But whether to return to an idealized pastoral past (like William Dean Howells) or to move forward to a gleaming industrial future of greater justice and equality (like Edward Bellamy) was less clear. 'The crucial difference between utopians and cataclysmists', according to Jaher, lay in 'their degrees of faith in the future of mankind.'[210]

The central figure in this debate, Bellamy, was amongst the greatest optimists of the era. He took this to some extremes. An early novel, *Dr. Heidenhoff's Process* (1880), concerns medical techniques to 'forget the past' through a 'Thought-Extirpation

[203] Nathaniel Beverley Tucker, *The Partisan Leader: A Tale of the Future* (1836; University of North Carolina Press, 1971), p. i.

[204] Savage, *The Amazonian Republic*, pp. 157, 163–4.

[205] For an assessment of these texts see Joel Nydahl, 'Early Fictional Futures', in Roemer, ed., *America as Utopia*, pp. 266–74.

[206] J. A. Mitchell, *The Last American: A Fragment from the Journal of Khan-Li, Prince of Dimph-Yoo-Chur and Admiral in the Persian Navy* (Frederick A. Stokes, 1889), p. 92.

[207] Roemer, *The Obsolete Necessity*, p. 21.

[208] Ismar Thiusen [John Macnie], *The Diothas or A Far Look Ahead* (G. Putnam's Sons, 1883), pp. 109, 112, 115.

[209] Frederic Cople Jaher, *Doubters and Dissenters: Cataclysmic Thought in America, 1885–1918* (Free Press, 1964), p. 21.

[210] Ibid., p. 22.

process', which would eliminate 'remembered sin' in order to promote a sense of well-being.[211] (This is sometimes conceived as a 'disturbingly similar' to many later dystopias.)[212]

Before *Looking Backward*, however, a reform movement sprang to life with Henry George's *Progress and Poverty* (1879), which warned of a possible regression 'back towards barbarism' under the 'vilest and most degrading' form of industrial plutocratic despotism.[213] George focused on inequality of landed wealth, the remedy for which was a single tax on land values.

Amongst the literary responses to this idea, the most important was Anna Bowman Dodd's *The Republic of the Future; or, Socialism a Reality* (1887). It imagines America in 2050 after a destructive revolution and a 'terrible reign of blood' have given way to 150 years of socialist peace. The old order has been destroyed. There is no more private property or war. The metropolis now consists of identical two-storey houses. The state brings up children, who spend one day per year at home. Equal to men, women occupy most important roles. Both sexes dress alike. Labour-saving machinery has eliminated degrading work. All work two hours daily. Food is supplied by a central board which assesses each household's needs monthly. It is portable, packaged in bottles or pellets, so cooking is unnecessary. Economic competition has ended, as the government runs all the shops. A pneumatic tube transports tourists beneath the Atlantic.[214]

But all this is actually a dystopia. The city is 'the very acme of dreariness', its 'total lack of contrast' resulting from 'the principle which has decreed that no man can have any finer house or better interior, or finer clothes than his neighbour'. Laws are passed 'forbidding mental or artistic development being carried beyond a certain fixed standard, a standard attainable by all'. This is 'common mediocrity'. So the more gifted are all exiled (we are not told where, but this clearly hints at a utopian enclave). Learning and the arts 'have gradually died out among this people'. Nothing beautiful or artistic is available in the shops. The population is listless, solemn, dull, and full of 'melancholy and dejection'. Though they have museums, clubs, shows, games, they seemingly spend much of their time wandering the streets with their hands in their pockets, or in the gymnasia—they are fitness fanatics. But 'all family life has died out', and with women's growing power, and the lack of any struggle to mate, much male sexual desire too. Yet 'the woman's vote' has also made wars illegal. Though travel is generally forbidden, this is not the dystopia of fear— except for intellectuals. But the majority suffer boredom rooted in regimentation and the suppression of difference. The author laments the decline of 'individual struggle' and 'incentives to personal activity'. Where 'all are equal, men are miserable because they are so; because all having equal claims to happiness, find

[211] Edward Bellamy, *Dr. Heidenhoff's Process* (1880; AMS Press, 1969), pp. 9, 99, 120–4.
[212] See Sylvia Strauss, 'Gender, Class and Race in Utopia', in Daphne Patai, ed., *Looking Backward* (University of Massachusetts Press, 1988), pp. 68–90, here, p. 85.
[213] Henry George, *Progress and Poverty* (1879; The Hogarth Press, 1953), pp. 202.
[214] Anna Bowman Dodd, *The Republic of the Future; or, Socialism a Reality* (Cassell & Co., 1887), pp. 8, 18, 20–2, 29, 35, 37–40, 43, 47–8.

life equally dull and aimless'. The projected equality of the socialists would thus be a dead end.[215]

A very different narrative would agitate the public's imagination for the next two decades. The *fin de siècle* epoch was dominated by Edward Bellamy's best-selling *Looking Backward 2000–1887* (1888).[216] Very much in the Saint-Simonian vein, this book placed industry at the core of human activity. It spawned not only a movement called Nationalism in the United States, but had a very substantial impact abroad.[217] Its success, one observer wrote, came because 'the majority of the thinking part of the public found in this book an echo of their own thought. In a simple and attractive way it set before the public mind the horrible iniquity of the present organization of society.'[218]

The scheme is described through the eyes of one Julian West, who falls asleep and awakens in Boston in 2000. Here, mostly through discussions with a Dr Leete and his obliging daughter, we see how the 'labour problem' has been solved. Following a lengthy concentration of the power of enormous syndicates or trusts, state management of industry and commerce and ownership of land commences. Effected without violence, a system emerges where all are educated to the age of twenty-one, then undergo three years of 'stringent discipline' at general labour, then work for twenty-one years more, and retire at forty-five, remaining available for emergencies until age fifty-five. The 'industrial army'—the concept is Saint-Simon's and Louis Blanc's, though the militarized ethos owes something to Carlyle's *Past and Present*—endeavours to match individual talents to positions.[219] Some changes of occupation are possible. But, despite the allure of lifelong employment, and the cornucopia of goods available, authoritarian elements clearly exist. If, in the existing society, Bellamy wrote, referring to the 'disciplinary and punitive side, the teeth and claws' of nationalism, there were 'many fine pleas for idleness', in 2000 the loafer 'would be stripped of all, and stand forth self-confessed'. Those refusing to work efficiently are,

---

[215] Dodd, *The Republic of the Future*, pp. 61, 66–8, 73, 75, 79, 83, 85. *Progress and Poverty* also features in Herman Hine Brinsmade's single-tax novel, *Utopia Achieved* (Broadway Publishing Co., 1912), which shows socialism failing in New Zealand, by contrast to the advantages of the single-tax system (p. 133.) See also Lewis Henry Behrens and Ignatius Singer, *The Story of My Dictatorship* (Henry George Foundation, 1934), where an elected dictatorship introduces George's land nationalization plans.

[216] On Bellamy see Sylvia E. Bowman, *The Year 2000: A Critical Biography of Edward Bellamy* (Bookman Associates, 1958). See also Patai, *Looking Backward 1988–1888*, and, on the text's reception, Kenneth M. Roemer, *Utopian Audiences: How Readers Locate Nowhere* (University of Massachusetts Press, 2003).

[217] See Sylvia E. Bowman et al., *Edward Bellamy Abroad: An American Prophet's Influence* (Twayne Publishers, 1962). Saint-Simon's likely influence is noted here (p. 55).

[218] Arthur Dudley Vinton, *Looking Further Backward* (Albany Book Co., 1890), p. 5.

[219] To its opponents, Blanc's organization of industry (1839) made government 'the Supreme Regulator of Industry', and invested it 'with great power' (*The Threatened Social Disintegration of France*, ed. James Ward (Richard Bentley, 1848), pp. 134, 156). The government was to set up social workshops which would eventually prevail over individual enterprises, but was not itself to benefit from their profits, or be a 'monopolist'. On Bellamy's knowledge of Blanc, see Sylvia Bowman, *Edward Bellamy* (Twayne, 1986), p. 53. Bellamy noted of Carlyle: 'Carlyle unfortunately no democrat and so a poor historian of Revolution, but must be read': Arthur E. Morgan, *Edward Bellamy* (Columbia University Press, 1944), p. 146. But Bellamy's idea of the 'industrial army' is clearly linked to Carlyle's 'organisation of labour' (p. 316).

in the spirit of many utopias of the period, 'sentenced to solitary imprisonment on bread and water' until they get the message. (This was altered in the second edition to the slightly less draconian 'cut off from all human society'.) Even the lame, blind, and crippled do something in the 'invalid corps', and no one can survive outside the system. It is not 'socialist', in this view—Bellamy wrote W. D. Howells that he 'never could well stomach' the word—but oriented, if anything, towards law and order and middle-class economic control. Nor is it 'democratic' insofar as universal suffrage has been replaced by a more elitist scheme. But it was intended to be 'wholly and enthusiastically American and patriotic' in outlook.[220]

Thus, 'Bellamy offered a collectivist alternative to working-class socialism which substituted bureaucratic order from above, government by an elite which abolished universal suffrage and imposed military discipline on the unruly workers.' (A group of retired military officers formed the first Bellamy club.)[221] In 2000, many live in great cities like Boston. Industrial pollution is a thing of the past. Money has been abolished, and bankers too. All use 'credit cards', which reflect an equal share corresponding to their proportion of the annual product, and some inheritance is permitted. But this credit is not otherwise transferable, and some spendthrifts have their expenditure controlled. The shops are full of goods, though no advertising is used. The society is highly advanced technically, with music piped into houses. Washing is done in public laundries, and cooking in public kitchens. All power is electric, and labour-saving inventions proliferate. There are no jails, there being no motive for most forms of crime, and 'atavism' is treated in hospitals.[222]

For the American working classes of 1890 this did not appear a bad deal at all. In the United States the Nationalist movement lasted until about 1894, when it merged into Populism and other fringe political trends. To its adherents, Bellamy represented justice for small capitalists and workers increasingly driven to the wall by all-powerful competitors. Its military ethos hinted at an ideal of self-sacrifice and camaraderie which appealed to many, 'The soldier's business' being, Bellamy thought, 'the only one in which, from the start, men throw away the purse and reject every sordid standard of merit and achievement.'[223]

To his critics, however, Bellamy's scheme hinted at disaster. Its mandatory labour system, restrictions on democracy, and quasi-military discipline would be read as anticipating National Socialism and Soviet state capitalism by writers like

[220] Bellamy to Howells, 17 June 1888, in 'Mutual Indebtedness: Unpublished Letters of Edward Bellamy to W. D. Howells', *Harvard Library Bulletin*, 12 (1958), 370; Edward Bellamy, *Looking Backward 2000–1887* (1st edn, George Routledge & Sons, 1890), p. 98; *Looking Backward 2000–1887* (2nd edn, Frederick Warne & Co., 1891), p. 75; Edward Bellamy, *Edward Bellamy Speaks Again!* (The Peerage Press, 1937), pp. 78, 80; Susan M. Matarese, *American Foreign Policy and the Utopian Imagination* (University of Massachusetts Press, 2001), p. 25 (which also details the utopian dimension of the American imperial vision of this period).

[221] Arthur Lipow, *Authoritarian Socialism in America: Edward Bellamy & the Nationalist Movement* (University of California Press, 1982), pp. 3, 16–17, 22, 30. Theosophists played a role in the movement too.

[222] Bellamy, *Looking Backward 2000–1887* (2nd edn), pp. 51–2, 58, 69, 71, 81, 115. A good modern edition which explains the changes made by Bellamy (pp. 198–220) is by Matthew Beaumont (Oxford University Press, 2007).

[223] Quoted in Lipow, *Authoritarian Socialism in America*, p. 85.

Lewis Mumford as late as the 1960s. Its authoritarian qualities are here epitomized in Bellamy's supposed assertion that 'If a man refuses to accept the authority of the state and the inevitability of industrial service, he loses all his rights as a human being.'[224] John Kasson thought Bellamy's system 'could rigidify into a prison'.[225] So it remains unclear as to which side of the utopia/dystopia divide Bellamy belongs.

At the time there were many types of response to Bellamy.[226] These are often portrayed as essentially reactionary, though given the authoritarian scheme proposed in *Looking Backward* some of its critics might seem less conservative than libertarian. Kenneth Roemer, who describes Bellamy as using fiction as 'only a sugarcoating for the author's realistic blueprints for the future', categorizes eight dystopias and nine anti-utopias in a period in which the utopian novel was perhaps the dominant genre in the United States, with over 150 novels having some form of utopian content.[227] Lyman Tower Sargent's indispensable bibliography, which lists journals as well as separately published titles for this period, indicates that perhaps sixty might be classed as dystopian.[228]

Amongst these works, Bellamy's imitators generally projected variations on a sequence of the existing system descending further into greater extremes of wealth and poverty, provoking substantial transformation, violent or otherwise, resulting in an improved system. Plutocracy and the ever-present ideological ethos of American individualism are key targets here. In Samuel Walker's *The Reign of Selfishness: A Story of Concentrated Wealth* (1891), for instance, the epoch's motto is 'every man for himself'. One giant corporation, the Great United Supply Company, dominates the nation until it is finally overthrown.[229] In Samuel Crocker's *That Island: A Political Romance* (1892), bankers exploit the working classes 'to a degree almost shameful and humiliating' before reforms occur.[230] *What's the World Coming To?* (1893) depicts all the world prospering after Bellamy's system is successfully adopted, except Ireland, which, having achieved Home Rule, refuses

---

[224] Mumford, *The Myth of the Machine*, vol. 2, p. 218. This quote is, in fact, not in Bellamy, but is from Marie Louise Berneri, *Journey through Utopia* (Routledge & Kegan Paul, 1950), p. 249.

[225] John F. Kasson, *Civilizing the Machine: Technology and Republican Values in America 1776–1900* (Viking Press, 1976), p. 202.

[226] See, generally, Francis Robert Shor, *Utopianism and Radicalism in a Reforming America 1888–1918* (Greenwood Press, 1997) (which sees dystopia in this period only as commencing with Jack London's *The Iron Heel* (Mills & Boon, 1908), p. 68) and Charles J. Rooney Jr, *Dreams and Visions: A Study of American Utopias 1865–1917* (Greenwood Press, 1985) (which describes no dystopias in this period). On technology in particular in this period see Howard P. Segal, *Technological Utopianism in American Culture* (University of Chicago Press, 1985), esp. pp. 19–44.

[227] Roemer, *America as Utopia*, pp. 329–30. See also Roemer, *The Obsolete Necessity*, pp. 3, 194–209, which offers an annotated bibliography of American utopias in this period; Edward Spann, *Brotherly Tomorrows: Movements for a Co-operative Society in America 1820–1920* (Columbia University Press, 1989); Vernon Lewis Parrington, *American Dreams: A Study of American Utopias* (Russell & Russell, 1964), pp. 69–97.

[228] The starting point for all work in this field, Lyman Tower Sargent's *British and American Utopian Literature, 1516–1985: An Annotated, Chronological Bibliography* (Garland, 1988), pp. 50–156, lists titles from 1850–1914. See <openpublishing.psu.edu/utopia>.

[229] [Samuel Walker], *The Reign of Selfishness: A Story of Concentrated Wealth* (M. K. Pelletreau, 1891), pp. 14, 372.

[230] Theodore Oceanic Islet [Samuel Crocker], *That Island: A Political Romance* (C. E. Streeter, 1892), p. 10.

to join the International Federation and finds no one will trade with her, resulting in economic collapse.[231] James Galloway's *John Harvey: A Tale of the Twentieth Century* (1897) portrays a growing and eventually victorious Nationality movement which triumphs after great trusts monopolize American business and the poor have become desperate.[232] In William Stanley Child's *The Legal Revolution of 1902* (1898), which covers only the fifteen years after 1897, the class despotism of the oligarchical trusts is finally overthrown, and an 'ideal and perfect Socialism' is established, though not before the plutocrats enlist Britain's help to suppress the radical movement. Here too a separate 'black republic' is organized.[233] In Albert Adams Merrill's *The Great Awakening* (1899) the 'Money Republic' is finally overthrown in 2021 after some forty years of a 'Chaotic Era' of destruction, discontent, and mob rule, and private property in land is abolished.[234]

The anti-Bellamy dystopias typically portray a revolution-gone-awry scenario where labour overthrowing capital is the starting point. Such texts usually aimed to demonstrate, as Arthur Dudley Vinton put it, 'wherein the Bellamy Nationalism would prove disastrously weak'. To Vinton, this was a projection of the 'whole tendency of Nationalism . . . to wipe out individualism and to train the individual to rely in all matters upon his rulers', leaving the nation so weakened that Chinese conquest results.[235] The United States collapses owing to an influx of foreign anarchists and socialists in John Bachelder's *A.D. 2050* (1890), and a communistic system introduced after a 'reign of riot and bloodshed' in the nineteenth century wastes resources, energy, and mental stamina in the name of the collective.[236] In W. W. Satterlee's *Looking Backward and What I Saw* (1890), the Nationalist system in the year 2101 emerges from a 'reign of terror' following a revolution in 1975 instigated by drunken foreign agitators. Satterlee conceded that the corporations' despotic power had resulted in little less than 'chattel slavery'. Nationalism introduces measures of economic justice, but the cities soon succumb to corruption and amusements 'provided on a magnificent scale by the government'. The system is overthrown. Then the narrative turns out to be a dream.[237] In H. B. Salisbury's *The Birth of Freedom* (1890) a wave of revolutionary destruction precedes the introduction of 'co-operative nationalism', clearly indicating, for some, nationalism's 'fear of the workers'.[238] In J. W. Roberts' *Looking Within* (1891), great wars have resulted

[231] W. Graham Moffat and John White, *What's the World Coming To? A Novel of the Twenty-First Century, Founded on the Fads, Facts, and Fiction of the Nineteenth* (Elliot Stock, 1893), pp. 112–13.
[232] [James M. Galloway], *John Harvey: A Tale of the Twentieth Century* (Charles H. Kerr, 1897), pp. 241, 253, 360, 406.
[233] William Stanley Child, *The Legal Revolution of 1902* (Charles H. Kerr & Co., 1898), pp. 122–4, 165, 198.
[234] Albert Adams Merrill, *The Great Awakening: The Story of the Twenty-Second Century* (George Book Publishing Co., 1899), pp. 49, 69, 131, 170.
[235] Vinton, *Looking Further Backward*, pp. 6, 28–9.
[236] [John Bachelder], *A.D. 2050: Electrical Development at Atlantis* (The Bancroft Co., 1890), pp. 6–7, 41.
[237] W. W. Satterlee, *Looking Backward and What I Saw* (Harrison & Smith, 1890), pp. 28, 42, 46, 159, 162.
[238] H. B. Salisbury, *The Birth of Freedom* (The Humboldt Publishing Co., 1890), p. 74; Lipow, *Authoritarian Socialism in America*, p. 210.

from revolutions in Europe.[239] 'Julian West''s *My Afterdream: A Sequel to the Late Mr. Edward Bellamy's Looking Backwards* (1900) portrays a successful Bellamy system as a paradise for working men, but not for those with higher aspirations, for whom it is more like a madhouse. It predicts overpopulation and overbureaucratization would ruin the scheme.[240] Originally published in German, Conrad Wilbrandt's *Mr. East's Experiences in Mr. Bellamy's World: Records of the Years 2001 and 2002* (1891) takes Bellamy's proposals to imply the maintenance of children by the state, and laments 'how cruel it is to rob parents of what is the source of their deepest happiness'. It also portrays increasing compulsion in the allocation of employment, since few want to be farmers or miners. The system verges on collapse by the end of the novel.[241]

One of the most influential of the anti-Bellamy tracts was Richard Michaelis' *A Sequel to Looking Backward* (1891). Here communism is portrayed as 'a failure whenever established without a religious basis'. Bellamy's system is accused of promoting favouritism, corruption, and 'an inequality in many respects more oppressive than the present state of things'. His scheme of equal pay, Michaelis alleged, would enrich 'the awkward, stupid, and lazy people, with the proceeds of the work of the clever and industrious'. The administrators of labour have 'well nigh absolute power' and naturally suppress dissent. Bellamy's doctrines have also encouraged more radical communists, who aim to abolish religion, marriage, and all personal property. Political influence has become 'the almighty factor in every affair of our lives'. Yet Michaelis did not favour the existing system. He provided instead his own utopia, where mutual production associations employ former owners as managers, as Mill had suggested. Landholding is restricted to forty acres. The government owns railways, telegraphs, and forests, thus uniting 'the few advantages of communism with the benefits of competition'.[242] So here dystopia criticizes utopia while proposing another, social democratic variant thereon.

And so the debate continued, as Michaelis, too, responded to his critics.[243] Bellamy's own late novel, *Equality* (1897), has been seen as moving towards a more democratic governmental ideal, and removing some of the punitive measures of *Looking Backward* by permitting the recalcitrant to withdraw to reservations to farm.[244] Elsewhere, he also proposed having all children reared by the state in order to eliminate the anxiety and sadness associated with parental love.[245] L. A. Geissler's *Looking Beyond* denied Michaelis' accusation that the system

[239] J. W. Roberts, *Looking Within: The Misleading Tendencies of 'Looking Backward'* (A. S. Barnes & Co., 1891), p. 97.
[240] Julian West, *My Afterdream: A Sequel to the Late Mr. Edward Bellamy's Looking Backwards* (T. Fisher Unwin, 1900), pp. 93, 101, 158, 239.
[241] Conrad Wilbrandt, *Mr. East's Experiences in Mr. Bellamy's World: Records of the Years 2001 and 2002* (Harper & Bros., 1891), pp. 32, 68–72, 237.
[242] Richard Michaelis, *A Sequel to Looking Backward, or, 'Looking Further Forward'* (William Reeves, 1891), p. iii, v, 34–5, 48, 50, 95–6, 108.
[243] E.g., L. A. Geissler, *Looking Beyond: A Sequel to 'Looking Backward', by Edward Bellamy, and An Answer to 'Looking Further Forward', by Richard Michaelis* (William Reeves, 1891), which revolves around denying Michaelis' assertion that more radical communist attacks on the family and religion would result from introducing Bellamy's system (p. 19).
[244] Edward Bellamy, *Equality* (Appleton-Century, 1937), p. 41; Bowman, *The Year 2000*, p. 143.
[245] Bowman, *The Year 2000*, p. 109.

would quickly become corrupt. It also envisioned some being permitted to live in the woods outside the system.[246] But for Bellamy's opponents, all the Bellamy and socialist utopias were, of course, dystopias, where collectivism is introduced and then inevitably fails.

Some anti-Bellamy novels had as their aim preserving something like the status quo. Yet others, following Michaelis, offer radical alternatives both to Bellamy and the existing system. In Frederick U. Adams' *President John Smith: The Story of a Peaceful Revolution* (1896), for instance, a new system avoids both the Bellamyite and anarchist extremes but abolishes middlemen and small factories, sells all produce through its own depots, and regulates wages.[247] In J. W. Roberts' *Looking Within: The Misleading Tendencies of 'Looking Backward' Made Manifest* (1893), revolutions have destroyed most European monarchies. America sinks into lawlessness, bribery, and drunkenness. Some profit-sharing enterprises, however, have avoided the worst aspects of the old capitalism as well as the new poverty and debauchery. It is explicitly denied that these are 'Utopia'. They are the humane capitalist alternative to exploitation on the one hand and socialistic expropriation on the other. Then, thirty-five years on, another war has killed 65 million people. Now a 'paternal government' owns all property, and restricts travel by reducing the rations of the peripatetic. 'Our people are strangers to each other', as a result, there being little intercourse between towns and regions. Poverty has notionally been abolished and most people are well fed, clothed, and housed. But there is still destitution and crime since some squander their wages and are 'selfish and sinful'. The poor drink, gamble, and indulge in orgies, producing 'the same old hell on earth of former times'. Human nature remains unaltered. 'Men cannot be reformed by either bread or law', we are told. Chastisements are offered to those who assumed that 'appliances which have no moral qualities or properties in themselves could, nonetheless, impart these to men'. One critic of the system describes it as 'a vast system of human slavery' in which 'manly independence' has been exchanged for food, clothing, and houses.[248]

Yet Roberts' alternative is not unrestricted capitalism, though it is perhaps the status quo before plutocracy. Roberts arranges for his narrator to meet Bellamy's Mr West at the Boston house of Dr Leete, who is described as neglecting the pitfalls of the new system (in *Looking Backward*). We see that foreigners are blamed for most of the 'discontent and hostilities' which produced bloodshed. Now, since the government owns all property, no incentives for new inventions or progress exist. Pay for mandatory equal work is low, which further restricts travel and encourages isolation. No one is allowed to visit anyone else during the eight working hours. Houses must be vacated when their chief productive occupant reaches the age of forty-five. The idle and indolent are rewarded equally with the diligent and industrious. In agriculture, about half are in each group, but the urban classes are

---

[246] Geissler, *Looking Beyond*, pp. 34, 40–1,

[247] Frederick U. Adams, *President John Smith: The Story of a Peaceful Revolution* (Charles H. Kerr & Co., 1896), pp. 275–7.

[248] Roberts, *Looking Within*, pp. 97, 109, 111–14, 140, 150–4, 161–2, 166–9, 171–7.

portrayed as parasitic 'pensioned paupers of the government'. Thus it is proposed that cities as currently composed be abolished (Morris would have approved), or converted into retirement areas, with paupers being compelled to become produ-cers, especially farmers. This is thus a radical agrarian counter-utopian proposal regarded as no 'more visionary or revolutionary than the one which makes the government owner of the man and the products of his labor'. So here we have dystopia, anti-utopia, and utopia all rolled into one thematic bundle.[249]

But then this system, too, threatens to crumble as the population increases, productivity falls, and the number of miners, fishermen, and farmers declines. The government is forced to compel movement into these occupations, thus abolishing the right to choose one's trade. This achieves temporary alleviation. Then a new radical group proposes a still more extreme equality in which men and women are 'molded' from infancy to be as similar as possible. Attempted in Massachusetts, this proves predictably disastrous. No one can tell anyone apart any more, and children, husbands, and wives become hopelessly intermixed. Finally, it is conceded that 'governmental care of all things removes all incentive to activity or desire to excel', and the system is abolished. In its place a new Constitution restricts landed property to twenty-five acres per family, introduces a progressive income tax, employs idlers in public works, and prohibits the very wealthy from attaining high judicial and political positions. Many public utilities are privatized, but not support for the aged.[250] Again, thus, utopia and dystopia are interwoven at a number of levels, evading simplistic classification, and making it difficult to speak of any 'classical' utopia or dystopia as such.

One of the more successful responses to Bellamy, Ignatius Donnelly's *Caesar's Column: A Story of the Twentieth Century* (1890), was more pessimistic than Ro-berts.[251] Set in 1988, it looked a century forward to a 'rotten age' riddled with corruption. The 'column' epitomizes the epoch's reversion to barbarism: it is a pyramid of corpses encased in concrete after the final battle in New York City, which now has 10 million inhabitants and stretches to Philadelphia. The narrator, Gabriel Weltstein, is a sheep farmer from Swiss-settled Uganda who endeavours to circumvent the wool monopoly by direct trade. Technologically the new society is sophisticated, with airship travel, electric mass transit systems, and cheap heating supplied from deep hot-water springs. Socially, however, it is extraordinarily oppres-sive. A 100 million-strong 'Brotherhood of Destruction' composed of anarchist revolutionaries led by Caesar Lomellini vies against a powerful consortium of 'almost all Hebrew' plutocrats (mostly bankers) known as the Oligarchy. The latter are evidently motivated in part by revenge for age-old persecution of their race. They are 'as merciless to the Christian as the Christian had been to them'. (But some of the Brotherhood's leaders are also Jews.) The women of this group are wanton, 'bold,

---

[249] Ibid., pp. 180–1, 184–7, 191, 193, 196, 221.
[250] Ibid., pp. 220–3, 239, 265–6, 269–71.
[251] Donnelly (1831–1901) was a Philadelphia-born Catholic who early lost his religious faith. He went on to become a lawyer and Minnesota state politician, becoming a congressman in 1863. In the 1870s, he was involved with a number of populist land movements and then in the 1880s became a best-selling author with *Atlantis: The Antediluvian World* ((Harper & Brothers, 1882).

penetrating, immodest'. The men are cunning and heartless, with 'all the marks of shrewdness and energy; a forceful and capable race'. They have corrupted the electoral process by bribery. They buy any women they choose; much of the novel's narrative is arranged around such an episode. They also propose eliminating 10 million of their opponents by poison bombs. 'Cruelty, craft and destruction' thus characterize the upper 30 per cent, and 'suffering, wretchedness, sin and shame' the lower 70 per cent of the population. 'Greed and gluttony' have destroyed the possibility of a more humane civilization, and are contrasted to 'the grand doctrine of brotherly love, enunciated by the gentle Nazarene'. The proletarian enemies of this system, too, are evidently beginning to regress, in Darwinian terms, towards cruder species types, 'the condition of the Australian savages'. But there is no suggestion that their overthrow of the system promises any utopia.[252]

As Nicholas Ruddick indicates, classifying Donnelly's novel is thus challenging. New York is the utopia only of the plutocratic few, many of whom live to be a hundred. Its streets swarm with ragged beggars who are often run over by the carriages of rich 'aristocrats'. A Social Darwinist pessimism pervades parts of the novel, though this is also the mentality, where it serves as an apology for plutocratic inhumanity, which Donnelly is keen to resist. A 'Darwin Hotel' is described as a kind of modern Babylon, a cornucopia of opulent consumption where hedonism reaches new peaks, or descends into new depths. Euthanasia clinics exist in every public square or park, where those ready to end their lives poison themselves. There is a hint, too, that in such a city much of the population is simply 'a superfluity'. 'The Garden in the Mountains' portrayed in the final chapter is a pastoral respite which, in many respects, epitomizes growing resentment of the east and city life by America's rural heartland. A chapter entitled 'Gabriel's Utopia' also hints at some solutions: abolishing interest on money and corporations; establishing a maximum on property in both money and land; great investment in public works; ending the gold and silver standards; and municipalizing all public services, including law and medicine. Marx is mentioned but dismissed. Religion, as such, is not a solution. The system is eventually over-thrown, though the leaders of the Brotherhood pillage the spoils. Caesar is killed, but the narrator is obliged to flee the 'barbarians' who have conquered Europe, and eventually kill three-quarters of humanity. In Africa, a high wall is erected to exclude the rest of the population. A new republic is founded on universal suffrage, compul-sory education, state ownership of roads, railways, and mines. It abolishes interest on money. A minimum wage compatible with a decent life is combined with some regulation of employment. All useful inventions are purchased for the good of the people. A new assembly is constructed composed of three branches, one representing the people, another the mercantile class, the third the educated. Trade is limited to nations with a similarly high standard of living.[253] So we end with a utopia, but it is again only for the very few. The rest of humanity must suffer its fate.

---

[252] But he did write a eutopia entitled *The Golden Bottle* (Sampson Low & Co., 1892).

[253] Edmund Boisgilbert [Ignatius Donnelly], *Caesar's Column* (1890; Wesleyan University Press, 2003), pp. xxxi, 15, 17, 19, 27–9, 33, 35, 56–7, 80–91, 112, 125, 128–9, 197, 211, 218, 223, 228, 231–5, 239. On Donnelly see David D. Anderson, *Ignatius Donnelly* (Twayne, 1980).

Donnelly inspired George Griffith's *The Angel of the Revolution: A Tale of the Coming Terror* (1893), which portrays a Russian tyranny threatening Europe. Aerial warfare has become common. A Brotherhood of Freedom, or Terrorists, aims to overthrow the Russian government. The town of Kronstadt is attacked with the narrator's air vessel with the aim of establishing peace on earth. After a vast war in 1904–5 which kills millions, and which Russia nearly wins, the Brotherhood seizes American military resources in a revolution. The great capitalists who compose the 'Ring' are tried along with the president and other officials, and sent into exile, their property being confiscated for the common good. The Russians invade Britain, but are finally repulsed by the Brotherhood's armies. Tsar Nicholas is sentenced to Siberian exile. All fortifications are destroyed and standing armies abolished. A new European Constitution recognizes the supremacy of the Anglo-Saxon Federation in foreign policy. All European land becomes state property and a progressive income tax is introduced. All rents are paid to the state, and none can live as landlords, only as cultivators.[254] Here we are back closer to Bellamy.

A late instance of the anti-Bellamy novel is David Parry's anti-collectivist satire, *The Scarlet Empire* (1906). This portrays a social democracy inhabited by the fish-people of Atlantis. Here clothing is identical, and the use of the arms and length of fingernails is standardized. The 'individual is merely one atom of the whole. The majority knows what is good for all, and when it speaks the individual must yield his opinion.' The population is restricted to speaking only 1,000 words per day because 'an unrestrained tongue leads frequently to crime and conspiracy'. 'Inspectors are everywhere' to ensure compliance; they are a quarter of the population. The system produces 'a dull, listless, lethargic race' without 'a glint of interest, hope or purpose' in their faces. So relentless is the pursuit of equality that it had 'founded a despotism so complete that it was stifling all the faculties which distinguish man from the brute'. Indeed, 'the people are no longer human beings—they are beasts'. The state itself is likened to 'a Frankenstein, which, while crushing in its grasp the souls of the people, was itself without a soul'. The introduction of Bellamy-like credit cards bring a tyranny of the frugal over the profligate. The historical antecedents of the modern dystopia are all trotted out here. The regime is compared to Satan's kingdom and 'the government of a prison', and savage mobs, the 'fiendish multitude', 'yell like a million demons' as they feed 'atavars' who rebel against the system to the kraken, 'a monster as big as a whale with huge tentacles'. This 'proves that there is a reversal of type in Atlantis, a return to the traits of ancient ancestry'. Children are raised in common 'like chickens in incubators', and the population subsist only by smoking the 'lethe weed'. Socialism, we are told, offers no 'pride of possession, the glory of attainment, the sharpening of wits against wits, the joys of true friendship, or the yearnings of love'.[255]

* * * *

[254] George Griffith, *The Angel of the Revolution: A Tale of the Coming Terror* (1893; Routledge, 1998), pp. 285, 368, 386–7.
[255] David M. Parry, *The Scarlet Empire* (The Bobbs-Merrill Co., 1906), pp. 9–10, 17–18, 29, 69, 80–1, 107, 120, 173, 206–7, 258, 262–4.

Texts speculating on dystopia thus portray a surprising range of options to the reader. In some novels, utopian spaces coexist spatially within dystopias or degraded normality. Others offer a sequence of events which mix utopian and dystopian possibilities. Often some rebellion occurs and the previous system is restored or some improved version thereof is introduced. Many texts portray a lengthy period of conflict, usually in the present and near future, out of which emerges a more just regime.[256] So a common narrative sequence is N (normality) → D (dystopia) → either U (utopia, a greatly improved state of affairs) or N+ (a somewhat or even considerably improved normality).

Bellamy provides a prototype for this trend. But there were many variants on the theme. In Walter Doty Reynolds' *Mr. Jonnemacher's Machine: The Port to which We Drifted* (1898), set in the twenty-first century, new machines are invented which displace much of the nation's labour but enrich a few capitalists. Then their inventor is assassinated and a new 'paternal form' of government, akin to 'a benign fatherhood providing for his whole family' is introduced, which regulates all work, and supply and demand.[257] In Thomas Dixon's *Comrades: A Story of Social Adventure in California* (1909), a socialist colony is established on an island off California, which degenerates into a dictatorship with prison-style labour and secret police. But the regime is overthrown by US troops from the mainland.[258] In Frank Rosewater's *'96: A Romance of Utopia* (1894), a new utopian order is imposed upon anarchic peoples whose economies have collapsed, usually through private greed.[259] In L. P. Gratacap's *The Mayor of New York: A Romance of Days to Come* (1910), an armed mob besieges the Pope in decadent Europe, so a disciple brings him to the United States to help thwart anarchist extremism but also to assist 'sane and moderate' socialists.[260] The present is also dystopian in George Allan England's *The Air Trust* (1915), which portrays an evil billionaire, the morphine addict Isaac Flint, who, with his partner Waldron, conspires to monopolize the very air people breathe by withdrawing oxygen from the air and then selling it back. Carrying, as the author described it, 'the monopolistic principle to its logical conclusion', the aim is thus to 'bring the human race wallowing to our feet in helpless bondage'. Yet the plans fall into the hands of the 'thoroughly class conscious' socialist Gabriel Armstrong. By coincidence he rescues Flint's daughter Catherine after a car crash, and converts her to socialism. They engineer a general strike, and the oxygen-extracting factory is destroyed. Flint and Waldron die and the promise of the 'Great Emancipation' looms.[261]

[256] E.g., H. Pereira Mendes, *Looking Ahead: Twentieth Century Happenings* (F. Tennyson Neely, 1899).
[257] Daedalus Haldane [Walter Doty Reynolds], *Mr. Jonnemacher's Machine: The Post to which We Drifted* (Knickerbocker Book Co., 1898), pp. 27, 165, 249–50.
[258] Thomas Dixon, *Comrades: A Story of Social Adventure in California* (Doubleday, Page & Co., 1909), pp. 118, 224, 306, 309, 318–19.
[259] E.g., Frank Rosewater, *'96: A Romance of Utopia: Presenting a Solution of the Labor Problem, a New God and a New Religion* (The Utopia Co., 1894), pp. 223–60.
[260] L. P. Gratacap, *The Mayor of New York: A Romance of Days to Come* (G. W. Dillingham Co., 1910), pp. 446–7, 457, 465.
[261] George Allan England, *The Air Trust* (Phil Wagner, 1915), pp. i, 18, 50, 71, 83, 128, 137–8, 209, 230, 235, 259, 317, 333.

Some texts hover ambiguously between praising and condemning collectivism. An interesting instance is A. P. Russell's *Sub-Coelum: A Sky-Built Human World* (1893), which describes an 'ideal republic' of small estates, general equality, and the discouragement of great wealth. Here, 'there was little of what might be called private life in the entire commonwealth'. The people

> discouraged if they did not prohibit privacy. Their remarkable individualism, ingenuousness and perception—almost prescience—revealed all and saw all. Mind and conduct reading had reached such perfection that wrong-doing was nearly impossible. Blinds on doors and windows were not so much to elude observation as to exclude and regulate the light.

And yet we are told, too, that 'Their greatest happiness was in intellectual and moral activity', that personal independence 'was a marked characteristic of the population', that 'Even the average man was not commonplace from conformity', and that 'no attempt was ever made to produce social equality; that had been left exclusively to self-regulation'.[262] We wonder if the great individualist/collectivist tension has finally been reconciled.

We can conclude this section by introducing another biting satire on the theme of equality, Paul Haedicke's *The Equalities of Para-Para* (1895). Here an African traveller discovers a land where the Equalites obsessively cultivate similarity, which includes disfiguring faces to produce warts, scars, and blemishes. They live entirely in public 'open to the views of all', and always walk in uneven numbers because 'the infallible vote of the majority' decides everything. Here, however, a group called 'Sophs' dwell as hermits, 'secretly countenance the crime of individuality', have to do the hard labour, and are not allowed to speak with the Equalites, whom they believe to be 'perfectly happy, after the manner in which brutes are'. The Equalite system emerges during the rule of the Trusts, when, during a great struggle between capital and labour, the workers become obsessed by the 'insane idea that nothing further was necessary to bring about human happiness than to make all goods common property'. When the labour organizations gain power, the economy collapses, and much of the population end up living like 'ragged beasts . . . among the rubbish in the cellars of the dismantled houses'. Eventually one Para emerges to found a new order, which includes prohibiting machines which take men's work as 'not compatible with equality; on the contrary the individuals who possessed it would have a natural advantage. His idea was to make the people into machines.' After twenty years he also has all books burned. From this order, the first Soph also emerges. The Equalites themselves are described as 'like a bag of rice' who do not even quarrel as there is nothing to argue about, for 'No one thought of anything, no one strove for any thing, either good or bad.' And 'Love and friendship were as unknown to the Equalites as hate and enmity.' Eventually, they kill all the Sophs and the narrator has to flee.[263] No hope here, then.

---

[262] A. P. Russell, *Sub-Coelum: A Sky-Built Human World* (Houghton, Mifflin & Co., 1893), pp. 59, 203, 206, 210, 213.

[263] Paul Haedicke, *The Equalities of Para-Para* (Schuldt-Gathmann Co., 1895), pp. 29, 33, 42, 58, 90, 98, 101, 106–9, 117, 136–7. A similar parody of egalitarianism in this period is offered in Paolo Mantegazza, *The Year 3000* (1897; University of Nebraska Press, 2010), pp. 68–72.

Dystopian Themes: Race, Eugenics, Empire, Feminism

Besides economics and politics, a number of other themes recur in dystopian texts of this period. The imperial expansionist theme is a common one now, implying dystopias for those so incorporated. Henry Hartshorne's *1931: A Glance at the Twentieth Century* (1881) has Canada, Mexico, and Cuba joining as US states.[264] In John Jacob Astor's *A Journey in Other Worlds: A Romance of the Future* (1894), Canada first merges with the United States, which no nation thinks of opposing as its 'moral power for good is tremendous'. Eventually, English speakers possess half the globe, with indigenous natives and the Spanish and Portuguese elements of the southern Americas conveniently dying out, their places being taken by 'the more progressive Anglo-Saxons'.[265] Stanley Waterloo's *Armageddon: A Tale of Love, War, and Invention* (1898) portrays a future Anglo-American alliance which ends war.[266]

Future war novels in the United States prior to 1914 tended to focus on the Chinese and Japanese. One of the earliest is Pierton Dooner's *Last Days of the Republic* (1880), where Chinese immigration results in a race war and eventual Chinese victory, with her flag floating over the Capitol.[267] In other novels, Britain is defeated by the United States for refusing to cede Canada to them, and the monarchy is overthrown.[268] Some of the imperial fantasies are extreme. Written during the Spanish–American War, Arthur Bird's *Looking Forward* (1899) announces that the United States, 'in years to come, will govern the entire western hemisphere', and further envisions Russia's conquest of China, Britain's rule over Africa and India continuing, and France, defeated by Germany in 1945, becoming virtually a province of the latter.[269] Racism in general is hardly uncommon in utopias of this period, and some utopias were anti-Semitic. In Alexander Craig's *Ionia, Land of Wise Men and Fair Women* (1898), for instance, a law is passed that 'no person of Jewish blood should ever be allowed to marry in Ionia, and so the whole tribe died out and passed away for ever'.[270]

Eugenics themes are perhaps slightly less evident in American novels than in British texts but are certainly still present. Racial segregation is certainly common. As early as 1836, the 'race problem' is solved in Mary Griffith's *Three Hundred Years Hence* by returning slaves to Africa after compensating their American

---

[264] Henry Hartshorne, *1931: A Glance at the Twentieth Century* (E. Claxton & Co., 1881), pp. 6–7.
[265] John Jacob Astor, *A Journey in Other Worlds: A Romance of the Future* (D. Appleton & Co., 1894), pp. 39, 42, 74.
[266] Stanley Waterloo, *Armageddon: A Tale of Love, War, and Invention* (Rand, McNally & Co., 1898), pp. 240, 259.
[267] Pierton W. Dooner, *Last Days of the Republic* (Alta California Publishing House, 1880), pp. 83–101, 256.
[268] Lieut. Alvarado M. Fuller, *A.D. 2000: A Novel* (Laird & Lee, 1890), pp. 203–4, 236.
[269] Arthur Bird, *Looking Forward: A Dream of the United States of the Americas in 1999* (L. C. Childs, 1899), pp. 3, 47, 113.
[270] Alexander Craig, *Ionia, Land of Wise Men and Fair Women* (E. A. Weeks, 1898), p. 222.

owners.[271] In John Jacob Astor's *A Journey in Other Worlds* (1894) the 'dark elements' die out or are deported to Jupiter, to be replaced by 'the more progressive Anglo-Saxons'.[272] In Chauncey Thomas' *The Crystal Button; or, Adventures of Paul Prognosis in the Forty-Ninth Century* (1891), we are told that there are few diseases left in the future. For no diseased or deformed people likely to communicate 'serious imperfection of any kind to offspring is ever allowed to marry', and they are in fact sterilized.[273] Similarly, in Will Harben's *The Land of the Changing Sun* (1894), each generation improves on the last, until no one remains who has a 'loathsome hereditary disease' or who is not 'thoroughly sound'. In this utopia, 'All our conveniences, the excellence of our products, our great inventions are the result.' And yet it is reported that the medical men who vote on 'fitness' have unjustly buried alive hundreds.[274] In John Bachelder's *A.D. 2050* (1890) the deaf, dumb, blind, and idiotic (as the text describes them) are not allowed to marry.[275] The Harvard philosopher William McDougall also projected the island of 'Eugenia', where, unlike Plato's *Republic*, the family would be preserved while 'persons of superior strains' would be matched, with their children then 'brought up with the noble ambition to serve the world'.[276]

Population control is also an issue in a number of other texts. In Alfred Denton Cridge's *Utopia: Or, The History of an Extinct Planet* (1884) a relatively benign form of socialism evolves, with liberties of speech, the press, and so on. But the population declines slowly and eventually the society dies out, apparently partly because of overzealous birth control.[277] In William Salisbury's satire, *The Squareheads: The Story of a Socialized State* (1929), where the garbage collectors are 'Socialism's chief ideal typified', eugenics is used to make people 'square', or undeviating from majority opinion (an interesting anticipation of the later beat generation term).[278] As late as 1933, too, in Robert Herrick's *Sometime*, a utopia which emerges out of the slavery of the Machine Age, only a small minority are permitted to bear children 200 years after a 'War to End Civilization' and the advance of an enormous ice cap.[279]

This is also the period in which feminism, usually treated as an aspect of utopia, makes its first prominent foray into dystopia. In some utopias women lose the vote when they marry.[280] But women wreak revenge for male tyranny elsewhere. In Mary E. Lane's *Mizora: A Prophecy* (1880–1), the narrator discovers a world

---

[271] As discussed by Jean Pfaelzer in Mary E. Bradley Lane, *Mizora: A Prophecy* (Syracuse University Press, 1990), p. xxxiii.

[272] Astor, *A Journey in Other Worlds*, p. 74.

[273] Chauncey Thomas, *The Crystal Button; or, Adventures of Paul Prognosis in the Forty-Ninth Century* (George Routledge & Sons, 1891), pp. 42–5.

[274] Will N. Harben, *The Land of the Changing Sun* (The Merriam Company, 1894), pp. 66, 79.

[275] [Bachelder], *A.D. 2050: Electrical Development at Atlantis*, p. 35.

[276] William McDougall, 'The Island of Eugenia; The Phantasy of a Foolish Philosopher', *Scribner's Magazine* (1921), 483–91.

[277] Alfred Denton Cridge, *Utopia: Or, The History of an Extinct Planet* (n.p., 1884), pp. 22–6.

[278] William Salisbury, *The Squareheads: The Story of a Socialized State* (The Independent Publishing Co., 1929), pp. 85, 116.

[279] Robert Herrick, *Sometime* (Farrar & Rinehart, 1933), pp. 69–70.

[280] E.g., Mendes, *Looking Ahead*, p. 219.

beneath the North Pole solely inhabited by blonde women. Men are extinct, their oppressive regime having been overthrown 3,000 years earlier. Scientific advances achieved over centuries enable women to reproduce asexually by themselves. But while the narrator returns to male society with a Mizoran, contemporary America finds little appealing in the new ideal. The Mizorans are clearly more civilized than their male predecessors or the rest of the contemporary world. But for men, of course, the ideal is a dystopian one, just as many male utopias had been dystopias for women. And the eugenicist Mizorans have also eliminated the darker-skinned races amongst them.[281]

* * * *

Early in the twentieth century, one further American text appeared which would become definitive of the genre as a whole.[282] Jack London's *The Iron Heel* is sometimes described as 'the first dystopian novel', and was a source for *Nineteen Eighty-Four*.[283] The title refers to an unprecedented worldwide oligarchical tyranny which, emerging from 1912–32 in the United States, has, over some three centuries, crushed all existing socialist governments. There is a great deal of quasi-philosophical dialogue of the sort modern readers find interminable, and an account of the crushing oppression and gross injustices of the existing capitalist system and 'the terrible wolf-struggle of those centuries'. The socialist cause is represented as a return to pure Christian teaching, with small capitalists helping to rebel against the great trusts. The reaction begins when mobs organized by the great capitalists destroy the socialist presses and burn their papers. The labour movement is crushed by strike-breakers. Socialist electoral victories do not prevent a war with Germany driven by economic competition. German socialists oppose the war and threaten a general strike, which spreads to the United States. War is avoided, but revolutions result, until the Iron Heel finally confronts commonwealths in many parts of the world. Driven underground, the American revolutionaries fight on, forced into terrorism in their unequal struggle. The story ends abruptly before their victory. This is broadly a description of what London saw happening in early twentieth-century America. As a dystopia it is chiefly a fictional commentary on the ruthless suppression of labour by capital. (Footnotes alert the reader to direct parallels with current events).[284]

[281] Lane, *Mizora*, p. 92.
[282] On the texts of this period see Howard P. Segal, 'Utopia Diversified: 1900–1949', in Roemer, ed., *America as Utopia*, pp. 333–46.
[283] Booker, *Critical Insights: Dystopia*, p. 8. For background see Jaher, *Doubters and Dissenters*, pp. 188–216.
[284] London, *The Iron Heel*, p. 55. A later post-apocalyptic work, *The Scarlet Plague* (Mills & Boon, 1912), portrayed the plague-induced collapse of civilization a century hence, following the near-enslavement of the workers. Humanity is reverting to savagery, and only a few small tribes remain. The young no longer respect the old. The human element here is represented chiefly in the proposition that in the ghettoes of the old society 'a race of barbarians, of savages', had been bred, who, during the plague, 'committed a thousand atrocities' (pp. 22, 88–9).

BRITAIN AND THE USA: DYSTOPIA TURNS
TOWARDS SCIENCE FICTION

While the dystopian literature of the 1880–1914 period was predominantly concerned with economics and politics, scientific themes nonetheless became increasingly common as everyday life promised to be revolutionized by new inventions and discoveries. Sometimes these are introduced almost at random, to spice up the plot, but without interfering with the narrative. (These we would not term 'science fiction' dystopias.) Some involve traditional mythology. In the sea voyage narrated in Hume Nisbet's *The Great Secret: A Tale of To-morrow* (1895), anarchists and others are shipwrecked on an island inhabited by 'disembodied demons', the spirits of murderers, who, like the undead, 'haunt the surface of the earth and incite mortals to crime'.[285] But, increasingly, it is newer science and technology which comes to the fore. Not uncommonly, science fiction motifs are employed to provide the same cognitive displacement or distancing from the reader's present that the remote island or lost world had previously done. In W. S. Harris' *Life in a Thousand Worlds* (1905), for instance, the exploration of different planets functions as a device for examining different relationships between rich and poor, including such extremes as monopolists charging for sunlight and water, and a triumph of labour bringing about 'many unreasonable laws' and widespread bribery by a wealthy minority.[286] Sometimes these scenarios are transposed to Mars or elsewhere, thereby making substantial changes appear less implausible by not having to explain just how they might be achieved on earth.[287] This, again, does not make such works 'science fiction' as such. The questions of realism and proportionality must determine this.

In other works, however, such themes are so central that we can describe them as dystopian science fiction. Three examples, one British, one American, and one Czech, which offer a particularly penetrating portrayal of future trends, may suffice to illustrate this trend, soon to become definitive of the genre.

E. M. Forster's short story 'The Machine Stops' (1909) is justly famous in the history of science fiction. It is much more relevant to our own age of the smartphone and a preference for mediated internet chatting over direct personal contact than to the early twentieth century. The surface of the earth has become a sterile environment and the population lives mainly underground. Video imaging, pneumatic post, and airships have dramatically increased the speed of communication. But to the narrator, Kuno, talking with his mother, a need for face-to-face contact still exists. For the Machine, as it is called, 'did not transmit *nuances* of expression. It only gave a general idea of people.' Food, music, clothing, and even literature are available at the touch of a button, all of which is explained in the operating manual, the Book of the Machine. But the food appears not to be very

---

[285] Hume Nisbet, *The Great Secret: A Tale of To-morrow* (F. V. White, 1895), pp. 118, 122, 137.
[286] W. S. Harris, *Life in a Thousand Worlds* (The Minter Co., 1905), pp. 54–5, 244–5.
[287] As in James Cowan, *Daybreak: A Romance of an Old World* (George H. Richmond, 1896), pp. 250–79.

good, and the population is increasingly irritable. When they say they are ill, a Chaplinesque machine descends from the ceiling to insert a thermometer into their mouths. Marriage is strictly regulated. Children are educated in public nurseries, then assigned virtually identical private rooms across the planet, where they might not see another person for months. It is regarded as unsuitable to be too strong, and the most fit are destroyed at birth. So technophilia or -holia has weakened humanity, rendering people increasingly sociophobic, with dependency replacing self-sufficiency. Non-mechanical creativity has nearly vanished. Authentic sociability in the sense of personal closeness, warmth, and affection has almost disappeared. Indeed, 'People never touched one another. The custom had become obsolete, owing to the Machine.'[288]

Kuno feels a need to escape this system of degeneration, where the stronger the Machine is, the weaker humanity becomes. His humanism (Forster elsewhere uses the term) is crudely expressed, and is ensconced in the unhelpfully vague phrase, 'man is the measure'. He flees to Wessex, on the surface, a place replete with English romantic associations of pre-Norman simplicity. The Machine, he reflects, 'has robbed us of the sense of space and of the sense of touch, it has blurred every human relation and narrowed down love to a carnal act, it has paralyzed our bodies and our wills, and now it compels us to worship it'. But he is recaptured, and further opportunities for others to visit the surface are curtailed. There is a hint that 'God' is an alternative to the Machine, and the body and soul are described as 'divine'. After Kuno's escape, religion is re-established, except that now the Machine is worshipped as quasi-Divine. Little by little, its servants become less and less capable of understanding 'the monster as a whole', becoming merely efficient cogs. Then the Machine begins to err and falter. Finally it breaks down. There is a hint that 'the homeless' will repopulate the earth, and that 'Humanity has learnt its lesson.' But the reader is left unsure.[289] A generation later, we will see, Huxley would revisit many of these themes.

Prior to this another extraordinary novel featured mechanical beings. In William Wallace Cook's *A Round Trip to the Year 2000* (1925), first published in *Argosy* in 1903, 'metal monsters' known as 'muglugs' do most of the work in a world where Trusts have monopolized the very air people need to breathe. Here, as in *Erewhon*, there are also allusions to humans becoming automatized in the present through quasi-hypnotic unconscious suggestion produced by systematic propaganda. 'The trouble with most of the people who live now', we are told,

> is that they have lost their nerve. Nine-tenths of them have become muglugs—living puppets who jump every time a trust flashes a thought-wave at them. The only real men are the buccaneers and the other outlaws. They have the courage to rebel against a condition of affairs to any one who has not been monopolized into a mere dummy.

---

[288] E. M. Forster, *The Machine Stops and Other Stories* (Andre Deutsch, 1997), pp. 87–118, here 89, 92, 97,

[289] Ibid., pp. 101, 105, 111, 117–18. In the essay, 'What I Believe', Forster said, 'The humanist has four leading characteristics—curiosity, a free mind, belief in good taste, and belief in the human race.'

The warning is made that 'the monster shall turn on Frankenstein'. But when the muglugs revolt they destroy only property, not people.[290] Whether they are the real working classes or actual machines readers may judge themselves. Worthy of mention in this context, too, is the account of the 'mechanized island' of Sarragalla in Alexander Moszkowski's little-known *The Isles of Wisdom* (1924). Here, saving time and maximizing effort and efficiency are carried to extremes, and 'the dominant idea is to transform the *nonchalant* worker into the *willing* worker'. Here, as elsewhere, as Dunn and Erlich have argued, the dominant dystopian metaphors become the beehive and the machine.[291]

Much better known is Karel Čapek's famous play *R.U.R.* (1920). *RUR*, meaning Rossum's Universal Robots (see Fig. 5.2), describes a world where organic manufactured beings, like Frankenstein's creature, rather than mechanical beings as such (confusingly they are nonetheless called machines), do the heavy labour, being two and a half times more efficient than 'human machines'.[292] Indebted to the Golem legend, this play, which gave the world the term *robot*, from the Czech, *robata*, meaning forced labour, beautifully illustrates the dehumanization of mankind by technology in the metaphor of the working classes becoming like machines, and manufactured on an assembly line.[293] Rossum aims 'to use science to knock God off his pedestal', and his products are almost human, lacking only a soul. His nephew, also Rossum, adds assembly-line manufacture. Like Wells' *The Time Machine*, the degradation of real workers, who are all rapidly becoming unemployed, is the satire's focus. The promise, however, is that all commodities will become so cheap that no human will need to do 'soul-destroying' work again. This thus looks like a paradise, where 'there's no need for man to work, because there's no need for him to suffer, because nowadays man needs nothing, nothing, nothing at all but to enjoy himself'. But then it becomes clear that 'the most terrible thing conceivable is to have given people paradise on earth!' No one makes any effort at anything anymore, and women cease having children. After the workers try to suppress them, the robots rise up, killing all but one human. Two robots, male and female, the new Adam and Eve, then set about perpetuating the new species.[294] This gives an optimistic ending which Andrew Milner terms 'essentially at odds

[290] William Wallace Cook, *A Round Trip to the Year 2000* (Street & Smith, 1925), pp. 43–5, 145, 239, 256. Mention can also be made here of Villier de L'Isle-Adam's *Tomorrow's Eve* (1886), in which an 'android' (this is the first literary use of the term) woman is constructed from artificial flesh, and animated by electricity, as a substitute for defective real women, with the hint that 'the facsimile may surpass the original' (tr. Robert Martin Adams (University of Illinois Press, 2001), pp. 60–1).

[291] Alexander Moszkowski, *The Isles of Wisdom* (George Routledge & Sons, 1924), pp. 147–80, here 169; Thomas P. Dunn and Richard D. Erlich, 'A Vision of Dystopia: Bee Hives and Mechanization', *Journal of General Education*, 33 (1981), 45–58.

[292] An illustrated account of their history is David Annan, *Robot: The Mechanical Monster* (Bounty Books, 1976).

[293] The term also referred to a much-hated system of land tenure before 1848, in which peasants were forced to exchange produce for the right of tenancy.

[294] Karel Čapek, *Rossum's Universal Robots (RUR)* (Hesperus Press, 2011), pp. 8, 10, 12, 37, 43,

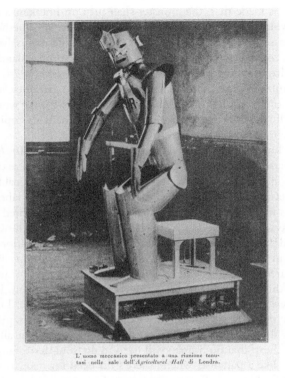

L' uomo meccanico presentato a una riunione tenu-
tasi nelle sale dell'*Agricoltural Hall* di Londra.

Fig. 5.2. Robot from Čapek play, 1929. © Mary Evans Picture Library 10006107.

with the play's main narrative'.[295] But the work itself is a powerful anti-utopian dystopia.

A Hungarian text of the same period, Frigyes Karinthy's *Voyage to Faremido Capillaria*, written in 1921, describes a land completely ruled by machines, who communicate through music. Inspired by both Swift and Wells, Karinthy recounts how machines became cleverer than mankind and finally compel the latter to imitate them, thus slowly declining in worth by comparison. The *solasis*, as the machines of Faremido are called, have inorganic brains but can deteriorate if infected by organic matter. Humans are as yahoos to the narrator, Gulliver, in fact organically like germs. Capillaria is an entirely female land at the bottom of the sea, and here the satire chiefly targets the 'war of the sexes' and the treatment of 'women as inanimate objects', thus establishing a thematic link between the two voyages. Also satirized here are those 'preoccupied with ideas that demanded individual self-sacrifice and selfless devotion for the sake of the community'.[296]

---

[295] Milner, 'Need It all End in Tears? p. 121. Čapek was also the author of a science fiction work, *War with the Newts* ((Allen & Unwin, 1937), in which some similar themes are explored.

[296] Frigyes Karinthy, *Voyage to Faremido Capillaria*, tr. Paul Tabori (Corvina Press, [1965]), pp. 14, 19, 30, 67, 84–5, 113.

And this theme leads us directly to consider the central political event of the epoch, the Russian Revolution.

ANTI-BOLSHEVISM AND ANTI-FASCISM, 1918–1940

The Bolshevik Revolution of 1917 was central to recrafting the dystopian literary genre, and to inspiring the individualist paradigm of revolt which defined the outlook of Zamyatin, Huxley, Orwell, Rand, and others. The revolution itself, of course, induced an explosion of utopian thinking and writing covering politics, society, art, architecture, and many other fields.[297] Marxism promised that humanity's ultimate stage, and the revolution's goal, communist society, would utterly transform social relations. Coercive political power would end, and a quasi-millenarian superseding of alienation between human beings both at work and vis-à-vis nature would occur. Like Christianity in the medieval world, this became the characteristic utopian vision of twentieth-century modernity at least until the collapse of the USSR in 1991. As we saw in Chapter 3, however, the revolution succumbed to accepting violent means and mass enslavement as a legitimate cost of achieving its industrial utopia. Soon the new collectivist mentality was being satirized, with Yevgeny Zamyatin's *We* becoming the most successful of the early twentieth-century dystopias. Before considering this, however, we should briefly touch upon a representative range of other immediately post-revolutionary texts.

In Owen Gregory's *Meccania: The Super-State* (1918)—the title is noteworthy—we view Europe in 1970 through the eyes of a Chinese. Travellers are now carefully controlled, and disinfected when they arrive. Seven social classes exist, including capitalists, with substantial differences of income between them, and a strict etiquette for saluting the higher ranks, violations of which are punished by death. Each class lives in a separate residential area, though none in the lowest resides in the capital, Mecco. Houses and flats are standardized and nearly identical. The men wear different-coloured uniforms, women being permitted more variety but still wearing class emblems. The women are all obliged to shop in person, at particular hours, and to remain with one dealer for a year at a time, to avoid congestion and wasting time. (But they are also protected from marital rape.) The shops are pretty dull as a result. Drinking is controlled and the three lowest classes are not allowed to imbibe at home. Marriage and the number of children are regulated, partially for eugenic ends. Censors regulate the press and the government publishes most books, reads all letters, and eavesdrops on conversations. Concert and theatre attendance is mandatory, while 'aimless amusement' has been nearly abolished.

As little is left to chance here as possible. There are not even queues for the theatre, for tickets are sold for pre-assigned times. Indeed, everyone must keep a diary showing how each half hour is used, submitting a plan every six months

---

[297] For the earlier period see Richard Stites, *Revolutionary Dreams: Utopian Vision and Experimental Life in the Bolshevik Revolution* (Oxford University Press, 1989), and for the later, Jerome M. Gilison, *The Soviet Image of Utopia* (The Johns Hopkins University Press, 1975).

which must be followed. This is accepted as conducive to efficiency. There are no organized sports like football, but there is mandatory military drill for men, and all workers spend five years as soldiers. Little crime occurs, so the police spend most of their time monitoring citizens' lives. The state employs half the population directly, but guarantees employment to all, and provides sickness insurance and old age pensions. The system is based on the principle that 'the private individual has no rights against the State'. 'The sense of orderliness is almost oppressive', and the 'machine seems to absorb everything; the individual counts for nothing'. The few disloyal citizens reside in lunatic asylums, but the young are not 'attacked by the disease'. The old state has been rescued from 'the false ideals of Liberty and Democracy', and the 'Super-State', resting on a military aristocracy, is the result. It is nearer to being proto-fascist (though race is not an issue) than communist-inspired. The lessons of socialism as well as Darwinism have been learnt, unity being regarded as 'the law of organic life'. And it acts aggressively towards some of its neighbours. 'The whole place is one gigantic prison', 'a community of slaves', says an asylum inmate. Here there is 'no hope from within: hope can only come from without'.[298]

The year 1918 also saw the publication of the Russian Symbolist Valery Brussof's (or Bryusov, 1873–1924) *The Republic of the Southern Cross*, which portrays a huge city at the South Pole several centuries in the future.[299] Life is dominated by state-owned mines, and metal-workers, who alone are fully enfranchised, make up 60 per cent of the population. They work short hours and live quite luxuriously. However, an inner 'purely autocratic tyranny' of a few shareholders and directors actually rules. It regulates 'mercilessly the whole life of the country', standardizing buildings, decorations, food, and clothing. The press is totally censored. The secret police are omnipresent. An epidemic of psychical 'contradiction' or mass psychosis breaks out, however, in which people wish one thing but do another ('intending to go to the left they turn to the right'). This results in massive depopulation and moral collapse, though at the end some revival occurs. Brussof supported the Bolsheviks at and after the revolution, but it is difficult not to see this rather strange tale as satirical.[300]

Socialist dictatorship is also the theme in Condé B. Pallen's *Crucible Island: A Romance, an Adventure and an Experiment* (1920). Here, the socialists are given their own island to work out their theories on the assumption that they will fail. Fifty years on, the state supervises and directs everything, including marriages. Peace and contentment reign. But on closer inspection we find dissenters being arrested for treason, and that socialism has 'fallen into a rut of commonplace and apathy'. There is an 'indifference to everything except the mere routine of living, this dead level of existence', an absence of 'the stimulus to progress . . . to strive for

---

[298] Owen Gregory, *Meccania: The Super-State* (Methuen & Co., 1918), pp. 10, 20–5, 28–9, 32, 40, 42, 45, 48–50, 53, 68, 70, 73–4, 78, 80, 84–5, 92, 113, 140, 152, 156, 158, 187, 196, 200, 221, 262–4, 267, 275, 283.
[299] On this and some earlier utopias, see Leland Fetzer, ed., *Pre-Revolutionary Russian Science Fiction: An Anthology (Seven Utopias and a Dream)* (Ardis, 1982).
[300] Valery Brussof, *The Republic of the Southern Cross* (Constable & Co., 1918), pp. 1–32.

something higher'. Once the 'love of individualism has practically atrophied', society tends to a 'common level for all', meaning 'in practice the plane of the average if not the lowest'. This is based upon the idea that 'Social redemption, that is, the total submergence of the individual in the welfare of the whole, is the only religion compatible with practical Socialism.' But the narrator concludes that

> true happiness does not consist in seeking the good of all by levelling us down to what Socialism brings us to, but in the possession of that happiness which we can find alone in each other, as individuals, and that when we destroy individuality and the family, we have torn up the roots of human joy.

He thus aims to escape to 'the land of liberty awaiting them beyond, America'.[301] In another dystopia of this period, P. Anderson Graham's *The Collapse of Homo Sapiens* (1923), such a recourse is not evident. Here, 200 years into the future, six months of rain first kills half the population, then a revolution leaves many of those who remain 'in the wild and reverted to barbarism', while a 'coloured army' lays waste to much of the country.[302] No hope here, again.

Yevgeny Zamyatin: *We* (1924)

We (1924) is rightly accounted one of the chief anti-utopian dystopian novels, even 'the first novel of literary importance that presented a relatively complete vision of the negative results involved in the realization of Utopia'.[303] A naval architect who built icebreakers, Yevgeny Zamyatin (1884–1937) was imprisoned under the Tsar. He spent some time in Britain before returning to Russia in 1917. A Bolshevik by 1905, he left the Party before 1917. Working in the House of the Arts in Petrograd in 1920, Zamyatin drew on Wells' fascination with cities and machines, especially the airplane, 'the symbol of the revolution taking place in man'. He described Wells' novels of 'socio-fantasy' as 'social pamphlets disguised as science fiction novels'. Zamyatin regarded Bolshevism as essentially a religion, in which the last 'ecclesiastical' period involved 'forcible salvation' where 'Christ becomes the Grand Inquisitor'. He remained gripped by the idea that the revolution, having negated yesterday, seemed fixated upon the sacrifice of today for tomorrow. He feared the destructive power involved, and invoked the trope of monstrosity, or Darwinian degeneration, writing that 'Man is dying. The proud *homo erectus* is getting down on all fours, is growing fangs and fur, the beast is conquering in man.' He was also greatly concerned with the effects of mechanization and technology. In many respects, his great work is a study of the machine and its effects upon industrial

[301] Condé B. Pallen, *Crucible Island: A Romance, an Adventure and an Experiment* (Harding & More, 1920), pp. 19, 23, 28, 47–8, 51–2, 110, 113–14, 215. Pallen was a Catholic journalist.
[302] Graham, *The Collapse of Homo Sapiens*, pp. 186, 258, 263.
[303] Alex Shane, *The Life and Works of Evgenij Zamjatin* (University of California Press, 1968), p. 140. A good study of the book is Brett Cooke, *Human Nature in Utopia: Zamyatin's We* (Northwestern University Press, 2002). A recent review of the literature is Peter Stillman's 'Rationalism, Revolution, and Utopia in Yevgeny Zamyatin's *We*', in Booker, ed., *Critical Insights: Dystopia*, pp. 160–74.

management. First published in English in 1924, an abridged Russian translation of *We* appeared in 1927 in Czechoslovakia, making Zamyatin's political position in Russia untenable. Nationwide attacks on him ensued in 1929, and in 1931 he asked Stalin for permission to go into exile. Remarkably, his request was granted. He died in poverty, evidently of a heart attack, in Paris in 1937.[304]

We is often described as an 'anti-Utopian novel', but anti-mechanistic or anti-uniformitarian would be as accurate.[305] It takes the form of a diary, and a manuscript entitled 'We', and opens with the commemoration of the thousand-year-old domination of the planet by the One State. All citizens are numbered. The narrator, D-503, is a mathematician and designer of the spacecraft, the 'Integral', a loosely disguised Comintern (Communist International) vehicle designed to extend the benefits of this society to the galaxy. The aim of the State is the 'endless equalization of all Creation'. After a 200-year war, a 'Green Wall' has been erected to shield humanity from the 'irrational world of trees, birds, animals'. The State is headed by the annually elected 'Benefactor', 'the new Jehovah'. But the outcome is known in advance, since all vote for him, and 'Guardians' preside to ensure no 'error' by voters occurs.[306] He also supervises the State's best doctors. The regime is entranced by, indeed enslaved to, technology, science, and the ethos of power surrounding them. The narrator describes these as resulting from an 'instinct of nonfreedom'. The population wears light-blue uniforms bearing their numbers, and walk in public in even ranks of four. They are regulated in general by the Taylor system of rationalized workflows aiming at increased efficiency, which at work makes them 'machine-perfect'.[307] No one is 'one', all are 'one of'. Two 'Personal Hours' daily are set aside for non-work activities. Food is reduced to one item, naphtha (a hydrocarbon mixture). 'Sexual Days' are determined by the rigorous science of the Sexual Bureau, and science aspires eventually to make even noses uniform. Pink coupons are issued for intercourse, which is linked to Maternal and Paternal Norms.

Erected like an icon on the walls of his room, the Table of Hourly Commandments dictates the course of D-503's daily life. This consists in arising at the same hour as everyone else, and doing much else exactly in common. In the transparent housing blocks, a Right of Blinds is permitted for use on Sexual Days only. The rest of the time all 'live in full sight of all, constantly bathed in light and surrounded by our glass walls'. There is 'nothing to conceal from one another', in any case. Yet this is not an utterly unhappy society. The omnipresence of fear has been mitigated by the provision of bodily comforts and pleasures. For many, thus, happiness without

[304] Yevgeny Zamyatin, 'H. G. Wells', in *A Soviet Heretic*, tr. Mirra Ginsberg (Quartet Books, 1991), pp. 259–90, here 285; Zamyatin, *We*, p. 12; Shane, *The Life and Works of Evgenij Zamjatin*, pp. 22–3, 50.

[305] Michael Glenny, in Zamyatin, *We*, p. 21. Max Eastman insisted it was not 'counter-revolutionary', and thought it addressed 'the unhappy situation of poetic people in that complete regimentation of life toward which science seems to lead the way': *Artists in Uniform: A Study of Literature and Bureaucratism* (George Allen & Unwin, 1934), pp. 83–4.

[306] Zamyatin, *We*, pp. 126, 178.

[307] Ibid., p. 115. This is doubtless named after the system of managerial efficiency and productivity devised by Frederick Winslow Taylor (1856–1915).

freedom is acceptable. Hunger has been conquered, and even love is only 'math-ematicized'. There are personal disagreements, anger, and deceit. The State en-deavours the surgical removal of fantasy by X-rays on a 'miserable little cerebral node' which will then put mankind 'on a par with machines', the implication being that only those made in the machine's image can become perfect. There is a nightly curfew at 22:30. The only 'right' is the right of punishment. All are obliged to report law-breakers to the Bureau of Guardians. Poets are sentenced to death for suggesting they are above the law, and are electrocuted publicly. The use of alcohol and tobacco is proscribed, but exists. There are rumours of plots against the State. Dissenters lurk in classrooms, and even emerge in public at times. But the narrator is not abnormal—he is not a rebel, except mentally. He thinks history has come full circle with the 'return to barbaric times' of tortures and execution. But this is mere musing.[308]

The plot here is driven by a love story. Following sex with the drinking and smoking rule-breaker, E-330, D-503 begins to disintegrate. Having made another girl pregnant, he becomes besotted with her. They illegally register as ill with a sympathetic doctor, stealing work time from the One State, and having sex without a pink coupon. D-503 begins to feel himself a criminal. Despondent, he is diagnosed with having a 'soul' formed within him, and is pronounced 'incurable'. 'Fantasiectomy'—a wonderful concept (we might add 'utopotomy' to it)—is pre-scribed. But he does not wish to rebel, and resists the 'pride' of rebellion, seeing that the 'consciousness of self, awareness of individuality' as akin to 'an infected finger, to an aching tooth': 'Abnormality and illness are one and the same.' Yet the system is not perfect. On the Day of Unanimity, when the Benefactor is to be re-elected, thousands suddenly raise their hands against. A brief riot ensues. Some flee beyond the Green Wall, where a race of naked survivors of the war is discovered. When D-503's diary is discovered, he is not arrested, though others, known as 'Mephis'—the devil image (Mephistopheles) linked to 'I'—are. To forestall further revolt, the State then proposes mass fantasiectomy, with those refusing becoming 'candidates for the machine of the Benefactor', that is, killed. After being 'operationed', columns march forth like 'humanoid tractors'. But D-503 does 'not want to be saved'. He escapes in the Integral, while his child and her mother flee beyond the Wall. But he apparently crashes.[309]

However, the escape was seemingly a dream. D-503 is called by the Benefactor, who reminds him that the all-powerful Christian God was also the great execu-tioner presiding in Hell. All men, the Benefactor tells him, have ever hoped and dreamed 'to have someone tell them, once and for all, just what happiness is—and then weld them to this happiness with chains'. This was 'the ancient dream of Heaven'. Here we are at the heart of a satire not only on utopia, but upon its great predecessor, Christianity, whose vision of Hell, we saw in Part I, was integral to that of Heaven. Nonetheless, 'they' blow up the Wall. As the novel closes, D-503 reports to the Bureau of Guardians to divulge his story. He rushes away as the 'most

[308] Zamyatin, *We*, pp. 24, 27–8, 30, 36, 38, 44, 48, 57, 62, 71–2, 77, 84, 87, 113, 152, 220.
[309] Ibid., pp. 104, 121, 123, 164–7, 181, 192–4, 208, 227, 230, 236, 258.

rational civilization in all history' collapses around him. The diary's last entry terms him 'perfectly well'. He has been seized, and the fantasiectomy performed. The 'soul sickness' is gone. He confesses the names of his co-conspirators, who are executed, along with many others. The last words of the novel are D-503's proclamation of the certainty that 'rationality must conquer'. It has already conquered him, in any case.[310]

We is an early literary refraction of Leninism. There is one road to the collectivist society. One leader prevails. Dissent becomes unthinkable. Yet this dictatorship has a purpose, or at any rate a rationale, which goes beyond personal power and beyond politics. It is mechano-intoxication incarnate. It seeks the perfectibility of scientific rationalism. Collectivism does not seek only to promote a uniform devotion to the common good. Mechanical uniformity and precision have become the paradigm of human rationality. Society aims to create people as efficient as machines by making society machine-like. The communist approach to democracy is satirized: previously the outcome of elections was unknown—to 'build a state upon utterly uncalculated chance happenings, blindly—what could be more senseless?' Here too there is a satire anticipating what would later be called *proletkult*, with poems on 'He Who Came Late to Work' and 'Stanzas on Sexual Hygiene'.

Yet *We* also penetrates to an apolitical ideal of hedonism as the philosophy of modernity as such. Its target is as much Bentham as Marx. The stark portrayal of the choices: 'either happiness without freedom or freedom without happiness', indicates what many later writers would concede to be modernity's cruel dilemma.[311] The pursuit of pleasure brings self-enslavement, the loss of freedom defined as self-command over the passions.

But we can easily see how the desire for pleasure trumps that for freedom. Freedom implies choice, uncertainty, contingency, all of which involve pain. Unfreedom is a superior guarantor of pleasure. And so, too, individuality implies separation and loneliness, while unity in the collective is soothing and reassuring. Hedonism, then, embraces uniformity with a vengeance, wholeheartedly. This is a stimulus-response causal relationship: the utopia of pleasure is the dystopia of similarity. Huxley, we will see, would reach almost exactly the same conclusion less than a decade later. Yet this 'unfreedom' is not the same as political dictatorship or the collectivist dystopia. It is more personal and philosophical. And it can be combined with other forms of regime.

A number of other anti-Bolshevik satires also merit mention here.[312] The Russian Mikhail Bulgakov's Wellsian fantasy, *The Fatal Eggs* (1925), set in 1928, recounts how, through the accidental adjustment of a microscope, the brilliant scientist Professor Persikov discovers a 'ray of life' which greatly accelerates breeding. Tadpoles become frogs in only a day, though they 'were so malevolent and voracious that half of them were immediately gobbled up by the other half'. (This is presumably a reference to the NEP introduction of some free-market activities in

---

[310] Ibid., pp. 259, 275–7, 281–2.   [311] Ibid., pp. 174, 99, 91.
[312] Still helpful is Peter Yershov, *Science Fiction and Utopian Fantasy in Soviet Literature* (Research Program on the U.S.S.R., 1954).

1920.) After the nation's chickens all die of plague, the ray is applied to imported German eggs. But these turn out to be snake eggs, and twelve-metre-long ana-condas and other snakes hatch. The resulting array of 'monstrous creatures' threatening Moscow are finally only defeated by a severe frost. Persikov is killed by an angry mob, and with him dies knowledge of how to build the ray. Given its central themes, its pointed comments about malnutrition resulting from war communism, its rude remarks about Marxists and glib references to the State Political Directorate (GPU) and illiterate officials, and its hints at people being shot for no reason, the novel was quickly recognized as an attack on Bolshevism. The author was lucky to escape with his life. (He died of natural causes in 1940.) The 'ray' which stimulates 'the vital processes of the lower organisms' is the regime's claim to be able to improve life dramatically as a result of communism, especially as a result of heroic efforts at labour, and of Soviet science's utopian potential as well.[313] Science fiction is here again only the disguise for a political tract of great power.

A somewhat later fictional treatment of Bolshevism is *Unborn Tomorrow* (1933), by Margaret Maud Brash, writing as John Kendall. This portrays a financial collapse followed by world war in 1938, which results in the Wellsian 'States of the United World'. Set in 1996, this is nonetheless a creaky dystopia/utopia at best. The new communist government, established after a Soviet invasion, has mottoes like 'All for the State and the State for All'. It is devoted to 'the abnegation of the individual to the needs of the state', and to 'equality of opportunity, in the glory of science, the service of machinery, in the beauty of sacrifice, in the limitless rights of the state, the infallible wisdom of its decrees'. Despite censorship, the regime is fairly mild, though some criminals end up dying as guinea pigs in medical experiments. Citizens are graded, but there is a privileged class immune from 'a host of regulations which pressed upon less favoured citizens'. The workday is only three hours long. Leisure, health, and comfort are universal. Eugenic breeding has eliminated 'defective types'. Some 'irreconcilables' from the old regime remain either in hiding or are permitted to die out on 'reservations' or 'closed land'. Some 'resisters' also flee to less populated areas. But there are still problems of race prejudice, for the Mongolian, Slavic, and Negro races are becoming predominant under a programme of planned miscegenation. This aims to produce an average 'State Stock' who will be placed in controlling positions, though the superiority of 'Nordic stock' is hinted at. Attempts to promote the arts have brought little result; creativity seems to require an individual and not a communal ethos. Compulsory sport also seems unappealing to many. The state tries to suppress religion, but outbreaks of religious hysteria occur. Food is often in short supply, and communal dining appears dreary. There is no respect for the old, worth being measured solely by 'use to the community'. So many prefer euthanasia to advancing age. The key problem is the rapidly declining birth rate. The new communal regime has eliminated family life as 'the root of all inequality and injustice', and raises children

---

[313] Mikhail Bulgakov, *The Fatal Eggs* (Oneworld Classics, 2011), pp. 5, 16, 18, 35, 75, 90, 99, 140.

in state nurseries. But this puts women off having children. Sex has been freed from 'sentimentalism', and love is suppressed, though people still marry.[314]

A love story divulges the psychological cracks in the system. An encounter with an old person reveals the view that the new order 'destroyed our religion, killed love, faith, pity on earth, all that was God in us, and left the physical only'. The new world of 'security, of efficiency [and] comfort, where the weak, the timid, the stupid, set the pace for the strong and the brave' has 'robbed man of God, of the world to come, of hope of developing in this life and of living again in life everlasting'. Having 'made the State God' has eliminated 'our natural instinct to worship, to love each other', these instincts being diverted to the State. The result of removing 'danger, pain, fear and worry' is 'infinite tedium, a grey monotony of comfortable security'. But the most 'unforgivable sin' is 'denying the divine in man'. Even the poor previously, we are told, 'knew more joy in life' than those now alive, and also 'suspense, hope, despair . . . the triumph of success, the agony of failure'. Now a 'dull apathy' prevails. As 'individualistic tendencies' are suppressed, life 'lacked colour, urge, hope'. 'Good fellowship' is encouraged, but 'close friendships' are not 'regarded as helpful to State interests', and 'suspicion of one's neighbour was now second nature'.[315]

So the lead character, Herek, rebels against the system. For assisting an 'irreconcilable' he is sentenced to serve three years in the Tropical Labour Corps, 'a tropical hell on earth'. Attempting to escape, he discovers a wider network of discontented 'Nordic stock' in northern Britain. Caught again, he is rescued by his girlfriend, who prays to the 'God of the old world'. They flee to an old house deep in the Lake District, where they recreate the old way of life. Five years later, communism collapses, 'at least in England', defeated by the Back to Nature Party, whose aims are described as a return of 'survival of the fittest', with religion aiding the less successful.[316]

A slightly later work, *The Strange Invaders* (1934), by Alun Llewellyn, is set in Russia, with fascism portrayed as imitating Stalin. There are climate change and science fiction motifs here. The novel also uses anti-mechanical imagery, notably in the assertion that: 'The machine was the child of his brain; the machine became his master . . . His mind was tried and found wanting. He surrendered it to the machine.' Here, however, the order is eventually overthrown.[317] After Labour's victory in the 1945 election, some right-wing critics used the dystopian form to insist 'how inevitably Social-Democracy must pave the way for Communism'.[318]

Ayn Rand: *Anthem* (1938)

A Russian-born émigré to the United States who became an author and screenwriter, Ayn Rand (1905–1982) was founder of the extreme libertarian philosophy

[314] John Kendall [Margaret Maud Brash], *Unborn Tomorrow* (W. Collins & Sons, 1933), pp. 6, 11, 13, 18–19, 37, 41, 43–5.
[315] Ibid., pp. 59, 76–7, 79–81, 86, 95, 123, 149, 200, 213, 215.
[316] Ibid., pp. 221–2, 265, 307, 316–19.
[317] Alun Llewellyn, *The Strange Invaders* (G. Bell & Sons, 1934), pp. 54, 58.
[318] Paul Faulconbridge, *Commissars over Britain* (The Beaufort Press, 1947), p. i.

known as Objectivism. Her *Anthem* (1938) is sometimes (mis)described as 'one of the earliest American dystopias'.[319] It is certainly one of the crudest examples of the genre, echoing Zamyatin but with little of his subtlety. Its target is squarely 'collectivism', here extraordinarily loosely defined as any proposal aiming at the 'common good'.

The story of Equality 7-2521, whose name appears on the iron bracelet all carry, is one of rebellion against the motto, '*We are one in all and all in one. There are no men but only the great WE, One, indivisible and forever.*' Since the Great Rebirth, a freely elected World Council has ruled. From the age of five, children are separated from their parents and educated in common. Employment is dictated by the Council of Vocations. The Council of Scholars teaches that the earth is flat and the sun revolves around it. For exhibiting signs of a rebellious spirit, Equality 7-2521 is chosen to be a street sweeper, and must live communally in the Home of the Street Sweepers. In the evenings there are mandatory social meetings and quasi-religious services praising brotherhood, equality, and the collective spirit. At forty all retire, worn out, to the Home of the Useless. Here they pretend to be happy, yet 'There is fear hanging in the air of the sleeping halls, and in the air of the streets. Fear walks through the City, fear without name, without shape. All men feel it and none dare to speak.' Some sob or scream in their sleep. Personal or private friendship is forbidden, 'since we must love all men and all men are our friends'. In this society men and women are forbidden to notice each other, except at the Time of Mating when all meet for one night at the City Palace of Meeting, where the Council of Eugenics chooses their mates. A friendship with International 4-8818 leads the narrator to explore a tunnel left over from the Unmentionable Times. It becomes their hiding place, where secret study takes place, and electricity is reinvented. Then Equality 7-2521 conceives a desire for Liberty 5-3000. He renames her the Golden One after her blonde hair, while she calls him the Unconquered. The only crime which is punishable by death is speaking the one Unspeakable Word, which is not explained until the end of the novel.[320]

Of course, the narrator and his friends are arrested and beaten for their unexplained absences. They escape, hoping to take their invention to the House of Scholars for reward. Instead they are accused of threatening ruin to the Department of Candles. They flee into the Uncharted Forest, followed by the Golden One. The individualist theme is restated. Having been taught that 'There is no life for men, save in useful toil for the good of all their brothers', the author concludes,

> But we lived not, when we toiled for our brothers, we were only weary. There is no joy for men, save the joy shared with all their brothers. But the only things which taught us joy were the power we created in our wires, and the Golden One. And both these joys belong to us alone, they come from us alone, they bear no relation to our brothers, and they do not concern our brothers in any way.

[319] Booker, *Critical Insights: Dystopia*, p. 9.
[320] Ayn Rand, *Anthem* (Signet Classics, 1946), pp. vii, 14, 21, 24, 27, 33, 37, 47, 59.

Discovering an old house deep in the mountains, the narrator reflects on the only three holy words, 'I will it.' We are told that 'My happiness is not the means to any end. It is the end. It is its own goal. It is its own purpose.' People cannot be 'the means to any end others may wish to accomplish'. All slavery and mastery, commanding and obeying, is thus set aside. The word 'We' 'crushes all beneath it', and is 'the word of serfdom, of plunder, of misery, falsehood and shame'. Thus we are left only with 'I', now the one 'god', the 'sacred word', 'Ego'.[321]

This is the classic statement of the hyperindividualistic argument, Hell as other people, or nearly my-opia, described in the Introduction here. All groups crush the individual, and only egotism and cooperation based solely upon self-interest can ever be justified. These themes would be extended in *The Fountainhead* (1943). Then came the mammoth *Atlas Shrugged* (1957), which focuses on the inevitable failure of governmental attempts to restrict private enterprise. Its hero, John Galt, denouncing the 'creed of sacrifice', exalts 'the independent mind that recognizes no authority higher than its own and no value higher than its judgment of truth', and proclaims that 'I will never live for the sake of another man, nor ask another man to live for mine.'[322] An extension of militant Protestantism worthy of a Stirner, this philosophy of extreme egoism has appealed to the libertarian right in the United States to the present day.

Anti-Fascism in the 1930s

Hitler's rise to power in the 1930s generated a new set of novels in Britain, the United States, and elsewhere which focused specifically on National Socialism. We can introduce about a dozen of these to give a sense of the contours of the genre.

We should first, however, briefly mention other subgenres which approach dystopia. Set on an imaginary planet, Patrick Hamilton's *Impromptu in Moribundia* (1939) is a light-hearted but caustic satire on the complacency of the British class system and the 'satanic' critique of it provided by Marxism, which includes a sustained dig at the sterile, inward-looking qualities of Wells and the pious 'Moribundian' viewpoint of Huxley.[323] Dystopias in this period also necessarily overlap with the future war novel. In *If Tomorrow Comes* (1934), for instance, the American Louis Aaron Reitmeister described anti-Semitic pogroms in Europe and a regime where 'habitual criminals, inclined to evil, lewd habits, degenerates, and other mental incurables, were sterilized and soon obliterated'. Here, by contrast, an alien from a planet called Jelabar is introduced to portray a regime where no law or compulsion exists, government is a mere 'self-supervising process', and each person 'retains his identity as an individual'.[324]

Stephen Southwold, writing as 'Neil Bell', was the author of an anti-Wellsian science fiction dystopia called *The Seventh Bowl* (1930), where the virulent Phosgas

[321] Ibid., pp. 97–8, 109–11, 113, 123.
[322] Ayn Rand, *Atlas Shrugged* (Signet Books, 1992), pp. 947, 676.
[323] Patrick Hamilton, *Impromptu in Moribundia* (Constable & Co., 1939), pp. 165, 245–52.
[324] Louis Aaron Reitmeister, *If Tomorrow Comes* (The Walden Press, 1934), pp. 147–8, 225, 229.

kills 150 million people in a week during the Great Gas War of 1940. One language and one elected world government of the League of Peoples prevail thereafter. Ectogenic alternative birth takes place in 1957, and in 1961 it is proposed that only a few thousand 'of the most perfect' women become mothers. Travel to the moon occurs. Alcohol has been replaced by an intoxicating drink which has no ill effects. Slums have disappeared and robots do much necessary labour. Most diseases have been conquered. In 1961, the possibility of extending life by up to 2,000 years and renewing any damaged organs is invented in the form of a serum named 'Plasm Alpha'. This is stolen by a group of politicians and their associates, who apply it to three or four hundred thousand of the most powerful people in the world. They aim to create a eugenic world dictatorship, abolishing child-rearing, sterilizing all who marry or having their children euthanized after birth, and reducing the world's population from 2.5 billion to 500 million. The World State assigns all work, and all personal property and money are abolished. Some 15 million die implementing these plans. By 1973 there are no young children left, and finally all toys are destroyed. One result is that far less labour is required, and it is reduced to 200 hours per year. Another is the growth in demand for euthanasia. Eventually the leaders become 'men like Gods', or Immortals, spending their days carousing in 'pleasure cities'. Unexpectedly, however, a rage for toys, children's stories, and all things childish begins in 1990. By the year 2000, a virtual 'Utopia Unlimited' has been achieved. But then a revolt occurs, led by non-whites, against 'this barren Utopianism, this sterile earthly paradise'. The Council insists that the future is only for whites. But a scientist in revolt accidentally alters the earth's orbit: it plunges towards the sun and all life is extinguished.[325]

Bell followed this with a future war novel, first published in 1931 under the title *Valiant Clay*, and later reprinted as *The Gas War of 1940*. Here, as the world 'drifted toward the catastrophe of war', Britain elects a dictator. Germany, having repudiated the Versailles Treaty, allies itself to the USSR in 1938 as Japan attacks the United States. Britain is eventually occupied by Germany and stable government disappears across the world; the global population falls by three-quarters.[326] Britain also gradually succumbs in Aelfrida Tillyard's *The Approaching Storm* (1932), where a Red Republic massacres the clergy in large numbers. After a long war, returning soldiers are afflicted with a dancing sickness which spreads to the rest of the population.[327]

Joseph O'Neill's *Land under England* (1935) is usually acknowledged as possessing greater literary merit than many such works. It recounts a man's metaphorical search for his father, who has returned from World War I a 'man without joy or laughter or life', but with an obsession with ancient Rome. Entering into a subterranean world, the narrator encounters strange monstrous creatures, and humans who appear to be descended from the Romans, but are also like

---

[325] 'Miles' [Stephen Southwold], *The Seventh Bowl* (Eric Partridge, 1930), pp. 21–4, 74–5, 92, 139–41, 149, 151, 162–7, 170–1, 181, 234, 243, 253–4. The author was born Stephen Henry Critten but assumed the name of Stephen Southwold.
[326] Neil Bell [Stephen Southwold], *The Gas War of 1940* (Collins, 1940), pp. 14, 23, 28, 43, 208, 240.
[327] Tillyard, *The Approaching Storm*, pp. 23–4, 262.

'automatons' or 'robots'. Exerting a 'group magnetism' on each other, they apparently communicate by telepathy, and then only where state business is at issue. He finds that his father has been 'remade' 'with all the warring elements left out', or 'absorbed' by the State. Physical violence has here been replaced by love of the common good, which is engineered by 'Masters' controlling the minds of the population. Having renounced individuality, they have become 'one great body, fused by one emotion, directed by one thought'. The narrator wonders whether this is not akin to a 'pulsation of feeling that had come from the mob', which could strike people 'like a wave', making them insane.[328]

The strength of the work thus lies in its delineation of the psychology of totalitarianism. This system, we are told, 'had arisen from the deep fear of the darkness, and the forces of destruction and death that they dreaded in the darkness'. Eventually, the 'mass-hysteria of the race' 'began to function for its own sake and to suppress, not merely irrelevant or unnecessary things, but all tendencies, emotions, actions, whether essential or not, so that it might control completely the social, mental, and emotional life of its people'. Their 'knowledge of tendencies, psychic reflexes, and the various automatic reactions of the mind, made it possible for them to turn into account the different forms of suggestion which produce an automatic functioning of this or that tendency'. The narrator marvels 'that such efficiency and such slavery could be produced in man even by the hysteria of overwhelming fear'. Here, 'under the influence of overwhelming defeat and the panic and hysteria that it brings, nations have been known to hand themselves over to the hypnotic suggestion of their leaders, and, under that hypnotic subjection, to take courses that are abhorrent to the normal instincts of humanity'. The narrator sees 'this underworld State clearly as the monstrous machine that it was—a blind thing, with no vision, no pity, no understanding, not even an understanding of that human need to love that it used to enslave its victims'. He describes his own role as making 'a stand for humanity against the Frankenstein's monster that, having devoured the highest as well as the lowest, now functioned mechanically in a world in which man, as we know him, had ceased to exist'. We are also warned that Britain might be invaded 'if a Fascist or Nazi section of her own citizens made common cause with the underearth invaders, because of the similarity of their doctrines'.[329]

In the United States the threat of a domestic fascist movement provoked a number of novels. As early as 1920 there were fantasies about coups which stabilized corporate capitalism under a benign dictatorship.[330] Sinclair Lewis' critically acclaimed *It Can't Happen Here* (1935) portrays a fascist revolution in America in which a 'clean and aggressive strength' is exerted by a populist senator who takes over the government and rules through a private army of 'Minute Men'. Aimed at the Louisiana politician Huey Long, who is mentioned, the novel satirizes

[328] Joseph O'Neill, *Land under England* (1935; Overlook Press, 1981), pp. 108, 115, 147, 149, 156.
[329] Ibid., pp. 243, 261, 122, 160–1, 176, 243–5.
[330] See [Edward Mandell House], *Philip Dru: Administrator. A Story of Tomorrow 1920–1935* (B. W. Huebsch, 1920).

anti-Semitism, anti-unionism, Red scares, evangelism, and the everyday intolerance evident over lengthy periods of American history. The fascist programme includes nationalizing finance, transport, mines, oilfields, and public utilities, and limiting wealth, disfranchising blacks, and hampering their education. Most women were to be returning to 'home-making', socialists and communists were to be imprisoned, and unions shackled. Once elected, 'the chief', named Berzelius Windrip, abolishes all parties except one. Concentration camps are opened. He is challenged by a liberal newspaper editor, Doremus Jessup, who forms a New Underground resistance movement. People are afraid to talk in public. Books are burnt and universities closed or replaced with new institutions. The brutality is as bad as the Nazis'. But new roads, hospitals, television stations, and the like are built. Finally, Windrip is overthrown by his own aide, and rebellious groups propose forming cooperative commonwealths. Windrip is exiled to Europe, where he has been amassing wealth in secret bank accounts. But his successor is then assassinated and someone even worse takes his place. The author's hope is clearly that 'the Liberals, the Tolerant, might in the long run preserve some of the arts of civilization'. Our hero, Jessup, escapes from the concentration camp he has been sent to for plotting against the regime, and war against Mexico provokes a rebellion against the regime. But this too falters and the country splits into rival factions.[331]

Margaret Storm Jameson's *In the Second Year* (1936) projects a similar downfall in Britain, which has succumbed to fascism following financial crises, strikes, and wage cuts under a Labour government. Amidst a continuing depression, Conservatives allow the victory of the charismatic 'Hillier', who provides the 'narcotic of belief', assisted by a private army of 'National Volunteers'. Labour Camps for the unemployed and brutal 'Training Camps' for political offenders have been set up. (German forerunners are mentioned.) A few communists have been shot. The repression 'makes people lie to themselves in the privacy of their own hearts ... And that is the worst thing of all. The awful isolation.' The regime aims at Spartan virtue and economic autarky, and avoiding Roman decline. Foreigners are demonized and excluded, though Jews are not singled out for mistreatment. 'There is no liberty', Hillier, says, echoing Carlyle, 'except in obedience' to a state which is mother and father to its people. But some Labour activists are not unhappy to see the defeat of 'the *real* enemy', communism, whose intolerance is also dismissed from a liberal viewpoint. There is, of course, a resistance, but the narrator is exiled rather than arrested. The novel closes with no prospect of the dictatorship being overthrown.[332]

Katharine Burdekin: *Swastika Night* (1937)

Written under the pseudonym of Murray Constantine, Katharine Burdekin's *Swastika Night* (1937) is generally viewed as the most significant English-language

---

[331] Sinclair Lewis, *It Can't Happen Here* (Jonathan Cape, 1935), pp. 16, 75–7, 153–4, 175, 242, 313, 369, 377, 390.

[332] [Margaret] Storm Jameson, *In the Second Year* (Cassell & Co, 1936), pp. 21, 41, 43, 89, 93, 111, 143, 148, 181–3, 260.

anti-Nazi novel. It also marks a milestone in the feminist turn in dystopian criticism, anticipating that treatment of gender themes which would become increasingly common in later dystopian writing.

The plot is set 720 years into the Year of the Lord Hitler. A dictatorship has enslaved most of Europe, including Britain. Books are strictly controlled. An ethos of brutal masculinity degrades women. Only strong sons, warriors, are valued, especially those called Knights, the most elite Nazi group. Women who bear girls are made to feel ashamed, and refer to themselves as 'dirt'. Much of the plot concerns the juxtaposition of the English character with the Nazi type, which is also portrayed in terms of a contrast in ideals of masculinity, a 'being of pride, courage, violence, brutality, ruthlessness' being juxtaposed to the idea of a man who 'is a mentally independent creature who thinks for himself and believes in himself, and who knows that no other creature that walks on the earth is superior to himself in anything *he can't alter*'. The contrast is between the idea of 'Blood as a mystery' and real manhood, which involves the Christian virtues of gentleness, mercy, and love. Thus, a Nazi is told, 'You hide behind the Blood because you don't really like yourselves, and you don't like yourselves because you can't be men.'[333] Nazism therefore appears as an immature, juvenile form of masculinity.[334]

There are some clearly satirical elements in the narrative. Women are forced to shave their heads and wear one 'dirty-brown' costume, which did not happen under Hitler. The word 'marriage' has disappeared. But other aspects are chillingly accurate. The Germans are described as having 'after a time killed all the Jews off', even in Palestine. There are hints of anti-imperial sentiment: 'Unshakable, impregnable Empire has always been the dream of virile nations, and now at last it's turned into a nightmare reality. A monster that is killing us.' A socialist perspective is offered of the ownership of the land and factories by those who work them. There is a resistance movement here too. We are told that: 'The scepticism will grow because it's a lively thing, full of growth, like an acorn. It will attack Germany in the end, Germans themselves will get sceptical about Hitler, and then your Empire will rot from within.' Burdekin added an optimistic note in 1940, stating that she thought that 'Nazism is too bad to be permanent, and that the appalling upheaval through which the world is passing is a symbol of birth, and that out of it will emerge a higher stage of humanity.'[335]

Arthur Koestler: *Darkness at Noon* (1940)

Arthur Koestler (1905–1983) was a Hungarian-born Marxist journalist who became a fervent anti-communist. *Darkness at Noon* (1940) is often rightly regarded as a prototype of the anti-Stalinist novel. Orwell regarded it as 'admirable in every way', and it is a key source for *Nineteen Eighty-Four*.[336] Its chief target is the 'closed system' embodied in the ideology of the Communist Party, against which no

[333] Murray Constantine [Katharine Burdekin], *Swastika Night* (Gollancz, 1940), p. 28
[334] Ibid., pp. 158, 161, 81, 69, 72.   [335] Ibid., pp. 81, 69, 72, 149, 78–9, 26, 3.
[336] George Orwell, *Smothered under Journalism 1946* (Secker & Warburg, 2001), p. 172.

criticism is even logically possible.[337] The work focuses on the transformation of guilt from a fixation on the old 'carnal knowledge' to one upon the new 'pure reason'. It is also a study in what Koestler called 'the problem of Ends and Means, the conflict between transcendental morality and social expediency'.[338] Almost the entire book, except for flashbacks, consists of denunciations, interrogations, nego-tiations, entrapments, logical contortions, the allegation of blatant falsehoods, the constant blurring of appearance and reality preceding the inevitable confession, show trial, and execution. Too realistic to be usually classified as a dystopia (we might call it a fictional carcerotopia), it chiefly assails Stalinist totalitarianism, though Hitler is mentioned.

Koestler's achievement, like Orwell's nine years later, lies in his penetration of totalitarian psychology. So deep-seated is the paranoia induced by the dictatorship that individuals dream about being arrested: this is where his protagonist Rubashov commences, in a dream, just prior to being actually arrested.[339] Koestler also exemplifies the moral desperation which dominates the mentality of the period. The proposition that the 'horror which No. 1 [Stalin] emanated above all consisted in the possibility that he was in the right, and that all those whom he killed had to admit, even with the bullet in the back of their necks, that he conceivably might be in the right'. In other words, the vast sacrifices justified in the name of abolishing 'senseless suffering' might eventuate in the promised workers' paradise after all, rather than 'a temporary enormous increase in the sum total' of suffering.[340] It was not to be the case. But if the end had been achieved, the means would have appeared justified, perhaps, particularly to those who had inherited, rather than been sacrificed for, its benefits. We have seen that imprisoned Party members often reasoned in this way.

In the meantime, the 'totalitarian principle' had triumphed in the east of Europe, and its method of persuasion was terror and torture. *Darkness at Noon* is thus, first and foremost, a novel of incarceration and interrogation. Anxiety is all-pervasive. Prisoners fear each other as potential informers, and they are haunted both by the sense of their own innocence and the plausibility of their 'objective' guilt. The ruthlessness and barbarity with which they are treated numbs and bewilders them. The degree to which truth is defined by Party resolutions, no matter how little bearing it has on reality, astonishes them. The Party 'cannot be mistaken' because it is 'the embodiment of the revolutionary idea in history. History knows no scruples and no hesitation ... History knows her way. She makes no mistakes. He who has not absolute faith in History does not belong in the Party's ranks.'[341]

These are not arguments which are easily countered. Their logic is imminent, overpowering, relentless. To defy them is the sole crime, and the sole punishment is

---

[337] Arthur Koestler, *Arrow in the Blue: An Autobiography* (Collins, 1952), pp. 230–1.

[338] Arthur Koestler, *Darkness at Noon* (Jonathan Cape, 1940), p. 146; Arthur Koestler, *The Invisible Writing* (Collins, 1954), p. 358, and generally 393–405, where the composition of the book is discussed.

[339] The character is based on Karl Radek and Nicolai Bukharin: Koester, *The Invisible Writing*, p. 155.

[340] Koestler, *Darkness at Noon*, pp. 21–2, 243.   [341] Ibid., p. 48.

'physical liquidation'. The 'Revolution' is like a 'house on fire', and there is no time to examine the niceties of doctrine. A surreal, dream-like sense of crisis and catastrophe pervades every act and every moment. (Here the psychological superiority of fiction to history writing really shows itself.) For the imprisoned, pain dominates every moment. For those outside, the fear of pain is almost as compelling. There is an air of indescribable moral confusion. Truth is indistinguishable from lies, freedom from slavery, the disease from the cure. There is no room here for 'humanitarian scruples': 'The individual was nothing, the Party was all.' The Party represented the laws of history, which were as certain as the laws of gravity and as impossible to defy. Every hint of disloyalty, of opposition, challenges this proclamation of infallibility. In this 'queer and ceremonious marionette-play', the actors speak only the official language of the latest Party proclamation, and the stage set is constantly altered by the disappearance of the portraits, photographs, and books of unpersons, and their replacement by substitutes. Rubashov even jokes that all is required to effect the complete rewriting of history is to publish a new and revised edition of the back numbers of old newspapers: here Orwell's Winston Smith has his work cut out for him.[342]

Koestler makes it clear that Catholicism is a chief model for communist persecution, quoting a fifteenth-century bishop to the effect that 'when the existence of the Church is threatened, she is released from the commandments of morality. With unity as the end, the use of every means is sanctified.' 'Neo-Machiavellism' is the philosophy which summarizes this viewpoint. The Inquisition is the model for its implementation. Yet the antidote, at the opposite ethical pole, is also a 'Christian and humane' ethics which 'declares the individual to be sacrosanct', and denies 'that the individual should be in every way subordinated and sacrificed to the community'. The problem is that no state has ever adopted such ideals.[343] Even if interrogators are themselves sometimes shot, there are few moments here of hope or levity. No romance stifles or embellishes the plot. Besides omnipresent violence, little action or movement occurs and there are few characters.

As the decade closed, several further novels echoed these concerns. In a bizarre mix of scientific and political themes, Howell Davies' *Minimum Man* (1938) imagines a fascist coup in Britain in 1950 which unleashes a wave of anti-Semitism, the suppression of unions and the Labour Party, and the setting up of concentration camps. A new human type of asexually conceived beings are then hatched, who plan to take over the world.[344] 'Clemence Dane''s [Winifred Ashton's] extreme fantasy of the scarecrow-come-to-life as dictator, *The Arrogant History of White Ben* (1939) portrays the killing of 700,000 crows and the incarceration of 1.6 million more in 'concentration cages'.[345] In Granville Hicks' *The First to Awaken* (1940), set in 2040, after dictatorship and civil war in the United States public industries

---

[342] Ibid., pp. 144, 134, 83, 116–17.   [343] Ibid., pp. 97–101, 153.
[344] Andrew Marvell [Jabez Burns], *Minimum Man, or, Time to Be Gone* (Victor Gollancz, 1939), pp. 5–6, 237.
[345] Clemence Dane [Winifred Ashton], *The Arrogant History of White Ben* (William Heinemann, 1939), pp. 19, 50, 363.

become 'so thoroughly disorganized that nationalization was an economic as well as a political necessity'. But while many cooperatives are formed, some 'individualists' subsist on abandoned farms without being disturbed. Eugenics ideas are discussed in the press, but there are no limits or restrictions on child-bearing. China has become more modern than the United States, but British industry has disintegrated, and without tourism 'the economy could not possibly be sustained'.[346]

Several 'German invasion' novels appeared at the beginning of the war. One was the compelling and well-written *If Hitler Comes*, by Douglas Brown (1940), which is set in the immediate present. Here anti-Semitism produces riots, and capitulation without resistance is followed by occupation. Press freedom is stifled, and the empire disintegrates. Daily life for the masses is 'very little altered', except by greater humiliation and fear. But after an attempt on Hitler's life three weeks of 'Terror' commences, with widespread arrests and concentration camp internments, including that of Winston Churchill. Thousands are killed in a few days. A 'slave state' or (German-defined) 'totalitarian state' is created, aided by a quisling group of 'time-servers and petty bullies' who assist Britain's transformation into a poor colony. Thousands are exported for labour abroad. Secret police monitor factories and villages. Medicine is twisted in the direction of 'National Socialist "eugenics"'. English is slowly abolished. Britain 'belongs to the past'. Perhaps its children will 'win their country back again'. There is some resistance and sabotage. At the end, the narrator flees to New Zealand, thence to embark for the United States to defend it against Germany. But there are already signs that the German Empire is overbloated and 'impeded by its own magnitude'. Britons are exhorted that only by 'denial of self and the sacrifice of personal ends' can their liberty be preserved.[347]

Margaret Storm Jameson's *Then We Shall Hear Singing* (1942), too, depicts an imaginary country (with enough Slavic names to deflect it from Britain) which has become a German Protectorate. The nation is enslaved. The intellectuals have been 'squeezed out'. People are forbidden to travel, change their work, even to sing. There has been much cruelty, and there are concentration camps. Medical experiments attempt to destroy the higher functions of the brain without harming the body. Destroying the remembrance of the past is partially the aim here. Memory is dangerous, especially the recollection of freedom. We are thrown the sop that decency, courage, pity might defeat this cruelty. But the prospects look unlikely.[348] In the purest type of non-dystopian future war novel Britain is simply defeated, sometimes with the United States attacked, though Vita Sackville-West, describing this, leaves the Empire State Building standing until explosions set off an earthquake.[349]

---

[346] Granville Hicks, *The First to Awaken* (Modern Age Books, 1940), pp. 190, 219, 330.

[347] Douglas Brown and Christopher Serpell, *If Hitler Comes: A Cautionary Tale* (Faber & Faber, 2009), pp. 39, 56–7, 85, 94–7, 102, 106, 111, 113, 138, 141.

[348] [Margaret] Storm Jameson, *Then We Shall Hear Singing* (Cassell & Co., 1942), pp. 17, 20, 26–7, 30, 58, 68, 224. On Jameson see Jennifer Birkett, *Margaret Storm Jameson: A Life* (Oxford University Press, 2009).

[349] V. Sackville-West, *Grand Canyon* (Michael Joseph, 1942), pp. 199, 203.

As World War II progressed, a few fantasies describing Britain's degeneration into totalitarianism appeared. Robin Maugham's *The 1946 Ms.* (1943) describes a coup by an enterprising general prepared by the suppression of liberties during the war.[350] J. D. Beresford and Esme Wynne-Tyson's *The Riddle of the Tower* (1944) conjectures that a 'permanent Totalitarian existence' emerges after the 'Third World War'. Critics of the system are 'removed' by a fatal soporific, without trial, genius is regarded as a form of madness, and the concept of parenthood has been abolished. Those who have outlived their usefulness go to 'the Hospital'. Under 'the mechanical system' people seem like automatons, even their laughter being a stimulus response. The population has 'no differences to discuss, because they were all in agreement, conforming so closely to the same pattern'. But in fact they are unhappy, and the narrator discovers that, while individual love has been 'pooled into communal love', 'Fear had been the "coherer" that had bound this race together to develop a common purpose.'[351] In Erwin Lessner's *Phantom Victory: The Fourth Reich: 1945–1960* (1944), Germany loses the war but Hitler goes into hiding, re-emerging in the 1950s to form a 'Fourth and Eternal Reich' which eventually conquers the United States.[352] Exploring the implications of a German victory would continue in the 1950s, with John William Wall's *The Sound of His Horn* (1952) imagining an airman awakening into a twenty-first-century Nazi hunting game where the prey are women (some are genetically modified to be crossed with leopards).

Finally, the immediate post-war era also saw a number of other, chiefly anti-Soviet, works published. Noteworthy amongst these was the Russian-born Vladimir Nabokov's wondrously quirky *Bend Sinister* (1947)—more Nabokov than dystopia—which describes a fictional European dictatorship run by a man named Paduk, leader of the Party of the Average Man and upholder of the vapid ideology of Ekwilism. This is described as an advance on both socialism and religion in its utopian philosophy of remoulding the individual to conform to a 'well-balanced pattern'. With the assistance of the Army and the State, individuals, 'by adjusting ideas and emotions to those of a harmonious majority', aim to 'dissolve in the virile oneness of the State'. The plot revolves around the philosopher Adam Krug, a former schoolmate of Paduk's, who is asked to help defend his university after its closure, and thus to collaborate with the regime. Krug believes himself secure, and refuses. Paduk summons him after four of his friends are arrested, and proposes making him president of the university, offering him also a cow, a bicycle, and other things, if he will but read a speech affirming his support for the regime. Of course, Krug refuses. Having a small child, he hopes to escape. Instead he is arrested, and agrees to support Ekwilism publicly if his son remains

350 Robin Maugham, *The 1946 Ms.* (War Facts Press, 1943), pp. 19, 35, 39.
351 J. D. Beresford and Esme Wynne-Tyson, *The Riddle of the Tower* (Hutchinson & Co., 1944), pp. 85–8, 93, 102, 110, 113.
352 Erwin Lessner, *Phantom Victory: The Fourth Reich: 1945–1960* (G. P. Putnam's Sons, 1944), pp. 7, 182, 224.

safe. But the boy dies, and then the lives of his friends are also threatened. Krug attacks Paduk, but is shot.[353]

CONCLUSION: THE CONTOURS OF THE LITERARY DYSTOPIA, 1792–1945

Born of satire, the literary dystopia assumed its earliest modern form following the French Revolution. It emerged into a fully formed genre in the United States and Britain in the last decades of the nineteenth century, when it was fuelled by industrialization, growing social inequality, and the increasing popularity of socialism and Social Darwinism. Dystopia defied the spirit of the day by asserting that retrogression as well as progression might define modernity. Scientific, technological, and productivist themes rapidly came to be central to dystopian visions of the future in the closing decades of the century. Now we witness the first abstract concerns that both have overtaken humanity's capacity to guard against their potentially evil consequences. Firstly, machines are seen only as enslaving the working classes. Eventually they come to dominate the species as a whole. Initially, their predominance is chiefly metaphorical: people come to act more like machines. Later, sometimes, it is literal: machines actually rule over us. And if first we come increasingly to think like machines, later the fear is that machines will come to think not just like us, but for us. Socially, a dystopian present, caused chiefly by an intense concentration of wealth in the hands of the few, looks, across this period, to many to be the natural outcome of modern economies. Frequently humans come to be valued only for their labour power, and then its efficient use alone.

One of the most obvious changes in dystopian literature after World War I is the seriousness of moral tone evident after 1918. Running through the 1930s, this makes lighter satire more difficult, and indicates that prophetic warnings of real nightmarish scenarios are much more realistic than the imaginative projections of the pre-war period. Many of the worst trends that the earlier dystopias had warned against now mature, and hint at real catastrophe. Despair now seems evident with regard to both capitalism and its alternatives; hence Max Eastman, writing in 1922, could describe a 'whole modern world of capitalism and Communism . . . rushing towards some enormous efficient machine-made doom of the true values of life'.[354] In such circumstances, satire increasingly seems a feeble weapon. As the battle lines in Europe divided between communist and fascist, the likelihood of one or the other eventually winning grew, and an atmosphere of grim despair haunts many works of the epoch. By the 1940s, Stalin's and Hitler's rise to power then offered further focus for dystopian themes.

---

[353] Vladimir Nabokov, *Bend Sinister* (Weidenfeld & Nicolson, 1960), pp. 44–5, 68–9, 80, 87, 124, 130, 132, 134, 160, 173, 189–90, 196–7, 202, 210–11.
[354] Quoted in Irving Howe, 'The Fiction of Anti-Utopia', in Irving Howe, ed., *Orwell's Nineteen Eighty-Four: Text, Sources, Criticism* (Harcourt, Brace & World, 1963), p. 303.

In the mid-twentieth century, two works would come to define the dystopian literary response to these developments more than any other: Huxley's *Brave New World* (1932) and Orwell's *Nineteen Eighty-Four* (1949). Though, as we will see, they are very different works, they take up the problematic of political dictatorship and the overpowering nature of machine civilization in some strikingly parallel ways.

6

The Huxleyan Conundrum
Brave New World as Anti-Utopia

INTRODUCTION: THE ROAD TO BRAVE NEW WORLD

World War I induced a profound rupture in European society, and proved the point that the science of destruction, when wedded to human ferocity, could easily outstrip progress in diplomacy and international sociability. Only a decade later, the Great Depression showed that the inherent instability of capitalist economies could generate colossal dislocation and suffering. The years from 1914 to 1945 represented, for Europeans in particular, an almost undiminished tale of woe. Most of the promises of eighteenth-century Enlightenment philosophical and nineteenth-century scientific and technological optimism seemed smashed. What now seems like a temporary recovery would take place in the second half of the twentieth century. But the road to dystopia was also now well signposted, as in the 1950s the threat of nuclear war, and in the 1960s and 1970s a looming demographic and environmental catastrophe, added to the growing sum of mankind's woes. Though the central themes of Brave New World began with Plato, eugenics ideas, as we saw in Chapter 5, became pronounced in utopian fiction as the debate over Darwin heated up in the 1870s. Once Wells in particular exploded upon the literary scene, imaginative leaps into the distant future were plentiful. But as science fiction emerged as a leading fictional genre, it tilted increasingly towards the portrayal of darker future scenarios. To many, indeed, it appeared that humanity's destructive powers were evolving faster than its creative and constructive capacities.

* * * *

It was against the backdrop of the catastrophe of World War I that Aldous Huxley grew to maturity. The grandson of 'Darwin's bulldog', the agnostic scientist T. H. Huxley, he was born on 26 July 1894 and died on 22 November 1963. He attended Eton, then Balliol College, Oxford. For a time, he returned to Eton as a master, and taught French briefly to the young Eric Blair, later to become George Orwell. He later worked briefly in a chemical plant, where his experience of 'an ordered universe in a world of planless incoherence' would be integrated into his later great work.[1] By his early twenties he had found his métier as a novelist,

---

[1] Aldous Huxley, Brave New World, ed. Margaret Atwood and David Bradshaw (Vintage Books, 2007), p. xxiii.

achieving early success with *Crome Yellow* (1921), whose setting is a country house party; a risqué satire on bohemian lifestyles, *Antic Hay* (1923); *Those Barren Leaves* (1925), another satire on the cultured elite, now set in an Italian villa; and *Point Counter Point* (1928). In the latter novel, if the communists seem to understand how dynamite and utopia can be wedded, the tortured intellects and insatiable libidos of the well-to-do now share the stage with wider politics, including the nascent fascist movement. This latter appeared as the green-uniformed Brother-hood of British Freemen, who claim to exist to 'keep the world safe for intelligence', and are 'banded to resist the dictatorship of the stupid', 'armed to protect indi-viduality from the mass man, the mob', and 'fighting for the recognition of natural superiority in every sphere'. This, in principle, means opposition to the 'dictator-ship of the proletariat' but mostly seems to consist in suppressing the workers. Its programme is described as 'Socialism without Political Democracy, combined with Nationalism without insularity', but these are seen as essentially meaningless slogans. They threaten, however, to render this precious, introverted, self-absorbed world utterly irrelevant. In an irritated outburst we are asked:

> Bolsheviks and Fascists, Radicals and Conservatives, Communists and British Freemen—what the devil are they all fighting about? I'll tell you. They're fighting to decide whether we shall go to hell by communist express train or capitalist racing motor car, by individualist 'bus or collectivist tram running on the rails of state control. The destination's the same in every case. They're all of them bound for hell, all headed for the same psychological impasse and the social collapse that results from psycho-logical collapse.[2]

Huxley's reluctance to take sides left him on the sidelines, damning the excesses of all parties, and condemning both communists and fascists as 'doomed to failure' for trying to create 'one single "right" ideal' of personality. And he mocked the communists in particular for believing that 'as soon as all incomes are equalized, men will stop being cruel. Also that all power will automatically find itself in the hands of the best people.'[3] Both *Eyeless in Gaza* (1936) and *Ends and Means* (1937) developed pacifist themes which would later mark Huxley's social and political thought. He now insisted that 'violent, unjust means' could never 'achieve peace and justice! Means determine ends; and must be like the ends proposed.'[4] Huxley went on to join the Peace Pledge Union, founded in 1934, which renounced war and promoted all steps to avoid it. It supported the appeasement of Hitler, in the hopes that sufficient recompense for the Versailles Treaty would assuage his territorial ambitions. Its propaganda became extremely pro-German. (Orwell was amongst its more strident critics.) Huxley's refusal to contemplate defending the United States would later cost him the possibility of citizenship there.

Moving to southern California in 1937 exposed Huxley both to the Hindu Vedanta philosophy, described in *The Perennial Philosophy* (1946), to which he

[2] Aldous Huxley, *Point Counter Point* (Chatto & Windus, 1947), pp. 55, 76, 201, 379, 381, 414–15.
[3] Aldous Huxley, *Eyeless in Gaza* (Chatto & Windus, 1936), pp. 143, 297.
[4] Ibid., p. 325.

became devoted, and also the extremes of hedonistic myth-making and propagandistic mass manipulation which defined Hollywood. He would from now on be
forever wrestling with the twin distractions of Ego and Eros, and grappling with
ultimate metaphysical questions of the sort which Orwell, a more political animal,
regarded as peripheral to the great concerns of humanity. *After Many a Summer*
(1939) was the first of Huxley's works to comment extensively on what he regarded
as the obsessive narcissism and superficiality of the 'democratic Far West', and his
increasingly introverted answers to the most fundamental problems. Here, a
concern with using science to achieve immortality, or at least prolong old age, is
evident, though this experiment results in the creation of a 'foetal ape'.[5] *Time Must
Have a Stop* (1944) continued the themes of cultured decadence and the meaninglessness of hedonism, with mysticism hinted at as a solution.

Such fundamental doubts to one side, Huxley did well in the New World. For a
time he was an immensely successful screenwriter, though he spent vast sums
assisting Nazi refugees to flee Germany. Hampered by near-blindness from the
age of seventeen, Huxley strove to attain sharper perceptions from inner circum-
spection. His interest in mysticism drove him to become a pioneering explorer with
psychedelic drugs, notably mescaline, later detailed most famously in *The Doors of
Perception* (1954), which later made him a prophet of the counter-culture.[6] This,
along with the *soma* and sex ecstasy of the world of *Brave New World*, rediscovered
during the spectacular later revival of Huxley's popularity, produced a new generation
of fans enamoured of the possibilities of boundless hedonism. In his later years, both
Vedanta and his inner journeys helped provide the setting for the utopian answer to
the problems outlined in *Brave New World*. Pushing the boundaries of self-
knowledge to the end, as he died he asked his wife to inject him with LSD.

Given this devotion to introspection, it is ironic that Huxley remains best known
for his most political novel. Yet a concern with the near-universal pressure to
collectivism was, of course, wedded to understanding the worth and meaning of
individualism, and its relation to birth regulation. The themes of Huxley's great
work were, however, already foreshadowed to some degree in earlier writings. This
is particularly the case with *Crome Yellow* (1921), where a character describes the
glorious future in which:

> An impersonal generation will take the place of Nature's hideous system. In vast state
> incubators, rows upon rows of gravid bottles will supply the world with the population
> it requires. The family system will disappear; society, sapped at its very base, will have
> to find new foundations; and Eros, beautifully and irresponsibly free, will flit like a gay
> butterfly from flower to flower through a sunlit world.[7]

* * * *

[5] Aldous Huxley, *After Many a Summer* (Chatto & Windus, 1939), pp. 3, 311.
[6] See also Aldous Huxley, *Heaven and Hell* (Chatto & Windus, 1956), and *Moksha: Writings on
Psychedelics and the Visionary Experience, 1931–1963* (Chatto & Windus, 1980).
[7] Aldous Huxley, *Crome Yellow* (Chatto & Windus, 1921), p. 31.

Brave New World (1932) would eventually prove second only to Orwell's *Nineteen Eighty-Four* in defining the emerging genre of dystopia.[8] As a work of fiction, George Woodcock has written, it departs from Huxley's earlier satires in being designed primarily to exhort.[9] Yet it is a highly ambiguous parody of several forms of utopia, for some of which Huxley retained varying degrees of sympathy despite his satire of the ideal as a whole. Huxley himself called the book a depiction of a 'utopia' in the 1946 introduction to the text, using the term neutrally in the sense of any imaginary projected vision of society, but clearly also implying that specific trends aiming at social amelioration could have the opposite effect.[10] But critics have also seen as its target contemporary America; the vulgarity of modern culture, 'progress' in general; and the cult of hedonism in particular, or a 'bourgeois dystopia',[11] as well as utopia as such, especially in its Wellsian variant; 'the modern worship of science',[12] 'the misuse by totalitarian government of science and technology, that is, scientism',[13] and also the growth of totalitarianism generally.

Huxley himself, in September 1931, described the progress of his 'difficult piece of work', 'a Swiftian novel about the future, showing the horrors of Utopia and the strange & appalling effects on feeling, "instincts" and general *Weltanschauung* of the application of psychological, physiological & mechanical knowledge to the fundamentals of human life'. Another letter portrayed his satire as focusing on 'the horror of the Wellsian utopia'.[14] Krishan Kumar consequently terms the book '*the* anti-utopia of science' and 'the most powerful denunciation of the scientific world-view that has ever been written'.[15] Yet Huxley, having in 1928 predicted that the 'achievements of civilisation will eventually bankrupt the world', had also decided by 1931 that, if utopia was to be possible, it depended upon two conditions: 'that the heritable qualities of the progressing population shall be improved (or at any rate changed in a specific direction) by deliberate breeding; and that the amount of

---

[8] A recent survey of the work and its context is given in M. Keith Booker, ed., *Critical Insights: Brave New World* (Salem Press, 2014), which includes my 'Huxley and Bolshevism' (pp. 91–107). Other essay collections on the book include David Garrett Izzo and Kim Kirkpatrick, eds., *Huxley's Brave New World: Essays* (McFarland & Co., 2008). This chapter also draws on my 'Malice in Wonderland: The Origins of Dystopia from Wells to Orwell', in *The Cambridge Companion to Utopian Literature* (Cambridge University Press, 2010), pp. 107–34.

[9] George Woodcock, *Dawn and the Darkest Hour: A Study of Aldous Huxley* (Faber & Faber, 1972), p. 175.

[10] Huxley, *Brave New World*, p. xliii. We recall that he quoted Nicolas Berdyaev's warning that 'Utopias seem much more likely than we had thought in the past. And now we are faced with a far more distressing question: How can their ultimate establishment be avoided? . . . Utopias are possible. Life marches toward Utopias. And yet a new age may be dawning, an age in which intellectuals and the educated classes will dream of ways to avoid Utopias and to return to a nonutopian, less "perfect", freer society' (p. v.).

[11] M. Keith Booker, *The Dystopian Impulse in Modern Literature: Fiction as Social Criticism* (Greenwood Press, 1994), p. 45.

[12] *Historical Dictionary of Utopianism*, ed. James M. Morris and Andrea L. Kross (The Scarecrow Press, 2004), p. 145.

[13] Richard C. S. Trahair, *Utopias and Utopians: An Historical Dictionary* (Fitzroy Dearborn Publishers, 1999), p. 47.

[14] Aldous Huxley, *Letters of Aldous Huxley* (Chatto & Windus, 1969), pp. 353, 348.

[15] Krishan Kumar, *Utopia and Anti-Utopia in Modern Times* (Basil Blackwell, 1987), p. 254.

population shall be reduced'.[16] These concerns would remain with him through the rest of his life, with overpopulation in particular being a constant theme.[17] So science, if a major part of the problem, was going to be integral to the solution.

THE BOOK

Brave New World stands as one logical extension of the Darwinian hint that science could assume control over human evolution and produce that mastery of the species which had eluded mankind from Plato onwards. It is a eugenicist's dream, wedded to what Huxley later called 'the completely controlled, collectivised society'.[18] The world envisioned follows, however, the human nightmare of global warfare and economic collapse. The juxtaposition of order to chaos remains a characteristically Huxleyan theme. The peculiar genius of this work, however, is its astute combination of utopian and dystopian themes, to the degree that readers today are still troubled as to how to classify the text.

The opening scenes and unfolding context seem to support the dystopian interpretation unreservedly. Set in the year A.F. (After Ford) 632, the narrative describes a World State of 2 billion standardized, scientifically bred beings who are 'hatched' like Model Ts in state factories in 'uniform batches'. Supervised by ten 'Controllers', who are 'Alpha Plus Intellectuals' bred from a single egg, the population is divided eugenically into 'castes' of Alphas, Betas, Gammas, Deltas, and Epsilons, echoing Plato's gold, silver, brass, and iron constitutions. These are cloned (as we would say today), as many as 17,000 from one egg, to fulfil different functions. In what may have been a satire on the existing class system (we have noted parallels in earlier texts), Epsilon embryos, amongst other things, are described as starved of oxygen to ensure 'semi-moron' stupidity. They are also bred to develop more quickly physically, and even conditioned for heat or cold depending on where they will work. Deltas are taught to hate books and flowers—superfluities for their caste. But we discover, with a hint at utopia, that their 'mild, unexhausting' work is limited to seven and a half hours a day—even less than what the nineteenth-century labour movement aspired to achieve. Further labour-saving devices are restricted only because extra leisure has been found only to increase tedium. This, in turn, has been found to promote excess use of the anti-depressant, bliss-inducing wonder drug *soma*, which is issued daily after work, and whose existence hints that some pain, if only tedium, disrupts this serenity—back to a dystopian motif. This class system is the best answer to the perennial problem of the search for perfectibility. Society could not be composed solely of Alphas, we are told, because they were capable of a degree of free choice and responsibility, and, not wanting to do

[16] Aldous Huxley, 'The Modern Doctrine of Progress', *Vogue* (21 March 1928), 55, 78; Aldous Huxley, 'Boundaries of Utopia', *Virginia Quarterly Review*, 7 (1931), 53.

[17] E.g., Aldous Huxley, *The Human Situation* (1959; Chatto & Windus, 1978), pp. 42–58.

[18] Aldous Huxley, *Collected Essays* (Harper & Brothers, 1958), p. 295. On the scientific background, see Jon Turney, *Frankenstein's Footsteps: Science, Genetics and Popular Culture* (Yale University Press, 1998), pp. 91–120.

menial work, would be miserable and unstable.[19] Like the characters in many of Huxley's early novels, a society composed of intellectuals would eventually dissolve into tedium, ennui, petty-mindedness, and mechanical hedonism.

In *Brave New World*, the institutions of marriage and the family have disappeared, and words like 'mother' are risible if not offensive. In what Adorno, in a brilliant essay, describes as a 'jaded official sexual regime',[20] mandatory sexual promiscuity—which Huxley called 'the truly revolutionary revolution'—prevents the attachments of emotional love, marriage, child-bearing, and the isolated family from eroding social cohesion.[21] (Orwell would portray an opposite regime aiming at the same end of repressing individual loyalties.) This represents an atavistic infantilism. Alphas, we are told, 'are so conditioned that they do not *have* to be infantile in their emotional behaviour. But that is all the more reason for their making a special effort to conform. It is their duty to be infantile, even against their inclination.'[22] This dutiful revelry, as Lewis Mumford recognized, is little else than the Saturnalia revived, if driven in the direction of 'an infantile dream state'.[23] The entire culture in which most partake indeed is overwhelmingly infantile—one can feel the self-confessed 'Highbrow' Huxley spitting out the word with infinite contempt.[24] The 'appalling dangers of family life' and the old damaging repressions have mostly disappeared. Even children engage in erotic play.[25] What Erich Fromm termed 'nonfrustration' is taken to its logical limits: we must never postpone the gratification of our wishes.[26] *Kinderland*, indeed, might well describe the new world. Frequent copulation diverts the passions from social or political criticism. So does shopping, for consuming commodities is strongly encouraged to keep industry active. In what Huxley called 'the conscription of consumption', every person is required to consume so much in a year, epitomized in the phrases, 'Ending is better than mending. The more stitches, the less riches.'

Not merely eroticism, but hedonism generally, thus suppress unsocial thought. Hypnopedia, or sleep-teaching (100 repetitions 3 nights a week for 4 years, or 62,400 in total), combined with a 'greatly improved technique of suggestion', encourages the sentiment that 'Everyone belongs to everyone else.'[27] Intensive group activities, like Solidarity Services where *soma* is passed around, hymns are sung, and rapturous dancing occurs, bond the population to a common ideal and outlook defined by class and function. To assist affiliation to the new the past has

[19] The text recounts the 'Cyprus experiment', where an Alpha society collapsed into civil war (*Brave New World*, pp. 196–7).

[20] Theodor Adorno, 'Aldous Huxley and Utopia', in Adorno, *Prisms* (MIT Press, 1983), p. 104.

[21] Huxley, *Brave New World*, p. xlv.

[22] Ibid., p. 84.

[23] Lewis Mumford, *The Myth of the Machine*, vol. 2: *The Pentagon of Power* (Secker & Warburg, 1964), p. 226.

[24] See 'I am a Highbrow', reprinted in the *Aldous Huxley Annual*, 7 (2003), 126–8.

[25] Huxley, *Brave New World*, p. 33. But in 1929 Huxley wrote that 'it appears to be impossible, as the Indians have discovered, to combine childish sexuality with intensive intellectual education' (*Selected Letters*, Ivan R. Dee, 2007, p. 219).

[26] Erich Fromm, *The Sane Society* (Routledge & Kegan Paul, 1956), p. 165.

[27] Huxley, *Brave New World*, p. xlviii.

been erased, echoing Henry Ford's famous description of history as 'bunk'.[28] All books, except those on technology, and, as in China's Cultural Revolution, all monuments relating to the former society have been destroyed. (This attitude Huxley detested as hostile to 'culture' in principle.)[29] Here, amusements, if limited and superficial, are plentiful. The 'Feelies' are a new form of cinema providing tactile amusement along with B-movie plots involving singing, dancing, and much action. There is electro-magnetic golf too. *Soma* ('One cubic centimetre cures ten gloomy sentiments') is always available to allay anxiety and alleviate boredom.[30] A monthly Violent Passion Surrogate treatment floods the system with adrenalin to release any residual tension. All this proves the superiority of conditioning over fear: 'Government's an affair of sitting, not hitting. You rule with the brains and the buttocks, never with the fists.' In the end, 'force was no good', one of the ten world controllers, Mustapha Mond, insists, compared to the 'slower but infinitely surer methods of ectogenesis, neo-Pavlovian conditioning and hypnopaedia'.[31]

Of course, someone must whinge at this great happiness-producing mechanism. Censorship prevents dissident literature appearing. A few deviants—evidently only Alphas—are transferred to St Helena and other remote locations. But overt physical repression is rare: it is not necessary. 'Community, Identity, Stability' are the proud mottoes of the new age. 'Stability', particularly, is 'the primal and ultimate need.' The old slogan, 'Liberty, Equality, Fraternity' is long forgotten. Conditioning has seemingly brought happiness, itself perhaps the goal of the old slogans combined. But it has been paid for, Huxley intimates, with the loss of freedom. This includes the freedom to be unhappy, to express passion, spontaneity, and real joy, to be irrational, and much else Huxley evidently valued. There are recurrent hints that the present 'happiness' does not deserve the name. Sex seems emotionless, mechanical. But this is deliberate: a leading slogan is: 'When the individual feels, the community reels.'[32] So mandatory promiscuity and prohibition of individual attachment are central to collective bonding.

While Huxley's narrative commences by regaling us with achievements of the new society, he soon hints that the system is not perfect. The problem lies mostly with the leaders. Several Alpha-Plus men, particularly Bernard Marx (other characters are named Engels, Bakunin, and Trotsky) and Helmholtz Watson, have slight defects (the former shorter than normal, the latter cleverer). This shows that some people still feel different, peculiarly individual, and outside the system. Not everyone can be a joiner. Private attachments do develop, despite the rules. The frustrations of unrequited desire still exist. The individualists typically are repelled

---

[28] He meant that 'it often happens that a man can think better if he is not hampered by the knowledge of the past', the past being useful 'only as it suggests ways and means of progress': Henry Ford, *My Life and Work* (William Heinemann, 1923), pp. 249, 273.

[29] See Aldous Huxley, *Music at Night* (Chatto & Windus, 1931), pp. 133–9. Ford epitomized the 'modern' outlook, which Huxley defined elsewhere as 'freedom from customary bonds and ancient prejudice, from tradition and vested interest, the freedom, in a word, from history' (*Aldous Huxley Annual*, 7 (2007), 79). But he liked Ford automobiles, and bought a new one in California. He was even a visiting Ford Professor at Berkeley. He had read Ford's 'Life' on a voyage to the USA and found it 'fascinating' (*Collected Essays*, vol. 2, p. 525).

[30] Huxley, *Brave New World*, p. 46.   [31] Ibid., pp. 49, 43.   [32] Ibid., p. 81.

by the rituals of groupism. Bernard Marx hates Solidarity Services and Community Sings, sometimes refuses *soma* offerings, and questions whether being 'enslaved by conditioning' destroys other forms of freedom, such as knowing 'what passion is'.[33] So there is still paranoia and anxiety, despair and humiliation, individuality and humanity, all in keeping with Huxley's view, as he put it in 1933, that, 'Even in the best regulated society, the individual will always have his private reasons for discontent and misery.'[34] But Marx's boss still warns him of his want of 'infantile decorum', threatens him with transfer to Iceland, and publicly humiliates him for his 'heretical views' on *soma*, sport, and sex.[35] And Helmholtz's fantasies about being alone nearly result in the same fate.

The plot of *Brave New World* thickens with the introduction of John, an inhabitant of one of the remaining 'Savage' reservations, whose old world descendants are surrounded by electrified fences. One of these is visited by Bernard and the 'wonderfully pneumatic', seductive Lenina Crowne, a Beta Plus and the embodiment of new world womanhood. John's mother Linda turns out to have been a civilized interloper, the girlfriend of Marx's boss, who had gotten lost on a similar visit years earlier. Though Huxley's portrayal of reservation life is not overly sympathetic, John's rebellious character partly embodies the less secure but more 'natural', romantic, and freer old world ways by contrast to the supposed superiority but obvious puerility of the new.[36] The Shakespeare-quoting John (who cites *The Tempest*'s immortal words, 'O brave new world that has such people in it') is brought out of the reservation as a kind of zoo specimen exhibiting how the environment affects character. Confronted with his offspring, Marx's boss is forced to resign. Linda then dies of a *soma* overdose and general surfeit of new world pleasures, with an expression of 'imbecile happiness' etched on her face. John is sickened by the mass production of human or less than human types. His engagement with Mustapha Mond notionally undermines the new ideals of 'civilized infantility' when juxtaposed to the 'authentic' liberty and 'real' experience of the old.[37] In a key scene, Mond explains the system to John:

> The world's stable now. People are happy; they get what they want, and they never want what they can't get. They're well off; they're safe; they're never ill; they're not afraid of death; they're blissfully ignorant of passion and old age; they're plagued with no mothers or fathers; they've got no wives, or children, or loves to feel strongly about; they're so conditioned that they practically can't help behaving as they ought to behave. And if anything should go wrong, there's *soma*.[38]

In perhaps the novel's definitive line, we are told that the alternative to the system involves recognizing 'that the purpose of life was not the maintenance of well-being, but some intensification and refining of consciousness, some enlargement of

---

[33] Ibid., pp. 79–81.
[34] *Aldous Huxley Annual*, 7 (2007), 105.   [35] Huxley, *Brave New World*, p. 129.
[36] Huxley's portrayal is indebted to his friend D. H. Lawrence's description of the effects of being liberated from the 'great era of material and mechanical development' in visiting New Mexico: *Brave New World*, p. xxv.
[37] Huxley, *Brave New World*, pp. 175–6, 138.   [38] Ibid., p. 173.

knowledge'. Mass production, however—not science as such—has engendered the shift to comfort and happiness, and away from engaging with truth, beauty, art, religion, even, to a degree, science, the too assiduous pursuit of which induces instability. Even the Controller muses, 'What fun it would be . . . if one didn't have to think about happiness.' There are hints that Huxley thinks the loss of religious belief to be a tragedy for the later moderns. In a lengthy passage, the Controller explains that belief in a God 'isn't compatible with machinery and scientific medicine and happiness', and why, accordingly, religious books can no longer be published. John's response that 'God's the reason for everything noble and fine and heroic' is met with the not unreasonable retort that: 'These things are symptoms of political efficiency', there being now no wars or intense individual love.[39]

But John doesn't want comfort. He wants God, poetry, danger, freedom, goodness, sin, 'the right to be unhappy', in the Controller's paraphrase, 'to grow old and ugly and impotent', to be struck down by disease and pain. He is doomed to lose this argument. He doesn't care. Nor does Mustapha Mond. Then John attempts an anti-*soma* rebellion, promising real 'freedom' instead, and is joined by Helmholtz, only to be defeated by *soma*-spraying police.[40] As a result, Bernard and Helmholtz are deported to islands of similar dissidents, where free discussion is allowed, and which seem to be the real utopias in the text, envied even by Mond. John is exiled to an old lighthouse, where in prayer and painful self-flagellation, his heroic qualities degenerating rapidly into neurosis, he tries to live up to the stern demands of his God and restrain his desires for Lenina. Persecuted by tourists, he hangs himself.

* * * *

Whether this broader scenario was intended to portray threat, promise, or prediction is unclear. It was seemingly equally unclear to Huxley at the time, and was veiled by constant irony in any case. Many aims have thus been associated with Huxley's greatest work. But he clearly had three main targets in 1932: the regime of mass-produced genetically engendered slavery; the totalitarian system of propagandistic behavioural training and manipulation; and the ideology of superficial hedonism which notionally supplants pre-Fordian value systems. Each of these requires treatment here.

SCIENCE AND *BRAVE NEW WORLD*

As Huxley later acknowledged, the book which 'started out as a parody of H. G. Wells's *Men Like Gods*' gradually 'got out of hand and turned into something quite different from what I'd originally intended'.[41] Though Wells wrote to

---

[39] Ibid., pp. 154–5, 209.   [40] Ibid., pp. 212, 186.
[41] Quoted in Donald Watt, ed., *Aldous Huxley: The Critical Heritage* (Routledge & Kegan Paul, 1975), p. 34. In *Men Like Gods*, a group of travellers accidentally enter another dimension, loosely described as utopia, where, after the 'Last Age of Confusion', population growth has been reduced from 2 billion to 250 million, births are regulated, and neither marriage nor maternity exist in the traditional

Huxley, describing his 'bitter satire on progressive ideas' as treason to science, Huxley said that the 'theme of *Brave New World* is not the advancement of science as such, it is the advancement of science as it affects human individuals'.[42] Many readers assume that this means eugenics in particular. Given Huxley's lifelong flirtation with such ideals, however, it is not at all clear that eugenics as such is portrayed negatively in *Brave New World*. Huxley clearly believed that science could benefit as well as degrade humanity. It was good 'if it facilitates liberation; indifferent if it neither helps nor hinders; bad if it makes liberation more difficult by intensifying the obsession with personality'.[43]

Huxley was, moreover, all in favour of intelligence leading the inert masses. The aristocracy, he wrote in 1922, were the only class 'impervious to general public opinion', slavery to which was 'among the evils begotten of our herding instinct'.[44] His 1927 comment that the ideal state was one in which 'material democracy controlled by an aristocracy of intellect—a state in which men and women are guaranteed a decent human existence and are given every opportunity to develop such talents as they possess, and where those with the greatest talent rule' seems to support this hypothesis.[45] He doubted in 1929 whether the modern world exhibited any 'improvements in individual virtue and intelligence'.[46] His enthusiasm for Wells' 'Samurai' ideal as late as 1935 has also been noted by David Bradshaw; Huxley wrote in 1934 that 'the Samurai idea is scientifically justified, inasmuch as it implies a recognition of the irreconcilable differences between human beings and a rejection of that wish-born theory of equality'.[47] Wells, Vilfredo Pareto, H. L. Mencken, Mencken's master, Nietzsche, and eugenics had all reinforced a near-inherited feeling of the value of an intellectual aristocracy in such schemes.[48] With the sense of the inevitability of a small governing elite, or 'ruling aristocracy of

---

sense, people propagating 'by fission' rather than by sexual intercourse. Private property has been abolished, along with police, prisons, lunacy and physical defects, and most diseases and pests, and all contribute to the common good without any central legislature or executive. Science, technology, and productive capacity, once monopolized by the rich, are now utilized for the good of all. Free discussion and criticism prevail, though lying is prohibited. Creativity is encouraged. But spite, vanity, and other human foibles still exist. There is, however, 'no crowd', and in each life individualism and collectivism are carefully balanced.

[42] H. G. Wells to A. W. Pickard, 1 October 1935, in *The Correspondence of H.G. Wells* (4 vols, Pickering & Chatto, 1998), vol. 4, p. 35; Watt, *Aldous Huxley*, p. 16; Huxley, *Brave New World*, p. xliv.

[43] Huxley, *After Many a Summer*, p. 110.

[44] David Bradshaw, ed., *The Hidden Huxley: Contempt and Compassion for the Masses 1920–36* (Faber & Faber, 1994), p. 36; *Aldous Huxley Annual*, 7 (2007), 63 ('Public Opinion and Personal Liberty').

[45] Bradshaw associates this with the 'Wellsian fellow-traveller': *The Hidden Huxley*, p. 37.

[46] Aldous Huxley, *Proper Studies* (Chatto & Windus, 1929), p. 13.

[47] Bradshaw, *The Hidden Huxley*, p. 41; *Aldous Huxley Annual*, 7 (2007), 109.

[48] Mencken's most relevant work here is *Notes on Democracy* (Jonathan Cape, 1927). Nietzsche, however, was also Huxley's great antagonist here, as having recognized, as Huxley himself expressed it in *Ends and Means* (Chatto & Windus, 1937), that the source of evil lay in the individual will, and then to deny (Buddhist) non-attachment as the antidote. Nietzsche's was sometimes understood as 'the egoistic philosophy'. See Robert S. Baker, *The Dark Historic Page: Social Satire and Historicism in the Novels of Aldous Huxley 1921–1939* (University of Wisconsin Press, 1982), p. 124.

mind', probably determined by eugenic criteria,[49] came the realization of the need for some new, superior religion to serve 'the cause of humanitarianism', like Comte's a century earlier.[50] Joined to this was the acceptance of the bankruptcy of the liberal mantra of the natural equality of mankind and of the herd-like nature of mass behaviour, dominated as it was by 'the newspaper-reading, advertisement-believing, propaganda-swallowing, demagogue-led man—the man who makes modern democracy the farce it is',[51] as *Proper Studies* (1927) so bitingly put it.

Many of the ideas surrounding artificial breeding which are central to *Brave New World* had been circulating for decades. At this time, Philip Gibbs' Wellsian *The Day after Tomorrow: What is Going to Happen in the World?* (1928), projecting fifty years into the future, discussed artificially producing 'ectogenic' children—the term Huxley, like J. D. Bernal, adopts from J. B. S. Haldane.[52] Huxley approved eugenics methods to further these ends in a radio interview on 'Science and Civilisation' two weeks before *Brave New World* appeared. The end point here may consequently have been much closer to Wells' own position than is often assumed.[53] Here Huxley stressed his interest in satirizing an essentially *dysgenic* aim of deliberately lowering 'the average mental standard' and, 'in a scientific civilisation', organizing society 'on a caste basis'.[54] What was clearly meant was not a criticism of eugenics as such, but of the application of scientific behavioural engineering to perpetuate and indeed deepen the existing class system by driving the most deprived into greater ignorance and stupidity.[55] This implies that the satire is chiefly about mass culture and the means by which most of the population is stupefied through propaganda and relentless hedonism, not about eugenics. If anything, Huxley was inclined to promote intelligent applications of the latter. So the 'cloning' of classes in *Brave New World*, despite the satire on Wells, is primarily a metaphor for expressing what was, for Huxley, the real problem: the application of psychology to propaganda as the key to understanding the future:

> Rulers have only to devise some scheme for laying their hands on new-born babies to be able to impose on their people almost any behaviour pattern they like. No serious practical difficulties stand in the way of such a plan. One of these days some apparently beneficent and humanitarian government will create a comprehensive system of State *creches* and baby-farms; and—with a little systematic conditioning of infant

[49] He later wrote, however, that he knew he 'should be proved wrong' about babies being generated artificially (*Complete Essays*, 6 vols, ed. Robert S. Baker and James Sexton (Ivan R. Dee, 2000–2), vol. 6, p. 189).

[50] Huxley. *Complete Essays*, vol. 2, p. 225 (*Proper Studies*, 1927). [51] Ibid., pp. 205–6.

[52] Philip Gibbs, *The Day after Tomorrow: What is Going to Happen in the World?* (Hutchinson & Co., 1928), p. 49; J. D. Bernal, *The World, the Flesh and the Devil* (Jonathan Cape, 1970), p. 37; Huxley, *Brave New World*, p. 39. Huxley probably knew of the utopia written by Haldane's second wife, Charlotte (*Man's World* (Chatto & Windus, 1926)), in which ectogenesis is used to reduce the number of women who breed until only the best remain (pp. 54–61). Her review of *Brave New World* described it as 'a very great book' (Watt, *Aldous Huxley*, p. 209).

[53] As Bradshaw, *The Hidden Huxley*, p. 34, infers. [54] Ibid., pp. 112–13.

[55] Bradley Hart shows that eugenicists did not regard the work as an attack on eugenics as such, and that Huxley continued to be involved in and to lend support for Eugenics Society events ('Aldous Huxley and the Twentieth-Century Eugenics Movement', in Booker, ed., *Critical Insights: Brave New World*, pp. 118–20).

reflexes—it will have the fate of its future subjects in its hands. From the baby-farm the already thoroughly-conditioned infant will pass to the State school. He will grow up reading State newspapers, listening to State wireless, looking at State cinemas and theatres. By the time he reaches what is somewhat ironically called the age of reason, he will be wholly unable to think for himself. None but the approved State ideas will ever even occur to him. This will make the overt use of force quite unnecessary. Dictatorship, as a form of government, may have, in the immediate future, a brief spell of popularity. In times of crisis like the present, strong government is probably necessary. But once the position has been stabilised and, above all, once our rulers have been educated up to the point of realising the extent of the power which psychological science has placed in their hands, strong government will cease to be necessary. When every member of the community has been conditioned from earliest childhood to think as his rulers desire him to think, dictatorship can be abandoned.[56]

Yet Huxley, adopting the standpoint of the 'humanist', was also clearly critical of such developments. What, he asked, would:

[B]e the attitude of the humanist towards scientific propaganda? Fundamentally, I think, he would be opposed to it. For if it were thoroughly scientific and efficient, scientific propaganda would obviously be quite incompatible with personal liberty. Now personal liberty is, for the humanist, something of the highest value. He believes that, on the whole, it is better to 'go wrong in freedom than to go right in chains'— even if the chains are imponderable, even if they are not felt by the prisoner to be chains. Nevertheless, it may be that circumstances will compel the humanist to resort to scientific propaganda, just as they may compel the liberal to resort to dictatorship. Any form of order is better than chaos. Our civilisation is menaced with total collapse. Dictatorship and scientific propaganda may provide the only means for saving humanity from the miseries of anarchy.

He added, too, that the

liberal and the humanist may have to choose the lesser of two evils and, sacrificing liberty, at any rate for a time, choose dictatorship and scientific propaganda as an alternative to collapse. Again, the humanist will have to remember that propaganda is a substitute for force in general and war in particular. It would certainly be worth forgoing a great deal of liberty for the sake of peace.[57]

Interestingly, too, Huxley here demonstrated that his target in *Brave New World* was less the eugenic engineers than the economists whose ideas dominated the debate about ending the Great Depression:

Eugenics are not yet practical politics. But propaganda could easily make them practical politics, while increase of knowledge will make them also purposive and far-sighted politics. The humanist would see in eugenics an instrument for giving to an ever-widening circle of men and women those heritable qualities of mind and body which are, by his highest standards, the most desirable. But what of the economist-ruler? Would he necessarily be anxious to improve the race? By no means necessarily.

---

[56] Bradshaw, *The Hidden Huxley*, pp. 109–10 ('Science and Civilisation', 1932).
[57] Ibid., p. 111.

He might actually wish to deteriorate it. His ideal, we must remember, is not the perfect all-round human being, but the perfect mass-producer and mass-consumer. Now perfect human beings probably make very bad mass-producers. It is quite on the cards that industrialists will find, as machinery is made more foolproof, that the great majority of jobs can be better performed by stupid people than by intelligent ones. Again, stupid people are probably the State's least troublesome subjects, and a society composed in the main of stupid people is more likely to be stable than one with a high proportion of intelligent people. The economist-ruler would therefore be tempted to use the knowledge of genetics, not for eugenic, but for dysgenic purposes—for the deliberate lowering of the average mental standard. True, this would have to be accompanied by the special breeding and training of a small caste of experts, without whom a scientific civilisation cannot exist. Here, incidentally, I may remark that in a scientific civilisation society must be organised on a caste basis. The rulers and their advisory experts will be a kind of Brahmins controlling, in virtue of a special and mysterious knowledge, vast hordes of the intellectual equivalents of Sudras and Untouchables.[58]

This passage makes it clear that the eugenic projection of class differences in *Brave New World* is a satire of non-eugenic trends in behavioural engineering. Thus, to conclude, with Wells, that Huxley was only 'one of the most brilliant' of the 'reactionary writers', is to ignore the politics of Huxley's condemnation of a capitalism which relentlessly bred stupidity.[59]

HUXLEY AND BOLSHEVISM

Though Judith Shklar thought Huxley's key work was 'not a political novel' and offered 'no insights into totalitarian systems',[60] *Brave New World* can in fact be understood as an (admittedly quirky) anti-totalitarian work.[61] The 'whole idea' of the novel, Huxley once said, was that if you could iron people 'into a kind of uniformity, if you were able to manipulate their genetic background . . . if you had a government sufficiently unscrupulous you could do these things without any doubt'.[62] Like Zamyatin, Koestler, Orwell, and others, Huxley focuses on antipathy to individualism in the collectivist state, and the decline of family and personal relationships.[63] To Krishan Kumar, these totalitarian features are secondary, and 'are really the offshoots

[58] Ibid., pp. 112–13.

[59] H. G. Wells, *The Shape of Things to Come* (Hutchinson & Co., 1933), p. 307.

[60] Judith Shklar, *After Utopia: The Decline of Political Faith* (Princeton University Press, 1957), p. 156. Peter Firchow, by contrast, insists that 'Orwell was profoundly influenced by Huxley's novel when he composed his own' (*The End of Utopia: A Study of Aldous Huxley's Brave New World* (Bucknell University Press, 1984), p. 128).

[61] E.g., in the entry in the *Historical Dictionary of Utopianism*, p. 46.

[62] Sybille Bedford, *Aldous Huxley: A Biography* (2 vols, Chatto & Windus, 1973), vol. 1, p. 244.

[63] But Huxley denied ever having read Zamyatin, and this supports the view that his anti-utopia was less anti-Bolshevik than Orwell's. Orwell later wrote that: 'It is this intuitive grasp of the irrational side of totalitarianism—human sacrifice, cruelty as an end in itself . . . that makes Zamiatin's book superior to Huxley's' (*Smothered under Journalism* (Secker & Warburg), 1998, p. 15). Huxley said that he had not encountered Zamyatin's *We* until the late 1950s: Alex Shane, *The Life and Works of Evgenij Zamjatin* (University of California Press, 1968), p. 140.

of more fundamental processes, in particular the laboratory production of children and their moral conditioning against strong individual feeling'.[64] They are attributes of what Huxley took to be the Wellsian state, where a Platonic caste system is underpinned by science. Yet they remain the means by which totalitarian aims might be, in Huxley's view, achieved. For the control of private life, of sexual desire, of individuality, are, as we have seen, central to collectivist regimes.

Few, too, have seen Huxley chiefly as specifically attacking Orwell's later chief target, *Bolshevik* totalitarianism.[65] What then can we say about Huxley's engagement with Bolshevism? As Bradshaw reminds us, Huxley flirted momentarily with socialism when he joined the Oxford Fabians in 1916.[66] Its levelling egalitarianism nonetheless probably quickly put him off. He regarded as 'repulsive' the fact that Bolshevism was 'a serious possibility' in November 1918: this was not a road he could contemplate taking.[67] Some of his early novels also hint at scepticism about the recent revolution, as well as the Wellsian utopia; in *Antic Hay* (1923),[68] the 'Red Guards' patrol the streets judging the class origins of people's accents—a peculiarly British obsession and a test the posh Huxley would have failed.[69] Yet he remained curious, planning a trip to the USSR in 1931 with his brother Julian, which eventually had to be aborted.[70]

There is some evidence of Huxley's admiration for the Soviet experiment by this point, however. In part this was deference to the emerging cult of science and expertise which the USSR exhibited, in which the Party might now be seen to be playing a leading role. Huxley had long been contemptuous of parliamentary democracies where propaganda by elites successfully manipulated the ignorant masses. He also admired planned economies, writing in 1931 that, 'I do feel more and more certain that unless the rest of the world adopts something on the lines of the Five Year Plan, it will break down. Modern industry is too huge and complicated to be left to individualistic enterprise.'[71] In 1932, he thus opposed the chaos of 'planless individualism'. He was also willing to 'believe that a lot of people

[64] Kumar, *Utopia and Anti-Utopia in Modern Times*, p. 260.
[65] Many studies of Huxley ignore the topic. A brief exception is M. D. Petre, 'An Argument against Bolshevik Ideals', which describes *Brave New World* as an exposition of Bolshevism, meaning, by this, principally an antagonism to the religious world-view (in Katie de Koster, ed., *Readings on Brave New World* (Greenhaven Press, 1999), pp. 33–42) (originally published as 'Bolshevist Ideals and the "Brave New World"', *Hibbert Journal* (October 1932)). Here, of course, the Savage, 'invincible by reason of that individuality which he alone, amongst them all, possesses', is the hero.
[66] Bradshaw, *The Hidden Huxley*, pp. viii–ix.
[67] Huxley, *Letters*, p. 169.
[68] This was one of Orwell's favourite books: see *A Kind of Compulsion 1903–1936* (Secker & Warburg, 2000), p. 308.
[69] An audio file exists (*c.*1962) of a talk given by Huxley at the University of California, Berkeley, called 'The Ultimate Revolution', which concerns the advantages of consent over force in ensuring the ability of a 'controlling oligarchy' to use 'scientific dictatorship' to ensure that a population loved its servitude. He again stressed the likelihood that the '*Brave New World* pattern' of dictatorship, notably through Pavlovian conditioning and the manipulation of suggestibility through 'pure persuasion', was a much more likely description of a stable and lasting future society than Orwell's. He thought here that about 20% of any population could be persuaded to believe almost anything. Huxley's accent was distinctly upper class. See Aldous Huxley. *The Ultimate Revolution* (YouTube).
[70] Huxley, *Letters*, pp. 348–9.   [71] Ibid., p. 351.

are happy in Russia—because happiness . . . is a by-product of something else and they've got a Cause . . . the working for which gives them happiness'. But, he conceded, 'it is always as history demonstrates, in the nature of a temporary intoxication'. So, 'In Russia where propaganda is more efficient, it may last a bit longer', but would probably end whether the 'Plan' failed or succeeded.[72] We get little sense here that Huxley, like the vehement anti-Bolshevik Nikolai Berdyaev, a writer he admired, regarded the Russian Revolution as the great caesura in modern development, particularly in religious terms.[73]

Huxley's knowledge of Bolshevism was based upon one key source. He wrote in December 1927 that:

> I have been much confirmed in my leanings towards aristocracy by the reading of a very interesting book on life, art and thought in modern Russia, called *The Mind and Face of Bolshevism*, by a German called [René] Fülöp-Miller. Do read it if you haven't already done so. It's really humiliating that human beings can be so stupid as these Russians seem to be. They really are the devil. Europeans must join together to resist all the enemies of our civilization—Russians, Americans, orientals—each in their own way a hideous menace. There are limits to toleration and they all overstep those limits![74]

Huxley would introduce Miller—who cited Le Bon—in *Music at Night* (1931) to define his portrait of Bolshevism.[75] He apparently took from him, amongst other things, the view that Bolshevism epitomized a mass society, a 'mighty and powerful organism' where the 'impersonal' 'mass man' was now 'lord of Russia'. This would have put paid to any notions that the Party represented some new form of intellectual and scientific aristocracy. Miller quoted a Soviet historian, Pokrovski, who suggested that,

> to us personality is only the instrument with which history works. Perhaps a time will come when these instruments will be artificially constructed, as today we make our electric accumulators. But we have not yet progressed so far; for the moment, these instruments through which history comes into being, these accumulators of the social process, are still begotten and born in an entirely elemental way.[76]

So Wells' hints at artificial breeding were here refined, and now wedded to propaganda. If anyone could make a human machine, it seemed the Soviets could.

Miller's account doubtless impressed Huxley because of its Fordist emphases.[77] Miller explored linkages between communist festivals devoted to 'the visible God', the machine, and the 'mechanical interpretation' of life, and the possible loss of the

---

[72] Bedford, *Aldous Huxley*, vol. 1, p. 262; Huxley, *Letters*, pp. 361–2.

[73] See, e.g., Nikolai Berdyaev, *The Russian Revolution* (Sheed & Ward, 1932).

[74] Huxley, *Letters*, p. 293.

[75] Huxley, *Music at Night*, p. 214. Peter Firchow briefly acknowledges Miller's impact on Huxley (*The End of Utopia*, pp. 96–7). Here the Savage is rejected as a hero figure because he represents a 'pure individualism' which is as flawed as the 'pure collectivism' of the Bolsheviks (p. 97).

[76] René Fülöp-Miller, *The Mind and Face of Bolshevism* (G. P. Putnam's Sons, 1927), pp. 1, 3, 7.

[77] Ford was, of course, anti-Bolshevik: see *My Life and Work*, pp. 4–5. He was, however, a 'figure of heroic proportions' in the USSR itself: Susan Buck-Morss, *Dreamworld and Catastrophe: The Passing of Mass Utopia in East and West* (MIT Press, 2000), p. 165.

value of individual personality. Huxley must have relished, while detesting, Miller's description of a communist future in which 'the last human remnants of everything organic will be sloughed off and replaced by mechanism [and] finally transformed into the mechanical component parts of a gigantic productive automaton which will function reliably, and thereby will be realized the ideal collective man, for whom the Bolsheviks are striving'. He doubtless paused at the observation that 'even Ford would certainly reject as a crazy scheme the ideal that this mechanization should be artificially extended from the factory to life itself'. He shared the conclusion that it was 'a perversity to see an ideal aim in automatization; the salvation of humanity lies rather in those remnants of the life of the soul which can never be entirely mechanized or standardized'. The 'idolatrous worship of the machine itself as the fullest expression of the mechanized mastery of life'[78] thus loomed large in Miller's description of Bolshevism.

Huxley clearly endorsed this account. This was not, in 1932, anything he associated with Hitler, whose global impact was yet to come. *Brave New World* is not in this sense a critique of 'totalitarianism', but, much more specifically, of Bolshevik modernity and its implications. Even more widely, it simply expressed the age of mechanization, which, in 1929, Huxley had seen most aptly described in 'the best and briefest summing-up of contemporary tendencies which has yet been made': Alphonse Séché's *La Morale de la Machine*. Here he read that: 'The machine murders fantasy and suppresses personal idiosyncrasies. Its slaves must work in the way (the, for most modern workers, senseless, monotonous, and imbecile way) which it finds suitable to its mechanical needs; they must consume the standardized objects it has created.' From now on he used 'Fordism' to denote 'the philosophy of industrialism'.[79] By this he meant in particular (quoting Ford) that, 'inasmuch as it "shifts the recurrent mental load from men in production to men in designing", the machine is our enemy; for it deprives the overwhelming majority of men and women of the possibility, the very hope, of even the most modest creative activity'.[80] Here then was the rebellion against Ford's assumption that 'the average worker . . . wants a job in which he does not have to think'.[81]

The Bolshevik 'machine cult', then, and not science as such, led Huxley towards the belief that freedom was the greatest casualty of this aspect of modernity. Miller also indicated that Bolshevism, and Lenin in particular, also epitomized an appeal to violence, and here too Huxley's opposition would have hardened. Miller saw Bolshevism as 'merely a change in the direction of the tyranny' of the old regime. The means of oppression were 'exactly the same', the *katorga* or system of Tsarist punishment and exile being merely replaced by its Chekist and then Joint State Political Directorate (OGPU) counterparts. But the latter were even more malevolent than that of the Tsarist secret police, the Okhrana, in being utterly free of judicial control, thus producing 'an arbitrary rule unknown in the rest of the world for centuries'—indeed, since the Inquisition. Yet Miller also indicated how far

---

[78] Fülöp-Miller, *The Mind and Face of Bolshevism*, pp. 13, 20–1, 24.
[79] Huxley, *Collected Essays*, vol. 3, pp. 222–4 (1929); p. 238 (1931).
[80] Ibid., p. 282.   [81] Ford, *My Life and Work*, p. 103.

America remained a bright ideal to the early Bolsheviks, and how far 'superamericanism' became synonymous with 'mechanical civilisation' in general. Miller's identification of Bolshevism and the United States is thus much closer than the Cold War literature on totalitarianism suggests. It is mirrored in Huxley's ambiguous account of a Fordist world which reveals dominant trends in both societies.[82]

Huxley would have here read the quote from Lenin that 'freedom is a bourgeois prejudice', perhaps pausing at the inference that 'human happiness can only be attained by lack of freedom, by slavish obedience'.[83] Miller regarded Bolshevism's denunciation of free will as essentially Jesuit in origin. Miller also taught, thought Huxley:

[T]hat the political doctrines elaborated by Lenin and his followers are the exact antithesis of the revolutionary liberalism preached by Godwin and dithyrambically chanted by Shelley a hundred years ago. Godwin and Shelley believed in pure individualism. The Bolsheviks believe in pure collectivism. One belief is as extravagantly romantic as the other. Men cannot live apart from society and without organization. But, equally, they cannot live without a certain modicum of privacy and personal liberty. The exclusive idealism of Shelley denies the obvious facts of human biology and economics. The exclusive materialism of Lenin denies the no less obvious and primary facts of men's immediate spiritual experiences. The revolutionary liberals were romantic in their refusal to admit that man was a social animal as well as an individual soul. The Bolsheviks are romantic in denying that man is anything more than a social animal, susceptible of being transformed by proper training into a perfect machine. Both are extravagant and one-sided.[84]

Faced with these two extremes, Huxley averred that an:

[E]xaggeration of the significance of the soul and the individual, at the expense of matter, society, machinery, and organization, seems to me an exaggeration in the right direction . . . if I had my way, I would not choose either of the romanticisms; I would vote for the adoption of a middle course between them. The only philosophy of life which has any prospect of being permanently valuable is a philosophy which takes in all the facts—the facts of mind *and* the facts of matter, of instinct *and* intellect, of individualism *and* of sociableness. The wise man will avoid both extremes of romanticism and choose the realistic golden mean.[85]

This indicates, amongst other things, that the ultra-individualist John could not be the hero of *Brave New World* a year later.

Yet to conserve some forms of individualism might well mean suppressing others. Here, the USSR might yet have lessons to teach. 'The Russians', Huxley thought:

[H]ave frankly avowed their intention of suppressing individualism in the interests of society. They are hardly less merciful to the family, because of its tendency to create an *imperium in imperio*. The State-paid professional educator is to take the place of the parents. There is an obvious tendency, all over the western world, to follow the lead of

Russia—not through any desire to imitate the Soviets but because circumstances are rendering it increasingly necessary for all States to guard against the dangers of insurgent individualism. Human standardisation will become a political necessity.[86]

This seems to indicate a sympathy for the view that benevolent dictatorship was increasingly necessary to restrain 'insurgent individualism' (including that fed by 'free-market' plutocracy). The trick, as ever, lay in getting the balance right between individualism and collectivism. In a similar vein, too, Huxley wrote in September 1931, advocating what Bradshaw describes as '*Soviet-style* planning', that:

> We may either persist in our present course, which is disastrous, or we must abandon democracy and allow ourselves to be ruled dictatorially by men who will compel us to do and suffer what a rational foresight demands.
>
> Or, if we preserve the democratic forms, we must invent some psychological technique for inducing the electorate to act before the crash rather than after; we must provide voters with bad emotional reasons for behaving with rational foresight.
>
> Or, finally, we may employ both these last methods together—compel and at the same time use propaganda to make the compulsion appear acceptable.
>
> This is the present Russian method. Refined and improved, it has a good chance of becoming universal.[87]

Huxley wrote in May 1931 that, if their Five-Year Plan succeeded, the Soviets might 'convert the whole world to her way of thinking'.[88] The scheme described in late 1931, then, looks broadly like *Brave New World*: overt coercion plays a negligible role and benevolent dictatorship is triumphant. *Music at Night* echoes this: 'Scientific psychology may succeed where Christianity and the political religions have failed. Let us hope so. In a world where most people had been taught to love their fellows there would be no difficulty in reconciling the claims of Grace with those of Justice, of universality with favouritism.' But Huxley also foresaw the possibility that, in 'the egalitarian state of the future all excessive accumulations of property will be abolished'. This implied 'the abolition of all excessive enjoyment of liberty', leaving everyone with the freedoms of 'the contemporary confidential clerk'.[89] It was not a life with which he could easily empathize.

Music at Night repeats the association of a mechanical world-view and machine worship to Bolshevism which would reappear in *Brave New World*:

> To the Bolshevik, there is something hideous and unseemly about the spectacle of anything so 'chaotically vital', so 'mystically organic' as an individual with a soul, with personal tastes, with special talents. Individuals must be organized out of existence; the Communist state requires not men but cogs and ratchets in the huge 'collective mechanism'. To the Bolshevik idealist, Utopia is indistinguishable from one of Mr. Henry Ford's factories. It is not enough, in their eyes, that men should spend only eight hours a day under the workshop discipline. Life outside the factory must be

[86] Bradshaw, *The Hidden Huxley*, p. 49 ('Babies: State Property', May 1930).
[87] Ibid., p. xviii.   [88] Ibid., pp. 62–3.
[89] Huxley, *Music at Night*, pp. 97, 121–2. John Atkins describes Huxley's views at this time as foreseeing 'a Bolshevik–Fordian Earthly Paradise which would be acceptable to communist and capitalist alike' (*Aldous Huxley: A Literary Study* (John Calder, 1956), p. 215).

exactly like life inside. Leisure must be as highly organized as toil. Into the Christian Kingdom of Heaven men may only enter if they have become like little children. The condition of their entry into the Bolsheviks' Earthly Paradise is that they shall have become like machines.[90]

We are not far from Le Bon's crowd here, but this mass is manufactured rather than spontaneous. There is no hint of atavism, or reversion: this is a new human, or perhaps somewhat less than, or more than, human type. Huxley added that:

[I]nterestingly, it is the new Soviet state, rather than America, which has shown the Fordian impulse in its clearest form . . . The Bolsheviks here are only indicating the tendencies apparent in all mass democracies, to organize the whole of society according to the dictates and the image of the machine.[91]

This passage indicates that the missing ingredient required for *Brave New World* was an account of how an ideal system of manipulation would function.

Huxley thus saw Bolshevism, through the Fülöp-Miller lens, as a specially nefarious instance of machine worship, and not solely as a totalitarian political dictatorship. The wider trend, Fordism run riot, was the ugly face of modernity. It is this trend towards a mechanical world-view, 'standardisation', not 'science' as such (except in the sense of 'scientific psychology'), which would become Huxley's chief target. His achievement here was to warn that the underlying psychology of manipulation might prove as devastating in societies where near-compulsory pleasure reigned as those where fear underpinned dictatorial power. There was, then, some ambiguity in Huxley's position in 1932. What Bradshaw has described as a 'sea change' in Huxley's attitudes towards authoritarianism only occurred after *Brave New World* appeared.[92]

HUXLEY AND HEDONISM: HIGH vs LOW UTILITARIANISM

In *Brave New World*, hedonism is both the predominant ethos and an obvious satirical target. Orwell wrote in 1940 that, in the book, 'the hedonistic principle is pushed to its utmost, the whole world has turned into a Riviera hotel'.[93] 'Everyone's happy now', says Lenina, repeating a phrase rehearsed a hundred and fifty times per night for twelve years during sleep indoctrination, affirming that

[90] Huxley, *Music at Night*, pp. 212–13.

[91] Cited by Erika Gottlieb (*Dystopian Fiction*, pp. 75–6, 293) as Huxley, 'The New Romanticism', pp. 213–14, in *Music at Night*. But the quote is not in this text.

[92] Quoted in Bradshaw, *The Hidden Huxley*, p. xxi.

[93] George Orwell, *The Collected Essays, Journalism and Letters of George Orwell* (Secker & Warburg, 1968), vol. 2, p. 32. Orwell also thought that 'though *Brave New World* was a brilliant caricature of the present (the present of 1930), it probably casts no light on the future. No society of that kind would last more than a couple of generations, because a ruling class which thought principally in terms of a "good time" would soon lose its vitality. A ruling class has got to have a strict morality, a quasi-religious belief in itself, a mystique' (Watt, *Aldous Huxley*, p. 333).

Epsilons, Betas, and Alphas were all satisfied with their existing position.[94] The amusements of the population, Huxley had earlier described, as including theatres where 'the egalitarians will enjoy the talkies, tasties, smellies and feelies, the Corner Houses where they will eat their synthetic poached eggs on toast-substitute and drink their surrogates of coffee'. These would be 'prodigiously much vaster and more splendid than anything we know to-day'.[95] They are so sumptuous by contemporary standards—we are in the Great Depression after all—that most would not take these pleasures as ersatz measures of happiness (if the distinction has any meaning). Yet, as Huxley explained in an essay on 'Modern Amusements', they still had to be condemned. For they rendered the public 'absolutely passive', mere onlookers, who formerly, even in the simple folk song or country dance, were 'potential performers', but who now instead merely looked and listened, and did not 'in any way create'.[96] So while such pleasures were an improvement on brutal poverty, they were far from ideal.

This is clearly intended to arouse the reader's suspicions: there is something false or artificial in this happiness. Is Huxley's a Potemkin-village world in which the 'happy' façade masks some awful inner distress, the smiles contorted to disguise some inner agony? Or is 'seven and a half hours of mild, unexhausting labour, and then the *soma* ration and games and unrestricted copulation and the feelies' just about as far as 'happiness' can ever take us, in Huxley's view—'pretty squalid' and 'never grand', but a perfectly plausible 'happiness' nonetheless?[97] Perhaps this is just what the human lot consists of, for the majority, and not that permanently dissatisfied snivelling group of intellectuals who cannot stand for or in the way of the rest. If people claim they are happy, they must be happy, the reasoning runs. And if they want to be happy more than anything else, who are we to tell them otherwise, and to insist that they are shamming and should join us in our misery, and in our obsessive, divisive and possible equally sham 'individuality'? 'What more do they want?', Mustapha Mond asks. What more would it be reasonable to expect? we might echo. Perhaps 'grandness' is just an illusion.

Most readers thus quickly sense that the contrast between the flashy, sexy new world and the drab, tired, miserable old one, as represented by the Savage reservation, is overdrawn and simplistic. The appeal of reservation life and noble savagery—whose description is coloured by Huxley's friendship with D. H. Lawrence—is actually pretty limited.[98] Asked in an interview whether he sympathized with this world or the brave new one, Huxley said 'neither'.[99] Huxley had never visited any

---

[94] Huxley, *Brave New World*, p. 65.
[95] Huxley, *Music at Night*, p. 123. In *Antic Hay* (Chatto & Windus, 1923, repr. 1973) Huxley had queried whether, if all had greater leisure, they would be freer: 'Cinemas, newspapers, magazines, gramophones, football matches, wireless, telephones—take them or leave them, if you want to amuse yourself. The ordinary man can't leave them. He takes; and what's that but slavery?' (p. 35).
[96] *Aldous Huxley Annual*, 3 (2003), 18–21.
[97] Huxley, *Brave New World*, p. 176.
[98] John's mother Linda is usually described as modelled on Lawrence's wife Frieda. Lawrence is often described as emphasizing to Huxley the need for everyone to become an artist, but also for artists to withdraw from society to express their genius (e.g., Atkins, *Aldous Huxley*, p. 38).
[99] *Aldous Huxley Annual*, 3 (2003), 123.

such reservation and relied on Smithsonian reports for inspiration.[100] He did not 'very much like primitive people', he remarked in *Beyond the Mexique Bay* (1934). He had no desire to become one. In 1933, he wrote that, 'back to Nature is not practical politics. The only cure for science is more science, not less.'[101]

Yet there are doubts here too, and these would grow. In 1935, he wrote about the Pueblo Indians that they seemed to exemplify the principle that 'no man shall have the power or even the desire to dominate his fellows'. Theirs was 'a society liberated from all sexual repressions, but overflowing with precisely those energies which seem to be the products of repression'.[102] Elsewhere he said 'primitives' possessed a 'human wholeness', the capacity to be 'a complete man, trained in all the skills of the community, able to fend for himself in all circumstances'. This, the moderns might emulate.[103] In lectures delivered in the 1950s, he described the small tribe of Arapesh people of New Guinea studied by Margaret Mead as a 'an essentially non-violent and co-operative society', noting that they 'set the highest value upon love and friendliness and have developed methods which are used from the earliest years for encouraging and implementing the ideals of love'.[104] Many of us readily identify with John, yet concede the attractions of ever-ready guiltless orgasms and euphoria on tap. We want, naturally, the best of both worlds, of reason and passion, the shallow and the deep, the individual and the group, stability and humanity, the material and the spiritual selves. We may mock the superficiality of hedonistic civilization. But we cannot escape it. To concede the intrinsic, deeply degrading, and highly anti-intellectual nature of much of our own popular culture risks ostracism or worse in a democratic society. So we remain impaled on the horns of Huxley's dilemma.

We cannot, however, doubt that the target of Huxley's critique includes the United States. Critics have accused Huxley of anti-American snobbism. He wrote of the outcome of World War I that: 'I dread the inevitable acceleration of American world domination.' In 1922, he regarded the United States as the country where the tyranny of public opinion was most powerful, adding that: 'That is part of the price that has to be paid for democracy and material progress.'[105] Yet he would soon regard America's future as 'the future of civilized man'.[106] In 1927, he described California as 'pure Rabelais', materially 'the nearest approach to Utopia yet seen on our planet', adding that 'After twenty-four hours of it, you begin to pine for the slums of Dostoievsky's Saint Petersburg!'[107] (Appropriately, the television adaptation of the book was set in brave new California rather than in London.) Yet Huxley spent most of the rest of his life in California, at the heart of the very industry which epitomized the shallowness of the new values, indeed profiting mightily from it. In what he termed in 1947 an 'Age of

---

[100] Modern readers are thus apt to object to his description: see Katherine Toy Miller, 'Pententes at the Snake Dance: Native Americans in *Brave New World*', in Booker, ed., *Critical Insights: Brave New World*, pp. 152–65.

[101] Bradshaw, *The Hidden Huxley*, p. 106. [102] *Aldous Huxley Annual*, 7 (2007), 124.

[103] Huxley, *Complete Essays*, vol. 3, p. 578. [104] Huxley, *The Human Situation*, p. 250.

[105] *Aldous Huxley Annual*, 7 (2007), 63. [106] Huxley, *Complete Essays*, vol. 3, p. 185.

[107] Huxley, *Selected Letters*, p. 189.

Nationalistic Idolatry, Organized Lying and Non-Stop Distractions', he was at the centre of it all, immersed, indeed, in promoting his own brand of what would become counter-cultural hedonism.[108]

Yet Huxley did later envision an alternative, 'higher' hedonism. In his later years as a visionary seer he approached, we will see momentarily, those utopias where intoxication and spiritual bliss intermix, bringing us back, on another level, to the festival, the wedding of utopia to euphoria, and the linkage of intoxication to the transcendence of social repression and insistence on equality. Here we see Fourier, too, and what is sometimes called 'utopian' socialism, not in satire but in reality.

HUXLEY AFTER *BRAVE NEW WORLD*

Following the great critical success of *Brave New World*, Huxley spent much of the rest of his life working through its implications, updating its predictions, and countering its evident pessimism. His enthusiasms concerning the potential benefits of dictatorships seem to have peaked in 1932. In 1934, reviewing the Federation of Progressive Societies and Individuals' *Manifesto*, Huxley still saw Communist Party members, 'trained up in habits of austere self-discipline', as functioning like Wells' Samurai. He reflected that,

> There is even a great deal to be said for the creation of a caste of Brahmins above the Samurai. Their immediate, political, propagandist value would be less than that of the more active Samurai; but ultimately, it seems to me, society can derive nothing but benefit from the existence of such a caste.[109]

But the existence of such a group was now firmly dissociated from political despotism. By late 1935, he termed any such form of rule 'intrinsically bad'. While his enthusiasm for such elites never waned, combining this with dictatorship was never again on his agenda. Huxley remained fascinated with the prospect of developing a 'science of propaganda'. He continued to feel that nationalistic propaganda produced by totalitarian states would possibly achieve short-term success, but then fail in the long term owing to the 'impossibility of reducing a huge, educated population to the spiritual homogeneity of a savage tribe'.[110] On this issue he greatly admired Vilfredo Pareto's work in particular.[111] (But he also

---

[108] Aldous Huxley, *Literature and Science; and Science, Liberty and Peace* (Chatto & Windus, 1970), p. 57.

[109] Quoted in Alexander Henderson, *Aldous Huxley* (Chatto & Windus, 1935), p. 196.

[110] 'Writers and Readers' (1936), in Huxley, *Collected Essays*, vol. 4, p. 18.

[111] He first read Pareto in Italian in 1926 (*Letters*, p. 275). In *Proper Studies* (1927), he wrote that: 'In his monumental *Sociologia Generale* I discovered many of my own still vague and inchoate notions methodically set down and learnedly documented, together with a host of new ideas and relevant facts. I have borrowed freely from this almost inexhaustible store' (*Collected Essays*, vol. 2, p. 149). The essay, 'Pareto and Society' (1934) (*Collected Essays*, vol., 3, pp. 386–7) indicates some of these debts, but hardly all of them. Huxley was likely most attracted to Pareto's idea that people were mainly persuaded through sentiment. See Vilfredo Pareto, *The Mind and Society* (Jonathan Cape, 1935), vol. 3, pp. 885–990.

worried that, while totalitarian systems of propaganda clearly let less truth in or out, 'Private, Plutocratic censorship' played a similar role in liberal democracies. Both, he wrote in 1935, were 'thoroughly vicious'.)[112]

So Huxley remained plagued by doubts about the incompatibility of industrial society with humanist aspirations. He deplored both the relations between man and machine and those between worker and boss. By 1937, he was a solid critic of the ruthless violence practised by the Soviet regime on an unprecedented scale.[113] His concerns grew as to the potential uses of controlled television, press, and other media as sources of propaganda.[114] His fascination with advertising was undiminished. Yet there was a growing sense that its exercise in all large states could not but be deleterious. He began moving swiftly and steadily towards the cooperative, decentralist principles which dominated his later social thought.[115] By 1937 he began to identify with an ideal of small-scale communitarianism 'composed of carefully selected individuals, united in a common belief and by fidelity to a shared ideal', where 'property and income should be held in common' and 'every member should assume unlimited liability for all other members'.[116] This was combined with a growing flirtation with Hinduism and Buddhism in the late 1930s, in search of a religious answer to modernity. Mixed with the ideal of self-sufficiency, which Huxley called 'Jeffersonian democracy' in 1939, Huxley's immersion in a personal search for Vedantist enlightenment and the 'Perennial Philosophy' resulted in the vision described in *Island* (1962), discussed below. Politically, by 1940, he was committed to the principle that 'economic independence', rather than 'centralized tyranny', was the only system upon which 'political democracy can be based'.[117]

By 1948, then, Huxley had little good to say about the Russian Revolution, which he characterized as 'two and a half times the population of London exterminated, in order that political power might be taken from one set of ruffians and given to another set; in order that a process of industrialization might be made a little more rapid and a great deal more ruthless than it otherwise would have been'.[118] Nationalization had not altered the principle of the management of resources in the least. The great 'state-controlled enterprises have been closely modelled upon those of capitalist big business'. Nor had 'the land and natural resources been nationalized with the purpose of giving individuals or co-operating groups free access to the means of small-scale production, personal liberty and self-government'. Here, 'gigantism' and 'centralisation' rendered the labour movement as prone to oligarchy as the bosses, and 'Self-government, which is the very essence of democratic freedom, is more or less completely absent from their professional lives.' In this process, greater size meant more power, the appetite for which was

---

[112] *Aldous Huxley Annual*, 7 (2007), 133 ('I am a Highbrow').
[113] See Huxley, *Collected Essays*, vol. 4, p. 174 (*Ends and Means*).
[114] E.g., Ibid., p. 288.   [115] E.g., Ibid., p. 153 (1936).
[116] Ibid., p. 174 (*Ends and Means*).
[117] Aldous Huxley, 'Introduction', in J. D. Unwin, *Hopousia: or the Sexual and Economic Foundations of a New Society* (George Allen & Unwin, 1940), p. 23.
[118] Aldous Huxley, *Time Must Have a Stop* (Chatto & Windus, 1948), p. 190. He thus estimated 20 million dead.

undiminished, and indeed grew into 'successive satisfaction of that most alluring and pernicious of all the lusts'. Yet the oppression indicated here was also a universal process in which, as Huxley stressed in 1947, 'every victory over Nature will inevitably serve only to increase that power and that oppression. This is what is actually happening.'[119]

And the pace of this process seemed to be increasing. In 1949, he worried that the revolution which would bring each individual's 'body, his mind, his whole private life directly under the control of the ruling oligarchy' was not likely to occur in five or six centuries, as *Brave New World* imagined, but much sooner, following Orwell, indeed, within thirty-five years. Ruling oligarchies both capitalist and totalitarian were gaining in power by applying science to propaganda. Preserving liberty under law seemed unlikely.[120] But Huxley continued to plump 'for the division and dispersal of power, the de-institutionalizing of politics and economics and the substitution, wherever possible, of regional co-operative self-help for centralized mass production and mass distribution, and of regional, co-operative self-government for state intervention and state control'.[121]

Unfortunately, there seemed ever less hope of achieving these goals. Huxley's description of how the Malthusian scenario promoted totalitarian tendencies, and 'the ravaging of his planet, the destruction of civilization, and the degradation of his species' gives readers today a striking contemporary application of his ideas.[122] Despotism driven by overpopulation was the face of the future. Unless the tide could be turned, the struggle for resources would ultimately trump all other considerations. As this intensified, the advanced countries would probably develop totalitarian institutions in order to exploit the less fortunate. (This scenario, as we have seen, can already be associated with Thomas More.) Overpopulation and overorganization would combine as *Brave New World* had loosely predicted.[123] The early years of Chinese communism seemed a halfway house between *Nineteen Eighty-Four* and *Brave New World*.[124]

Fascism, Stalinism, World War II, and nuclear weapons all had a bearing on the main themes of *Brave New World*. So the book appeared still more relevant as the destructive power of science loomed ever larger after 1945. In a 1946 preface to *Brave New World*, Huxley proposed that a better world might be imagined in which science and technology were 'made for man, not . . . as though man were to be adapted and enslaved to them'. More than anything else, he now saw *Brave New World* as a vision of a world driven by propaganda. Huxley tell us that:

> The love of servitude cannot be established except as the result of a deep, personal revolution in human minds and bodies. To bring about that revolution we require, among others, the following discoveries and inventions. First, a greatly improved technique of suggestion—through infant conditioning and, later, with the aid of

[119] Huxley, *Literature and Science*, p. 105, 114–15, 141–2.
[120] Huxley, *Collected Essays*, vol. 5, pp. 109, 256, 260 (1946).   [121] Ibid., p. 272.
[122] Ibid., p. 132. The world's population was then about 2.7 billion. See also Aldous Huxley, *The Politics of Ecology* (Center for the Study of Democratic Institutions, 1963), pp. 2–5.
[123] Huxley, *Collected Essays*, vol. 6, pp. 229, 235.   [124] Ibid., pp. 261–2.

drugs, such as scopolamine. Second, a fully developed science of human differences, enabling government managers to assign any given individual to his or her proper place in the social and economic hierarchy. (Round pegs in square holes tend to have dangerous thoughts about the social system and to infect others with their discontents.) Third (since reality, however Utopian, is something from which people feel the need of taking pretty frequent holidays), a substitute for alcohol and the other narcotics, something at once less harmful and more pleasure-giving than gin or heroin. And fourth (but this would be a long-term project, which would take generations of totalitarian control to bring to a successful conclusion), a foolproof system of eugenics, designed to standardize the human product and so to facilitate the task of the managers. In *Brave New World* this standardization of the human product has been pushed to fantastic, though not perhaps impossible, extremes.[125]

He added that:

The people who govern the Brave New World may not be sane (in what may be called the absolute sense of that word); but they are not madmen and their aim is not anarchy but social stability. It is in order to achieve stability that they carry out, by scientific means, the ultimate, personal, really revolutionary revolution.[126]

In the first instance, this stability was to be attained through greater centralization and the creation of totalitarian governments, which Huxley believed would inevitably emerge on a large scale in the near future. The 'immediate future', he thought, was:

[L]ikely to resemble the immediate past, and in the immediate past rapid technological changes, taking place in a mass-producing economy and among a population predominantly propertyless, have always tended to produce economic and social confusion. To deal with confusion, power has been centralized and government control increased. It is probable that all the world's governments will be more or less completely totalitarian even before the harnessing of atomic energy; that they will be totalitarian during and after the harnessing seems almost certain. Only a large-scale popular movement toward decentralization and self-help can arrest the present tendency toward statism.[127]

So the first problem of *Brave New World* was that of scale: the World State was now not viable, even in principle. The larger groups were, the more totalitarian they became, and the largest groups were the most dangerous. Yet population growth inexorably pushed towards their creation.

By 1946, Huxley viewed the book's second great difficulty as the simplistic juxtaposition of alternative world-views offered there, which he called 'the most serious defect in the story'. He now wrote of John's character that:

The Savage is offered only two alternatives, an insane life in Utopia, or the life of a primitive in an Indian village, a life more human in some respects, but in others hardly less queer and abnormal. At the time the book was written this idea, that human beings are given free will in order to choose between insanity on the one hand and lunacy on the other, was one that I found amusing and regarded as quite possibly true.[128]

[125] Huxley, *Brave New World*, p. xlix.   [126] Ibid., p. xlv (1946 introduction).
[127] Ibid., pp. xlvii (1946 introduction).   [128] Ibid., p. xlii.

He added:

> If I were now to rewrite the book, I would offer the Savage a third alternative. Between the Utopian and the primitive horns of his dilemma would lie the possibility of sanity—a possibility already actualized, to some extent, in a community of exiles and refugees from the Brave New World, living within the borders of the Reservation. In this community economics would be decentralist and Henry-Georgian, politics Kropotkinesque and co-operative. Science and technology would be used as though, like the Sabbath, they had been made for man, not (as at present and still more so in the Brave New World) as though man were to be adapted and enslaved to them. Religion would be the conscious and intelligent pursuit of man's Final End, the unitive knowledge of the immanent Tao or Logos, the transcendent Godhead or Brahman. And the prevailing philosophy of life would be a kind of High Utilitarianism, in which the Greatest Happiness principle would be secondary to the Final End principle—the first question to be asked and answered in every contingency of life being: 'How will this thought or action contribute to, or interfere with, the achievement, by me and the greatest possible number of other individuals, of man's Final End?'
>
> Brought up among the primitives, the Savage (in this hypothetical new version of the book) would not be transported to Utopia until he had had an opportunity of learning something at first hand about the nature of a society composed of freely co-operating individuals devoted to the pursuit of sanity. Thus altered, *Brave New World* would possess an artistic and (if it is permissible to use so large a word in connection with a work of fiction) a philosophical completeness, which in its present form it evidently lacks.[129]

Yet Huxley was in fact growing more, not less, pessimistic, particularly about overpopulation. He also wondered in 1946 whether 'the Brave New World is only a couple of generations away, with really scientific dictatorships using all the resources of applied psychology and biology to make their subjects like the slavery to which they have been reduced'. He expressed concern in 1948 that

> there will be at the end of this century twice as many feeble-minded children in the schools as there are now and half as many children of outstanding ability. Moreover the average intelligence of the community will have declined by 5 IQ points on the Binet scale. The question arises: can one have a democratic way of life in a population which is, biologically speaking, degenerating?[130]

The twin concerns of overpopulation and eugenics were thus still united.

At this point Huxley published a second dystopia, which remains much less well known than *Brave New World*. *Ape and Essence* (1949) again raised fears of both science and leaders, particularly in combination, gone awry, with 'progress' portrayed like an uncontrollable genie released from the bottle. Though set in the immediate present, a film script is recovered which concerns a world where humans, who walk on all fours, are the pets of baboons, who dress like humans. (Film buffs will recognize a *Planet of the Apes* scenario.) The first such human we meet is Michael Faraday. But it is soon evident that the key theme is one of the

---

[129] Ibid., pp. xlii–xliv.   [130] Huxley, *Letters*, pp. 539, 587.

ignorance of a consumerist society, and of blind humanity generally, and the need for knowledge of higher things and of our 'Essence'. We move to the year 2108, after the Third World War, where we encounter not one but two Einsteins led by apes, who conspire to infect humanity with diseases which will kill them all. Los Angeles is a nearly abandoned wasteland where the radiation has finally subsided sufficiently to allow those living in the wilderness to plunder the city. New Zealand has survived the wars, and its explorers send a group, which lands in Los Angeles. Here many children deformed by radiation—'monsters'—are killed. Belial, the Devil, thought to have punished man, is worshipped. Mating is restricted to two weeks a year, and the 'Hots' who break the rules play the role of enemies here, taking all the blame for the society's woes. Huxley explains that 'If you want social solidarity, you've got to either have an external enemy or an oppressed minority.' (But small communities of 'Hots' exist, towards one of which the lead characters flee at the end.)[131]

These catastrophes have resulted chiefly from the worship of science, which results in flesh being 'subordinated to iron' and mind 'made the slave of wheels'. It also brought overpopulation, then finally 'the deserts spreading, the forests dwindling'. 'Progress and nationalism' are the two key ideas which bring about humanity's destruction. (We will see Orwell reaching exactly the same conclusion in Chapter 7.) Progress includes the 'theory that utopia lies just ahead and that, since ideal ends justify the most abominable means' we may eliminate those who 'obstruct the onward march to the earthly paradise'. Nationalism means 'that the state you happen to be subject to is the only true god, and that all other states are false gods'. The Belial, the demoniac, in humanity is responsible for all this, and gave us fascism, communism, persecution, death camps, and more. Huxley's dystopia is a lament of the power of the Unholy Spirit, the loss of the 'old beliefs in the value of the individual soul', and the rising tide of violence and sadism which seems to pervade the entire culture, which inures even children to atrocities. The moral laid bare is that 'Eastern mysticism' might ensure the wise use of Western science, with 'the Eastern art of living refining Western energy' and 'Western individualism tempering Eastern totalitarianism'. This would remain Huxley's refrain for the rest of his life.[132]

Overpopulation was now a constant concern for Huxley. He worried in 1950 that the world might reach 3 billion before stabilizing: it is obvious what he would have said about our world, twice as large and still unstoppably expanding.[133] He also deepened his historical sense of the origins of mass psychology in a 1952 study entitled *The Devils of Loudun*, which revealed plentiful evidence of the power of suggestion in early modern ideas of demonical possession.[134] Here he reiterated that 'the incessant suggestions of bewitchment, the daily warnings against the devil,

---

[131] Aldous Huxley, *Ape and Essence: A Novel* (Chatto & Windus, 1949), pp. 25, 29, 49–50, 68, 77, 90.
[132] Ibid., pp. 91–4, 97, 103, 138, 152–3.
[133] Aldous Huxley, *Themes and Variations* (Chatto & Windus, 1950), p. 247.
[134] Huxley's ideas are discussed in J. A. C. Brown, *Techniques of Persuasion: From Propaganda to Brainwashing* (Penguin Books, 1963), pp. 301–2.

had a disastrous effect'. He regarded this process as analogous to hypnosis. The combination of fasting, meditating, and contemplating the demonic, the suggestion that the Devil was active amongst a given group, and the accusation of possession combined powerfully to create hysteria. Both autosuggestion and deliberate fraud were at work here.[135] This then was a prototype of later mass behavioural manipulation.

In Huxley's failed and seemingly improbable attempt to turn *Brave New World* in to a musical in 1956, we see some movement forward on the themes of the original novel along with some dumbing down of key themes. There is more interaction between the castes here, and seemingly more contempt on the part of the Alphas, one of whom, colliding with an underling, swears, 'Can't you dumb Epsilons even look where you're going?' Bernard Marx is centrally categorized as 'an Individualist', and is described as being investigated for 'unsocial activities'. We see that Mustapha Mond is guarded by death-ray-wielding Gammas: this is more overtly totalitarian than the original. The central theme of the book is restated: 'Except for a few members of the upper castes, everybody *is* happy—and in consequence of it there's no art, no religion, no literature, or music, or philosophy... Universal contentment, but at the price of unrelieved monotony, of irremediable second-rateness, of the most revolting vulgarity.' It is clearer here than in the original book that *soma* is used as a method of direct control, since rations are denied unproductive workers and 'that's enough to keep them on their toes'. So we can see that Huxley meant us to feel the discontent seething beneath the surface of everyday life, even for the workers. And the ending is completely altered, with John being sent to Tahiti, where a civil war rages, with both sides 'fighting for God and true religion'.[136] This version we can easily see working for present-day audiences.

The essays published as *Brave New World Revisited* (1958) make it clear that Huxley remained concerned with capitalism's tendency to produce a moronic conformism based on consumerism and to undermine the personality by advertising. Whether a 'power elite' or the state engaged in such censorship and manipulation was to him, by this point, a lesser concern.[137] Self-control and regulation are presented as always more effective than surveillance by authority. Considering the issue of 'freedom and its enemies', Huxley admitted that the very desire for freedom seemed to be 'on the wane'. While paying homage to Orwell, Huxley insisted that behavioural engineering in both Soviet-style and Western regimes was enormously threatening. He wrote Orwell in 1949 that:

---

[135] Aldous Huxley, *The Devils of Loudun* (Chatto & Windus, 1952), pp. 146, 185–6, 219.

[136] *Aldous Huxley Annual*, 3, pp. 41, 43, 54, 80, 85, 96,

[137] Aldous Huxley, *Brave New World Revisited* (Harper & Row, 1965), p. 35: 'In the totalitarian East there is political censorship, and the media of mass communication are controlled by the State. In the democratic West there is economic censorship and the media of mass communication are controlled by members of the Power Elite.' And p. 56: ' "Both parties", we were told in 1966 by the editor of a leading business journal, "will merchandize their candidates and issues by the same methods that business has developed to sell goods. These include scientific selection of appeals and planned repetition... Radio spot announcements and ads will repeat phrases with a planned intensity. Billboards will push slogans of proven power... Candidates need, in addition to rich voices and good diction, to be able to look 'sincerely' at the TV camera." '

The philosophy of the ruling minority in *Nineteen Eighty-Four* is a sadism which has been carried to its logical conclusion by going beyond sex and denying it. Whether in actual fact the policy of the boot-on-the-face can go on indefinitely seems doubtful. My own belief is that the ruling oligarchy will find less arduous and wasteful ways of governing and of satisfying its lust for power, and that these ways will resemble those which I described in *Brave New World*.[138]

He also still maintained that the greatest danger promoting such trends was world overpopulation, the probability of which 'leading through unrest to dictatorship becomes a virtual certainty'.[139] Huxley further thought that uncontrolled population growth would result in the ultimate triumph of world communism because declining resources would produce social instability.[140] Degeneration into uniformity through loss of the sense of freedom is thus still a key theme. The fewer the numbers, the smaller the scale, the more liberty might thrive.

Was religion still an antidote? To an impressive degree, Huxley now opted for freedom of information as the key to withstanding mass manipulation and a capitalist ethos of conditioned consumption. 'Democracy', in the sense of collective, conscious self-government, was now more explicitly pitted against capitalist hedonism. Huxley still worried about drugs, and about communism. But the most insidious enemy lay in the application of the techniques of mind control to advertising, to politics, to undermining the sense of reality, to reinforcing egotism and hedonism. Democracy would drown in an ocean of popcorn and toothpaste, cola and designer handbags. Citizenship would be debased to a mere feel-good commodity like all the rest, marketed with cheap slogans, patriotic symbols, and glitzy jingles. It would not be crushed under the Hitlerian jackboot. Huxley proposed limiting political campaign spending, and even banning 'anti-rational propaganda' in election campaigns. The answer, then, was not religion: it was birth control—requiring an attack on some religions—and democratic rationalism in politics. But Orwell's scenario, Huxley now thought, seemed actually to be in retreat. He now considered that:

George Orwell's *1984* was a magnified projection into the future of a present that contained Stalinism and an immediate past that had witnessed the flowering of Nazism. *Brave New World* was written before the rise of Hitler to supreme power in Germany and when the Russian tyrant had not yet got into his stride. In 1931 systematic terrorism was not the obsessive contemporary fact which it had become in 1948, and the future dictatorship of my imaginary world was a good deal less brutal than the future dictatorship so brilliantly portrayed by Orwell. In the context of 1948, *1984* seemed dreadfully convincing. But tyrants, after all, are mortal and circumstances change. Recent developments in Russia and recent advances in science and technology have robbed Orwell's book of some of its gruesome verisimilitude. A nuclear war will, of course, make nonsense of everybody's predictions. But, assuming for the moment that the Great Powers can somehow refrain from destroying us, we can say that it now

[138] Huxley, *Letters*, p. 604.   [139] Huxley, *Brave New World Revisited*, pp. 4, 13.
[140] Aldous Huxley, *Tomorrow and Tomorrow and Tomorrow* (Harper & Brothers, 1952) (*Adonis and the Alphabet*), pp. 300–1.

looks as though the odds were more in favor of something like *Brave New World* than of something like *1984*.[141]

By contrast to *Nineteen Eighty-Four*, then, the odds were much more likely that

> control through the punishment of undesirable behavior is less effective, in the long run, than control through the reinforcement of desirable behavior by rewards, and that government through terror works on the whole less well than government through the non-violent manipulation of the environment and of the thoughts and feelings of individual men, women and children.[142]

Huxley later wrote that the 'society described in *1984* is a society controlled almost exclusively by punishment and the fear of punishment. In the imaginary world of my own fable punishment is infrequent and generally mild.'[143] Yet even he thought this contrast was less extreme than it seemed. For if, in *Nineteen Eighty-Four*, the 'lust for power is satisfied by inflicting pain; in *Brave New World*, it is by inflicting a hardly less humiliating pleasure'.[144] This comment, perhaps more than any other, indicates just how subtle and pervasive Huxley's critique of modernity was. But most of us, of course, also find enduring the humiliation even of 'inflicted' unlimited pleasure a great deal easier than suffering any pain at all. Decadence is fun too, after all.

A final reckoning, the novel *Island* (1962), which ostensibly proposes a utopia to counter the dystopia, is generally accounted as less successful from both the literary and intellectual viewpoints. Often regarded as considerably more optimistic than its more famous predecessor, it can also be read as marking a retreat from the suggestion that mankind's great problems could be solved humanely on a global scale. It is a retreat, idyllic, perhaps, but not an alternative and better world state.

Island describes Pala, a Buddhist-, sex-, and drug-defined utopia whose manifest spirituality was evidently intended to compensate for the moral impasse of *Brave New World*. Huxley himself described it as 'a kind of reverse *Brave New World* ... a Topian rather than a Utopian phantasy, a phantasy dealing with a place, a *real* place and *time*, rather than a phantasy dealing with *no* place and time'.[145] Here violence, crime, hunger, overpopulation, and inhumanity have been conquered. *Island* indicates that, far from having abandoned his support for a eugenically defined aristocracy, Huxley remained a committed utopian on this issue. In Pala, every third child resulted from artificial breeding. A race of 'superior stocks' was slowly being created who would possess an IQ of 115, while the rest of the world was

---

[141] Huxley, *Brave New World Revisited*, pp. 110, 4–5.   [142] Ibid., p. 5.
[143] Huxley, *Collected Essays*, vol. 6, p. 224.
[144] Huxley, *Brave New World Revisited*, p. 27. A debt to Pareto seems evident here, for Pareto distinguished between bureaucratic, idealistic, and conservative elites who normally aimed to conserve what had been established, and who ruled by force; and mercantile elites, where an instinct for combining was predominant, who ruled by guile, and for whom propaganda was an invaluable tool. Pareto also argued that ruling elites normally became reluctant to utilize force to uphold their rule, thus fatally weakening their position and leading to their displacement by other elites. Those able to recognize the value of persuasion were more likely to enjoy longevity of rule.
[145] Bedford, *Aldous Huxley*, vol. 2, p. 241.

becoming stupider. 'Family servitude' has been replaced by 'mutual adoption clubs' which give every child twenty homes. None is more than a few times richer than anyone else. 'The pleasures of vanity and the pleasures of bullying' associated with nationalism and aggression have been surpassed. The love of power has been canalized and deflected 'away from people and on to things'. Paraphrasing Lenin's 'electricity plus socialism equals communism', we are told: 'Electricity minus heavy industry plus birth control equals democracy and plenty. Electricity plus heavy industry minus birth control equals misery, totalitarianism and war.' But *Island* is ultimately a pessimistic work. Humanity's woes have been solved in one place, not on the planet as a whole, where 'armaments, universal debt and planned obsolescence' proliferate.[146] Here then we have the utopia of the few, with the many left to shift for themselves outside the gates.[147] Utopia on a large scale seems impossible as such, for large-group dynamics prohibit it. The book lacks the degree of confrontation with the problems of hedonism and mass manipulation which mark Huxley's chief work. Pavlov makes an appearance; the problem is still collective somnambulism. But the response is not on a scale sufficient to answer the questions left begging in *Brave New World*. And so it is closer to More's *Utopia* than we might imagine.

Though it is not obvious here, Huxley, nonetheless, had not retreated from the view that world government was 'obviously infinitely desirable'.[148] Yet the religious answer here is private and individual, the product of inner self-mastery. It is at best bounded by a small community like John Humphrey Noyes' Oneida, which Huxley admired to some degree, while still (in 1956) disparaging 'life in a community' as 'life in a crowd—the same old crowd, day in, day out'. *Island* does not represent a mass collective bond of public worship, not a Nazi or Stalinist political religion.[149] Sensing the exacerbated problems of large-scale groupism, Huxley indeed now disparaged large groups entirely on principle, insisting that, in industry, twenty-five to thirty people working together ought to be the maximum, and where mental work was dominant, a mere twelve.[150] Yet this still lay within the bounds of possibility. For Huxley had no faith in utopias where people were portrayed 'radically unlike human beings...quite different from what they are and from what, throughout recorded history, they have always been'.[151] (He condemned Swift's obsessive reluctance to acknowledge the realistic humanity of the Yahoos in *Gulliver's Travels*.) The answer, then, lay in a more 'rational mode' of democracy, where 'a ruling aristocracy of mind', still based on eugenics, had a prominent role, and balanced self-interest, demagoguery, and corruption by practising the 'disinterested virtues'. This was what religion, aiming at 'non-attachment' to material things and desire in general, ought to seek as its secular end. Here too Huxley

---

[146] Aldous Huxley, *Island* (Chatto & Windus, 1962), pp. 92, 109, 144–6, 154, 188.
[147] See Huxley, *After Many a Summer*, pp. 115–23. Here Huxley clearly states his preference for American over Soviet collectivism of any type (p. 132). The course of the Spanish Civil War clearly played a major role here.
[148] Huxley, *The Human Situation*, p. 101.
[149] Huxley, *Tomorrow and Tomorrow and Tomorrow*, pp. 95, 99.
[150] Woodcock, *Dawn and the Darkest Hour*, p. 212.   [151] Huxley, *Proper Studies*, p. ix.

worried that the worship of man, with 'all the virtues and perfections of God . . . lodged in humanity', posed a significant danger, as did equivalent devotion to party, state, nation, or race. These encouraged immersion in 'the sub-human world of crowd emotion'—back to Le Bon—which was the most effective totalitarian tool. Yet Huxley was not opposed to intelligent planning for the future. He may have lacked Orwell's commitment to a socialist variation on collectivism. But he praised Roosevelt's and others' attempts to anticipate the results of technological developments, so long as they were 'carried out by the right sort of means and in the right sort of governmental, administrative and educational contexts', that is to say, in an ethically sound manner, and through 'decentralization and responsible self-government'. And he retained an enduring interest in whether small-scale communities of intelligent, like-minded individuals could further such ends.[152]

CONCLUSION

Huxley's chief work has remained a critical success to the present day. There are echoes of it in many later dystopias where medication is used for psychological domination, including the Swedish poet Karin Boye's *Kallocain* (1940), in which the discovery of a truth serum renders obsolete the last vestige of privacy in a totalitarian state.[153] It finds support in the many later dystopias which take manipulation via advertising as a theme, notably Frederik Pohl and Cyril Kornbluth's *The Space Merchants* (1952), discussed in Chapter 8. If we must reduce negative futures to two key visions, most readers will usually juxtapose this one to Orwell's.

Yet the jury is still out, to some degree, as to how we are meant to read the text. Margaret Atwood describes *Brave New World* as 'either a perfect world utopia or its nasty opposite, a dystopia, depending on your point of view'.[154] But it is also neither. It defies the generic dystopian definition used here insofar as both literary and real dystopias are typically dominated by fear. The hedonistic dystopia presents a special category. Fear is present in Huxley's tale, but not in the usual combinations of cruelty, pain, mass murder, and slave labour. Most of these would have been superseded scientifically. The persistent need for the mood-enhancing *soma* admittedly betrays a widespread moderate anxiety, depression, even neurosis, especially because it is withheld for misbehaviour. But *soma* is readily available and, unlike its historical and contemporary antecedents, has no side effects beyond psychological addiction.

Huxley well recognized the role of fear in everyday life in the modern world, terming it 'the very basis and foundation of modern life'.[155] Perhaps for this reason he chose to minimize and disguise it here. But as the most distinctive attribute of

---

[152] Ibid., pp. 157, 215; Huxley, *Ends and Means*, pp. 3, 59, 62; Huxley, *Collected Essays*, p. 257; Huxley, *Ends and Means*, pp. 59, 62.
[153] Karin Boye, *Kallocain* (1940; University of Wisconsin Press, 1966).
[154] Huxley, *Brave New World*, p. ix.   [155] Huxley, *Ape and Essence*, p. 37.

Brave New World as a dystopia, this challenges the application of the term to the text.[156] The book is not, as such, a critique of totalitarianism. It represents instead a form of post- or 'perfected' totalitarian analysis in which technological modernity and psychological manipulation are the key targets. In it, the ideals of totalitarian social efficiency had indeed been achieved in 'the completely controlled, collectivized industrial society'.[157] But they were maintained by a much more psychologically sophisticated system than anything evident in Huxley's life. This essentially benevolent global dictatorship, Huxley later acknowledged, had been a false prediction, but again because the pressure of population made oppressive dictatorships more likely.[158]

The enduring strength of *Brave New World*, then, lies in the fact that it does not satirize totalitarianism alone. Instead, it takes as its target certain strands which Huxley regarded as inherent in modernity as such, especially the scientific application of the psychology of propaganda, indoctrination or the manipulation of behaviour. The propensity to view this suggestibility as inherently dangerous we have associated here with the theory of the crowd from at least Le Bon onwards. It reappears in Freud and later in mass psychology. It would result, as we have seen in this chapter, in Huxley rejecting large groups as such, seeing them as inherently restrictive of individuality and liberty. Despite their differences, as we will see in Chapter 7, Orwell would reach some very similar conclusions.

---

[156] According to Richard Layard, for instance, 'the best state of society is the one where there is the most happiness and the least misery' (*Guardian*, 21 July 2012, 38).

[157] Huxley's description of *Brave New World*, in Huxley, *Collected Essays*, vol. 5, p. 313.

[158] Huxley, *Complete Essays*, vol. 6, p. 189.

7

Vaporizing the Soviet Myth
Orwell's *Nineteen Eighty-Four*

England is lacking...in what one might call concentration-camp literature. The special world created by secret police forces, censorship of opinion, torture and frame-up trials is, of course, known about and to some extent disapproved of, but it has made very little emotional impact. One result of this is that there exists in England almost no literature of disillusionment about the Soviet Union.

(George Orwell, *I Have Tried to Tell the Truth*, 1944)

I belong to the Left and must work inside it, much as I hate Russian totalitarianism.

(George Orwell, *I Belong to the Left*, 1945)

[N]othing has contributed so much to the corruption of the original idea of Socialism as the belief that Russia is a Socialist country and that every act of its rulers must be excused, if not imitated. And so for the past ten years I have been convinced that the destruction of the Soviet myth was essential if we wanted a revival of the socialist movement.

(George Orwell, *It is What I Think*, 1947)

Who controls the past controls the future: who controls the present controls the past.

(George Orwell, *Nineteen Eighty-Four*, 1948)

INTRODUCTION

Nineteen Eighty-Four is a book draped in the blackest black.[1] The pall of death—not least its author's—hangs over it. Its eerie gloom depresses even the most stalwart reader. Yet this in part also explains its enormous success. Orwell wrote in 1948 that his great work 'isn't a book I would gamble on for a big sale'. But the

---

[1] References to the Secker & Warburg 2000–2 edition of George Orwell's writings are by Roman numerals. The vols used here are: X. *A Kind of Compulsion 1903–1936*; XI. *Facing Unpleasant Facts 1937–9*; XII. *A Patriot after All 1940–1*; XIII. *All Propaganda is Lies 1941–2*; XIV. *Keeping Our Little Corner Clean 1942–3*; XV. *Two Wasted Years 1943*; XVI. *I Have Tried to Tell the Truth 1943–4*; XVII. *I Belong to the Left 1945*; XVIII. *Smothered under Journalism 1946*; XIX. *It is What I Think 1947–8*; XX. *Our Job is to Make Life Worth Living 1949–50*.

'Utopia in the form of a novel' became the one literary dystopia everyone knows.[2] Big Brother, thoughtcrime, doublethink, the telescreen, Newspeak: this 'Orwellian' vocabulary is almost identical with how we imagine 'totalitarianism' and other forms of the surveillance state. With its remarkable precursor, *Animal Farm* (1945), it has probably outsold all the rest of the utopias and dystopias ever written put together.[3] Anthony Burgess termed *Nineteen Eighty-Four* 'one of the few dystopian visions to have changed men's habits of thought'.[4] Orwell has even been called 'the most influential political writer of the twentieth century'.[5]

The power of this book lies chiefly in its ability to entice the reader into a world defined by paranoia, oppression, fear, and pain. Here, fiction does the work of which history can scarcely dream. Orwell's masterpiece horrifies: it makes the flesh crawl. His anti-hero, Winston Smith, is a weak, whimsical, forgetful, unappealing figure. Like most of Orwell's central male characters, and often their creator, he is habitually despondent, and exudes failure. Yet he becomes us and we him.[6] His very ordinariness becomes heroic. His defiance of Big Brother becomes the rebellion of every (wo)man who was ever crushed by life, by love, by work, physical frailty, gender, oppression. An early reader thought Orwell had 'done what Wells never did, created a fantasy world which yet is horribly real so that you *mind* what happens to the characters which inhabit it'.[7] Yet this is also an intellectually engaging book which works alike as a piece of political theory, history, and future projection. It is one of the most important accounts ever written about power and corruption, and far more penetrating than most of the canon of political theory we usually advert to in exploring these themes. Often referred to as a 'vision of the future', it is as much an acute portrait of a very real world which so few studies of the novel actually explore. So that must be one of our aims here.

This chapter will assess the development of the key themes which distinguish the text, and provide a context for understanding it as Orwell himself wanted it to be understood: as an attack on Stalinism, and, behind this, the 'gramophone mind'.[8] There is a large secondary literature here, though much of it appeared before Peter

---

[2] Orwell, XX, p. 35; XIX, p. 486. For biographical background see, in particular, Bernard Crick, *George Orwell: A Life* (Penguin Books, 1982), Michael Shelden, *George Orwell: The Authorised Biography* (Heinemann, 1991), Peter Davison, *George Orwell: A Literary Life* (Macmillan, 1996), Gordon Bowker, *George Orwell* (Abacus Books, 2003), and, most recently, Robert Colls, *George Orwell: English Rebel* (Oxford University Press, 2013) (which gives a good summary of Orwell's later reputation). A recent thematic introduction is John Rodden, ed., *The Cambridge Companion to George Orwell* (Cambridge University Press, 2007). The range of interpretations of Orwell is surveyed in Jeffrey Meyers, ed., *George Orwell: The Critical Heritage* (Routledge & Kegan Paul, 1975), John Rodden, *The Politics of Literary Reputation: The Making and Claiming of 'St. George' Orwell* (Oxford University Press, 1989), and John Rodden, *The Unexamined Orwell* (University of Texas Press, 2011). For Orwell's politics the best starting point is William Steinhoff, *The Road to 1984* (Weidenfeld & Nicolson, 1975).

[3] Both *Nineteen Eighty-Four* and *Animal Farm* have sold perhaps 20 million copies.

[4] Anthony Burgess, *The Novel Now* (Faber & Faber, 1967), p. 43.

[5] Timothy Garton Ash, cited in Vladimir Shlapentokh, 'George Orwell: Russia's Tocqueville', in Thomas Cushman and John Rodden, eds., *George Orwell: Into the Twenty-First Century* (Paradigm Publishers, 2004), p. 281.

[6] 'Every book is a failure', Orwell once remarked (XVIII, p. 320).

[7] Orwell, XIX, p. 482.   [8] Orwell, XVII, p. 259.

Davison's magnificent edition of the *Complete Works* (2000–2), which greatly augments the Orwell we can study.[9] New light on his ideas has been shed by the opening up of the archives of the Stalinist period, as well as new information about Mao, Pol Pot, and other communist dictators. It is also evident that, towards the end of his life, Orwell began to conceive of the central political problems of modernity in terms familiar to us here from our previous discussion of group psychology and of the mechanization of society. We will see that Orwell poses the problem of how writers can safeguard their intellectual and moral integrity in the face of the need for partisan political identity in a novel and intriguing way. He also personified the difficulties of being on the left, yet anti-Stalinist.

PRELUDE

The ideas behind his last work first gelled in Orwell's mind in 1943, but had been percolating for many years beforehand.[10] Orwell was born as Eric Arthur Blair at Motihari in India in 1903, the son of a lowly official in the imperial Opium Department. He died of tuberculosis in London in 1950. He is sometimes portrayed as a rebel from youth onwards, and as working out in later life the psychological implications of the bullying and humiliation he suffered as a child.[11] Living in England with his mother, he spent some happy years just outside London, and would later idealize the timeless sense of certainty of the pre-war epoch. Sent away to preparatory school at St Cyprian's on the south coast, however, he was 'flung into a world of force and fraud and secrecy, like a goldfish into a tank of pike'. He described 'the pattern of school life' as 'a continuous triumph of the strong over the weak'. It was his first experience as an inferior and outsider. He hated it, and this anticipated much of his later relation to groups. He saw himself as poor, weak, ugly, unpopular, in every way inadequate. 'Failure, failure, failure' was 'by far the deepest conviction that I carried away'. The anxiety haunted much of his own life and all his later chief literary characters.[12] He remained characteristically lonely, isolated, resentful of privilege, a quintessential outsider. He despised arbitrary punishment and cruelty, and was frustrated at their persistence. These tendencies were, to some degree, reinforced by his time as a scholarship boy at Eton, where

---

[9] See, e.g., Samuel Hynes, ed., *Twentieth-Century Interpretations of 1984* (Prentice Hall, 1971); Peter Stansky, ed., *On Nineteen Eighty-Four* (W. H. Freeman & Co., 1983); Ejner J. Jensen, ed., *The Future of* Nineteen Eighty-Four (University of Michigan Press, 1984); Irving Howe, ed., *1984 Revisited: Totalitarianism in Our Century* (Harper & Row, 1983); Abbott Gleason, Jack Goldsmith, and Martha C. Nussbaum, eds., *On Nineteen Eighty-Four: Orwell and Our Future* (Princeton University Press, 2005); Patrick Reilly, *Nineteen Eighty-Four: Past, Present and Future* (Twayne, 1989).

[10] The notes for the book from this period correspond closely to its final structure: George Orwell, *Nineteen Eighty-Four*, ed. Bernard Crick (Clarendon Press, 1984), pp. 111, 137–8.

[11] An extreme formulation of this thesis is offered in Michael Carter, *George Orwell and the Problem of Authentic Existence* (Croom Helm, 1985). Anthony West's charge is that most of the things which terrified Orwell were 'of an infantile character' and 'clearly derive from the experience described in *Such, Such Were the Joys*' (*Principles and Persuasions* (Eyre & Spottiswoode, 1958), p. 156). This is a gross oversimplification: see Tosco Fyvel's comments in Stephen Wadhams, comp., *Remembering Orwell* (Penguin Books, 1984), p. 206.

[12] Orwell, XIX, pp. 370, 378, 382.

class privileges were ubiquitous but the possibility of joining the establishment by merit also existed. The challenge of Orwell's later life involved belonging to privileged groups and yet detesting what they stood for: exploiting others. Orwell developed what appears in retrospect to have been an almost instinctive feeling for the underdog. For reasons that remain unclear, his life would become devoted to the downtrodden. As Eric Blair he would be, for a time, their oppressor. In George Orwell he became their champion.

Orwell, still Blair, perhaps accidentally cast himself in the role of the exploiter when he went to Burma as an imperial policeman (1922–7). He had been an indifferent student, so Oxford, otherwise a natural destination, was not an option.[13] He told a contemporary that he wanted to 'go back' to 'the east'.[14] Whether he expected what Burma delivered is another matter. The climate was deadly, the country dangerous, crime-ridden, and isolated, the population sullen and resentful of British rule. At his first landfall in Asia, stopping at Columbo, he saw a 'sub-human' coolie being kicked by a white police sergeant as other passengers looked on approvingly. Yet he too lost his temper at least once in Burma and hit, with his walking stick, a young man who had knocked him over accidentally. The temptation to succumb to brutality soon collided with what Orwell later called his 'natural hatred of authority' and 'hatred of oppression'. A revulsion set in—clearly against one side of himself—which would eventually reach the 'extraordinary lengths' of regarding only failure as virtuous and every attempt to 'succeed' in life as 'spiritually ugly, a species of bullying'. And so one of his later fictional anti-heroes, Gordon Comstock in *Keep the Aspidistra Flying*, makes it his 'especial purpose *not* to "succeed"'.[15]

In Burma, then, Orwell's native rebelliousness, already evident at school, took shape and flourished, perhaps in part by becoming 'hated by large numbers of people' for the first time in his life.[16] He had already determined to become a writer, and was possessed by the writer's inner daemon.[17] But he found the atmosphere there 'a stifling, stultifying world in which to live'. Here, 'every word and every thought is censored . . . even friendship can hardly exist when every white man is a cog in the wheels of despotism. Free speech is unthinkable.' Burma was 'essentially despotic'.[18] Orwell soon concluded that imperialism was 'an evil thing'. He realized that 'when the white man turns tyrant it is his own freedom that he destroys', his shame burning hot when forced to shoot an elephant to avoid losing

---

[13] To Michael Shelden this was not an act of rebellion, however, but a lack of support from his family to get to Oxford, possibly mixed with a romantic view of imperial administration (*Orwell*, pp. 85–6).

[14] Crick, *Orwell*, p. 136.

[15] Orwell, XII, p. 121; Shelden, *Orwell*, p. 114; Orwell, XVIII, p. 319; George Orwell, *The Road to Wigan Pier* (1937) (Secker & Warburg, 1959), p. 150; *The Penguin Complete Novels of George Orwell* (Penguin Books, 1983), p. 603.

[16] Orwell, X, p. 501. He later described British rule in India as 'just as bad as German Fascism' (XI, p. 80).

[17] 'Writing a book is a horrible, exhausting struggle, like a long bout of some painful illness. One would never undertake such a thing if one were not driven on by some demon whom one can neither resist nor understand' (XVIII, p. 320).

[18] Orwell, *Complete Novels*, p. 113; Orwell, X, p. 144.

face before a crowd of natives. His novel, *Burmese Days* (1934), is the first moment
when he portrays the juxtaposition of individual moral rectitude to group conformity as a central theme. Here, too, we find the first inklings of Orwell as a critic
of modernity or 'progress' as such, in the narrator's reflection that, if Britain
continued to 'modernize' Burma:

> [I]n two hundred years all this . . . all this will be gone—forests, villages, monasteries,
> pagodas all vanished. And instead, pink villas fifty yards apart; all over those hills, as far
> as you can see, villa after villa, with all the gramophones playing the same tune. And all
> the forests shaved flat-chewed into wood-pulp for the *News of the World*, or sawn up
> into gramophone cases.[19]

On his return to England, 'conscious of an immense weight of guilt that I had got to
expiate', Orwell readily transferred his sympathies from the Burmese to the poor of
the capital's East End and elsewhere.[20] Like Jack London before him, Orwell
immersed himself amongst the poor in Paris and London in 1928–9 in an attempt
to feel as they felt, without possessions, on the earthen floor of society.[21] He became a
dishwasher, then a tramp, briefly a Kentish hop-picker, and Billingsgate market
porter in 1931. His first novel, *Down and Out in Paris and London* (1933), written
under the pseudonym of George Orwell, recounts these experiences with characteristic sympathy and humanity, though its allusion to some 'dismal Marxist utopia' as
an alternative to the present is prescient.[22] There is no doubt that, driven by guilt and
a sense of injustice, he consciously sought out poverty in order to understand it: 'I had
got to escape not merely from imperialism but from every form of man's dominion
over man.' He now 'reduced everything to the simple theory that the oppressed are
always right and the oppressors are always wrong: a mistaken theory, but the natural
result of being one of the oppressors yourself'. Those receiving unemployment
benefit lived wretchedly, or became 'tramps' moving daily between workhouses.
'[H]aggard, unshaven, filthy and tattered', they were sunk in degradation well
below Burmese levels. The prison atmosphere of the workhouses included taking
away clothes and personal possessions, and feeding inmates grey, stale bread. The
alternative, 'Doss houses', 'horrible fetid dens' packed with up to a hundred men
goaded by a jail-like discipline, was scarcely an improvement.[23] The worst-paid fared
little better. But to all this Orwell had no answer, only commiseration.

Orwell's other early novels also shed little light on his mature political thought.
Most readers rarely encounter two works Orwell himself later dismissed as inferior,

---

[19] Orwell, *Complete Novels*, p. 96.
[20] Orwell, *The Road to Wigan Pier*, p. 149; Orwell, X, pp. 501, 504, 123–5. Alan Sandison
describes him as being religiously inclined, and 'in search of absolution . . . amongst the despised and
destitute' (*George Orwell after 1984* (Longwood Academic, 1986), p. 67). (This is a revised edition of
Sandison's *The Last Man in Europe: An Essay on George Orwell* (Macmillan, 1974)). Richard Rees said
he was 'haggard with social guilt . . . he possessed, or was possessed by, a moral force which drove him
to violent extremes of expiation' (quoted in Jeffrey Meyers, *Orwell: Wintry Conscience of a Generation*
(W. W. Norton, 2000), p. 70).
[21] London published *The People of the Abyss* (Isbister, 1903) on the basis of his experiences.
[22] George Orwell, *Down and Out in Paris and London* (Penguin Books, 1966), p. 107.
[23] Orwell, *The Road to Wigan Pier*, pp. 149–50; X, pp. 129–30, 265.

The Clergyman's Daughter (1935) and *Keep the Aspidistra Flying* (1936). The former, however, treats of the loss of religious belief, later a central theme for Orwell, while the latter is a fine study in the perils of being impoverished, lower middle class, and desperately squeezed by the system.[24] Psychologically, too, they are interesting, populated as they are by shy, solitary, maladjusted characters ill-adapted to meeting the challenges of the age, chips off the Blair block.

Orwell's engagement with poverty was taken to another level in *The Road to Wigan Pier* (1937). Commissioned by Victor Gollancz in 1936 to survey Britain's industrial poverty in its heartland, the book led Orwell to find the poor still wearing wooden and steel 'clogs' for shoes. The squalor, the dilapidation, the smells, the dejection and degradation are acutely felt and recounted. Orwell would later write that 'I became pro-Socialist more out of disgust with the way the poorer section of the industrial workers were oppressed and neglected than out of any theoretical admiration for a planned society.'[25] Yet he was still grappling with the magnitude of the problem and the entwinement of poverty with modernity. He became aware that mass production had helped to avert revolution. The 'post-war development of cheap luxuries has been a very fortunate thing for our rulers', he thought, for it was 'quite likely that fish-and-chips, art-silk stockings, tinned salmon, cut-price chocolate (five two-ounce bars for sixpence), the movies, the radio, strong tea and the Football Pools have between them averted revolution'.[26]

In 1937, Orwell also looked beyond poverty to consider the wider effects of mechanical civilization. In an Erewhonian vein he lamented its tendency 'to make life safe and soft; and yet you are striving to keep yourself brave and hard'. In aiming to eliminate physical labour and make everything easier, mechanical progress removed 'the human need for effort and creation', atrophying the physical senses. Thus, the 'logical end of mechanical progress' was 'to reduce the human being to something resembling a brain in a bottle'.[27] With, perhaps, Huxley mentally before him, but in a spirit which evokes William Cobbett still more, Orwell lamented 'the frightful debauchery of taste that has already been effected by a century of mechanisation'.[28] He early gleaned the meaning of the triumph of form over content. In the case of food:

> In the highly mechanised countries, thanks to tinned food, cold storage, synthetic flavouring matters, etc., the palate is almost a dead organ...what the majority of English people mean by an apple is a lump of highly-coloured cotton wool from America or Australia; they will devour these things, apparently with pleasure, and let the English apples rot under the trees. It is the shiny, standardised, machine-made look of the American apple that appeals to them; the superior taste of the English apple is something they simply do not notice.

---

[24] The latter, in turn, contains a portrait of a wealthy socialist litterateur, Ravelston, which gives an excellent sense of Orwell's attitude towards the class problem at this point. See *Complete Novels*, p. 628.
[25] Orwell, X, p. 421; Orwell, XIX, p. 87. On Blair's development into Orwell in this period, see Peter Stansky and William Abrahams, *Orwell: The Transformation* (Constable, 1979), pp. 119–84.
[26] Orwell, *The Road to Wigan Pier*, p. 91.   [27] Ibid., pp. 193, 200.
[28] Colls identifies Orwell with an 'English Tory radical tradition' (*Orwell*, p. 97).

The same thing, he thought, was equally true of 'furniture, houses, clothes, books, amusements and everything else that makes up our environment'. If only taste were 'uncorrupted' then

> most of the products of the machine would be simply unwanted. In a healthy world there would be no demand for tinned food, aspirins, gramophones, gaspipe chairs, machine guns, daily newspapers, telephones, motor-cars, etc., etc.; and on the other hand there would be a constant demand for the things the machine cannot produce.[29]

This lament for a world passing away was thus mixed with resignation. In the long run, Orwell reluctantly conceded, the machine had

> to be accepted . . . rather as one accepts a drug—that is, grudgingly and suspiciously. Like a drug, the machine is useful, dangerous and habit-forming. The oftener one surrenders to it the tighter its grip becomes. You have only to look about you at this moment to realise with what sinister speed the machine is getting us into its power.[30]

(Would Orwell have reverted to an ink pen after learning to type? No: he later took up the newly invented biro with enthusiasm.)

Politically, though Orwell was moving leftwards, *Wigan Pier* is surprisingly cranky and irritated. The reason for this, he wrote, was that socialism

> *in the form in which it is now presented*, appeals chiefly to unsatisfactory or even inhuman types. On the one hand you have the warm-hearted unthinking Socialist, the typical working-class Socialist, who only wants to abolish poverty and does not always grasp what this implies. On the other hand, you have the intellectual, book-trained Socialist, who understands that it is necessary to throw our present civilisation down the sink and is quite willing to do so. And this type is drawn, to begin with, entirely from the middle class, and from a rootless town-bred section of the middle class at that.[31]

And so Orwell proclaimed that 'in order to defend Socialism it is necessary to start by attacking it'. His subsequent now-famous parody of the socialist intelligentsia as faddists, fruit-juice drinkers, nudists, sandal-wearers, Quakers, pacifists, and quacks, and, even worse, the 'Bolshevik commissars' amongst them as 'half gangster, half gramophone', betrayed all his own prejudices. It was so biting that his left-wing publisher, Gollancz, had to write a special preface distancing himself from the text.[32] But Orwell, with Wells in mind, saw the appeal of socialism as 'bound up, more or less inextricably, with the idea of machine-production'. It was defined by airplanes and gleaming glass-and-concrete towers piercing the sky, the polar opposite of Wigan's squalor. As a creed, socialism had grown out of urbanism and industrialization. Its future was 'always pictured as a completely mechanised, immensely organised world, depending on the machine as the civilisations of

---

[29] Orwell, *The Road to Wigan Pier*, p. 203.   [30] Ibid., p. 202.   [31] Ibid., pp. 181–2.
[32] Ibid., pp. 151, 173–4. On this theme see Alex Zwerdling, *Orwell and the Left* (Yale University Press, 1974), pp. 38–61. At this point Orwell himself admitted he knew 'nothing' of Russia, though there is some evidence from the late 1920s of his defending its revolution. See Wadhams, *Remembering Orwell*, p. 42.

antiquity depend on the slave'. But, consequently, socialists regarded 'the idea of mechanical progress, not merely as a necessary development but as an end in itself, almost as a kind of religion'. This, he thought, Čapek had captured in 'the horrible ending of *R.U.R.*, when the Robots, having slaughtered the last human being, announce their intention to "build many houses" (just for the sake of building houses, you see)'.[33] He thought Zamyatin had got this right as well.[34]

This worried Orwell exceedingly. He sensed minds enthralled to machines. The underlying motive of many socialists, he insisted, seemed to be 'simply a hypertrophied sense of order. The present state of affairs offends them not because it causes misery, still less because it makes freedom impossible, but because it is untidy; what they desire, basically, is to reduce the world to something resembling a chess-board.' Thus, the

> kind of person who most readily accepts Socialism is also the kind of person who views mechanical progress, *as such*, with enthusiasm. And this is so much the case that Socialists are often unable to grasp that the opposite opinion exists. As a rule the most persuasive argument they can think of is to tell you that the present mechanisation of the world is as nothing to what we shall see when Socialism is established. Where there is one aeroplane now, in those days there will be fifty! All the work that is now done by hand will then be done by machinery: everything that is now made of leather, wood or stone will be made of rubber, glass or steel; there will be no disorder, no loose ends, no wildernesses, no wild animals, no weeds, no disease, no poverty, no pain—and so on and so forth. The Socialist world is to be above all things an *ordered* world, an *efficient* world.

But, Orwell concluded, 'it is precisely from that vision of the future as a sort of glittering Wells-world that sensitive minds recoil. Please notice that this essentially fat-bellied version of "progress" is not an integral part of Socialist doctrine.' What needed to be resisted, in the short term, then, was the socialist tendency towards 'that nexus of thought, "Socialism-progress-machinery-Russia-tractor-hygiene-machinery-progress"'.[35]

His own alternative was epitomized in the delicious English apple rotting on the ground while tasteless foreign imports were munched to the tune of an advertising jingle. But this *was*, to a degree, wishful thinking, and a wistful nostalgia which Orwell knew he could not indulge in for long. Wells and Morris would have to meet somewhere, and so they met, to a degree, in Orwell.[36] Machinery might be

---

[33] Orwell, *The Road to Wigan Pier*, p. 188.

[34] Orwell said that 'what Zamyatin seems to be aiming at is not any particular country but the implied aims of industrial civilisation' (XVIII, p. 16).

[35] Orwell, *The Road to Wigan Pier*, pp. 187–9, 178, 207.

[36] In a manner of speaking: when they finally met Orwell and Wells fell out, and the latter termed Orwell a 'Trotskyite with big feet'. Orwell referred to Morris inter alia in *The Road to Wigan Pier* as a 'dull, empty windbag' (p. 161). Morris' answer did not really suit him either. Why, Orwell asked, 'not retain the machine *and* retain "creative work"? Why not cultivate anachronisms as a spare-time hobby? Many people have played with this idea; it seems to solve with such beautiful ease the problems set by the machine. The citizen of Utopia, we are told, coming home from his daily two hours of turning a handle in the tomato-canning factory, will deliberately revert to a more primitive way of life and solace his creative instincts with a bit of *fretwork*, pottery-glazing or handloom-weaving. And why is this

placed at arm's length, and used for what it could produce. It needed always to be balanced against the simpler pleasures. It should not be allowed to displace that respect for nature, for the local, for the raw rather than the processed, which links the rural radical tradition of Cobbett to modern ecologism. Orwell loved the countryside and animals, and after his work enjoyed gardening most. Mucking about and getting his hands dirty appealed to him. The remote Scottish island of Jura, where he spent much of his last few years, became his rural idyll and utopian retreat, remote from the nuclear war he thought probable. In London, he took to carpentry as a distraction. Here there are strong echoes of Ruskin and Morris, and latterly, R. H. Tawney, whom he befriended.[37] We get a sense of work valuing 'in one's own time and after one's own fashion . . . something that needs skill and can be a source of pride'. Man, Orwell thought,

> is a working animal, his work is and must be the central factor in his life, and those whose work is soul-destroying tend to seek mechanical, mass-produced amusements (the film and the radio) in their spare time. This point has never been satisfactorily met by the defenders of either Socialism or of large-scale Capitalism.[38]

So there was a clear linkage here between work, leisure, and the dehumanization of machine civilization, with Bellamy and Wells on one side and Morris and Orwell on the other. Marx, whose influence over socialism Orwell would come greatly to lament, was left out of the equation.

SPAIN AND SOCIALISM

History stopped in 1936.
(Orwell to Koestler, *All Propaganda is Lies* (1942), p. 16)

It took the Spanish Civil War to turn Orwell away from modernity as such and towards practical politics. His enlistment in the republican cause against Franco's fascists is recounted in *Homage to Catalonia* (1938). His experiences in Spain included a once-in-a-lifetime moment of catharsis. Experiencing comradeship in Barcelona in 1937 led him to confess that he had 'seen wonderful things, and at last really believe in Socialism, which I never did before'. He now had 'an accurate political orientation', had reached 'a firm decision' and 'knew where I stood'.[39] What socialism meant was the real brotherhood of those bonded by a recognition of mutual humanity. This belief was fused and driven by an intensely emotional experience. In a few key moments of quintessentially utopian personal intimacy,

---

picture an absurdity—as it is, of course? Because of a principle that is not always recognised, though always acted upon: that so long as the machine *is there*, one is under an obligation to use it' (p. 198).

[37] Orwell knew Ruskin's *Sesame and Lilies* (*Complete Novels*, p. 501).

[38] Orwell, XVII, p. 28. Richard Rees, amongst others, links Orwell to Morris (*George Orwell: Fugitive from the Camp of Victory* (Secker & Warburg, 1961), p. 55).

[39] Orwell, XI, p. 28; Orwell, XVIII, p. 319.

Orwell found that complete strangers were suddenly friends.[40] The core loneliness of his own personality dissipated for the first time as seemingly impenetrable barriers between people vanished. He was astonished 'what human beings are like when they are trying to behave as human beings and not as cogs in a capitalist machine'. Bootblacks refused tips. Even the brothels had signs pleading for respect: 'Please treat the women as comrades'. For several months,

> large blocks of people believed that all men are equal and were able to act on their belief. The result was a feeling of liberation and hope that is difficult to conceive in our money-tainted atmosphere... No one who was in Spain during the months when people still believed in the revolution will ever forget that strange and moving experience.[41]

Orwell had glimpsed utopia, and he liked it. He embraced the group of humanity wholeheartedly. Spain left him, he later wrote, with 'not less but more belief in the decency of human beings'.[42] It was the highest compliment he could pay his species.

Spain also taught Orwell a second great lesson. He was, by 1936, alive to political extremism, wary of the analytical inflexibilities of communist orthodoxy, alert to 'dishonest' propaganda of left and right alike, but equally apprehensive about a peculiarly British snobbery which might 'pave the way for some form of Fascism'. In Catalonia in 1937 he experienced a 'horrible atmosphere of political suspicion and hatred'. Here, 'the notion of "liquidating" or "eliminating" everyone who happens to disagree with you' seemed natural. He saw people arrested, and disappearing, on mere suspicion of heresy, while other well-meaning people refused to acknowledge it or, worse still, thought the price worth paying. Orwell served with the militia attached to the Partido Obrero de Unificación Marxista, or POUM, a left party which had British supporters in the Independent Labour Party (ILP), but which Moscow, attempting to dominate the republic's strategy, soon condemned as 'part of Franco's "fifth column"'. POUM members were arrested by People's Commissariat for Internal Affairs (NKVD) agents in Spain, tried secretly, and sometimes executed.[43] When his associates were imprisoned, Orwell quickly learnt how 'confessions' were extracted, how the prisoners were 'half-starved, beaten, and insulted', and how little legality mattered. He became himself a suspected 'Trotskyist', and had his papers confiscated. He still resisted the 'vulgar lie, now so popular' (1936) that fascism and communism were the same thing. But, by mid-1937, he saw them as 'different in degree, not in kind' in their suppression of liberty and free speech, and in imprisonment without trial.[44]

---

[40] Most notably the Italian militiaman to whom he took 'an immediate liking'; they shook hands, and Orwell later wrote, 'Queer, the affection you can feel for a stranger! It was as though his spirit and mine had momentarily succeeded in bridging the gulf of language and tradition and meeting in utter intimacy' (*Homage to Catalonia* (1938, Penguin Books, 1962), p. 7). 'Everybody is friends with everybody in a minute, knowing that in twenty-four or forty-eight hours one will have to separate again', reported Franz Borkenau in August 1936: *The Spanish Cockpit* (Faber & Faber, 1937), p. 73.
[41] Orwell, XI, p. 87.   [42] Orwell, *Homage to Catalonia*, p. 220.
[43] Orwell, X, pp. 534, 477; Orwell, *Homage to Catalonia*, pp. 189–90; Orwell, XI, pp. 12, 32, 117.
[44] Orwell, X, pp. 534; Orwell, XI, p. 76.

So the feeling of betrayal became overwhelming. 'So far from pushing the Spanish Government further towards the Left', Orwell now thought, 'the Communist influence has pulled it violently towards the Right.' The communists, it seemed, would rather see the fascists win than let their allies on the left gain the upper hand. And in fact they had no 'allies'—every non-Stalinist was an enemy. It was clear that the 'logical end' of this process was 'a regime in which every opposition party and newspaper is suppressed and every dissentient of any importance is in jail'. Even when 'operated by Communists and Liberals', this regime had 'more points of resemblance to Fascism than points of difference'.[45]

By July 1937, then, Orwell proclaimed that 'Communism is now a counter-revolutionary force' which aimed to destroy 'any party that shows signs of revolutionary tendencies'. The only antidote to this was 'for the workers to keep the power in their own hands'.[46] He now began reading left-wing publications more seriously. Marx he never engaged with at length; he probably read the *Manifesto* but little else. After he began collecting political pamphlets in 1935, however, he studied a great deal of contemporary Marxist debate, surprising onlookers with his mastery of detail.[47] The 'main weakness' of Marxism he regarded as 'its failure to interpret human motives'.[48] In 1937 he named a poodle puppy Marx 'to remind us that we had never read Marx and now we have read a little and taken so strong a personal dislike to the man that we can't look the dog in the face when we speak to him'.[49] (The irony being that his great ambition in life was, of course, to avoid being Marx's poodle.) But he did loosely accept Marx's account of the bourgeoisie's exploitation of the proletariat.[50]

His Spanish experience thus simultaneously had an immense impact both on Orwell's sense of what socialism promised and what Soviet domination of international communism threatened. 'Every line of serious work that I have written since 1936', he later said, 'has been written, directly or indirectly, *against* totalitarianism and *for* democratic Socialism, as I understand it.'[51] Arrests, torture, and executions became increasingly common—some 500 members of the communist International Brigade, which Orwell sought to join, were killed by their own secret police.[52] Then, returning to Britain, he found that fellow travellers refused to publish his more critical accounts and reviews respecting the conflict. He often wondered, subsequently, to the end of his life, when he kept a loaded pistol to hand, whether the communists might not kill him too.

---

[45] Ibid., pp. 51–2, 59. A summary of the ILP position on POUM which helps flesh out Orwell's views is given in Tom Taylor, *Defend Socialism from the Communists* (ILP, 1942).

[46] Orwell, XI, pp. 41–2, 45, 59, 76.

[47] Davison, *George Orwell*, p. 90; Rees, *Orwell*, p. 147.   [48] Orwell, XII, p. 244.

[49] Peter Davison, ed., *The Lost Orwell: Being a Supplement to* The Complete Works of George Orwell (Timewell Press, 2006), p. 72 (*c.*16 February 1937).

[50] E.g., Orwell, XIX, p. 88. See generally Philip Bounds, *Orwell and Marxism: The Political and Cultural Thinking of George Orwell* (I.B. Tauris, 2009).

[51] Orwell, XVIII, p. 319.

[52] Davison, *George Orwell*, p. 84. Their total numbers were about 35,000, so 1 in 70 was executed by their own side.

Having thus learned how central propaganda and disinformation were to communist aims first-hand during the 'reign of terror' in Barcelona (his phrase), Orwell now began to comprehend both the scale of Stalinist repression and its peculiar ferocity. Boris Souvarine's anti-Stalinist account of the 1937 show trials was a key source here.[53] This indicated how little truth mattered in the trials, and how far the State Political Directorate (GPU) 'equals or surpasses the Inquisition' in its methods. (Both Souvarine and the Austrian socialist Felix Adler compared the proceedings to medieval sorcery trials.)[54] Soon Orwell feared communism would render the whole socialist movement 'perverted'. When, in 1938, he reviewed Lyons' *Assignment in Utopia* it was clear he had followed the Moscow show trials carefully. In the USSR, Orwell wrote, 'the G.P.U. are everywhere, everyone lives in constant terror of denunciation, freedom of speech and the press are obliterated to an extent we can hardly imagine'. Communist writers were 'obliged to claim infallibility for their party chiefs'. They believed 'Anything is right which advances the cause of the Party', so that the 'unquestionable doctrine of Monday may become the damnable heresy of Tuesday, and so on'. In 1942, he recalled that the propaganda of this period made him feel that 'the very concept of objective truth is fading out of the world'.[55] The former Comintern functionary Franz Borkenau helped him see that communist parties taught 'a contempt for democratic methods' and 'a belief in violence and double-crossing'.[56] He began to see 'totalitarian' dictatorships as 'something entirely unprecedented'.[57] Yet he still conceded in 1939 that 'humanity must move in the direction of Communism or perish'.[58] So 'communism' and 'totalitarianism' were not yet identical.

Orwell's last pre-war novel, *Coming Up for Air* (1939), shows that his wider concerns had not disappeared. It evidences his continuing unease with the cult of success, the worship of the money-god, the grinding pressure to conform to the bourgeois class norms, and the relentless subordination of human being to machine, which he increasingly saw as epitomizing modern life. A world disappears before our eyes, much of it valuable. Another, defined by war and brutality, looms on the horizon. The narrator, George Bowling—another failure—reflects on 'the way we're going nowadays. Everything slick and streamlined . . . Celluloid, rubber, chromium-steel everywhere, arc-lamps blazing all night, glass roofs over your head, radios all playing the same tune, no vegetation left, everything cemented over, mock turtles grazing under the neutral fruit-trees.' An anti-fascist lecturer he encounters, preaches

---

[53] Boris Souvarine, *Cauchemar en URSS* [Nightmare in the USSR] (Revue de Paris, 1937), which Orwell owned.

[54] Steinhoff, *The Road to 1984*, pp. 32–4. Orwell regarded Koestler's novel as 'rather like an expanded imaginative version of Souvarine's pamphlet' (XII, p. 359). See also Boris Souvarine, *Stalin* (Secker & Warburg, 1939). Soviet prison life is also recounted in Iulia de Beausobre's *The Woman Who Could Not Die* (1938; Victor Gollancz, 1948), the 1948 edition of which Orwell owned.

[55] Orwell, XI, pp. 58, 67, 112–13; 163; Orwell, XII, p. 101; Orwell, XIII, p. 504.

[56] Orwell, XI, p. 203. See esp. F. Borkenau, *The Communist International* (Faber & Faber Ltd, 1938), pp. 401–29.

[57] He first used the word 'dictatorship' in 1938 (Orwell, XI, p. 247).

[58] Orwell, XI, pp. 317, 327.

Hate, hate, hate. Let's all get together and have a good hate. Over and over . . . I felt
what he was feeling . . . I saw the vision that he was seeing . . . It's a picture of himself
smashing people's faces in with a spanner. Fascist faces, of course.

So he envisions 'the crowds of a million people all cheering for the Leader till
they deafen themselves into thinking that they really worship him, and all the time,
underneath, they hate him so that they want to puke'. In a milk bar he enters,
everything is

> slick and shiny and streamlined; mirrors, enamel, and chromium plate whichever
> direction you look in. Everything spent on the decorations and nothing on the food.
> No real food at all. Just lists of stuff with American names, sort of phantom stuff that
> you can't taste and can hardly believe in the existence of. Everything comes out of a
> carton or a tin, or it's hauled out of a refrigerator or squirted out of a tap or squeezed
> out of a tube. No comfort, no privacy. Tall stools to sit on, a kind of narrow ledge to
> eat off, mirrors all round you. A sort of propaganda floating round, mixed up with the
> noise of the radio, to the effect that food doesn't matter, comfort doesn't matter,
> nothing matters except slickness and shininess and streamlining.[59]

Orwell could not but lament the loss and deliberate destruction of ways of life to
which he was attached. He had lived in this now pastel, ethereal, disappearing
world in Henley and elsewhere. In *Coming Up for Air* it is Lower Binfield which is
'swallowed' by progress. Here, the narrator briefly imagines the war just coming,
which will smash this world to pieces, and substitute one dominated by 'air-raid
sirens blowing and the loud-speakers bellowing that our glorious troops have taken
a hundred thousand prisoners . . . I see the posters and the food-queues, and the
castor oil and the rubber truncheons and the machine-guns squirting out of
bedroom windows.'[60] Here we are close to the Oceania of *Nineteen Eighty-Four*.
So dystopia is also the degeneration of modernity as such, an attitude and mental
world derived from mechanization and urbanization. After his political immersion
in Spain, Orwell had come up for air, only to emerge into the foul stench of the
modern swamp—'the machine age'.

WORLD WAR II AND SOCIALISM

During the war, Orwell's political ideas developed in three distinctive ways: he
crafted a concept of revolutionary patriotism; he engaged with James Burnham's
theories respecting the inevitability of oligarchy; and he grappled with the metaphysical problems of finding a basis for his moral beliefs, as an alternative to power
worship.

Orwell's initial response to the war was to propose uniting a peculiar type of
patriotism rooted in specifically British/English virtues (he used these terms interchangeably) with an agenda of socialist revolution. The war clarified for Orwell
what the generation of the 1930s had wavered over constantly: whether the choice

---

[59] Orwell, *Complete Novels*, pp. 519, 242–3, 518.   [60] Ibid., pp. 443–4.

was really between a capitalism naturally evolving into fascism, and communism. His answer, characteristically, was neither. 'Patriots and Revolutionaries' (January 1941) declared that Britain was 'on the road to revolution'. In February, 'Fascism and Democracy' stressed 'an all-important English trait: the respect for constitutionalism and legality, the belief in "the law" as something above the State and above the individual'. The law itself was cruel, stupid, and unjust, designed for the rich and against the poor. It did, however, instil a sense of fairness lacking in systems rooted only in naked power.[61] But how could this be combined with a revolutionary political strategy?

The answer came that month, February 1941, in *The Lion and the Unicorn*, subtitled as 'Socialism and the English Genius'. Here Orwell contrasted totalitarianism to the 'privateness of English life', belief in 'liberty of the individual', and a quiet, anti-militarist patriotism and dislike of regimentation.[62] In Britain, 'the totalitarian idea that there is no such thing as law, there is only power, has never taken root. Even the intelligentsia have accepted it only in theory'. 'The power-worship which is the new religion of Europe, and which has infected the English intelligentsia, has never touched the common people. They have never caught up with power politics.' Patriotism to Orwell had 'nothing to do with Conservatism. It is actually the opposite of Conservatism, since it is a devotion to something that is always changing and yet is felt to be mystically the same. It is the bridge between the future and the past. No real revolutionary has ever been an internationalist.' Amongst the middle class, Orwell thought, 'patriotism, when it comes to the pinch, is stronger than their sense of self-interest'. Those of the 'Europeanized' intelligentsia who took their 'cookery from Paris and their opinions from Moscow' came out badly in this account. But so did the rich: England was 'a family with the wrong members in control'. So the burden of expectation rested on the working classes, who would make the greatest sacrifices, but who would, Orwell thought, then demand fundamental changes. They, more than their rulers, believed in 'bourgeois Democracy' and freedom. The war was helping to break down class barriers: the 'Blitz' spirit had a radical, egalitarian aspect.[63] So Orwell proposed a programme which included nationalizing the land, mines, banks, railways, and major industries, and abolishing land ownership in towns, to persuade the common people that their sacrifices were worthwhile.

The second major development of Orwell's wartime thought came through engaging with the ex-Trotskyist James Burnham's ideas, notably as expressed in

---

[61] Orwell, XII, pp. 343, 397.

[62] See my '*The Lion and the Unicorn*, Patriotism, and Orwell's Politics', *Review of Politics*, 47 (1985), 186–211.

[63] Contemporaries like Angus Calder observed, about the early months of World War II in Britain, that, 'In the buses, the trains and pubs of Britain, strangers were speaking to one another.' Orwell's friend Julian Symons also noted that 'life in London at the time gave us a hint of it as life in Russia must have done in the months after the Revolution . . . Living became a matter of the next meal, the next drink. The way in which people behaved to each other relaxed strangely. Barriers of class and circumstances disappeared, so that London was more nearly an equalitarian city than it has ever been in the last quarter of a century' (quoted in Alok Rai, *Orwell and the Politics of Despair* (Cambridge University Press, 1988), p. 93).

The Managerial Revolution (1941). Many such ideas would appear in *Nineteen Eighty-Four*. They focused on the inevitable emergence of a new managerial ruling class and of three great super-states, and were indebted to Robert Michels' 'iron law of oligarchy', amongst other sources. Like other anti-Stalinist works which foresaw a bureaucratic despotism arising from collectivism, Burnham hinted that proletarian revolutions inevitably failed. Burnham, Orwell wrote in 1946, thought 'All talk about democracy, liberty, equality, fraternity, all revolutionary movements, all visions of Utopia... are humbug... The English Puritans, the Jacobins, the Bolsheviks, were in each case simply power-seekers using the hopes of the masses in order to win a privileged place for themselves.' Orwell dissented, insisting that 'Burnham and his fellow thinkers are wrong... in trying to spread the idea that totalitarianism is *unavoidable*, and that we must therefore do nothing about it.' Suppose, Orwell thought,

> he is wrong. Suppose the ship is not sinking, only leaking. Suppose that Communism is not yet strong enough to swallow the world and that the danger of war can be staved off for twenty years or more: then we don't have to accept Burnham's remedy—or, at least, we don't have to accept it immediately and without question.

Thus it was only the case that the '"managerial" class *might* get control of our society'.[64] In 1946, Orwell wrote that

> It is too early to say in just what way the Russian regime will destroy itself. If I had to make a prophecy, I should say that a continuation of the Russian policies of the last fifteen years—and internal and external policy, of course, are merely two facets of the same thing—can only lead to a war conducted with atomic bombs, which will make Hitler's invasion look like a tea-party. But at any rate, the Russian regime will either democratise itself, or it will perish. The huge, invincible, everlasting slave empire of which Burnham appears to dream will not be established, or, if established, will not endure, because slavery is no longer a stable basis for human society.[65]

Orwell willingly conceded that 'it has always been obvious that a planned and centralised society is liable to develop into an oligarchy or a dictatorship'. He admitted that if socialism 'was supposed to connote political democracy, social equality, and internationalism' there was 'not the slightest sign that any of these things is in a way to being established anywhere'. Burnham's theory was thus 'extremely plausible' as an account of what '*is happening*', particularly relative to the USSR since 1940 or so. Yet Orwell clearly did not consider 'Communism and Fascism to be *the same thing*', and dissociated himself from those who did.[66] He also

---

[64] Orwell, XVI, p. 61. Burnham replied that he thought totalitarianism 'probable' (p. 62). On his influence on Orwell, see Steinhoff, *The Road to 1984*, pp. 43–55, and Michael Maddison, '*1984*: A Burnhamite Fantasy?', *Political Quarterly*, 32 (1961), 71–9. Several writers had indicated the possibility of a bureaucratic dictatorship emerging from socialist revolutions, including Mikhail Bakunin (against Marx, in *Statism and Anarchy*, 1873), Waclaw Machajski (*The Evolution of Social Democracy*, 1899), and Bruno Rizzi (*The Bureaucratization of the World* (1939; Tavistock, 1985)). For a general account of Burnham, see Samuel Francis, 'Power and History: The Political Thought of James Burnham', *Political Science Reviewer*, 12 (1982), 265–313.

[65] Orwell, XVIII, p. 283.   [66] Ibid., p. 279.

probed the 'general drift . . . towards oligarchy'. Burnham insisted that all politics was 'the struggle for power' by particular groups, 'especially among dissatisfied groups whose talents do not get free play under the existing form of society'. Yet Burnham, Orwell averred, never explained '*why* people want power' and why the peculiar power worship of the present age was expressed as it was. In particular, the English intelligentsia became sympathetic to the USSR only *after* it had become totalitarian, doubtless imagining its own self-advancement in similar circumstances. But 'fortunately', Orwell thought, the 'managers' were 'not so invincible as Burnham believes'. Meanwhile, however, he worried about communist infiltration in Britain itself, given the fact that the 'USSR is and must be implacably hostile to a social-democratic government of the British type'.[67]

'NOTES ON NATIONALISM' AND GROUP IDENTITY

Though hastily composed, Orwell's brief 'Notes on Nationalism' (October 1945) is a key text for understanding *Nineteen Eighty-Four*.[68] Here Orwell generalized from his earlier assessment of communism. Terming it the 'patriotism of the deracinated' in 'Inside the Whale' (1940), Orwell had asserted that communism's appeal lay in its being 'something to believe in. Here was a church, an army, an orthodoxy, a discipline. Here was a Fatherland . . . All the loyalties and superstitions that the intellect had seemingly banished could come rushing back under the thinnest of disguises.' Now he returned to this theme. The collapse of religious belief and disconcerting decay of other loyalties had left an aching unfulfilled desire for group attachment and identity. This was intensified by the pressure of circumstances. The need to satisfy this longing Orwell described as a 'habit of mind . . . now become so widespread' that it affected 'our thinking on nearly every subject'. It had, he thought, 'not been given a name'. So, awkwardly, he called it 'nationalism'. We might recognize it as a peculiar form of groupism.[69]

'Nationalism' meant, centrally, 'power hunger tempered by self-deception'. It would define the mental world of Oceania's rulers. It included 'the habit of assuming that human beings can be classified like insects and that whole blocks of people can be confidently labelled "good" or "bad"'. And, 'much more important', it meant 'the habit of identifying oneself with a single nation or other unit, placing it beyond good and evil and recognizing no other duty than advancing its interests'. Nationalism is contrasted to patriotism, a devotion to particular places

[67] Ibid., pp. 269–72, 279, 282–3, 287.

[68] Orwell, XVII, pp. 141–57. The essay was first published in *Polemic: A Magazine of Philosophy, Psychology & Aesthetics*. Orwell later wrote that it was 'written in bad circumstances and could do with revision' (XX, p. 228). It has been discussed (e.g. William Steinhoff, *The Road to 1984* (Weidenfeld and Nicolson, 1975) pp. 165–6), but its significance is largely underlooked. George Kateb, however, recognizes that the theme of 'the immersion of the self in something larger than the self' is 'most forcefully articulated here, prior to *Nineteen Eighty-Four*' ('The Road to 1984', *Political Science Quarterly*, 81 (1966), 569). See further my 'Orwell's "Notes on Nationalism" and *Nineteen Eighty-Four*', in Thomas Horan, ed., *Critical Insights: Nineteen Eighty-Four* (The Salem Press, 2016).

[69] Orwell, XII, p. 103; Orwell, XVII, p. 141.

and ways of life which one had 'no wish to force on other people', and was 'inseparable from the desire for power'. The 'abiding purpose of every nationalist' was 'to secure more power and more prestige, not for himself but for the nation or other unit in which he has chosen to sink his own nationality'. This could be a purely negative feeling. A nationalist, Orwell insisted, 'is one who thinks solely, or mainly, in terms of competitive prestige. He may be a positive or a negative nationalist ... but at any rate his thoughts always turn on victories, defeats, triumphs and humiliations.' This habit of mind was 'widespread among the English intelligentsia, and more widespread there than among the mass of the people'.[70]

Here we see Orwell defining what he saw as the moral rot infecting the intelligentsia from *c.*1936 onwards. To them, the 'dominant form of nationalism is Communism', which meant justifying Russian policy and interests. But all forms of nationalism shared certain qualities. These included, firstly, a tendency to dwell obsessively on the 'superiority of his own power unit'—we note group psychology now comes to the fore. Secondly, 'nationalist' loyalties were transferable and elastic, which the term 'nationalism' in its original meaning hardly suggests to later readers. Loyalties could move from country to country or entity to entity, the constant being the state of mind, the desire for loyalty and identity as such. This was a much more extreme process, and one more prone to dishonesty than a patriotism focused on one's own country. Thirdly, nationalists were indifferent to reality, or prone to inconsistency. Whatever 'our side' did was acceptable. Atrocities committed by the other side were reprehensible. 'Indifference to objective truth' occurred as a result of the sacrifices required by loyalty. Past events were 'omitted' from current accounts; the Russians were already removing references to the Russo-German Pact of 1939–41 from their histories. What was crucial was the willingness 'to *feel* that his own unit is getting the better of some other unit, and he can more easily do this by scoring off an adversary than by examining the facts'. So, at one level, this is just a feel-good narrative written to make present readers comfortable—a perspective we can readily identify, if not identify with. Orwell then offered an account of what he termed Positive, Transferred, and Negative nationalisms. The former included neo-Toryism and Zionism. Transferred types included communism, political Catholicism, colour and class feelings (a 'belief in the superiority of the proletariat' being quite compatible with 'ordinary snobbishness in everyday life'), and pacifism. Negative nationalism included Anglophobia, anti-Semitism, and Trotskyism.

Orwell's analysis here indicates that 'nationalism' is a misleading term when used to describe these phenomena. The 'monomania' or 'obsessive fixation on a single subject, the same inability to form a genuinely rational opinion based on probabilities', are qualities associated with political religion, and particular forms of group and crowd psychology. Orwell's term, 'power unit', is particularly telling here, for it goes to the emotional and irrational core of group identity. Such groups replace traditional affiliations, including 'nationalism' as usually conceived. The emotions are crucial here: 'as soon as fear, hatred, jealousy and power-worship are involved,

---

[70] Ibid., pp. 141–2.

the sense of reality becomes unhinged' and 'the sense of right and wrong becomes unhinged also'. (*The Lion and the Unicorn* had asserted of the individual that the nation had 'the power to absolve him from evil'.)[71] Orwell fought shy of exploring the causes of these phenomena, describing this as 'too big a question to be raised here'. He concluded, instead, with a plea for a *'moral* effort' to struggle against 'nationalistic loves and hatreds'. So he did think these tendencies could be combated. This was 'a question first of all of discovering what one really is, what one's own feelings really are, and then of making allowance for the inevitable bias'. He added that the 'emotional urges which are inescapable, and perhaps even necessary for political action, should be able to exist side by side with an acceptance of reality'.[72] Thus, one could be committed to a just cause without being swallowed by the group's demand that truth be renounced in favour of dogma. This theme would haunt *Nineteen Eighty-Four*.

ANIMAL FARM

Orwell's great work of the wartime period was *Animal Farm*, which was completed in early 1944. Terming it 'strongly anti-Stalin in tendency', he correctly foresaw that Gollancz would not publish it.[73] In this 'fairy story'—his own subtitle—farm animals led by pigs, including Napoleon (Stalin), eject Mr Jones from Manor Farm.[74] The exuberant charm of the animals' triumph is short-lived. The philosophy of Animalism is defined by the formula 'Four legs good, two legs bad.' But the pigs quickly learn to read and write, and soon lord it over the proletarian chickens, sheep, donkeys, and goats. Snowball (Trotsky), Napoleon's competitor, is forced to flee after trained dogs are set on him. Some animals object, but are reminded of the importance of loyalty, obedience, and 'iron discipline'.[75] The point of the tale, Orwell wrote, was to avoid revolutions led by 'unconsciously power-hungry people'. Revolutions would 'only effect a radical improvement when the masses are alert and know how to chuck out their leaders as soon as the latter have done their job'. 'The turning point of the story', he added, 'was supposed to be when the pigs kept the milk and apples for themselves.'[76]

---

[71] George Orwell, *The Lion and the Unicorn* (1941, Penguin Books, 1979), p. 35.
[72] Orwell, XVII, pp. 143–55.   [73] Orwell, XVI, pp. 126, 142.
[74] The symbolism of the characters is explained in J. R. Hammond, ed., *A George Orwell Companion* (Macmillan, 1962), p. 161. Orwell found real pigs the 'most annoying destructive animals, and hard to keep out of anywhere because they are so strong and cunning' (XIX, p. 451).
[75] Orwell, *Complete Novels*, p. 33.
[76] Orwell, XVIII. p. 507. See Orwell, *Complete Novels*, pp. 25–6. When the story was dramatized for radio he added the lines:

CLOVER: Do you think that is quite fair [the appropriation of the apples]?
MOLLY: What, keep all the apples for themselves?
MURIEL: Aren't we to have any?
COW: I thought they were going to be shared equally.

The producer cut this out. See Davison, *George Orwell*, p. 128. T. S. Eliot, who had fascist sympathies, rejected the MS at Faber & Faber, reasoning that, as the most intelligent animals, the pigs

Many of the themes of *Nineteen Eighty-Four* are explored here. Animals are found to be conniving at a human restoration. So there are purges and executions, privation and propaganda, nobility, sacrifice, and tragedy. Clover the carthorse, a leader amongst the lower animals, has 'no thought of rebellion or disobedience in her mind' despite the purges. For she is convinced that they are better off than under human rule, 'and that before all else it was needful to prevent the return of the human beings'. Party lines waver incessantly: 'No animal shall kill any other animal' becomes 'No animal shall kill any other animal *without cause.*' 'No animal shall sleep in a bed' becomes 'No animal shall sleep in a bed *with sheets.*' 'No animals shall drink alcohol' becomes 'No animal shall drink alcohol *to excess.*' When the animals suffer privation, they are told life is better than ever, though in reality only the pigs and their guardian dogs enjoy good rations. When, after many years, the farm grows richer, only the latter really prosper. Whatever goes wrong is blamed on the banished Snowball, whose role in the rebellion is suppressed. But some animals do object to the pigs, and attempt to save the great carthorse Boxer before he is butchered. Some sense the betrayal of the revolution, and yet, we are told, they 'lacked the words to express' their dissent. Gradually they forget what happened at the revolution: 'There was nothing with which they could compare their present lives: they had nothing to go upon except Squealer's lists of figures, which invariably demonstrated that everything was getting better. The animals found the problem insoluble; in any case, they had little time for speculating on such things now.' 'And yet the animals never gave up hope', we are told:

> None of the old dreams had been abandoned. The Republic of the Animals which Major had foretold, when the green fields of England should be untrodden by human feet, was still believed in. Some day it was coming: it might not be soon, it might not be within the lifetime of any animal now living, but still it was coming.

And some indeed secretly hum now-forbidden tunes which none dare sing aloud.[77]

But finally Napoleon and the other pigs learn to walk on their hind legs. They begin consorting with the neighbouring farmers. As they play cards together, both the pigs and humans cheat; the other animals peering in from 'outside looked from pig to man, and from man to pig, and from pig to man again; but already it was impossible to say which was which'. The human analogy is complete. The chant 'Four legs good two legs bad' becomes 'Four legs good two legs *better*'. And all the original principles are reduced to one:

ALL ANIMALS ARE EQUAL
BUT SOME ANIMALS ARE MORE
EQUAL THAN OTHERS.[78]

'Equal Comrade' Duch, two pens protruding, would have well understood.

---

were most qualified to run the farm (Frederic Warburg, *All Authors are Equal: The Publishing Life of Frederic Warburg, 1936–1971* (Hutchinson, 1973), p. 43).

[77] Orwell, *Complete Novels*, pp. 45–6, 61–2.   [78] Ibid., p. 66.

NINETEEN EIGHTY-FOUR

'It was a bright cold day in April, and the clocks were striking thirteen.' So opens Orwell's great work. It is set in London, a city in Oceania, one of the three great states apparently constantly at war with one another—apparently, because despite an earlier atomic war, the conflicts now may well only be staged by the three governments to distract and suppress their populations. Oceania's dominant ideology is called Ingsoc. It is derived originally from English socialism, but is not, we must note, identical with it.[79] It masks a brutal dictatorship. The one ruling Party deliberately keeps most people relatively deprived. Many of its own functionaries constantly fear arrest, forced confession, execution, or imprisonment in labour camps. The working-class majority, or 'proles', know of no alternative to the system: they have no collective memory.[80] There is no law, only power: this we recall was the definitive feature of totalitarianism for Orwell. For Party members, fear penetrates every crevice of everyday life. 'Facecrime' might betray a quaver of doubt.[81] Looking aside, or disinterested, or too interested at the wrong moment, is dangerous. Talking in one's sleep might invite denunciation even by one's children, who, still more than their parents, are deformed by sadism and paranoia but adore (as Orwell expressed it in a passage struck out) the 'vicious gang loyalty' encouraged by the Party.[82] (Little wretches, they beg to attend the monthly hangings of prisoners of war in the park.) 'Newspeak''s domination of language reduces the possibility of even thinking oppositionally. The word 'free', for instance, is used only in the sense of 'this dog is free from lice'—exactly how, as we saw in Chapter 4, the Khmer Rouge used it. Its overall aim, quite in keeping with Stalinist practice, was to '*diminish* the range of thought'.[83]

'Ownlife', or personal privacy, is thus, for Outer Party members, practically non-existent, and very dangerous. Most avoid it. Katherine, for example, is the estranged wife of the novel's protagonist, Winston Smith. Ultraconventional and frigid, a walking gramophone of slogans and a victim of the Party's anti-sex propaganda, she feels 'very uneasy' when separated from one of the incessant collective activities at the Community Centre. Such persons are rooted in and sustained by the crowd.[84] They are group persons, 'We'. They think groupthink. They fear isolation and being alone—they fear themselves, for the self itself is, of course, suspect. And yet these groups also symbolize estrangement. In another passage struck out, Orwell

[79] Ingsoc is about as close to English socialism as National Socialism was to German Social Democracy.

[80] Crick records an intriguing MS note by Orwell which reads: 'Impossibility of detecting similar memories in anyone else. Non-memory [?] of the proles' (*Orwell*, p. 585).

[81] Meyers quite wrongly interprets this as 'having pronounced Semitic features', *A Reader's Guide to George Orwell* (Thames and Hudson, 1975), p. 147.

[82] George Orwell, *Nineteen Eighty-Four: The Facsimile of the Extant Manuscript*, ed. Peter Davison (Secker & Warburg, 1984), p. 62. Also struck out: 'All their gang loyalty had been captured by the Party.' And: 'All their ferocity had been turned outwards against imaginary enemies [rewritten: 'the enemies of the state']—against foreigners, traitors, saboteurs, thought-criminals.' To those interested in Orwell's intentions this edition is extremely useful.

[83] Orwell, *Nineteen Eighty-Four*, p. 242.   [84] Ibid., p. 111.

describes them as living in 'locked loneliness'.[85] We now know dystopia when we see it.

Winston Smith is somehow detached from and even above these pressures. This must, we sense from the outset, prove his undoing. The novel commences as he leaves his soulless abode in Victory Mansions for his post at the Ministry of Truth. Here, taking up Zamyatin's hint, he rewrites old newspapers to accord with the latest shifts in the Party line, so that the past never varies from it.[86] The city itself, London, is a kind of inverted Wellsian futuristic landscape mostly drawn from the London of 1948. Almost every aspect of this world, from the permanently invasive smell of boiled cabbage and old rag mats in Winston's hallway, is foetid, dingy, drab, dreary, dirty, crumbling. (Few writers do squalor better than Orwell.)[87] At the end of this hallway is a large poster of 'a man of about forty-five, with a heavy black moustache and ruggedly handsome features'. This is Big Brother. His image is everywhere: socialism with a human face, as Heller and Nekrich mockingly put it.[88] The caption beneath it runs: 'BIG BROTHER IS WATCHING YOU.' The eyes seem to follow you. They may not belong to a real person. It does not matter. Big Brother does not need to exist. He functions as a 'focussing point for love, fear, and reverence, emotions more easily directed towards an individual than an organisation'.[89] He stands for a system in which uniformity and solitude have replaced privacy, love, and friendship. 'You did not have friends nowadays, you had comrades.'[90] (What a telling comment on Orwell's Spanish experience, where the two were synonymous. Here is the distance between utopian enhanced sociability and dystopian coerced sociability or compulsory solidarity.)

For Outer Party members, life is nearly as transparent as in the description of Zamyatin's glass houses which Orwell so admired.[91] Paranoia is omnipresent. The emotions are militarized, and wedded to sadism. Constant war communiqués have as 'their sole purpose the whipping-up of fear and hatred'.[92] Daily rants like the Two Minutes Hate sustain this spirit. In prolonged campaigns of antagonism like Hate Week, enemy prisoners are slaughtered. In frenzied meetings, a 'hideous ecstasy of fear and vindictiveness, a desire to kill, to torture, to smash faces in with a

---

[85] Orwell, *Nineteen Eighty-Four: The Facsimile*, p. 72.

[86] Modern historians of the USSR quote Orwell as to the accuracy of this trend: Mikhail Heller and Aleksandr Nekrich, *Utopia in Power: The History of the Soviet Union from 1917 to the Present* (Hutchinson, 1986), p. 294.

[87] Compare this with the opening passages in *The Road to Wigan Pier*, for instance.

[88] Heller and Nekrich, *Utopia in Power*, p. 281. An author Orwell met during his BBC years, Amabel Williams-Ellis, had used 'Big Brother' to describe a communist figure in her dystopia, *To Tell the Truth* (Jonathan Cape, 1933), p. 46.

[89] Orwell, *Nineteen Eighty-Four*, pp. 5, 167. A deleted passage reads: 'Big Brother reigned in the hearts of the people because he saved them from imaginary perils and because he flattered their vanity by winning imaginary victories. In place of liberty they had the sense of deliverance, and in place of physical well-being they had military glory' (Orwell, *Nineteen Eighty-Four: The Facsimile*, p. 202). And so too 'Heresy will never die out. Goldstein will live for ever. Over and over we shall create the heretic' (p. 328).

[90] Orwell, *Nineteen Eighty-Four*, p. 42.

[91] He described *We* as, 'in effect a study of the Machine . . . the genie that man has thoughtlessly let out of its bottle and cannot put back again' (XVIII, p. 16).

[92] Deleted passage: Orwell, *Nineteen Eighty-Four: The Facsimile*, p. 208.

sledge-hammer, seemed to flow through the whole group of people like an electric current, turning one even against one's will into a grimacing, screaming lunatic'.[93] This is (rightly) described as sublimated eroticism.[94] There was, we are told,

a direct intimate connexion between chastity and political orthodoxy. For how could the fear, the hatred, and the lunatic credulity which the Party needed in its members be kept at the right pitch, except by bottling down some powerful instinct and using it as a driving force? The sex impulse was dangerous to the Party, and the Party had turned it to account.[95]

So in Newspeak 'goodsex' means only pleasureless, dutiful intercourse between man and wife, all other sex being 'sexcrime'. Eventually, it is hoped that 'artsem', or artificial insemination, would prevail (Huxley was partly in mind here, but again we have seen that there was a direct Stalinist parallel).[96]

Many commentators have found this account heavy-handed and the psychology feeble.[97] Who could abolish the family? But remember both medieval Catholicism in its most extreme forms, re: sex, some moments in Bolshevism; and then Pol Pot, re: the family.[98] Thus, what in fiction seems psychologically unreal, extreme, and distended turns out historically to be spot on, exactly depicting the most extreme perversions of this mentality.

Winston Smith's downfall commences when, for some reason, he risks death by buying (from a police spy, we discover) an old-fashioned diary. He can write in it by hiding in a small alcove in his apartment, unseen by the ubiquitous telescreen which monitors all Outer Party members. (This device, nonetheless, keeps up a constant nonsensical cacophony of propaganda about the wars, rations, and production figures in a 'fruity voice'—doubtless Orwell had some BBC announcer in mind—thus effectively sustaining both hysteria levels and the confusion caused by constant disinformation. This, with the occasional sound of rocket bombs going off, is the book's soundtrack. The telescreen is probably inspired by the generally anti-machine film 'Modern Times', where the factory boss uses a TV to spy on his employee, Charlie Chaplin—Orwell's favourite actor.) On paper, Winston pours out his minimal political consciousness. Mostly this is just letting off steam. Worse still, Winston then has a furtive affair with another Outer Party member, Julia. She works in a propaganda section where machines assist in writing the cheap books which help distract the proles. This forbidden relationship must clearly terminate with their arrest, torture, and utter extinction.[99] It transpires soon enough that in

[93] Orwell, *Nineteen Eighty-Four*, p. 15.
[94] On this theme see George Mosse, *Nationalism and Sexuality* (Howard Fertig, 1997).
[95] Orwell, *Nineteen Eighty-Four*, p. 109.   [96] Ibid., p. 56.
[97] Raymond Williams, for instance, who knew enough about Stalinism, finds it to be the weakest part of the novel, and notes 'that it seems to have been taken from Zamyatin's *We* is relevant but secondary' (*Orwell* (Viking Press, 1971), p. 81).
[98] The parallels between Orwell's description of Big Brother and Pol Pot's Cambodia have been adequately established. See Henri Locard, *Pol Pot's Little Red Book: The Sayings of Angkar* (Silkworm Books, 2004), p. 113.
[99] Shelden notes parallels between this and a Cyril Connolly short story called 'Year Nine', which was reprinted in 1945 (*Orwell*, p. 355). Written in 1938, this story hints at Newspeak-type terms but is

Oceania only the Thought Police are efficient.[100] Almost from the outset we know that they will suck Winston in and spit him out again, and then 'vapourise' him, in the parlance of the epoch (a nice substitute for 'liquidate'). He is as doomed as the certainty of the clocks striking thirteen. He feels it. We feel it. It sets the tone and provides the tempo of the book.

This sense of inevitability darkens and gains momentum as we proceed. We learn that Julia, patronizingly called a 'rebel from the waist downwards' by Winston, fornicates with Party members but cannot envision revolting in any wider sense. Orwell is often faulted for the weakness of his female characters, and has even been labelled misogynistic.[101] But quite another view of Julia's character is possible. She is as brave a rebel as Winston, and has virtues he lacks. 'In some ways', we are told, 'she was far more acute than Winston, and far less susceptible to Party propaganda.' She ventures that 'the war was not happening', even that the rocket bombs are launched by Oceania against its own people, before Winston, who has access to many more facts, understands this. She cannot accept 'that the individual is always defeated'.[102] She denies that 'there was no such thing as happiness, that the only victory lay in the far future, long after you were dead, that from the moment of declaring war on the Party it was better to think of yourself as a corpse'.[103] She is, admittedly, the kind of person on whom 'the world-view of the Party imposed itself most successfully' because they were 'incapable of understanding it . . . By lack of understanding they remained sane.'[104] (How many are there?) This is why she has to doze off while Winston reads to her from 'the Book' which discloses the regime's inner secrets: it exhibits her impenetrability. She thus represents one of Orwell's key themes here, the instinctive continuity of the human, 'a pragmatic instinct for survival', in Anne Mellor's phrase, which the proles also embody. (This is also why he makes her clever with machinery.) This corresponds in part to Orwell's conception of nature, as does the large prole woman Winston observes frequently washing, and singing as she works, who is also a crucial symbol.[105] Julia's humanity is expressed through her animality. It is more material, more real than Winston's

extremely brief and not overtly anti-Stalinist, being more concerned with Nazi ideas of degenerate art (*The Condemned Playground* (Routledge, 1945), pp. 154–9).

[100] 'The only efficient organ of Soviet power was the Cheka-GPU': Heller and Nekrich, *Utopia in Power*, p. 203.

[101] Notably in Daphne Patai's *The Orwell Mystique: A Study of Male Ideology* (University of Massachusetts Press, 1984), the key study of Orwell's attitude towards gender. To Patai, Julia 'is not held up for our admiration' (p. 244). Some of Orwell's friends agreed about his misogyny. See Bowker, *George Orwell*, pp. 128, 132.

[102] In a deleted passage, Julia says all the confessions are 'a fraud', and adds 'Who does believe it?': Orwell, *Nineteen Eighty-Four: The Facsimile*, p. 104.

[103] Orwell, *Nineteen Eighty-Four*, pp. 111, 127.

[104] Ibid., p. 128. A passage struck out reads: 'He perceived that even people hostile to the Party, & intellectually unequal to doublethink, could be made to accept plain violations of reality, because they were not sufficiently interested in public events to notice what was happening' (Orwell, *Nineteen Eighty-Four: The Facsimile*, p. 102).

[105] Anne Mellor, ' "You're Only a Rebel from the Waist Downwards": Orwell's View of Women', in Stansky, ed., *On Nineteen Eighty-Four*, p. 121. She needs to be contrasted directly to the portrayal of the 'desolate, hopeless' woman defeated by drudgery and exhaustion whom Orwell glimpses from a train, as recounted in *The Road to Wigan Pier*, p. 16.

whimsical abstractions and metaphysical conundrums. Her loyalty is also personal: if Winston chose to rebel, she says (in a deleted passage) 'I'll do it for *you*, dear . . . not for Goldstein' (the supposed leader of the resistance).[106] Julia is here close to Orwell's delineation of the proles, and accordingly plays a more important part than most accounts suggest.[107] Yet Winston's pessimism, or realism, prevails.

The central theme of *Nineteen Eighty-Four* is the fragility of memory. The Party constantly rewrites the past so that no points of comparison betray whether life had ever been better or worse. Winston does not quite grasp this: 'What most afflicted him with the sense of nightmare was that he had never clearly understood *why* the huge imposture was undertaken. The immediate advantages of falsifying the past were obvious, but the ultimate motive was mysterious.' Within twenty years, we learn, all alternate variations of memory will be eliminated. 'The past is a curious thing,' George Bowling had reflected in *Coming Up for Air*, 'It's with you all the time.' Winston Smith was devoted to ensuring this did not happen in Oceania.[108] His job enables him to *know* that constant alterations are made in the written record. He does not fall prey to the implication that proving the necessary infallibility of Big Brother and the Party is for the good of all. Yet he comes to question his own ability to recall different moments in the past which contradict the current line.

So, constantly, we are told that his sense of an 'objective' truth lying 'out there' or 'back then' can be erased by the Party. Orwell's own greatest concern was that this 'truth' might actually be mutable if enough effort was devoted to the task. His single most powerful plea is thus for the balanced writing of history. This concept of objective truth is contrasted to his torturer O'Brien's insistence that 2 + 2 = 5 if the Party says so.[109] And Winston is obliged to give much more than mere lip service to this untruth. He must really believe it. Under prolonged torture he finally does. (It seems . . .) Out goes the humdrum empiricism of everyday history. In comes Total Propaganda, the view that only what people perceive to be true is actually true. Postmodernists feel quite at home.

Once broken, Winston symbolizes 'the last man' in Europe (the original title of the book), 'outside history', 'non-existent', the fossil, or, literally, skeletal exhibit of a now-extinct world-view. Under torture, he ventures, rather hesitantly, that 'the spirit of man' will defeat the Party. But we see he is clutching at straws. Indeed, this

---

[106] Orwell, *Nineteen Eighty-Four: The Facsimile*, p. 116. And later, when both go to visit O'Brien, Julia repeats, in another deleted passage: 'It's *your* conspiracy so far as I'm concerned, dear, not O'Brien's or Goldstein's' (p. 132).

[107] Shelden sees her as modelled in part on Orwell's second wife, Sonia Brownell, whom he greatly admired (*Orwell*, p. 448).

[108] Orwell, *Complete Novels*, p. 445.

[109] As we saw in Part II, 2 + 2 of course made 5—the Five-Year Plan completed in four years, because the Party said so. He had asserted that it was 'quite possible that we are descending into an age in which two and two will make five when the Leader says so' in 1939 (Orwell, XI, p. 311). The assertion was repeated in 1942 (Orwell, XIII, p. 504). But the '5' was cut from early editions, leaving '2+2 ='. Peter Davison notes: 'The English hard-back editions lost the 5 from 1951 onwards and the Penguin paperback editions followed suit. Even the special reprintings for Nineteen Eighty-Four—by Secker's *and* Penguin—lack the 5' (*George Orwell and Nineteen Eighty-Four* (Library of Congress, 1985), p. 12). It is in, e.g., Crick's *Nineteen Eighty-Four* edition and the 1987 edition.

is the 'last man in Europe's' last straw. The 'guardian of the human spirit,' Winston dies, spiritually. By contrast, the Party, O'Brien assures him, 'is immortal'.[110] But O'Brien—to some a popish, perhaps a Satanic figure, though he also 'saves' Winston—is mad.[111] Intoxicated with power, he too cannot see clearly, or at least clearly beyond power—and for a few moments—we grasp his own inner weakness. Winston's body is destroyed by torture, and reduced to a pathetic caricature of humanity. He too eventually is seemingly driven mad, saying that if the Party says the 'law of gravity was nonsense', and that nothing happens outside the mind, it must be true.[112] But we are not meant to believe this. It is not clear he does either.

Worse, perhaps, Winston is defeated morally from the moment he abandons the high ground of his private humanity by agreeing (to O'Brien, who entraps him by initially pretending to oppose the Party) 'to lie, to steal, to forge, to murder, to encourage drug-taking and prostitution, to disseminate venereal diseases, to throw vitriol in a child's face' if the oppositional Brotherhood calls for it, all of which he recalls under torture. Here, we see, he accepts that any means can be justified if the end is sacred enough. He is compromised and ambiguous thereafter. But this makes the book more interesting. He is so weak, in the face of so much strength, that we feel he must fail, has failed from the outset. And we feel, too, that we would all fail and fall with him, would undergo the 'cure' and welcome the bullet as he does, almost demanding it, and receiving O'Brien's mocking reply, 'don't give up hope. Everyone is cured sooner or later. In the end we shall shoot you.'[113]

Orwell has chosen this sad little character carefully: black versus white, a bland fetishized hope and Hollywood superheroism pitted against monstrous villainy would not have worked nearly as well. Yet after he seems utterly broken, Winston realizes in his cell, momentarily fantasizing about Julia, that 'he still hated the Party'.[114] His reward is the still worse torture of Room 101, where a cage filled with rats—Winston's and Orwell's own most loathed creature—is placed upon his face.[115] The intensity of this moment is the book's crescendo. We can scarcely believe what we read. (Yet everything in the description of Winston's torture and multiple confessions is true, in the sense of having exact parallels Orwell possibly knew of— even the rats.) Winston buckles. 'Do it to Julia', he screams, in the final act of betrayal, in the ultimate renunciation of own life. Is he beaten now? He has collapsed in the face of pain. But has his hatred of the Party been eradicated? In the final few pages Winston sits in the Chestnut Tree café. His mind meanders, flitting between true and false memories. We see that they have got inside him. So does he. We feel that he has lost his soul, the last shred of his moral fibre. So does he. So we are not too surprised with the last line, amidst the telescreen's announcement of a great military

---

[110] Orwell, *Nineteen Eighty-Four*, p. 216.

[111] E.g., Christopher Small, *The Road to Miniluv: George Orwell, the State, and God* (Victor Gollancz, 1975), p. 161. In the draft MS his real name is Watson (Orwell, *Nineteen Eighty-Four: The Facsimile*, p. 240).

[112] Orwell, *Nineteen Eighty-Four*, p. 223.   [113] Ibid., p. 220.   [114] Ibid., p. 225.

[115] A similar torture is described in a book Orwell would have known, George Kitchin's *Prisoner of the OGPU* (Longmans, Green & Co., 1935), p. 126.

victory, and his own fantasy of finally being shot. His struggle has ended. Ingsoc has finally mastered him (or: *Winston bellyfeel Ingsoc*). 'He loved Big Brother.'[116]

* * * *

The book thus falls neatly into three segments: the introduction, which positions Winston Smith and commences his rebellion; the unfolding of this revolt through his affair with Julia; and their capture, interrogation, confession, and conversion.

The narrative is broken by a middle section, the book within the book, 'The Theory and Practice of Oligarchical Collectivism'. Many readers initially find this perplexing if not irritating.[117] As in many utopias, however, it fulfils the vital function of offering a much more complex explanation of the regime's principles than the plot itself could ever convey. The power of the novel is not, however, diminished by this potentially awkward interpolation of a lengthy explanation as to how the world has degenerated so far. This tract supposedly emanates from the leader of the 'Brotherhood' or resistance movement, Emmanuel Goldstein, modelled on Trotsky.[118] The political theory it describes is remarkably sophisticated. But it transpires that the book was dreamt up by a group which includes O'Brien: this job can't be trusted to a machine. But then neither can the book be trusted. Or at least, we sense, what it says is only partly what Orwell believes. (It is mostly a parody of Burnham, with whom he had various disagreements.)

Goldstein explains the planet's division into three great totalitarian states, Oceania, Eurasia, and Eastasia.[119] They are notionally at war with one another, but only in order to maintain the 'social atmosphere' of a 'besieged city . . . the mentality appropriate to a state of war'.[120] Concentrated feelings of hatred and sacrifice assist the destruction, through war, of the produce of machines which would otherwise lead to a higher standard of living, increasing intelligence and the eventual realization that these systems were essentially fraudulent. Opulence would induce resistance because it generates equality and gives greater scope and time for independent thought. So living on the margins—'austerity' (sound familiar?)—keeps the proles' focus on daily life constant.

Oceania's ideology rests on three great mottoes:

WAR IS PEACE
FREEDOM IS SLAVERY
IGNORANCE IS STRENGTH.

---

[116] In the first film version Winston shouts 'Down with Big Brother' at the end, thus entirely defeating the point of the novel. On the film versions of *Animal Farm* and *Nineteen Eighty-Four*, see Erika Gottlieb, 'Orwell's Satirical Version on the Screen: The Film Versions of *Animal Farm* and *Nineteen Eighty-Four*', in Cushman and Rodden, eds., *George Orwell: Into the Twenty-First Century*, pp. 252–63.

[117] Kubal describes it as a 'serious structural defect': David L. Kubal, *Outside the Whale: George Orwell's Art and Politics* (University of Notre Dame Press, 1972), p. 130.

[118] Steinhoff, *The Road to 1984*, p. 34. Orwell, however, felt that the USSR 'would not have been substantially different if Lenin or Trotsky had remained in control' (XVII, p. 343), and that 'Well before 1923 the seeds of a totalitarian society were quite plainly there' (XVIII, p. 274).

[119] 'What it is really meant to do is to discuss the implications of dividing the world up into "Zones of influence"', Orwell reflected in late 1948, noting the origins of this concept in the 1944 Teheran conference (Orwell, XIX, p. 487).

[120] Orwell, *Nineteen Eighty-Four*, p. 155.

They mean, via doublethink: the pretence of constant war ensures domestic peace insofar as the Party's rule is not threatened; that the 'free' epoch prior to Party rule had been one of working-class enslavement by capitalists; and that as knowledge of the truth (of the past in particular) would weaken the regime (recall Ford's 'bunk'), so ignorance of it props it up.

Internally, Oceania is composed of three groups. At the top is the Inner Party, modelled on the British intelligentsia.[121] Its functionaries, less than 2 per cent of the population, have servants and luxury goods.[122] The more numerous Outer Party members, about 15 per cent, like Winston Smith, endure dull work, privation, and an endlessly dreary, listless, and exhausting life, as well as the constant threat of being eliminated for even dreaming of rebellion. Victory Gin, freely available, dulls their senses. Then there are the proles.

The point of the system, we are told, is to preserve the Party's power. Its ideology, Ingsoc, grew out of earlier forms of British socialism, to which some lip service is still paid. But the old ideals of liberty and equality have been superseded. In a classic passage O'Brien tells Winston *why* the system works this way, and what motivates its rulers:

> The Party seeks power entirely for its own sake. We are not interested in the good of others; we are interested solely in power. Not wealth or luxury or long life or happiness: only power, pure power . . . We are different from all the oligarchies of the past, in that we know what we are doing. All the others, even those who resembled ourselves, were cowards and hypocrites. The German Nazis and the Russian Communists came very close to us in their methods, but they never had the courage to recognize their own motives. They pretended, perhaps they even believed, that they had seized power unwillingly and for a limited time, and that just round the corner there lay a paradise where human beings would be free and equal. We are not like that. We know that no one ever seizes power with the intention of relinquishing it. Power is not a means, it is an end. One does not establish a dictatorship in order to safeguard a revolution; one makes the revolution in order to establish the dictatorship. The object of persecution is persecution. The object of torture is torture. The object of power is power.[123]

And so O'Brien describes the 'religion of power . . . the last religion, which destroys all others'.[124] Its aim, ultimately, is to make hatred all-pervasive, and to destroy all 'emotions except fear, rage, triumph, and self-abasement'. Everything else, he

---

[121] A deleted passage terms it 'virtually a priesthood': Orwell, *Nineteen Eighty-Four: The Facsimile*, p. 210.

[122] He wrote in 1941 that 'The thing that always strikes one about the British intelligentsia is its extraordinarily negative outlook, its lack of any firm beliefs or positive aims, and its power of harbouring illusions that would not be possible to people in less sheltered places' (XIII, p. 71). Accused of 'intellectual-hunting' by Alex Comfort in 1942, his response was 'It is just because I do take the function of the intelligentsia seriously that I don't like the sneers, libels, parrot phrases and financially profitable back-scratching which flourish in our English literary world' (XIII, p. 399). This description also echoed anarchist descriptions of Bolshevik power as 'a despotism of the intelligentsia' (Igal Halfin, *From Darkness to Light: Class, Consciousness and Salvation in Revolutionary Russia* (University of Pittsburgh Press, 2000), p. 368).

[123] Orwell, *Complete Novels*, p. 895.

[124] Deleted passage: Orwell, *Nineteen Eighty-Four: The Facsimile*, p. 316.

boasts, would be destroyed, including 'the links between child and parent, and between man and man, and between man and woman'. Already no 'one dares trust a wife or a child or a friend any longer'. But in the future

> there will be no wives and no friends. Children will be taken from their mothers at birth, as one takes eggs from a hen. The sex instinct will be eradicated. Procreation will be an annual formality like the renewal of a ration card. We shall abolish the orgasm. Our neurologists are at work upon it now. There will be no loyalty, except loyalty towards the Party. There will be no love, except the love of Big Brother. There will be no laughter, except the laugh of triumph over a defeated enemy . . . But always . . . there will be the intoxication of power, constantly increasing and constantly growing subtler. Always, at every moment, there will be the thrill of victory, the sensation of trampling on an enemy who is helpless. If you want a picture of the future, imagine a boot stamping on a human face—for ever.[125]

For his part, Winston agrees, after torture, that 'God is Power'. But this parroting of Burnham, whose view Orwell summarized as 'Politics is, can be, nothing except a struggle for power', does not, as Zwerdling indicates, by any means necessarily represent Orwell's own position. Indeed, it is the very argument he seeks to refute.[126] Nor, Crick contends, does this passage adequately characterize Hitler's or Stalin's personalities: both were much more complex and ideologically driven. So here Orwell is probably satirizing Burnham rather than admitting that power worship alone could be a supreme motive sustaining long-term regimes.[127] And there are clearly echoes here of the anarchist critique of Marxism, as similar themes had been mooted by Bakunin in the late nineteenth century.[128]

The third and largest part of Oceania's population is the 'proles', whose portrayal is pivotal to the entire narrative. Orwell's description of them is perhaps the most contentious aspect of the book. We learn at the outset that they are not completely docile. A woman complains out loud in the cinema about the sadism displayed in a newsreel. An old man laments in an air raid shelter that 'We didn't ought to 'ave trusted them . . . We didn't ought to have trusted the buggers' (but *which* buggers, Winston never learns).[129] Most of the time they have to endure widespread criminality and a constant struggle for existence: half are barefoot, and they suffer many food shortages. Occasionally they are roused to brief frenzies of patriotism.[130]

---

[125] Orwell, *Complete Novels*, p. 898. The 'boot' image draws on Orwell's description of the goose step as 'the vision of a boot crashing down on a face', 'simply an affirmation of naked power' (*The Lion and the Unicorn*, p. 43).

[126] Orwell, XVI, p. 73; Zwerdling, *Orwell and the Left*, p. 104. Drucker, too, asserted that '"Power is its own justification" is regarded as self-evident' (*The End of Economic Man: A Study of the New Totalitarianism* (Harper & Row, 1969), p. 14).

[127] Orwell, *Nineteen Eighty-Four*, pp. 65, 86–91. Burnham seems to have conceded this point by 1947.

[128] Mikhail Bakunin wrote that 'no dictatorship can have any other aim except to perpetuate itself' (*Selected Writings*, ed. Arthur Lehning (Grove Press, 1974), p. 270).

[129] Orwell, *Complete Novels*, p. 762.

[130] A deleted passage adds: 'frenzies in which they lynched Negroes and looted Jewish shops': Orwell, *Nineteen Eighty-Four: The Facsimile*, p. 209. Anthony Burgess unaccountably describes the proles as 'untroubled by crime and violence' (*1985* (Arrow Books, 1980), p. 47).

Most of the time they are left alone. They cannot join the Outer Party; the clever ones are killed off.[131] 'Proles and animals are free' because their 'freedom' means nothing in any earlier sense. Most have no telescreens: they are not needed.[132] The Party regards them contemptuously: one of Winston's workplace comrades, Syme, even blurts out, 'the proles are not human beings'.[133]

To keep the proles content, the Party tolerates or provides gambling, pornography, films, football, beer, and the occasional bottle of Victory Gin, to aid their forgetfulness. But their lives are, by the standards of London in 1948, passably normal. Prole women use scent and makeup—Outer Party women cannot. Proles use pens and ink—this is how Winston gets his. Even in prison they are irreverent and not cowed by their guards or the system, unlike party members. They have friendships, affection, a measure of individuality. They preserve personal bonds, as in the society of two generations ago, when (in a passage struck out) 'private life came first. What mattered was not any public achievement, but loyalty to individuals.'[134] They 'were not loyal to a party or a country or an idea, they were loyal to each other . . . The proles had stayed human. They had not become hardened inside.'[135]

Once Winston recognizes this, he cease to see them as 'simply an inert force which would one day become conscious [penultimate draft: spring to life] and regenerate the world'.[136] And yet there are clues as to their own slide towards inhumanity. In a passage struck out from the final MS, Orwell wrote of Winston's response to complaint by the woman in the cinema: 'Typical prole reaction—not to care about the thing itself, only about its being shown in front of the children.' And he added another anecdote to the same effect.[137] So the proles are hardly cast in the heroic mould. Over the long term they too are vulnerable. Yet, fundamentally, they are decent: personal loyalty, not loyalty to an ideal or a class, defines their lives.

So, to Winston, Syme was completely wrong. The proles are the *only* humans left. The rest of the society are gramophone machines. So while Winston and Julia might talk 'endlessly of engaging in active, violent rebellion against the party', only the proles might really overthrow it.[138] In one of the most famous, if puzzling, passages of *Nineteen Eighty-Four*, Winston reflects that

> If there was hope, it *must* lie in the proles, because only there, in those swarming disregarded masses, 85 per cent of the population of Oceania, could the force to destroy the Party ever be generated. The Party could not be overthrown from within. Its enemies, if it had any enemies, had no way of coming together or even of identifying

---

[131] Thus it is not the case that 'the proles can speak freely' (Lynette Hunter, *George Orwell: The Search for a Voice* (Open University Press, 1984), p. 200).

[132] Orwell, *Nineteen Eighty-Four*, pp. 11, 122, 135.

[133] Orwell, *Complete Novels*, p. 774. The MS note on this theme reads: 'Inaccessibility of the proles' (Orwell, *Nineteen Eighty-Four*, p. 142.) In a deleted passage Orwell has O'Brien saying: 'They are animals: we keep them animals. Humanity is the Party. The others are outside—irrelevant': Orwell, *Nineteen Eighty-Four: The Facsimile*, p. 332.

[134] Orwell, *Nineteen Eighty-Four: The Facsimile*, pp. 22, 130.

[135] Orwell, *Nineteen Eighty-Four*, p. 135.

[136] Orwell, *Nineteen Eighty-Four: The Facsimile*, p. 130.   [137] Ibid., p. 28.

[138] Ibid., p. 94. This passage was struck out.

one another. Even if the legendary Brotherhood existed, as just possibly it might, it was inconceivable that its members could ever assemble in larger numbers than twos and threes. Rebellion meant a look in the eyes, an inflexion of the voice; at the most, an occasional whispered word. But the proles, if only they could somehow become conscious of their own strength, would have no need to conspire. They needed only to rise up and shake themselves like a horse shaking off flies. If they chose they could blow the Party to pieces tomorrow morning. Surely sooner or later it must occur to them to do it? And yet—![139]

Much turns on this 'yet'. Winston concludes that 'Until they become conscious they will never rebel, and until after they have rebelled they cannot become conscious.' And yet... One prole woman whom Winston routinely observes from his hideout with Julia has a 'solid, contourless body, like a block of granite'. She embodies a future which 'belonged to the proles', who would eventually awaken 'though it might be a thousand years' hence, who stayed alive 'against all the odds... passing on from body to body the vitality which the Party did not share and could not kill'. So there is a hint here that 'hope' lies not in the proles' capacity for rebellion as such, but in their impenetrability, which might put history on their side. Yet... Winston is prone to confusion and self-delusion, cannot distinguish between lost and phantom memories, and barely knows his present from his past. The hints laid down in 'the Book' as to a possible prole rebellion are negated by the fact that O'Brien & Co. are its authors. To drive the point home, while torturing him, O'Brien assures Winston that 'The proletarians will never revolt, not in a thousand years or a million. They cannot... The rule of the Party is for ever.'[140] And O'Brien, Winston knows, is a great deal cleverer than he is. But he is mad too.

Winston himself is proven to be so deluded so often that we can reasonably be chary of his judgement. Crucially he wrongly assumes, with Julia, that even under torture 'they can't get inside you'. They do, easily. They not only *can* get inside you. They *become* you, and you them.[141] That's the whole point: the group swallows the individual. This is one of the system's great achievements. They mark its improvements on even the considerable efforts of twentieth-century totalitarian regimes. Individual identity is tentative, fragile, and contingent on memory. This is why the

---

[139] Orwell, *Nineteen Eighty-Four*, p. 59. The extant early draft does not cover this section of the book. The whole issue clearly vexed him greatly: notes for the book include the comments: 'If there is hope', and 'why shd. they revolt? Perfectly satisfied' (p. 143).

[140] Orwell, *Nineteen Eighty-Four*, pp. 175, 210. In a deleted passage O'Brien suggests to Winston that the 'theoretical possibility that the animals might one day revolt against mankind and conquer the earth', as an equally unlikely prospect: Orwell, *Nineteen Eighty-Four: The Facsimile*, p. 308.

[141] 'We shall squeeze you empty, and then we shall fill you with ourselves', says O'Brien (Orwell, *Nineteen Eighty-Four*, p. 380). Actually Orwell had already answered this in 1944, writing that it was a 'fallacy... to believe that under a dictatorial government you can be free *inside*... Why is this idea false? I pass over the fact that modern dictatorships don't, in fact, leave the loopholes that the old-fashioned despotisms did; and also the probable weakening of the *desire* for intellectual liberty owing to totalitarian methods of education. The greatest mistake is to imagine that the human being is an autonomous individual. The secret freedom which you can supposedly enjoy under a despotic Government is nonsense, because your thoughts are never entirely your own' (XVI, p. 172.) The MS note for this section reads: 'They can't get inside you—but they can' (Orwell, *Nineteen Eighty-Four*, p. 141).

Party expends so much effort reinventing it. The Party has learned from past regimes. Even the Russian purges, we learn, left 'rebellion locked up' in the victim's skull as he walked down the passage waiting for the bullet. The Thought Police go further. Now 'Everyone is washed clean.' Complete, sincere inner penitence is required. Torture can elicit it. And so Winston, in Max Cosman's phrase, is 'turned into a robot'.[142]

Orwell has been accused of exaggerating the pursuit of power beyond 'hardheaded reason', inducing 'incredulity'. Thus, 'no historical experience would bear Orwell out' respecting the predominance of cruelty and sadism described in *Nineteen Eighty-Four*.[143] 'Abandoning rationalism', the 'masochistic-sadistic' Orwell views 'reality through the dark glasses of a quasi-mystical pessimism.'[144] Really? Readers of Part II will query whether this is at all preposterous. Victims now 'begged to be shot quickly, so that they could die while their minds were still clean'. O'Brien tells Winston that:

> We do not destroy the heretic because he resists us: so long as he resists us we never destroy him. We convert him, we capture his inner mind, we reshape him. We burn all evil and all illusion out of him; we bring him over to our side, not in appearance, but genuinely, heart and soul. We make him one of ourselves before we kill him. It is intolerable to us that an erroneous thought should exist anywhere in the world, however secret and powerless it may be.[145]

This 'penitence' requires an overwhelming sense of guilt, whence deliverance is achieved through confession. Parallels with Catholicism—which Orwell despised—are evident throughout.[146] When Winston meets O'Brien, for instance, there is a ceremony involving wine and a wafer at his apartment. Then Winston comes to love O'Brien himself, and thence Big Brother, partly in a parody of the uselessness of loving God while forgetting humanity, and partly to exhibit the masochism which was, for Orwell, the flip side of the sadism which epitomized the system. All of this is entirely commensurate with Stalinist experience.

Winston finally loses himself in what might appear to be the masochistic embrace of the extreme group symbol, swallowed up by O'Brien's greater intellect.[147] The final portrayal of O'Brien reveals the intoxicating, self-deluding

---

[142] Max Cosman, 'George Orwell and the Autonomous Individual', *Pacific Spectator*, 9 (1955), 83.

[143] Kateb, 'The Road to 1984', 565–6.

[144] Isaac Deutscher, *Heretics and Renegades* (Hamish Hamilton, 1955), pp. 46, 40.

[145] Orwell, *Nineteen Eighty-Four*, pp. 204–5. A passage struck out is: 'It is the minds of our enemies that we seek to conquer, not their bodies': Orwell, *Nineteen Eighty-Four: The Facsimile*, p. 286.

[146] He regarded Graham Greene's 'cult of the sanctified sinner' as frivolous (Orwell, XIX, p. 405). He was always disdainful of anything 'popish', thinking Catholicism childish. But he also warned that 'if it is allowed to survive as a powerful organization, it will make the establishment of true socialism impossible, because its influence is and always must be against freedom of thought, against human equality' (p. 166).

[147] In a moment of torture Winston reflects: 'He had never loved him so deeply as at this moment, and not merely because he had stopped the pain. The old feeling, that at bottom it did not matter whether O'Brien was a friend or an enemy, had come back... In some sense that went deeper than friendship, they were intimates' (Orwell, *Nineteen Eighty-Four*, p. 376). Compare Bukharin's letter to Stalin while in prison in 1937, addressing him as 'Koba', saying 'now I feel you so close to me' (Igal

madness which absolute power induces. Yet O'Brien does not *believe* 2 + 2 = 5: the Party's power requires knowing that it is 4.[148] Let us leave aside Orwell's boarding-school and Eton experiences, and the moral erosion which infects the British rulers of Burma. The relentless desire to extract voluntary confessions from all heretics is, if anything, the legacy of the Inquisition. O'Brien is the modern Grand Inquisitor.

'I DO NOT UNDERSTAND WHY': INTERPRETING *NINETEEN EIGHTY-FOUR*

By no means as straightforward as it appears, this narrative leaves us with various problems. All appear magnified by its reception history. *Nineteen Eighty-Four* erupted—no other term captures the effect of its publication—just as the Cold War began. Interpretations of the book have consequently always been highly politicized. Resentful of its Cold War hijacking by American conservatives, the Marxisant 'left'—mostly, for Orwell, 'right' in the wrong sense—were and remain shrill in their hostility to it. Some of them, moreover, actually appear glad that the right *did* take Orwell up. It proves their suspicions about his heresies, thus reinforcing their own orthodoxies. In the nearly seventy years since 1949 some (few) have conceded that recognizing the calamity of left-wing totalitarianism does not make one 'reactionary', 'conservative', 'counter-revolutionary', or 'anti-utopian'.[149] For others, still, as in the 1930s, it is 'our cause or nothing', 'our utopia but no-one else's'. It would be helpful if we could finally move beyond this perspective. But we have not yet done so.

Thus, even before Isaac Deutscher's well-known essay, 'The Mysticism of Cruelty' (1954),[150] considerable invective was heaped on Orwell for supposedly abandoning his left-wing origins for 'a disillusionment not only with Stalinism but with every form and shade of socialism' by creating a 'giant Bogy-cum-Scapegoat'.[151] Even his publisher, Fredric Warburg, called the book a 'deliberate and sadistic attack on socialism and socialist parties generally'. (Later he withdrew the

Halfin, *Stalinist Confessions: Messianism and Terror at the Leningrad Communist University* (University of Pittsburgh Press, 2009), p. 147).

[148] In 1942 he wrote that: 'Against that shifting phantasmagoric world in which black may be white tomorrow and yesterday's weather can be changed by decree, there are in reality only two safeguards. One is that however much you deny the truth, the truth goes on existing, as it were, behind your back, and you consequently can't violate it in ways that impair military efficiency. The other is that so long as some parts of the earth remain unconquered, the liberal tradition can be kept alive' (Orwell, XIII, p. 505).

[149] See the enmity heaped on Orwell in Christopher Norris, ed., *Inside the Myth: Orwell: Views from the Left* (Lawrence & Wishart, 1984).

[150] In Deutscher, *Heretics and Renegades*, pp. 35–50.

[151] Ibid., pp. 49–50. This is addressed in Bounds, *Orwell and Marxism*, esp. pp. 139–41, 174. The thrust of Deutscher's criticism was that Orwell portrayed the party as 'a phantom-like emanation of all that is foul in human nature. It is the metaphysical, made and triumphant, Ghost of Evil.' It does not help that Deutscher asserted that a 'book like *1984* may be used without much regard for the author's intention' (p. 35).

judgement.)[152] The ex-Stalinist Raymond Williams (whose dislike of Orwell was pronounced) asserted that 'in his last fiction he discarded the apparently positive element of the illusion—the belief in the imminence of social democracy—and was left with only its negative effects. He could see only authoritarian communism, in the future, with no alternative or countervailing social forces.'[153] The communist historian A. L. Morton thought *Nineteen Eighty-Four* aimed to prove that 'any attempt to realize socialism must lead to a world of corruption, torture and insecurity'.[154] To E. P. Thompson, the 'denial of hope had the force of an irrational taboo' which 'contaminated all confidence in social man and imprisoned Orwell in the negations of *1984*'.[155]

Even more extreme is the judgement of the pro-Stalinist journalist Alaric Jacob, who called the novel 'one of the most disgusting books ever written—a book smelling of fear, hatred, lies and self-disgust by comparison with which the works of the Marquis de Sade are no more than the bad dreams of a sick mind'. Similarly, the communist journalist Samuel Sillen thought Orwell's 'sickness' had produced a 'diatribe against the human race'. In a wondrous contortion, the Soviet newspaper *Pravda* in 1950 said that Orwell 'imputes every evil to the people'.[156] In another recent un- or anti-contextual reading, again without appraising his other writings, Fredric Jameson says of Orwell's 'anti-utopian' work that 'the force of the text . . . springs from a conviction about human nature itself, whose corruption and lust for power are inevitable, and not to be remedied by new social measures or programs, nor by heightened consciousness of the impending dangers'. Orwell, he continues, has projected out of the history of Stalinism 'a baleful vision of human nature as an insatiable and lucid hunger for power'.[157]

The earlier amongst these judgements seem pardonable, or at least explicable, in a Cold War environment. The later defy comprehension. For there is no evidence for these conclusions. They reek of sour grapes: who would rather not shoot the messenger than confront the message? We sense, too, a visceral reaction here. Orwell is a heretic, an enemy. He has defiled the temple, broken from the group's magic circle. He thinks he is telling the truth: in fact the myth or fetish of

---

[152] Warburg, *All Authors are Equal*, pp. 104–6.

[153] Williams, *Orwell*, p. 96. On his hardening view, see Rodden, *The Politics of Literary Reputation*, pp. 188–200. Williams in 1979 also declared Orwell to have been an 'ex-Socialist' in 1949 (John Newsinger, *Orwell's Politics* (Macmillan, 1999), p. 124) whilst expressing his own solidarity with both the Chinese Cultural Revolution and the Khmer Rouge. An interesting account of just how Orwellian the former was is offered in F. Quei Quo, 'Orwell's *Nineteen Eighty-Four* and Mao's Cultural Revolution', in Peter Buitenhuis and Ira B. Nadel, eds., *George Orwell: A Reassessment* (Macmillan, 1988), pp. 126–38.

[154] Miriam Gross, ed., *The World of George Orwell* (Weidenfeld & Nicolson, 1971), p. 274.

[155] E. P. Thompson, 'Inside *Which* Whale?', in Raymond Williams, ed., *George Orwell: A Collection of Critical Essays* (Prentice Hall, 1974), p. 83.

[156] Norris, *Inside the Myth*, p. 81; Meyers, *Orwell: The Critical Heritage*, pp. 274, 282.

[157] Fredric Jameson, *Archaeologies of the Future: The Desire for Utopia and Other Science Fictions* (Verso, 2005), pp. 198–200. This positions Orwell much closer to his favourite author, Swift, than the evidence indicates—Orwell thought he had been 'too hard on humanity' (XIV, p. 157). Jameson also asserts that Orwell is 'anti-Utopian, given the way in which they are informed by a central passion to denounce and to warn against Utopian programs in the political realm' (*Archaeologies*, pp. 198–9).

'hope'—rather ironically championed by supposed materialists (though it was a mainstay of official propaganda in the period)[158]—was necessary for 'progress'. So such critics deny any need to study Orwell in detail. They 'know' him because he is a class enemy. To read him carefully would be contemptible, perhaps dangerous: his sentiments might be contagious. In the debate over who 'owns' Orwell those who wish to defend the USSR (notwithstanding Stalinism) tried, in particular as the actual date of 1984 was reached, to monopolize the concept of the 'left' entirely, as they had done in the 1930s and 1940s.[159] Orwell himself always resisted these attempts to capture the trademark brand of the 'left'. He viewed Stalinists as reactionaries bent on destroying every real revolutionary sentiment, using 'hope' for the future to justify anything now. 'The grotesque feature', he wrote of the Spanish conflict, 'which very few people outside Spain have yet grasped, is that the Communists stood furthest of all to the Right, and were more anxious even than the liberals to hunt down the revolutionaries and stamp out all revolutionary ideas.' He told Victor Gollancz that he was 'not criticizing the Soviet regime from the Right', adding quite correctly that 'in my experience the other kind of criticism gets one into even worse trouble'.[160]

So, curiously, both right-wing conservatives and Stalinists agree here that Orwell was no socialist. He understood this coalescence: both were conservative. But, shortly before he died, Orwell distanced himself completely from such interpretations. To clarify his intentions he stated that:

> It has been suggested by some of the reviewers of NINETEEN EIGHTY-FOUR that it is the author's view that this, or something like this, is what will happen inside the next forty years in the Western world. This is not correct. I think that, allowing for the book being after all a parody, something like NINETEEN EIGHTY-FOUR *could* happen. This is the direction in which the world is going at the present time, and the trend lies deep in the political, social and economic foundations of the contemporary world situation.
>
> Specifically the danger lies in the structure imposed on Socialist and on Liberal capitalist communities by the necessity to prepare for total war with the U.S.S.R. and the new weapons, of which of course the atomic bomb is the most powerful and the most publicized. But danger lies also in the acceptance of a totalitarian outlook by intellectuals of all colours.
>
> The moral to be drawn from this dangerous nightmare situation is a simple one: *Don't let it happen. It depends on you.*[161]

He added shortly after:

> My novel *Nineteen Eighty-four* is *not* intended as an attack on socialism, or on the British Labor party, but as a show-up of the perversions to which a centralized

---

[158] So argues Anne Applebaum, *Iron Curtain: The Crushing of Eastern Europe* (Penguin Books, 2012), p. 426.

[159] Hence the title, *Inside the Myth: Orwell: Views from the Left*, ed. Christopher Norris. Andrew Milner reaches substantially similar conclusions about this perspective: *Locating Science Fiction* (Liverpool University Press, 2012), pp. 120–3.

[160] Quoted in Crick, *Orwell*, pp. 350, 453.   [161] Orwell, XX, p. 134.

economy is liable, and which have already been partly realized in Communism and fascism. I do not believe that the kind of society I describe necessarily *will* arrive, but I believe (allowing of course for the fact that the book is a satire) that something resembling it *could* arrive. I believe also that totalitarian ideas have taken root in the minds of intellectuals everywhere, and I have tried to draw these ideas out to their logical consequences.[162]

* * * *

Sorting out the interpretations of *Nineteen Eighty-Four* requires that we pose two questions: what are we asking about the book, and what types of evidence will we consider to answer this query? Two main ways of approaching the text are the internal and the external. We may privilege the book *qua* book by asking what it delivers and implies, and how it impresses us, as if it were a picture hanging in a gallery. Here we take the book's first and last pages as logical/semantic/historical/ hermeneutic/narrative boundaries. Or we may decipher it contextually on the basis of what we know of Orwell's life and times, sources and influences, as well as the meanings lent to the book by generations of readers. The former approach relies on an analytical, textual exposition of key themes, and asks a series of questions about coherence and consistency, mood and tone. The latter strategy, requiring *in addition* as much detail for interpreting meaning as can be provided, is adopted here. Much commentary on *Nineteen Eighty-Four* either remains internalist, mostly assessing the novel itself, or considers a very narrow range of Orwell's works and biography and a few other key literary sources. An unhistorical and uncontextual reading of *Nineteen Eighty-Four*—often shared with Orwell's critics on both right and left—usually produces quite pessimistic conclusions respecting Orwell's intentions and the aims of the text. By contrast, contextual or externalist readings, taking in as much additional information as space and time permit, result in a quite different account. In order to weigh both approaches we need first to provide some background detail respecting Orwell's development in the 1940s.

Orwell's Politics 1942–9

Orwell's enthusiasm about the possibility of revolution in Britain had retreated by 1942. With the USSR now Britain's ally, pro-Soviet propaganda reached its peak. (In 1942 even Americans were being denounced to the FBI for making anti-Russian comments.)[163] Orwell was alarmed that other nations might drift into the Soviet camp. But in this period he also recrafted his own socialist ideals into an anti-communist social democratic ideal. Then, during the immediate post-war years, he hoped that Europe could become a middle ground between American capitalism and Soviet communism.

---

[162] Ibid., p. 135. He added that: 'The name suggested in NINETEEN EIGHTY-FOUR is of course Ingsoc, but in practice a wide range of choices is open. In the U.S.A. the phrase "Americanism" or "hundred per cent Americanism" is suitable and the qualifying adjective is as totalitarian as anyone could wish.'

[163] Robert A. Vogeler, *I Was Stalin's Prisoner* (W. H. Allen, 1952), p. 22.

Such a position was neither pessimistic nor conservative as such. In fact, Orwell positioned himself quite clearly against both outlooks. This did not make him 'hopeful'; though sometimes he was. In 1942 he wrote that: 'The struggle of the working class is like the growth of a plant. The plant is blind and stupid, but it knows enough to keep pushing upwards towards the light, and it will do this in the face of endless discouragements.' Sometimes he was not. 'The danger of ignoring the neo-pessimists', he argued in 1943, 'lies in the fact that up to a point they are right. So long as one thinks in short periods it is wise not to be hopeful about the future.' And there are bleak moments too—after all, it was by no means clear that Hitler would be defeated. Orwell conceded (in 1944) that:

> Since about 1930 the world has given no reason for optimism whatever. Nothing is in sight except a welter of lies, hatred, cruelty and ignorance, and beyond our present troubles loom vaster ones which are only now entering into European consciousness. It is quite possible that man's major problems will *never* be solved. But it is also unthinkable![164]

But Orwell did not shift ideologically rightwards. In 1944 he wrote: 'I believe very deeply . . . in the English people and in their capacity to centralise their economy without destroying freedom in doing so.' So he described Arthur Koestler's position as 'not far removed from pessimistic Conservatism', meaning that he came 'near to claiming that revolutions are of their nature bad . . . all efforts to regenerate society by violent means lead to the Ogpu'. This—again the allegation of Marxists against *Nineteen Eighty-Four*—was a position from which he specifically distanced himself. Orwell never adopted Koestler's outlook or concluded that all revolutions must fail. There was always the possibility of altering course—the issue was the odds that this would happen. In 1944 he wrote, with his novel underway, that

> if the sort of world that I am afraid of arrives, a world of two or three great superstates which are unable to conquer one another, two and two could become five if the fuhrer wished it. That, so far as I can see, is the direction in which we are actually moving, though, of course, the process is reversible.[165]

In 1946, revisiting the theme, Orwell listed a number of main groupings in contemporary thought: pessimists (including Peter Drucker, Friedrich von Hayek, and James Burnham); democratic socialists (Arthur Koestler, Franz Borkenau, and Orwell himself) whose goal was 'a planned society which is also democratic'; Christian reformers; and Pacifists (Huxley was here).[166] He restated these categories, now describing them as:

1. The Pessimists.—Those who deny that a planned society can lead either to happiness or to true progress.

---

[164] Orwell, XIII, p. 506; Orwell, XVI, pp. 35, 393, 397.   [165] Ibid., pp. 190–1.
[166] Orwell, XVIII, p. 41. Reviewing Hayek in 1945, Orwell stated that: 'By bringing the whole of life under the control of the State, Socialism necessarily gives power to an inner ring of bureaucrats, who in almost every case will be men who want power for its own sake and will stick at nothing in order to retain it' (XVI, p. 149).

2. The Left-wing Socialists.—Those who accept the principle of planning, but are chiefly concerned to combine it with individual liberty.

3. The Christian Reformers.—Those who wish to combine revolutionary social change with adherence to Christian doctrine.

4. The Pacifists.—Those who wish to get away from the centralised State and from the whole principle of government by coercion.[167]

The 'best expression of the pessimistic viewpoint' was a work by F. A. Voigt, *Unto Caesar* (1938), 'written round the thesis that societies which set out to establish the "earthly paradise" always end in tyranny'. This was again what Marxists would usually allege against *Nineteen Eighty-Four*'s perspective. But, thought Orwell, Voigt's description of Nazism and Stalinism as 'for practical purposes the same thing' was 'certainly an over-simplification'. Others who had adopted the 'whole problem of Utopian aims, and their tendency to end in tyranny', like Bertrand Russell, Drucker, and Burnham, were also included under the 'pessimistic' rubric, and described as mostly 'romantic Conservatives'. Orwell, then, did not become (what he called Drucker in 1946) one of the 'pessimistic conservative school of sociologists' who 'disbelieves in all Utopias, and maintains that only a "mixed society" can be the guardian of our liberties'. Instead he clearly implied that he saw himself amongst the 'Left-wing Socialists'.[168]

But did Orwell become more pessimistic in his last few years? At the war's end the Labour Party swept to power in the 1945 election. Orwell's views at the time were, in Crick's words, 'Tribune socialism': 'egalitarian, libertarian, suspicious of the Government and the party, non-theoretical, an odd historical amalgam of the intellectual and the populist'.[169] Fenner Brockway, recalling a lengthy conversation with Orwell about whether a collectivist society and liberty could be reconciled, termed him a 'libertarian socialist' who wanted 'industrial democracy, local democracy' rather than merely a state-centralized bureaucratic system.[170] He supported, albeit critically, the Labour government. He hoped it would abolish the House of Lords, public schools, and titles first. (It did not.) He wanted top incomes not to exceed the bottom by more than ten times. There is no evidence that he regarded it as embodying a 'creeping totalitarianism'.[171] In 1945 Orwell drafted a two-page manifesto for a 'League for the Dignity and Rights of Man', which also indicates his politics in this period. Here he described the state's functions as being:

(1) To guarantee the newborn citizen his equality of chance.

(2) To protect him against economic exploitation by individuals or groups.

---

[167] Orwell, XVIII, p. 57.

[168] Ibid., p. 9. 'If people think I am defending the status quo', he wrote, 'that is, I think, because they have grown pessimistic and assume that there is no alternative except dictatorship or laissez-faire capitalism' (XVIII, p. 507).

[169] Orwell, *Nineteen Eighty-Four*, p. 114.   [170] Wadhams, *Remembering Orwell*, p. 150.

[171] As Jameson, *Archaeologies*, p. 198, suggests.

(3) To protect him against the fettering or misappropriation of his creative faculties and achievements.

(4) To fulfil these tasks with maximum efficiency and a minimum of interference.[172]

Many statements from this period indicate a cautious optimism after the Nazis' defeat. In 1946, Orwell reflected that, for 'some years past, orthodoxy . . . has consisted in not criticising Stalin, and the resulting corruption has been such that the bulk of the English intelligentsia has looked on torture, massacre and aggression without expressing disapproval, and perhaps in the long run without feeling it'. But he added: 'This may change, and in my opinion probably will change.'[173] As late as 1948 he wrote that

> The most encouraging thing about revolutionary activity is that, although it always fails, it always continues. The vision of a world of free and equal human beings, living together in a state of brotherhood—in one age it is called the Kingdom of Heaven, in another the classless society—never materialises, but the belief in it never seems to die out.[174]

We recall here Orwell's assertion that while 'all revolutions are failures'—because they never achieve perfection—they were 'not the same failure'. This is not 'conservatism': it is acknowledging that failing in a just cause is noble.[175]

But constant struggle was required to avoid contamination by totalitarian ideals. And the masses often failed to see this. Writing in 1944, Orwell said that: 'One can't be sure . . . that the common people won't think ten years hence as the intellectuals do now. I *hope* they won't, I even trust they won't, but if so it will be at the cost of a struggle.'[176] A year later he added, to the same effect, that 'Tolerance and decency are deeply rooted in England, but they are not indestructible, and they have to be kept alive partly by conscious effort.'[177]

But he remained nagged by doubts. In 1946 he wrote that

> Today the whole world is moving towards a tightly planned society in which personal liberty is being abolished and social equality unrealised. This is what the masses want, for to them security is more important than anything else . . . Those intellectuals who today are rebels do not suffer economic hardship because almost every intellectual is better off than before. As soon as his most urgent needs are met he discovers that it is not so much money and status he lacks as liberty and a world not wrecked and made soulless by the machine: those are the things that really matter. In seeking such things, he is of course swimming against the tide. The question is, will the masses ever rebel in this way? Will the man in the street ever feel that freedom of the mind is as important and as much in need of being defended as his daily bread?[178]

---

[172] Quoted in Crick, *Orwell*, pp. 497–8.   [173] Orwell, XVIII, p. 443.

[174] Introduction to George Orwell and Reginald Reynolds, eds., *British Pamphleteers* (Alan Wingate, 1948), vol. 1, p. 10.

[175] Orwell, XVI, p. 400.   [176] Ibid., p. 191.

[177] Orwell, XVII, p. 258 (1945, in the original preface to *Animal Farm* entitled 'The Freedom of the Press').

[178] Orwell, XVIII, p. 71.

In the post-war period Orwell also hoped that, on the Continent, a social democratic bloc might be created with sufficient weight to balance its antagonists. In mid-1947 he proposed, in 'Toward European Unity', that throughout Europe there were still 'large numbers of people to whom the word "Socialism" has some appeal and for whom it is bound up with liberty, equality, and internationalism'. 'Social Democracy', he thought, 'unlike capitalism, offers an alternative to Communism, and if somewhere or other it can be made to work on a big scale . . . then the excuse for dictatorship vanishes.'[179]

Respecting the USSR, however, Orwell struck a more pessimistic note. Three years after the end of the war, the former ally was rapidly becoming an enemy. (Churchill's 'Iron Curtain' speech was given in March 1946.) Czechoslovakia and Hungary succumbed to coups in 1948, and Hungary's western border was mined. As the Cold War commenced, many feared imminent nuclear conflict. Orwell's growing paranoia was not unreasonable and was widely shared.

A key question throughout this period was how long Orwell thought Stalin's regime might last. Basily's *Russia under Soviet Rule*, which Orwell reviewed in 1939, did not anticipate an early demise. Basily thought the 'spirit of freedom' was

> bound to revive sooner or later. He even believes that this is happening already: "The thirst for liberty, the notion of self-respect . . . all these features and characteristics of the old Russian elite are beginning to be appropriated by the intellectuals of to-day . . . The moment the Soviet elite opens its fight for emancipation of the human individual, the vast popular masses will be at its side."

But, asked a rightly sceptical Orwell:

> [W]ill they? The terrifying thing about the modern dictatorships is that they are something entirely unprecedented. Their end cannot be foreseen. In the past every tyranny was sooner or later overthrown, or at least resisted, because of 'human nature', which as a matter of course desired liberty. But we cannot be at all certain that 'human nature' is constant. It may be just as possible to produce a breed of men who do not wish for liberty as to produce a breed of hornless cows. The Inquisition failed, but then the Inquisition had not the resources of the modern state. The radio, press-censorship, standardised education and the secret police have altered everything. Mass-suggestion is a science of the last twenty years, and we do not yet know how successful it will be.[180]

In 1948 Orwell acknowledged that the Russian Revolution had not realized Marx's predicted course of democratic government by the proletariat. Instead, what resulted was 'the seizure of power by a small body of classless professional revolutionaries, who claimed to represent the common people but were not chosen by them or genuinely answerable to them'. 'Placed as they were, the Russian Communists necessarily developed into a permanent ruling caste . . . the dictatorship of a handful of intellectuals, ruling through terrorism.' Again we are in Oceania. Could the USSR reform itself? Orwell did not know. Asking in February 1948 'whether

---

[179] Orwell, XIX, pp. 464, 181.   [180] Orwell, XI, pp. 315–17.

Russian regime will grow more liberal', his response was, 'for lack of precedents one can only guess at the answer'. (He did not live to see revolts in Poland, Hungary, the German Democratic Republic (GDR), Czechoslovakia, and elsewhere.) Yet even under Stalin, he thought, it was possible, if one generation rejected 'the ideas of the last . . . which even the NKVD will be unable to eradicate', that by 1960 millions of Russians might be 'bored by dictatorship and loyalty parades, eager for more freedom, and friendly in their attitude toward the West'. But he was guessing. In his literary notebook of this period, he wrote: 'Is there any mechanism by which the Russian regime can become more liberal?'[181] The question remained unanswered.

So did Orwell become more pessimistic in his last years? The answer is clearly yes. His bleakest remark, perhaps, came in 1947, when he commented that:

> A socialist today is in the position of treating an all but hopeless case. As a doctor, it is his duty to keep the patient alive, and therefore to assume that the patient has at least a chance of recovery. As a scientist, it is his duty to face the facts, and therefore to admit that the patient will probably die. Our activities as socialists only have meaning if we assume that socialism *can* be established, but if we stop to consider what probably *will* happen, then we must admit, I think, that the chances are against us.

He added 'I would give odds against the survival of civilization within the next few hundred years.' He also considered whether the fear of using atomic weapons would be so great that no one would use them, Orwell comments:

> This seems to me to be the worst possibility of all. It would mean the division of the world among two or three vast superstates, unable to conquer one another and unable to be overthrown by any internal rebellion. In all probability their structure would be hierarchic, with a semidivine caste at the top and outright slavery at the bottom, and the crushing out of liberty would exceed anything the world has yet seen. Within each state the necessary psychological atmosphere would be kept up by a continuous phony war against rival states. Civilizations of this type might remain static for thousands of years.

This 'worst possibility'—not, we note, the only one—is *Nineteen Eighty-Four*. Yet Orwell continued that 'the only way of avoiding' this was 'to present somehow or other, on a large scale, the spectacle of a community where people are relatively free and happy and where the main motive in life is not the pursuit of money or power. In other words, democratic socialism must be made to work throughout some large area.'[182] This, he thought, could only occur in Western Europe, in the form of a 'socialist United States of Europe', the prospects for which, however, he admitted 'seems to me a very unlikely event'.[183]

Orwell and Utopia

We have already seen that a second aspect of the allegation that Orwell was 'pessimistic' or 'conservative' in 1949 respects his supposedly 'anti-utopian' stance. (Some Marxists, curiously, style attacks on the Soviet system 'anti-utopian'.)

---

[181] Orwell, XIX, pp. 269, 167, 270.   [182] Ibid., pp. 163–4.   [183] Ibid., p. 166.

There are two ways of approaching this question. The first is to acknowledge that Orwell clearly targeted Wells' vision as *the* modern utopian ideal, the 'perfect', machine-made society. Much of this he found reprehensible. In *The Road to Wigan Pier*, Orwell wrote of Wells that 'The thought he dare not face... is that the machine itself may be the enemy.'[184] Wells, machinery, and irritation were fused in Orwell's mind. In 1940, Orwell wrote that 'The whole concept of progress (meaning aeroplanes and steel-and-concrete buildings), the vision of a Utopia in which machines do the work for you, which is definitely a part of the modern mind, owes an immense amount to him.' But the trouble was 'his confusion of mechanical progress with justice, liberty and common decency. The kind of mind that accepts the machine and despises the past is supposed to be, automatically, the kind of mind that longs for a world of free and equal human beings.' This was not the case. Yet Orwell also averred in 1941 that Wells was 'probably right that a "reasonable", planned form of society with scientists rather than witch-doctors in control will prevail sooner or later'. But he continued to reject the idea that 'progress is inevitable', writing in 1945 that it was 'logical to condone tyranny and massacre if one assumes that progress is inevitable', since Stalin or Henry VIII, or any other dictator could be excused this way.[185]

Another aspect of utopianism Orwell rejected was its supposed quest for perfection. Reviewing Herbert Samuel's *An Unknown Land* in 1942, he saw it as failing 'at just the same point as all other books of this type—that is, in being unable to describe a society which is anywhere near perfection and which any normal human being would want to live in'. He added that 'One is driven to conclude that fully human life is not thinkable without a considerable intermixture of evil. It is obvious, to take only one instance, that humour and the sense of fun, ultimately dependent on the existence of evil, have no place in any Utopia.' This is close to Huxley's position in *Brave New World*. If 'utopia' meant the 'perfect society', Orwell wanted nothing to do with it. Thus in 1943 he reiterated that the

real answer is to dissociate Socialism from Utopianism. Nearly all neo-pessimistic apologetics consists in putting up a man of straw and knocking him down again. The man of straw is called Human Perfectibility [but] Socialists don't claim to be able to make the world perfect: they claim to be able to make it better.[186]

'Perhaps', he reflected, 'some degree of suffering is ineradicable from human life, perhaps the choice before Man is always a choice of evils, perhaps even the aim of Socialism is not to make the world perfect but to make it better.' He continued:

I suggest that the real objective of Socialism is not happiness. Happiness hitherto has been a by-product, and for all we know may always remain so. The real objective of Socialism is human brotherhood.... Men use up their lives in heart-breaking political struggles... not in order to establish some central-heated, air-conditioned,

184 Orwell, *The Road to Wigan Pier*, pp. 201–2.
185 Orwell, XII, p. 191; Orwell, XII, p. 539; Orwell, XVII, p. 343.
186 Orwell, XIV, p. 254; Orwell, XVI, p. 35.

strip-lighted Paradise, but because they want a world in which human beings love one another instead of swindling and murdering one another.[187]

So the utopia of enhanced sociability, as we have termed it here, and which he had glimpsed in Barcelona, Orwell still found appealing. Here he again hoped that 'the need for planned societies and . . . a high level of industrial development' might be combined with liberty, equality, and greater brotherhood. Generally, he thought, a 'threecornered struggle is always going on between Machiavellianism, bureaucracy, and Utopianism'. 'At this moment', however, it was 'difficult for Utopianism to take shape in a definite political movement. The masses everywhere want security much more than they want equality, and do not generally realise that freedom of speech and of the Press are of urgent importance to themselves.' Here, crucially, we thus see Orwell aligning 'Utopianism' with the struggle for freedom of speech and the press, which were the great themes of both *Animal Farm* and *Nineteen Eighty-Four*. The 'Utopians', he insisted, were indeed, if 'at present a scattered minority', 'the true upholders of Socialist tradition'. So here, as Crick puts it, Orwell clearly came 'down on the side of the Utopians' in seeing that 'Utopianism, if not immediately realistic, yet must be preserved as an ideal.'[188]

The Proles and the Problem of 'Hope'

Much of Orwell's success lay precisely in the fact that he did not fall prey to a happy ending syndrome, and whisk away by wishful thinking what he thought history would not deliver. Philip Rahv rightly observed that if *Nineteen Eighty-Four* 'inspired dread above all, that is precisely because its materials are taken from the real world'.[189] Realism was one of Orwell's strong points. Pessimism might result. This might prove depressing. So what? If you want hope, go to church or Hollywood, Orwell would probably have said. The writer's function is to tell the truth, not to sell dreams. And even if we assign utopia the latter task, dystopia's is surely the former.

Nonetheless, readers continue to ransack the text for optimistic clues dropped like breadcrumbs in the forest. Returning to *Nineteen Eighty-Four*, we can see that resolving how pessimistic or 'hopeful' both author and book are requires both internal and external forms of evidence. Some have found scarcely a glimmer of hope. His publisher Fredric Warburg wrote that Orwell's MS was 'amongst the most terrifying books I have ever read', adding that 'Orwell has no hope, or at least he allows his reader no hope, no tiny flickering candlelight of hope.'[190] Robert Lee describes it as 'an unbearably gloomy work . . . unequalled in modern literature'.[191] Stephen Spender attacked Orwell because '*1984* offers so little hope for the

[187] Ibid., pp. 400, 42–3.
[188] Orwell, XVIII, pp. 60–2; Crick, *Orwell*, p. 507; Orwell, *Nineteen Eighty-Four*, p. 445.
[189] Meyers, *George Orwell: The Critical Heritage*, p. 268.
[190] Warburg, *All Authors are Equal*, p. 103; Orwell, XIX, p. 479.
[191] Robert A. Lee, *Orwell's Fiction* (University of Notre Dame Press, 1969), p. 128.

future'.[192] To Hammond, it is 'sombre, despairing, almost unrelievedly pessimistic. It is the work of a man who has lost hope, not merely in politicians and causes but in mankind itself.'[193] Even sympathizers thought it extended 'no comfort of any kind'.[194] More controversially, writing in 1954, John Atkins said bluntly of the conviction that the English people could resist totalitarian principles, 'In *1984* it is clear that he had given up this hope', adding that 'In his earlier work we can find hints in abundance of the malevolent superstate that might be building, but not until the end do we have the conviction that the worst must triumph.'[195] Anthony Burgess adds that he had 'dropped all pretence of believing in the working class'.[196] Patronizing Orwell as a 'simple-minded anarchist' who found 'dialectical-materialist philosophy . . . too abstract', Isaac Deutscher not only accused him of lifting much of his book from *We*, but thought 'the warning defeats itself because of its underlying boundless despair'. This, he imagined, resulted from Orwell's 'convulsive reaction to his defeated rationalism'.[197]

Yet others fundamentally reject these interpretations. Crick terms the book 'a warning, not a prophecy, a cry of "danger" not "despair"'.[198] Thus it portrays what *might* happen, not what *will* happen, which accords better with Orwell's own explanations. To John Wain, who knew Orwell, the latter's spirits actually rose after Hitler's defeat through the courage of 'common humanity'. *Nineteen Eighty-Four* was pessimistic, but it was 'constructive', and Orwell 'never sank under his load of despair'.[199] To David Kubal, the book is not 'a satire on socialism, but . . . a picture of what will occur if Orwell's concept of socialism is not adopted'.[200] To Erich Fromm, Orwell was 'not a prophet of disaster. He wants to warn and to awaken us. He still hopes—but in contrast to the writers of utopias in the earlier phases of Western society, his hope is a desperate one.'[201] And to George Woodcock, a close friend, the book 'poses a final question which is almost an assertion on the self-destructive nature of caste systems'.[202] This is a much more positive gloss.

[192] Stephen Spender, 'Introduction to *1984*', in Hynes, ed., *Twentieth Century Interpretations of 1984*, p. 65.

[193] Hammond, *A George Orwell Companion*, p. 177.

[194] Peter Lewis, *George Orwell: The Road to 1984* (Heinemann Quixote Press, 1981), p. 112.

[195] John Atkins, *George Orwell. A Literary Study* (Calder & Boyars, 1954), pp. 28, 237.

[196] Burgess, *1985*, p. 102.

[197] Deutscher, *Heretics and Renegades*, pp. 45, 49. The case against overemphasizing Zamyatin's influence is presented in James Connors, 'Zamyatin's *We* and the Genesis of *1984*', *Modern Fiction Studies*, 21 (1975), 107–24. See also Gorman Beauchamp, 'Of Man's Last Disobedience: Zamiatin's *We* and Orwell's *1984*', *Comparative Literature Studies*, 10 (1973), 285–301.

[198] Orwell, *Nineteen Eighty-Four*, p. 112. This remains the best brief introduction to the book. See generally Steinhoff, *Orwell*, pp. 193–204, which summarizes views on both side of this argument.

[199] Gross, *The World of George Orwell*, pp. 89–90.

[200] David L. Kubal, *Outside the Whale: Orwell's Art and Politics* (University of Notre Dame Press, 1972), p. 46.

[201] Erich Fromm, 'Afterward on *1984*', in Irving Howe, ed., *Orwell's Nineteen Eighty-Four: Text, Sources, Criticism* (Harcourt, Brace & World, 1963), pp. 209–10.

[202] George Woodcock, *The Crystal Spirit. A Study of George Orwell* (Jonathan Cape, 1967), p. 176. He does not, as Zwerdling suggests, describe it as a 'statement of faith in humanity', which refers to the essay 'Looking Back on the Spanish Civil War' (Zwerdling, *Orwell*, p. 105). On the theme of despair here, see Erika Gottlieb, *The Orwell Conundrum: A Cry of Despair or Faith in the Spirit of Man?* (Carleton University Press, 1992).

Returning to the textual evidence, we see that, internally, clues of various kinds as to the possible instability of the system are indeed scattered throughout the book. Some of these we have touched on already. Another worth noting is the intriguing fact that in the Appendix on 'Newspeak', Orwell shifts tenses into the past and the perfect continuous conditional. He writes, 'When Oldspeak had been once and for all superseded, the last link with the past would have been superseded', an event previously described as likely to occur around 2050, or some sixty-six years later than the narrative.[203] This is puzzling. For it might imply, looking from a more distant future, that this never happened, making Orwell a 'secret optimist'.[204] Indeed, for Margaret Atwood, we are thus assured that 'the world of *1984* is over'.[205]

Yet for most readers the characterization of the 'proles' is the key question. And most view Winston's wistful optimism on this point as essentially illusory. To Patrick Reilly,

> the text makes it plain that the proles are hopeless—that is the inescapable internal conclusion . . . The *action* of *Nineteen Eighty-Four* does nothing to confirm this faith in democratic invincibility; we can dream of a prole victory if we wish, but there is nothing in the text to justify, and much to discredit, it.[206]

To Daphne Patai, 'Orwell cannot imagine any possibility for social progress because he views the "other" as lacking in consciousness and hence incapable of action.'[207] Tom Moylan adds that because 'there is no meaningful possibility of movement or resistance, much less radical change, embedded in any of the iconic elements of the text'.[208]

Many support this view. But the more *faux naïf* uncontextual readings have clear limitations. They are, by definition, ill-supported. They do not approach Orwell's ideas historically or contextually, or examine the more nuanced statements evident in the reviews and letters. They rarely investigate what Orwell knew about totalitarianism, or what he might be reasonably expected to know. They do not acknowledge that at the time it was perfectly plausible to hold, as Nadezhda Mandelstam recalled, 'the belief that the victory was final, and that the victors were here to stay for all eternity'.[209] Burnham, perhaps Koestler, sometimes Zamyatin—or at any rate what Orwell says about them—is about as far as the known world usually goes here. So we cannot really separate fact from fiction or what is contrived and unrealistic, however powerful its effects may be, from what rings true. In one well-known instance, Podhoretz's equally uncontextual case for

[203] Orwell, *Nineteen Eighty-Four*, p. 250.
[204] Frank Winter, 'Was Orwell a Secret Optimist? The Narrative Function of the "Appendix" to Nineteen Eighty-Four', in Benoit J. Suykerburk, ed., *Essays from Oceania and Eurasia: George Orwell and 1984* (Progreff, 1984), pp. 79–89.
[205] Margaret Atwood, *Curious Pursuits: Occasional Writing 1970–2005* (Virago, 2005), p. 337.
[206] Patrick Reilly, *George Orwell: The Age's Adversary* (Macmillan, 1986), p. 295.
[207] Patai, *The Orwell Mystique*, p. 265.
[208] Tom Moylan, *Scraps of the Untainted Sky: Science Fiction, Utopia, Dystopia* (Westview Press, 2000), pp. 161–2.
[209] Nadezhda Mandelstam, *Hope against Hope: A Memoir* (Collins & Harvill, 1971), p. 166.

the conservative Orwell rests on alleging that 'neither in *Animal Farm* nor in *Nineteen Eighty-Four* was there any trace of the idea that a socialist revolution could be accomplished without a betrayal of the ideals of liberty and equality to whose full realization socialism was in theory committed'.[210] But as Crick notes, not 'to be explicitly socialist is not the same as being implicitly anti-socialist'.[211] Indeed, there is no connection between the two positions. Orwell would most likely have said today that the right was right about communism but wrong about capitalism.

It is possible to go round in circles on this issue ad infinitum. And that indeed is what much Orwell scholarship has done, without ever breaking out. If, however, bearing in mind that the text's setting is Britain, we juxtapose its representations of the proles to Soviet reality a somewhat different reading emerges. The portrayal of Party life was indeed realistic; as Czesław Miłosz put it: 'Even those who know Orwell only by hearsay are amazed that a writer who never lived in Russia should have so keen a perception into its life.'[212] That of the proles has no similar correspondence. In *Nineteen Eighty-Four*, the proles are prohibited from entering the Party, and the able amongst them who might pose a challenge are simply eliminated. They are also not generally subject to or victims of the Party's relentless propaganda. Under Stalin, neither of these occurred. After the purges of the old Bolsheviks and the old intelligentsia, workers were recruited by the thousands into high party positions on the sole basis of their class background. Over 61 per cent of party members were from proletarian backgrounds by 1929, versus only 16.9 per cent from the intelligentsia.[213] Soviet ideology permeated both education and work, and a 'proletarian intelligentsia' was created to replace the old educated elite.[214] Much of the brutality of the real system indeed emanated in part from the inadequate education and intense class hostility of this group towards the better educated.

As we have also seen, the working classes were also the victims of terror to a very considerable extent. They were the majority of the Gulag's population. They had witnessed and participated in massive collectivization movements since the early days of the revolution. The standards of behaviour set for the working classes generally, it is true, were not, under Stalin, as rigid or demanding as those imposed on party members. They had more freedom of speech, at least privately, than the intelligentsia. But the effort to break their humanity, to render them subservient even mentally to the system, was much more persistent and widespread than in Orwell's portrayal of life in totalitarian London. In *Nineteen Eighty-Four* there are no *kulaks* in sight, indeed no sign of the peasantry at all; perhaps they had already

---

[210] Norman Podhoretz, 'If Orwell Were Alive Today', *Harper's Magazine* (January 1983), 32.
[211] Orwell, *Nineteen Eighty-Four*, p. 4.
[212] Czesław Miłosz. *The Captive Mind* (Secker & Warburg, 1953), p. 42. For a similar Russian account, see Vladimir Shlapentokh, 'George Orwell: Russia's Tocqueville', pp. 267–85, where one Russian describes Orwell as 'probably the single Western author who understood the nature of the Soviet world' (p. 274).
[213] Neil Wood, *Communism and the British Intellectuals* (Victor Gollancz, 1959), p. 19.
[214] Halfin, *From Darkness to Light*, p. 32.

been vapourized.[215] There are many poor people. But we do not see entire categories of workers being exterminated in principle. Oceania, in fact, is recognisably a satire on totalitarianism in Britain, not in the USSR. And in this sense the reality of Stalinism was much worse than the world of *Nineteen Eighty-Four*. The psychological world of Party members in the book is much the same as that under Stalin in the late 1930s. Here, the parallel is a recognisably exact one. But for the proles it was not: here the parallel ends.

Yet Orwell *knew* that his own scenario differed greatly from that of the USSR. Various sources he had seen—Kravchenko (himself a proletarian), Souvarine, Lyons, Ciliga, Beausobre, and others—furnished abundant evidence as to the reality of *mass* oppression in the USSR.[216] Souvarine had indicated that not only had millions been sent to the camps, but millions more 'in relative liberty' had been interrogated, and that 'la majeure partie de la population citadine' was 'surveillé au travil et au domicile'—which is very different from *Nineteen Eighty-Four*.[217] Orwell knew something of the Gulag system, as Tchernavin's, Utley's, Ciliga's, and other accounts had been available since 1935.[218] Ciliga, amongst others, made it clear that 'all social strata were represented' in Soviet prisons, including 'discontented workmen', soldiers and sailors, and *kulaks*.[219] This was not merely the cleverest being eliminated. It was mass repression, whose victims included many proletarian political activists. And Orwell was well aware that many who made up what Djilas would shortly term the 'new class' of rulers were originally workers.[220]

His own sources, then, show that Orwell's portrayal of the proles in *Nineteen Eighty-Four* was not meant to mirror Soviet reality. Notwithstanding Orwell's defensive claim that the book was set 'in Britain in order to show that the English-speaking races are not innately better than anyone else and that totalitarianism, if not fought against, could triumph anywhere', he was fully aware that the British working classes possessed a potential resilience which was a key source of

---

[215] We do learn that the fields are 'cultivated with horse-ploughs', but not who does the ploughing.

[216] He reviewed Lyons at length and owned works by the first three. They were: de Beausobre, *The Woman Who Could Not Die*, Souvarine's *Cauchemar*, and Victor Kravchenko's *I Chose Freedom: The Personal and Political Life of a Soviet Official* (Robert Hale, 1947). The latter was an extremely influential account which turned many against Stalinism.

[217] Souvarine, *Cauchemar*, p. 37. Souvarine's *Stalin* also spoke of a 'permanent civil war' waged by the GPU on 'the supposedly intractable population who were, in reality, perfectly submissive' (p. 603). Some of these works are discussed in Steinhoff, *The Road to 1984*, pp. 30–41.

[218] Orwell, XIV, p. 234. He had been studying the camps in Morocco in 1940, according to Eileen Shelden (*Orwell*, p. 331). Orwell reported as early as 1942 that well over a million Polish Jews had been killed by the Nazis. On the German camps he knew David Rousset's *A World Apart* (Secker & Warburg, 1951), though he lamented that it fell short of being 'a scholarly work on concentration and forced-labour camps' of the type he wanted: Orwell, XIX, pp. 330–1, 337–8. Rousset's account focuses on Buchenwald. *Krematoria* are mentioned (*A World Apart*, pp. 4, 9), but the emphasis here is on brutality rather than mass murder. However, Birkenau is discussed as a 'city of death' where 'tens of thousands were gassed each day' (pp. 26–7), and the role of the *Sonderkommando* is noted. As far as the Soviet camps were concerned, Orwell's main source was probably Anton Ciliga's *The Russian Enigma* (George Routledge & Sons, 1940), which estimated 5 million prisoners in 1940 (p. 136).

[219] Ciliga, *The Russian Enigma*, pp. 152, 168–9. 234–5, 245.

[220] Milovan Djilas, *The New Class: An Analysis of the Communist System* (Thames & Hudson, 1957), p. 41: 'The social origin of the new class lies in the proletariat'.

their strength.[221] He might well have suspected, too, that this quality had been substantially undermined or even eradicated in the USSR. If so, then, he may have been more pessimistic about the USSR by contrast with the fictional world of *Nineteen Eighty-Four.*

The disjunction between Soviet reality and the literary portrayal of the proles in the book, then, was evidently deliberate. Why? The issue has troubled or irritated some readers. The fact that the regime made 'no attempt to indoctrinate the working class' was an 'omission', Deutscher notes, which 'Orwell would have been the last to ascribe to Stalinism'.[222] To Rahv, describing the proles as left alone 'appears to me to run contrary to the basic tendencies of totalitarianism', which 'necessitates the domination of all citizens, of whatever class'.[223] Kumar queries, too, why Orwell did 'not try to imagine the impact of totalitarian rule on the common people', as London and Zamyatin had done. He concludes thus that 'Crick is probably right in arguing that here—more damagingly perhaps than at any other point in the novel—the satiric purpose overwhelms the imaginative portrayal of a totalitarian world.'[224] Crick notes that 'the sociology of the Proles, considering their importance as the sole vehicle of hope, is sketchy and, as it stands, implausible'. This apparent disjuncture between fiction and reality occurred 'because their main function in the story is to serve as a satire of what the mass media, poor schools, and the selfishness of the intelligentsia were doing to the actual working class of Orwell's time'. This helps account for his description of the book as a 'flawed masterpiece'.[225]

These deductions miss entirely a vital point. Orwell's description allowed him to avoid the much more pessimistic conclusion which a fictional portrayal of the Soviet proletariat would have entailed. This became his chief means of ensuring that a hopeful perspective *was* somehow maintained in the novel. The Soviet proletariat, for aught Orwell knew, may not have been able to survive Stalinism. By contrast, the British proletariat were the gambling, beer-swilling, don't-give-a-damn heirs of Wigan's working classes. If it was Orwell's deliberate strategy to describe the latter in *Nineteen Eighty-Four* in order to leave the scope for working-class impenetrability and thus the hope of the overthrow of the system, the effect is highly ironic. Winston must expire following 'the final consciousness of failure'.[226] But the proles are made to live on organically because to show them as shaped by the system—as they really were in the USSR—would have virtually removed the chance of their revolting against it. Orwell has left a space for hope quite deliberately, where few have found it, by locating the novel in Britain.

---

[221] Orwell, XX, p. 135.   [222] Deutscher, *Heretics and Renegades*, p. 43.

[223] Philip Rahv, 'The Unfuture of Utopia', in Howe, ed., *Orwell's Nineteen Eighty-Four*, p. 315.

[224] Krishan Kumar, *Utopia and Anti-Utopia in Modern Times* (Basil Blackwell, 1987), p. 335.

[225] Crick, *Orwell*, pp. 570–1, 551. Crick thus describes the book's portrayal as the 'exact opposite of what was, in Orwell's view (expressed in essays and book reviews) the very mark of totalitarianism' (Orwell, *Nineteen Eighty-Four*, p. 30). 'We need to know why hope lies in the proles' is one aspect of the book's 'flawed' quality for Crick.

[226] An MS note respecting the plot, from 1943: Orwell, *Nineteen Eighty-Four*, p. 138.

NINETEEN EIGHTY-FOUR AND GROUP IDENTITY

Nineteen Eighty-Four, then, represents neither a hopelessly pessimistic nor an anti-revolutionary, anti-utopian, or 'conservative' perspective. Its chief accomplishment, in light of our discussion in Parts I and II, is to delineate with breathtaking clarity how some kinds of totalitarian group functioned. What made the mentality of the Inner Party possible, Orwell thought, was its denial of a conception of objective truth. 'Truth' meant what was good for 'progress', as defined by the latest party 'line'. The power worship which underpinned this perspective was, in turn, for Orwell, rooted in the decline of religious belief, and in the relativism and histori-cism which resulted from it. It was also linked to his sense of the decline of the 'autonomous individual'. Such ideas permeated the intelligentsia, but not the English working classes nor the proles of *Nineteen Eighty-Four*, who are substan-tially identical. We need here briefly to ascertain how, for Orwell, machine worship had enabled hedonism to fill some of this vacuum, why this was an inadequate world-view, and how it was connected to power worship. We also need to consider why Orwell felt that his own value system, focused on the idea of 'decency', was a viable alternative to both hedonism and power worship, and to see how this was linked to his love of nature. Both, in turn, would underpin his sense of the virtues of individual autonomy. Finally, returning to group psychology, we can conclude by examining how Orwell felt that his personal position as a writer was crucial to the issues explored in the novel.

Hedonism and Republicanism

Orwell felt that power and machine worship were interwoven with a hedonistic world-view which he also rejected. Crude hedonism, he thought, ignored the value of work as a creative activity. In *Wigan Pier* he had asserted that

> a human being is not eating, drinking, sleeping, making love, talking, playing games or merely lounging about—and these things will not fill up a lifetime—he needs work and usually looks for it . . . man is not, as the vulgarer hedonists seem to suppose, a kind of walking stomach; he has also got a hand, an eye and a brain.[227]

Secondly, hedonism undermined both national morale and military capacity. Here we see Orwell adopting a standpoint traditionally associated with a republican tradition of hostility to the corrosive effects of luxury. 'Man needs warmth, society, leisure, comfort and security', Orwell conceded. But he also needed 'solitude, creative work and the sense of wonder'. Recognizing this, 'he could use the products of science and industrialism eclectically, applying always the same test: does this make me more human or less human? He would then learn that the highest happiness does *not* lie in relaxing, resting, playing poker, drinking and making love simultaneously.' Thus,

[227] Orwell, *The Road to Wigan Pier*, p. 196.

the instinctive horror which all sensitive people feel at the progressive mechanisation of life would be seen not to be a mere sentimental archaism, but to be fully justified. For man only stays human by preserving large patches of simplicity in his life, while the tendency of many modern inventions—in particular the film, the radio and the aeroplane—is to weaken his consciousness, dull his curiosity, and, in general, drive him nearer to the animals.[228]

(Or perhaps, rather, the machines?)

But hedonism also had political implications: some politics addressed non-hedonistic needs. Condemning what he termed the 'falsity of the hedonistic attitude to life' in 1940, Orwell wrote that people '*don't* only want comfort, safety, short working hours, hygiene, birth control, and, in general, common sense; they also, at least intermittently, want struggle and self-sacrifice, not to mention drums, flags and loyalty parades'. The pursuit of happiness, paradoxically, did not neces-sarily make people happier. This made fascism 'psychologically far sounder than any hedonistic conception of life'.[229] A year later he reiterated that

> During the past twenty years the negative, fainéant outlook which has been fashionable among English left-wingers, the sniggering of the intellectuals at patriotism and physical courage, the persistent effort to chip away English morale and spread a hedonistic, what-do-I-get-out-of-it attitude to life, has done nothing but harm. It would have been harmful even if we had been living in the squashy League of Nations universe that these people imagined. In an age of fuehrers and bombing planes it was a disaster. However little we may like it, toughness is the price of survival. A nation trained to think hedonistically cannot survive amid peoples who work like slaves and breed like rabbits, and whose chief national industry is war.[230]

Nineteen Eighty-Four was thus, to some degree, a reckoning with Huxley's projec-tion of a hedonistic future. Orwell wrote in 1940 that while

> *Brave New World* was a brilliant caricature of the present (the present of 1930), it probably casts no light on the future. No society of that kind would last more than a couple of generations, because a ruling class which thought principally in terms of a 'good time' would soon lose its vitality. A ruling class has got to have a strict morality, a quasi-religious belief in itself, a *mystique*.[231]

For this reason, he thought Jack London's description in *The Iron Heel* of a 'caste of plutocrats who rule the world for seven centuries as inhuman monsters', who were not 'idlers or sensualists', was 'a truer prophecy of the future than either *Brave New World* or *The Shape of Things to Come*'. It indicated that 'hedonistic societies cannot endure'.[232] In 1943 he also wrote privately to a *Tribune* reader that

---

[228] Orwell, XVIII, p. 32.
[229] Orwell, XII, p. 118. In a brief piece entitled 'Will Freedom Die with Capitalism?' (1941) Orwell insisted that 'there is not much doubt that primitive peoples, untouched by capitalism and industrialism, are happier than civilised men. Almost anyone who has travelled will confirm this. Among primitive peoples, at any rate in warm climates, the faces that you see are predominantly happy; in no great city of the West is this true' (Orwell, XII, p. 460).
[230] Orwell, *The Lion and the Unicorn*, p. 115.   [231] Orwell, XII, p. 211.
[232] Orwell, XV, pp. 4–6.

I think you overestimate the danger of a 'Brave New World'—i.e. a completely materialistic vulgar civilization based on hedonism. I would say that the danger of that kind of thing is past and that we are in danger of quite a different kind of world, the centralized slave state, ruled over by a small clique who are in effect a new ruling class, though they might be adoptive rather than hereditary. Such a state would not be hedonistic, on the contrary its dynamic would come from some kind of rabid nationalism and leader-worship kept going by literally continuous war, and its average standard of living would probably be low . . . I see no safeguard against this except (a) war-weariness and distaste for authoritarianism which may follow the present war, and (b) the survival of democratic values among the intelligentsia.[233]

In a similar vein, Orwell later wrote that here Zamyatin was the realist, 'on the whole more relevant to our own situation', while Huxley was merely misguided. Zamyatin portrayed public executions as human sacrifices, providing, Orwell thought, an 'intuitive grasp of the irrational side of totalitarianism—human sacrifice, cruelty as an end in itself, the worship of a Leader who is credited with divine attributes'. These qualities made 'Zamyatin's book superior to Huxley's'.[234] So the world of *Nineteen Eighty-Four* is 'the exact opposite of the stupid hedonistic Utopias that the old reformers imagined'. But this refers to the leaders. For the proles are indeed still distracted by their simple pleasures, which the Party releases in just the right doses so as to ensure neither deprivation nor saturation. So we are much closer to Wigan than to Huxley. And Julia, too, is, at one level, hedonism incarnate: 'Life as she saw it', Winston learns, 'was quite simple. You wanted a good time; "they", meaning the Party, wanted to stop you having it; you broke the rules as best you could.'[235]

The Religion of Power

The hedonistic world-view thrived, of course, thought Orwell, because of a declining belief in the afterlife. Power worship came from the same source. As early as *Homage to Catalonia*, Orwell had written that: 'The major problem of our time is the decay in the belief in personal immortality, and it cannot be dealt with while the average human being is either drudging like an ox or shivering in fear of the secret police.'[236] 'The real problem', he reiterated in 1944, 'is how to restore the religious attitude while accepting death as final. Men can only be happy when they do not assume that the object of life is happiness.' The same year Orwell stressed that it was necessary to find a 'much-needed alternative' to 'Russian authoritarianism on the one hand and American materialism on the other'. This was only possible, however, if 'a planned economy can be somehow combined with the freedom of the intellect, which can only happen if the concept of right and wrong is restored to politics'.[237] In 1945 he again asserted that

[233] Orwell, XII, pp. 211, 540; quoted in Crick, *Orwell*, p. 468.   [234] Orwell, XVIII, p. 15.
[235] Orwell, *Nineteen Eighty-Four*, pp. 389, 269.
[236] Orwell, *Homage to Catalonia*, p. 245. This is reiterated word for word in 1942: Orwell, XIII, p. 510.
[237] Orwell, XVI, pp. 398, 150.

As long as supernatural beliefs persist, men can be exploited by cunning priests and oligarchs, and the technical progress which is the prerequisite of a just society cannot be achieved. On the other hand, when men stop worshipping God they promptly start worshipping Man, with disastrous results. The humanist has to decide whether what is needed is re-education and a 'change of heart', or whether the indispensable first step is the abolition of poverty.[238]

The 'decay of the belief in absolute good and evil' was thus bound up with both hedonism and power worship. 'There is very little doubt', Orwell wrote in 1944, that 'the modern cult of power-worship is bound up with the modern man's feeling that life here and now is the only life there is.' Thus,

> If death ends everything, it becomes much harder to believe that you can be in the right even if you are defeated. Statesmen, nations, theories, causes are judged almost inevitably by the test of material success. Supposing that one can separate the two phenomena, I would say that the decay of the belief in personal immortality has been as important as the rise of machine civilisation.

But he added: 'I do not want belief in life after death to return, and in any case it is not likely to return. What I do point out is that its disappearance has left a big hole, and that we ought to take notice of that fact.'[239]

This was, for Orwell, largely a problem for the intelligentsia. Thus, in 1943, he noted that 'The English left-wing intelligentsia worship Stalin because they have lost their patriotism and their religious belief without losing the need for a god and a Fatherland.'[240] By contrast, he felt that 'the English common people ... have failed to catch up with power politics, "realism", *sacro egoismo* and the doctrine that the end justifies the means'.[241] In 1944 he added that

> there is one sense in which the English common people have remained more Christian than the upper classes, and probably than any other European nation. This is in their non-acceptance of the modern cult of power-worship ... It is significant that in this country, unlike most others, the Marxist version of Socialism has found its warmest adherents in the middle class. Its methods, if not its theories, obviously conflict with what is called "*bourgeois* morality" (i.e., common decency), and in moral matters it is the proletarians who are "*bourgeois*".[242]

The antidote to godless hedonism was, according to Orwell, a godless 'humanism' based upon two qualities: an ideal of decency and a love of nature.[243] Salvaging civilization, Orwell wrote in 1944, required reinventing 'a system of good and evil which is independent of heaven and hell'.[244] The term 'decency' summed up a core

---

[238] Orwell, XVII, p. 227.   [239] Orwell, XVI, pp. 105–6, 112–13.

[240] Orwell, XV, p. 107. He added: 'I have always held that many of them would transfer their allegiance to Hitler if Germany won.'

[241] Orwell, XVI, p. 206. He also referred to 'realism' as 'the doctrine that might is right' (p. 354).

[242] Orwell, XVI, p. 205.

[243] 'The basis of Socialism is humanism', he wrote in 1946, adding that 'It can co-exist with religious belief, but not with the belief that man is a limited creature who will always misbehave himself if he gets half a chance' (Orwell, XVIII, p. 60).

[244] Orwell, XVIII, p. 113.

of values: common sense, humanity, and respect for others. The virtues he respected were working class, Peter Lewis notes, including 'hard work, fair dealing, thrift, endurance and cheap and common pleasures'.[245] He once wrote that Charlie Chaplin's 'peculiar gift' was 'his power to stand for a sort of concentrated essence of the common man, for the ineradicable belief in decency that exists in the hearts of ordinary people'. He even described 'intellectual decency' as 'responsible for all true progress for centuries past', with its loss implying that the 'very continuance of civilized life is by no means certain'.[246] This Davison terms the substance of his 'religionless Christianity', and Sandison, 'a personal secular and ultimately indefinable moral standard'. It is a transparent concept analogous to Orwell's famous description of good English prose, as akin to a window pane.[247] It is a primitive, intuitive, and emotional expression of sympathy for others who share life's burdens and woes. It may be regarded as a fundamentally optimistic, ontological statement about the human spirit, or a sociologically grounded assessment of a particular strata of society not corroded by external influences, or a nostalgic incantation of a childhood mantra, or some combination of all three. At one extreme, it suggests that all of Orwell's outlook was fundamentally moral rather than political. But it does not follow that he 'was never really a socialist at any time in his life'.[248]

Love of nature was also required to counterbalance machine worship. The relationship between machine civilization and power worship was that machines symbolize, indeed epitomize, power—either of us over nature, or over other people, or over us. The logical chain is: the death of God reveals hedonism to be the sole viable life philosophy; this opens up the way for power and machine worship and the worship of man because they promise us unbounded happiness; totalitarianism exacerbates the worst tendencies which result; we need to reinstate some form of humanism to counter these; but we don't know how.

Orwell detested machine worship, and disliked much of modern urban life which inevitably accompanied it. He feared that the entire drift of life spent in public was towards an undifferentiated pleasure consciousness where constant artificial stimuli bombarded and mesmerized the senses, turning human beings into something resembling fish in an aquarium.[249] He preferred to garden, to

[245] Lewis, *George Orwell*, p. 8. This insightful study is one of the better short introductions to Orwell.

[246] Orwell, XII, p. 315; Orwell, XVIII, p. 268.

[247] Davison, *George Orwell*, p. 65; Sandison, *George Orwell after 1984*, p. 96. See also Stephen Ingle, *George Orwell. A Political Life* (Manchester University Press, 1993), pp. 35–55. On Orwell and religion see Christopher Small, *The Road to Miniluv: George Orwell, the State, and God* (Victor Gollancz, 1975), James Connors, '"Who Dies If England Live?" Christianity and the Moral Vision of George Orwell', in W. W. Wagar, ed., *The Secular Mind* (Holmes & Meier, 1982), pp. 169–96, and Gordon B. Beadle, 'George Orwell and the Death of God', *Colorado Quarterly*, 23 (1974), 51–63. W. H. Auden considered him a 'true Christian' (Ingle, *Orwell*, p. 109).

[248] S. J. Ingle, 'The Politics of George Orwell: A Reappraisal', *Queen's Quarterly*, 80 (1973), 31.

[249] In 1946, Orwell returned to the theme of the dehumanization of leisure in a remarkable essay entitled 'Pleasure Spots'. This described schemes for establishing mass holiday resorts which epitomized almost everything he disliked about modern life. 'Pleasure' would be concentrated in a complex of bars, restaurants, bowling alleys, lagoons, cinemas, and huge car parks. The underlying motif of this 'future paradise', he thought, could be expressed in five principles: '(a) One is never alone.;

'muck about' with his hands, to listen to bird calls, to go fishing. He liked to watch clouds. He did not like crowds. He liked isolation.[250] There was a clear, conscious purpose in this. In a telling passage in his 1946 essay, 'Some Thoughts on the Common Toad', he wrote that

> I think that by retaining one's childhood love of such things as trees, fishes, butterflies and ... toads, one makes a peaceful and decent future a little more probable, and that by preaching the doctrine that nothing is to be admired except steel and concrete, one merely makes it a little surer that human beings will have no outlet for their surplus energy except in hatred and leader-worship.[251]

The retreat, as his life drew to a close, to Jura and a nearly pre-industrial world—'Orwell's Utopia', Warburg called it—thus symbolized this need for an inner respite from modernity.[252] Nature provided a balance, a contrast, a way of showing how tawdry was the sparkling allure of the noisy milk-bar and machine culture generally. (It does not take much imagination to see his eyes rolling at our world.) But this life clearly could only serve as a universal model with great difficulty.

This exposes the great tension at the core of Orwell's personality, and one which was perhaps inevitably unresolved. The freedom of Jura could never be accessible to the majority, who would probably not want it anyway. The blare of music, the flashing lights, the slick chrome countertops of milk bars and glitzy modern public houses was too alluring. (Ditto the tablet, the laptop, the mobile phone.) Orwell was the last man, indeed, not to be swallowed up by the great whale of the modern crowd. Winston Smith is the last humanist, the last adherent to solid moral values emanating from material existence empirically observed, the last to believe in an autonomy which was being everywhere lost.[253] So in *Nineteen Eighty-Four*, 'The Last Man in Europe' presented in this small measure, at least, his own dilemma: to be embraced by the warmth of fraternal brotherhood, as in Barcelona, or to flee the suffocating crowd for a life of inner peace and personal autonomy.

(b) One never does anything for oneself.; (c) One is never within sight of wild vegetation or natural objects of any kind.; (d) Light and temperature are always artificially regulated.; (e) One is never out of the sound of music.' The music was particularly important here; it was, he thought, 'the most important ingredient. Its function is to prevent thought and conversation, and to shut out any natural sound, such as the song of birds or the whistling of the wind, that might otherwise intrude.' Hazarding a (not unreasonable) psychological generalization, he reflected that: 'It is difficult not to feel that the unconscious aim in the most typical modern pleasure resorts is a return to the womb. For there, too, one was never alone, one never saw daylight, the temperature was always regulated, one did not have to worry about work or food, and one's thoughts, if any, were drowned by a continuous rhythmic throbbing' (Orwell, XVIII, p. 31).

[250] He once remarked that if it were not for his son Richard he would like to live in a lighthouse (Shelden, *Orwell*, p. 424).

[251] Orwell, XVIII, p. 240.   [252] Warburg, *All Authors are Equal*, p. 94.

[253] See Ian Watt, 'Winston Smith: The Last Humanist', in Stansky, ed., *On Nineteen Eighty-Four*, pp. 103–13.

Totalitarian Groups and the Humanist Writer

The essence of being human is that one does not seek perfection, that one *is* sometimes willing to commit sins for the sake of loyalty, that one does not push asceticism to the point where it makes friendly intercourse impossible, and that one is prepared in the end to be defeated and broken up by life, which is the inevitable price of fastening one's love upon other human individuals.[254]

How could Orwell project this outlook without himself falling prey to the partisan demands of the struggle for socialism? From 1937 onward, he gradually came to see that the position of the writer in an intensely politicized milieu was an awkward, difficult, and inevitably a partly detached one. The words 'loyalty' and 'groups' pervade his writings in these years as they did the politics of the epoch. It is deeply ironic that, about the time Orwell began to equate brotherhood with socialism, he also came most deeply to appreciate the need for the 'autonomous individual', particularly in the writer's perspective. Resistance to communism in the name of socialism required a delicate balancing act. As a socialist, Orwell remained committed to propaganda. As a writer, he was equally committed to truth-telling and to an idea of objective truth as such, both of which served the end of decency. This entailed keeping a distance from political groups, given their tendency to distort truth.

This issue emerged out of Orwell's ILP–POUM experience in Spain. 'In sentiment I am definitely "left"', he wrote in 1940, adding that, nonetheless, 'What I saw in Spain, and what I have seen since of the inner workings of left-wing political parties, have given me a horror of politics . . . I believe that a writer can only remain honest if he keeps free of party labels.'[255] He understood, then, why some, like Henry Miller, chose to withdraw from politics, and stay 'outside the whale', terming this 'honest', though E. P. Thompson thought it promoted quietism.[256] In an age of dictatorships, isolation was one means of preserving intellectual independence. It was hardly ideal, but it was better than choosing the wrong side.

Such a position indeed came easily to Orwell, for it matched his own personality. Almost permanently an outsider, he was more sensitive to the nuances of group pressure than most. 'I am by nature not gregarious', he wrote in 'Such, Such Were the Joys'.[257] He had felt the pressure to conform often enough to be able to resist it, and this remained crucial to his relentless and distinguishing intellectual honesty. He never left the bourgeoisie, a class in which he had no faith.[258] Yet he was never of it.[259] He chafed at the bit working amidst the 'huge bureaucratic machine' of the

---

[254] Orwell, XX, p. 8.   [255] Orwell, XII, p. 148.
[256] Rodden, *The Politics of Literary Reputation*, p. 192.   [257] Orwell, XIX, p. 370.
[258] He met a working-class communist who cheerfully told him he would shoot him if he had the chance. But he gave as good as he got, telling another who was vilifying the bourgeoisie, 'Look here, I'm a bourgeois and my family are bourgeois. If you talk about them like that I'll punch your head' (Rees, *Orwell*, p. 146).
[259] Crick, *Orwell*, p. 419. On the use of Cockney and its potential oppositional status in Oceania, see Roger Fowler, *The Language of George Orwell* (Macmillan, 1995), esp. pp. 207–11. But did Orwell really think that Cockney was 'the linguistic underdog, a shame even to those who spoke it' (W. F. Bolton, *The Language of 1984* (Basil Blackwell, 1984), p. 93). Orwell was known occasionally to drink tea from the saucer and to affect a working-class accent ('formalized Cockney', according to

BBC during the war.[260] Victor Pritchett said of him that 'He belongs to no group, he joins no side; if he dallies with the idea, he turns out to be a liability to his party. He is entirely on his own.' David Astor called him 'a great individualist'. This brings to the fore the interpretation of Orwell as an 'anarchist' or 'tory anarchist', a view often associated with the Canadian anarchist George Woodcock, his friend and the author of what Crick calls 'perhaps the best account of Orwell's politics yet written'.[261]

As we saw in Part I, the anarchists—notably William Godwin—have often targeted group identity as the root of other forms of collectivist tyranny, and warned of the dangers of group mentalities corroding moral and intellectual judgement. In Spain, Orwell viewed 'their hatred of privilege and injustice' as 'perfectly genuine'.[262] Yet he also realized that his own early belief, based on his Burmese experience, in an 'anarchistic theory that all government is evil, that the punishment always does more harm than the crime and that people can be trusted to behave decently if only you will let them alone', was 'sentimental nonsense'. Instead, it was 'always necessary to protect people from violence'.[263]

For this, a complicated state was necessary, and if 'the trend is towards centralism and planning' then more safeguards than ever were needed to protect against a new class of power-hungry centralizing bureaucrats and planners. But these came from the intelligentsia, who, he worried, were naturally a kind of club anyway, partly dependent on the Establishment, partly wishing to replace it with themselves. As a group they exuded their own orthodoxy and intolerance. Literary cliques worked the same way, and the more political they were, the stronger the tendencies, with the communists the worst of the lot. All, in Zwerdling's words, operated as a 'closed world . . . addicted to coterie loyalty and exclusion', and constantly tempted their members 'to blunt honest criticism in the name of civility'.[264] These groups perverted the possibility of more ethical individual behaviour. Thus, in 1946, again reflecting on Burnham, Orwell toyed with the conclusion at which 'Notes on Nationalism' had hinted, that intellectual honesty and group membership were, as such, virtually incompatible. Man was 'an animal that can act morally when he acts as an individual, but becomes unmoral when he acts collectively'.[265] This

one) in order to taunt middle-class colleagues. He knew that, in Britain, an 'h' *deliberately* dropped in a single word epitomized a world-view and defined a chasm between rulers and ruled. But he never engaged sufficiently in ritualized class humiliation to emerge a convert and mimic on the other side.

[260] Orwell, XIII, p. 426.

[261] Audrey Coppard and Bernard Crick, *Orwell Remembered* (Facts on File Publications, 1984), pp. 165, 191, 199. Rees terms him a 'Bohemian tory anarchist' until about 1939 (*Orwell*, p. 48).

[262] Orwell, *Homage to Catalonia*, p. 61. Curiously enough, George Woodcock, also a biographer of Godwin, never linked the two. He does not tease out the argument of 'Notes on Nationalism' in *The Crystal Spirit*, pp. 202–3.

[263] Orwell, *The Road to Wigan Pier*, p. 148. Others have here identified Orwell with the existentialists, to the degree that the latter share, as Michael Carter puts it, 'a denial of group identity': Carter, *George Orwell and the Problem of Authentic Existence*, p. 29. But Orwell himself found this perspective unimpressive.

[264] Zwerdling, *Orwell and the Left*, p. 41.

[265] Orwell, XVIII, p. 281. But the comment, on Burnham's *The Machiavellians*, also insisted that this referred only to 'the higher groups', and was less applicable to the masses.

implied that the writer had always to be an individual first and foremost. The group had always to remain subservient, secondary, and suspect. We return thus, thematically, to Crusoe and Sartre, for here the dilemmas revealed in Part I are clearly central.

In his last years Orwell approached these themes several times. In 'Why I Write' (1946), he explored the tension between political affiliation and personal independence, stating that

> What I have most wanted to do throughout the past ten years is to make political writing into an art. My starting point is always a feeling of partisanship, a sense of injustice. When I sit down to write a book, I do not say to myself, 'I am going to produce a work of art.' I write it because there is some lie that I want to expose, some fact to which I want to draw attention, and my initial concern is to get a hearing.[266]

But partisanship did not have to be totalitarian. 'It is at the point where literature and politics cross', Orwell now thought, 'that totalitarianism exerts its greatest pressure on the intellectual.' One therefore had to reject the proposition that 'freedom is undesirable and that intellectual honesty is a form of anti-social selfishness'.[267] In 1948, he reiterated that

> acceptance of *any* political discipline seems to be incompatible with literary integrity ... Group loyalties are necessary, and yet they are poisonous to literature, so long as literature is the product of individuals. As long as they are allowed to have any influence, even a negative one, on creative writing, the result is not only falsification, but often the actual drying-up of the creative faculties.

This did not mean avoiding politics. But we should recognize that 'a willingness to *do* certain distasteful but necessary things does not carry with it the obligation to swallow the beliefs that usually go with them'. Relative to a political movement, a writer was 'an individual, an outsider, at the most an unwelcome guerrilla on the flank of a regular army', an awkward position indeed, but not an impossible one.[268] The paradox was that, while only committed, passionate writing was good, this was the moment when truth was most at risk. So perhaps the best position to adopt was standing at the edge of the group, ready to bolt when necessary.

CONCLUSION

> People sacrifice themselves for the sake of fragmentary communities—nation, race, creed, class—and only become aware that they are not individuals in the very moment when they are facing bullets. A very slight increase of consciousness, and their sense of loyalty could be transferred to humanity itself, which is not an abstraction.[269]

---

[266] Orwell, XVIII, pp. 319–20.   [267] Orwell, XVII, pp. 374, 372.
[268] Orwell, XIX, pp. 291–2.   [269] Orwell, XII, p. 126.

Readers of Part II here know that most of what Orwell described in *Nineteen Eighty-Four* not only happened. It did so on a vast scale and at a psychological depth as intense, and hence much more frightening—just *because* it is real,—than in the novel. There was nothing quixotic about Orwell's aim of puncturing the Soviet myth: Saint George was not Don Quixote, even if Stalin was perhaps the dragon.

The book did, in many ways, summarize Orwell's political experiences from 1936 to 1948. From his conversion to socialism in Barcelona onwards he did not abandon the cause. Yet from the beginning he came to see Stalinism as a great danger, not only for other socialists but for civilization more generally. He identified, moreover, some mental traits of socialist intellectuals with a wider infatuation with a Wellsian machine civilization which he had always disliked. The destruction of the Soviet myth became the great object of his later years. But Orwell retained the hope that democracy and socialist collectivism could be combined. He ventured, on occasion, in the last years, that this might be a hope against hope. But even in the depths of his final illness there is no evidence that he abandoned it.

8

The Post-Totalitarian Dystopia, 1950–2015

INTRODUCTION

The reshaping of dystopian writing in the aftermath of World War II was dominated by five themes. Firstly, humanity entered the nuclear age on 16 July 1945. By the mid-1950s we could destroy ourselves completely, and there were good reasons to assume we would. Secondly, the spectre of environmental degeneration, later transmuted into a discourse on climate change, with a potentially catastrophic outcome, emerged in the 1970s. Thirdly, the progress of mechanization threatened ever more subordination of people to machines, and an increasing blurring of human/machine identity. Fourthly, liberal non-totalitarian societies showed serious signs of cultural degeneration into intellectual senility and enslavement to a mindless ethos of hedonistic consumption. Finally, anxiety regarding the 'War on Terror' came to dominate the news.

These currents have been counterbalanced by the continuous promises of improvement which scientific and technological innovation have offered throughout this period. From the 1950s, expansion into space has been accompanied with startling discoveries and innovations in robotics, computing, electronics, medicine, and genetics in particular. Much of what was science fiction to earlier generations is science fact now. These developments have provided a substantial utopian impulse. But this has been increasingly outweighed by the threat of catastrophe. So as we near the present, the mood turns increasingly dystopian, until it appears to define the temper and outlook of the later moderns, as we begin to sense, if still in denial, that the end times may really be nigh.

So many dystopias consequently now appear that analysing or categorizing them is extremely difficult.[1] Insufficient time has passed to produce an agreed canon of key, intellectually superior texts. A survey of this kind can but scratch the surface of the rich melange of themes, ideas, and images this genre presents. Some hundreds of books might have been considered, and many of the texts introduced here could themselves be the subject of chapters or even books.

---

[1] On American texts of this period see Lyman Tower Sargent, 'Eutopias and Dystopias in Science Fiction: 1950–75', in Kenneth Roemer, ed., *America as Utopia* (Burt Franklin & Co., 1981), pp. 347–66. Numerous works discussed in this section have been analysed in articles in *Utopian Studies*, the indispensable journal for this field generally. Reasonable Wikipedia articles also exist for most authors.

In keeping with our concern so far with the more political and anti-utopian literary dystopias, however, we will here focus chiefly on British and American novels with thick social and political content and historical understanding. The plausibility test introduced here in Chapter 5, as defended by Margaret Atwood, prevails again here. Our chief interest is with historical narrative—the sense of the future and the description of actual phenomena—which these works reveal, and how the negative aspects of this are accentuated. Our focus is thus upon content rather than form. How do later modern dystopias come to terms with the crises of later modernity? What projections do they offer, and what solutions, if any? How do they alter the genre we understand as 'dystopia'? What does the literary focus on the individual provide which the historical focus on the collective does not?

Yet if we leave the analysis of the literary character of these works to literary critics, we need, nonetheless, to recall how the dystopian genre is distinguished from other literary forms. If, as Michel Houellebecq has recently asserted, entertainment is the general purpose of the novel, Margaret Atwood nevertheless insists that the specific function of dystopias is to warn us of societies we do not wish to inhabit.[2] Formally, some types of novel may accomplish this better than others— Atwood thinks so at any rate. For lack of space some types of texts are omitted here, including most young adult fiction, the most overtly science fiction-oriented dystopias. (There are hundreds of such works.) The presence of dystopian motifs in computer games, another important development, is similarly ignored. Fictional depictions of the Holocaust and Gulag are also not discussed. We will also have to abandon the more intensively contextual analysis of Chapters 6 and 7 on Huxley and Orwell, opting instead, given the large number of texts under discussion, for a more thematic approach, explored first chronologically and then theoretically, and concentrating on the sixty or so most important dystopian works of the past seventy years. A brief discussion of dystopian films is included at the end. Film adaptations of the novels are marked throughout with an (F).

* * * *

THE LEADING TEXTS

In the Shadow of the Bomb: The 1940s

B. F. Skinner's *Walden Two* (1948) has been described as perhaps 'the most influential American literary utopia' after Bellamy.[3] But some have suggested it is actually a dystopia. Invoking the isolated Walden Pond narrative of the American individualist Henry David Thoreau, Skinner describes a 'utopian community' 'of about a thousand people who are living a Good Life'.[4] The problem here—familiar

---

[2] Both cited in *The Guardian*, 6 September 2015 and 23 September 2015, respectively. Houellebecq's novel under discussion here is *Submission*; Atwood's is *The Heart Goes Last*.

[3] Roemer, *America as Utopia*, p. 18.

[4] B. F. Skinner, 'Utopia as an Experimental Culture', in ibid., p. 28; B. F. Skinner, *Walden Two* (1948; Macmillan, 1962), p. 6.

to us from Huxley—is that the scheme is founded on principles of behavioural psychology which treat human beings essentially as laboratory rats or pigeons whose actions are susceptible to modification by means of 'conditioned reflex' and 'stimulus-response'. The aim is to 'control human behaviour', a phrase rich in ambiguity and more than overtly threatening, forcing us minimally to rethink what we mean by and how and why we value 'freedom'. Clearly we all want food, sex, affection, security, the approval of others, art, and culture. If all these were provided without coercion, and with minimal effort, what objection could there be merely to the fact that they were 'designed', provided consciously rather than chaotically or spontaneously? The analogy with market-based needs satisfaction and systems of rational planning is obvious. Surely a 'scientific' approach trumps one which is merely haphazard, archaic, and invariably biased by religion, ethnicity, and a hundred other prejudices. Skinner acknowledges that 'Design implies control', implying benevolent dictatorship, and that this is the heart of most objections to his scheme. But if we are happy, he responds, and not harmed in any way, the means appear justified. His techniques are manifestly superior to, and are a conscious substitute for, punishing 'bad' behaviour. Chiefly this is because we aim only to use positive reinforcement to improve behaviour.[5] In being educated only to desire what is good for us (as members of a community) and to reject what is bad for us, we achieve the utopian core of every religious and moral system.

Much of this is to be accomplished through mimicry, which is for Skinner at the core of reshaping pigeon behaviour, though we might contend that it is groupism, and not merely the categorization of the group as a 'behaving unit', which needs addressing. We do what the group does through imitation, akin for Skinner to the 'instinct of the herd'. Skinner concedes that the individual may suffer 'temporary disadvantage' due to 'group control', while seeing this as counterbalanced by the advantages of group strength. But just what the individual loses thereby, and what the group does to other groups, and how, for example, it defines its superiority by their inferiority, and how groups and crowds should be differentiated, he does not investi-gate.[6] Yet Skinner manifestly defends humane aims shared by many later modern readers, notably the avoidance of overpopulation, pollution, and the exhaustion of resources. Many might concede that attaining these goals requires ceding a 'thorough-going individualism' in favour of 'a particular kind of social environment'.[7]

So does Skinner's novel represent a dystopia with cult-like qualities? Dystopias, we have conjectured, generally require not only manipulation, but undue coercion. Where, here, is any liberal conception of autonomy? Likening it to an institution whose inmates commit themselves voluntarily, Joseph Wood Krutch called *Walden Two* an 'ignoble utopia', and contends that its conditioning short-circuits the reasoning process which education aims to cultivate. Here goals or outcomes freely

---

[5] B. F. Skinner, *Science and Human Behavior* (Free Press, 1953), pp. 47–8; Skinner, 'Utopia as an Experimental Culture', p. 37.
[6] Skinner, *Science and Human Behavior*, pp. 119–22, 297–329, here 327; B. F. Skinner. *About Behaviourism* (Jonathan Cape, 1974), p. 42.
[7] Skinner, *About Behaviourism*, p. 201.

chosen are superior to those which are merely inculcated. Skinner retorted that the 'scientific conception of man', involving 'effective cultural design' based on behavioural engineering, was merely an improved version of every other effort to solve 'the psychological problems of group living'. Manners, customs, and religion functioned in the same way, only erratically and unscientifically. All culture 'controls the behaviour of the members of the group that practices it'.[8] So free choice is, in any case, an illusion: we are always 'conditioned'. Yet this does not render all forms of 'control' equal.

Walden Two recounts the creation of a thousand-strong rural colony established on behavioural principles. This seems idyllic enough at first sight. We are reminded of the Fourierist and Owenite communities of the nineteenth century. Art flourishes. The people are 'pleasant and well-mannered, yet perfectly candid'. They are 'lively, but not boisterous; affectionate, but not effusive'. The women are beautiful, the dress demure. The children are 'well-behaved'. The community is exceedingly conscious of its size, and of being a group as such. Very significantly, crowds are regarded as 'unpleasant and unhealthful', even dangerous. Here the 'mob rushes in where individuals fear to tread', and *führers* emerge. (Skinner has read his Le Bon, we surmise: 'How does a group behave?', he asks himself in a notebook.) Lectures and large assemblies are avoided, and dining schedules staggered to avoid crowding. Labour-saving devices have reduced drudgery. Inspired by Bellamy, a labour-credit scheme has replaced money, and all work an average of four hours daily, with harder tasks receiving more credit. All must perform some manual labour, even the scientists. Men and women do similar tasks everywhere. Less work as such is necessary because there is no drunkenness, no crime, no leisure class, vastly less unproductive labour, and far fewer possessions per capita than elsewhere. But the organizers do not 'propagandize' to make particular tasks more appealing. There is little personal jealousy because there are many attractive alternatives, in mates as well as jobs. Government is by a Board of six Planners, three men, three women, who may serve only ten years. They are chosen by the dozens of managers of the main community activities, and are not elected by the members, who, we are told, have no wish for such control.[9] (Why not?)

Here we thus encounter the same 'dystopian' objection we saw levelled against Bellamy: that direct democracy has been abolished. What about shirkers, also a problem, we recall, with Bellamy? There seem to be none, though incompetents are replaced, without blame being assigned. (What if they refuse?) What then about the regime of conditioned reflexes? Even musicians lack rivalry and jealousy thanks to 'cultural engineering'. The 'right conditions' prevail again to produce good. Marriages often occur early and may be postponed if the Manager of Marriages advises against them. (More not so subtle coercion.) Men and women are

---

[8] Joseph Krutch, *The Measure of Man* (Alvin Redman, 1956), p. 57; B. F. Skinner, *Cumulative Record* (Appleton-Century-Crofts, 1959), pp. 3–17; Skinner, *About Behaviourism*, p. 203. Harold L. Berger also writes of the 'dystopian virus in *Walden Two*' (*Science Fiction and the New Dark Age* (Bowling Green University Popular Press, 1976), p. 52).

[9] Skinner, *Walden Two*, pp. 23, 28, 35–7, 41–4, 54; B. F. Skinner, *Notebooks* (Prentice Hall, 1981), p. 111.

encouraged to enjoy 'simple friendship', but mere sexual desire, or seeing sex as merely amusing, is regarded as a sign of 'malaise or instability'. (Skinner abandons Fourier and Huxley here—but most less repressive later moderns do not.) Children are raised in a group but embraced by all, and see their parents for a few minutes every day or two. Undue affection for one's own children is frowned on. Young people move to adult buildings at thirteen, and are sometimes parents by sixteen. (But husbands and wives retain separate rooms.) Childbearing by the 'unfit' is discouraged. The possibility of future 'experimental breeding', following the 'weakening of the family structure', is hinted at. Children are taught self-control through deferred gratification. Food is presented to them when they are hungry but they must wait to eat. Thus they are gradually raised to cope with frustrations, annoyances, and discouragements, sometimes, like laboratory pigeons and rats, by music or flashing lights. Just why this makes them more sociable and less aggressive, and what specific techniques are applied, is not clear, however. Nor is there any sense of the failure of positive reinforcement techniques aiming at similar ends in the past (in Christianity, for instance).[10]

Skinner denies that his engineers are 'subtle sadists'. There is no punishment in this experimental system, which, we are told, owes nothing to history, a discipline fit only for entertainment. (We see Ford nodding.) The teaching of all subjects is very relaxed, with a focus only on learning and thinking as such, not a common curriculum. No uniform personality results, and there is a great range of aptitudes and abilities. To the charge that this involves 'tyrannical control', Skinner, through his literary persona, Frazier, 'quite the contrary' of the historian, replies that *Walden Two* does indeed replace the family both as an economic and social and psychological unit, since the group functions far more effectively than any pair of parents. With a goal of 'general tolerance and affection', considerable leisure, and many freedoms, and the desire for fame, fortune, and personal distinction greatly reduced, eutopia seems indeed to have been achieved. There are no 'politics', though a Political Manager studies candidates for elections in the wider society, and indicates how members should vote. There are rules, admittedly, for example against gossip. The teaching of history is rejected as too emotive and susceptible to manipulation, so we are condemned to live in an eternal (ignorant) present. As in More's *Utopia*, the Walden Code as a whole cannot be discussed amongst members, only by Managers and Planners, who alone can change its Constitution. So freedom of speech and thought are limited. But this is portrayed as a small price to pay for what is gained.[11]

Walden Two thus offers one of the most important challenges to the distinction between utopia and dystopia. Overtly positivistic and experimental, it elevates behaviourism to the queen of the human sciences, and demotes the historian to the role of court jester. The 'dystopian' charges against *Walden Two* amount to four: the removal of children from their parents and their subjection to collective education; the system of behavioural stimulus-response with which children are

---

[10] Skinner, *Walden Two*, pp. 55–62, 90, 92, 96, 99, 108–11, 137.
[11] Ibid., pp. 111–15, 119, 124, 127–8, 132, 135, 138, 140, 143, 161, 163–4, 172, 196, 226, 270.

educated; the possibility of considerable loss of individuality resulting, with an attendant mediocrity; and the elite nature of the management system. For Skinner, 'group care is better than parental care'. (Russia is criticized for having abandoned this.) No 'force' as such is employed. But most parents in fact do not wish to surrender their children or to forego the affection and love which the private family permits. Relinquishing such love may also harm individual growth in many circumstances. Restrictions exist here also on freedom of discussion. The structure is overtly if mildly authoritarian, elite control being justified as 'necessary for the proper functioning of the community', as the 'unskilled' cannot manage their own affairs, and indeed become less capable 'as the science of government advances'. This is, one observer here suggests, a 'limited Fascism', in which the holding of power by a few could not but eventually result in a new caste. But there is no 'leader principle'.[12]

Some readers might envision such a structure becoming ossified, and see personal initiative shrinking, as another bystander here suggests. The future of behaviourism, it is alleged, lies particularly in its exploration of the 'special capacities of the group', and the creation of 'efficient group structure', with the promise that we 'can construct groups of artists and scientists who will act as smoothly and efficiently as champion football teams'. Just why these will not be 'unpleasant and unhealthful' groups is unclear. Reducing sexual desire seems unrealistic. Skinner's retort is that the experiment should be made. And 'freedom' is not a worry since all behaviour is determined, and people will generally do what positive reinforcement indicates they should do. Real freedom only comes from satisfying everyone's needs, by planning, guided by experts, but without force. Political democracy is mere majority tyranny: the majority do not choose experts, and only end up exercising their own inferior despotism. Real freedom also consists in choosing what you want to do, but only choosing what is 'best for themselves and the community'.[13]

Most of these issues were later explored in Skinner's *Beyond Freedom and Dignity* (1971), which met with much criticism. This again challenges the idea of freedom as autonomy, and of dignity as possible only if actions are free and not determined. It contends that if 'we cannot now design a successful culture as a whole . . . we can design better practices in a piecemeal fashion'.[14] In a new introduction to *Walden Two* (1976), Skinner credited advances of 'behavioral modification' in the 1950s and 1960s with fuelling the success of the novel. He insisted upon the plausibility of small-scale experimentation, the futility of political action, and the failure of cities to nurture human fulfilment, seen now in terms of less pollution, less consumption, birth control, and crime reduction.[15] He continued to be caustic of those still clinging to 'half-analyzed ideas of individual responsibility'. Having achieved sales of only 250 in 1955, some 2.5 million copies of the novel had been

[12] Ibid., pp. 142, 162, 174, 233, 235, 237, 239, 259–60, 263, 266, 268, 275, 281.
[13] Ibid., pp. 293, 297.
[14] B. F. Skinner, *Beyond Freedom and Dignity* (Penguin Books, 1971), pp. 24–6, 153.
[15] Ibid., pp. vi, ix–xi, xvi.

sold by the time Skinner died in 1990. And he had the additional gratification of seeing several communities founded on the principle of using positive reinforcement to stimulate non-competitive ethics.[16]

Capitalist and Communist Evils: The 1950s

In the early 1950s, conventional anti-Soviet dystopias, often pale imitations of Orwell, poured from the presses. An anti-utopia written from a liberal economic standpoint (it is dedicated to Ludwig von Mises) is Henry Hazlitt's *The Great Idea* (1951). This portrays Wonworld, ruled by the dictator Stalenin, with its capital in Moscow, in the year 2100, 282 years AM (After Marx). Society is divided into four groups: Protectors (1 per cent), who wear black; Deputies (10 per cent), clad in navy blue; proletarians, with grey uniforms (*c.*70%); and at the bottom, Social Unreliables (*c.*20 per cent), who 'are assigned to labor camps, or starve'. People are usually known by their numbers. Most books have been burnt, and the rest are restricted to only a few people. Parades in Red Square include *kulak* families in steel cages who are to be guillotined. Leisure time is chiefly spent in Organized Recreation Platoons, and most apartments are shared by two families, divided by a curtain, this being 'all the privacy that a socialist society needs'. Propaganda is dominated by the principle that 'The truth is whatever is good for communism.' Then the son of the dictator undergoes a change of heart. He introduces free-market principles, then goes to America, which he names Freeworld, and raises a force to overthrow the dictatorship.[17]

Ronald Matthews' *Red Sky at Night* (1951) (F) follows a similar pattern. Set in Moscow in 1974, the story is recounted of the overthrow of the 'Tyranny' after a Crusade by the Pope brought about the Rising and the Great Deliverance. The narrative recounts purges from the late 1920s onwards; of the alliance with the 'almost worse regime' of Hitler, with whom, it is implied, anti-Soviet groups rightly rallied in 1941; of the hundreds of thousands convicted without guilt or reason; of Eastern Europe swallowed up by the Soviet system; and of the fervour of the Stalinist 'religious believer'. It is assumed that a few millions between rulers and masses possess a faith akin to Christianity, and would not become 'selfish monopoly capitalists'. There are Ukrainian and Lithuanian rebels, who rescue People's Commissariat for Internal Affairs (NKVD) prisoners. Many Soviet deserters have fled to the West and are described as revolutionaries who believed it was 'possible to make mankind permanently happy', but who felt betrayed by their leaders. There is an insistence that 'freedom is everywhere where God is there to make men free', but this is not the 'equivalent of 1917 . . . embodied in a living person, whom they call God'. All that is required is to transmute Bolshevik idealism back into religion. The rebellion commences with a supposed miracle in a small Slovakian town, when a man arises from the dead. Soon thousands believe Christ reigns again. The Crusade

---

[16] Daniel W. Bjork, *B.F. Skinner: A Life* (American Psychological Association, 1997), pp. 151, 162.
[17] Henry Hazlitt, *The Great Idea* (Appleton-Century-Crofts, 1951), pp. 3, 7, 10, 19, 23, 25, 70, 190, 259, 364.

sweeps across Western Europe, then America. Even Muslims join in. Avenging himself upon the atheists, God sends a great fog in the shape of a cross to deter action against the massed pilgrims as they reach the Soviet frontier. Many border guards join them. The Crusaders sweep all before them. The USSR breaks up. But a Christian spirit inspires a treaty of friendship between Russia, Europe, and the United States, and the Pope plans the 'Great Reunion' of faiths.[18]

We return to an Erewhonian take on technological dystopia with Kurt Vonnegut Jr's acclaimed *Player Piano* (1952). Set in a post-Third World War New York town named Ilium in the near future, this explores the damage wrought by progressive mechanization from the standpoint of humanism, the 'main business of humanity' being 'to do a good job of being human beings'. Machines owned by great companies do much of the work, but an elite of managers, scientists, and engineers mostly benefits. A computer named EIPCAC XIV supervises most things, including the supply and demand of commodities and labour. Many of the former industrial workforce are employed by the government, often in the Reconstruction and Reclamation Corps, like Depression-era public works projects. There is no substantial political repression. Citizens have 'free speech, freedom of worship, the right to vote', and a higher average standard of living than before, as well as health care and social insurance. But those competing with machines are plagued by feelings of depression, suicide, a declining sense of self-worth, and the loss of 'a feeling of participation, the feeling of being needed on earth—hell, dignity'. People 'have no choice but to become second-rate machines themselves, or wards of the machines'.[19]

Personal relations have not deteriorated substantially, however, and environmental problems seem negligible. Still, the streets are patrolled by armoured cars, and there is a huge standing army, partly to keep the unemployed young out of trouble. There are also hints of simmering discontent, sabotage, and a 'threat of revolution' from the mysterious Ghost Shirt Society (named after the nineteenth-century Native American Ghost Dance resistance). This aims 'to give America back to the people', to make people control machines, and to judge all new mechanisms by their effect on 'life patterns'. People, it is proclaimed, cannot be happy 'unless engaged in enterprises that make them feel useful'. Norbert Wiener's philosophy is discussed in relation to the threat that machines may come to 'devaluate human thinking'. By and large, this is a satire on corporate life, and a 'realistic dystopia' of a particularly mild type. At the end a revolution does occur. For a short time in the temporary 'Utopia' of the Ghost Shirts, people destroy machines, revert to wood fires, and read books instead of watching TV, before the 'experiment' collapses.[20]

---

[18] Ronald Matthews, *Red Sky at Night* (Hollis & Carter, 1951), pp. 3, 8–9, 12, 16, 23–4, 29, 55–6, 61, 77, 98, 113, 127, 130, 165, 173, 216. The real-life instance of the bleeding Madonna of Lublin in 1949 makes this tale less fanciful. See Anne Applebaum, *Iron Curtain: The Crushing of Eastern Europe* (Penguin Books, 2012), pp. 452–4.

[19] Kurt Vonnegut, Jr, *Player Piano* (1952; Macmillan, 1967), pp. 12–13, 18, 20, 79–80, 100–1, 113, 179, 219, 251,

[20] Ibid., pp. 258, 261, 273, 291. Studies of Vonnegut include: James Lindquist, *Kurt Vonnegut* (Ungar, 1977) and Jerome Klinkowitz, *Kurt Vonnegut* (Methuen, 1982). Also of note is Vonnegut's

A more traditional anti-totalitarian dystopia, written during the McCarthyite communist witch-hunts, David Karp's *One* (1953), focuses on a lustful lip-reading academic, Professor Burden. He is a spy for the Department of Internal Examination of the American 'benevolent state', the United States being the twentieth-century Rome within a World Federation. Burden is charged with rooting out heresy, the regime's aim being to 'erase the concept of individuality' so that 'the individual good is completely and utterly identified with the national good'. Some older people complain that the new society, created some thirty years earlier, has 'no zest, no verve, no drive, no sense of excitement'. Though private property seems untouched, there is a 'Church of State' religion which is overtaking all others. Describing adherents as 'a crowd' whose references are always to 'us', 'we', and 'ours', it 'teaches people to be obedient sheep' who are part of 'some sort of mass soul of which everyone has a share'. Though some heretics are 'destroyed', most are 'adjusted' by 'therapy, psychoanalysis, instruction and understanding' until 'social conformity' results. Suspected of heresy himself, Burden is injected with a truth serum which reveals a fondness for 'people with souls . . . who understand what a lie means'. He links the idea of an individual soul with a 'debt to God to retain our separate, personal identities'. Yet some 'heretics' also work for the state, where their 'independence of judgment' is still required. So they must forego that happiness which 'comes from conformity—comes from being exactly like your fellows'. For having one's hopes, dreams, joys, and sorrows 'shared and felt by others make[s] for happiness'. Burden thus must be 'purged'. 'You must only love it', he is told of the state. He is shown that only lunatics 'do not believe as all others do' and do not see that 'what everyone believes to be reality is reality'. Declared dead to his wife and family, who bury someone else's corpse, his memory expunged, he is given a new identity as Mr 'Hughes'. Yet Hughes, too, languishes after individuality. This failure challenges the entire system, and his execution is ordered.[21]

Often described as a work of science fiction, Frederick Pohl and Cyril M. Kornbluth's *The Space Merchants* (1953) not only unfolds a perfectly plausible vision, but foreshadows many later neo-liberal dystopias. A century hence, a vastly overpopulated world is dominated by giant multinational corporations who outwit moronic consumers by subliminal advertising and by lacing foods with habit-forming substances. They pay politicians to fail to regulate them adequately, but are opposed by the 'Consies' (Conservationists), who oppose 'reckless exploitation of natural resources' and believe 'that continued exploitation will mean the end of human life on Earth'. A few names are dropped in the text to give us theoretical orientation: Malthus, Ricardo, Pareto. The plot unfolds with a rocket being built to send 1,800 people to Venus, but this is a mere distraction from the satire. The

brief short story, 'Harrison Bergeron', set in 2081, which satirizes egalomania through the insistence that no one be allowed to appear any better than anyone else (in *Welcome to the Monkey House* (Vintage, 1994), pp. 7–13).

[21] David Karp, *One: A Novel* (Victor Gollancz, 1954), pp. 7, 9, 11, 18, 21, 48, 54–5, 82, 87–9, 92, 96, 101–2, 111, 129–30, 139, 141, 180, 195, 198, 214, 245–6, 252–6. On the confession genre, see David Seed, *Brainwashing: The Fictions of Mind Control* (Kent State University Press, 2004).

narrator, Mitchell Courtenay, is an advertising executive tasked with selling the concept of the new settlement and then overseeing its exploitation. On earth, real food is scarce, and protein substitutes common. Pollution is terrible. Even the well-to-do live in small apartments where beds have to be set up and taken down every day. The United States has 800 million people. The police have been privatized and are only available to subscribers. Corporations routinely assassinate their competitors. Rockets take visitors to the North Pole. But the trip is accompanied by continuous advertising, which includes olfactory stimulation. The narrator has his death faked and identity altered on such an expedition, and is kidnapped and sent to Costa Rica for near-slave employment with the Chlorella Corp., which virtually runs the country. Here, workers are permanently indebted to the company and can never leave, even children becoming indentured to it. Consies help Mitchell to escape, however. He concludes that 'The interests of producers and consumers are not identical; Most of the world is unhappy; Workmen don't automatically find the job they do best; Entrepreneurs don't play a hard, fair game by the rules; The Consies are sane, intelligent, and well-organized.' Mitchell is eventually outed as a Consie, and deported on the Venus expedition.[22]

We revert back to the anti-collectivist dystopia in one of the better-known texts of this period, a penetrating critique of democratic mass culture and group conformism. The title of Ray Bradbury's *Fahrenheit 451* (1953) (F) refers to the temperature at which paper burns, for the novel describes a regime which systematically destroys a million forbidden books, including the Bible. 'Firemen' do the dirty deed here, burning houses which contain books and sometimes their owners too. They trace their pedigree to 1790, when the first fireman, Benjamin Franklin, burnt 'English-influenced books in the Colonies', thus inaugurating 'the terrible tyranny of the majority'. There are the usual household gadgets—machines which deliver buttered toast, and mechanical guard dogs, and TV advertisements which address you by name. There is an atmosphere of imminent conflict, after two atomic wars since 1960. America is rich; most of the rest of the world is poor. But overpopulated America is also supremely intolerant. Culture in the age of the masses is 'levelled down to a sort of paste pudding norm', until classics become a two-minute book column or ten-line dictionary résumé: 'More sports for everyone, group spirits, fun, and you don't have to think'. Mesmerizing TV programmes deaden thought. The movement to destroy books did not come from the government: it came from the people, the comic-book, sex magazine-loving people whose pressure banned every reference to any minority. Controversy disappears. 'We must be all alike', they proclaim, 'everyone made equal.' So 'intellectual' became 'the swear word it deserved to be'. The firemen came to be custodians of 'our understandable and rightful dread of being inferior', and of the right to happiness, which means not being insulted by any book, and of feeling part of 'the family'. The system is 'happiness': 'Fun is everything.' Amusement means popular contests, clubs, parties, magicians, jet cars, sex, heroin: 'solid entertainment'. 'Don't give

---

[22] Frederick Pohl and Cyril M. Kornbluth, *The Space Merchants* (1953; Penguin Books, 1965), pp. 7–11, 37, 40, 47, 66, 69, 78, 82–3, 115, 126, 137, 165–6.

them any slippery stuff like philosophy or sociology to tie things up. That way lies melancholy.' Both friendship and knowledge are discouraged. Front porches, gardens, and rocking chairs have been abolished because they encourage 'the wrong *kind* of social life'. The new sociability replaces intimacy with group identity. Then one fireman, Guy Montag, begins to feel qualms about his job. He keeps twenty books he should have burnt, then plans a rebellion, even subverting the firemen by planting books in their houses. But his ideas get the better of him. He blurts out that he sees his wife and her 'normal' friends as 'monsters'. She denounces him and he flees to a hobo camp full of ex-academics who memorize books to preserve their contents. In the docile and welcoming countryside, as the bombs flatten the cities into baking powder, they are the hope of the future.[23]

A less successful satirical variant in the realistic genre, Evelyn Waugh's *Love among the Ruins* (1953) (F) is a slender light-hearted take on the idea of the blameless criminal under the future People's State. Strikes and power outages are common. Workers live in ghastly, shoddy hostels filled with gloom. 'Progress' has arrived. Euthanasia is available on the National Health System, though the queues for the gas chamber are so long patients often die while waiting. The love of a bearded ballerina and an orphaned ex-prisoner is ill-fated. For no particular reason the latter burns his former prison to the ground. The state assigns him the task of designing another and, for respectability's sake, marries him to his now beardless love.[24]

One-time secretary to Leon Trotsky, the American author Bernard Wolfe's *Limbo '90* (1953) commences alarmingly but is happily resolved. After three great atomic wars have destroyed most cities, a doctor experiments on an island in the Indian Ocean, trying to remove aggression from humanity. He has ended child mortality and many infectious diseases. A secondary plot line concerns the mechanization of warfare. Both Russia and the United States epitomize 'the managerial society' where technicians run the state. Both get EMSIACS (Electronic Military Strategy Integrator and Computer), or 'god-machines', which control warfare. Humanity's insect-like existence is dominated by compulsion, the 'characteristic of modern life in general' being subjection to 'vast impersonal forces, agencies beyond their reach'. EMSIAC is nonetheless finally overthrown in what is described as 'an affirmation of life and human goodness . . . an assertion of free will, of self-determination, of decision and decisiveness as against all steamrollers'.[25]

Maximizing freedom, however, proves disastrous in William Golding's classic, *Lord of the Flies* (1954) (F) (the name is from a biblical description of Beelzebub), a study in group psychology in a setting akin to a Hobbesian robinsonade. During a

[23] Ray Bradbury, *Fahrenheit 451* (Rupert Hart-Davis, 1953), pp. 22, 27, 35–7, 42, 52, 55, 57–61, 64–5, 71, 73, 95, 98, 105, 113, 116, 139, 152, 155–6. On Bradbury see Wayne L. Johnson, *Ray Bradbury* (Ungar, 1980) and David Mogen, *Ray Bradbury* (Twayne, 1986).

[24] Evelyn Waugh, *Love among the Ruins: A Romance of the Near Future* (Chapman & Hall, 1953), pp. 17–18, 21, 41, 49–51. On Waugh see David Lodge, *Evelyn Waugh* (Columbia University Press, 1971) and Jacqueline McDonnell, *Evelyn Waugh* (Macmillan, 1988).

[25] Bernard Wolfe, *Limbo '90* (Secker & Warburg, 1953), pp. 13–14, 40, 139, 200, 203–4, 211, 221, 224. On Wolfe see Caroline Geduld, *Bernard Wolfe* (Twayne, 1972).

nuclear war some schoolboys are stranded on a remote tropical island. Lacking adult leaders, they attempt to organize themselves, but soon revert to barbarism, their 'devils' re-emerging as the brutal underside of human nature reveals itself. From the outset, one boy, nicknamed Piggy, is 'the centre of social derision'. The aggressive bullies soon come to the fore, as the head boy and choir leader, Jack Merridew, nominates himself to be 'chief', only to be challenged by the conch-blowing Ralph. At first the boys can scarcely kill wild pigs for food, and the 'littluns' are plagued by fears of beasts in the forest. They are very English and very middle class, and mimic the regimen of boarding school, whose 'rules' are judged to separate them from the 'savages'. In face of chaos, however, squabbling begins. A parachutist provides the illusion that a 'beast' really exists, and precipitates a split in the group, with factions forming around two chiefs. One 'tribe' now becomes 'savages'. They put on war paint, and exult in 'the liberation into savagery that the concealing paint brought'. They must steal fire from the other. The 'Lord of the Flies' is the head of a pig which has been killed and is covered with flies. But now one boy, Simon, begins to identify with it, and soon is given this title by the author. Precipitated by lightning and thunder, the boys begin a frenzied, murderous dance, acting as 'a single organism' intent on killing the beast. The violence accelerates, egged on: 'they made us . . . they hurt us . . . it's a tribe . . . we couldn't help it'. Then a naval vessel suddenly arrives. An officer laments that a 'pack of British boys' should have 'put up a better show than that'.[26]

Englishness also features in Robert Kee's *A Sign of the Times* (1955). Here the mass 'regroupment' into slave labour of 'maladjusted persons', which includes large ethnic groupings like the Australian aborigines, is part of a near-future American/Russian dictatorship. This emerges after a nuclear attack on Taiwan, followed by a week-long war and the reconciliation of the two great ideological systems. Fascists are still a risk, at least in Germany, whose borders are sealed. Gentlemen still call each other 'old boy' and dine comfortably in their London clubs, however, and much of English life seemingly goes on as before. The protagonist here, the bureaucrat Arthur Crowther, amidst a dying marriage, moves towards a nervous breakdown after he kills the office pet peacock and then faces blackmail after he is observed. He is forced to hand over a list of those whose activities might be 'sickening to the body politics' who will be placed 'in care' (deported), including artists, churchmen, philosophers, and politicians (among them is one 'Freddie' Ayer, i.e., the philosopher A. J. Ayer). Down at the local pub, as in *Nineteen Eighty-Four*, people are interested only in beer, films, and sport. They are oblivious to the 'maladjusts'. Arthur and others flee the country for Germany, only to be killed at the frontier.[27]

[26] William Golding, *Lord of the Flies* (Faber & Faber, 1954), pp. 12–13, 28–30, 41, 55, 89, 118–19, 158–9, 171–4, 179, 184, 187–8, 198, 206, 212, 223, 231, 246, 248. Film adaptations: 1963, 1990. On Golding, see, e.g., Bernard F. Dick, *William Golding* (Twayne, 1987) and James Gindin, *William Golding* (Macmillan, 1988).

[27] Robert Kee, *A Sign of the Times* (Eyre & Spottiswoode, 1955), pp. 13–14, 18, 21, 32, 50, 59, 63, 71, 79, 83–8, 107, 110, 141, 207, 247, 252.

At the borders of dystopia and futurology is Michael Young's *The Rise of the Meritocracy 1870–2033* (1958). It aims chiefly to satirize the potential outcome of educational streaming by projecting an ascending meritocracy contrasted to a declining manual working class. In the progress of more than a century it has been discovered that intelligence is distributed fairly randomly through the population. The ascent of some makes 'casualties of progress' out of many more. Yet the net political effect is rule by 'a true meritocracy of talent', the notional aim of socialists critical of nepotism and inherited power. Much of the detailed account of the vices of Britain's educational system will strike readers as parochial and outdated. Dystopian fiction enters here, however, in the projection of discernible trends in real social and economic decline amongst the most marginalized. If here the causes of decline are inadvertent, the consequences remain the same. There is no need for the unskilled here; a third of all adults are unemployed by 1988. Domestic service increases. The labour movement and Labour Party suffer a decline as the concept of the 'worker' is discredited. Finally a populist revolt aspiring to an egalitarian, classless society and led by women challenges the system, but its outcome is unclear.[28]

Gradual descent into dystopia in this period is less frequent than its catastrophic arrival. Science fiction meets old world supernatural in one of many post-nuclear war narratives, Walter Miller's *A Canticle for Leibowitz* (1959) (F). Set in Leibowitz Abbey in the south-western United States, which houses the relics of Leibowitz, a twentieth-century radio technician, the novel describes the process of rebuilding civilization 600 years later. It dwells on the themes of repentance, the loss of religious faith, the parallels between the biblical 'deluge' and its nuclear equivalent, and the failure of the 'Age of Enlightenment'. 'New Rome' is the revived Catholic Church, a beacon of reason in a desert of primitive heathenism, once again busying itself with theological niceties like Eve's power before the Fall. Much of North America is now thinly populated by 'simple clanfolk loosely organized into small communities' who live by hunting, fishing, primitive agriculture, and warfare. Witchcraft is the most promising road to fame and fortune, and is persecuted again by the Church, which maintains armies against the heathen. Beforehand, during the great 'Simplification', rulers, scientists, technicians, and teachers were killed for having nearly destroyed the earth by 'the maddened mobs' who proudly called themselves 'simpletons'. The new Church like the old seems mainly concerned with enhancing its power, both temporal and spiritual, by validating relics and miracles, promoting canonizations, and extracting confessions. There is a vague reference to Stalin here: an 'Antipope' is named Vissarion. Otherwise there are few twentieth-century reference points. In the year 3781, nuclear war erupts again and the monastery is destroyed, but twenty-seven monks flee the planet. Bewilderingly, we are told that 'Too much hope for Earth had led men to try to make it Eden'—the original anti-utopian argument: 'The closer men came to perfecting for themselves a paradise, the more impatient they seemed to be with it, and with

---

[28] Michael Young, *The Rise of the Meritocracy 1870–2033* (Penguin Books, 1961), pp. 14–15, 21, 103–5, 118, 120, 122, 140, 162, 164–9.

themselves as well.' Instead we are enjoined to have 'hope for the soul and substance of Man somewhere'—but not on earth: a deeply pessimistic conclusion, rendered more preposterous by the inference that this scenario somehow reflects God's will.[29] (We recall the rabbi at Auschwitz.)

Nuclear war also dominates Mordecai Roshwald's acclaimed novel, *Level 7* (1959) (F).[30] Here a diary records the life of officer X-127, guarding the Bomb 4,000 feet underground in an entirely self-sufficient underground world. His relatives are told he has been killed in an accident. Amongst his associates, there is initially no fraternity of the kind 'which is supposed to spring up when . . . people are shipwrecked together. Instead there was a curious lack of interest in other people; perhaps even some resentment, as if each thought the others were responsible for his present state.' In fact, the officers have been chosen because they are loners, making Level 7 an 'unsocial society', a 'hive of monsters'. The use of numbers rather than names encourages this. But some friendships grow. This is not a political dystopia, for we learn little about the regimes above ground. Nor is it even really science fiction. It is rather a combination of carcerotopia and the groupist dystopia, underground; and above, the nightmare of total atomic destruction. There is interesting speculation as to how such groups would evolve over time. One other level (2) has all of society's 'maladjusted people', misfits including 'peacemongers', 'critics of society and other cranks'—a million of them anyway. X-127 starts to lose his mind. Then missiles begin to be launched—accidentally, with automatic retaliation. In less than three hours most of the world is devastated. Radiation seeps down as far as Level 2, then deeper. Finally 7's own reactor leaks. The narrator dies on the last page.[31]

A slightly less bleak nuclear Apocalypse is portrayed in Pat Frank's gripping *Alas Babylon* (1959). City after city disappears under mushroom clouds during an atomic war begun accidentally during a Middle Eastern conflict. Fort Repose in Florida becomes an island cut off from the destruction. Disorder soon reigns. Food and fuel disappear quickly. Money is useless. 'If the dollar was worthless, everything was worthless', a banker reflects: 'Civilization was ended.' So he shoots himself. Looting commences. Drug addicts run amok. Without insulin, diabetics die quickly. Pet cats eat pet birds as food becomes scarce, then go wild and eat chickens. Soon people start eating dogs too. The central characters quickly lose weight. Shoes wear thin. The men grow beards. The town is segregated, with drinking fountains marked 'Whites Only' and 'Colored Only'. But the barriers disappear quickly as barter becomes crucial to all. Some kindness, and a sense of mutual need, remain. But highwaymen also infest the roads. We discover that others have survived,

[29] Walter Miller, *A Canticle for Leibowitz* (Corgi Books, 1959), pp. 17, 22, 26, 46–7, 51–3, 58, 119, 157, 184, 190, 198–9, 202, 216–17, 220–2, 233–7, 276–7.
[30] On the subgenre see David Dowling, *Fictions of Nuclear Disaster* (University of Iowa Press, 1987) and David Seed, *Under the Shadow: The Atomic Bomb and Cold War Narratives* (Kent State University Press, 2013).
[31] Mordecai Roshwald, *Level 7* (Signet Books, 1959), pp. 14, 23, 28–30, 33, 47–8, 69, 84–7, 93–4, 97, 112–13, 126–7, 143. Similar themes are explored in Eugene Burdick and Harvey Wheeler's *Fail-Safe* (Hutchinson, 1962).

though the population has been greatly reduced. At the end we learn America has 'won' the war, 'Not that it matters.'[32] Similar future nuclear war scenarios are portrayed in the 1960s in such works as John Wyndham and Lucas Parkes' *The Outward Urge* (1959–61), where the destruction of the northern hemisphere in 2044 leaves Brazil the remaining world power, with Australia as a rival for the conquest of space. By and large, however, as the 1960s dawned, the genre was making way for other scenarios, or being combined with them.

Ends in Sight: The 1960s

A brilliant satire on consciousness of class, status, and egalomania, L. P. Hartley's *Facial Justice* (1960) is set in 'the not very distant future, after the Third World War'. This has killed all but 20 million people, most of whom live underground until a rebellion leads many back to the surface. A Dictator has ruled for fifteen years, but is often satirized and criticized. 'Justice', we are told, has 'made great strides', chiefly in the sphere of 'equalisation', especially of faces. These are surgically altered to reduce envy. The New State above ground embodies the ideal of equality, but is embraced on the basis of Free Will, not torture and mass executions. Citizens are ranked from alpha to gamma, but can move between categories by altering their appearance at the Ministry of Facial Justice. The former have the most privileges, but are regarded as anti-social and thus are not envied. Each group indeed is taught to be satisfied with its position, and has Huxleyan slogans reflecting its claims to well-being ('How gloriously gamma!', or 'How absolutely alpha!') Marriage is slowly disappearing and most children are reared in common. Isolation and 'pairing off' are discouraged, even by the married. Work is light, and recreation is obligatory. Incomes are equal, but black marketeers deal in scarce goods and are fined by Inspectors, and the civil service is corrupt. Nuclear war has altered the climate and turned the countryside from green to brown. Towns are small and isolated, and travel is discouraged. Other countries can only be described positively, and there are fines for not knowing the latest ever-changing mandatory alliterative epithet ('beautiful Belgium'). The plot is driven by one Jael 97, a Failed Alpha who refuses to be 'betafied', thereby exhibiting an unhealthy 'Voluntary Principle'. She joins a group of conspirators who aim to assassinate the Dictator, who eventually abdicates after a new outbreak of equality leads everyone to want to make mistakes, in fairness to those who do.[33]

By the 1960s, the spectre of world overpopulation was beginning to filter seriously into dystopian fiction. The prologue to Harry Harrison's *Make Room! Make Room!* (1966) (F) indicates that this is intended as a realistic projection to 1999, when the world has 7 billion inhabitants (sixteen years before it actually

---

[32] Pat Frank, *Alas Babylon* (Constable & Co., 1959), pp. 9, 11, 19, 24, 63, 91, 100–3, 120, 128, 131, 137, 145, 148–50, 156, 161, 164, 168, 172, 189, 200, 208, 232, 241, 251–4.

[33] L. P. Hartley, *Facial Justice* (Hamish Hamilton, 1960), pp. 9, 12–13, 20, 24, 29, 38, 46, 53–4, 65, 84, 125, 132, 139, 149, 177, 181–3, 230, 235–6, 254–6. On Hartley see Peter Bien, *L. P. Hartley* (Chatto & Windus, 1963) and Edward T. Jones, *L.P. Hartley* (Twayne, 1978).

reached that number). The 'oil is gone, the topsoil is depleted and washed away, the trees chopped down, the animals extinct, the earth poisoned'; 'all our troubles come from only one reason'—overpopulation. New York City contains 35 million people, and suffers from food, water, and electricity shortages—people have pedal-operated generators for their refrigerators. Many live a hand-to-mouth existence on welfare. Dogs are eaten. The United States consumes nearly all the world's resources. There are hints at parallels to the Christian Armageddon. Family planning is indicated as the means of preventing all this, though only in the form of giving mothers 'birth control information'. Most of the novel focuses on individual characters coping with such circumstances. But as the book progresses the shortages worsen. Hungry mobs begin to riot. The 'Save Our Babies nuts', chiefly Catholics, protest at any birth restraints. A 2008 Afterward laments that many of these forecasts have proven 'too horribly correct'.[34]

A better-known account of the breakdown of social order, set in the near future, is Anthony Burgess' *A Clockwork Orange* (1962) (F), a study in gratuitous gang violence whose anti-hero, Alex, personifies mindless drug-addled delinquent viciousness. After an astonishing series of brutal acts, Alex is subjected to 'Reclamation' via aversion therapy, being shown violent films while pumped with drugs which make him ill, making his new self evidently less violent. Here, as with Huxley and Skinner, the free will/determinism issue is central. Burgess described the book (in 1972) as a 'sermon . . . on the importance of power of choice' whose chief aim was 'to state that it is preferable to have a world of violence undertaken in full awareness—violence chosen as an act of will—than a world conditioned to be good or harmless'. A key target here, thus, is Skinner's scheme of behavioural engineering, which Burgess described as 'the death of autonomous man', the 'wish to diminish free will' even being 'the sin against the Holy Ghost'. Burgess' Catholicism is central here: 'essential good' is described as an 'aspect of God'. The main underlying themes are Original Sin (perhaps 'some devil . . . crawls inside' Alex) and the need for free will. ('Goodness is something chosen. When a man cannot choose he ceases to be a man.' 'What does God want?' we are asked, 'Does God want goodness or the choice of goodness?' Reclamation provides only the former: to be human beings we need the power of choice.) A potent symbol of the turn towards violence in popular culture, especially film, from this period onwards, the novel has been termed an 'inverted utopia'. It is not a dystopia as such. Its violence is not the result of a particular regime, though a shortage of police is noted, and the first victim is a 'boorjoyce' schoolmaster, implying a link between political and gang violence. Burgess admired Huxley and Orwell. But he chose to offer no political explanations here, no chronology of deterioration, no prospect of alternatives. Alex's working-class parents get no blame. 'Badness', for Burgess, 'is of the self, the one', always in rebellion against 'big machines'. The blame lies with 'the adult world . . . with their wars and bombs and nonsense'. 'The ultra-violent' outlook is simply a hatred of middle-class domesticity, of youth for age, of meaninglessness for

---

[34] Harry Harrison, *Make Room! Make Room!* (Penguin Books, 1967), pp. 5, 22, 43, 52, 138, 158, 166, 172–3, 178, 181, 230, 232. The film is entitled *Soylent Green* (1973).

conventionality and respectability, of arrant hedonism for humdrum workaday enslavement. Besides, Alex is violent just because he likes it.[35]

Overpopulation is the focus of another Anthony Burgess novel, *The Wanting Seed* (1962), which is set in London, which now stretches from the south coast to Birmingham. Children are rationed—one birth per family is allowed, even if twins or triplets result, though the proletariat and 'God-followers' break the rules frequently. The dead are recycled as fertilizer. Homosexuality is encouraged, 'anything to divert sex from its natural end'. Indeed, the 'homos' virtually run the country, being given preference because they have no children. So some pretend to be gay to advance themselves (one such instance is central to the plot). Misogyny is growing too. The state discredits 'the whole notion of family' to the extent even of encouraging fraternal enmity. The Poppol, or Population Police, maintains vigilance over family size. The world is at peace, dominated by two great empires, English- and Russian-speaking. It is grouped according to language, rather than ethnicity, racial integration having been successfully achieved. Much of the philosophic debate juxtaposes a Pelagian desire for perfectibility against an Augustinian conception of Original Sin. It is also suggested that all art revolves around fertility and reproduction. Parliamentary government has given way to non-partisan administration. Religion is illegal. There is still labour unrest. Nearly all are non-smoking, non-drinking vegetarians, for land is not available for alcohol or tobacco, and artificial food is common. As the book progresses, the population problem worsens and the food supply shrinks. China has become 'almost standing room only', and people are executed for disobeying the birth-control laws. An illegal pregnancy becomes integral to rebellion against the system, this corresponding to God's will to 'go forth and multiply'. For unclear reasons, a regime championing fertility also returns. We are left with the Catholic query as to 'man's ability to organize the good life' without God's grace.[36]

Fictional global warming scenarios also begin to appear in the 1960s. In one of the earliest inundation dystopias, J. G. Ballard's *The Drowned World* (1963), solar flares, not human activity, are the cause. The book commences with the relentless heat of the rising sun above a tropical lagoon where a United Nations biological research station is located. Its crew are the focus of the book. Many of earth's great cities have disappeared. The sea washes over the tops of five- or six-storey structures. The former great wheatfields of North America and Europe are underwater. The heat, abetted by vast tropical rainstorms, has bred enormous clouds of mosquitoes the size of dragonflies. Bats, snakes, spiders, and iguana proliferate. Two-thousand-strong

---

[35] Anthony Burgess, *A Clockwork Orange* (1962; William Heinemann, 2012), pp. 11, 25, 45–7, 92, 104–5, 114, 137, 169, 173, 198, 247–8, 279. Burgess thought Skinner's view was that 'we must give up certain rights and privileges so that we do not obtrude ourselves upon our neighbours. We must exercise control; we must limit our freedom for society's sake. This means we relinquish our freedom of choice', adding that 'The artist is a rebel who defies control through his work' (p. 255), a clear statement of the Crusoe hypothesis. Burgess positions himself in the utopian tradition in *The Novel Now* (Faber & Faber, 1967), pp. 38–47.

[36] Anthony Burgess, *The Wanting Seed* (Heinemann, 1962), pp. 3, 5–6, 11, 13, 16–17, 29–30, 38, 42, 44, 48, 59, 65, 67, 100–1, 120, 130, 253, 282–3. On Burgess see, e.g., A. A. Devitis, *Anthony Burgess* (Twayne, 1972) and Samuel Coale, *Anthony Burgess* (Frederick Ungar, 1981).

packs of alligators represent 'a massive group incarnation of reptilian evil'. Malaria is rife. Many living in the sinking cities become 'either psychopaths or suffering from malnutrition and radiation sickness'. Temperatures at the Equator are heading towards 200°F, while the Arctic is 85°. The population of the tropical regions has long since migrated north or south from temperatures of 130–140°. With the melting of the polar icecaps and glaciers vast amounts of silt have poured into the sea. Eventually only the poles are habitable, and here 5 million people remain, few children being born any longer. (Just how the rest have died is unclear, which prevents the natural dystopia from becoming a political one.) All forms of organism are mutating backwards, including humanity, which is reverting towards ancient drives and taboos. As reptiles proliferate, nightmares are increasingly common in which phantoms shift imperceptibly from reality to sleep, and psychic landscapes invoke Hiroshima, Auschwitz, Golgotha and Gomorrah, and 'ancient organic memories' millions of years old. An extraordinarily improbable plot detracts only slightly from the sombreness of the setting, into which the hero sinks, lost, at the end.[37]

Some dystopian novels approach a purer form of science fiction. Adapted to film as *The Blade Runner*, Philip K. Dick's justly renowned novel, *Do Androids Dream of Electric Sheep?* (1968), is a post-Apocalypse science fiction dystopia which focuses on the spectrum and meaning of human/mechanical identity. World War Terminus, which no one seems to have won, has left few humans on earth, though others have migrated to Mars or elsewhere. Radiation has killed off most animals, so 'electric sheep' and other substitutes (including rather inferior wheezing cats) have been introduced. 'Andys', or android servants, are also common. The plot centres on six Nexus-6 andys who have escaped and are pursued by a bounty hunter, Rick Deckard. Androids differ from humans, we are told, in that they lack empathy with both humans and animals. (In the twentieth century this hardly counts as a definitive human characteristic either—hence the satire here: 'Mankind needs more empathy.') The errant androids are solitary predators who have killed their masters (perhaps for good reason) and pose as humans. They can only be detected by an empathy test, which some may pass (and some humans are misclassified as androids). Aside from the predominance of a few large corporations, we learn remarkably little about human–human social relations here, or how survival is possible in this environment, or what caused the war to start with. This is a machine–human confrontation. People don't usually feel empathy for androids, though a few have (dreary, illegal) sex with them. But some do. And these andys are in fact not very unsympathetic, and one helps Deckard catch the others. She is 'certainly as human as any girl he had known', after sex, anyway. So there is moral density and ambiguity here. And indeed the 'fact' of human empathy is challenged

---

[37] J. G. Ballard, *The Drowned World* (Victor Gollancz, 1963), pp. 9–10, 12, 15, 17, 19, 21, 23, 42, 44, 74, 85, 87, 91, 175. A film version was being planned in 2013. On Ballard see, e.g., A. Gasiorek, *J. G. Ballard* (Manchester University Press, 2005) and John Baxter, *The Inner Man: The Life of J. G. Ballard* (Weidenfeld & Nicolson, 2011).

too, as being merely a social or ideological construct. By the end, our sympathies have been seriously challenged, and perhaps the animals come off best.[38]

Dick also wedded science fiction and dystopian narratives in other novels, including *Flow My Tears, the Policeman Said* (1974). Here a TV star in 1988, whose ID number is tattooed on his arm, wakes up in a world he was not born into. The United States has become a police state where students are the special prey, so they mostly live underground to avoid the forced labour camps. But we learn little as to how this has come to pass, beyond the fact that eugenic experiments have rendered some groups (with six or seven fingers) superior to others, and that a Second Civil War has vastly reduced the black population. At the end, most students voluntarily enter the camps and renounce their underground lives. But such events merely decorate the narrative, which does not hinge upon them.[39] Sometimes described as dystopian, Dick's *A Scanner Darkly* (1977) (F), set in Orange County in 1994, features the drug-induced obsessions and manic mentality of users and pushers as a central theme. Shopping malls are surrounded by electronic walls which admit only those with valid credit cards. Rape and robbery are widespread. Most of the science here is pharmaceutical, though a suit has been invented for undercover police work which makes its wearer unidentifiable. This is not a dystopia, just a magnification of crazed modernity, dedicated, on the last page, to fifteen victims of drug abuse.[40]

We return to overpopulation with John Brunner's *Stand on Zanzibar* (1968), classed as dystopian science fiction, which projects a world of 7 billion people in the year 2010 (erring by only four years). The narrative is experimental, fragmentary, dense, and itself overpopulated with characters. It is constantly interspersed with commercial advertising. 'So far' the earth can still sustain its population. In developed countries, eugenics legislation has nearly eliminated deformed children. Family size has shrunk, though some 'Right Catholics' still resist birth control. Some US states ban immigrants or force them to become sterilized. In some countries, those denied parenthood rights kill themselves, while in others selected 'optimisation' programmes aim to 'breed supermen', possibly through cloning. Enormous corporations dominate the economy, but political systems everywhere remain much as they were in the 1960s. Detroit is 'like a ghost town', its car factories abandoned. In Frankfurt and London the streets have been built over with high rises. In less developed countries huge cities are 'swarming antheaps' of 'riot, armed robbery, and pure directionless vandalism' where police enter reluctantly. Group solidarity is weakened by shortage of territory, which induces widespread

[38] Philip K. Dick, *Four Novels of the 1960s* (Library of America, 2007), pp. 431–608; here 436–9, 444–5, 450, 455–6, 461, 469, 471, 484, 488, 535, 537, 558, 572, 574, 584–5.

[39] Philip K. Dick, 'Flow My Tears, the Policeman Said', in *Five Novels of the 1960s and 1970s* (The Library of America, 2008), pp. 687, 692, 776, 797, 856. Also worth mention is Dick's *The Man in the High Castle* (Victor Gollancz, 1975), where the Nazis and Japan win World War II and conquer the United States. It includes a variant on the real history as an alternate history within the book (pp. 60–1).

[40] Philip K. Dick, 'A Scanner Darkly', *Five Novels of the 1960s and 1970s*, pp. 867–70, 877–8, 1098. On Dick, see, e.g., Kim Stanley Robinson, *The Novels of Philip K. Dick* (UMI Research Press, 1989), Lejla Kucukalic, *Philip K. Dick: Canonical Writer of the Digital Age* (Routledge, 2008).

aggressiveness. Lack of privacy increasingly breeds psychosis. Millions take tran-
quillizers. Others randomly grab guns or axes and murder anyone around them.
(*You: Beast* is the title of a book describing this. *You're an Ignorant Idiot* is by the
same author.) Manhattan sits under a dome in which cars are banned. It too has
hundreds of homeless people. This is the dystopia of everyday life projected
forwards, minus ecological catastrophe. It is 'anti-utopian' if we assume the universal consumerist paradigm of modernity to be utopian. There is not much science
fiction in it beyond advanced domestic appliances. This world does not alter
substantially in the course of the novel, beyond edging towards greater eugenic
manipulation and the further exploitation of natural resources, in one instance
requiring complete corporate control over a nation, mostly by a computer. The
general trend of modernity is indicated as: '*First you use machines, then you wear
machines, and then . . .* you serve machines.' This is a degenerative condition, and
one which by now we are very familiar with.[41]

A very different approach to growing numbers and a prescient anticipation of the
world of virtual sociability, or possibly my-opia, Michael Frayn's *A Very Private Life*
(1968), envisions a world where everyone has withdrawn into the utmost privacy,
or what we in the Introduction here termed hyperinteriority. People wear dark
glasses so as not to expose their feelings to others through their naked eyes. In the
old world everyone 'ate in crowds, worked in crowds, relaxed in crowds', and
constantly gave each other diseases. There was some danger of complete control by
central authority, and the whole of life becoming public and communal. So
reaction occurred: 'People recognised the corruption of indiscriminate social contact, and one by one they withdrew from it.' Crowding has nearly been abolished.
All the earlier public freedoms were recognized to impinge upon the public
freedoms of others. But utterly private freedom does not. In houses, reality is
filtered through electronic media and chemical mediation. Most life is lived inside
one's head. Virtual reality provides vastly superior stimulation to the outside world,
with three-dimensional holovision systems. People remain indoors for years at a
time, for food and everything else is piped in, even babies. Virtual relationships of
every imaginable type exist, with orgasms medically initiated. Exercising machines
prevent people from deteriorating physically. When they need to move, 'travelling
houses' transport them to other areas, and there are also rockets. The main
character, a rebellious young girl named Uncumber, contrives to explore the
outside world, which in past times was intensely hot. Only technicians and
maintenance men, members of the 'outside classes' who have to work, seem to
be there, but they sometimes riot against the 'Kind People'. She also refuses to take
the standard drugs which regulate behaviour. But she is eventually rehabilitated
and, restored to her family, looks forward to a life of several hundred years.[42]

---

[41] John Brunner, *Stand on Zanzibar* (1968; Millennium, 1999), pp. 4, 12, 24, 39, 52–3, 57, 75–9,
104, 230, 233, 243, 248, 263, 318, 320–1, 353, 502, 607, 633.
[42] Michael Frayn, *A Very Private Life* (Collins, 1968), pp. 5–6, 9, 20, 23, 25–6, 31–2, 35–9, 44,
46, 50, 69, 73, 102, 153, 184, 192. On Frayn see Michael Frayn, *My Father's Fortune: A Life*
(Windsor, 2011).

Environmental Catastrophe Looms: The 1970s

Control by medication in an overpopulated world also occurs in another anti-totalitarian anti-utopia, Ira Levin's *This Perfect Day* (1970). The regime, 'the Family', promotes love and mutual assistance, and opposes selfishness, aggressiveness, and greed. Its symbol is a gold cross and sickle. (A key holiday is called Marxmas.) The population of 8 billion is controlled by a computer, UniComp. It decides what people do, where they live, who they marry, and whether they have children (two at most per couple, but none to some, so the population is declining). Movements are monitored via wrist bracelets which can be scanned to determine location. Monthly drug 'treatments' keep people happy, and minimize aggressiveness, but also joy. They aim to enhance 'helpfulness and docility and gratitude', and produce contented smiles. There are four names for boys and four for girls, and the population has been eugenically homogenized to create uniform eye and hair colour, height and so on, like 'peas in a pod'. After 'Unification', some 160 years earlier, certain 'incurables' fled the system and live in deep caves. 'Pre-U' thoughts, like classifying oneself, are forbidden as manifestations of 'selfishness'. Some who remain dislike UniComp. One such deviant is Chip, who finds others who complain that treatments 'make us into machines', without feelings. They want to make their own choices and live their own lives, to be 'people' rather than 'members', to have children if they want. They reject 'universal mechanical efficiency'. They believe that, in the past, 'members seem to have felt stronger and happier than we do. Going where they wanted, doing what they wanted, "earning" things, "owning" things, choosing, always choosing—it made them somehow more *alive* than members today.' He comes to believe that the host of non-productive people in the past helped to maintain freedom. They 'gave up efficiency—in exchange for freedom', whilst their successors did the reverse. So they plot to reduce their treatments, and discover that groups do exist, living like savages, with hunger, religion, and alcohol. They both live longer and die younger. Like Huxley's John, they have 'true freedom' to do things, rather than just freedom from want, war, hunger, crime, and violence. Chip is caught and cured, but escapes and, by destroying the system, emerges the victorious hero at the end.[43]

A more plausibly realistic dystopia is Adrian Mitchell's *The Bodyguard* (1970), set in Britain in the mid-1980s. Here informers and the European Riot Police or 'Yellows' help contain 'the Rot', which mostly consists of strikes and violence instigated by subversive movements. The police are taught that all forms of protest are dangerous because they 'erode general confidence'. The narrator, Len Rossman, is trained as an agent provocateur and infiltrates left-wing groups, and then becomes a bodyguard (BG). Police stations are built like fortresses and Rehabilitation Camps house captured members of 'subvert' groups, of which there are many. Surgical experiments on prisoners sometimes occur here. Amongst themselves, the

[43] Ira Levin, *This Perfect Day* (Fawcett Crest, 1970), pp. 8–9, 16–17, 22, 27–8, 38, 40, 49, 56, 64–6, 74, 82, 92, 113–14, 121, 126, 135–6, 142, 153, 161, 177, 207, 210, 213–14, 219, 230, 236, 245, 284–5, 314.

Yellows are friends, mates, chums, pals, but in a world of paranoid people. Len is a hard man, as a BG must be, practically Action Man, and we learn much of his aptitudes and ambitions, and of the 'special race' of his calling. But as dissent and the threat of revolution grow, Rossman dies in the line of duty. The last line notes that revolution has triumphed for some five years.[44]

We return to overpopulation in *The Edict* (1971) by Max Ehrlich, which began life as a screenplay. The future World Government broadcasts propaganda in three languages by satellite ('Big Mouth') to its 'trapped and surly', 'captive and long-suffering populations' through the wallscreens of everyone's personal cubicle. A pollution crisis decades ago induced a revolution which 'smashed the military-industrial complex and outlawed the entire profit system'. The official daily calorie ration is announced by WorldGov to be 652 when the novel commences. (Privileged officials lead a much better life.) This is not enough to maintain life in a world of some 20 billion, where there are teeming crowds everywhere, and no work, since machinery does everything important. Zero Population Growth programmes, in place since the 1970s, have failed, because the poor and ignorant fail to heed the norm of one to two children per family set by the well-to-do. Even algae farms and plankton plantations and squeezing nutrients from rocks are not sufficient to produce enough food. There are no birds, few trees, little grass. Pets have all long since been consumed at the end of the Meat Age, though a few stuffed specimens exist in museums, which people book years in advance to see. Cannibalism and food riots are common. Population density has generated extreme selfishness. There is no trust, and constant betrayal, with even best friends informing on each other to gain a bit more space. Thus 'nobody really touched each other, nobody really *loved* each other'. Extreme isolation does not require totalitarianism: compression in the crowd is sufficient. So WorldGov proposes putting all over seventy, who 'contribute nothing', to death, painlessly. Their Senior cities take up half of humanity's living space, since some live to 150, with organ transplants and grafts and medical advances. Some object, however, that this is genocide. So a new plan is hatched. No baby will be born for thirty years, under penalty of death (strangulation in public), with all born before the Edict branded electronically. In a population where sex with many partners is common this might be challenging. Moreover, child-rearing habits need to be maintained, so robot babies are given to selected potential parents, with drugs and therapy to render the experience realistic. The rebel figure here, Carole, bears a real child, the act of rebellion giving her and her mate, as in Levin's *This Perfect Day*, the sense for the first time that they are free, that they are living like human beings. But they are eventually forced to flee to a desolate island which is a dumping ground for unused nuclear weapons. Others have taken sanctuary there, and life begins anew. But of course their rebellion only enlarges the population further.[45]

---

[44] Adrian Mitchell, *The Bodyguard* (Jonathan Cape, 1970), pp. 15, 23, 28–33, 44–5, 61, 81, 116, 132, 142–3, 153, 155, 165, 170, 172–3, 185, 187.
[45] Max Ehrlich, *The Edict* (Bantam Books, 1972), pp. 3–8, 13, 18, 22, 24, 29, 36, 39, 41, 43–5, 48, 68, 82, 89, 111, 114, 135, 173, 176, 179, 215. Ehrlich wrote a screenplay in 1972 entitled *Z.P.G.*

While its central premise is science fictional, Ursula Le Guin's 1971 novel, *The Lathe of Heaven* (F), set in Portland, Oregon, in 2012, includes socio-political–environmental themes like overpopulation, global warming, epidemics, crime waves, food shortages, and war (in the Middle East). But it is suggested that overpopulation is not so severe a problem, that Americans can adjust to a reduced standard of living, and that much of the 'excessive dread of overpopulation—overcrowding' is 'an inward state of mind'. Much of the novel focuses upon the ability of one central character, George Orr, to alter reality through dreams. His psychiatrist, William Haber, encourages him to improve the world with this power. The dreams thus function as a kind of utopian projection, a literal social dreaming. But the results are less than successful—Orr dreams the reduction of population and a plague wipes out much of humanity. Then Haber's megalomania gets the better of him. Multiple alternative realities are introduced, including alien invasion (dreamt up to make humans fight something else), such that science fiction displaces dystopia in much of the novel.[46]

Environmental destruction looms more forcefully in John Brunner's *The Sheep Look Up* (1972), often described as dystopian science fiction, though it is mostly a dystopia. The narrative stretches across a year in the very near future. Large multinationals appear to control much of the economy, and sometimes assassinate their critics. The water is badly polluted with lead and plastic by-products, arsenic, and insecticides. The Great Lakes, the Caspian Sea, and the Baltic are dead or dying. Many food sources are depleted. In Los Angeles the air is thick and poisonous, and the sun is rarely seen. Oxygen is sold from machines. Traffic is bumper to bumper. Crime is rampant. Private compounds and high rises policed by private armies guard the well-to-do, who can cushion themselves even from the environment to some degree. The rest inhabit rat-ridden rabbit-warren slums where life expectancy is declining and starvation in the winter is common. The followers of one Austin Train, called 'Trainites', are sceptical about modern technology. They live in communes, resist traffic pollution, and protest other forms of degradation. Resistance movements elsewhere are becoming increasingly violent. Martial law is declared in many cities. As the book progresses, hordes of starving refugees from southern countries head northwards, and some borders are closed against them. Finally Trainite principles become widely accepted, and there are promises to restore ecological balance. Whether this is too late is unclear.[47]

In the 1970s we also begin to see a turn towards feminism and emerging concern with gender relations and misogyny which would become increasingly central to the genre. Such issues are at the core of Suzy McKee Charnas' *Walk to the End of the World* (1974). This commences with a cataclysm: 'pollution, exhaustion and

[46] Ursula Le Guin, *The Lathe of Heaven* (Grafton Books, 1974), pp. 9, 28–9, 54–5, 61–2, 70–2, 76–7, 87, 98, 105, 125–6. Neither Le Guin's *The Dispossessed* (1974) nor *The Left Hand of Darkness* (1969) are dystopias. Studies of Le Guin include Elizabeth Cummins, *Understanding Ursula K. Le Guin* (University of South Carolina Press, 1993) and Mike Cadden, *Ursula K. Le Guin beyond Genre: Fiction for Children and Adults* (Routledge, 2005).
[47] John Brunner, *The Sheep Look Up* (1972; Benbella Books, 2003), pp. 4–8, 11, 13, 15, 34, 44, 66, 110, 128, 141, 166, 184, 194–5, 207, 210, 225, 287, 355, 362–3.

inevitable wars among swollen, impoverished populations have devastated the world, leaving it to the wild weeds'. A few high officials emerge from their shelters and live mainly on seaweed, competing with a race of 'beasts', 'monsters', or mutants who have survived outside. All men are regarded as brothers, and blood ties are not recognized. But there are social ranks, denoted by tattoos on shoulders, and differences in wealth. A cult of masculinity is central to male identity. Boys are brought up to believe that: 'In discipline is belonging . . . In discipline is solidarity.' This involves resisting the 'fem-fat' in their own spirits, and becoming toughened into 'rugged individualism'. 'Manly love' is homosexual, as opposed to the 'counterfeit kind represented by a fem's bewitchments'. Much of the novel concerns the interrelations of a small group, where the men are bonded in part by oppressing 'fems'. Women have 'masters', are trained to complete slave-like subservience, and are treated like breeding animals. It is the fashion to cut their tongues out. They are believed not to have souls, and their deaths are of no significance. Some are reputed to 'change shapes, steal souls, control weather' and are burned as witches. (Men who believe such things are 'duped by their ideology'.) As a food shortage looms some are eaten. But cells of young rebels calling themselves The Pledged plot to escape their servitude, hoping to join the legendary 'free fems' who have escaped this tyranny. At the end one finally flees.[48]

One of the best-known novels of this epoch was written by the British-born author Doris Lessing (1919–2013), perhaps the only dystopian writer to have been awarded the Nobel Prize for Literature (2007). *The Memoirs of a Survivor* (1974) (F) is centrally concerned with group psychology. Set in Britain in the near future, society is collapsing following some unspecified disaster, probably an epidemic. Many cities are drained of people. Food rationing exists and public services are rapidly deteriorating, though there are still prisons, reform schools, and old age homes. Gangs of hooligans roam the streets, and move from district to district, pillaging; they are 'the gang, the crowd, the team, the pack'. The 'higher levels', the 'administrating class', still have food, amenities, even luxuries. Most people have to adjust to 'the ordinariness of the extraordinary'. Up 'to the end', citizens' groups form for mutual assistance, and to try to maintain moral standards, like not eating dogs and cats. The wealth of meticulously observed and beautifully portrayed detail and depth of character and emotional sensitivity mark this novel.[49]

The plot, centring on an abandoned child and her caretaker, does not, however, take us far into the structure of dystopia. There is a yearning for 'utopia', 'safety, refuge, peace', perhaps on a Welsh farm. There is some sense here that any disaster—earthquake, comet strike, climate change, 'a tyranny that twists men's minds, the savagery of a religion', could have brought about this state of affairs. But socially the focus here is not on the causes but the process of degeneracy as manifested in personal feeling, and then in the decay of civilized individualism back to tribalism. Everywhere 'young people were gathering in admiration and then

---

[48] Suzy McKee Charnas, *Walk to the End of the World* (1974; Victor Gollancz, 1979), pp. 3–4, 22, 45, 53, 55–7, 96, 102, 107–9, 121, 143–7, 159, 173, 202, 204, 212–14.
[49] Doris Lessing, *The Memoirs of a Survivor* (The Octagon Press, 1974), pp. 9, 14, 19, 21.

emulation of the migrating tribes'. In the face of disaster, strength lies in the group. These 'chattering noisy groups' always 'seemed lit with an inner violence of excitement or of readiness for excitement'. Excitement is displacement of anxiety, as the group is displacement of individual weakness. In the groups there is still some tenderness towards the distressed and forlorn, even though this 'softness... was superfluous to the demands of survival'. So 'mutual aid and self-sacrifice went side by side with the callousness'. The sense of the communal, 'this act of mingling constantly with others', and also a relearning of 'the pecking order', are key themes here. Some groups of younger children have never known parents and 'the softening of the family'. They band together, but 'only for the sake of protection in numbers. They had no loyalty to each other, or, if so, a fitful and unpredictable loyalty.' They are 'savages', representing humanity's lowest level. One girl who joins them is 'Beauty', 'wrapped in beast's clothing... surviving as one'. So this is survival: 'We had returned to an earlier time of man's condition.' The future bodes ill here, though errant children join a trusted leader to flee the city as the book closes.[50]

Inspired in part by Alvin Toffler's *Future Shock* (1970)—Toffler's law being that 'the future arrives too soon and in the wrong order'—John Brunner's *The Shockwave Rider* (1975) is at the science fiction end of the genre. The setting, the United States in the early twenty-first century, includes a shadowy oligarchy linked to organized crime from which the hero, Nick Haflinger, flees. The government uses behavioural psychology to play up the dystope of threat and trauma it needs to survive. The society is rife with religious conflict, riots, and crime. Large numbers of people live in poverty. Starvation occurs in other countries. San Francisco has been destroyed by an earthquake, the survivors of which are plagued by irrational cults who feed on their fears. A vast computer network ('the net') links individuals, and monitors their desires, tastes, and locations. But it is full of worms (the term was invented here). Our hero adapts it to recreate his identity continuously and to avoid the ubiquitous surveillance. People also use machines as proxies to avoid personal contact with others, though the big corporations are wary of their excessive use. Many governments have secret centres 'dedicated to exploiting genius' in a highly competitive international 'brain race'. They produce 'the top end of a series of cultural subgroupings' which have evolved to deal with 'the complexity and dazzling variety of twenty-first-century existence' because 'We prefer to identify with small, easily isolable fractions of the total culture.'[51]

These institutions, however, seem to lack any moral compass. Their graduates are 'convinced they were incapable of error'. So our hero opts out of his. There are many hints at the source of the problem. One is that 'you've decided machines are our superiors and you want to imitate them', particularly in the area of stimulus

---

[50] Ibid., pp. 31, 34, 44, 49, 54, 64–5, 73–4, 83, 85, 91–2, 102, 112, 130, 132, 147–8, 154, 156, 166, 182. On Lessing see Carole Klein, *Doris Lessing: A Biography* (Duckworth, 2000) and Susan Watkins, *Doris Lessing* (University of Manchester Press, 2010).

[51] John Brunner, *The Shockwave Rider* (J. M. Dent, 1975), pp. 7, 11, 26, 28, 39–40, 43–4, 52, 66–7, 103, 105, 107–10, 126–7, 134.

response. Another is that the 'new conformity' of the constant flux of modern urban life is producing anxiety neuroses and 'personality shock' because of the overload of opportunities it presents and the breakdown of families it encourages. Another is that the new intellectual elite only crave power. A few eco-friendly 'village'-style communities exist outside the net in 'paid-avoidance zones' which have low population turnover and therefore high stability. Here people 'knew how to idle', and most have several occupations, but doing things they like. Here 'everybody is ready to help everybody else'. We are clearly in utopia. Of course, the government finds such communities outside its control intolerable. But Haflinger helps them to remain independent, and in the end engineers a digital referendum to abolish poverty.[52]

We return to the threat of overpopulation in Naomi Mitchison's *Solution Three* (1975), also at the science fiction end of the dystopian spectrum. Here gender restructuring is portrayed as potentially central to solving mankind's problems. Aggression has destroyed much of the earth's populated and food-producing spaces. After various policies, including contraception, abortion, and the rising cost of living fail to stem overpopulation, the world government introduces cloning to produce a new generation of homosexual and mixed race He and She humans destined to control the world. This, with other stress reduction schemes, like abolishing exams for children, appears to diminish anger and hate, even to the extent of making the eating of animals repugnant. Mothers who bear clones must relinquish their children for social conditioning. But several women conspire to give birth the old way, and the system is thrown into question by the erratic behaviour of some clones. The question arises as to whether creating 'excellence' of this kind leads to imbalance, and the loss of other useful or even vital qualities in the cloning process seems evident. The hint is evident that greater love of and care for children is one of them.[53]

We ought at least to consider one still purer work of science fiction if only to compare how dystopian themes are treated in such a context. A worthy instance is Samuel R. Delany's *Triton* (1976), later published as *Trouble on Triton: An Ambiguous Heterotopia*, which responds in part to Ursula Le Guin's *The Dispossessed*. Here gender identity and science fiction meet in a setting on one of Jupiter's moons, where a libertarian regime permits extensive experimentation in private life in selected 'unlicensed' city sectors. Technology assists the process by enabling considerable personal modification of appearance, gender, and even personal taste. Much of the novel speculates about the private lives of the leading characters, the experimental nature of their living arrangements (most live in cooperatives), their varied sex acts, and the problem of the meaninglessness even of such an apparently free life. Gender identity is again a key theme; the lead character changes from male

---

[52] Ibid., pp. 137–8, 140, 143, 146, 162–3, 168–71, 197, 214, 219, 225, 256, 265, 268, 273, 281.
[53] Naomi Mitchison, *Solution Three* (Dennis Dobson, 1975), pp. 7, 30, 34, 39, 52, 61, 137–8, 144, 153–4, 160. Further into science fiction is Joanna Russ' *The Female Man* (Bantam Books, 1975), which uses the idea of parallel worlds to explore concepts of womanhood. On Mitchison see Jill Benton, *Naomi Mitchison: A Century of Experiment in Life and Letters* (Pandora, 1990).

to female about two-thirds into the narrative. There are both utopian and dystopian aspects to the social system. Basic food, shelter, and limited transport are provided for free, while a system of labour credit operates to finance further consumption. But the government gathers substantial information on its citizens, and crime, mental health problems, sects, violence, and economic crises are common. Less than 20 per cent of the population chooses to reproduce. The same number are 'frozen' on welfare. But they are not markedly more or less happy than us. Earth, on the other hand, warring with Triton as the novel progresses, seems to be a police state where torture is routine and dissidents are 'hauled off for resocialization'. It has far more people on welfare, and a much less fair tax system (in Triton, taxes which users do not benefit from are objected to). The war brings it great distress, including cannibalism. The location of plot and dramatic developments on other planets, then, does not necessarily diminish such works' utility for dystopian projections. It merely makes them less realistic.[54]

A notional realism is at the core of Anthony Burgess' *1985* (1978), which is a direct continuation of Orwell's novel, first as an engaging commentary on the text, then updating the narrative in an often reactionary rant (particularly against unions) of a very 1970s Tory but un-Orwellian kind. We are back in Britain, which has had a Labour government more or less since 1945. Nuclear wars have wrought great destruction. London has a large Muslim population, and the Arabs own North Sea oil and much else. Swahili-speaking gangs roam the streets. Charles III is king. There are strikes, and the unions have both the nation and the protagonist, Bev, in a stranglehold. His wife dies in a hospital fire while the firefighters are on strike. He loses his job for defying the union, joins a resistance group funded by Muslims, and allows his daughter to become a sheikh's concubine. After a general strike commences the government falls. Some of the Channel Islands are placed under Islamic law. Bev is incarcerated in a mental home as the US economy collapses and a Middle East war looms.[55]

We return to gender as a central theme in Sally Gearhart's *The Wanderground: Stories of the Hill Women* (1978), which is a work of fantasy as well as science fiction and dystopia. It portrays separatist groups of lesbians who have fled both cities and men. Those who remain face a deteriorating society where male oppression is increasing. There is some New Age spiritualism here. The women possess 'unique female powers' which they use to communicate and negotiate with animals as well as each other. Some have learnt to float above the ground. 'Outlaw women' are portrayed as 'the only hope for the earth's survival'. Misandry—hatred of men—is promoted in the narrative. (Gearhart once asserted that men should be reduced to no more than 10 per cent of the population.) All male–female sex is portrayed as

---

[54] Samuel R. Delany, *Triton* (Bantam Books, 1976), pp. 4–5, 8, 54, 72, 132, 161, 178, 291. 'Heterotopia' is a term adopted here from Michel Foucault to indicate transient spaces like trains, or moments of 'otherness', which lie outside formal or hegemonic social mores. Delany is the subject of Douglas Barbour, *Worlds Out of Words: The SF Novels of Samuel R. Delany* (Bran's Head Books Ltd, 1979).

[55] Anthony Burgess, *1985* (Arrow Books, 1980), pp. 13, 105, 108, 120, 127, 137, 153, 175, 180, 205, 217–18.

rape. Letting men die is encouraged, for 'the madness of power' possesses them. Some women have visions of 'manslaying, of man-mangling'. The political narrative commences with a backlash against feminism, and accusations against women of witchcraft. Laws are introduced requiring women to be married, even polygamously, and to wear dresses. So they flee to the country, pursued by men trying to rape them. The cities are full of slums, and crime is rampant. Technology seems to be becoming less efficient, and chemical substitutes supplant natural foods. But this could be present-day America. There is no degeneration narrative, nor any hint at gender reconciliation. In the cities there are still women who are 'the only edition acceptable to men, streamlined to his exact specifications', with thick makeup and flimsy clothes, either whores or housewives. The only 'gentle', good men here are gay, and they are persecuted by Christian vigilante groups.[56]

Towards Feminist Dystopias: The 1980s

More traditional themes predominate in Russell Hoban's *Riddley Walker* (1980), a post-apocalyptic tale set in Kent, which is virtually separated from the rest of England, two thousand years after nuclear wars in the late 1990s have destroyed much of the world. Survivors subsist at Iron Age levels of civilization, hunting with bows and spears, salvaging metals from old machines and speaking a dialect based on Kentish, in which the entire book is written. Order is maintained by a quasi-religious organization which uses mythology and a creative interpretation of the past to explain the 'Bad Time'. Cannibalism occurs, and packs of wild dogs attack people. The plague has returned. The inhabitants have only a dim idea of how all this has come about. Nuclear war is elliptically linked with EUSA (the United States).[57]

Experiments in style also mark Alasdair Gray's *Lanark: A Life in Four Books* (1981), which portrays both Glasgow and a future city modelled on it named Unthank, whose residents suffer from a variety of inexplicable illnesses, and which, by the novel's end, after some thirty years, is nearing social, political, and economic collapse. The tone of life here is contemporary rather than futuristic. The central character, 'Lanark' (not his real name), is a writer with an awkward skin disease evidently caused by sun deprivation—the sun in Unthank shines only a few minutes a day. This has produced a dragon-claw-like deformity on one hand. He lives in a dreary tenement, where people disappear for no particular reason. The city is decrepit. Many shops are boarded up, and its population is shrinking. A small minority own most of the property. He goes to a welfare centre, but has no sense of the value of money. An indeterminate war seems to be going on. People often speak elliptically, and seemingly without purpose. Lanark is operated on in a hospital under a mountain, where they try to make him a doctor, and interest him in the variety of dragons confined there, some with wings, horns, and spikes. These

[56] Sally Gearhart, *The Wanderground: Stories of the Hill Women* (1978; The Women's Press, 1985), pp. 2, 60–1, 68–9, 92, 96, 131, 138, 145–6, 164–5, 171, 174, 194.
[57] Russell Hoban, *Riddley Walker* (Jonathan Cape, 1980), pp. 2–3, 12, 91, 125, 177.

absurdities are heaped up until dystopia is submerged in an Alice in Wonderland-style fantasy which perhaps hints at the incomprehensibility of it all. This confusion is encouraged by the ordering of the book (Books 3–1–2–4, and a prologue and epilogue also out of sequence), which is explained by the author when he intrudes to introduce himself and proclaim his literary sources. The moral of the story, glimpsed where it is not overwhelmed by a Swiftian experimental form and abandonment of linear time, seems to be that the world is 'mad with greed' for profit and busily destroying itself. Governments are 'plundering their neighbours and planning to atom bomb each other'. Food, fuel, space, are all in short supply. The world is failing because it is 'bad at loving'. There are occasional digs at a bureaucratized Stalinism as no answer to these problems.[58]

One of the most self-consciously realistic, and indisputably the most influential, of contemporary dystopian writers is the Canadian Margaret Atwood, who has consistently produced gripping, relevant, alarming visions of the future for thirty years. The first and most famous of these, *The Handmaid's Tale* (1986) (F), is not, in the author's own view, science fiction and not beyond the bounds of plausibility, a position adhered to in varying degrees in later works and which we have termed the Atwood principle.[59] This updating of the totalitarian model (Patrick Parrinder terms it a 'postmodern utopia') portrays a Christian fundamentalist dictatorship in which female uniformed birth slaves, the red-clad Handmaids, and servants, the green-robed Marthas, cater to the needs of the elite which governs the Republic of Gilead, formerly part of the United States.[60] Handmaids wear veils, and expose as little of their bare flesh as possible. They are tattooed on the ankles with numbers. Their old names are banned, and they are named after their masters, 'Offred' being 'Of Fred'. They must bear children to Commanders whose wives cannot. They live in compounds, while the general population is confined within a large wall. Those attempting to flee, like doctors who formerly performed abortions, which are now illegal, are killed, though some forge passports and visas to escape.[61]

We are not told much as to how the 'time before' progressed to the present. A few decades ago the 'sect wars' commenced, and there has been environmental destruction resulting in birth defects and the extinction of many animal species. 'Islamic fanatics' are blamed for killing the president and Congress. The Constitution was suspended thereafter, and a puritanical crackdown begun on what was evidently an extremely sexualized decadent culture, albeit one in which an 'inability to feel' was increasing. (Ironically, thus, both Christian and Muslim zealots coalesce in condemning women's rights.) Then a ban on women holding property is introduced.

---

[58] Alasdair Gray, *Lanark: A Life in Four Books* (Canongate Publishing, 1981), pp. 6–7, 12–13, 19–23, 29–30, 32, 38, 41, 43, 58, 61, 66, 78, 102, 104, 295, 307, 354, 410, 482–4, 546. Studies of Gray include Stephen Bernstein, *Alasdair Gray* (Bucknell University Press, 1999) and Gavin Miller, *Alasdair Gray: The Fiction of Communion* (Rodopi, 2005).

[59] Margaret Atwood, *Curious Pursuits: Occasional Writing 1970–2005* (Virago, 2005), p. 85.

[60] Patrick Parrinder, *Utopian Literature and Science: From the Scientific Revolution to* Brave New World *and Beyond* (Palgrave Macmillan, 2015), p. 5.

[61] Margaret Atwood, *The Handmaid's Tale* (Houghton Mifflin, 1986), pp. 9–11, 14, 20, 22–5, 31, 43, 50, 59, 61, 65, 71, 83–5.

Soon neighbours are 'careful to exchange nothing more than the ordinary greetings', and denunciations for disloyalty begin. Jews and others who refuse to convert are persecuted. 'Unwomen' live in impoverished places called the 'colonies', some of which are toxic dumps.[62]

The Handmaids are separated into groups according to function and wear clothes coloured accordingly. They are not supposed to 'sororize' with each other, and 'Friendships were suspicious.' Secret Police called the Eyes make arrests occasionally. There is no money, but a black market gives the narrator hope for improvement. There are various wars going on against rebels, some of whom are Baptists. Magazines and films, lawyers and universities no longer exist. Many books have been burnt. Poor women are allowed to become 'econowives', and can wear what they like. Women are not harassed in the street, as in the old days. Other countries, however, have not been affected by these changes, though their TV broadcasts are jammed. Ruthless transparency is a definitive quality of this world. The narrator laments the loss of 'that freedom from being seen'. Dehumanization is the essence of the Handmaid's life; 'I want to be held and told my name. I want to be valued, in ways that I am not; I want to be more than valuable', laments the narrator, who wonders if she is dying from lack of love. There is furtive desire and stolen love here too, however. Rules are broken, and a large 'club' of old-fashioned sexual thrill-seekers made up of senior officials even exists. There is a network of resistance. But the memory of the past is slowly being erased and people are being taught not to 'want things they can't have'. The narrator comes to have feelings for her Commander, who ceases to be 'a thing' to her. She ends up arrested. Men do not come off well in this account, though the narrator hints that people who think they can 'create Utopia' in women-only enclaves are mistaken.[63]

Reversion to an identifiable past dominates Paul Auster's powerfully gloomy 1987 *In the Country of Last Things*. This follows the fate of a young woman named Anna Blume who searches for her brother William in the chaos of a post-apocalyptic, rubble-, corpse-, and pothole-strewn city. It is a portrait straight out of, and seemingly partly drawn from, one of the Jewish ghettoes in wartime Poland, early in the Holocaust. (Anna is Jewish; the currency is called 'glots', similar to the Polish *zloty*. Auster's parents were Polish Jews.) The city is populated chiefly by cart-hauling scavengers and 'object hunters'. Barricades are guarded by gangs who demand money, food, sex. There is little food in the few legal public markets, which are guarded by police, and thieves often steal what is bought anyway. Most buildings are not owned and tenancy is fragile. There are no schools. The last movie was five years ago. Even the memory of airplanes is fading, indeed is encouraged to fade, and the words for many other things, like flowerpots, are disappearing too. The disaster which took place some ten years earlier has taken a great psychological toll too. People run in groups hoping their hearts will give out,

---

[62] Ibid., pp. 94–5, 97, 112, 117, 161, 169, 172, 174, 178, 180.
[63] Ibid., pp. 201, 210, 235, 294. Accounts of Atwood include Coral Ann Howells, *Margaret Atwood* (St. Martin's Press, 1996) and Coral Ann Howells, ed., *The Cambridge Companion to Margaret Atwood* (Cambridge University Press, 2006).

or jump from tall buildings, or hire assassins to do them in. Euthanasia clinics do a brisk business. Most just die on the street, and the main expense of government is clearing their corpses away. Few babies are born. There are some rules, though: scavenging without a licence might get you a one-way ticket to a labour camp. People have 'all become monsters' in the face of so much misery, and sadists too. Deterioration into superstition is common. The 'Smilers' are a sect who insist that bad weather results from bad thoughts, while the Crawlers prostrate themselves in perpetual penance and shame. Just why this disintegration has occurred, and how much of the rest of the world suffers a similar fate, is unclear. (England seems secure.) Chiefly we follow a small group as they plot a grim course of survival, burning library books for warmth, until an injury lands Anna in the relative haven of Woburn House, where she is cared for, the food is good, and some sense of civility remains. But when this too collapses, Anna and a few friends plan to flee the city.[64]

Towards a New Millennium: The 1990s

Best known for her utopian *Woman on the Edge of Time* (1976), the American writer Marge Piercy offered a partial recasting of the Golem legend, along with recollections of medieval anti-Semitism, in *He, She and It* (1991). Set mainly in North America in 2059, where 2 billion have died through famine and plague, society is dominated by twenty-three great corporations called Multis, who have maintained peace since a two-week nuclear war in 2017 which destroyed Israel. The planet is hot, the polar caps are melting, and the Amazon is a desert. In privileged enclaves, some in air-conditioned domes, houses have intelligent computers which protect them, and cosmetic beautification is the norm. The society is hierarchical, and ranked by technical aptitude. Lower ranking women have fewer rights. Population is controlled by implants in women at puberty to prevent pregnancy, though radiation has left many infertile anyway. Most of the society lives in far worse, hot, crime- and disease-ridden, oppressive conditions in the 'Glop' outside, where the UN or eco-police hold sway where gangs do not. Here many are addicted to realistic computer games. Some free towns exist as enclaves. The main character, Shira, becomes involved with a cyborg named Yod who has been created illegally to guard her home, the Jewish free town Tikva (created like Golem to protect the Jews). This world contains a spectrum of humanoid types. 'Apes' are genetically modified humans with greater strength and speed. Robots do not look like humans since cyber-riots attacked many for taking jobs away. They do most of the housework. Some are pets. Some, like Yod, are partly organic and partly mechanical.[65]

---

[64] Paul Auster, *In the Country of Last Things* (Viking Penguin, 1987), pp. 1–8, 12–14, 17, 20, 26–9, 31, 66, 83, 87, 89, 115, 128, 136, 139, 171, 186. A film adaptation was reported in progress in 2013.
[65] Marge Piercy, *He, She and It* (Alfred A. Knopf, 1991), pp. 3–5, 7, 15, 21–2, 30.

This is one of the chief novels of this period to consider human–AI interfaces. The Golem query is asking what it means 'to push yourself beyond the human' by assuming God's functions. But we also encounter the question of post-human identity as such: what is distinctive about the 'human' where so many variants and intermixtures exist? (And what would 'humanism' entail when juxtaposed to mechanism as an 'ism'?) Many people here have artificial organs. So there is a spectrum of human–cyborg–machine life. Yod is 'considered a person', though 'not a human person', by his maker; 'he'—not 'it'—is good company, and feels 'the desire for companionship'. But Yod is also capable of disobeying orders. He makes clumsy mistakes, destroying a rosebush because it is 'armed'. When he kills humans, defending Shira, he reports a feeling 'as intense as sexual pleasure or mastering a new skill'. He is uninterested in sex initially. How then might he 'feel'? He is programmed; but is socializing children not programming too? we are asked—back to Skinner. But when Shira, aged seventy-two, seduces him, 'he discovered he liked sex better than almost anything'. Being programmed 'for intimacy, connection', and to satisfy, he is tirelessly unselfish in bed, a cross between 'a person and a large fine toy'. Women who have had affairs with 'hairy objects far less human than Yod' are encouraged to sympathize: virtual relationships are so much easier, since all the personal awkwardness is removed. Yod's emotions grow with use, too. Yet when he reads *Frankenstein* he is embarrassed to be a 'monster' himself.[66]

So as the story moves forward he is 'working heroically to be human'. Since 'Men so often try to be inhumanly powerful, efficient, unfeeling, to perform like a machine', this is ironic. And there is doubt that cyborgs could ever be attracted to other cyborgs. Still, Shira hints that her animal side is in some sense also inferior, 'messy and biological'. Since human–non-human interactions are the central theme, this is more science fiction than dystopia by the criteria discussed in Chapter 5. The machines have not done badly in the comparison, however, and perhaps better than the humans. It is possible to create one which might love us as we want to be loved. Yet, of course, this is also simply an exercise in narcissistic solipsism. So the story closes with the suggestion that it is 'better to make people into partial machines than to create machines that feel and are yet still controlled like cleaning robots'.[67] It seems a resigned rather than a healthy choice.

The Nazi victory novel of the 1930s and 1940s made a reappearance as alternative history in Robert Harris' best-selling novel *Fatherland* (1992) (F). Set in 1964, it is a not implausible historical projection in which the Nazis win World War II in Europe and Russia and make peace with the United States. (Britain's Queen flees to Canada with Churchill.) It is told through the eyes of a detective, Xavier March, investigating the murder of a leading architect of the Holocaust, Josef Buhler, who has 'the face of a machine man'. The novel describes the continuation of the war against American-backed Soviet guerrillas, and ongoing 'terrorism' against the Third Reich. Hitler, Goebbels, Heydrich, and other leading

---

[66] Ibid., pp. 33, 35–6, 44, 48, 50, 73, 80–1, 93, 95, 98, 105, 111, 121, 125, 155.
[67] Ibid., pp. 168, 176–7, 204, 248, 333, 338, 353, 364, 426, 442.

Nazis are still alive. The Nazis plough on, loving hatred and enjoining, 'Let the beast in man devour man.' A European Union, created by Germany, exists, where everyone speaks German as a second language. But Xavier March is a sceptic who makes jokes about the Party. As the novel progresses, the murder mystery unfolds. It concerns covering up the 'final solution', the execution of which is accurately detailed. Xavier is betrayed by his son, a model Hitler Youth. This is not a dystopia in the sense of a society we wish to avoid, but rather one we perhaps only narrowly escaped.[68]

But more likely disastrous futures were also lurking close by in this period. In P. D. James' *The Children of Men* (1992) (F), mass infertility is the central theme, as the earth's population verges on extinction—seen through the eyes of an Oxford don. In the mid-1990s the sperm count starts to drop dramatically. The last human being is born in 1995, and dies in a pub brawl in 2021. The last generation born in England, the spoilt, arrogant, cruel, and violent 'Omegas', enjoy varied privileges, but are ruled by a despot, the narrator's cousin, Xan Lyppiatt, whose ideology is nonetheless egalitarian. Guest workers called Sojourners are imported, then expelled at the age of sixty, the same age most face euthanasia. Suicides are common, and depression grips much of the population. Groups of flagellants expiate their sins publicly. Some women demonstrate the psychological strain by wheeling dolls in prams, and feigning pregnancy. Criminals are sent to the Isle of Man where many starve or are tortured by vicious gangs. Slowly the population congregates in towns to conserve power and public services. The plot revolves around a group of Christian pro-democratic dissidents called the Five Fishes, one of whom bears a boy seemingly fated to become the country's future leader. The dictator arrives to seize the child, 'the hope of the world'. But the narrator kills him, assumes his powers, and in the last line baptises the child, underscoring the Christian religious subtext.[69]

Religion also comes to the fore in Octavia E. Butler's *The Parable of the Sower* (1993), which is on the border of dystopia, young adult fiction, and science fiction, with some New Age philosophy thrown in. Los Angeles in 2024–7 is disintegrating into widespread violence. The sixteen-year-old narrator, Lauren Olamina, has 'hyperempathy', which heightens her sense of feelings in others. Sceptical about Christianity, she invents a religion called Earthseed, which consists chiefly in bland platitudes (the 'destiny of Earthseed is to take root among the stars', 'God is Change', which is endlessly repeated). She is poor, and lives in a walled town surrounded by drug users, drunkards, and the homeless, who are sometimes eaten by dogs. The heavily armed town dwellers associate in tight-knit groups, often based on race, and avoid 'outsiders'. Old hates and new combine to increase enmity. Wild roving mobs with painted faces burn down entire communities.

---

[68] Robert Harris, *Fatherland* (Hutchinson, 1992), pp. 3, 5, 17, 22, 24, 28, 30, 37, 39, 46, 48, 74, 83, 203–4, 333. Josef Bühler (1904–48) was a real person.

[69] P. D. James, *The Children of Men* (Faber & Faber, 1992), pp. 3–4, 7–10, 33, 46, 61, 69, 89, 98, 114, 143, 146, 177, 184, 226, 230, 235–9. James (1920–2014) was an active Anglican. On her work see Norma Siebenheller, *P. D. James* (Ungar, 1981) and Richard B. Gidez, *P. D. James* (Twayne, 1986).

Cruelty, meaningless torture, and mutilation are common. The police and fire departments charge fees for their services, so many don't use them. Companies are beginning to manage some cities. Yet there are still missions to Mars, and radios, TVs, and computers. For the unskilled who can find work, debt slavery is common. The rich still live well, and have private armies of well-armed security guards. Epidemics, droughts and tornados, and rising sea levels indicate the advance of global warming. The protagonists feel they cannot change the state of society, and consider survivalism (an increasingly dominant American motif in this period), retreating from the city to live off the land. When their 'island community, fragile, and yet a fortress' is finally assaulted and burnt out, they flee. An earthquake adds to the chaos. Cannibalism occurs. 'A group is strong', Lauren insists. Hers finally reaches sanctuary in the far north of California, and begins to eke out a subsistence life.[70]

Similar locations form the backdrop to William Gibson's *Virtual Light* (1993), usually classified in style as cyberpunk (high-tech/low-life dystopia). It takes place in 2006 in the San Francisco Bay area after an earthquake. Powerful corporations enrich a small monopolistic elite who have privatized almost everything, including the formerly public parks. Here, and in other countries, larger unities have disintegrated into smaller, and there are many more countries in the world. The middle class has nearly disappeared, at least here. The marginalized majority make do with deteriorating social and economic conditions, crime and violence, and the occasional pandemic. There have been civil wars in Europe. AIDS continues rampant. There are strange sects, like the First Church of Jesus, Survivalist. The dystopian elements are an everyday background of tired normality like bad weather, to be suffered rather than resisted. Interspersed with several other plots, the main story revolves around a juvenile centre runaway turned bicycle messenger named Chevette, who steals a pair of virtual light glasses which contain valuable plans to rebuild the city using nanotechnology. Suspected of murder, she is captured by two Russian policeman, but is rescued by a private detective with whom she becomes involved.[71]

The corporate dystopia is also at the heart of David Foster Wallace's massive tome, *Infinite Jest* (1996), set in a future united American superstate incorporating the United States, Canada, and Mexico. Companies are so powerful that they name years after their products ('the Year of the Whopper'). A large part of the north-eastern United States and south-eastern Canada has been set aside for storing hazardous waste. The narrative takes place chiefly at a tennis academy, and centres on the retrieval of a film, *Infinite Jest*, which is so mesmerizing that people die because they do nothing else than view it. The cast of characters here and in a

[70] Octavia E. Butler, *The Parable of the Sower* (1993; The Women's Press, 1995), pp. 8, 14, 17, 39, 47, 51, 64, 71, 77, 95, 102, 109, 124–5, 142, 192, 250, 268, 276, 285. On Butler as a dystopian writer see Hoda Zaki, 'Utopia, Dystopia, and Ideology in the Science Fiction of Octavia Butler', *Science-Fiction Studies* 17 (1990), 239–51.

[71] William Gibson, *Virtual Light* (Penguin, 1993), pp. 35, 47, 71–2, 112–13, 123, 125, 181, 222, 230, 239, 249. Studies of Gibson include Lance Olsen, *William Gibson* (Borgo Press, 1992) and Dani Cavallaro, *Cyberpunk and Cyberculture: Science Fiction and the Work of William Gibson* (Athlone Press, 2000).

substance abuse recovery centre is frighteningly large, and the reader is virtually flooded in the minutiae of their personal everyday lives and their intricately wacky psychological contortions, drug habits, sex lives, and devotion to 'maximum pleasure'. The dystopian element here is consequently submerged if not drowned in this veritable tsunami of detail and stream-of-consciousness prose in ten-page paragraphs, most of which is recognisably here and now, albeit weirder.[72]

Much more plausible is the vision unfolded in Maggie Gee's 1998 novel, *The Ice People*, usually described as a work of science fiction, though its central theme is entirely realistic. Here global warming has reversed, producing an ice age in which the world's population is much reduced and life expectancy drops dramatically. (Evidently 10–12,000-year warming periods not uncommonly precede ice ages of 100,000 years or more.) Scarcity predominates. The narrator, Saul, a mixed-race man of sixty, born in 2005, just as the Tropical Time is beginning, recalls his past. Sea levels are rising, and the army is required to stem the flow of immigrants. In the 2020s the world's population is 8 billion, and plague has engendered civil disorder and the collapse of governments, affecting the poor much more than the rich, who are protected by private contractors. Identities shift: the genders move apart, and each closer to its own members, partly to dispel loneliness, partly because of growing resentment of the other gender. As groupism advances, each begins to adopt a uniform to mark its distinctiveness. Sex becomes less frequent, and fertility drops, leading to more gender hatred. The trajectory of technological improvement produces home robots called Doves who do the cleaning, say 'I love you', and have sex with men. Soon able to reproduce themselves, they mutate, and begin to eat cats and attack babies. Then, in only twenty years, a new ice age commences, the temperature dropping by 1–2° a year. Little can be done to prevent it; there was 'no money for science, or support, or time'. In Britain, feminist 'Wicca' leaders promote resistance to the Doves, whom the men defend, forming a 'Manguard' resistance group. A massive volcanic eruption hastens the cooling process, and forces migration southwards. Some African countries refuse to admit European 'ice people'—those who were so icy to them for the last thousand years: 'Serve them right.' Here the narrator's origins give him an edge. Kidnapping his son from his estranged wife, whose Wicca group feeds him oestrogen to feminize him, he attempts vainly to reach this haven.[73]

Our Present Discontents: 2000 and After

A trilogy of dystopias in the new century confirmed Margaret Atwood's position as the premier writer in this field. *Oryx and Crake* (2003) and its prequel, *The Year of*

---

[72] David Foster Wallace, *Infinite Jest* (Little, Brown & Co., 1996), pp. 58–9, 90, 126, 223, 318–19, 382–6, 424. On Wallace see Marshall Boswell and Stephen Burn, eds., *A Companion to David Foster Wallace Studies* (Palgrave Macmillan, 2013).

[73] Maggie Gee, *The Ice People* (Richard Cohen Books, 1998), pp. 3, 6–7, 11–12, 25, 28, 40, 46, 57, 66, 69, 75, 83, 94, 100, 102, 104, 106–9, 111, 115, 119–22, 136, 146, 164, 222, 234, 241. On Gee see Mine Özyurt Kiliç, *Maggie Gee: Writing the Condition of England Novel* (Bloomsbury Academic, 2013).

the Flood (2009) both portray a world where a new wonder drug called BlyssPluss, designed to protect against all STDs, provide unlimited libido and sexual prowess, and prolong youth, has caused a global epidemic, the 'waterless flood'. This was followed by *MaddAddam* (2013), which gave its name to the trilogy.

Modelled in part on *Brave New World*, *Oryx and Crake* projects the scenarios of corporate dictatorship, global warming, and collapsing civilization fifty years into the future. This is identifiably still North America, with high school drug problems, computer gaming, live executions on the Internet, a euthanasia website, and pornography aplenty. Life in the walled corporate compounds is reasonably prosperous, with air purifiers and microclimate management, though travel permits are required to move about. In the pleeblands or cities security is poor and crime rife. There are science fiction components here, including human organs grown in animals (already underway); the evolution of women into different mating patterns (they turn blue when ready); talking toasters and shoes that change colour to match clothes; and solar cars and ray guns. The Crakers are clones, programmed to die at thirty, but capable of reproducing themselves. But the more familiar plagues, famines, droughts, floods, and wars result chiefly from overpopulation. By the conclusion this world is falling apart, instigated in part by a plague introduced by a drug company.[74]

Sustaining her insistence on realism, Atwood describes *The Year of the Flood* as 'fiction, but the general tendencies and many of the details in it are alarmingly close to fact'. Set before this disaster, a corporate dictatorship governs, and focuses on inventing new species and selling new drugs. News is controlled by the media Corps, though the Internet still functions. The 'pleebs' are often gang-ridden, run-down slums, though there is a middle class here too. The 'affluents', mostly scientists and corporation workers, live in luxurious gated corporate compounds. A powerful and corrupt police force, CorpSeCorps, monopolizes new weapons, even turning bees into spy drones, supervises the army, and disarms most of the population. It also encourages denunciations. But the corporations don't impose 'overt totalitarian rule' because it would ruin their image. Various small cult-like groups oppose them, but ineffectually, though some, like the survivalist Gardeners joined by the narrator of 'Flood', have utopic qualities in their 'ultra-green' dedication to preserving the environment. The world is headed towards destruction owing to overpopulation, resource depletion, and global warming before the epidemic commences. Genetic modification is a central theme here, along with environmental collapse. A variety of monsters are created as substitutes for or improvements on extinct species. This world verges on being both post-animal and post-human.[75]

MaddAddam is described on the Atwood principle as a work of fiction which 'does not include any technologies or biobeings that do not already exist, are not under construction, or are not possible in theory'. It is the location of an enclave of

[74] Margaret Atwood, *Oryx and Crake* (Bloomsbury, 2003), pp. 24, 27, 120, 196, 250, 258, 279, 291, 302, 340.
[75] Margaret Atwood, *The Year of the Flood* (Bloomsbury, 2009), p. 433.

flood survivors, the marooned good guys, bonded and bounded by 'groupthink walls'. Outside rove the bad guys, cult-gangs like the Painballers, robbing and raping, along with many predator animals. But so do the 'brave new humans', the tender, purring, bewildered, flower-picking, leaf-eating Crakers, who have had aggression bred out of them, but with it, seemingly, much of their intelligence, leaving them 'walking potatoes'. They are the caricature of utopia's excesses: Crake 'thought he could perfect humanity'; others liken them to 'indigenous peoples', by contrast to the 'greedy, rapacious Conquistadors'. The pandemic buried in the BlyssPluss pills has killed almost everyone. There is not much humanity in what is left of humanity. Food, shelter, 'who and what to kill'—these are the basics. Foraging amongst the remnants of civilization is still possible. There are occasional flashbacks to pre-flood warnings of imminent Apocalypse, which compete on TV with live executions or suicides and kiddie porn for increasingly jaded, stupefied audiences. There are soul-savers too, though Atwood never gives them much credence, and parodies some as oil worshippers and global warming deniers. Even the eco-babblers are sent up to some degree here. Powerful corporations hack one another endlessly, eavesdrop on their own employees, run the press, and are busy 'bulldozing the planet flat and grabbing anything of real value'. Long flashbacks take us into the seedy pleebland shantytowns and gated Corps compounds of yore, the privatized public security, the pervasive gang violence. The present is deteriorating. As for the future—it might be worse. But a number of the MaddAddam women give birth to Craker hybrids, thus superior humans. This is the promise of new life.[76]

We return to counterfactual alternative history with Philip Roth's *The Plot against America* (2004), in which Franklin Delano Roosevelt loses the 1940 presidential election to the famed aviator and isolationist Charles Lindbergh, setting in motion a wave of anti-Semitism. (In 1940, the Republican candidate for president was, in fact, Wendell Willkie.) The plot covers only June 1940 to October 1942, seen through the eyes of Roth himself. Here Lindbergh wins by a barnstorming campaign, flying to the forty-eight states and hammering home an anti-war message. He gains key Jewish support from a rabbi who stresses that he is an '*American* Jew'. After Lindbergh wins, he meets Hitler in Iceland to offer assurances about American policy, then does the same with Japan. Soon the Roth family begins to encounter anti-Semitism. Then selected Jews, including Philip's father, are offered the 'once in a lifetime opportunity' to settle on farms in the American interior, as homesteaders, to 'enrich their Americanness', but really to dilute their influence, as non-Jews take their places. When the newspaper columnist Walter Winchell begins an anti-Lindbergh campaign, anti-Semitic agitators disrupt his meetings. Rioting targets Jewish neighbourhoods and shops in Detroit, where hundreds flee to Canada. Copycat riots follow elsewhere. Winchell is assassinated. Then Lindbergh flees to Germany, and the kidnapping of Lindbergh's infant son in 1932 is revealed to have been a Nazi plot to blackmail the father, who

[76] Margaret Atwood, *MaddAddam* (Bloomsbury, 2013), pp. 9, 14, 19–20, 26, 32, 43, 57–9, 69, 89, 98, 112–13, 117, 126, 131, 140, 247, 255, 342, 352, 377, 393.

was then forced to support America First while the son remained in Germany. Or so it is rumoured. In the event, the Nazis are defeated.[77]

More illustrative of the mainstream dystopian preoccupation with science, Kazuo Ishiguro's *Never Let Me Go* (2005) (F), set in the 1990s, is a much-acclaimed account of a boarding school, Hailsham, whose students are clones created for organ transplants. Told through the eyes of Kathy H., initially as adolescent recollections, and very young adult in tone and focus, we learn much of the personal lives and interactions of the students at the notional arts school. They are aware, through their Guardians, that they will give 'donations'. But there does not seem to be anything particular odd about the arrangement, except that they must remain exceptionally healthy. There is no inkling as to how all this came about, except that cloning began after 'the war' and the system is widely applauded as helping the majority to avoid many serious diseases. More extreme eugenic variants, such as creating 'superior' children, have been rejected. So by sacrificing one group for the rest by organ farming, the society is consensually dystopian.[78]

The issue of group identity is again central to Rupert Thomson's *Divided Kingdom* (2005). Britain's recent history has been defined by 'acquisition and celebrity ... envy, misery and greed'. The family declines. Violence and racism slowly degenerated into downright barbarism as habits of civility engrained over centuries dropped off. So the decision was taken to divide the country by psychological type into four colour-coded groups. The English are red, the colour associated with being sanguine and with blood; the Irish are yellow, associated with bile and being choleric; the Scots are green (phlegmatic, phlegm); and the Welsh blue (melancholic, black bile). (The scheme corresponds to Greek theories about character resulting from the absence or presence of these fluids in the body.) People cannot move from one area to another, and antagonism is nurtured; the 'new racism is psychological'. New loyalties are quickly built, based on the ideal of 'a new family' as 'a group of people who shared a psychological affinity', 'people who got on'. Some boys mix their blood together to affirm brotherhood for eternity. Others marry. Some who fail to integrate are mysteriously removed to unknown places.[79]

We follow a young boy who undergoes 'rearrangement' and moves to a new family in the 5 million-strong Red Zone. Riots and social unrest continue, but within a year the borders are sealed to prevent 'psychological contamination'. In all four quarters anyone suspected of 'undermining the fabric of society' can be imprisoned without trial for up to two years. Some years later, attending a conference in the Blue Quarter, renowned for its ecological awareness and opposition

---

[77] Philip Roth, *The Plot against America* (Jonathan Cape, 2004), pp. 3–5, 13–14, 30–1, 36, 53–4, 78, 83, 170, 174, 195, 204–5, 250, 254, 264–6, 272–3, 280, 309–13, 316, 321–6, 330. A film adaptation is reported in progress. On Roth see Steven Milowitz, *Philip Roth Considered: The Concentrationary Universe of the American Writer* (Routledge, 2000) and Timothy Parrish, *The Cambridge Companion to Philip Roth* (Cambridge University Press, 2007).

[78] Kazuo Ishiguro, *Never Let Me Go* (Faber & Faber, 2005), pp. 28, 63, 73, 140, 152, 189, 194, 239–41.

[79] Rupert Thomson, *Divided Kingdom* (Bloomsbury, 2005), pp. 5, 7–11, 14–15, 17, 19.

to violence, he breaks the rules and mixes with the locals. (When he wishes to return here, he worries about being charged with Article 58 of the Internal Security Act, 'undermining the state', a clear reference to Stalinism.) Increasingly his hopes are focused on the nomadic White People he meets. They have 'no concept of property or ownership' and are 'incapable of suspicion... sealed in an eternal condition of trust'. They are flawed utopian types, floating islands of cosmopolitanism in a world of extreme groupism, but illustrating a deviant inversion of sociability. Travelling with a woman, they encounter a group of football fans, who are 'like the divided kingdom in miniature—the same tribalism, the same need to belong'. We end with the thought that he and the woman may live together and have a child. Since this is not an overpopulation dystopia this is presumably not ironic.[80]

The new century has given rise to many overtly post-apocalyptic works. One of the most successful has been Cormac McCarthy's *The Road* (2006) (F). Defined by its sparse, stark, economical, transparent prose, the account follows the travels of a man and his son across a bleak and violated landscape following an unspecified disaster which has killed most of the population (apparently a nuclear war, followed by epidemics). Ruined houses, corpses, decay, and grey ash are everywhere. The book is a political dystopia only insofar as the social relations of substantial groups play a role. Most survivors are armed, some only with spears. Some groups of 'bad guys' have slaves who are harnessed to draw wagons. Some are cannibals. All are slowly reverting to animality; one man they encounter after seeing no one for a year has 'reptilian calculations' in his 'cold and shifting eyes'. 'Phantoms not heard from in a thousand years' loom into consciousness as terror and paranoia become all-consuming. The struggle for food predominates here. People have become 'the walking dead in a horror film'. Only their dreams are pleasant, resplendent with long lost treasures. Yet these too are interspersed with nightmares. When they discover a stock of food, 'the richness of a vanished world', matters improve. Then the father dies. But the boy finds another family and lives on.[81]

In similar post-apocalyptic vision, Jim Crace's *The Pesthouse* (2007), set in an indeterminate future in America, we again get little sense of how civilization collapsed. A group of refugees heads eastwards, mostly on foot, some with horses and carts, with little food, robbed by bandits, in a kind of conquest of the west in reverse. There are rumours of naked cannibals, ugly dwarves, monstrous animals, impenetrable swamps and forests to be encountered, the primordial dystopian nightmare, in other words. Two brothers, Franklin and Jackson, reach the Pesthouse, a respite for the sick, where Franklin meets a woman, Margaret. As they move on, disease, hunger, slavery, fear, and hostility are omnipresent. They fantasize about reaching the sea, and taking a ship somewhere—but where? Margaret encounters a

---

[80] Ibid., pp. 24, 28, 31, 36, 38, 47, 60, 65, 112, 125, 130, 151–2, 168, 174, 183, 192, 196, 213, 236, 242–5, 263, 274, 283, 297–8, 375, 305, 317, 335, 346, 379, 382–4, 395.

[81] Cormac McCarthy, *The Road* (Picador, 2006), pp. 45, 47, 52, 56, 64, 78, 98, 111, 117, 181, 194, 237–8. On McCarthy see Steven Frye, *Understanding Cormac McCarthy* (University of South Carolina Press, 2009) and Steven Frye, ed., *The Cambridge Companion to Cormac McCarthy* (Cambridge University Press, 2013).

group of 'Finger Baptists' who dwell in the 'Ark' community and reject metal as the cause of greed and war. Franklin and Margaret reach the ocean and see a sailing ship, but fear piracy, mutinies, disease, disaster. Various ships ply the seas, and emigrants are offered free passage in exchange for a year's free work, as was the case centuries earlier. Just why life should be better overseas we do not learn. So they turn westwards, and return to the Pesthouse where, after a fashion, they are free.[82]

The causes of dystopian catastrophe are much more clearly outlined in Alex Scarrow's *Last Light* (2007), set in 1999, which portrays Britain starved of oil after disorder in the Middle East interrupts supplies. With terrorist threats to boot, civil society unravels remarkably quickly, people becoming aggressive, menacing, and violent simply in the face of supermarket shortages. Within days normality disappears in the midst of riots, plunder, and rape, and a general decline into savagery. There are limited nuclear wars involving China, Russia, and India over oil fields. The author's antidote is a world 'less greedy; less obsessed with having things; trinkets and baubles, gadgets and bling'.[83]

A mixture of biting anti-evangelical social satire and global warming dystopia, Ben Elton's *Blind Faith* (2007) foresees a future fifty years after much of the world has been submerged. The population, led by The Temple, have turned against science and reverted to an updated and now mandatory Christian faith. An Inquisition arrests people for incitement to religious hatred. Privacy has become 'a blasphemy' since 'only perverts do things in private'. Vaccination and abortion are illegal. But public nudity is common, and women in particular are hypersexualized, with immense social pressure for breast enlargement and having many sexual partners. Most TV programmes are pornographic. A law is also passed making everyone famous. Much of this appears to be the natural effect of mass society. A leading character exclaims: 'I hate people. Well, I hate most of them anyway. And I hate all of them when they're in a crowd.' The heroic opposition here are the Humanists, who promote scepticism and Darwinism. Most are killed at the end of the novel.[84]

Proving the resilience of the subgenre, C. J. Sansom's *Dominion* (2012) is one of the most recent of alternative history 'if Hitler won' novels. Britain has been defeated in 1940, and in 1952 the prime minister is Lord Beaverbrook, the right-wing tabloid press baron, who owns half the country's newspapers, and leads a coalition which includes the Home Secretary Mosley's fascists. Enoch Powell is Minister for India, which seethes with rebellion. War with the USSR continues, with 5 million Germans dead and no end in sight. East of the Volga the communists share power with other parties, including capitalists, but fight on. Stalin has been captured. Hitler is virtually disabled with Parkinson's disease, then dies of a

[82] Jim Crace, *The Pesthouse* (Picador, 2007), pp. 9, 25, 43, 124, 142–4, 147, 184, 192, 196, 213–14, 224–5, 245–7, 267, 285, 309. On Crace see Philip Tew, *Jim Crace* (Manchester University Press, 2006).
[83] Alex Scarrow, *Last Light* (Orion, 2007), pp. 25, 137, 143, 397–8.
[84] Ben Elton, *Blind Faith* (Bantam Press, 2007), pp. 23, 31, 35, 98, 108, 154, 168, 317, 320.

heart attack. British Jews are forced to wear the yellow star, then are arrested and moved to camps outside the cities, with plans to send them to Eastern Europe. The police are already greedily eying their possessions. In 'the right set of circumstances' many Britons have become fascists (some Scottish nationalists are sympathizers), and life goes on much as before. Germany does not rule Britain as such, occupying only the Isle of Wight. Senate House at the University of London is their embassy, with the Gestapo housed in the basement, and Rommel as ambassador. There is TV and rock and roll, but feminism has not advanced. An isolationist United States is still ahead of Germany in nuclear weapons research, which figures centrally in the plot. There is a resistance movement, and Churchill returns to power. Beaverbrook's newspaper empire is broken up, and Russia becomes a corrupt capitalist state.[85]

Corporate totalitarianism in the digital age defines one of the most stimulating of recent dystopias, Dave Eggers' *The Circle* (2013). Set in a crumbling present, it focuses upon the not implausible development of thumb-sized portable camera technology called SeeChange by a Google-like company named the Circle, which has already ended internet anonymity. Seen through the eyes of a young executive, Mae Holland, this project both takes up the age-old utopian bid for total transparency and the later modern narcissistic obsession with documenting every movement in our lives, the Facebook, Twitter, and selfie culture. Described here as an answer to crime and immorality generally, SeeChange may potentially eliminate all secrecy and privacy. 'All that happens must be known' becomes the slogan of the Second Enlightenment. There are also plans to develop tracker chips to implant in children, to produce 'an age without worry' for parents. Inside the company everything is monitored, producing a dizzying volume of digital contact and information about everyone, not just to monetize the information (which is described critically), but for its own sake (hinting at an anti-utopian dystopia).[86]

Eggers' satire on the corporate ethos is telling. Everyone is encouraged to be happy, to like, to hug, to feel constantly a part of the 'Circle community', to document digitally virtually their entire lives— recording everything, by corporate mandate deleting nothing—all of which contributes to their ratings and corporate assessment. Total commitment and complete integration into the Circle is mandatory. A US Congresswoman readily adopts SeeChange in the name of transparency, and other politicians follow. As the cameras proliferate outdoors their crime-reducing qualities also become more obvious. Indoors, their ability to reduce anti-social behaviour is mooted. If we were all watched, a Circle executive contends, 'we would lead to a more moral way of life'. In 'a world where bad choices are no longer an option, we have no choice *but* to be good', putting us on the road to 'perfectibility'. As Mae is sucked into this world, a friend objects that she is becoming 'socially autistic', that 'a world of ever-present daylight . . . will burn us all alive', but vainly. Instead, Mae accepts the view that 'secrets are lies', that 'sharing is caring', that 'privacy is theft'. The world rapidly starts becoming 'transparent' as the Circle aims at 'Completion'. But then the

[85] C. J. Sansom, *Dominion* (Mantle, 2012), pp. 1, 5, 9, 13, 15, 18, 21, 24, 27, 34, 43, 67, 80, 86, 93, 101, 138, 164, 201, 239, 247, 255, 336, 382, 470, 563–7.
[86] Dave Eggers, *The Circle* (Hamish Hamilton, 2013), pp. 21, 30, 62, 65–7, 90, 96–7.

consequences of transparency begin to show: embarrassing intimacies, crimes not prevented, skeletons in family closets, when history becomes digitized. An inventor of the system now warns us that 'Completion' is 'a totalitarian nightmare', that Demoxie, internet-driven participatory 'democracy', is mere 'mob rule'. Here, then, is the near-immediate future as dystopia—or is it utopia? Either way it feels ominously and unstoppably imminent.[87]

While we have generally avoided pure futurology here, a persuasive blend of fact and fiction, Naomi Oreskes and Erik M. Conway's *The Collapse of Western Civilization: A View from the Future* (2014) merits mention. This assumes the shape of a commentary by a future historian on the twenty-first century's incapacity to understand and react to threats of environmental catastrophe. Blinded by an obsession with 'free markets', or what is termed 'market fundamentalism', driven by those who profit by fossil fuel consumption, the world enters a stage called the 'Great Collapse and Mass Migration', which lasts from 2073 to 2093. Many coastal nations, including the Netherlands, are largely submerged. The accumulation of carbon dioxide and the resulting global warming had been well understood scientifically beforehand. But climate change deniers neutralized this message. The actual reduction of greenhouse gas emissions and population growth was led by China, but not followed by others, as ignorance and belligerent denial triumph over common sense. Scientists are actually prosecuted for suggesting imminent threats. By 2040 temperatures have risen by nearly 4° C—well above sustainable levels (but in keeping with many predictions in 2016). Unprecedented heat waves destroy crops worldwide, producing panic, mass migration, unparalleled growth in insect populations, and widespread social disorder and political breakdown. Sea level rises of eight metres produce a 20 per cent movement in world population. A second Black Death kills half of Europe. Global temperature rises of 11° then kill off the inhabitants of Africa and Australia. But China successfully relocates 250 million people to higher ground, thanks to an interventionist governmental strategy which makes neo-liberal ideas of laissez-faire seem suicidal.[88]

* * * *

THEMATIC SYNOPSIS

While its thematic breadth makes generalization difficult, several salient trends are discernible in late twentieth- and early twenty-first-century literary dystopian writing. Most obvious is the shift from a concentration on political collectivism to that of the impact of technology, population growth, and environmental degradation. The more realistic narratives begin with nuclear war in the 1950s

[87] Ibid., pp. 98–100, 108, 124, 134, 178–9, 204, 208, 238, 240, 261–2, 280, 284–91, 297, 301–3, 311, 329, 366–7, 392, 431–2, 439–40, 459, 481, 483. On Eggers see Timothy W. Galow, *Understanding Dave Eggers* (University of South Carolina Press, 2014).
[88] Naomi Oreskes and Erik M. Conway, *The Collapse of Western Civilization: A View from the Future* (Columbia University Press, 2014), pp. ix, 2–6, 12, 24–5, 30–3, 35–6, 51–2.

and move through overpopulation to environmental collapse in the 2000s. In most cases these dangers do not produce the great worry of the twentieth century: totalitarian dictatorship. Instead, centralized states are increasingly depicted as destroyed by neo-liberal ideological assaults. They allow the wealthy to retreat into enclaves, leaving most of humanity to their unfortunate fate (one shared in many late nineteenth-century texts). Selfishness, viciousness, violence, scarcity for the many, but bare, breadline survival for the few, define the future. The plutocratic dystopia edges ahead of its collectivist counterpart.

Two attributes of the later dystopian novel diminish confrontations with the reality of these threats. While our concerns here have been chiefly with more plausible texts, or occasionally the realistic wing of dystopian science fiction, the latter has occasioned a deflection from the central political themes of the 1930s and 1940s by displacing our focus onto extreme fantasy. We worry less about poverty depicted on Mars than in Detroit. Here we see the relevance of the Atwood principle: realism is meant to bring these problems home rather than to estrange us further from them.

Secondly, while dystopian novels as fiction necessarily deal with individuals, characters, and relationships with whom we are supposed to identify, they are often overly zealous in their insistence on the necessity for happy endings, imagining deviant rebels who beat the system, implausibly rescuing their central characters, and providing 'hope' in the persistence of utopian enclaves, the birth of children, and the like. This tendency, however, diminishes in recent decades with an increasing trend towards post-apocalyptic despair and away from 'critical dystopia'. Combined with increasingly experimental styles, and a much richer sense of character, these factors have diminished the political content of many later novels while encouraging their flourishing as a richer literary genre than ever before. From the 1990s, then, dystopias are often less concerned with how plutocratic or collectivist regimes emerge and function, and more focused on how the Apocalypse feels, and whether it brings out our better or (as commonly) our less desirable attributes, both individually, when the monsters within are released, and in the groups which increasingly dominate us. A concern with the latter, as we have seen, and the loss or destruction of our individuality, remains a central element gluing together the historical, sociological, and literary emanations of dystopia. Until there are no more groups, group identity remains at the core of the dystopian problematic.

Continuity with nineteenth- and early twentieth-century texts exists in other areas. The concern with machines and their increasing domination of humanity centrally shared by both science fiction and dystopia results in a growing focus on the human/machine identity spectrum. The human–machine interface is quintessentially what Patricia Warrick has called 'the transforming relationship of the twentieth century'.[89] We began this chapter by looking at B. F. Skinner's modifications of Huxley's assumptions about controlling behaviour through

---

[89] Patricia Warrick, 'The Man–Machine Intelligence Relationship', in Thomas Clareson, ed., *Many Futures Many Worlds: Theme and Form in Science Fiction* (Kent State University Press, 1977), p. 184.

psychological engineering. The many critics of this approach echoed much earlier concerns, expressed by Samuel Butler among others, about the reshaping of human consciousness and the dangers of various forms of estrangement through contact with machines. The freedom not to be increasingly driven by mechanical ideas of efficiency weds Victorian with anti-collectivist and later modern concerns. The propensity for technology to render social relations increasingly transparent equally links both traditional dystopian concerns with concentration on surveillance, and the Internet, and modern techniques of observing and monitoring individuals. Critics still regard the imitation of machines as implying uniformity, standardization, enforced efficiency, power worship, identity with if not enslavement to machines themselves, and the loss of or alienation from some fundamental human essence as well as freedom. We are Fordified, Taylorized, and processed like chunks of data, until we feel like mere cogs in a gigantic social machine, cells in the glass and concrete hive, ants in the swarm. Anti-collectivist authors posed a 'humanist' standpoint to critically defend the value of individuality in face of the absolute transparency and universal supervision of totalitarianism. Increasingly, the same perspective was offered to identify quintessential qualities which differentiate humans from machines, or from mixtures of both, now also by contrast with new regimes of universal observation and monitoring. For the religiously minded, the existence of a 'soul' is central here. To secularists, human dignity sometimes works as a substitute.

More novel is the increasingly central role played by gender from the 1980s and after, in the form of both claims of right, queries about the identities of masculinity and femininity, and statements of historical oppression. Enslavement to corporate dictatorships, however, seems to differ little from that to the collectivist state, notwithstanding the former's consumerist ideology of freedom and choice. The mediocrity, relentless egalitarianism, and mindless conformity of late capitalism, too, seems at some levels little superior to more direct forms of traditional oppression. Submitting to the dictates of technology and the ethos of efficiency seemingly leaves us with as little free will as historical necessity or racial destiny ever permitted. If the choice is between Skinnerian behavioural manipulation and the preservation of a God-given freedom to do evil (Burgess), we can only despair. Yet mass poverty and neglect are, nonetheless, still superior to carcerotopia, if only because we may still retain the semblance of private humanity and sociability.

But let us let the machine have the last word. The most important dystopian trend lies in the depiction of scientific and technical advancement, as what was once science fiction becomes increasingly viable. The twentieth century became the age of robotics, cyborgs, organ replacement, the mechanical substitution of limbs and other physical bodily components, and genetically modified implantations, and the androidist blurring of human–machine boundaries. The twenty-first century will probably witness the creation of the first post-human generation of people. Despite the promise of longevity and health implied here, many later authors are indisputably wary about these developments. We come to see the machine as the ideal, perfected human, and anything less as inferior. Robots who obey Asimov's three laws of robotics appear 'incapable of harming humans, incapable of tyranny, of corruption, or stupidity, or prejudice'.[90] This implies—vis-à-vis Skinner—that 'consciousness' and 'free will' are less valuable than moral behaviour. But humans cannot perform at these levels, or exhibit so much virtue. We have seen what demanding perfect workers and selfless comrades entails. And if enhanced sociability, the more close-knit community, is a central aim of utopianism, the perfect human machine, the robot, stands as the asocial symbol par excellence of human alienation in a technological society. Robots don't chat, don't socialize, don't express emotional warmth and mutual sustenance. They don't 'think'. (Do they?) They cannot love, or hate, or mate.[91] (Yet.) They are surprisingly like totalitarian citizens, as we have seen, isolated, mute, obedient. As automatons they do not freely choose their behaviour. They do what they are programmed to do. But so do Skinner's pigeon-citizens . . .

APPENDIX: A FEW WORDS ON FILM

Dystopia and cinema are a marriage made in Heaven, for both are in love with high drama, exaggeration, and special effects. As a medium, however, film differs from written narrative, both fictional and otherwise, in many ways.[92] Its purpose—documentaries aside—is primarily entertainment rather than edification. By definition, plot and character are secondary to action and visual effect. We may be willing to learn something from a novel. Preaching in a film destroys the effect. The moral to the story may be a blunt and unpleasant one, but we cannot dally long explaining why. The feel-good impulse often demands a simplified version of life: black and white, valiant heroes and despicable villains, and the exoneration of our ideals, usually, when portrayed by Hollywood, the American Way of Life, preferably in Los Angeles, and a happy ending, boy meets (robot) girl, with some humour, suspense, drama, and fear stirred in. And then action, movement, noise, massed symbols of power: guns, airplanes, helicopters, aircraft carriers, missiles, more and bigger guns, blood, explosions, car chases, sweat, tears, still more and still bigger guns. Much of this involves that cult of violence and sadism which Orwell had already deplored in the early 1940s, but which, thanks to an inured population jaded by computer gaming, has become vastly gorier. In dystopia, sometimes, there is no happy ending: perhaps LA is destroyed (*Escape from Los Angeles*). Yet we still arise, brush off the popcorn, feeling relieved: this can't happen here. So our anxieties are purged for the moment.

[90] Susan Calvin, quoted in Patricia S. Warrick, *The Cybernetic Imagination in Science Fiction* (MIT Press, 1980), p. 66.

[91] Some novels do portray them as more moral than people, however: in Jack Williamson's *The Humanoids* (Science Fiction Club, 1953) they prevent scientists from developing more destructive weapons.

[92] Two recent surveys here are Artur Blaim and Ludmiła Gruzsewska-Blaim, eds., *Imperfect Worlds and Dystopian Narratives in Contemporary Cinema* (Peter Lang, 2011), and Artur Blaim and Ludmiła Gruzsewska-Blaim, eds., *Mediated Utopias: From Literature to Cinema* (Peter Lang, 2015). These include analyses of virtually every major film based on dystopian novels, including many not discussed here.

Nowadays, however, film is, for many, the primary entry point into dystopia. So a very brief survey of the cinematic encounter with dystopia is better than none at all. As with literature, we must here exclude science fiction, the most popular of all modern cinematic genres, in favour of more realistic projections into the future. So out go aliens, zombies, and monsters, and the whole range of superheroes from Batman and Superman to Iron Man. Out goes space, the 'final frontier', in the memorable words of the *Star Trek* series, the 'Wagon Train to the stars', extending the imperial western frontier motif, yet often acknowledging, in the launching of earth's problems into orbit, the failure to solve them here. So having wrecked one country/planet, we go on to steal someone else's. Nor can we discuss the extraordinarily popular subgenre of young adult dystopian film adaptations. (Here *The Hunger Games* trilogy, portraying twenty-four young adults are chosen annually as 'tributes' from each district of a state called Panem to fight in gladiatorial combat to the death on commercially sponsored TV, is an outstanding example. A large proportion of these films is simply violence, with a sharp contrast presented between high-tech video game management and primitivist survivalism.)[93] But robots and environmental catastrophe, nuclear war and mechanized worlds, remain our concern.

The more serious instances of the genre tend to be literary adaptations. We have noted in this chapter many such attempts, including *Brave New World* (1990, 1998, the former superior) and *Nineteen Eighty-Four* (1956, wooden but still viewable, 1984, superb). (A fine satire is Terry Gilliam's *Brazil* (1985).) From at least Fritz Lang's film noir classic *Metropolis* (1927), many of the leading nineteenth-century dystopian themes have come together in film. Here we have a robot, Maria, the great towering modern city of skyscrapers, the romance between a wealthy man and a poor woman, the warning of the revolt of the teeming masses living underground, who through Maria vow 'Death to the machines!'[94] The interwar future war scenario is ingeniously represented in the adaptation of H. G. Wells' ideas in *Things to Come* (1936), which traces a long history (1940–2036) in which much of the world's population is killed or dies of disease. Amongst Hollywood's braver (and more successful) efforts in the period, *On the Beach* (1958), presents a plausible post-nuclear war scenario, with the lines, 'There is hope, there's always hope' ironically offered as the prospect of the complete annihilation of humanity looms. (The nuclear war theme is satirized brilliantly in *Dr. Strangelove* (1964)). *City of Ember* (2008) illustrates the post-Apocalypse underground survivor scenario. There are a few more narrowly political dystopias later in this period, such as the Orwellian *V for Vendetta* (2005), based on a 1988 novel, and portraying resistance to a future British police state. Amongst the overpopulation novels to be dramatized, *Logan's Run* (1976), set in 2274, is one of the best-known portrayals of resistance to mandatory euthanasia at age thirty. *Fortress* (1992) depicts a future mandatory one-child society where a couple rebels.

---

[93] Thematic variations include *Rollerball* (1978), set in a corporate-dominated world in 2018, *The Running Man* (1987), and *Death Race 2000* (1975).

[94] Thea von Harbou, *Metropolis* (1929; Gregg Press, 1975), p. 179.

The Island (2005) concentrates on the themes of cloning and organ-harvesting. (Wells' *The Island of Doctor Moreau* was the subject of a 1996 film.) *Gattaca* (1997) similarly explores the idea of genetic engineering to create an 'invalid' menial class. In *Repo Men* (2010), artificial organs are reclaimed by those who fail to keep up their payments. Occasionally notable, daring, experimental films emerge not based on novels, like Jean-Luc Godard's *Alphaville* (1965), set in a futuristic dictatorship which seeks to abolish individualism by computerized mind control. In *THX 1138* (1971), too, George Lucas began his career as a director with the portrayal of a world where android police and emotion-suppressing drugs dominate the population. The complete inhibition of emotions is also a central theme in *Equilibrium* (2002), where books, music, and art are prohibited.

While aliens, for the time being, still count as science fiction, in 2016 robots are at the forefront in the science fiction/dystopian genres. *Blade Runner* (1982), we saw, portrays robots used to explore other planets, who revolt. Works like *I, Robot* (2004) and *Ex Machina* (2015) indicate growing alarm at the shrinking AI–human gap. Films like the *Terminator* series and *RoboCop* move such themes further into the science fiction genre, but often return to the Frankenstein motif (creature rebels against creator).

Equal success, too, has been achieved with environmental catastrophe. *The Day after Tomorrow* (2004) introduces a serious and well-argued global warming/cooling narrative succeeded by spectacular special effects and a hopelessly improbable plot, topped with the mandatory message of hope, that mankind might well survive a new ice age. The film *2012* (2009) follows a similar scenario, with arks provided to rescue the super-rich. *Snowpiercer* (2013) imagines a train carrying rich and poor survivors across a frozen globe. Extermination by viruses is the theme of *Æon Flux* (2005), set in the twenty-fifth century, where an oppressive 'perfect society' is also featured. In *I am Legend* (2007) a supposed cure for cancer wipes out the world. But these are the tip of the (melting) iceberg, so to speak; hundreds more might be instanced.

Considering the centrality of the genre, however, it might be contended that Hollywood has done scant justice to much of the dystopian scenario outlined in this book. Art has failed life miserably. Disaster films are easily made and readily lend themselves to those forms of computer-generated imaging which make audiences gasp. *Schindler's List* is depressingly realistic, but sanitized. But until *Son of Saul* (2015) there was, for a long time, at least in English, no film of a gas chamber being emptied in Auschwitz.[95] For Cambodia, *The Killing Fields* (1984) remains chilling, but again the documentary, *S21: The Khmer Rouge Killing Machine* (2003) is vastly more informative as to the horrors of Tuol Sleng. There is no classic film of Stalin's great purges of 1937–8. If the purpose of film is (usually) to allow hope to trump realism, these are—outside of documentaries—almost unfilmable subjects, for we know the ending will go badly. Nonetheless, students of dystopia should

---

[95] Yet even this brilliantly harrowing film, by the Hungarian filmmaker László Nemes, does not portray the victims actually being murdered within the gas chambers, or the horrors evident just after the doors were opened. Perhaps this proves it cannot be done.

watch Claude Lanzmann's riveting nine-hour Holocaust narrative, *Shoah*. They should also see Angus McQueen's excellent documentary *Gulag* (BBC, 1999).[96] Here film surpasses itself as a medium capable of clarifying the savagery of the twentieth century.

CONCLUSION TO PART III

The dystopian literary tradition is now some two centuries old. Born out of satire, it grew, by the 1890s, into an established means of confronting, promoting, and assailing the prospects of revolutionary social, political, and economic transformation. By 1900, a growing engagement with the impact of machinery upon all aspects of human existence, combined with scientific discovery, had also come to the fore as a central theme in the genre. Between 1917 and 1950, the spectres of Bolshevik and fascist totalitarianism agitated most dystopian authors. Yet warnings also appeared, most notably with Huxley, as to the potential for collectivism to adopt hedonistic strategies familiar to capitalist society, and possibly to emerge out of mass culture. Huxley brilliantly caricatured the deliberate, manipulative production of mass identity using the techniques of mass hypnosis as well as mass advertising to form personality as such. Both Huxley and Orwell juxtaposed the rational individual to the mass robotic creature of propagandistic suggestion and enforced imitation. Both, if in quite different ways, reinforced the idea that the mass or crowd was linked with dystopia in a number of ways, and flirted with the romantic individualist (or Stirnerian anarchist) postulate that dystopia is the rule of the group over the individual. From 1950 to the present, nuclear warfare, overpopulation, and the threat of the scientific and technological domination of mankind have come to define the ever-mutating and increasingly popular genre. Fears concerning extreme egalitarianism and collectivism retreated in the 1960s and 1970s. In an intermediary period they were replaced by a focus on overpopulation (Pohl/Kornbluth; Harrison; Burgess; Ehrlich; Mitchison). Thereafter, catastrophist scenarios mostly focused on climate change predominate.

A number of qualities distinguish the development of dystopian writing across this period. Firstly, perhaps the most marked discontinuity in the development of the genre is a relative disengagement with everyday politics which characterized so many later nineteenth-century texts. The Bellamy phenomenon involved a close assessment of the actual state of capitalism in late nineteenth-century America, and particularly its monopolistic tendencies. Many texts envisioned, for both better and worse, the development of these immediate characteristics into the near future, sometimes involving the revolutionary overthrow of the system, and then perhaps a return to the *status quo ante*, or some improvement thereon. Most, though not all, dystopias include such elements of 'hope'—the 'critical dystopia' is hardly a rarity.

---

[96] See, however, the film of Solzhenitsyn's *One Day in the Life of Ivan Denisovich* (1970).

Others, however, close with defeat, calamity, suicide, and are no less edifying in their pessimism.

By the twenty-first century, however, projections in this linear form are rare. While the gradual degeneration of capitalism is a common theme, the revolutionary overthrow of the system, for either better or worse, is rarely ever encountered in literary form. A paler and less reassuring hope lies instead, commonly, in charting the fate of a few survivors of any number of kinds of catastrophe. The relative scarcity of collectivist solutions coincides with the decline in projections from the immediate present into the future. Instead, most dystopias today take us into the future without substantial explanations as to how we have descended into the dismal state we encounter. Our real potential fate is so complicated as, seemingly, often to defy literary imagination. Despotism we can understand. How having children could bring about the end of the world seemingly defeats us.

Secondly, the spectre of totalitarian despotism dies out as the central target of dystopia by the 1980s. Taking its place, commonly, is corporate dictatorship in various guises, with the privatization, marketization, and monetization of all available resources, to the benefit of the wealthy. With this comes the gradual evaporation of centralized state power and collapse of civil order into gangland criminality for the majority, with the wealthy minority protecting themselves in well-guarded enclaves. Here, a spiralling downwards into violence and the war of all against all is the most common future predicted by literary projectors. The physical vision we have of dystopia now looks more like Detroit than Moscow. We also accordingly witness a decline in specifically anti-utopian dystopias. Perhaps surprisingly, and with a few notable exceptions, neither fascist nor communist collectivist dictatorships appear, to many later modern authors, as genuine outcomes of overpopulation or environmental degradation. The threat of universal surveillance remains a constant here, however, and is clearly reinforced by the growth of the Internet and the capacity for universal monitoring which current technologies permit. George Orwell would immediately recognize, and loathe, the world described by Dave Eggers.

The most obvious development in the dystopian genre in the past century in particular is the growing predominance of science and technology. Both the Frankenstein motif, which in turn drew upon ancient tropes on monstrosity, and its application to eugenics in particular, are extended into the present in various forms. As we have seen, science fiction looms increasingly large in these narratives, despite the assertion of the necessity for realist projections by authors like Atwood and Brunner. Human–machine interfaces, and the threat they pose for a humanist world-view, are now near the centre of our concerns. There is some continuity here with nineteenth- and twentieth-century discussions as to whether our increasing submission both to machines and to the scientific techniques associated with managing them would remove any freedom of will or sense of control over our lives. Centrally explored in Huxley's *Brave New World*, these concerns were renewed in the controversy over Skinner's *Walden Two*, and would remain crucial in works like *Limbo '90* and *A Clockwork Orange*.

Yet these more philosophical questions also show signs of being increasingly outpaced by the dramatic threats of real environmental and demographic catastrophe, accompanied by the further displacement of many traditional jobs by machines. We worry less now about free will than we do about physical survival. The net effect of this focus is to negate the dominant ideology of progress of the later modern period, and to force us to confront the possibility that colossal tragedies yet lie ahead of humanity. The late nineteenth and early twentieth centuries were intoxicated by science and technology, with people seeing in them the solution to all mankind's woes. Technophiles still harbour this view, seeing salvation renewed in each new generation of mobile phone. Dystopians rarely do.

The range of themes emerging recently is tending to displace that central concern with group identity which, as we saw in relation to Orwell, could be construed as the quintessential dystopian theme by the mid-1940s. We no longer fear the political parties lurking behind Big Brother. The face of plutocratic corporate governance is invisible. Complex financial institutions whose failure brings global market and then social and political chaos are nearly incomprehensible to most. The jackboot we can understand. Concepts like 'collateralized debt obligations' leave our heads swimming. And we sense that these 'products' are as little under the control of the masters of the universes as they are of the rest of us.

The fragmentation of civil society, of voluntary associative groups, was a central element in totalitarianism. Here, the absolute alienation of individuals, to the point of asociability, was a key result. This theme is resurgent in the post-apocalyptic scenarios which increasingly populate our own imagination. Yet we no longer fear (it seems) collectivism overwhelming of the individual. What we fear are plutocratic post-statist orders which abandon most of us to crime, disease, hunger, and global warming. Golding's *Lord of the Flies* and Burgess' *Clockwork Orange* hint at the violence lying just beneath the surface, the monster awaiting the moment to strike. The distinctly realistic possibility that the latter conditions will be conducive to creating massive new dictatorships, while occasionally encountered, is not at the moment central to our literary projections of the future. But this will clearly change.

Conclusion
Dystopia in the Twenty-First Century

The natural history of dystopia commences with a metaphorical Apocalypse. An angry god punishes humanity's wickedness with a flood, leaving only Noah, his family, and the animals to commence anew. It ends, seemingly, with various real dystopias created by humanity's aggression against itself and against nature. Again a flood may submerge us. Here the resemblance ends, however. The first Apocalypse was evidently a threat used to regulate behaviour, to keep us morally in line, and to ensure our faith. The second represents an imminent real catastrophe. Many, perhaps most, or even all the people will perish. No Noah will save them, and no God will save Noah.

* * * *

Besides these outcomes, as we have seen throughout this book, dystopia has functioned to project many other variants on mankind's fate. We saw in Part I that the earliest psychological dystopia of a *terra incognita* teeming with monsters and irritable spirits gave way, in the medieval and early modern period, to the imagined rule of the Devil over mankind above ground and in Hell beneath. From the First Crusade there commenced terror *cognita*, the large-scale persecution of Jews, heretics, witches, and deviant minorities. Here the rationale for persecution was often defined by particularly paranoid groups, whose need to conjure up enemies as scapegoats and to assert their own purity became all-consuming in moments of crisis, then continued as a means of perpetrating power. The Inquisition was one of the most important of such organizations.

Part II examined the principal forms of the twentieth-century totalitarian political dystopia. Both Hitler and Stalin promised new utopias which, however, required the enslavement or murder of millions. Both exhibited the most paranoid and aggressive forms of groupism described in Part I. Despite the ferocity of the Holocaust, persecution based on class ultimately caused even more bloodshed than that based on race.[1] Both forms of despotism shared a Social Darwinist obsession with struggle and a disdain for pity. Both believed the survival of their groups entailed killing millions of others. Their justification for persecution was interwoven with millenarian assumptions from the outset, and with an ideal of secular grace, historical or racial necessity, and/or group morality which boldly excused their actions. Auschwitz, the Gulag, and much further mass killing were a result of these anxieties.

---

[1] From 1500 to 1980 both come out about even.

Part III described how the literary dystopia, first born as a reaction to popular revolutionism, came to satirize the excesses of capitalist exploitation, the projections of machine-centred civilization, and the extremes of utopian ambition. The Bellamy controversy debated whether capitalist monopoly or utopian alternatives would serve humanity best. The coalescence of World War I and Bolshevism began the wedding of the fears of technology worship and extreme political collectivism which we first associate with Zamyatin's *We*. The leading subsequent authors of literary dystopias, notably Huxley, Orwell, and Skinner, all recognized the centrality of both groupism and technophilia to modern oppression. Free will was increasingly seen as displaced by overwhelming forces and both capitalist and communist ideologies and systems of manipulation. Humanity, it was feared, was being supplanted by mechanism. After 1945, visions of Apocalypse often involved atomic weapons. Robots, surveillance, and corporate domination also loomed ever larger. Then environmental collapse moved to the forefront. So the natural history of dystopia ends both with the death of nature, and the commencement of, and then too in turn perhaps the conclusion of, the artificial and mechanical history of mankind.

* * * *

Dystopia thus describes negative pasts and places we reject as deeply inhuman and oppressive, and projects negative futures we do not want but may get anyway. In so doing it raises perennial problems of human identity. Shall we be monsters, humans, or machines? Shall we be enslaved or free? *Can* we be 'free' or only conditioned in varying degrees? Shall we preserve our individuality or be swallowed by the collective? For us, these are mostly modern questions, and the story of dystopia presented here, by and large, asks them in the context of a highly complex, technologically driven world. This history exposes, above all, the paradox of the impotence of an apparently omnipotent humanity. We now possess the powers which once only the gods wielded. And yet, finally apparently in control of our own destiny, and seemingly infatuated with our own inventiveness, we lose or relinquish our self-command to elites, machines, and systems. In the oscillation between our aspirations to regenerate humanity in millenarian form and our tendency to revert to monstrosity, the latter seems too often to triumph, sometimes as a result of the former.

And thus dystopia increasingly defines the spirit of our times. Now, though terrorism captures the headlines more frequently, our long-term anxieties increasingly focus on climate change. Blessed with a wondrous planet, we have contrived to ruin it. Even the more dire predictions of a decade ago begin to look increasingly likely. International agreements do nothing to stem the warming process. (CO_2 emissions continue to rise at *c*.4.5 per cent per annum.) Population growth is undiminished, and surpasses our capacity to provide a decent standard of living for all. The scenario of having more children as a rebellion against 'the system' (Burgess, Levin, Ehrlich) is no longer a plausible one. As we devour the earth, species losses are frighteningly large and swift. Resources decline constantly. The threat of nuclear war remains. We are, the philosopher Slavoj Žižek writes, approaching an 'apocalyptic zero-point' where ecological crisis and struggles over raw materials, along with other factors, threaten complete collapse.[2] The eminent scientist Martin Rees terms the present mankind's 'final century'.[3] There is no reason to dispute his judgement.

* * * *

How might such a future unfold? We may, for a moment, abandon history for futurology. If the past is anything to go by, here are some not implausible scenarios for the late twenty-first century.

The polar icecaps have nearly melted, and much of the Siberian tundra. It is extremely hot, 4–6° C above present temperatures, or even more. But that will be in the more temperate regions. Nearer the equator, the home of many billions of the world's fastest-growing populations now, the land will become uninhabitable. Its peoples will have to move, like many in the great seaside cities everywhere. Rising sea levels, crop failures, and desertification will make resources increasingly scarce. Every attempt to conserve or renew energy will be negated by the numbers requiring its use. With some 20 billion human beings on the planet, wars over water and land will be constant. Raging storms will wreak great devastation. Tropical insects and diseases will run rampant. The Great Burning and the Great Thirst will drive swarming masses north or south up to the protective walls, which stretch for thousands of miles, isolating the more temperate climes. Here the billions locked out, increasingly thinking and acting as crowds, will swelter in poverty. They will clamour and importune until they can tolerate it no longer. Then they will come crashing through.

Initially the well-to-do—the 1 per cent or the 'One', who will possess three-quarters or more of the world's wealth—will, of course, be less affected by this process. As conditions worsen, the rich, in the comfortable regions, will retreat further into the luxurious isolation of their fortified compounds. Here they will watch the strange weather in air-conditioned comfort through layers of glass. TV cameras and security reports will keep them informed about life beyond the walls. With little sympathy, they will blame the feckless masses for overbreeding. Their own lives, meanwhile, will lengthen through many advances in science. They will be diverted by infinite forms of multidimensional amusement.

But, even so cushioned, they too will eventually sense the end times. Many will begin sinking into a reckless *fin de l'histoire* decadence. A cult of Apocalypse will promote wild lovemaking and carnivalesque abandon. While rising sea levels inundate millions, thousands will drown their anxieties in baths of champagne. The intellectuals will once again lose their way and seek guidance in a new Nietzsche. His doctrines, unsurprisingly, will resemble his predecessor's. He—or she—will reach back to Darwin, and even further to Malthus.

Outside these enclaves, in the wider world, poverty will confront prodigality as never before. The brainwashing mass media will, for a time, hold sway in

---

[2] Slavoj Žižek, *Living in the End Times* (Verso, 2010), p. x.
[3] Martin Rees, *Our Final Century: A Scientist's Warning. How Terror, Error and Environmental Disaster Threaten Humankind's Future in this Century—on Earth and Beyond* (Heinemann, 2003).

perpetuating, through corporate propaganda, the myths of progress, growth, and infinite expansion, production, and consumption. When this ideology finally expires there will be a moral, intellectual, and emotional free-for-all. Having failed to provide the answers, science will fall into disrepute. Messiahs and lunatics will swarm like woodlice, quoting scriptures, Joachim of Fiore, or Nostradamus. Some will proclaim a return to the purity of a lost golden age, be it a caliphate or a Christian Jerusalem. Many will claim we have lost our 'soul', and that they have found it. Mysticism will sprout everywhere. Some will claim to be Dr Frankenstein, and others, his monster. Neo-Antinomians will proclaim themselves free of sin, and act accordingly.

Eventually, great sweeping psychic epidemics will produce mass frenzies like the Tarantella. The scapegoating will commence. As numbers grow, cults of sexual abstinence will arise just as complete promiscuity becomes a norm. A renewal of misogyny may accompany such efforts as women are blamed for overpopulation: seeing sex once again as Original Sin, we may hunt witches again. Hatreds will burn as never before. Intense fantasies of power, violence, and sadism will attempt to displace the growing lack of real power. A profound reaction against capitalism, which will be linked to sin and desire, will commence. Many will reject the utopia of universal plenitude, novelty, and luxury. Making a virtue of necessity, abstinence, piety, and stoicism will revive. Neo-pagan asceticism and nature worship will trump hedonism as expressed through material possession. Survivalist cults will flourish. Satan will make an astonishing comeback. But Brahma, Buddha, Christ, and Marx will also all reappear. The symbols of opulence will be attacked publicly. And then these countercultures too will be commodified and marketized.

Amidst this chaos, various groups will seek world domination, promising order, restraint, and a return to the good old times—at a price. They will contend that, in order for 'Us' to survive, 'They' must perish. They will start with immigrants and those on welfare. Most of the remaining middle classes will edge towards authoritarian solutions, worshipping the One and aspiring to membership within it. But the poor will eventually blame the rich, and storm their bastions. The masses will gratefully accept Austrian corporals who will again rise from the trenches, or failed seminarians who abandon prayer beads for handouts from media moguls. The Hitler of 2080 or the Stalin of 2100 will again demand total loyalty. Millions of ordinary followers will grant it. Restrictions on family size will finally be accepted, though reluctantly and too late. They will be policed with violence, and flouted nonetheless. Despairing neo-Augustinians will blame humanity as such, invoking Original Sin and expecting the worst, which they will likely get. The Holocaust may come to seem like a rehearsal for what follows. Having failed the first test, humanity, a lazy student, is unlikely to pass the resit.

Machines will play a central role in all this. Neo-Erewhonians in colourful homespun woollen costumes will arise to destroy our metal friends or 'comrades', seeing robots as the new witches. Invoking a new ideal of pure humanity and unmediated sociability, they will assail the creeping mechanization of human relations which only validates experience filtered through machines. Others, however, will still seek the salvation of their increasingly mechanical souls and bodies in new and cleverer inventions. In increasing numbers they will prefer robot to human company. A cult of robot worship will appear. And these machines will certainly proliferate. They will be doing all the work in the uninhabitable regions. They will also develop their own cultures. Let us hope they are sufficiently diverted by chess clubs, robo-reality TV (watch it eat lizards), and geeky gameshows. When they begin to form groups, look out. If they take up politics, we are in for trouble. If they get religion and are taught equality we are doomed. So when the Robot Party begins to speak of social hygiene, you can guess who will be the 'virus', the 'parasite', and the 'monster'. Will a robot Lenin shout 'death to humanity' to the metal proletarians? Perhaps. But will they be as cruel as humans are to humans? No. That is impossible. (Unless of course they learn this from us too . . .)

* * * *

However fanciful such scenarios appear, all are plausible. They are not predictions, and not science fiction, but projections, on the Atwood principle, of some worst-case scenarios. But neither are they inevitable: many factors might forestall or divert their development.

Such nightmares nonetheless clearly indicate the centrality of dystopia to our times. Dystopian literature may have fallen short, in the face of so much horror, in describing the genocides of the twentieth century. But now, particularly where science and technology are central, its projections have much to offer. The new, it warns us, is not always the better. 'Progress' is not automatic, and may be dangerous. What benefits the few may harm the many. Machines may devour us. So may corporations or revolutionaries. Hurtling towards an uncertain but clearly perilous future, we need visions of alternatives—even utopias—to delineate which paths suggest the greater and which the lesser evils. We need the long view, not the short-termism which politics and the desire for ever-more-instant gratification force upon us.

The task of the literary dystopia, then, is to warn us against and educate us about real-life dystopias. It need not furnish a happy ending to do so: pessimism has its place. But it may envision rational and collective solutions where irrationality and panic loom. Entertainment plays a role in this process. But the task at hand is serious. It gains daily in importance. Here, then, is a genre, and a concept, whose hour has come. May it flourish.

Bibliography

BOOKS

Abel, Theodore. *Why Hitler Came to Power* (Harvard University Press, 1986).

Acworth, Andrew. *A New Eden* (Ward & Lock, 1896).

Adams, Frederick U. *President John Smith: The Story of a Peaceful Revolution* (Charles H. Kerr & Co., 1896).

Addison, Hugh. *The Battle of London* (Herbert Jenkins Ltd, 1924).

Adler, Nanci. *Keeping Faith with the Party: Communist Believers Return from the Gulag* (Indiana University Press, 2012).

Adorno, T. W., Else Frenkel-Brunswik, Daniel Levinson, and Nevitt Sanford. *The Authoritarian Personality* (Harper, 1950).

Agabekov, Georges. *OGPU: The Russian Secret Terror* (Hyperion Press, 1975).

Aldridge, Alexandra. *The Scientific World-View in Dystopia* (UMI Research Press, 1978).

Alford, C. Fred. *Group Psychology and Political Theory* (Yale University Press, 1994).

Allen, Grant. *The Evolution of the Idea of God* (Grant Richards, 1904).

Allott, Kenneth, and Stephen Tait. *The Rhubarb Tree* (The Cresset Press, 1937).

Allport, Gordon. *The Nature of Prejudice* (Addison-Wesley Publishing Co., 1954).

Aly, Götz, and Susanne Heim. *Architects of Annihilation: Auschwitz and the Logic of Destruction* (Weidenfeld & Nicolson, 2002).

Amis, Kingsley. *New Maps of Hell: A Survey of Science Fiction* (Victor Gollancz, 1963).

Anderson, Andrew Runni. *Alexander's Gate, Gog and Magog, and the Inclosed Nations* (Medieval Academy of America, 1932).

Anderson, Benedict. *Imagined Communities: Reflections on the Origin and Spread of Nationalism* (Verso, 1991).

Anderson, David D. *Ignatius Donnelly* (Twayne, 1980).

An Ex-M.P. *A Radical Nightmare: Or, England Forty Years Hence* (Field & Tuer, 1885).

An Ex-Revolutionist. *'England's Downfall;' or, The Last Great Revolution* (Digby & Long, 1893).

Anissimov, Myriam. *Primo Levi: The Tragedy of an Optimist* (Aurum Press, 1998).

Annan, David. *Robot: The Mechanical Monster* (Bounty Books, 1976).

Applebaum, Anne, ed. *Gulag Voices: An Anthology* (Yale University Press, 2011).

Applebaum, Anne. *Iron Curtain: The Crushing of Eastern Europe* (Penguin Books, 2012).

Arendt, Hannah. *The Origins of Totalitarianism* (2nd edn, George Allen & Unwin, 1958).

Arendt, Hannah. *Eichmann in Jerusalem: A Report on the Banality of Evil* (Faber & Faber, 1963).

Arendt, Hannah. *On Violence* (Allen Lane, 1970).

[Ashton, Winifred]. Clemence Dane. *The Arrogant History of White Ben* (William Heinemann, 1939).

Asma, Stephen T. *On Monsters* (Oxford University Press, 2009).

Astor, John Jacob. *A Journey in Other Worlds: A Romance of the Future* (D. Appleton & Co., 1894).

Atkins, John. *George Orwell. A Literary Study* (Calder & Boyars, 1954).

Atkins, John. *Aldous Huxley: A Literary Study* (John Calder, 1956).

Atwood, Margaret. *The Handmaid's Tale* (Houghton Mifflin, 1986).

Atwood, Margaret. *Oryx and Crake* (Bloomsbury, 2003).

Atwood, Margaret. *Curious Pursuits: Occasional Writing 1970–2005* (Virago, 2005).

Atwood, Margaret. *The Year of the Flood* (Bloomsbury, 2009).

Atwood, Margaret. *MaddAddam* (Bloomsbury, 2013).

Audisio, Gabriel. *The Waldensian Dissent: Persecution and Survival c. 1170–c. 1570* (Cambridge University Press, 1999).

Auster, Paul. *In the Country of Last Things* (Viking Penguin, 1987).

Baccolini, Raffaella, and Tom Moylan, eds. *Dark Horizons: Science Fiction and the Dystopian Imagination* (Routledge, 2003).

[Bachelder, John]. *A.D. 2050: Electrical Development at Atlantis* (The Bancroft Co., 1890).

Bacon, Edwin. *The Gulag at War: Stalin's Forced Labour System in the Light of the Archives* (Macmillan, 1994).

Baczko, Bronisław. *Utopian Lights: The Evolution of the Idea of Social Progress* (Paragon House, 1989).

Baczko, Bronisław. *Ending the Terror: The French Revolution after Robespierre* (Cambridge University Press, 1994).

Bagchi, Barnita, ed. *The Politics of the (Im)possible: Utopia and Dystopia Reconsidered* (Sage, 2012).

Bailey, Michael D. *Battling Demons: Witchcraft, Heresy and Reform in the Late Middle Ages* (Penn State University Press, 2003).

Baker, Robert S. *The Dark Historic Page: Social Satire and Historicism in the Novels of Aldous Huxley 1921–1939* (University of Wisconsin Press, 1982).

Baker-Smith, Dominic, and C. C. Barfoot, eds. *Between Dream and Nature: Essays on Utopia and Dystopia* (Rodopi, 1987).

Baldick, Chris. *In Frankenstein's Shadow: Myth, Monstrosity, and Nineteenth-Century Writing* (Clarendon Press, 1987).

Ballard, J. G. *The Drowned World* (Victor Gollancz, 1963).

Bardach, Janusz. *Man is Wolf to Man: Surviving the Gulag* (Scribner, 2003).

Baring-Gould, S. *Curious Myths of the Middle Ages* (Rivington, 1868).

Baring-Gould, Sabine. *The Book of Were-Wolves* (Smith, Elder & Co., 1865).

Barkun, Michael. *Disaster and the Millennium* (Yale University Press, 1974).

Barmine, Alexander. *One Who Survived: The Life Story of a Russian under the Soviets* (G. P. Putnam's Sons, 1945).

Barnes, Steven A. *Death and Redemption: The Gulag and the Shaping of Soviet Society* (Princeton University Press, 2011).

Barnouin, Barbara, and Yu Changgen. *Ten Years of Turbulence: The Chinese Cultural Revolution* (Kegan Paul International, 1993).

Barrett, David V. *The New Believers: A Survey of Sects, Cults and Alternative Religions* (Cassell & Co., 2001).

Barron, John, and Anthony Paul. *Murder of a Gentle Land: The Untold Story of Communist Genocide in Cambodia* (Reader's Digest Press, 1977).

Barrows, Susanna. *Distorting Mirrors: Visions of the Crowd in Late Nineteenth-Century France* (Yale University Press, 1981).

Bartlett, F. C. *Psychology and Primitive Culture* (Cambridge University Press, 1923).

Barton, Carlin A. *The Sorrows of the Ancient Romans: Gladiator and Monster* (Princeton University Press, 1993).

Bauer, Raymond A. *The New Man in Soviet Psychology* (Harvard University Press, 1952).

Bauman, Zygmunt. *Modernity and the Holocaust* (Polity Press, 1989).

Baxter, John. *The Inner Man: The Life of J. G. Ballard* (Weidenfeld & Nicolson, 2011).

Beaumont, Matthew. *Utopia Ltd.: Ideologies of Social Dreaming in England 1870–1900* (E. J. Brill, 2005).

Beaumont, Matthew. *The Spectre of Utopia: Utopian and Science Fictions at the Fin-de-Siècle* (Peter Lang, 2012).

Beausobre, Iulia de. *The Woman Who Could Not Die* (Victor Gollancz, 1948).

Beck, F., and W. Godin. *Russian Purge and the Extraction of Confession* (Hurst & Blackett, 1951).

Becker, Elizabeth. *When the War was Over: The Voices of Cambodia's Revolution and Its People* (Simon & Schuster, 1986).

Bedford, Sybille. *Aldous Huxley: A Biography* (2 vols, Chatto & Windus, 1973).

Behrens, Lewis Henry, and Ignatius Singer. *The Story of My Dictatorship* (Henry George Foundation, 1934).

Bellamy, Edward. *Dr. Heidenhoff's Process* (1880; AMS Press, 1969).

Bellamy, Edward. *Looking Backward 2000–1887* (repr. of 1st edn; George Routledge & Sons, 1890).

Bellamy, Edward. *Looking Backward 2000–1887* (repr. of 2nd edn; Frederick Warne & Co., 1891).

Bellamy, Edward. *Edward Bellamy Speaks Again!* (The Peerage Press, 1937).

Bellamy, Edward. *Equality* (1897; Appleton-Century, 1937).

Benedict, Ruth. *Patterns of Culture* (1934; Routledge & Kegan Paul, 1952).

Benton, Jill. *Naomi Mitchison: A Century of Experiment in Life and Letters* (Pandora, 1990).

Berdyaev, Nikolai. *The Russian Revolution* (Sheed & Ward, 1932).

Berdyaev, Nicolas. *The Destiny of Man* (The Centenary Press, 1939).

Beresford, J. D. *Revolution: A Novel* (W. Collins Sons & Co., 1921).

Beresford, J. D., and Esme Wynne-Tyson. *The Riddle of the Tower* (Hutchinson & Co., 1944).

Berger, Harold L. *Science Fiction and the New Dark Age* (Bowling Green University Popular Press, 1976).

Berger, Joseph. *Shipwreck of a Generation: The Memoirs of Joseph Berger* (Harvill Press, 1971).

Bernal, J. D. *The World, the Flesh and the Devil* (Jonathan Cape, 1970).

Bernard, John. *The New Race of Devils* (Anglo-Eastern Publishing Co., 1921).

Bernheimer, Richard. *Wild Men in the Middle Ages* (Harvard University Press, 1952).

Bernstein, Alan E. *The Formation of Hell: Death and Retribution in the Ancient and Early Christian Worlds* (UCL Press, 1993).

Bernstein, Stephen. *Alasdair Gray* (Bucknell University Press, 1999).

Besançon, Alain. *The Intellectual Origins of Leninism* (Basil Blackwell, 1981).

Besant, Walter. *The Inner House* (Bernhard Tauchnitz, 1888).

Bethencourt, Francisco. *The Inquisition: A Global History, 1478–1834* (Cambridge University Press, 2009).

Bettelheim, Bruno. *The Informed Heart: The Human Condition in Modern Mass Society* (Thames & Hudson, 1960).

Bettelheim, Bruno. *The Uses of Enchantment: The Meaning and Importance of Fairy Tales* (Alfred A. Knopf, 1977).

Bettelheim, Bruno. *Surviving and Other Essays* (Thames & Hudson, 1979).

Bien, Peter. *L. P. Hartley* (Chatto & Windus, 1963).

Billig, Michael. *Social Psychology and Intergroup Relations* (Academic Press, 1976).

Billington, James H. *Fire in the Minds of Men: Origins of the Revolutionary Faith* (Temple Smith, 1980).

Bion, Wilfred. *Experiences in Groups* (Tavistock Publications, 1961).

Bird, Arthur. *Looking Forward: A Dream of the United States of the Americas in 1999* (L. C. Childs, 1899).

Birkett, Jennifer. *Margaret Storm Jameson: A Life* (Oxford University Press, 2009).

Bizot, François. *The Gate* (The Harvill Press, 2003).

Bjork, Daniel W. *B. F. Skinner: A Life* (American Psychological Association, 1997).

Blaim, Artur, and Ludmiła Gruszewska-Blaim, eds. *Imperfect Worlds and Dystopian Narratives in Contemporary Cinema* (Peter Lang, 2011).

Blaim, Artur, and Ludmiła Gruszewska-Blaim, eds. *Mediated Utopias: From Literature to Cinema* (Peter Lang, 2015).

Blakemore, Felix J. *The Coming Hour (?)* (Sands & Co., 1927).

Blanc, Louis. *The Threatened Social Disintegration of France*, ed. James Ward (Richard Bentley, 1848).

Bleackley, Horace. *Anymoon* (The Bodley Head, 1919).

Bodmer, Beatriz Pastor. *The Armature of Conquest: Spanish Accounts of the Discovery of America, 1492–1589* (Stanford University Press, 1992).

Booker, M. Keith. *The Dystopian Impulse in Modern Literature: Fiction as Social Criticism* (Greenwood Press, 1994).

Booker, M. Keith. *Dystopian Literature: A Theory and Research Guide* (Greenwood Press, 1994).

Booker, M. Keith, ed. *Critical Insights: Dystopia* (Salem Press, 2013).

Booker, M. Keith, ed. *Critical Insights: Brave New World* (Salem Press, 2014).

Borkenau, F. *The Communist International* (Faber & Faber, 1938).

Borkenau, F. *The Totalitarian Enemy* (Faber & Faber, 1940).

Borkenau, Franz. *The Spanish Cockpit: An Eye-Witness Account of the Political and Social Conflicts of the Spanish Civil War* (Faber & Faber, 1937).

Boswell, Diane. *Posterity: A Novel* (Jonathan Cape, 1926).

Boswell, Marshall, and Stephen Burn, eds. *A Companion to David Foster Wallace Studies* (Palgrave Macmillan, 2013).

Bounds, Philip. *Orwell and Marxism: The Political and Cultural Thinking of George Orwell* (I.B. Tauris, 2009).

Bourdieu, Pierre. *Outline of a Theory of Practice* (Cambridge University Press, 1977).

Bourke, Joanna. *Fear: A Cultural History* (Virago, 2005).

Bourke, Joanna. *What It Means to Be Human* (Virago, 2011).

Bowker, Gordon. *George Orwell* (Abacus Books, 2003).

Bowman, Sylvia. *Edward Bellamy* (Twayne, 1986).

Bowman, Sylvia E. *The Year 2000: A Critical Biography of Edward Bellamy* (Bookman Associates, 1958).

Bowman, Sylvia E. et al. *Edward Bellamy Abroad: An American Prophet's Influence* (Twayne Publishers, 1962).

Boye, Karin. *Kallocain* (1940; University of Wisconsin Press, 1966).

Bradbury, Ray. *Fahrenheit 451* (Rupert Hart-Davis, 1953).

Bradshaw, David, ed. *The Hidden Huxley: Contempt and Compassion for the Masses 1920–36* (Faber & Faber, 1994).

Brady, Robert A. *The Spirit and Structure of German Fascism* (Victor Gollancz, 1937).

Bramah, Ernest. *The Secret of the League: The Story of a Social War* (Thomas Nelson & Sons, 1909).

Bramstedt, E. K. *Dictatorship and Political Police: The Technique of Control by Fear* (Kegan Paul, Trench, Trubner & Co., 1945).

[Brash, Margaret Maud]. John Kendall. *Unborn Tomorrow* (W. Collins & Sons, 1933).

Braunthal, Julius. *In Search of the Millennium* (Victor Gollancz, 1945).

Brewer, Keagan, ed. *Prester John: The Legend and Its Sources* (Ashgate, 2015).

Brinsmade, Herman Hine. *Utopia Achieved* (Broadway Publishing Co., 1912).

Bromage, Bernard. *Man of Terror: Dzherzhynski* (Peter Owen Ltd, 1956).

Brookfield, Arthur. *Simiocracy: A Fragment from Future History* (Blackwood & Sons, 1884).

Brown, Douglas, and Christopher Serpell. *If Hitler Comes: A Cautionary Tale* (Faber & Faber, 2009).

Brown, E. J. *Brave New World, 1984, and We: An Essay on Anti-Utopia* (Ardis, 1976).

Brown, J. A. C. *Techniques of Persuasion: From Propaganda to Brainwashing* (Penguin Books, 1963).

Brown, Norman O. *Life against Death: The Psychoanalytic Meaning of History* (Vintage Books, 1959).

Brown, Peter. *The Body and Society: Men, Women and Sexual Renunciation in Early Christianity* (Faber & Faber, 1989).

Brown, Rupert. *Group Processes: Dynamics Within and Between Groups* (Blackwell, 2000).

Browning, Christopher R. *Ordinary Men: Reserve Police Battalion 101 and the Final Solution in Poland* (HarperCollins, 1992).

Brunner, John. *Stand on Zanzibar* (1968; Millennium, 1999).

Brunner, John. *The Sheep Look Up* (1972; Benbella Books, 2003).

Brunner, John. *The Shockwave Rider* (J. M. Dent, 1975).

Brussof, Valery. *The Republic of the Southern Cross* (Constable & Co., 1918).

Brustein, William I. *Roots of Hate: Anti-Semitism in Europe before the Holocaust* (Cambridge University Press, 2003).

Buber, Margarete. *Under Two Dictators* (Victor Gollancz, 1949).

Buber, Martin. *Paths in Utopia* (Beacon Press, 1949).

Buca, Edward. *Vorkuta* (Constable, 1976).

Buck-Morss, Susan. *Dreamworld and Catastrophe: The Passing of Mass Utopia in East and West* (MIT Press, 2000).

Buckingham, James Silk. *Letters to a Clergyman* (Chapman & Hall, 1846).

Bulgakov, Mikhail. *The Fatal Eggs* (Oneworld Classics, 2011).

Buller, Erik. *Metamorphoses of the Vampire in Literature and Film: Cultural Transformations in Europe 1732–1933* (Camden House, 2010).

Bulwer-Lytton, Edward. *The Coming Race* (George Routledge & Sons, 1872).

[Burdekin, Katharine] Murray Constantine. *Swastika Night* (Victor Gollancz, 1940).

Burdick, Eugene, and Harvey Wheeler. *Fail-Safe* (Hutchinson, 1962).

Burgess, Anthony. *A Clockwork Orange* (1962; William Heinemann, 2012).

Burgess, Anthony. *The Wanting Seed* (Heinemann, 1962).

Burgess, Anthony. *The Novel Now* (Faber & Faber, 1967).

Burgess, Anthony. *1985* (Arrow Books, 1980).

Burgess, Percy. *Born of those Years: An Autobiography* (J. M. Dent, 1952).

Burke, Edmund. *The Works of the Right Hon. Edmund Burke* (12 vols, John C. Nimmo, 1899).

Burleigh, Michael. *The Racial State: Germany 1933–1945* (Cambridge University Press, 1991).

Burleigh, Michael. *Death and Deliverance: 'Euthanasia' in Nazi Germany* (Cambridge University Press, 1994).

Burleigh, Michael. *Ethics and Extermination: Reflections on Nazi Genocide* (Cambridge University Press, 1997).

Burleigh, Michael. *The Third Reich: A New History* (Pan Books, 2000).

Burleigh, Michael. *Sacred Causes: Religion and Politics from the European Dictators to Al Qaeda* (HarperPress, 2006).

Burman, Edward. *The Inquisition* (The Aquarian Press, 1984).

Butler, Octavia E. *The Parable of the Sower* (1993; The Women's Press, 1995).

Butler, Samuel. *Erewhon and Erewhon Revisited* (The Modern Library, 1927).

Cadden, Mike. *Ursula K. Le Guin: Beyond Genre: Fiction for Children and Adults* (Routledge, 2005).

Campbell, Charlie. *Scapegoat: A History of Blaming Other People* (Duckworth Overlook, 2011).

Canetti, Elias. *Crowds and Power* (Penguin Books, 1992).

Cantril, Hadley. *The Psychology of Social Movements* (John Wiley & Sons, 1941).

Čapek, Karel. *War with the Newts* (Allen & Unwin, 1937).

Čapek, Karel. *Rossum's Universal Robots (RUR)* (Hesperus Press, 2011).

Carlson, Elof Axel. *The Unfit: The History of a Bad Idea* (Cold Spring Harbor Laboratory Press, 2001).

Carlyle, Thomas. *On Heroes, Hero-Worship and the Heroic in History* (Chapman & Hall, 1841).

Carlyle, Thomas. *Sartor Resartus* (Chapman & Hall, 1885).

Carlyle, Thomas. *The French Revolution: A History* (2 vols, Chapman & Hall, 1898).

Carlyle, Thomas. 'The Signs of the Times', in *Works* (30 vols, Chapman & Hall, 1899), vol. 27.

Carne-Ross, Joseph. *Quintura: Its Singular People and Remarkable Customs* (J. & R. Maxwell, 1886).

Carney, Timothy Michael, ed. *Communist Party Power in Kampuchea (Cambodia): Documents and Discussion* (Data Paper no. 106, Department of Asian Studies, Cornell University, 1977).

Carter, Michael. *George Orwell and the Problem of Authentic Existence* (Croom Helm, 1985).

Carter, Paul A. *The Creation of Tomorrow: Fifty Years of Science Fiction* (Columbia University Press, 1977).

Cassinelli, C. W. *Total Revolution: A Comparative Study of Germany under Hitler, the Soviet Union under Stalin, and China under Mao* (Clio Books, 1976).

Cavallaro, Dani. *Cyberpunk and Cyberculture: Science Fiction and the Work of William Gibson* (Athlone Press, 2000).

Cavendish, Richard. *The Powers of Evil in Western Religion, Magic and Folk Belief* (Routledge & Kegan Paul, 1975).

Cervantes, Fernando. *The Devil in the New World: The Influence of Diabolism in New Spain* (Yale University Press, 1994).

Chakotin, Serge. *The Rape of the Masses: The Psychology of Totalitarian Political Propaganda* (George Routledge & Sons, 1940).

Chamberlin, William Henry. *Russia's Iron Age* (Duckworth, 1935).

Chandler, David. *Voices from S-21: Terror and History in Pol Pot's Secret Prison* (Silkworm Books, 2000).

Chandler, David P. *Brother Number One: A Political Biography of Pol Pot* (Silkworm Books, 1999).

Chapman, Brian. *Police State* (Pall Mall Press, 1970).

Charnas, Suzy McKee. *Walk to the End of the World* (1974; Victor Gollancz, 1979).

Chen, Jack. *Inside the Cultural Revolution* (Sheldon Press, 1976).

Child, William Stanley. *The Legal Revolution of 1902* (Charles H. Kerr & Co., 1898).

Chirot, Daniel. *Modern Tyrants: The Power and Prevalence of Evil in Our Age* (Free Press, 1994).

Chol-hwan, Kang, and Pierre Rigoulot. *The Aquariums of Pyongyang: Ten Years in the North Korean Gulag* (Atlantic Books, 2006).

Ciliga, Anton. *The Russian Enigma* (George Routledge & Sons, 1940).

Ciszek, Walter J. *With God in Russia* (Peter Davies, 1965).

Claeys, Gregory. *Machinery, Money and the Millennium: From Moral Economy to Socialism, 1815–1860* (Princeton University Press, 1987).

Claeys, Gregory. *Citizens and Saints: Politics and Anti-Politics in Early British Socialism* (Cambridge University Press, 1989).

Claeys, Gregory, ed. *Modern British Utopias* (8 vols, Pickering & Chatto, 1993).

Claeys, Gregory, ed. *Utopias of the British Enlightenment* (Cambridge University Press, 1994).

Claeys, Gregory, ed. *Political Writings of the 1790s* (8 vols, Pickering & Chatto, 1995).

Claeys, Gregory. *The French Revolution Debate in Britain* (Palgrave Macmillan, 2007).

Claeys, Gregory, ed. *Late Victorian Utopias* (6 vols, Pickering & Chatto, 2008).

Claeys, Gregory. *Mill and Paternalism* (Cambridge University Press, 2013).

Clark, Paul. *The Chinese Cultural Revolution: A History* (Cambridge University Press, 2008).

Clark, Stuart. *Thinking with Demons: The Idea of Witchcraft in Early Modern Europe* (Oxford University Press, 1997).

Clarke, Percy. *The Valley Council; or, Leaves from the Journal of Thomas Bateman of Canbelego Station, N.S.W.* (Sampson Low & Co., 1891).

Clasen, Claus-Peter. *Anabaptism: A Social History 1525–1618* (Cornell University Press, 1972).

Coale, Samuel. *Anthony Burgess* (Frederick Ungar, 1981).

Cohen, Elie A. *Human Behaviour in the Concentration Camp* (Jonathan Cape, 1954).

Cohen, Jeffrey Jerome, ed. *Monster Theory* (University of Minnesota Press, 1996).

Cohen, Jeffrey Jerome. *Of Giants: Sex, Monsters, and the Middle Ages* (University of Minnesota Press, 1999).

Cohen, John. *Human Robots in Myth and Fiction* (George Allen & Unwin, 1966).

Cohen, Stephen F. *The Victims Return: Survivors of the Gulag after Stalin* (I.B. Taurus, 2011).

Cohn, Norman. *Warrant for Genocide* (Eyre & Spottiswoode, 1967).

Cohn, Norman. *The Pursuit of the Millennium: Revolutionary Millenarians and Mystical Anarchists of the Middle Ages* (Paladin Books, 1970).

Cohn, Norman. *Europe's Inner Demons: An Enquiry Inspired by the Great Witch-Hunt* (Chatto-Heinemann, 1975).

Cohn, Norman. *Cosmos, Chaos, and the World to Come: The Ancient Roots of Apocalyptic Faith* (Yale University Press, 1993).

Cole, Robert William. *The Struggle for Empire: A Story of the Year 2236* (Elliot Stock, 1900).

Colls, Robert. *George Orwell: English Rebel* (Oxford University Press, 2013).

Connolly, Cyril. *The Condemned Playground* (Routledge, 1945).

Conquest, Robert. *The Great Terror: Stalin's Purge of the Thirties* (Macmillan, 1968).

Conquest, Robert. *Kolyma* (Macmillan, 1978).

Conquest, Robert. *Inside Stalin's Secret Police: NKVD Politics, 1936–9* (Macmillan, 1985).

Conquest, Robert. *Reflections on a Ravaged Century* (John Murray, 1999).

Conquest, Robert. *The Harvest of Sorrow: Soviet Collectivisation and the Terror-Famine* (Pimlico Books, 2002).

Cook, William Wallace. *A Round Trip to the Year 2000* (Street & Smith, 1925).

Cooke, Brett. *Human Nature in Utopia: Zamyatin's* We (Northwestern University Press, 2002).

Coppard, Audrey, and Bernard Crick. *Orwell Remembered* (Facts on File Publications, 1984).

Corbet, Mrs George. *New Amazonia: A Foretaste of the Future* (Power Publishing Co., 1889).

Cornwell, John. *The Dark Box: A Secret History of Confession* (Profile Books, 2014).

Coulton, G. C. *Inquisition and Liberty* (Heinemann, 1958).

Cournos, John. *London under the Bolsheviks: A Londoner's Dream on Returning from Petrograd* (Russian Liberation Committee, 1919).

Courtois, Stéphane, Nicolas Werth, Jean-Louis Panné, Andrzej Paczkowski, Karel Bartošek, and Jean-Louis Margolin. *The Black Book of Communism: Crimes, Terror, Repression* (Harvard University Press, 1999).

Cowan, James. *Daybreak: A Romance of an Old World* (George H. Richmond, 1896).

Crace, Jim. *The Pesthouse* (Picador, 2007).

Craig, Alexander. *Ionia, Land of Wise Men and Fair Women* (E. A. Weeks, 1898).

Crawley, Ernest. *The Mystic Rose: A Study of Primitive Marriage and of Primitive Thought in Its Bearing on Marriage* (Watts & Co., 1932).

Crick, Bernard. *George Orwell: A Life* (Penguin Books, 1982).

Cridge, Alfred Denton. *Utopia: Or, The History of an Extinct Planet* (n.p., 1884).

Critchley, Simon. *The Faith of the Faithless: Experiments in Political Theology* (Verso, 2012).

[Crocker, Samuel] Theodore Oceanic Islet. *That Island: A Political Romance* (C. E. Streeter, 1892).

Cumings, Bruce. *North Korea: Another Country* (The New Press, 2004).

Cummins, Elizabeth. *Understanding Ursula K. Le Guin* (University of South Carolina Press, 1993).

Curtis, Michael. *Totalitarianism* (Transaction Books, 1979).

[Davies, Howell] Andrew Marvell. *Minimum Man, or, Time to Be Gone* (Victor Gollancz, 1939).

Davies, Nigel. *Human Sacrifice in History and Today* (Macmillan, 1981).

Davies, Sarah. *Popular Opinion in Stalin's Russia: Terror, Propaganda and Dissent, 1934–1941* (Cambridge University Press, 1997).

Davis, E. J. *Pyrna: A Commune; or, Under the Ice* (Bickers and Son, 1875).

Davis, J. C. *Utopia and the Ideal Society: A Study of English Utopian Writing 1516–1700* (Cambridge University Press, 1981).

Davison, Peter. *George Orwell: A Literary Life* (Macmillan, 1996).

Davison, Peter, ed. *The Lost Orwell: Being a Supplement to* The Complete Works of George Orwell (Timewell Press, 2006).

De L'Isle-Adam, Villier. *Tomorrow's Eve* (1886), tr. Robert Martin Adams (University of Illinois Press, 2001).

Delany, Samuel R. *Triton* (Bantam Books, 1976).

Delarue, Jacques. *The History of the Gestapo* (Macdonald, 1964).

Delumeau, Jean. *Sin and Fear: The Emergence of a Western Guilt Culture 13th–18th Centuries* (St. Martin's Press, 1990).

Delumeau, Jean. *History of Paradise* (Continuum, 1995).

Demick, Barbara. *Nothing to Envy: Real Lives in North Korea* (Granta, 2010).

Depaul, Kim, ed. *Children of Cambodia's Killing Fields* (Yale University Press, 1997).

Des Pres, Terence. *The Survivor: An Anatomy of Life in the Death Camps* (Oxford University Press, 1976).

Desborough, Robert. *State Contentment: An Allegory* (Newsagents' & Publishing Co., 1870).

Detmer, David. *Sartre Explained* (Open Court, 2008).

Deutscher, Isaac. *Heretics and Renegades* (Hamish Hamilton, 1955).

Devitis, A. A. *Anthony Burgess* (Twayne, 1972).

Dick, Bernard F. *William Golding* (Twayne, 1987).

Dick, Philip K. *The Man in the High Castle* (Victor Gollancz, 1975).

Dick, Philip K. *Four Novels of the 1960s* (Library of America, 2007).

Dick, Philip K. *Five Novels of the 1960s and 1970s* (The Library of America, 2008).

Dietzgen, Joseph. *Some of the Philosophical Essays* (Charles H. Kerr, 1906).

Dikötter, Frank. *Mao's Great Famine: The History of China's Most Devastating Catastrophe, 1958–62* (Bloomsbury, 2010).

Dikötter, Frank. *The Tragedy of Liberation: A History of the Chinese Revolution, 1945–57* (Bloomsbury, 2013).

Dixon, Thomas. *Comrades: A Story of Social Adventure in California* (Doubleday, Page & Co., 1909).

Djilas, Milovan. *The New Class: An Analysis of the Communist System* (Thames & Hudson, 1957).

Dodd, Anna Bowman. *The Republic of the Future; or, Socialism a Reality* (Cassell & Co., 1887).

Dolgun, Alexander. *Alexander Dolgun's Story: An American in the Gulag* (Alfred A. Knopf, 1975).

Donnelly, Ignatius. *Atlantis: The Antediluvian World* (Harper & Brothers, 1882).

[Donnelly, Ignatius]. Edmund Boisgilbert. *Caesar's Column* (1890; Wesleyan University Press, 2003).

Donnelly, Ignatius. *The Golden Bottle* (Sampson Low & Co., 1892).

Dooner, Pierton W. *Last Days of the Republic* (Alta California Publishing House, 1880).

Dostoevsky, Fyodor. *The House of the Dead* (William Heinemann, 1915).

Douglas, Mary, ed. *Witchcraft Confessions and Accusations* (Tavistock Publications, 1970).

Douglas, Mary. *Collected Works*, vol. 2: *Purity and Danger: An Analysis of the Concepts of Pollution and Taboo* (Routledge, 2003).

Douthwaite, Julia V. *The Wild Girl, Natural Man and the Monster: Dangerous Experiments in the Age of Enlightenment* (University of Chicago Press, 1992).

Dowling, David. *Fictions of Nuclear Disaster* (University of Iowa Press, 1987).

Doxiadis, Constantinos. *Between Dystopia and Utopia* (Faber & Faber, 1966).

Drucker, Peter. *The End of Economic Man: A Study of the New Totalitarianism* (Harper & Row, 1969).

[Dudgeon, Robert Ellis]. *Colymbia* (Trübner & Co., 1873).

Dudley, Edward, and Maximilian E. Novak, eds., *The Wild Man Within: An Image in Western Thought from the Renaissance to Romanticism* (University of Pittsburgh Press, 1972).

Dunlop, Nic. *The Lost Executioner: A Story of the Khmer Rouge* (Bloomsbury, 2005).

Dunn, Thomas P., and Richard D. Erlich, eds. *The Mechanical God: Machines in Science Fiction* (Greenwood Press, 1982).

Dunn, Thomas P., and Richard D. Erlich, eds. *Clockwork Worlds: Mechanized Environments in SF* (Greenwood Press, 1983).

Durkheim, Emile. *The Elementary Forms of the Religious Life* (Allen & Unwin, 1915).

Dziak, John K. *Chekisty: A History of the KGB* (Lexington Books, 1988).

Ea, Meng-Try. *The Chain of Terror: The Khmer Rouge Southwest Zone Security System* (DC-Cam, 2005).

Eastman, Max. *Artists in Uniform: A Study of Literature and Bureaucratism* (George Allen & Unwin, 1934).

Eastman, Max. *Love and Revolution: My Journey through an Epoch* (Random House, 1964).

Edwards, Lyford P. *The Natural History of Revolution* (University of Chicago Press, 1970).

Eggers, Dave. *The Circle* (Hamish Hamilton, 2013).

Ehrlich, Max. *The Edict* (Bantam Books, 1972).

Eibl-Eibesfeldt, Irenäus. *Love and Hate: On the Natural History of Basic Behaviour Patterns* (Methuen & Co., 1971).

Eisenstadt, S. N. *Fundamentalism, Sectarianism and Revolution: The Jacobin Dimension of Modernity* (Cambridge University Press, 1999).

Eisler, Robert. *Man into Wolf: An Anthropological Interpretation of Sadism, Masochism, and Lycanthropy* (Routledge & Kegan Paul, 1951).

Elias, Norbert. *The Society of Individuals* (University College Dublin Press, 2010).

Elias, Norbert, and John L. Scotson. *The Established and the Outsiders* (University College Dublin Press, 2008).

Elliot, Robert C. *The Shape of Utopia: Studies in a Literary Genre* (University of Chicago Press, 1970).

Elliott, Dyan. *Fallen Bodies: Pollution, Sexuality, and Demonology in the Middle Ages* (University of Pennsylvania Press, 1999).

Ellul, Jacques. *The Technological Society* (Vintage Books, 1964).

Elster, Jon. *Strong Feelings: Emotion, Addiction, and Human Behavior* (MIT Press, 1999).

Elton, Ben. *Blind Faith* (Bantam Press, 2007).

[Emanuel, Victor]. Victor Rousseau. *The Messiah of the Cylinder* (Curtis Brown, 1917).

Emmerson, Richard Kenneth. *Antichrist in the Middle Ages: A Study of Medieval Apocalypticism, Art, and Literature* (Manchester University Press, 1981).

England, George Allan. *The Air Trust* (Phil Wagner, 1915).

Erdman, Carl. *The Origin of the Idea of Crusade* (Princeton University Press, 1977).

Etcheson, Craig. *After the Killing Fields: Lessons from the Cambodian Genocide* (Praeger, 2015).

Etymonia (Samuel Tinsley, 1875).

Eurich, Nell. *Science in Utopia: A Mighty Design* (Harvard University Press, 1967).

Evans, Richard. *The Third Reich at War: How the Nazis Led Germany from Conquest to Disaster* (Penguin Books, 2008).

Evans-Pritchard, E. *Theories of Primitive Religion* (Clarendon Press, 1965).

Everitt, Graham. *Guillotine the Great and Her Successors* (Ward and Downey, 1890).

[Fairchild, Charles]. *The Socialist Revolution of 1888* (Harrison & Sons, 1884).

Fanon, Frantz. *The Wretched of the Earth* (Grove Press, 1968).

Faulconbridge, Paul. *Commissars over Britain* (The Beaufort Press, 1947).

Fehér, Ferenc, ed. *The French Revolution and the Birth of Modernity* (University of California Press, 1990).

Ferguson, Adam. *An Essay on the History of Civil Society* (1767; Edinburgh University Press, 1966).

Fetzer, Leland, ed. *Pre-Revolutionary Russian Science Fiction: An Anthology* (*Seven Utopias and a Dream*) (Ardis, 1982).

Fifty Adventures into the Unknown (Odhams Press, 1938).

Figes, Orlando. *A People's Tragedy: The Russian Revolution 1891–1924* (Pimlico, 1997).

Figes, Orlando. *The Whisperers: Private Life in Stalin's Russia* (Allen Lane, 2007).

Firchow, Peter. *The End of Utopia: A Study of Aldous Huxley's Brave New World* (Bucknell University Press, 1984).

Fiske, Susan T. *Social Beings: Core Motives in Social Psychology* (John Wiley, 2010).

Fitzpatrick, Sheila. *Everyday Stalinism: Ordinary Life in Extraordinary Times. Soviet Russia in the 1930s* (Oxford University Press, 1999).

Florinsky, Michael T. *Fascism and National Socialism* (Macmillan, 1936).

Foigny, Gabriel de. *The Southern Land Known* (1676), ed. David Fausett (Syracuse University Press, 1993).

Follingsby, Kenneth. *Meda: A Tale of the Future* (Printed for Private Circulation, 1891).

Ford, Henry. *My Life and Work* (William Heinemann, 1923).

Forrest, W. G. *A History of Sparta 950–152 BC* (Hutchinson, 1968).

Forster, E. M. *The Machine Stops and Other Stories* (Andre Deutsch, 1997).

Forsyth, Neil. *The Old Enemy: Satan and the Combat Myth* (Princeton University Press, 1987).

Foucault, Michel. *Discipline and Punish: The Birth of the Prison* (Penguin Books, 1979).

Fowler, Roger. *The Language of George Orwell* (Macmillan, 1995).

Fraenkel, Ernst. *The Dual State: A Contribution to the Theory of Dictatorship* (Oxford University Press, 1941).

France, Anatole. *The Gods are Athirst* (The Bodley Head, 1913).

Frank, Pat. *Alas Babylon* (Constable & Co., 1959).

Franklin, H. Bruce. *Future Perfect: American Science Fiction of the Nineteenth Century* (Oxford University Press, 1978).

Frayn, Michael. *A Very Private Life* (Collins, 1968).

Frayn, Michael. *My Father's Fortune: A Life* (Windsor, 2011).

Frazer, Shamus. *A Shroud as Well as a Shirt* (Chapman & Hall, 1935).

Freud, Sigmund. *Group Psychology and the Analysis of the Ego* (Bantam Books, 1960).

Freud, Sigmund. *Totem and Taboo: Some Points of Agreement between the Mental Lives of Savages and Neurotics* (Routledge & Kegan Paul, 1960).

Freud, Sigmund. *Civilization and Its Discontents* (W. W. Norton, 1961).

Freud, Sigmund. *The Future of an Illusion* (Anchor Books, 1964).

Friedländer, Saul, Gerald Holton, Leo Marx, and Eugene Skolnikoff, eds. *Visions of Apocalypse: End or Rebirth?* (Holmes & Meier, 1985).

Friedman, John B. *The Monstrous Races in Medieval Art and Thought* (Harvard University Press, 1981).

Friedrich, Carl J., and Zbigniew K. Brzezinski. *Totalitarian Dictatorship and Autocracy* (Harvard University Press, 1956).

Friedrich, Carl J., Michael Curtis, and Benjamin R. Barber. *Totalitarianism in Perspective: Three Views* (Pall Mall Press, 1969).

Friesen, Abraham. *Thomas Muentzer: A Destroyer of the Godless* (University of California Press, 1990).

Fritzsche, Peter. *Life and Death in the Third Reich* (Harvard University Press, 2008).

Fromm, Erich. *Escape from Freedom* (Holt, Rinehart & Winston, 1941).

Fromm, Erich. *The Sane Society* (Routledge & Kegan Paul, 1956).

Fromm, Erich. *The Anatomy of Human Destructiveness* (Fawcett Crest, 1973).

Fromm, Erich. *On Disobedience and Other Essays* (Routledge & Kegan Paul, 1984).

Frye, Steven. *Understanding Cormac McCarthy* (University of South Carolina Press, 2009).

Frye, Steven, ed. *The Cambridge Companion to Cormac McCarthy* (Cambridge University Press, 2013).

Fuller, Lieut. Alvarado M. *A.D. 2000: A Novel* (Laird & Lee, 1890).

Fülöp-Miller, Rene. *The Mind and Face of Bolshevism* (G. P. Putnam's Sons, 1927).

Furet, François. *Interpreting the French Revolution* (Cambridge University Press, 1981).

Furet, François. *The Passing of an Illusion: The Idea of Communism in the Twentieth Century* (University of Chicago Press, 1999).

Galow, Timothy W. *Understanding Dave Eggers* (University of South Carolina Press, 2014).

[Galloway, James M.]. *John Harvey: A Tale of the Twentieth Century* (Charles H. Kerr, 1897).

Gasiorek, A. *J. G. Ballard* (Manchester University Press, 2005).

Gearhart, Sally. *The Wanderground: Stories of the Hill Women* (1978; The Women's Press, 1985).

Gedulde, Caroline. *Bernard Wolfe* (Twayne, 1972).

Gee, Maggie. *The Ice People* (Richard Cohen Books, 1998).

Geifman, Anna. *Thou Shalt Kill: Revolutionary Terrorism in Russia, 1894–1917* (Princeton University Press, 1993).

Geiger, H. Kent. *The Family in Soviet Russia* (Harvard University Press, 1968).

Geissler, L. A. *Looking Beyond: A Sequel to 'Looking Backward', by Edward Bellamy, and An Answer to 'Looking Further Forward', by Richard Michaelis* (William Reeves, 1891).

Geldern, James von. *Bolshevik Festivals 1917–1920* (University of California Press, 1993).

Gellately, Robert. *The Gestapo and German Society* (Clarendon Press, 1990).

Gellately, Robert. *Lenin, Stalin, and Hitler: The Age of Social Catastrophe* (Jonathan Cape, 2007).

Gentile, Emilio. *Politics as Religion* (Princeton University Press, 2006).

George Orwell and Nineteen Eighty-Four (Library of Congress, 1985).

George, Henry. *Progress and Poverty* (1879; The Hogarth Press, 1953).

Getty, J. Arch, and Roberta T. Manning, eds. *Stalinist Terror: New Perspectives* (Cambridge University Press, 1993).

Getty, J. Arch, and Oleg V. Naumov. *The Road to Terror: Stalin and the Self-Destruction of the Bolsheviks, 1932–1939* (Yale University Press, 1999).

Geyer, Michael, and Sheila Fitzpatrick. *Beyond Totalitarianism: Stalinism and Nazism Compared* (Cambridge University Press, 2009).

Gibbon, Edwarda. *History of the Decline and Fall of the British Empire* (Field & Tuer, 1884).

Gibbs, Philip. *The Day after Tomorrow: What is Going to Happen in the World?* (Hutchinson & Co., 1928).

Gibson, William. *Virtual Light* (Penguin, 1993).

Gidez, Richard B. *P. D. James* (Twayne, 1986).

Gilbert, Geoffrey, ed. *Malthus: Critical Responses* (4 vols, Routledge, 1998).

Gilison, Jerome M. *The Soviet Image of Utopia* (Johns Hopkins University Press, 1975).

Gilmore, David D. *Monsters: Evil Beings, Mythical Beasts, and All Manner of Imaginary Terrors* (University of Pennsylvania Press, 2003).

Gindin, James. *William Golding* (Macmillan, 1988).

Ginsborg, Paul. *Family Politics: Domestic Life, Devastation and Survival 1900–1950* (Yale University Press, 2014).

Ginzburg, Carlo. *The Night Battles: Witchcraft and Agrarian Cults in the Sixteenth and Seventeenth Centuries* (Routledge & Kegan Paul, 1983).

Ginzburg, Evgenia Semyonova. *Into the Whirlwind* (Collins/Harvill, 1967).

Girard, René. *Violence and the Sacred* (Johns Hopkins University Press, 1977).

Girard, René. *The Scapegoat* (The Athlone Press, 1986).

Gleason, Abbott. *Totalitarianism: The Inner History of the Cold War* (Oxford University Press, 1995).

Gleason, Abbott, Jack Goldsmith, and Martha C. Nussbaum, eds. *On Nineteen Eighty-Four: Orwell and Our Future* (Princeton University Press, 2005).

Glover, Edward. *War, Sadism and Pacifism: Further Essays on Group Psychology and War* (George Allen & Unwin, 1946).

Glover, Jonathan. *Alien Landscapes? Interpreting Disordered Minds* (Harvard University Press, 2014).

Godbeer, Richard. *The Devil's Dominion: Magic and Religion in Early New England* (Cambridge University Press, 1992).

Goffman, Erving. *Asylums: Essays on the Social Situation of Mental Patients and Other Inmates* (Doubleday & Co., 1961).

Goffman, Erving. *Relations in Public: Microstudies of the Public Order* (Penguin Books, 1971).

Goldhagen, Daniel Jonah. *Hitler's Willing Executioners: Ordinary Germans and the Holocaust* (Little, Brown & Co., 1996).

Goldhammer, Jesse. *The Headless Republic: Sacrificial Violence in Modern French Thought* (Cornell University Press, 2005).

Golding, William. *Lord of the Flies* (Faber & Faber, 1954).

Goldman, Wendy Z. *Terror and Democracy in the Age of Stalin* (Cambridge University Press, 2007).

Gorabatov, A. V. *Years Off My Life: The Memoirs of General of the Soviet Army* (Constable, 1964).

Gordin, Michael D., Helen Tilley, and Gyan Prakash, eds. *Utopia/Dystopia: Conditions of Historical Possibility* (Princeton University Press, 2010).

Gottlieb, Erika. *The Orwell Conundrum: A Cry of Despair or Faith in the Spirit of Man?* (Carleton University Press, 1992).

Gottlieb, Erika. *Dystopian Fiction East and West* (McGill-Queen's University Press, 2001).

Graf, Arturo. *The Story of the Devil* (Macmillan & Co., 1931).

Graham, Elaine L. *Representations of the Post/Human: Monsters, Aliens and Others in Popular Culture* (Manchester University Press, 2012).

Graham, P. Anderson. *The Collapse of Homo Sapiens* (G. P. Putnam's Sons, 1923).

Grant, I. F. *A Candle in the Hills* (Hodder & Stoughton, 1926).

Gratacap, L. P. *The Mayor of New York: A Romance of Days to Come* (G. W. Dillingham Co., 1910).

Gray, Alasdair. *Lanark: A Life in Four Books* (Canongate Publishing, 1981).

Gray, John. *Black Mass: Apocalyptic Religion and the Death of Utopia* (Allen Lane, 2007).

Gray, John. *The Soul of the Marionette: A Short Inquiry into Human Freedom* (Allen Lane, 2015).

Green, Toby. *Inquisition: The Reign of Fear* (Macmillan, 2007).

Gregory, Owen. *Meccania: The Super-State* (Methuen & Co., 1918).

Gregory, Paul R. *Terror by Quota: State Security from Lenin to Stalin* (Yale University Press, 2009).

Greif, Gideon. *We Wept without Tears: Testimonies of the Jewish Sonderkommando from Auschwitz* (Yale University Press, 2005).

Grierson, Francis D. *Heart of the Moon* (Alston Rivers Ltd, 1928).

Griffin, Roger, ed. *Fascism, Totalitarianism and Political Religion* (Routledge, 2005).

Griffith, George. *The Angel of the Revolution: A Tale of the Coming Terror* (1893; Routledge, 1998).

Gross, Miriam, ed. *The World of George Orwell* (Weidenfeld & Nicolson, 1971).

Gutman, Yisrael, and Michael Berenbaum, eds. *Anatomy of the Auschwitz Deathcamp* (Indiana University Press, 1994).

Hackett, David A., ed. *The Buchenwald Report* (Westview Press, 1995).

Haedicke, Paul. *The Equalities of Para-Para* (Schuldt-Gathmann Co., 1895).

Haffner, Sebastian. *Germany: Jekyll and Hyde* (Secker & Warburg, 1940).

Hagenloh, Paul. *Public Order and Mass Repression in the USSR, 1926–1941* (Johns Hopkins University Press, 2009).

Haldane, Charlotte. *Man's World* (Chatto & Windus, 1926).

Halfin, Igal. *From Darkness to Light: Class, Consciousness and Salvation in Revolutionary Russia* (University of Pittsburgh Press, 2000).

Halfin, Igal. *Terror in My Soul: Communist Autobiographies on Trial* (Harvard University Press, 2003).

Halfin, Igal. *Stalinist Confessions: Messianism and Terror at the Leningrad Communist University* (University of Pittsburgh Press, 2009).

Hall, Frederic T. *The Pedigree of the Devil* (Trübner & Co., 1883).

Hambrook, Emerson C. *The Red To-Morrow* (The Proletarian Press, 1920).

Hamerton-Kelly, Robert G., ed. *Violent Origins: Robert Burkert, René Girard, and Jonathan Z. Smith on Ritual Killing and Cultural Formation* (Stanford University Press, 1987).

Hamilton, Patrick. *Impromptu in Moribundia* (Constable & Co., 1939).

Hammond, J. R., ed. *A George Orwell Companion* (Macmillan, 1962).

Hanke, Lewis. *All Mankind is One: A Study of the Disputation between Bartolomé de las Casas and Juan Ginés de Sepúlveda in 1550 on the Intellectual and Religious Capacity of the American Indians* (Northern Illinois University Press, 1974).

Harben, Will N. *The Land of the Changing Sun* (The Merriam Company, 1894).

Harris, Robert. *Fatherland* (Hutchinson, 1992).

Harris, W. S. *Life in a Thousand Worlds* (The Minter Co., 1905).

Harrison, Harry. *Make Room! Make Room!* (Penguin Books, 1967).

Hartland, Edwin Sidney. *The Science of Fairy Tales* (Walter Scott, 1891).

Hartley, L. P. *Facial Justice* (Hamish Hamilton, 1960).

Hartshorne, Henry. *1931: A Glance at the Twentieth Century* (E. Claxton & Co., 1881).

Hastings, Milo M. *The City of Endless Night* (1920; Hesperus Books, 2014).

Hay, William Delisle. *Three Hundred Years Hence* (Newman & Co., 1881).

Hayek, Friedrich von. *The Road to Serfdom* (University of Chicago Press, 1944).

Hayes, Frederick W. *The Great Revolution of 1905; or, the Story of the Phalanx* (R. Forder, 1893).

Hazlitt, Henry. *The Great Idea* (Appleton-Century-Crofts, 1951).

Hellbeck, Jochen. *Revolution on My Mind: Writing a Diary under Stalin* (Harvard University Press, 2006).

Heller, Mikhail, and Aleksandr Nekrich. *Utopia in Power: The History of the Soviet Union from 1917 to the Present* (Hutchinson, 1986).

Henderson, Alexander. *Aldous Huxley* (Chatto & Windus, 1935).

[Henham, Ernest George]. *John Trevena: The Reign of the Saints* (Alson Rivers, 1911).

Herbert, William. *The World Grown Young* (W. H. Allen & Co., 1892).

Herf, Jeffrey. *The Jewish Enemy: Nazi Propaganda during World War II and the Holocaust* (Harvard University Press, 2006).

Herling, Gustav. *A World Apart* (William Heinemann, 1951).

Hermand, Jost. *Old Dreams of a New Reich: Volkish Utopias and National Socialism* (Indiana University Press, 1992).

Herrick, Robert. *Sometime* (Farrar & Rinehart, 1933).

Hertzler, Joyce. *The History of Utopian Thought* (George Allen & Unwin, 1923).

Hesdin, Raoul. *The Journal of a Spy in Paris during the Reign of Terror* (John Murray, 1895).

Hester, Marianne. *Lewd Women and Wicked Witches: A Study of the Dynamics of Male Domination* (Routledge, 1992).

Hicks, Granville. *The First to Awaken* (Modern Age Books, 1940).

Higonnet, Patrice. *Goodness beyond Virtue: Jacobins during the French Revolution* (Harvard University Press, 1998).

Hill, Christopher. *Antichrist in Seventeenth-Century England* (Oxford University Press, 1971).

Hillegas, Mark. *The Future as Nightmare: H.G. Wells and the Anti-Utopians* (Southern Illinois University Press, 1967).

Him, Chanrithy. *When Broken Glass Floats: Growing Up under the Khmer Rouge* (W. W. Norton, 2000).

Hinton, Alexander Laban. *Why Did They Kill? Cambodia in the Age of Genocide* (University of California Press, 2005).

Hitler, Adolf. *Mein Kampf* (Hurst & Blackett, 1939).

Hitler, Adolf. *The Speeches of Adolf Hitler 1922–39* (2 vols, Oxford University Press, 1942).

Hitler, Adolf. *Hitler's Table-Talk 1941–1944* (Weidenfeld & Nicolson, 1953).

Hoban, Russell. *Riddley Walker* (Jonathan Cape, 1980).

Hobsbawm, Eric. *Primitive Rebels: Studies in Archaic Form of Social Movement in the 19th and 20th Centuries* (Manchester University Press, 1959).

Hobsbawm, Eric. *Interesting Times: A Twentieth Century Life* (Abacus Books, 2002).

Hochschild, Adam. *The Unquiet Ghost: Russians Remember Stalin* (Viking Penguin, 1994).

Hodgen, Margaret T. *Early Anthropology in the Sixteenth and Seventeenth Centuries* (University of Pennsylvania Press, 1964).

Hoess, Rudolf. *Commandant of Auschwitz: The Autobiography of Rudolf Hoess* (Phoenix Press, 2000).

Holland, Jack. *A Brief History of Misogyny* (Constable & Robinson, 2006).

Hollander, Paul, ed. *From the Gulag to the Killing Fields: Personal Accounts of Political Violence and Repression in Communist States* (ISI Books, 2006).

[House, Edward Mandell]. *Philip Dru: Administrator, A Story of Tomorrow 1920–1935* (B. W. Huebsch, 1920).

Howe, Irving. *Decline of the New* (Victor Gollancz, 1971).

Howe, Irving, ed. *1984 Revisited: Totalitarianism in Our Century* (Harper & Row, 1983).

Howells, Coral Ann. *Margaret Atwood* (St. Martin's Press, 1996).

Howells, Coral Ann, ed. *The Cambridge Companion to Margaret Atwood* (Cambridge University Press, 2006).

Hubert, Henri, and Marcel Mauss. *Sacrifice: Its Nature and Function* (University of Chicago Press, 1964).

Hunter, Lynette. *George Orwell: The Search for a Voice* (Open University Press, 1984).

Hutschnecker, Arnold A. *Love and Hate in Human Nature* (Skeffington, 1956).

Huxley, Aldous. *Crome Yellow* (Chatto & Windus, 1921).

Huxley, Aldous. *Proper Studies* (Chatto & Windus, 1929).

Huxley, Aldous. *Antic Hay* (Chatto & Windus, 1923; repr. 1973).

Huxley, Aldous. *Music at Night* (Chatto & Windus, 1931).

Huxley, Aldous. *Ends and Means. An Enquiry into the Nature of Ideals and into the Methods Employed for their Realization* (Chatto & Windus, 1937).

Huxley, Aldous. *After Many a Summer* (Chatto & Windus, 1939).

Huxley, Aldous. *Point Counter Point* (Chatto & Windus, 1947).

Huxley, Aldous. *Ape and Essence: A Novel* (Chatto & Windus, 1949).

Huxley, Aldous. *Time Must Have A Stop* (Chatto & Windus, 1948).

Huxley, Aldous. *Themes and Variations* (Chatto & Windus, 1950).

Huxley, Aldous. *The Devils of Loudun* (Chatto & Windus, 1952).

Huxley, Aldous. *Tomorrow and Tomorrow and Tomorrow* (Harper & Brothers, 1952).

Huxley, Aldous. *Heaven and Hell* (Chatto & Windus, 1956).

Huxley, Aldous. *Collected Essays* (Harper & Brothers, 1958).

Huxley, Aldous. *Island* (Chatto & Windus, 1962).

Huxley, Aldous. *Brave New World Revisited* (Harper & Row, 1965).

Huxley, Aldous. *Letters of Aldous Huxley*, ed. Grover Smith (Chatto & Windus, 1969).

Huxley, Aldous. *Literature and Science; and, Science, Liberty and Peace* (Chatto & Windus, 1970).

Huxley, Aldous. *The Human Situation* (1959; Chatto & Windus, 1978).

Huxley, Adous. *The Politics of Ecology* (Center for the Study of Democratic Institutions, 1963).

Huxley, Aldous. *Moksha: Writings on Psychedelics and the Visionary Experience, 1931–1963* (Chatto & Windus, 1980).

Huxley, Aldous. *Complete Essays*, 6 vols, ed. Robert S. Baker and James Sexton, (Ivan R. Dee, 2000–2002).

Huxley, Aldous. *Brave New World*, intro. by Margaret Atwood and David Bradshaw (Vintage, 2007).

Huxley, Aldous. *Selected Letters* (Ivan R. Dee, 2007).

Huxley, Julian, ed. *Aldous Huxley* (Chatto & Windus, 1965).

Hynes, Samuel, ed. *Twentieth-Century Interpretations of 1984* (Prentice Hall, 1971).

In the Future: A Sketch in Ten Chapters (Hampstead, 1875).

Ingle, Stephen. *George Orwell. A Political Life* (Manchester University Press, 1993).

Inkeles, Alex, and Raymond A. Bauer. *The Soviet Citizen: Daily Life in a Totalitarian Society* (Harvard University Press, 1959).

Isaacs, Harold R. *Idols of the Tribe: Group Identity and Political Change* (Harvard University Press, 1989).

Ishiguro, Kazuo. *Never Let Me Go* (Faber & Faber, 2005).

Izzo, David Garrett, and Kim Kirkpatrick, eds. *Huxley's Brave New World: Essays* (McFarland & Co., 2008).

J. J. J. *The Blue Shirts* (Simpkin, Marshall, Hamilton, Kent & Co., 1926).

Jackson, Karl D., ed. *Cambodia 1975–1978* (Princeton University Press, 1989).

Jaher, Frederic Cople. *Doubters and Dissenters: Cataclysmic Thought in America, 1885–1918* (Free Press, 1964).

James, P. D. *The Children of Men* (Faber & Faber, 1992).

Jameson, Fredric. *Marxism and Form: Twentieth-Century Dialectical Theories of Literature* (Princeton University Press, 1971).

Jameson, Fredric. *The Political Unconscious: Narrative as a Socially Symbolic Act* (Routledge, 1983).

Jameson, Fredric. *Archaeologies of the Future: The Desire for Utopia and Other Science Fictions* (Verso, 2005).

Jameson, [Margaret] Storm. *Then We Shall Hear Singing* (Cassell & Co., 1942).

Jameson, Storm. *In the Second Year* (Cassell & Co, 1936).

Ja'szi, Oscar, and John D. Lewis. *Against the Tyrant: The Tradition and Theory of Tyrannicide* (Free Press, 1957).

Jefferies, Richard. *After London* (Cassell & Co., 1885).

Jenks, Gregory C. *The Origins and Early Development of the Antichrist Myth* (Walter de Gruyter, 1991).

Jensen, David, and Claus-Christian W. Szejnmann, eds. *Ordinary People as Mass Murderers: Perpetrators in Comparative Perspective* (Palgrave Macmillan, 2008).

Jensen, Ejner J., ed. *The Future of* Nineteen Eighty-Four (University of Michigan Press, 1984).

Jiaqi, Yan, and Gao Gao. *Turbulent Decade: A History of the Cultural Revolution* (University of Hawaii Press, 1996).

Jiehong, Jiang. *Red: China's Cultural Revolution* (Jonathan Cape, 2010).

Jisheng, Yang. *Tombstone: The Untold Story of Mao's Great Famine* (Allen Lane, 2012).

Johnson, Eric A. *Nazi Terror: The Gestapo, Jews, and Ordinary Germans* (John Murray, 1999).

Johnson, Eric A., and Karl-Heinz Reuband. *What We Knew: Terror, Mass Murder, and Everyday Life in Nazi Germany: An Oral History* (John Murray, 2005).

Johnson, Wayne L. *Ray Bradbury* (Ungar, 1980).

Jones, Edward T. *L. P. Hartley* (Twayne, 1978).

Jones, Ernest. *On the Nightmare* (The Hogarth Press, 1931).

Jouvenel, Bertrand de. *Sovereignty* (Cambridge University Press, 1957).

Jung, Carl. *Psychological Types or the Psychology of Individuation* (Kegan Paul, Trench, Trubner & Co., 1923).

Kafka, Franz. *The Trial* (Everyman's Library, 1992).

Kamm, Henry. *Cambodia: Report from a Stricken Land* (Arcade Publishing, 1998).

Kaplan, Matt. *The Science of Monsters* (Constable, 2013).

Kardiner, Abram. *The Individual and His Society: The Psychodynamics of Primitive Social Organization* (Columbia University Press, 1939).

Karinthy, Frigyes. *Voyage to Faremido Capillaria*, tr. Paul Tabori (Corvina Press, 1965).

Karp, David. *One: A Novel* (Victor Gollancz, 1954).

Kasson, John F. *Civilizing the Machine: Technology and Republican Values in America 1776–1900* (Viking Press, 1976).

Kateb, George. *Utopia and Its Enemies* (Schocken Books, 1972).

Kautsky, Karl. *Terrorism and Communism* (George Allen & Unwin, 1920).

Kearney, Richard. *Strangers, Gods and Monsters: Interpreting Otherness* (Routledge, 2003).

Kee, Robert. *A Sign of the Times* (Eyre & Spottiswoode, 1955).

Keith, W. J. *Richard Jefferies: A Critical Study* (University of Toronto Press, 1965).

Kelly, Henry Ansgar. *Satan: A Biography* (Cambridge University Press, 2006).

Kelsen, Hans. *Secular Religion: A Polemic against the Misinterpretation of Modern Social Philosophy, Science and Politics as 'New Religions'* (Springer, 2012).

Kerr, Wilfred B. *The Reign of Terror 1793–4* (University of Toronto Press, 1927).

Kershaw, Ian. *The Nazi Dictatorship: Problems of Perspective and Interpretation* (Arnold, 2000).

Kershaw, Ian. *Hitler, the Germans, and the Final Solution* (Yale University Press, 2008).

Kerslake, Patricia. *Science Fiction and Empire* (Liverpool University Press, 2007).

Ketterer, David. *New Worlds for Old: The Apocalyptic Imagination, Science Fiction, and American Literature* (Anchor Press, 1974).

Kharkhordin, Oleg. *The Collective and the Individual in Russia: A Study of Practices* (University of California Press, 1999).

Khlevniuk, Oleg V. *The History of the Gulag* (Yale University Press, 2004).

Kierkegaard, Søren. *The Concept of Dread* (Princeton University Press, 1957).

Kiernan, Ben. *The Pol Pot Regime: Race, Power and Genocide in Cambodia under the Khmer Rouge, 1975–79* (2nd edn, Yale University Press, 2004).

Kiliç, Mine Özyurt. *Maggie Gee: Writing the Condition of England Novel* (Bloomsbury Academic, 2013).

Kim, Sathavy. *A Shattered Youth: Surviving the Khmer Rouge* (Maverick House, 2010).

Kitchin, George. *Prisoner of the OGPU* (Longmans, Green & Co., 1935).

Klaits, Joseph. *Servants of Satan: The Age of the Witch Hunts* (Indiana University Press, 1985).

Klein, Carole. *Doris Lessing: A Biography* (Duckworth, 2000).

Klinkowitz, Jerome. *Kurt Vonnegut* (Methuen, 1982).

Knox, R. A. *Enthusiasm: A Chapter in the History of Religion* (Clarendon Press, 1950).

Koestler, Arthur. *Darkness at Noon* (Jonathan Cape, 1940).

Koestler, Arthur. *The Yogi and the Commissar* (Jonathan Cape, 1945).

Koestler, Arthur. *Arrow in the Blue: An Autobiography* (Collins, 1952).

Koestler, Arthur. *The Invisible Writing* (Collins, 1954).

Koestler, Arthur. *The Ghost in the Machine* (Hutchinson, 1967).

Koestler, Arthur. *The God that Failed: Six Studies in Communism* (Hamish Hamilton, 1950).

Kogon, Eugen. *The Theory and Practice of Hell: The German Concentration Camps and the System behind Them* (Octagon Books, 1973).

Kołakowski, Leszek. *The Death of Utopia Reconsidered* (Cambridge University Press, 1983).

Kolnai, Aurel. *The War against the West* (Victor Gollancz, 1938).

Koonz, Claudia. *Mothers in the Fatherland: Women, the Family and Nazi Politics* (Jonathan Cape, 1987).

Kopelev, Lev. *No Jail for Thought* (Secker & Warburg, 1977).

Kopelev, Lev. *The Education of a True Believer* (Wildwood House, 1981).

Koselleck, R. *The Practice of Conceptual History* (Stanford University Press, 2002).

Koselleck, Reinhart. *Futures Past: On the Semantics of Historical Time*, tr. Keith Tribe (Columbia University Press, 2004).

Kotkin, Stephen. *Magnetic Mountain: Stalinism as a Civilization* (University of California Press, 1995).

Kotkin, Stephen. *Stalin*, vol. 1: *Paradoxes of Power, 1878–1928* (Allen Lane, 2014).

Krivitsky, W. G. *In Stalin's Secret Service* (1938; Enigma Books, 2000).

Krutch, Joseph. *The Measure of Man* (Alvin Redman, 1956).

Kubal, David L. *Outside the Whale: Orwell's Art and Politics* (University of Notre Dame Press, 1972).

Kubizek, August. *Young Hitler: The Story of Our Friendship* (Mann, 1973).

Kucukalic, Lejla. *Philip K. Dick: Canonical Writer of the Digital Age* (Routledge, 2008).

Kuehling, Susanne. *Dobu: Ethics of Exchange on a Massim Island, Papua New Guinea* (University of Hawaii Press, 2005).

Kumar, Krishan. *Utopia and Anti-Utopia in Modern Times* (Basil Blackwell, 1987).

Kumar, Krishan. *Utopianism* (Open University Press, 1991).

Kune, N. *The Need to Belong: Rediscovering Maslow's Hierarchy of Needs* (Paul H. Brookes Publishers, 2011).

La Mettrie, Julien Offray de. *Man a Machine* (The Open Court Publishing Co., 1927).

Landes, Richard. *Heaven on Earth: The Varieties of the Millennial Experience* (Oxford University Press, 2011).

Lane, Mary E. Bradley. *Mizora: A Prophecy* (Syracuse University Press, 1990).

Langbein, Hermann. *People in Auschwitz* (University of North Carolina Press, 2004).

Larina, Anna. *This I Cannot Forget: The Memoirs of Nicolai Bukharin's Widow* (W. W. Norton, 1993).

Larner, Christina. *Witchcraft and Religion* (Basil Blackwell, 1984).

Lasky, Melvin. *Utopia and Revolution* (University of Chicago Press, 1976).

Lazarus, Henry. *The English Revolution of the Twentieth Century: A Prospective History* (T. F. Unwin, 1894).

Le Bon, Gustave. *The Crowd: A Study of the Popular Mind* (T. Fisher Unwin, 1896).

Le Bon, Gustave. *The Psychology of Socialism* (T. Fisher Unwin, 1899).

Le Bon, Gustave. *The Psychology of Revolution* (T. Fisher Unwin, 1913).

Le Bon, Gustave. *The World in Revolt: A Psychological Study of Our Times* (T. Fisher Unwin, 1921).

Le Guin, Ursula. *The Lathe of Heaven* (Grafton Books, 1974).

Le Queux, William. *The Great War in England in 1897* (Tower Publishing Co., 1894).

Le Queux, William. *The Invasion of 1910* (Eveleigh Nash, 1906).

Le Queux, William. *The Unknown Tomorrow: How the Rich Fared at the Hands of the Poor, Together with a Full Account of the Social Revolution in England* (F. V. White, 1910).

Lea, Henry Charles. *The Inquisition of the Middle Ages* (Eyre & Spottiswood, 1963).

Lederer, Emil. *State of the Masses: The Threat of the Classless Society* (W. W. Norton, 1940).

Lederer, Wolfgang. *The Fear of Women* (Grune & Stratton, 1968).

Lee, Robert A. *Orwell's Fiction* (University of Notre Dame Press, 1969).

Leese, Daniel. *Mao Cult: Rhetoric and Revolution in China's Cultural Revolution* (Cambridge University Press, 2011).

Lefebvre, Georges. *The Great Fear of 1789: Rural Panic in Revolutionary France* (NLB, 1973).

Leff, Gordon. *Heresy in the Later Middle Ages* (Manchester University Press, 1967).

Lenin, V. I. *The State and Revolution* (2nd edn, Communist Party of Great Britain, 1925).

Lenin, V. I. *The Proletarian Revolution and Kautsky the Renegade* (Modern Books, 1929).

Lenotre, G. *The September Massacres* (Hutchinson & Co., 1929).

Lerner, Robert E. *The Heresy of the Free Spirit in the Later Middle Ages* (University of California Press, 1972).

Lessing, Doris. *The Memoirs of a Survivor* (The Octagon Press, 1974).

Lessner, Erwin. *Phantom Victory: The Fourth Reich: 1945–1960* (G. P. Putnam's Sons, 1944).

Levene, Mark. *Genocide in the Age of the Nation-State*, vol. 1: *The Meaning of Genocide* (I.B. Taurus, 2005).

Levi, Primo. *The Reawakening* (Little, Brown & Company, 1965).

Levi, Primo. *If This is a Man* and *The Truce* (Penguin Books, 1979).

Levi, Primo. *Moments of Reprieve* (Abacus Books, 1987).

Levi, Primo. *The Drowned and the Saved* (Abacus Books, 1988).

Levin, Ira. *This Perfect Day* (Fawcett Crest, 1970).

Levitas, Ruth. *The Concept of Utopia* (Syracuse University Press, 1990).

Lévy-Bruhl, Lucien. *How Natives Think* (George Allen & Unwin, 1926).

Lévy-Bruhl, Lucien. *The 'Soul' of the Primitive* (George Allen & Unwin, 1928).

Lévy-Bruhl, Lucien. *Primitives and the Supernatural* (George Allen & Unwin, 1936).

Lewis, Arthur O., ed. *American Utopias: Selected Short Fiction* (Arno Press, 1971).

Lewis, Peter. *George Orwell: The Road to 1984* (Heinemann Quixote Press, 1981).

Lewis, Sinclair. *It Can't Happen Here* (Jonathan Cape, 1935).

Li, Zhisui. *The Private Life of Chairman Mao* (Chatto & Windus, 1994).

Lianke, Yan. *The Four Books* (Chatto & Windus, 2015).

Lifton, Robert Jay. *Thought Reform and the Psychology of Totalism: A Study of 'Brainwashing' in China* (Penguin Books, 1967).

Lindquist, James. *Kurt Vonnegut* (Ungar, 1977).

Lipow, Arthur. *Authoritarian Socialism in America: Edward Bellamy and the Nationalist Movement* (University of California Press, 1982).

Lipper, Elinor. *Eleven Years in Soviet Prison Camps* (Hollis & Carter, 1951).

Llewellyn, Alun. *The Strange Invaders* (G. Bell & Sons, 1934).

Locard, Henri. *Pol Pot's Little Red Book: The Sayings of Angkar* (Silkworm Books, 2004).

Lodge, David. *Evelyn Waugh* (Columbia University Press, 1971).

London, Artur. *The Confession* (William Morrow & Company, 1970).

London, Jack. *The People of the Abyss* (Isbister, 1903).

London, Jack. *The Iron Heel* (Mills & Boon, 1908).

London, Jack. *The Scarlet Plague* (Mills & Boon, 1912).

Longerich, Peter. *Holocaust: The Nazi Persecution and Murder of the Jews* (Oxford University Press, 2010).

Loomis, Stanley. *Paris in the Terror* (Jonathan Cape, 1964).

Lüthi, Max. *Once upon a Time: On the Nature of Fairy Tales* (Indiana University Press, 1966).

Lyons, Eugene. *Assignment in Utopia* (George G. Harrap & Co., 1938).

Macaulay, Rose. *What Not: A Prophetic Comedy* (Constable & Co., 1919).

McCarthy, Cormac. *The Road* (Picador, 2006).

McCrindle, J. W. *Ancient India as Described by Megasthenes and Arrian* (Trübner & Co., 1877).

McCrindle, J. W. *Ancient India as Described in Classical Literature* (Philo Press, 1971).

McDonnell, Jacqueline. *Evelyn Waugh* (Macmillan, 1988).

McDougall, William. *The Group Mind: A Sketch of the Principles of Collective Psychology* (Cambridge University Press, 1920).

Machajski, Waclaw. *The Evolution of Social Democracy* (1899).

Mackail, J. W. *The Life of William Morris* (2 vols, Longmans, Green & Co., 1899).

Mackay, Charles. *Memoirs of Extraordinary Popular Delusions* (3 vols, Richard Bentley, 1841).

[Macnie, John]. Ismar Thiusen. *The Diothas or A Far Look Ahead* (G. Putnam's Sons, 1883).

Maguire, Peter. *Facing Death in Cambodia* (Columbia University Press, 2005).

Maier, Hans, and Michael Schäfer, eds. *Totalitarianism and Political Religion* (3 vols, Routledge, 2007).

Malinowski, Bronisław. *Freedom and Civilization* (George Allen & Unwin, 1947).

Malinowski, Bronisław. *Magic, Science and Religion and Other Essays* (Free Press, 1948).

Mandelstam, Nadezhda. *Hope against Hope: A Memoir* (Collins & Harvill, 1971).

Mandelstam, Nadezhda. *Hope Abandoned: A Memoir* (Collins & Harvill, 1974).

Mandeville, Sir John. *The Travels of Sir John Mandeville* (Penguin Books, 1983).

Manguel, Alberto, and Gianni Guadalupe. *The Dictionary of Imaginary Places* (Alfred A. Knopf, 1999).

Mannheim, Karl. *Ideology and Utopia* (Kegan Paul, Trench, Trubner & Co., 1936).

Mannheim, Karl. *Diagnosis of Our Time* (Kegan Paul, Trench, Trubner & Co., 1943).

Mantegazza, Paolo. *The Year 3000* (1897; University of Nebraska Press, 2010).

Manuel, Frank. *Freedom from History* (New York University Press, 1971).

Manuel, Frank, ed. *French Utopias* (Schocken Books, 1971).

Maple, Eric. *The Domain of Devils* (Robert Hale, 1966).

Marcel, Gabriel. *Homo Viator: Introduction to a Metaphysic of Hope*, tr. Emma Crauford (Victor Gollancz, 1951).

Marchenko, Anatoly. *My Testimony* (Pall Mall Press, 1969).

Mark, Ber. *The Scrolls of Auschwitz* (Am Oved Publishers, 1985).

Marx, Karl, and Frederick Engels. *Karl Marx-Frederick Engels Collected Works* (50 vols, Lawrence & Wishart, 1975–2004).

Marx, Leo. *The Machine in the Garden: Technology and the Pastoral Ideal in America* (Oxford University Press, 2000).

Maslow, Abraham H. *Religions, Values, and Peak-Experiences* (Ohio State University Press, 1964).

Matarese, Susan M. *American Foreign Policy and the Utopian Imagination* (University of Massachusetts Press, 2001).

Matthews, Ronald. *Red Sky at Night* (Hollis & Carter, 1951).

Maugham, Robin. *The 1946 Ms.* (War Facts Press, 1943).

Mayer, Arno J. *The Furies: Violence and Terror in the French and Russian Revolutions* (Princeton University Press, 2000).

Mayne, John D. *The Triumph of Socialism, and How It Succeeded* (Swan Sonnenschein & Co., 1908).

Mayor, Adrienne. *The First Fossil Hunters: Paleontology in Greek and Roman Times* (Princeton University Press, 2000).

Medvedev, Roy. *Let History Judge: The Origins and Consequences of Stalinism* (Vintage Books, 1973).

Meissner, Maurice. *Marxism, Maoism and Utopianism* (University of Wisconsin Press, 1982).

Melgounov, Sergey Petrovich. *The Red Terror in Russia* (J. M. Dent, 1926).

Mencken, H. L. *Notes on Democracy* (Jonathan Cape, 1927).

Mendelsohn, Everett, and Helga Nowotny, eds. *Nineteen Eighty-Four: Science between Utopia and Dystopia* (D. Reidel, 1984).

Mendes, H. Pereira. *Looking Ahead: Twentieth Century Happenings* (F. Tennyson Neely, 1899).

Merrill, Albert Adams. *The Great Awakening: The Story of the Twenty-Second Century* (George Book Publishing Co., 1899).

Mey, Chum. *Survivor: The Triumph of an Ordinary Man in the Khmer Rouge Genocide* (DC-Cam, 2012).

Meyers, Jeffrey, ed. *George Orwell: The Critical Heritage* (Routledge & Kegan Paul, 1975).

Meyers, Jeffrey. *Orwell: Wintry Conscience of a Generation* (W. W. Norton, 2000).

Meyers, Jeffrey. *A Reader's Guide to George Orwell* (Thames & Hudson, 1975).

Meynell, Laurence. *Storm against the Wall* (Hutchinson & Co., 1931).

Michael, Robert. *Holy Hatred: Christianity, Antisemitism, and the Holocaust* (Palgrave Macmillan, 2006).

Michaelis, Richard. *A Sequel to Looking Backward, or, 'Looking Further Forward'* (William Reeves, 1891).

Michelet, Jules. *The People* (Whittaker & Co., 1846).

Mill, John Stuart. *On Liberty* (3rd edn, Longman, Green, Longman, Roberts & Green, 1864).

Mill, John Stuart. *The Collected Works of John Stuart Mill* (33 vols, Routledge & Kegan Paul, 1965–91), vol. 28.

Miller, Gavin. *Alasdair Gray: The Fiction of Communion* (Rodopi, 2005).

Miller, Walter. *A Canticle for Leibowitz* (Corgi Books, 1959).

Milner, Andrew. *Locating Science Fiction* (Liverpool University Press, 2012).

Milowitz, Steven. *Philip Roth Considered: The Concentrationary Universe of the American Writer* (Routledge, 2000).

Mitchell, Adrian. *The Bodyguard* (Jonathan Cape, 1970).

Mitchell, J. A. *The Last American: A Fragment from the Journal of Khan-Li, Prince of Dimph-Yoo-Chur and Admiral in the Persian Navy* (Frederick A. Stokes, 1889).

Mitchell, J. Leslie. *Three Go Back* (Jarrolds, 1932).

Mitchison, Naomi. *Solution Three* (Dennis Dobson, 1975).

Moffat, W. Graham, and John White. *What's the World Coming To? A Novel of the Twenty-First Century, Founded on the Fads, Facts, and Fiction of the Nineteenth* (Elliot Stock, 1893).

Mogen, David. *Ray Bradbury* (Twayne, 1986).

Monnerot, Jules. *Sociology of Communism* (George Allen & Unwin, 1953).

Montefiore, Simon Sebag. *Stalin: The Court of the Red Czar* (Phoenix, 2007).

Montesquieu, Baron de. *The Spirit of the Laws* (Hafner Publishing Co., 1949).

Moore, Barrington, Jr. *Moral Purity and Persecution in History* (Princeton University Press, 2000).

Moore, R. I. *The Origins of European Dissent* (University of Toronto Press, 1977).

Moore, R. I. *The Formation of a Persecuting Society: Power and Deviance in Western Europe, 950–1250* (Blackwell, 1987).

More, Thomas. *Utopia*, ed. David Wootton (Hackett Publishing Co., 1999).

Morgan, Arthur E. *Edward Bellamy* (Columbia University Press, 1944).

Morgan, Chris. *The Shape of Futures Past: The Story of Prediction* (Webb & Bower, 1980).

[Morris, Alfred]. *Looking Ahead: A Tale of Adventure* (Henry & Co., 1892).

Morris, James M., and Andrea L. Kross, eds. *Historical Dictionary of Utopianism* (The Scarecrow Press, 2004).

Morris, William. *Political Writings: Contributions to Justice and Commonweal 1883–1890*, ed. Nicholas Salmon (Thoemmes Press, 1994).

Morson, Gary. *The Boundaries of Genre: Dostoevsky's Diary of a Writer and the Traditions of Literary Utopia* (Northwestern University Press, 1981).

Mosse, George. *Nationalism and Sexuality* (Howard Fertig, 1997).

Mosse, George L. *The Nationalization of the Masses: Political Symbolism and Mass Movements in Germany from the Napoleonic Wars through the Third Reich* (Howard Fertig, 1975).

Moszkowski, Alexander. *The Isles of Wisdom* (George Routledge & Sons, 1924).

Moylan, Tom. *Demand the Impossible: Science Fiction and the Utopian Imagination* (Methuen, 1986).

Moylan, Tom. *Scraps of the Unpainted Sky: Science Fiction, Utopia, Dystopia* (Westview Press, 2000).

'Mr. Dick'. *James Ingleton: The History of a Social State. A.D. 2000* (James Blackwood & Co., 1893).

Muchembled, Robert. *A History of the Devil: From the Middle Ages to the Present* (Polity Press, 2003).

Müller, Filip. *Eyewitness Auschwitz: Three Years in the Gas Chambers* (Ivan R. Dee, 1979).

Mumford, Lewis. *The Culture of Cities* (Secker & Warburg, 1938).

Mumford, Lewis. *Technics and Civilization* (George Routledge & Sons, 1947).

Mumford, Lewis. *The Story of Utopia* (1922; The Viking Press, 1962).

Mumford, Lewis. *The Myth of the Machine*, vol. 2: *The Pentagon of Power* (Secker & Warburg, 1964).

Munro, H. H. *When William Came: The Story of London under the Hohenzollerns* (John Lane, 1913).

Murphy, Cullen. *God's Jury: The Inquisition and the Making of the Modern World* (Allen Lane, 2012).

Murphy, G. Read. *Beyond the Ice: Being a Story of the Newly Discovered Region Round the North Pole* (Sampson Low & Co., 1894).

Murray, Margaret Alice. *The Witch-Cult in Western Europe* (Clarendon Press, 1921).

Mussolini, Benito. *The Doctrine of Fascism* (Vellecchi Editore, 1936).

Nabokov, Vladimir. *Bend Sinister* (Weidenfeld & Nicolson, 1960).

Naimark, Norman M. *Stalin's Genocides* (Princeton University Press, 2010).

Nauman, Bernd. *Auschwitz: A Report on the Proceedings against Robert Karl Ludwig Mulka and Others before the Court at Frankfurt* (Pall Mall Press, 1966).

Negley, Glenn, and J. Max Patrick, eds. *The Quest for Utopia* (Henry Schuman, 1952).

Neugroschel, Joachim, ed. *The Golem* (W. W. Norton, 2006).

Neumann, Franz. *Behemoth: The Structure and Practice of National Socialism* (Victor Gollancz, 1942).

Neumann, Sigmund. *Permanent Revolution: The Total State in a World at War* (Harper & Brothers, 1942).

Newsinger, John. *Orwell's Politics* (Macmillan, 1999).

Newte, Horace W. C. *The Master Beast: Being a True Account of the Ruthless Tyranny Inflicted on the British People by Socialism, A.D. 1888–2020* (Rebman, 1907).

[Newton, Alex]. *Posterity, Its Verdicts and Its Methods, or, of Democracy A.D. 2100* (Williams & Norgate, 1897).

Newton, Michael. *Savage Girls and Wild Boys: A History of Feral Children* (Faber & Faber, 2002).

Ngor, Haing S. *Surviving the Killing Fields: The Cambodian Odyssey of Haing S. Ngor* (Pan Books, 1989).

Nickerson, Hoffman. *The Inquisition* (John Bale, Sons & Danielsson, 1923).

Niemann, August. *The Coming Conquest of England* (George Routledge & Sons, 1904).

Niemeyer, Gerhart. *Between Nothingness and Paradise* (Louisiana State University Press, 1971).

Nietzsche, Friedrich. *The Twilight of the Idols* (T. N. Fouis, 1911).

Niewyk, Donald L., ed. *Fresh Wounds: Early Narratives of Holocaust Survival* (University of North Carolina Press, 1998).

Nisbet, Hume. *The Great Secret: A Tale of To-morrow* (F. V. White, 1895).

Noonan, F. Thomas. *The Road to Jerusalem: Pilgrimage and Travel in the Age of Discovery* (University of Pennsylvania Press, 2007).

Norris, Christopher, ed. *Inside the Myth: Orwell: Views from the Left* (Lawrence & Wishart, 1984).

Nugent, Christopher. *Masks of Satan: The Demonic in History* (Sheed & Ward, 1983).

Nye, Louis A. *The Origins of Crowd Psychology: Gustave Le Bon and the Crisis of Mass Democracy in the Third Republic* (Sage Publications, 1975).

O'Den, Daniel. *Crimson Courage* (Frederick Muller Ltd, 1940).

[O'Grady, Standish James]. *The Queen of the World; or, Under the Tyranny* (Lawrence & Bullen, 1900).

O'Kane, Rosemary. *The Revolutionary Reign of Terror: The Role of Violence in Political Change* (Edward Elgar, 1991).

Olsen, Lance. *William Gibson* (Borgo Press, 1992).

Olusoga, David, and Casper W. Erichsen. *The Kaiser's Holocaust: Germany's Forgotten Genocide* (Faber & Faber, 2010).

O'Neill, Joseph. *Land under England* (1935; Overlook Press, 1981).

Oplinger, Jon. *The Politics of Demonology: The European Witchcraze and the Mass Production of Deviance* (Associated University Presses, 1990).

Oreskes, Naomi, and Erik M. Conway. *The Collapse of Western Civilization: A View from the Future* (Columbia University Press, 2014).

Ortega y Gasset, José. *Man and People* (George Allen & Unwin, 1959).

Ortega y Gasset, José. *The Revolt of the Masses* (George Allen & Unwin, 1972).

Orwell, George. *Down and Out in Paris and London* (1933; Penguin Books, 1966).

Orwell, George. *The Road to Wigan Pier* (1937) (Secker & Warburg, 1959).

Orwell, George. *Homage to Catalonia* (1938) (Penguin Books, 1962).

Orwell, George. *The Lion and the Unicorn* (1941) (Penguin Books, 1970).

Orwell, George. *Nineteen Eighty-Four: The Facsimile of the Extant Manuscript*, ed. Peter Davison (Secker & Warburg, 1984).

Orwell, George. *The Penguin Complete Novels of George Orwell* (Penguin Books, 1983).

Orwell, George. *Collected Writings* (Secker & Warburg 2000–2): X. *A Kind of Compulsion 1903–36*; XI. *Facing Unpleasant Facts 1937–9*; XII. *A Patriot after All 1940–1*; XIII. *All Propaganda is Lies 1941–2*; XIV. *Keeping Our Little Corner Clean 1942–3*; XV. *Two Wasted Years 1943*; XVI. *I Have Tried to Tell the Truth 1943–4*; XVII. *I Belong to the Left 1945*; XVIII. *Smothered under Journalism 1946*; XIX. *It is What I Think 1947–8*; XX. *Our Job is to Make Life Worth Living, 1949–50*.

Orwell, George, and Reginald Reynolds, eds. *British Pamphleteers*, vol. 1 (Alan Wingate, 1948).

Osman, Ysa. *The Cham Rebellion: Survivors' Stories from the Villages* (DC-Cam, 2006).

Ozouf, Mona. *Festivals and the French Revolution* (Harvard University Press, 1988).

Pagden, Anthony. *The Fall of Natural Man: The American Indian and the Origins of Comparative Ethnology* (Cambridge University Press, 1982).

Pagels, Elaine. *Adam, Eve, and the Serpent* (Vintage Books, 1989).

Paine, Lauran. *Witches in Fact and Fantasy* (Robert Hale, 1971).

Pallen, Condé B. *Crucible Island: A Romance, an Adventure and an Experiment* (Harding & More, 1920).

Palmer, John. *The Hesperides: A Looking-Glass Fugue* (Martin Secker & Warburg, 1936).

Pan, David. *Sacrifice in the Modern World: On the Particularity and Generality of Nazi Myth* (Northwestern University Press, 2012).

Panh, Rithy. *The Elimination: A Survivor of the Khmer Rouge Confronts His Past and the Commandant of the Killing Fields* (The Clerkenwell Press, 2013).

Paré, Ambroise. *On Monsters and Marvels* (University of Chicago Press, 1982).

Pareto, Vilfredo. *The Mind and Society* (Jonathan Cape, 1935).

Park, Robert E. *The Crowd and the Public and Other Essays* (University of Chicago Press, 1972).

[Parnell, John]. *Cromwell the Third; or the the Jubilee of Liberty* (John Parnell, 1886).

Parrinder, Patrick, ed. *Learning from Other Worlds: Estrangement, Cognition, and the Politics of Science Fiction and Utopia* (Duke University Press, 2001).

Parrinder, Patrick. *Utopian Literature and Science: From the Scientific Revolution to* Brave New World *and Beyond* (Palgrave Macmillan, 2015).

Parrington, Vernon Lewis. *American Dreams: A Study of American Utopias* (Russell & Russell, 1964).

Parrish, Timothy, ed. *The Cambridge Companion to Philip Roth* (Cambridge University Press, 2007).

Parry, David M. *The Scarlet Empire* (Bobbs-Merrill Co., 1906).

Parvilahti, Unto. *Beria's Gardens: Ten Years' Captivity in Russia and Siberia* (Hutchinson, 1959).

Patai, Daphne. *The Orwell Mystique: A Study of Male Ideology* (University of Massachusetts Press, 1984).

Patai, Daphne, ed. *Looking Backward 1988–1888* (University of Massachusetts Press, 1988).

Paulding, [J. R.]. *The Merry Tales of the Three Wise Men of Gotham* (Harper & Brothers, 1839).

Perez, Joseph. *The Spanish Inquisition* (Profile Books, 2004).

Pfaelzer, Jean. *The Utopian Novel in America 1886–1896* (University of Pittsburgh Press, 1984).

Philmus, Robert. *Into the Unknown: The Evolution of Science Fiction from Francis Godwin to H.G. Wells* (University of California Press, 1970).

Pick, Daniel. *The Pursuit of the Nazi Mind: Hitler, Hess and the Analysts* (Oxford University Press, 2012).

Piercy, Marge. *He, She and It* (Alfred A. Knopf, 1991).

Pinker, Steven. *The Blank Slate: The Modern Denial of Human Nature* (Penguin Books, 2002).

Pintar, Judith, and Steven Jay Lynn. *Hypnosis: A Brief History* (Wiley-Blackwell, 2008).

Pipes, Richard, ed. *The Unknown Lenin* (Yale University Press, 1996).

Pliny. *Natural History* (10 vols, William Heinemann, 1940).

Plutarch. *Moralia* (15 vols, William Heinemann, 1968).

Pohl, Frederick, and Cyril M. Kornbluth. *The Space Merchants* (1953; Penguin Books, 1965).

Pol Pot Plans the Future: Confidential Leadership Documents from Democratic Kampuchea, 1976–77, tr. David P. Chandler, Ben Kiernan, and Chanthou Boua (Yale University Southeast Asia Studies, 1988).

Polak, Fred L. *The Image of the Future* (2 vols, Oceana Publications, 1961).

Polak, Fred L. *Prognostics: A Science in the Making Surveys and Creates the Future* (Elsevier Publishing Co., 1971).

Ponchaud, François. *Cambodia Year Zero* (Holt, Rinehart & Winston, 1978).

Popper, Karl. *The Open Society and Its Enemies* (2 vols, Princeton University Press, 1966).

Posner, Gerald L., and John Ware. *Mengele: The Complete Story* (Queen Anne Press, 1986).

Prince, Edward. *Wake Up, England! Being the Amazing Story of John Bull, Socialist* (St. Stephen's Press, 1910).

Puddington, Arch. *Failed Utopias: Methods of Coercion in Communist Regimes* (ICS Press, 1988).

Rabkin, Eric S., Martin H. Greenberg, and Joseph D. Olander, eds. *No Place Else: Explorations in Utopian and Dystopian Fiction* (Southern Illinois University Press, 1983).

Rai, Alok. *Orwell and the Politics of Despair* (Cambridge University Press, 1988).

Ramsay, Clay. *The Ideology of the Great Fear: The Soissonais in 1789* (Johns Hopkins University Press, 1992).

Rand, Ayn. *The Fountainhead* (Bobbs-Merrill, 1943).

Rand, Ayn. *Anthem* (Signet Classics, 1946).

Rand, Ayn. *Atlas Shrugged* (Signet Books, 1992).

Rapoport, David C., and Yonah Alexander, eds. *The Morality of Terrorism: Religious and Secular Justifications* (Columbia University Press, 1989).

Rauschning, Hermann. *Germany's Revolution of Destruction* (William Heinemann, 1939).

Rauschning, Hermann. *Hitler Speaks: A Series of Political Conversations with Adolf Hitler on His Real Aims* (Thornton Butterworth, 1940).

Razgon, Lev. *True Stories* (Ardis, 1997).

Reade, Winwood. *The Martyrdom of Man* (15th edn, Kegan Paul, Trench, Trübner & Co., 1896).

Rees, Richard. *George Orwell: Fugitive from the Camp of Victory* (Secker & Warburg, 1961).

Rees, Valery. *From Gabriel to Lucifer: A Cultural History of Angels* (I.B. Taurus, 2013).

[Reeves, John]. *Publicola. A Sketch of the Times and Prevailing Opinions, from the Revolution in 1800 to the Present Year 1810* (J. Wright, 1810).

Reilly, Patrick. *George Orwell: The Age's Adversary* (Macmillan, 1986).

Reilly, Patrick. *Nineteen Eighty-Four: Past, Present and Future* (Twayne, 1989).

Reitmeister, Louis Aaron. *If Tomorrow Comes* (The Walden Press, 1934).

Report of the Court Proceedings in the Case of the Anti-Soviet 'Bloc of Rights and Trotskyites' (People's Commissariat of Justice of the USSR, 1938).

[Reynolds, Walter Doty]. Daedalus Haldane. *Mr. Jonnemacher's Machine: The Post to which We Drifted* (Knickerbocker Book Co., 1898).

Rhodes, James M. *The Hitler Movement: A Modern Millenarian Revolution* (Hoover Institution Press, 1980).

Ribot, Théodule. *The Psychology of the Emotions* (Walter Scott, 1897).

Richards, Jeffrey. *Sex, Dissidence and Damnation: Minority Groups in the Middle Ages* (Routledge, 1991).

Richter, Peyton, ed. *Utopia/Dystopia?* (Schenkman Publishing Co., 1975).

Rieder, John. *Colonialism and the Emergence of Science Fiction* (Wesleyan University Press, 2008).

Riesman, David. *The Lonely Crowd* (Yale University Press, 1950).

Ritter, Gerhard. *The Corrupting Influence of Power* (Tower Bridge Publications, 1952).

Rivers, W. H. R. *Psychology and Politics and Other Essays* (Kegan Paul, Trench, Trubner & Co. 1923).

Rizzi, Bruno. *The Bureaucratization of the World* (1939; Tavistock, 1985).

Roberts, J. W. *Looking Within: The Misleading Tendencies of 'Looking Backward'* (A. S. Barnes & Co., 1891).

Roberts, Penny, and William G. Naphy, eds. *Fear in Early Modern Society* (Manchester University Press, 1997).

Robin, Corey. *Fear: The History of a Political Idea* (Oxford University Press, 2004).

Robins, Robert S., and Jerrold M. Post. *Political Paranoia: The Psychopolitics of Hatred* (Yale University Press, 1997).

Robinson, Kim Stanley. *The Novels of Philip K. Dick* (Umi Research Press, 1989).

Rodden, John. *The Politics of Literary Reputation: The Making and Claiming of 'St George' Orwell* (Oxford University Press, 1989).

Rodden, John, ed. *The Cambridge Companion to George Orwell* (Cambridge University Press, 2007).

Rodden, John. *The Unexamined Orwell* (University of Texas Press, 2011).

Roemer, Kenneth, ed. *America as Utopia* (Burt Franklin & Co., 1981).

Roemer, Kenneth. *The Obsolete Necessity. America in Utopian Writings, 1888–1900* (Kent State University Press, 1976).

Roemer, Kenneth M. *Utopian Audiences: How Readers Locate Nowhere* (University of Massachusetts Press, 2003).

Rogers, Katharine M. *The Troublesome Helpmate: A History of Misogyny in Literature* (University of Washington Press, 1966).

Rogovin, Vadim Z. *1937: Stalin's Year of Terror* (Mehring Books, 1998).

Roland, Alan. *In Search of the Self in India and Japan* (Princeton University Press, 1988).

Rooney, Charles J., Jr. *Dreams and Visions: A Study of American Utopias 1865–1917* (Greenwood Press, 1985).

Roper, Lyndal. *Oedipus and the Devil: Witchcraft, Sexuality, and Religion in Early Modern Europe* (Routledge, 1994).

Roper, Lyndal. *Witch Craze: Terror and Fantasy in Baroque Germany* (Yale University Press, 2004).

Rosefielde, Steven. *Red Holocaust* (Routledge, 2010).

Rosenbaum, Alan S., ed. *Is the Holocaust Unique? Perspectives on Comparative Genocide* (2nd edn, Westview Press, 2001).

Rosenberg, Yudl. *The Golem and the Wondrous Deeds of the Maharal of Prague* (Yale University Press, 2007).

Rosenberg, William G., ed. *Bolshevik Visions: First Phase of the Cultural Revolution in Russia* (University of Michigan Press, 1990).

Rosenfield, Leonora Cohen. *From Beast-Machine to Man-Machine: Animal Soul in French Letters from Descartes to La Mettrie* (2nd edn, Octagon Books, 1968).

Rosewater, Frank. *'96: A Romance of Utopia: Presenting a Solution of the Labor Problem, a New God and a New Religion* (The Utopia Co., 1894).

Roshwald, Mordecai. *Level 7* (Signet Books, 1959).

Ross, Harry. *Utopias Old and New* (Nicholson & Watson, 1938).

Roth, Jack J. *The Cult of Violence: Sorel and the Sorelians* (University of California Press, 1980).

Roth, Michael S. *Memory, Trauma, and History* (Columbia University Press, 2012).

Roth, Philip. *The Plot against America* (Jonathan Cape, 2004).

Rousseau, Jean-Jacques. *Discourse on the Origins of Inequality*, ed. Roger D. Masters and Christopher Kelly (University Press of New England, 1992).

Rousseau, Jean-Jacques. *The Social Contract and Discourses* (J. M. Dent, 1973).

Rubin, Miri. *Gentile Tales: The Narrative Assault on Late Medieval Jews* (Yale University Press, 1999).

Rudé, George. *The Crowd in the French Revolution* (Clarendon Press, 1959).

Rudé, George. *The Crowd in History: A Study of Popular Disturbances in France and England 1730–1848* (John Wiley, 1964).

Rummel, Rudy. *Lethal Politics: Soviet Genocide and Mass Murder since 1917* (Transaction Publishers, 1990).

Rummel, Rudy. *China's Bloody Century: Genocide and Mass Murder since 1900* (Transaction Books, 1991).

Russell, A. P. *Sub-Coelum: A Sky-Built Human World* (Houghton, Mifflin & Co., 1893).

Russell, Francis. *Touring Utopia: The Realm of Constructive Criticism* (The Dial Press, 1932).

Russell, Jeffrey Burton. *Witchcraft in the Middle Ages* (Cornell University Press, 1972).

Russell, Jeffrey Burton. *Lucifer: The Devil in the Middle Ages* (Cornell University Press, 1984).

Rustoff, Michael. *What Will Mrs Grundy Say? Or, A Calamity on Two Legs (A Book for Men)* (Simpkin & Marshall, 1891).

Rybakov, Anatoli. *Fear* (Hutchinson, 1993).

Sackville-West, V. *Grand Canyon* (Michael Joseph, 1942).

Sagan, Eli. *Cannibalism: Human Aggression and Cultural Form* (Harper Torchbooks, 1974).

Sagan, Eli. *Citizens and Cannibals: The French Revolution, the Struggle for Modernity, and the Origins of Ideological Terror* (Rowman & Littlefield, 2001).

Salisbury, H. B. *The Birth of Freedom* (The Humboldt Publishing Co., 1890).

Salisbury, William. *The Squareheads: The Story of a Socialized State* (The Independent Publishing Co., 1929).

Salverte, Eusebe. *The Occult Sciences* (2 vols, Richard Bentley, 1846).

Sanderson, Alan, and Robert Dingley, eds. *Histories of the Future: Studies in Fact, Fantasy and Science Fiction* (Palgrave, 2000).

Sandison, Alan. *George Orwell after 1984* (Longwood Academic, 1986).

Sansom, C. J. *Dominion* (Mantle, 2012).

Sargent, Lyman Tower. *British and American Utopian Literature, 1516–1985: An Annotated, Chronological Bibliography* (Garland, 1988).

Sargent, Lyman Tower. *Utopianism* (Oxford University Press, 2010).

Satterlee, W. W. *Looking Backward and What I Saw* (Harrison & Smith, 1890).

Saunders, Kate. *Eighteen Layers of Hell: Stories from the Chinese Gulag* (Cassell, 1996).

Saunders, W. J. *Kalomera: The Story of a Remarkable Community* (Elliot Stock, 1911).

Savage, Timothy. *The Amazonian Republic* (1842; Scholars' Facsimiles & Reprints, 1976).

Scarrow, Alex. *Last Light* (Orion, 2007).

Schmitt, Carl. *Political Theology* (MIT Press, 1985).

Schmitt, Carl. *The Concept of the Political* (University of Chicago Press, 1996).

Scholmer, Joseph. *Vorkuta* (Weidenfeld & Nicolson, 1954).

Sconduto, Leslie A. *The Metamorphoses of the Werewolf: A Literary Study from Antiquity through the Renaissance* (McFarland & Co., 2008).

Scott, William. *Terror and Repression in Revolutionary Marseilles* (Macmillan, 1973).

Seed, David. *Brainwashing: The Fictions of Mind Control* (Kent State University Press, 2004).

Seed, David. *Science Fiction* (Oxford University Press, 2011).

Seed, David. *Under the Shadow: The Atomic Bomb and Cold War Narratives* (Kent State University Press, 2013).

Segal, Howard P. *Technological Utopianism in American Culture* (University of Chicago Press, 1985).

Sennett, Richard. *The Uses of Disorder: Personal Identity and City Life* (Faber & Faber, 1996).

Sereny, Gitta. *Into that Darkness: From Mercy Killing to Mass Murder* (Andre Deutsch, 1974).

Shalamov, Varlam. *Kolyma Tales* (W. W. Norton & Co., 1980).

Shane, Alex. *The Life and Works of Evgenij Zamjatin* (University of California Press, 1968).

Shanks, Edward. *The People of the Ruins: A Story of the English Revolution and After* (W. Collins & Sons, 1920).

Shelden, Michael. *George Orwell: The Authorised Biography* (Heinemann, 1991).

Shelley, Mary. *The Last Man* (University of Nebraska Press, 1993).

Shiel, M. P. *The Purple Cloud* (Chatto & Windus, 1901).

Shklar, Judith. *After Utopia: The Decline of Political Faith* (Princeton University Press, 1957).

Shor, Francis Robert. *Utopianism and Radicalism in a Reforming America 1888–1918* (Greenwood Press, 1997).

Showalter, Elaine. *Hystories: Hysterical Epidemics and Modern Culture* (Picador, 1977).

Sidis, Boris. *The Psychology of Suggestion: A Research into the Subconscious Nature of Man and Society* (D. Appleton & Co., 1924).

Siebenheller, Norma. *P. D. James* (Ungar, 1981).

Siegelbaum, Lewis, and Andrei Sokolov, eds. *Stalinism as a Way of Life: A Narrative in Documents* (Yale University Press, 2000).

Sighele, Scipio. *La Fou Criminelle: Essai de Psychologie Collective* (Félix Alcan, 1901).

Sikes, Wirt. *British Goblins: Welsh Folk-Lore, Fairy Mythology, Legends and Traditions* (Sampson Lowe, Marston, Searle & Rivington, 1880).

Simmel, Georg. *The Sociology of Georg Simmel*, ed. Kurt H. Wolff (Free Press, 1950).

Simmel, Georg. *On Individuality and Social Forms* (University of Chicago Press, 1971).

Sisk, David W. *Transformations of Language in Modern Dystopias* (Greenwood Press, 1997).

Skinner, B. F. *Walden Two* (1948; Macmillan, 1962).

Skinner, B. F. *Science and Human Behavior* (Free Press, 1953).

Skinner, B. F. *Cumulative Record* (Appleton-Century-Crofts, 1959).

Skinner, B. F. *Beyond Freedom and Dignity* (Penguin Books, 1971).

Skinner, B. F. *About Behaviourism* (Jonathan Cape, 1974).

Skinner, B. F. *Notebooks* (Prentice Hall, 1981).

Slessarev, Vsevolod. *Prester John: The Letter and the Legend* (University of Minnesota Press, 1959).

Small, Christopher. *The Road to Miniluv: George Orwell, the State, and God* (Victor Gollancz, 1975).

Smith, Adam. *Theory of Moral Sentiments* (Henry G. Bohn, 1853).

Snyder, Timothy. *Bloodlands: Europe between Hitler and Stalin* (The Bodley Head, 2010).

So, Farina. *The Hijab of Cambodia: Memories of Cham Muslim Women after the Khmer Rouge* (DC-Cam, 2011).

Sobchack, Vivian. *Screening Space: The American Science Fiction Film* (Rutgers University Press, 1997).

Sofsky, Wolfgang. *The Order of Terror: The Concentration Camp* (Princeton University Press, 1997).

Solonevich, Ivan. *Escape from Russian Chains* (Williams & Norgate, 1938).

Solonevich, Ivan. *Russia in Chains* (Williams & Norgate, 1938).

Solzhenitsyn, Alexander. *The Gulag Archipelago 1918–1956* (3 vols, Collins & Harvill Press, 1974).

Søndergaard, Leif, and Rasmus Thorning Hansen, eds. *Monsters, Marvels and Miracles: Imaginary Journeys and Landscapes in the Middle Ages* (University Press of Southern Denmark, 2005).

Sonn, Moeung, with Henri Locard. *Prisoner of the Khmer Rouge* (Editions Funan, 2007).

Sontag, Susan. *Illness as Metaphor* (Penguin Books, 1987).

Sorel, George. *Reflections on Violence* (Collier Books, 1950).

[Southwold, Stephen]. 'Miles'. *The Seventh Bowl* (Eric Partridge, 1930).

[Southwold, Stephen]. Bell, Neil. *The Gas War of 1940* (Collins, 1940).

Souvarine, Boris. *Cauchemar en URSS* (Revue de Paris, 1937).

Souvarine, Boris. *Stalin* (Secker & Warburg, 1939).

Souvestre, Emile. *The World as It Shall Be*, ed. I. F. Clarke (Wesleyan University Press, 2004).

Spann, Edward. *Brotherly Tomorrows: Movements for a Co-operative Society in America 1820–1920* (Columbia University Press, 1989).

Spencer, Herbert. *Principles of Sociology* (3 vols, D. Appleton & Co., 1905).

Sprott, W. J. H. *Human Groups* (Penguin Books, 1963).

Stansky, Peter, ed. *On Nineteen Eighty-Four* (W. H. Freeman & Co., 1983).

Stansky, Peter, and William Abrahams. *Orwell: The Transformation* (Constable, 1979).

Stargardt, Nicholas. *The German War: A Nation under Arms* (The Bodley Head, 2015).

Steed, Wickham. *The Meaning of Hitlerism* (Nisbet & Co., 1934).

Steinberg, Paul. *Speak You Also: A Survivor's Reckoning* (Penguin Books, 2000).

Steiner, Jean-François. *Treblinka* (Weidenfeld & Nicolson, 1967).

Steinhoff, William. *The Road to 1984* (Weidenfeld & Nicolson, 1975).

Sternberg, Robert J., and Karin Sternberg. *The Nature of Hate* (Cambridge University Press, 2008).

Stevenson, Robert Lewis. *The Strange Case of Dr Jekyll and Mr Hyde* (Longmans, Green, & Co., 1897).

Stirner, Max. *The Ego and Its Own* (A. C. Fifield, 1913).

Stites, Richard. *Revolutionary Dreams: Utopian Vision and Experimental Life in the Bolshevik Revolution* (Oxford University Press, 1989).

Stoker, Bram. *Dracula* (Oxford University Press, 1983).

Stone, Dan. *Constructing the Holocaust: A Study in Historiography* (Vallentine-Mitchell, 2003).

Stone, Dan. *Histories of the Holocaust* (Oxford University Press, 2010).

Stone, Dan, ed. *The Historiography of Genocide* (Palgrave Macmillan, 2010).

Stone, Dan, ed. *The Holocaust and Historical Methodology* (Berghahn, 2012).

Stone, Dan. *The Holocaust, Fascism and Memory* (Palgrave Macmillan, 2013).

Stoneman, Richard, ed. *Legends of Alexander the Great* (J. M. Dent, 1994).

Sturt, Mary. *The Psychology of Time* (Kegan Paul, Trench, Trubner & Co., 1925).

Summers, Montague. *The Vampire in Europe* (Kegan Paul, Trench, Trubner & Co., 1929).

Sussman, Herbert S. *Victorians and the Machine: The Literary Response to Technology* (Harvard University Press, 1968).

Sutherland, Morris. *Second Storm* (Thornton Butterworth, 1930).

Suttie, Ian D. *The Origins of Love and Hate* (Kegan Paul, Trench, Trubner & Co., 1935).

Suvin, Darko. *Victorian Science Fiction in the U.K.: Discourses of Knowledge and of Power* (G. K. Hall, 1983).

Suvin, Darko. *Metamorphoses of Science Fiction* (Macmillan, 1988).

Swain, Jon. *River of Time* (Heinemann, 1995).

Talmon, Jacob. *The Origins of Totalitarian Democracy* (Secker & Warburg, 1960).

Talmon, Jacob. *Political Messianism: The Romantic Phase* (Secker & Warburg, 1960).

Talmon, Jacob. *The Unique and the Universal: Some Historical Reflections* (Secker & Warburg, 1965).

Talmon, Jacob. *The Myth of the Nation and the Vision of Revolution* (Secker & Warburg, 1981).

Tarde, Gabriel. *On Communication and Social Influence* (University of Chicago Press, 2010).

Tayler, J. Lionel. *Social Life and the Crowd* (Leonard Parsons, 1923).

Taylor, Tom. *Defend Socialism from the Communists* (ILP, 1942).

Tchernavin, Tatiana. *Escape from the Soviets* (Hamish Hamilton, 1933).

Tchernavin, Vladimir V. *I Speak for the Silent: Prisoners of the Soviets* (Hamish Hamilton, 1935).

Tew, Philip. *Jim Crace* (Manchester University Press, 2006).

Theweleit, Klaus. *Male Fantasies* (2 vols, Polity Press, 1989).

Thibault, John W., and Harold H. Kelley. *The Social Psychology of Groups* (John Wiley & Sons, 1959).

Thomas, Chauncey. *The Crystal Button; or, Adventures of Paul Prognosis in the Forty-Ninth Century* (George Routledge & Sons, 1891).

Thomas, Keith. *Religion and the Decline of Magic* (Penguin Books, 1991).

Thompson, E. P. *The Making of the English Working Class* (Victor Gollancz, 1963).

Thomson, Rupert. *Divided Kingdom* (Bloomsbury, 2005).

Thurston, Anne F. *Enemies of the People* (Alfred Knopf, 1987).

Thurston, Robert. *Life and Terror in Stalin's Russia, 1934–1941* (Yale University Press, 1996).

Tillyard, Aelfrida. *Concrete: A Story of Two Hundred Years Hence* (Hutchinson & Co., 1930).

Tillyard, Aelfrida. *The Approaching Storm* (Hutchinson & Co., 1932).

Tismaneanu, Vladimir. *The Devil in History: Communism, Fascism, and Some Lessons of the Twentieth Century* (University of California Press, 2012).

Toch, Hans. *Violent Men: An Inquiry into the Psychology of Violence* (Aldine Publishing Co., 1969).

Tocqueville, Alexis de. *Democracy in America* (2 vols, Longmans, Green & Co., 1875).

Tocqueville, Alexis de. *The Ancien Régime and the French Revolution* (Cambridge University Press, 2011).

Todorov, Tzvetan. *Facing the Extreme: Moral Life in the Concentration Camps* (Henry Holt and Co., 1996).

Toker, Leona. *Return from the Archipelago: Narratives of Gulag Survivors* (Indiana University Press, 2000).

Tönnies, Ferdinand. *Community and Civil Society*, ed. José Harris (1887; Cambridge University Press, 2001).

Tormey, Simon. *Making Sense of Tyranny: Interpretations of Totalitarianism* (Manchester University Press, 1995).

Toscano, Alberto. *Fanaticism: On the Uses of an Idea* (Verso, 2010).

Trachtenberg, Joshua. *The Devil and the Jews: The Medieval Conception of the Jew and Its Relation to Modern Antisemitism* (Yale University Press, 1943).

Trahair, Richard C. S. *Utopias and Utopians: An Historical Dictionary* (Fitzroy Dearborn Publishers, 1999).

Trollope, Anthony. *The Fixed Period* (2 vols, Bernhard Tauchnitz, 1882).

Trotsky, Leon. *The Defence of Terrorism* (Labour Publishing Co., 1921).

Trotsky, Leon. *My Life* (Grosset & Dunlap, 1960).

Trotsky, Leon. *Literature and Revolution* (University of Michigan Press, 1975).

Trotter, W. *Instincts of the Herd in Peace and War* (T. Fisher Unwin, 1916).

Truitt, E. R. *Medieval Robots: Mechanism, Magic, Nature, and Art* (University of Pennsylvania Press, 2015).

Tucker, Nathaniel Beverley. *The Partisan Leader: A Tale of the Future* (1836; University of North Carolina Press, 1971).

Turney, Jon. *Frankenstein's Footsteps: Science, Genetics and Popular Culture* (Yale University Press, 1998).

Tuveson, Ernest Lee. *Millennium and Utopia: A Study in the Background of the Idea of Progress* (Harper Torchbook, 1964).

Ulianov, V. I. [Lenin]. *The State and Revolution* (2nd edn, Communist Party of Great Britain, 1925).

Ung, Loung. *First They Killed My Father* (Harper Perennial, 2006).

[Upward, Allen]. *Romance of Politics: The Fourth Conquest of England: A Sequel to 'Treason'* (The Tyndale Press, 1904).

Utley, Freda. *The Dream We Lost: Soviet Russia Then and Now* (The John Day Co., 1940).

Valentino, Benjamin. *Final Solutions: Mass Killing and Genocide in the Twentieth Century* (Cornell University Press, 2004).

Van Ginnekin, Jaap. *Crowds, Psychology and Politics 1871–1899* (Cambridge University Press, 1992).

Van Schaack, Beth, Daryn Reicherter, and Youk Chhang, eds. *Cambodia's Hidden Scars: Trauma Psychology in the Wake of the Khmer Rouge* (DC-Cam, 2011).

Vaneigem, Raoul. *The Movement of the Free Spirit* (Zone Books, 1994).

Veith, Ilza. *Hysteria: The History of a Disease* (University of Chicago Press, 1965).

Venezia, Shlomo. *Inside the Gas Chambers: Eight Months in the Sonderkommando of Auschwitz* (Polity Press, 2009).

Verhoeven, Wil. *Americomania and the French Revolution Debate in Britain, 1789–1802* (Cambridge University Press, 2013).

Verne, Jules. *The Masterless Man: Part One of The Survivors of the 'Jonathan'* (Arco Publications, 1962).

Verne, Jules. *The Unwilling Dictator: Part Two of The Survivors of the 'Jonathan'* (Arco Publications, 1962).

Verner, Lisa. *The Epistemology of the Monstrous in the Middle Ages* (Routledge, 2005).

Vickery, Michael. *Cambodia 1975–1982* (George Allen & Unwin, 1982).

Vinton, Arthur Dudley. *Looking Further Backward* (Albany Book Co., 1890).

Viola, Lynne. *The Unknown Gulag: The Lost World of Stalin's Special Settlements* (Oxford University Press, 2007).

Voegelin, Eric. *The New Science of Politics* (University of Chicago Press, 1952).

Voegelin, Eric. *Political Religions* (Edwin Mellen Press, 1986).

Voegelin, Eric. *Hitler and the Germans* (University of Missouri Press, 1999).

Vogeler, Robert A. *I Was Stalin's Prisoner* (W. H. Allen, 1952).

Voigt, F. A. *Unto Caesar* (Constable & Co., 1938).

[Von Kuehnelt-Leddihn, Erik and Christiane]. Campbell, Francis S. *The Menace of the Herd* (The Bruce Publishing Co., 1943).

Von Kuehnelt-Leddihn, Erik and Christiane. *Moscow 1979* (Sheed & Ward, 1946).

Vonnegut, Kurt, Jr. *Player Piano* (1952; Macmillan, 1967).

Vonnegut, Kurt, Jr. *Welcome to the Monkey House* (Vintage, 1994).

Voragine. *The Golden Legend of Jacobus de Voragine* ([*c.*1290]; Longmans, Green & Co., 1941).

W[aterhouse], E[lizabeth]. *The Island of Anarchy* (Lovejoy's Library, 1887).

Wachsmann, Nikolaus. *Hitler's Prisons: Legal Terror in Nazi Germany* (Yale University Press, 2004).

Wadhams, Stephen, comp. *Remembering Orwell* (Penguin Books, 1984).

Wagar, Warren. *Terminal Visions: The Literature of Last Things* (Indiana University Press, 1982).

Waite, Gary K. *Heresy, Magic and Witchcraft in Early Modern Europe* (Palgrave, 2003).

Walicki, Andrzej. *Marxism and the Leap to the Kingdom of Freedom* (Stanford University Press, 1995).

Walker, D. P. *The Decline of Hell. Seventeenth-Century Discussions of Eternal Torment* (Routledge and Kegan Paul, 1964).

Walker, J. Bernard. *America Fallen! The Sequel to the European War* (G. P. Putnam's Sons, 1915).

[Walker, Samuel]. *The Reign of Selfishness: A Story of Concentrated Wealth* (M. K. Pelletreau, 1891).

Wallace, David Foster. *Infinite Jest* (Little, Brown & Co., 1996).

Wallas, Graham. *Human Nature in Politics* (Constable & Co., 1919).

Walsh, Chad. *From Utopia to Nightmare* (Geoffrey Bles, 1962).

Walter, Eugene Victor. *Terror and Resistance: A Study of Political Violence* (Oxford University Press, 1969).

Warburg, Frederic. *All Authors Are Equal: The Publishing Life of Frederic Warburg, 1936–1971* (Hutchinson, 1973).

Ward, Capt. Will J. *Shanghaied Socialists: A Romance* (The Maritime Review, 1911).

Ward, Richard Heron. *The Sun Shall Rise* (Ivor Nicholson & Watson, 1935).

Warner, Rex. *The Wild Goose Chase* (Boriswood, 1937).

Warrick, Patricia S. *The Cybernetic Imagination in Science Fiction* (MIT Press, 1980).

Waterloo, Stanley. *Armageddon: A Tale of Love, War, and Invention* (Rand, McNally & Co., 1898).

Watkins, Susan. *Doris Lessing* (University of Manchester Press, 2010).

Watlock, W. A. *The Next 'Ninety-Three, or Crown, Commune and Colony* (Field & Tuer, 1893).

Watson, H. C. R. *Erchomenon; or, The Republic of Materialism* (S. Low, 1879).

Watt, Donald, ed. *Aldous Huxley: The Critical Heritage* (Routledge & Kegan Paul, 1975).

Watts, Sheldon. *Epidemics and History: Disease, Power and Imperialism* (Yale University Press, 1997).

Waugh, Evelyn. *Love Among the Ruins: A Romance of the Near Future* (Chapman & Hall, 1953).

Webb, Sidney and Beatrice. *Soviet Communism: A New Civilisation* (2 vols, Longmans, Green & Co., 1941).

Weeks, Albert L. *The First Bolshevik: A Political Biography of Peter Tkachev* (New York University Press, 1968).

Wegner, Phillip E. *Imaginary Communities: Utopia, the Nation, and the Spatial Histories of Modernity* (University of California Press, 2002).

Weiss, Reska. *Journey through Hell: A Woman's Account of Her Experiences at the Hands of the Nazis* (Vallentine-Mitchell, 1961).

Weissberg, Alex. *Conspiracy of Silence* (Hamish Hamilton, 1952).

Wells, H. G. *The Island of Doctor Moreau* (William Heinemann, 1896).

Wells, H. G. *When the Sleeper Awakes* (Harper & Bros., 1899).

Wells, H. G. *Anticipations* (Chapman & Hall, 1902).

Wells, H. G. *Tales of Space and Time* (Macmillan, 1906).

Wells, H. G. *First and Last Things* (Archibald Constable & Co., 1908).

Wells, H. G. *The Dream* (Jonathan Cape, 1924).

Wells, H. G. *The Autocracy of Mr Parnham: His Remarkable Adventures in this Changing World* (William Heinemann, 1930).

Wells, H. G. *The Shape of Things to Come* (Hutchinson & Co., 1933).

Wells, H. G. *The Correspondence of H.G. Wells*, ed. David C. Smith (4 vols, Pickering & Chatto, 1998).

Wells, H. G. *A Modern Utopia* (Collins, n.d.).

Werth, Nicolas. *Cannibal Island: Death in a Siberian Gulag* (Princeton University Press, 2007).

Wesson, Robert G. *Soviet Communes* (Rutgers University Press, 1963).

West, Anthony. *Principles and Persuasions* (Eyre & Spottiswoode, 1958).

West, Julian. *My Afterdream: A Sequel to the Late Mr Edward Bellamy's Looking Backwards* (T. Fisher Unwin, 1900).

Wheatley, Dennis. *Black August: A Novel* (Hutchinson & Co., 1934).

White, Osmar. *Green Armour* (George Allen & Unwin, 1945).

Wieland, Christina. *The Fascist State of Mind and the Manufacturing of Masculinity* (Routledge, 2015).

Wiener, Norbert. *Cybernetics: Or Control and Communication in the Animal and the Machine* (John Wiley & Sons, 1957).

Wiesel, Elie. *Night* (Penguin Books, 1981).

Wiesner-Hanks, Merry E. *Christianity and Sexuality in the Early Modern World* (Routledge, 2000).

Wilbrandt, Conrad. *Mr East's Experiences in Mr Bellamy's World: Records of the Years 2001 and 2002* (Harper & Bros., 1891).

Williams, Raymond. *Orwell* (Viking Press, 1971).

Williams-Ellis, Amabel. *To Tell The Truth* (Jonathan Cape, 1933).

Wilson, Stephen. *The Magical Universe: Everyday Ritual and Magic in Pre-Modern Europe* (Hambledon, 2000).

Winner, Langdon. *Autonomous Technology: Technics-Out-of-Control as a Theme in Political Thought* (MIT Press, 1977).

Wittke, Carl. *Against the Current: The Life of Karl Heinzen* (University of Chicago Press, 1945).

Wolfe, Bernard. *Limbo '90* (Secker & Warburg, 1953).

Wood, Neil. *Communism and the British Intellectuals* (Victor Gollancz, 1959).

Woodcock, George. *The Crystal Spirit: A Study of George Orwell* (Jonathan Cape, 1967).

Woodcock, George. *Dawn and the Darkest Hour: A Study of Aldous Huxley* (Faber & Faber, 1972).

Wright, Dudley. *Vampires and Vampirism* (William Rider & Son, 1924).

Wright, Henry. *Mental Travel in Imagined Lands* (Trübner & Co., 1878).

Wright, Henry. *Depopulation: A Romance of the Unlikely* (George Allen, 1899).

Wu, Harry, and Carolyn Wakeman. *Bitter Winds: A Memoir of My Life in China's Gulags* (John Wiley & Sons, 1994).

Wu, Hongda Harry. *Laogai: The Chinese Gulag* (Westview Press, 1992).

Yathay, Pin. *L'Utopie Meurtrière: Une rescape du genocide cambodgien temoigne* (Editions Robert Laffont, 1980).

Yathay, Pin. *Stay Alive, My Son* (Silkworm Books, 2000).

Yelverton, Christopher. *Oneiros, or, Some Questions of the Day* (Kegan Paul & Co., 1889).

Yershov, Peter. *Science Fiction and Utopian Fantasy in Soviet Literature* (Research Program on the U.S.S.R., 1954).

Young, Michael. *The Rise of the Meritocracy 1870–2033* (Penguin Books, 1961).

Yu, Frederick T. C. *Mass Persuasion in Communist China* (Pall Mall Press, 1964).

[Zajdlerowa, Zoë]. *The Dark Side of the Moon* (Faber & Faber, 1946).

Zamyatin, Yevgeny. *We*, tr. Bernard Guilbert Guerney (Jonathan Cape, 1970).

Zamyatin, Yevgeny. *A Soviet Heretic*, tr. Mirra Ginsberg (Quartet Books, 1991).

Zarod, Kazimierz. *Inside Stalin's Gulag: A True Story of Survival* (The Book Guild, 1990).

Zenker, E. V. *Anarchism: A Criticism and History of the Anarchist Theory* (Methuen & Co., 1898).

Zipes, Jack. *The Irresistible Fairy Tale* (Princeton University Press, 2012).

Zwerdling, Alex. *Orwell and the Left* (Yale University Press, 1974).

Articles and Chapters

Abensour, Miguel. 'Saint Just and the Problem of Heroism in the French Revolution', in Ferenc Fehér, ed. *The French Revolution and the Birth of Modernity* (University of California Press, 1990), pp. 133–49.

Adorno, Theodor. 'Aldous Huxley and Utopia', in Adorno. *Prisms* (MIT Press, 1983), pp. 95–118.

Angenendt, Arnold. 'Relics and their Veneration in the Middle Ages', in Anneke B. Mulder-Bakker, ed. *The Invention of Saintliness* (Routledge, 2002), pp. 27–37.

Baczko, Bronisław. 'The Terror before the Terror?', in Keith Michael Baker, ed. *The French Revolution and the Creation of Modern Political Culture*, vol. 4: *The Terror* (Pergamon, 1994), pp. 19–38.

Beadle, Gordon B. 'George Orwell and the Death of God', *Colorado Quarterly*, 23 (1974), 51–63.

Beauchamp, Gorman. 'Of Man's Last Disobedience: Zamiatin's *We* and Orwell's *1984*', *Comparative Literature Studies*, 10 (1973), 285–301.

Beauchamp, Gorman. 'Cultural Primitivism as Norm in the Dystopian Novel', *Extrapolation*, 19 (1977), 88–96.

Behrens, Mathias. ' "Political Religion"—a Religion? Some Remarks on the Concept of Religion', in Hans Maier and Michael Schäfer, eds. *Totalitarianism and Political Religion* (3 vols, Routledge, 2007), vol. 2, pp. 225–45.

Bellamy, Edward. 'Mutual Indebtedness: Unpublished Letters of Edward Bellamy to W.D. Howells', *Harvard Library Bulletin*, 12 (1958), 363–74.

Bildhauer, Bettina. 'Blood, Jews and Monsters in Medieval Culture', in Bettina Bildhauer and Robert Mills, eds. *The Monstrous Middle Ages* (University of Wales Press, 2003), pp. 75–96.

Blaim, Artur. 'Hell upon a Hill: Reflections on Anti-Utopia and Dystopia', in Fátima Vieira, ed. *Dystopia Matters* (Cambridge Scholars Publishing, 2013), pp. 80–91.

Browning, Gordon. 'Towards a Set of Standards for Everlasting Anti-Utopian Fiction', *Cithara*, 10 (1970), 18–32.

Budakov, V. M. 'Dystopia: An Earlier Eighteenth Century Use', *Notes and Queries*, 57 (2010), 86–8.

Claeys, Gregory. '*The Lion and the Unicorn*, Patriotism, and Orwell's Politics', *Review of Politics*, 47 (1985), 186–211.

Claeys, Gregory. 'Malice in Wonderland: The Origins of Dystopia from Wells to Orwell', in Claeys, ed. *The Cambridge Companion to Utopian Literature* (Cambridge University Press, 2010), pp. 107–34.

Claeys, Gregory. 'The Five Languages of Utopia: Their Respective Advantages and Deficiencies; With a Plea for Prioritising Social Realism', in Artur Blaim and Ludmiła Gruszewska-Blaim, eds. *Spectres of Utopia* (Peter Lang, 2012), pp. 26–31.

Claeys, Gregory. 'News from Somewhere: Enhanced Sociability and the Composite Definition of Utopia and Dystopia', *History*, 98 (2013), 145–73.

Claeys, Gregory. 'Huxley and Bolshevism', in M. Keith Booker, ed. *Critical Insights: Brave New World* (Salem Press, 2014), pp. 91–107.

Claeys, Gregory. 'Paine and the Religiosity of Rights', in Rachel Hammersley, ed. *Revolutionary Moments* (Bloomsbury, 2015), pp. 85–92.

Claeys, Gregory. 'Socialism and the Language of Rights', in Miia Halme-Tuomisaari and Pamela Slotte, eds. *Revisiting the Origins of Human Rights: Genealogy of a European Idea* (Cambridge University Press, 2015), pp. 206–36.

Claeys, Gregory. 'Orwell's "Notes on Nationalism" and *Nineteen Eighty-Four*', in Thomas Horan, ed. *Critical Insights: Nineteen Eighty-Four* (The Salem Press, 2016).

Claeys, Gregory. 'When Does Utopianism Produce Dystopia?' in Zsolt Czigányik, ed. *Utopian Horizons: The Interaction of Political and Utopian Thought* (CEU Press, 2016).

Claeys, Gregory, and Christine Lattek. 'Radicalism, Republicanism, and Revolutionism: From the Principles of '89 to Modern Terrorism', in Gareth Stedman Jones and Gregory Claeys, eds. *The Cambridge History of Nineteenth-Century Political Thought* (Cambridge University Press, 2011), pp. 200–54.

Cohn, Norman. 'How Time Acquired a Consummation', in Malcolm Bull, ed. *Apocalypse Theory and the Ends of the World* (Blackwell, 1985), pp. 21–37.

Connors, James. 'Zamyatin's *We* and the Genesis of *1984*', *Modern Fiction Studies*, 21 (1975), 107–24.

Connors, James. ' "Who Dies If England Live?" Christianity and the Moral Vision of George Orwell', in W. W. Wagar, ed. *The Secular Mind* (Holmes & Meier, 1982), pp. 169–96.

Cosman, Max. 'George Orwell and the Autonomous Individual', *Pacific Spectator*, 9 (1955), 74–84.

Disch, Thomas M. 'Buck Rogers in the New Jerusalem', in Kenneth Roemer, ed. *America as Utopia* (Burt Franklin & Co., 1981), pp. 52–6.

Dresen-Coenders, Lène. 'Witches as Devils' Concubines: On the Origin of Fear of Witches and Protection against Witchcraft', in Lène Dresen-Coenders, ed., *Images of Women in the 15th and 16th Centuries* (The Rubicon Press, 1987), pp. 59–82.

Dunn, John. 'Totalitarian Democracy and the Legacy of Modern Revolutions: Explanation or Indictment?', in Yehoshua Arieli and Nathan Rotenstreich, eds. *Totalitarian Democracy and After* (Frank Cass, 1984), pp. 37–55.

Dunn, Thomas P., and Richard D. Erlich. 'A Vision of Dystopia: Bee Hives and Mechanization', *Journal of General Education*, 33 (1981), 45–58.

Fitzpatrick, Sheila. 'Everyday Stalinism: Ordinary Life in Extraordinary Times', in David L. Hoffmann, ed. *Stalinism* (Blackwell, 2003), pp. 161–78.

Forrest, Alan. 'The Local Politics of Repression', in Keith Michael Baker, ed. *The French Revolution and the Creation of Modern Political Culture*, vol. 4: *The Terror* (Pergamon, 1994), pp. 81–98.

Francis, Samuel. 'Power and History: The Political Thought of James Burnham', *Political Science Reviewer*, 12 (1982), 265–313.

Freedman, Carl. 'Science Fiction and Utopia: A Historico-Philosophical Overview', in Patrick Parrinder, ed. *Learning from Other Worlds: Estrangement, Cognition, and the Politics of Science Fiction and Utopia* (Duke University Press, 2001), pp. 72–97.

Friedländer, Saul. 'Themes of Decline and End in Nineteenth Century Western Imagination', in Saul Friedländer, Gerald Holton, Leo Marx, and Eugene Skolnikoff, eds. *Visions of Apocalypse: End or Rebirth?* (Holmes & Meier, 1985), pp. 61–83.

Fromm, Erich. 'Afterward on *1984*', in Irving Howe, ed. *Orwell's Nineteen Eighty-Four: Text, Sources, Criticism* (Harcourt, Brace & World, 1963), pp. 204–10.

Frye, Northrop. 'Varieties of Literary Utopia', in Frank E. Manuel, ed. *Utopias and Utopian Thought* (Beacon Press, 1967), pp. 25–49.

Furedi, Frank. 'Towards a Sociology of Fear', in Kate Hebblethwaite and Elizabeth McCarthy, eds. *Fear: Essays on the Meaning and Experience of Fear* (Four Courts Press, 2007), pp. 18–30.

Gaskell, Malcolm. 'Fear Made Flesh: The English Witch-Panic of 1645-7', in David Lemmings and Claire Walker, eds. *Moral Panics, the Media and the Law in Early Modern England* (Palgrave Macmillan, 2009), pp. 78–96.

Gentile, Emilio. 'The Sacralisation of Politics: Definitions, Interpretations and Reflections on the Question of Secular Religion and Totalitarianism', *Totalitarian Movements and Political Religions*, 1 (2000), 18–55.

Gnuse, Robert. 'Ancient Near Eastern Millennialism', in Catherine Wessinger, ed. *The Oxford Handbook of Millennialism* (Oxford University Press, 2011), pp. 235–51.

Gottlieb, Erika. 'Orwell's Satirical Version on the Screen: The Film Versions of *Animal Farm* and *Nineteen Eighty-Four*', in Thomas Cushman and John Rodden, eds. *George Orwell: Into the Twenty-First Century* (Paradigm Publishers, 2004), pp. 252–63.

Gregor, Neil. 'Nazism: A Political Religion? Rethinking the Voluntarist Turn', in Neil Gregor, ed. *Nazism, War and Genocide* (University of Exeter Press, 2005), pp. 1–22.

Guilhaumou, Jacques. 'A Discourse of Denunciation', in Keith Michael Baker, ed. *The French Revolution and the Creation of Modern Political Culture*, vol. 4: *The Terror* (Pergamon, 1994), pp. 139–56.

Halfin, Igor. 'Stalinist Confessions in an Age of Terror: Messianic Times at the Leningrad Communist Universities', in Michael D. Gordin, Helen Tilley, and Gyan Prakash, eds. *Utopia/Dystopia* (Princeton University Press, 2010), pp. 231–49.

Hall, Alexander Charles Oliver. 'A *Nineteen Eighty-Four* for the Twenty-First Century: John Twelve Hawss's Four Realm Trilogy as Critical Dystopia', in M. Keith Booker, ed. *Critical Insights: Dystopia* (Salem Press, 2013), pp. 209–22.

Harrison, J. F. C. 'Millennium and Utopia', in Peter Alexander and Roger Gill, eds. *Utopias* (Duckworth, 1984), pp. 61–8.

Hart, Bradley W. 'Aldous Huxley and the Twentieth-Century Eugenics Movement', in M. Keith Booker, ed. *Critical Insights: Brave New World* (Salem Press, 2014), pp. 108–22.

Hillegas, Mark. 'The Literary Background to Science Fiction', in Patrick Parrinder, ed. *Science Fiction: A Critical Guide* (Longman, 1979), pp. 2–17.

Hooper, Cynthia. 'Terror of Intimacy: Family Politics in the 1930s Soviet Union', in Christina Kaier and Eric Naiman, eds. *Everyday Life in Early Soviet Russia* (Indiana University Press, 2006), pp. 61–92.

Huxley, Aldous. 'The Modern Doctrine of Progress', *Vogue* (21 March 1928), 55, 78.

Huxley, Aldous, 'Boundaries of Utopia', *Virginia Quarterly Review*, 7 (1931), 49.

Huxley, Aldous. 'Introduction', in J. D. Unwin, *Hopousia: or the Sexual and Economic Foundations of a New Society* (George Allen & Unwin, 1940), pp. 13–29.

Huxley, Aldous. 'I am a Highbrow', *Aldous Huxley Annual*, 7 (2003), 126–8.

Huxley, Aldous. 'Public Opinion and Personal Liberty', *Aldous Huxley Annual*, 7 (2007), 63.

Ingle, S. J. 'The Politics of George Orwell: A Reappraisal', *Queen's Quarterly*, 80 (1973), 22–34.

Kamenetsky, Ihor. 'Totalitarianism and Utopia', *Chicago Review*, 4 (1964), 114–59.

Kateb, George. 'The Road to 1984', *Political Science Quarterly*, 81 (1966), 564–80.

Kessler, M. 'Power and the Perfect State: A Study of Disillusionment as Reflected in Orwell's *Nineteen Eighty-Four* and Huxley's *Brave New World*', *Political Science Quarterly*, 72 (1957), 565–77.

Ketterer, David. 'Utopian Fantasy as Millennial Motive and Science-Fictional Motif', *Studies in the Literary Imagination*, 6 (1973), 79–101.

Kołakowski, Leszek. 'Need of Utopia, Fear of Utopia', in Dick Howard, Leszek Kolakowski, Maurice Meisner, Robert Nisbet, Bertell Ollman, and Marcus Raskin, *Radicalism in the Contemporary Age*, vol. 2: *Radical Visions of the Future* (Westview Press, 1977), pp. 3–12.

Lewis, Arthur O., Jr. 'The Anti-Utopian Novel: Preliminary Notes and Checklist', *Extrapolation*, 2 (1961), 27–32.

Lowe, Scott. 'Chinese Millennial Movements', in Catherine Wessinger, ed. *The Oxford Handbook of Millennialism* (Oxford University Press, 2011), pp. 307–25.

Lucas, Colin. 'Revolutionary Violence, the People and the Terror', in Keith Michael Baker, ed. *The French Revolution and the Creation of Modern Political Culture*, vol. 4: *The Terror* (Pergamon, 1994), pp. 57–80.

Lucas, Colin. 'The Theory and Practice of Denunciation in the French Revolution', in Sheila Fitzpatrick and Robert Gellately, eds. *Accusatory Practices: Denunciation in Modern European History, 1789–1989* (University of Chicago Press, 1997), pp. 22–39.

McDougall, William. 'The Island of Eugenia; The Phantasy of a Foolish Philosopher', *Scribner's Magazine*, 70 (1921), 483–91.

Maddison, Michael. '*1984*: A Burnhamite Fantasy?', *Political Quarterly*, 32 (1961), 71–9.

Mansfield, Harvey C. 'The Unfinished Revolution', in Ralph C. Hancock and L. Gary Lambert, eds. *The Legacy of the French Revolution* (Rowman & Littlefield, 1996), pp. 19–42.

Margolin, Jean-Louis. 'Mao's China: The Worst Non-Genocidal Regime?', in Dan Stone, ed. *The Historiography of Genocide* (Palgrave Macmillan, 2010), pp. 438–67.

Mellor, Anne. '"You're Only a Rebel from the Waist Downwards": Orwell's View of Women', in Peter Stansky, ed. *On Nineteen Eighty-Four* (W. H. Freeman & Co., 1983), pp. 115–25.

Miller, Katherine Toy. 'Penitentes at the Snake Dance: Native Americans in *Brave New World*', in M. Keith Booker, ed. *Critical Insights: Brave New World* (Salem Press, 2014), pp. 152–65.

Milner, Andrew. 'Need It All End in Tears? The Problem of Ending in Four Classic Dystopias', in M. Keith Booker, ed. *Critical Insights: Dystopia* (Salem Press, 2013), pp. 109–24.

Moylan, Tom. 'Beyond Negation: The Critical Utopias of Ursula K. Le Guin and Samuel R. Delany', *Extrapolation: A Journal of Science Fiction and Fantasy*, 21 (1980), 236–53.

Moylan, Tom. '"Look into the Dark": On Dystopia and the Novum', in Patrick Parrinder, ed. *Learning from Other Worlds: Estrangement, Cognition, and the Politics of Science Fiction and Utopia* (Duke University Press, 2001), pp. 51–71.

Nydahl, Joel. 'Early Fictional Futures', in Kenneth Roemer, ed. *America as Utopia* (Burt Franklin & Co., 1981), pp. 266–74.

Ozouf, Mona. 'The Terror after the Terror: An Immediate History', in Keith Michael Baker, ed. *The French Revolution and the Creation of Modern Political Culture*, vol. 4: *The Terror* (Pergamon, 1994), pp. 3–18.

Panafieu, Christine Woesler de. 'Automata: A Masculine Utopia', in Everett Mendelsohn and Helga Nowotny, eds. *Nineteen Eighty-Four: Science between Utopia and Dystopia* (D. Reidel, 1984), pp. 127–46.

Parrinder, Patrick. 'Science Fiction and the Scientific World-View', in Patrick Parrinder, ed. *Science Fiction: A Critical Guide* (Longman, 1979), pp. 67–89.

Petre, M. D. 'An Argument against Bolshevik Ideals', in Katie de Koster, ed. *Readings on Brave New World* (Greenhaven Press, 1999), pp. 33–42.

Philmus, Robert. 'The Language of Utopia', *Studies in the Literary Imagination*, 6 (1973), 61–78.

Podhoretz, Norman. 'If Orwell Were Alive Today', *Harper's Magazine* (January 1983), 32.

Pohl, Frederick. 'The Politics of Prophecy', in Donald M. Hassler and Clyde Wilcox, eds. *Political Science Fiction* (University of South Carolina Press, 1997), pp. 7–17.

Quo, F. Quei. 'Orwell's *Nineteen Eighty-Four* and Mao's Cultural Revolution', in Peter Buitenhuis and Ira B. Nadel, eds. *George Orwell: A Reassessment* (Macmillan, 1988), pp. 126–38.

Rahv, Philip. 'The Unfuture of Utopia', in Irving Howe, ed. *Orwell's Nineteen Eighty-Four: Text, Sources, Criticism* (Harcourt, Brace & World, 1963), pp. 181–5.

Redles, David. 'National Socialist Millennialism', in Catherine Wessinger, ed. *The Oxford Handbook of Millennialism* (Oxford University Press, 2011), pp. 529–48.

Rohatyn, Dennis. 'Hell and Dystopia: A Comparison and Literary Case Study', in Michael S. Cummings and Nicholas D. Smith, eds. *Utopian Studies 2* (University Press of America, 1989), pp. 94–101.

Russell, Jeffrey Burton. *Satan: The Early Christian Tradition* (Cornell University Press, 1981).

Sargent, Lyman Tower. 'The Three Faces of Utopianism', *Minnesota Review*, 7 (1967), 222–30.

Sargent, Lyman Tower. 'Utopia: The Problem of Definition', *Extrapolation*, 16 (1975), 137–48.

Sargent, Lyman Tower. 'Eutopias and Dystopias in Science Fiction: 1950–75', in Kenneth Roemer, ed. *America as Utopia* (Burt Franklin & Co., 1981), pp. 347–66.

Sargent, Lyman Tower. 'The Three Faces of Utopianism Revisited', *Utopian Studies*, 5 (1994), 1–37.

Sargent, Lyman Tower. 'The Problem of the "Flawed Utopia": A Note on the Costs of Eutopia', in Tom Moylan and Raffaella Baccolini, eds. *Dark Horizons: Science Fiction and the Dystopian Imagination* (Routledge, 2003), pp. 225–32.

Sargent, Lyman Tower. 'Theorizing Utopia/Utopianism in the Twenty-First Century', in Artur Blaim and Ludmila Gruszewska-Blaim, eds. *Spectres of Utopia* (Peter Lang, 2012), pp. 13–26.

Schofield, Philip. 'Reeves, John (1752–1829)', *Oxford Dictionary of National Biography* (online edn, 2008).

Segal, Howard P. 'Utopia Diversified: 1900–1949', in Kenneth Roemer, ed. *America as Utopia* (Burt Franklin & Co., 1981), pp. 333–46.

Shlapentokh, Vladimir. 'George Orwell: Russia's Tocqueville', in Thomas Cushman and John Rodden, eds. *George Orwell: Into the Twenty-First Century* (Paradigm Publishers, 2004), pp. 267–85.

Singer, Brian. 'Violence in the French Revolution: Forms of Ingestion/Forms of Expulsion', in Ferenc Fehér, ed. *The French Revolution and the Birth of Modernity* (University of California Press, 1990), pp. 150–73.

Spender, Stephen. 'Introduction to *1984*', in Samuel Hynes, ed. *Twentieth Century Interpretations of* 1984 (Prentice Hall, 1971), pp. 62–72.

Stedman Jones, Gareth. 'Religion and the Origin of Socialism', in Ira Katznelson and Stedman Jones, eds. *Religion and the Political Imagination* (Cambridge University Press, 2010), pp. 171–89.

Stillman, Peter. 'Rationalism, Revolution, and Utopia in Yevgeny Zamyatin's *We*', in M. Keith Booker, ed. *Critical Insights: Dystopia* (Salem Press, 2013), pp. 160–74.

Stone, Dan. 'Nazism as Modern Magic: Bronislaw Malinowski's Political Anthropology', *History and Anthropology*, 14 (2003), 203–18.

Stone, Dan. 'The Uses and Abuses of "Secular Religion": Jules Monnerot's Path from Communism to Fascism', *History of European Ideas*, 37 (2011), 466–74.

Strauss, Sylvia. 'Gender, Class and Race in Utopia', in Daphne Patai, ed. *Looking Backward 1988–1888* (University of Massachusetts Press, 1988), pp. 68–90.

Su, Yang. 'Mass Killings in the Cultural Revolution: A Study of Three Provinces', in Joseph W. Esherick, Paul G. Pickowicz, and Andrew G. Walder, eds. *The Chinese Cultural Revolution as History* (Stanford University Press, 2006), pp. 96–123.

Talmon, Jacob. 'Utopianism and Politics', in George Kateb, ed. *Utopia* (Atherton Press, 1971), pp. 91–102.

Tausiet, Maria. 'Witchcraft as Metaphor: Infanticide and Its Translations in Aragón', in Stuart Clark, ed. *Languages of Witchcraft: Narrative, Ideology and Meaning in Early Modern Culture* (St. Martin's Press, 2001), pp. 179–96.

Thiess, Derek. 'Critical Reception', in M. Keith Booker, ed. *Critical Insights: Dystopia* (Salem Press, 2013), pp. 19–36.

Thompson, E. P. 'Inside *Which* Whale?', in Raymond Williams, ed. *George Orwell: A Collection of Critical Essays* (Prentice Hall, 1974), pp. 80–8.

Warrick, Patricia. 'The Man–Machine Intelligence Relationship', in Thomas Clareson, ed. *Many Futures Many Worlds: Theme and Form in Science Fiction* (Kent State University Press, 1977), pp. 182–223.

Watt, Ian. 'Winston Smith: The Last Humanist', in Peter Stansky, ed. *On Nineteen Eighty-Four* (W. H. Freeman & Co., 1983), pp. 103–13.

Weingart, Peter. 'Eugenic Utopias: Blueprints for Rationalization of Human Evolution', in Everett Mendelsohn and Helga Nowotny, eds. *Nineteen Eighty-Four: Science between Utopia and Dystopia* (D. Reidel, 1984), pp. 175–87.

Weisbrod, Bernd. 'Religious Language of Violence', in Stuart Carroll, ed. *Cultures of Violence: Interpersonal Violence in Historical Perspective* (Palgrave Macmillan, 2007), pp. 64–78.

Werth, Nicolas. 'The Crimes of the Stalin Regime', in Dan Stone, ed. *The Historiography of Genocide* (Palgrave Macmillan, 2010), pp. 400–19.

Williams, Raymond. 'Utopia and Science Fiction', in Patrick Parrinder, ed. *Science Fiction: A Critical Guide* (Longman, 1979), pp. 52–66.

Winter, Frank. 'Was Orwell a Secret Optimist? The Narrative Function of the "Appendix" to Nineteen Eighty-Four', in Benoit J. Suykerburk, ed. *Essays from Oceania and Eurasia: George Orwell and 1984* (Progreff, 1984), pp. 79–89.

Wittkower, Rudolf. 'Marvels of the East: A Study in the History of Monsters', *Journal of the Warburg and Courtauld Institutes*, 5 (1942), 159–97.

Woodcock, George. 'Utopias in Negative', *Sewanee Review*, 64 (1956), 81–97.

Wooden, Warren W. 'Utopia and Dystopia: The Paradigm of Thomas More's *Utopia*', *Southern Humanities Review*, 14 (1980), 91–100.

Zaki, Hoda. 'Utopia, Dystopia, and Ideology in the Science Fiction of Octavia Butler', *Science-Fiction Studies*, 17 (1990), 239–51.

Index

Printed and bound by CPI Group (UK) Ltd, Croydon, CR0 4YY